HISTORY AND DEVELOPMENT OF PRAKRIT LITERATURE

History and Development of Prakrit Literature

J.C. JAIN

MANOHAR
2004

First published 2004

© Anil J. Jain, 2004

All rights reserved. No part of this publication may be reproduced or transmitted, in any form or by any means, without prior permission of Anil J. Jain and the publisher

ISBN 81-7304-537-2

Published by
Ajay Kumar Jain for
Manohar Publishers & Distributors
4753/23 Ansari Road, Daryaganj
New Delhi 110002

Typeset by
A J Software Publishing Co. Pvt. Ltd.
New Delhi 110005

Printed at
Lordson Publishers Pvt. Ltd.
Delhi 110007

‘त्वदीयं वस्तु गोविन्द तुभ्यमेव समर्पये’

O Govinda! the creation which is really yours is being dedicated to you!

Contents

Foreword

The late Prof. Jagdish Chandra Jain does not require any introduction from a less competent man like myself. It was his greatness to count me as one of his friends, and it was in 1994 when he was 83 years of age that I was able to bring out his felicitation volume under the title *Jainism and Prakrit in Ancient and Medieval India: Essays for Prof. J.C. Jain.* In the preface of the volume the following was written: 'In the scholarly world Prof. Jagdish Chandra Jain is known as a great historian and as an authority in Prakrit language and literature. But basically he is a creative artist, a philosopher whose approach towards life is conducive to the welfare of mankind as a whole. The wealth of experience which he acquired in his chequered career through many ups and downs, poverty and hardship, toil and turmoil, has given him a heroic magnificence, a rare insight and a power to transcend human frailties and limitations. The story of his life reads like an epic—though it lacks epic grandeur, it is not devoid of epic qualities.'

Here I shall say a few words about his contribution to Prakrit language and literature. Earlier Western writers were interested in Sanskrit and specially Vedic Sanskrit because of its Indo-European affiliation. Subsequently, however, scholars became interested in the study of Prakrit and regional languages. Though a kind of simple Sanskrit served as the occasional spoken language of the elitist and scholarly class all over the country, the language of the masses was Prakrit. R. Pischel writes:

'The basis (*prakṛti*) of Prakrit is the natural current language of the people that cannot be fashioned according to the rules of the grammar.' Keith says: 'It is impossible to decide what was the process which led to the use of the term; perhaps speeches other than Sanskrit received the name from being the common or vulgar speech.' Besides there are many similarities between Prakrit and Vedic languages. Prakrit could not have been developed out of Sanskrit. The presence of *prakritism* in the Vedas proves that there were spoken Prakrits even in the Vedic age and that later literary

Prakrits must have descended from these earlier spoken Prakrits and not from classical Sanskrit.

According to Prof. Jain the Middle Indo-Aryan consists of all Prakrit languages which incorporates the Prakrit inscribed in Aśokan edicts, Niya Prakrit and the Prakrit of the *Dhammapada* discovered in Chinese Turkestan. The first stage of the Middle Indo-Aryan (600 BC-AD 200) contains Pali, Prakrit of the inscriptions, the oldest Jain Ardhamāgadhī canons, the Śaurasenī canonical literature of the Digambaras and the Prakrit of the Sanskrit dramas of Aśvaghoṣa. The second stage (200 BC- AD 600) comprises Prakrits of classical Sanskrit dramas, Hāla's *Sattasai* and Guṇādhya's *Bṛhatkathā* and the Prakrit grammars and includes the Jain Ardhamāgadhī, Śaurasenī, Mahārāṣṭrī, Māgadhī and their sub-dialects. The third stage (AD 600-1000) comprises Apabhraṃśa while the next stage of New Indo-Aryan (AD 1000 onwards) comprises the modern Indo-Aryan languages such as Hindi, Gujarati, Marathi, Bengali, Punjabi, Sindhi and so on.

Throughout his long life Prof. Jain had written numerous books, booklets and articles on different aspects of Prakrit and his history of Prakrit literature in Hindi has been regarded as a classic. Other scholars also contributed to the study of Prakrit language and literature. Though their works are by no means insignificant, and some of them have supplied a great deal of source-material, Prof. Jain's life-long study has a different value. The credit of Prof. Jain lies in the fact that he has taken into account all the traditional views of ancient authors and grammarians and compared them with the modern views in order to present the clearest aspect of the situation. He has shown the similarity between the Prakrit and Vedic language and held that though the popular and regional pronunciation and formation of Sanskrit words formed a part of Prakrit vocabulary, the basic Prakrit had its source in the living and not in the sacerdotal tradition of the Vedic language which, in his opinion, was not a one-way traffic.

In this very big and comprehensive work Prof. J.C. Jain has highlighted the importance of the indigenous words forming the substratum of Prakrit and classified the Indo-Aryan languages to show the emergence of the major Prakrit dialects like the Ardhamāgadhī, Śaurasenī, Mahāraṣṭrī, Paiśācī, etc., and their subdivisions. He has dealt elaborately with the Ardhamāgadhī of the Jain canonical literature and its transformation into other forms of

Prakrit in the religious literature of the Digambaras and post-canonical literature of the Śvetāṃbaras. Apart from religious literature, the Prakrit language contains epic poetry, lyrical poetry, gnomic poetry and religious lyrics, besides various types of poetical anthologies. There is a vast didactic and narrative literature in Prakrit. In fact, in story telling, the contributions of Prakrit are unique. These are mostly of Jain inspiration and form part of the mercantile literature which is why many of them have made their way even in European literature like *Gesta Romanorum*. Prof. Jain has ably demonstrated how various forms of Prakrit have been used in Sanskrit dramas. Actually the *Nāṭyaśāstra* itself lays down the injunction that certain dramatic characters are to speak in Prakrit.

In the present history of Prakrit Prof. Jain has also laid stress on the inner strength of the Prakrit languages which is why eminent grammarians and literary critics of the past were serious about them. There are many independent works on grammar, prosody, lexicography and poetics. There is no dearth of Prakrit works on secular subjects like astronomy, astrology, ensnaring, omens and portents, medicine, art of warfare, erotica, taming, music, mining, testing of jewels, science of coins, architecture, knowledge of horses, training of elephants and even the art of stealing. All these have been treated in details in this work. Moreover, in his fairly long academic life Prof. Jain had the opportunity of visiting many libraries, archives and *grantha-bhāṇḍāras* and he had the occasion to see, examine and note the contents of numerous unpublished Prakrit works. He had collected not only a great deal of materials but also employed a modern and historical mind to work on them.

It would have been a matter of great pleasure for all of us if Prof. Jain were alive to see this great volume printed and brought to light. Our affectionate Sri Anil Jain, worthy son of the late Prof. Jain, should be congratulated for collecting all the relevant papers and writings of which the present volume is constituted. I specially thank Sri Ajay Jain, who is the son of my esteemed friend Sri Ramesh Jain, of Manohar Publishers & Distributors for bringing out this volume as a tribute to the memory of Prof. Jain.

N.N. BHATTACHARYYA

Joraghat
Chinsurah 712101
West Bengal

1

Evolution of the Prakrit Languages

Language is a method of communicating ideas. 'Language is a social fact', writes Calvert Watkins. He says, 'Languages are not spoken in a vacuum but by human beings living in a society.' Elaborating his statement, he writes, 'Language is intimately linked to culture in a complex fashion; it is at once the expression of culture and part of it. Especially the lexicon of a language, its dictionary is a face turned towards culture. Though by no means a perfect mirror, the lexicon of a language remains the single most effective way of approaching and understanding the culture of its speakers. As such the contents of the Indo-European lexicon provide a remarkably clear view of the whole culture of an otherwise unknown prehistoric society.'[1]

The Indo-European Family of Languages

The Indo-European family of languages, comprising Indic (Sanskrit, Prakrit and Dardic) and Iranian, Greek, Armenian, Slavic, Baltic, Albanian, Celtic, Italic, Germanic, Hittite and Tokharian, is descended from a prehistoric language, Proto-Indo-European, spoken in the fifth millennium BC in a region that has not been identified. The similarities among the different Indo-European languages require us to suppose that they are the continuation of a simple prehistoric language, called Indo-European or Proto-Indo-European.

There are several thousand languages around the world. Language goes on changing from place to place, from time to time, according to geographical, historical and other aspects of human life. No language is static: it always changes and grows. It is always in a state of flux. It has been pointed out that just as in mathematics, the line is the flux of a point, so 'language is the flux of the mind'.[2] Take the instance of Avesta, the oldest attested group in the Indo-Iranian branch of Indo-European. It has undergone several historical forms such as Old Persian, Avestan, Pahlavi, Middle Persian and modern Persian. The Old Persian was the ancient form of Persian, the language of the inscriptions of Darius from the sixth to the fifth century BC. Avesta was the language of sacred writing of the ancient Persians. Pahlavi was a south-western dialect of Middle Persian, the language of the commentaries. Middle Persian was the language of the Sassanians, from the third to the seventh century AD. Besides, economy of effort, progressive refinement in courts and cities, softening influence of a semi-tropical climate and the influence of the speech-habits of non-Āryan people can be mentioned as the causes of such changes.[3] Thus no language remains pure even though meant for sacred ritualistic purposes.

A large number of Indo-European terms relating to time, weather, seasons and natural surroundings can be reconstructed from the daughter languages.[4] Some of these terms permit certain inferences about the homeland of the Indo-European speaking people before the period of their migration to the different localities where they appear historically. This 'cradle' of the Indo-Europeans may never be known. Where the primitive Indo-Āryan developed into the oldest Indo-European speeches—Vedic and Gāthā, Avesta and Homeric Greek—is not known. It is also not known when exactly the linguistic forefathers of all modern peoples, diverse in origin and mental make-up, were living as a single undivided people.[5] Contact with non-Āryan people and natural developments brought about changes into the Āryans' language. It changed slowly from the Āryan or Indo-Iranian, which is represented in its latest phase by the language of the *Ṛgveda.* Thus the language of the Āryan tribes underwent new sets of changes in phonetics, in grammar and in vocabulary. Cerebral sounds were developed, which was the most marked change in phonetics. This may be due to extraneous non-Āryan influence. In the lexicon new words were created, many of them borrowed. In this way, Āryan or Indo-Iranian became Indo-Āryan among those who brought into India the language and some of the Vedic hymns and the Vedic traditions in religion and culture. These Indian Āryans laid the foundation of a remarkable synthesis of race, religion and civilization, including a synthesis of speech.[6]

The Āryans brought their language and possibly also a portion of Vedic hymns which it possessed as an inheritance from their Indo-European ancestors and this inheritance would appear to have been remarkably well preserved by the Āryan immigrants, without much conscious effort on their part. But in course of time, as the spoken language changed from the Vedic norm and as foreigners began to adopt the Āryan speech, spontaneous transmission of language, retaining its fundamental traits, became translated to the plane of academic attainment. The result was the scholarly effort to preserve the text correctly in order to retain its correct pronunciation.[7]

The Basic Dialect of the *Ṛgveda*

The behaviour of *r* and *l* plays an important role in the Ṛgvedic dialect. The basic dialect of the *Ṛgveda* was one that had only *r* and not *l*. It spirantized internal voiced aspirants such as *gh, jh, dh, bh* ultimately to change them to *h*; and turned intervocal *ḍ, ḍh* to the liquids *ḷ ḷh*. It is to be noted that in its preference for *r* the Ṛgvedic dialect agrees with Avestan. It is assumed that in the Indo-Iranian period the Indo-European sound *l* had been replaced by *r*. In this connection, a quotation from the *Satapatha Brāhmaṇa* (III, 2, 1, 23) is noteworthy: it is stated that the Asuras who initiated the Brāhmaṇas in performing the sacrifice often misused words or misplaced the accent. Instead of putting a lengthened accent *(pluta)* on *he* and pronouncing the word *arayaḥ* after it, they used the words *helaya helaya.* Thus deprived of speech they were vanquished, for they could not get the benefit of the sacrifice for victory. It has been stated that a Brāhmaṇa should not mispronounce the word as did the *Mlecchas.*

The Origin of Prakrit

The word Prakrit means 'original', 'natural', 'normal'. It has been used in this sense in the Vedic literature, in the *Prātiśākhyas,* the *Śrautasūtras* and also in Patañjali's *Mahābhāsya.* Prakrit or Prakrit *bhāsā* indicates the common or ordinary speech of the common people. The word literally means 'non-artificial' which is different from the literary or ceremonial language that was thought to be artificial. The term Prakrit has been employed by ancient grammarians and literary critics to denote a multitude of languages and dialects whose common origin is attributed to Sanskrit. Orthodox grammarians like Hemacandra (AD 1088-1172) derive the word from *prakrti,* 'element', 'basis' and according to them this basis is Sanskrit. Hemacandra has stated, 'Sanskrit is the basis, what originated from it or what is derived from it, is called Prakrta'. (प्रकृतिः संस्कृतम् तत्र भवम् तत्र आगतम् वा प्राकृतम्.)[8]

This view is contradicted by Nami Sādhu, another Jain scholar of the eleventh century. Commenting on Rudraṭa's *Kāvyālaṅkāra* (2.12), he explains the word Prakrit as follows:

> The basis of Prakrit is the natural language of intercourse of all beings of the world which is not refined by grammar, rhetoric etc.; and a speech is called Prakrit because it is derived from this language or is itself the same. . . . Or it may be that Prakrit means first produced (*prāk pūrvaṃ kṛtaṃ prākṛtaṃ*). Prakrit is the speech easily intelligible to children, women and others and the source of all other speeches. It is of a homogeneous character like rain water falling from the clouds; the same speech being distributed in different localities and being specialised by refinement is later differentiated into Sanskrit and other speeches. For this reason the author of the text (Rudrata) first mentions Prakrit and then Sanskrit and other speeches. It is called Sanskrit on account of being refined by Pāṇinī and others, in the rules of their grammar.[9]

Vākpatirāja (*c.* AD 750), dealing with Prakrit as a prominent speech, has stated in his *Gauḍavaho* (93): 'All speeches merge into it (Prakrit) and spring out of it just as all waves merge into the ocean and spring out of it.'[10]

We have seen that there are two different views about the origin of the Prakrit language. The one is traditional or derivative, according to which the primary source of Prakrit is Sanskrit. This view is generally held by Indian grammarians. The other view is that *Prakṛti* is not merely a corrupt form of Sanskrit, but a natural flow of human speech, derived from *prakṛti* or nature, what all people without special instruction easily understand and speak. Explaining the significance of the term Prakrit, Keith writes, 'It is impossible to decide what was the process which led to the use of the term; perhaps speeches other than Sanskrit received the name from being the common or vulgar speech, the language of the humble man as opposed to him of education who could talk the pure language.'[11]

Discussing the origin of the Prakrit language, Dinesh Chandra Sirkar has said in his *Grammar of the Prakrit Language*'[12] 'The common speech of the Vedic Āryan which apparently differed in some respects from the literary language of the *Saṃhitās* (that was gradually becoming archaic) is no doubt the origin of the so-called Prakrit language.' In his opinion the language of the common people of the early Vedic age changed continually and after several centuries assumed the form of Prakrit. Sanskrit is the reformed, literary and elegant form of this language, at an early stage of development. This refined language was based on the speech of the cultured people (*śiṣṭa*). It was standardized by grammarians and the great Pāṇinī (fifth century BC) gave it a final and stereotyped form.

Pischel argues that Sanskrit was not the basis of the Prakrit dialects. He considers Prakrit to be a folk language, acquired without special instruction. According to him, these dialects go back to a certain popular spoken dialect, which on political or religious grounds was raised to the status of a literary medium. He writes, 'But the difficulty is that it does not seem probable that all the Prakrit dialects sprang out from one and the same source. At least they could not have developed out of Sanskrit as is generally held by Indian scholars and Höffer, Lassen, Bhandarkar and Jacobi (according to Jacobi, Pali and Prakrit are essentially a later form of Sanskrit).'[13]

In his *Linguistic Survey of India* Grierson classifies Prakrit in three great stages: (i) Primary Prakrit dialects of the Vedic age from which the Vedic language and the classical Sanskrit, which is its lineal descendant, are to be derived. The classical Sanskrit is fixed in its existing form by the labours of grammarians, especially by Pāṇinī; (ii) Secondary Prakrit: The Primary Prakrits having no extant literature of their own are now lost. Out of these sprung literary Prakrits, represented in literature by Pali, Jain Ardhamāgadhī, the edicts of Asoka, the Prakrit dialects of the dramas and Jain Mahārāṣṭrī and the last stage of the Apabhraṃsa of the grammarians; (iii) Tertiary Prakrits which include modern Āryan vernaculars that arose about the tenth century AD.

Presenting a comparative study of Vedic and Sanskrit words (such as ऋजुप उडुप, तलित् तडित्, कृत्रिम कुहिम, मर्त मट्ट, यहि, कृत कुट, etc.), P.V. Gune in his *An Introduction to Comparative Philology* has stated that the Prakrit origin of these words cannot be denied. He concludes that the linguals in the Vedic and later Sanskrit are due to the influence of old Prakrit, which therefore must have existed side by side with the Vedic dialects.[14]

SIMILARITY BETWEEN PRAKRIT AND VEDIC LANGUAGES

There are a number of grammatical and lexical characteristics common to Prakrit and Vedic, but significantly missing from Sanskrit. Nātyāyana has discussed the divergent irregularities in the Vedic language. He observes that suffixes, both declensional and conjugational, ātmanepada, parasmaipada, genders, persons, tenses, vowels, consonants, voices and frequentatives are used in the Vedic languages without observing hard and fast rules, unlike the Classical Sanskrit. Such divergent forms were possible in the language spoken by the Āryans of the Vedic period as it was not bound by the rules of grammar. The Prakrit languages too did not have a standard speech. Let us consider certain similarities between the two languages:

(i) Retention of Prakrit forms in the language of the Vedas, the Brāhmaṇas and in early Classical Sanskrit: for example, vikṛta=vikaṭa; kiṃ kṛta=kikaṭa; dandra=daṇḍa; srīra=slīla; srithira=sithira; kṣudra=kṣulla; grath=ghaṭ[15] and so on. This indicates that the Vedic priests while pronouncing these words, regarded them as possible forms of the same language and did not distinguish between one and the other.

(ii) In the following Vedic words the voiced aspirate changes into *h*, and so is the case with Prakrit: for example, *dhā=hita*; *dhi=hi*; *gṛdha=gṛha*; *grabh=grah*; *ghnanti=hanti*; *argha=arha*; *dhadh=dah* and so on.[16]

(iii) scarcity of *visarga* and the substitution of *o* in the nominative singular of stems ending in *a*.

(iv) Retention of suffix '*bhis*' in the instrumental plural.

(v) The omission of final consonants.

(vi) Scarcity of dative case and the replacement of the genitive.

(vii) The hiatus or absence of *sandhi.*[17]

(viii) The loss of dual number. In the *Ṛgveda* the dual had a restricted use. In Avestan it is rare and in Old Persian practically lost.[18]

According to scholars the presence of Prakritisms in the Vedic texts shows that there were spoken Prakrits even in that age. Perhaps these spoken dialects were lost as they could not be preserved in literature. And the later literary Prakrits descended from the early spoken dialects of Prakrit, and not from later Classical Sanskrit.[19]

Indian grammarians have approached the study of Prakrit from the viewpoint of Sanskrit grammar. The formation of their rules of Prakrit grammar are framed after the pattern of Sanskrit grammar, written in Sanskrit. Some of the Prakrit grammar books like those of Hemacandra and Kramadīśvara are composed as mere supplements of their Sanskrit grammar. These words were also meant for the students of Sanskrit drama who were expected to have a fair knowledge of Sanskrit language and grammar. The classification of *tatsama, tadbhava* and *desī* words are based on the orthodox view of the origin of Prakrit from Sanskrit. The *tatsama* words and roots were identical with those of Sanskrit, the *tadbhava* were derived from Sanskrit, and the *desī* words and roots were those which have no real or apparent relationship with Sanskrit.[20]

The Classification of Indo-Āryan Languages

From the linguistic point of view the Indo-Āryan languages can be classified into languages of three periods: the Old Indo-Āryan, the Middle Indo-Āryan and the New Indo-Āryan. The Old Indo-Āryan (OIA) period (from 2000 or 1500 to 600 or 500 BC) is represented by the dialects current among the Vedic Āryans in that period; the language of the *Vedas* and Classical Sanskrit as defined by Pāṇinī and Patañjali. The language of this period was similar to the Vedic language in the pronunciation of vowels and consonants, and the use of case-terminations. The Middle Indo-Āryan (MIA) period (from the sixth or the fifth century BC to the tenth or eleventh century AD) consists of all the Prakrit languages as defined by grammarians in the widest sense of the term Prakrit. This period is represented by Pali and Prakrit comprising all dialects of the age beginning with the time when certain phonetic changes and grammatic variations had produced a language different from the OIA. This is an important period of the Indo-Iranian branch of Indo-European which is closely associated with the Old Indo-Āryan and Classical Sanskrit on the one hand, and with Indo-Iranian at some distance and Indo-European at a greater distance, on the other. This period incorporates not only those Prakrits described by Indian grammarians and rhetoricians but also the Prakrit inscribed in the edicts of Asoka and others, Niya Prakrit written in Kharoṣṭhī script and the Prakrit of the *Dhammapada*, discovered in Chinese Turkestan. During this period various phonetic, morphological and conjugational changes gathered force as the language advanced.

Phonetic changes: (i) *ṛ* transformed into *a, u* and *i*, (ii) the reduction of long dipthongs to *e* and *o*, (iii) simplification of consonant groups by assimilation (*kk, dd, tt, mh*, etc.), (iv) final consonants and *visarga* dropped, (v) tendency towards cerebralization of dental stops and aspirants in connection with *r*, (vi) *s ṣ s* reduced generally to one sibilant, *s* or *s*, (vii) the difference between *ṇ* and *n* often more orthographical than phonetic.

Morphological changes: (i) considerable simplification of the declensional system, (ii) move towards standardizing *-a* declension, (iii) the dual number lost although it continued to exist for a time in certain dialect-groups, (iv) the dative merged into the genetive (v) the forms of the pronominal declension extended to the noun.

Conjugational changes: Prakrit verbs have undergone greater changes than the noun. There has been the same tendency as in the case of declension, to reduce all verbs to one type. (i) The *ātmanepada* voice almost gone, (ii) apart from scattered remnants, the wealth of perfects, imperfects and aorists lost, (iii) the past tense expressed by a participle with or without an auxiliary verb, (iv) imperative and optative remain, but the subjunctive, found in a few rare cases, lost, (v) middle voice, preserved as a remnant in the early period, disappeared, (vi) of the derived forms, causative alone a living form, (vii) verbal nouns and gerunds become fewer, though more used, (viii) wider use of the passive participle for the past tense, (ix) few propositional particles.[21]

Middle Indo-Āryan is further divided into three stages, the Early Stage (600 to 200 BC), comprised Pali, and the Prakrit of the inscriptions, the oldest Jain *Sūtras* and the Prakrit of the early Sanskrit dramas like those of Aśvaghoṣa. The Middle Stage (200 BC to AD 600), comprised Prakrit passages in the classical Sanskrit dramas, works like Hāla's *Sattasaī* and Guṇāḍhya's *Bṛhatkathā* and the Prakrit grammars. These Prakrits include Śaurasenī, Mahārāṣṭrī, Māgadhī and Jain Ardhamāgadhī with their sub-dialects. The third Stage (AD 600 to 1000) comprises Apabhraṃśa. The literary dialect of Apabhraṃśa is known from the sixth or the seventh century but the full-fledged Apabhraṃśa stage was reached by the ordinary colloquial speech when the Prakrit of the dramas and grammars had become archaic and stereotyped. This was the beginning of the modern Indo-Āryan languages.

The last period (after AD 1000) of the Indo-Āryan languages is represented by the New Indo-Āryan (NIA) languages such as Hindi, Gujarati, Marathi, Bengali, Panjabi, Sindhi and so on.

Prakrit Dialects and Their Treatment

The oldest Vedic manuscripts extant are not even a thousand years old, yet it is significant that the Vedic hymns have been faithfully preserved with the same *sikṣā* (the science of proper articulation and pronunciation), *chandas* (metre), *vyākaraṇa* (linguistic analysis), *nirukta* (explanation of difficult words), and *jyotiṣa* (astronomy) as they were 5000 years ago. This helped in the preservation of the authenticity of the Vedas which are said to be revelation orally communicated by the Deity, and heard but not composed or written down by men. These hymns were important as they contained words of prayer and adoration often addressed to deities for granting health, wealth, long life, cattle, offspring or victory over enemy. Such was not the case with Prakrit. Prakrit was known to be the natural language of intercourse of common people, easily intelligible to children, women and the aged. It went on changing from region to region and from time to time.

Yet in that case there also developed certain problems. As Sunitikumar Chatterji pointed out in *Origin and Development of Bengali Language,* the Prakrits (and Apabhraṃśas) are literary and to a great extent artificial languages, standing to some extent off from the general current of development of MIA as spoken. Our other authorities, the Prakrit grammarians, are not reliable guides, themselves influencing as much as being influenced by the texts and theories. Also, there has been intermixture among the various dialects to an extent which makes their affiliation to forms of MIA, as in our records, at times rather problematic.

As indicated earlier, Middle Indo-Āryan had taken various forms and shapes. It developed into Ardhamāgadhī, the Prakrit of the Śvetāmbara Jain canonical literature, Śaurasenī, the Prakrit of the Digambara canonical literature, Maharaṣṭrī, the Prakrit of Jain narrative literature, the Prakrit of Sanskrit dramas in various forms, the Prakrit of lyrical poetry such as of the *Gāhāsattasaī,* the Paisācī Prakrit of Guṇāḍhya's *Bṛhatkathā,* the Prakrit of Asoka's inscriptions, the Niyā Prakrit, the Prakrit of *Dhammapada* written in Kharoṣṭhī and so on. They are all Prakrits, though the grammarians have called them by different names. As these dialects belong to different regions, and were spoken by different people, there could not be any uniformity amongst them. Hence there is no standard Prakrit grammar to explain the rules as there is for Sanskrit. As we have seen, the study of Sanskrit grammar has a unique place in the history of human culture, but that was not the case with Prakrit. Since Prakrit was the language of current use it was difficult to check it by *sikṣā* and *vyākaraṇa,* and Prakrit has not produced grammarians like Pāṇinī, Kātyāyana and Patañjali. The rules of Prakrit grammar were composed very late as an aid to comprehension of old Prakrit works such as the Jain canonical text, old dramas and the new Prakrit poems and plays.

These rules were based on texts accessible to the grammarians. For example, Vararuci and Hemacaṇdra were not in a position to provide authentic information about the Prakrit of Aśvaghoṣa's dramas or of the Kharoṣṭhī *Dhammapada* or of the Paisācī Prakrit of Guṇāḍhya's *Baḍḍakahā* or of the Svetambara Jain canonical literature in Ardhamāgadhī of the fifth century BC. As a good deal of the canonical literature had gone into oblivion, various councils were convened to set the canon right, the last council being convened at Valabhi in Saurashtra in the fifth century. Thus we see that the grammars of Prakrit languages were composed when the different languages described in them had already assumed the literary form and were more or less standardized by usage and were no longer in the process of formation. The Prakrit inscriptions too, which play a very important role in the study of Prakrit, and which are widely scattered all over India, ranging from about the middle of the third century BC to the end of the fourth century AD, could not find place in the works of Prakrit grammarians.

The Eastern and Western Schools

It has been indicated that the Prakrit grammars which we have before us were written under the influence of Sanskrit. It has also been stated that there is no homogeneity in the rules of Prakrit grammar laid down by grammarians. As rightly said by S.M. Katre in his *Prakrit Languages and their Contribution to Indian Culture*, 'The differential of grammatical rules are indication of an artificial canalising of probable tendencies, exaggerating the minor idiosyncracies of the different languages with which they deal. It is this same tendency which makes Mārkaṇḍeya record 27 varieties of Apabhraṃsa or 11 varieties of Paisācī.' There are two schools of Prakrit grammarians, the eastern and the western. The former is represented by Vararuci and the later by Hemacandra. The earliest commentaries on Vararuci's *Prākṛtaprakāṣa* are *Prākṛtamañjarī* by Kātyāyana (sixth-seventh century) and the *Manoramā* by Kashmirian Bhāmaha (seventh-eighth century). Later important works of this school are the *Prākṛtakāmadhenu* or *Prākṛtalaṅkesvavararāvana* by Laṅkesvara, the *Prākṛtapāda*, as the last chapter of the *Saṃkṣiptasāra* of Kramadīsvara (twelfth-thirteenth century), the *Prākṛtasaṃjīvanī*, the commentary on the *Prākṛtaprakāsa* by Vasantarāja (fourteenth-fifteenth century), the *Prākrtānusāsana* by Puruṣottama (twelfth century) of Bengal, on which is based the *Prākṛtalakpataru* by Rāmasarmā Tarkavāgīsa (seventeenth century) of Bengal, which again was used by Mārkaṇḍeya (around the seventeenth century) of Orissa. The western school is also called the school of Vālmīki. The *Vālmīki Sūtras* are lost in their original and are only presented in an extended late version. Besides Hemacandra's *Siddhahemasabdānusāsana*, other important works of this school are the *Prākṛtasabdānusāsana* of Trivikrama (thirteenth century), who uses the terminology of the *Vālmīki Sūtras*, the *Prākṛtarūpāvatara* of Siṃharāja (fifteenth century), the *Prākṛtamaṇidīpa* of Appayadīkṣita (sixteenth-seventeenth century) and the *Saḍbhāsācandrikā* of Lakṣmīdhara (sixteenth century), who has followed Trivikrama's commentary on his *Prākṛtasabdānusāsana*.

It is significant that the eastern and the western schools of Prakrit grammar differ from each other in many respects. The *gaṇas* of each school rarely agree and their accounts of Paisācī Prakrit are mutually inconsistent. Besides, the eastern school lists numerous major and minor Prakrit dialects, which are wanting in the grammar of the western school. Vararuci, the earliest Prakrit grammarian, in his *Prākṛtaprakāsa* deals with Mahārāṣṭrī, Paisācī, Māgadhī and Śaurasenī as four major Prakrit dialects. He does not expressly mention Mahārāṣṭrī by name until शेषं महाराष्ट्रीवत् XII. 32, which happens to be the last *Sūtra* of the last chapter of his work. This chapter is conspicuous by its absence in Bhāmaha's commentary, Manoramā. Then, Caṇḍa in his *Prākṛtalakṣaṇa* mentions Mahārāṣṭrī as the main dialect and among others he speaks of Apabhraṃśa, Paisācikā, Māgadhikā, Ārṣa and Śaurasenī. He also covers Ardhamāgadhī, Jain Māgadhī and Jain Śaurasenī. Hemacandra (twelfth century) in the eighth chapter of his *Siddhahema* deals with seven dialects, Prakrit (equivalent to Mahārāṣṭrī), Ārṣa, Māgadhī, Śaurasenī, Paisācī, Cūlikā Paisācī and Apabhraṃśa. Hemacandra is followed by Trivikrama, Simharāja, Narasiṃha (his work is the *Prākṛtasabdadīpikā*) and Laksmīdhara, with the difference that Trivikrama excludes Ārṣa, whereas Siṃharāja, Narasiṃha and Lakṣmīdhara take no notice of it. Like Hemacandra's *Siddhahema*, Kramadisvara composed the *Saṃkṣiptasāra*, a work on Sanskrit grammar; in the eighth chapter of this work, he gives a brief treatment to Prakrit as indicated. He mainly deals with Mahārāṣṭrī and Apabhraṃśa. He also recognizes Māgadhī, Paisācikā , Ardhamāgadhī and Sābarī as other dialects. He refers to three main varieties of Apabhraṃśa, i.e. Nāgara, Upanāgara and Vrācaṭa.

Puruṣottama, Rāmasarmā and Mārkaṇḍeya, the followers of the eastern school, also have the same view. Mārkaṇḍeya along with Puruṣottama and Rāmasarmā divides Prakrit into Bhāṣā, Vibhāṣā, Apabhraṃsa and Paisācikā. They deal with Mahārāṣṭrī, Śaurasenī, Prācyā, Āvantī and Māgadhī under Bhāṣā; both reject Ardhamāgadhī, calling it a form of Māgadhī which is not distant from Śaurasenī. Vālhīkī is a form of Āvantī according to both. Like Ardhamāgadhī, Dākṣiṇātyā is also not considered a separate dialect by Mārkaṇḍeya. Under Vibhāṣā, he includes Sākārī, Cāṇḍālī, Sābarī, Ābhīrī and Ṭakkī. He denies the status of Vibhāṣā to Oḍrī and Drāviḍī. The Ṭakkī is considered as mixing of Sanskrit and Śaurasenī; according to Mārkaṇḍeya and Rāmasarmā, it has been influenced by Drāviḍī, the latter considered a form of Māgadhī. Since this dialect has very few illustrations, the grammarians have found it difficult to ascertain its characteristics. According to Mārkaṇḍeya, Oḍrī and Sābarī are one and the same dialect. Further, Vararuci does not mention Apabhraṃśa at all—he does not consider it to be Prakrit. Nami Sādhu mentions three languages: Prakrit, Sanskrit and Apabhraṃśa. Daṇḍī also mentions Apabhraṃśa under which are included the languages of groups like the Ābhīras.

As Prakrit was a dead language when the Prakrit grammars were written, the authors are often mutually inconsistent and sometime unable to point out the actual difference between two dialects. While explaining the rules of grammar, Hemacandra, Trivikrama and others have used the expressions such as 'often', 'sometimes', 'occasionally', 'generally', 'at times' (*prāyaḥ, bahula, kvacit, vā,* etc.) which indicates that the rules were not uniform. There is no uniformity of rules with regard to *ya-sruti,* use of *na* and *ṇa,* and *anusvāra* (the nasal sound which is marked by a dot above the line) and *anunāsika* (nasal uttered through the nose).

Ya-sruti is not accepted by Vararuci and his commentator Bhāmaha (2.2), whereas other commentators like Vasantarāja and Sadānanda reject it (*Prākṛtaprakāsa,* Benaras, 1927, pp. 44f). Caṇḍa in his *Prākṛtalakṣaṇa* (Calcutta, 1880, pp. 32, 51) prescribes it between *a* and *ā*. According to Hemacandra (*Siddhahema,* 8.1.180), when *ka, ga, ca, ja,* etc., are elided, the remaining *avarṇa,* viz., *a* or *ā* if preceded by *a* or *ā,* is pronounced like *ya* (e.g. *nagara=nayara*). Thus *ya-sruti* according to Hemacandra is possible only after *avarṇa,* but in the old manuscripts of the *Kalpasūtra* there is exception to the rule; here we have a variety of usages: *titthayara, āaana, caiṃ* (instead of *cayaṃ*).

Among the eastern grammarians, it is only Mārkaṇḍeya who refers to the phenomenon. According to him (*Prākṛtasarvasva* 2.2), non-initial *a* and *i* should be pronounced like *ya.*[22]

Regarding *ya-sruti,* A.M. Ghatge noted:

> The rules laid down by Hemacandra in this respect are neglected by the writers of the Mss and also by modern scholars while editing the works in Ardhamāgadhī, Jain Ardhamāgadhī, Jain Śaurasenī and Apabhraṃśa. It was only Pischel who tried to follow them in his edition of the *Desīnāmamālā,* by discarding the Mss evidence on the basis that the explicit teaching of a grammarian must be given due weight against the chaotic writings of the scribes. . . . This is regarded as a writing contention of the Jain scribes. In purely non-Jain works like the *Gahāsattasāi,* the *Rāvaṇavaho,* the *Gauḍavaho,* the *Līlāvaī* and other later works like the *Kaṃsavahi,* the *Usaṇiruddhaṃ* and some of the *Saṭṭakas* no *ya-sruti* is used. In the case of the *Gauḍavaho* when all the Mss come from Jain *Bhandaras* and use *ya* throughout, the new edition of Prof. Suru drops this *ya* in all cases, while others like Prof. Patwardhan and Dr. Upadhya continue to use it in non-Jain works when the Mss show it. The same holds good of a large number of Sanskrit dramas written by Jain and non-Jain writers. This practice is thus taken to be a writing method and is treated as such and no phonetic value is attached to it. Hence also the complete neglect of the restrictions imposed on it by Hemacandra. (Presidential Address, First National Prakrit Conference, Bangalore, 1990)

Vararuci (2.42) always prefers *ṇa* instead of *na.* Hemacandra (*Siddhahema,* 8.1.228-30) prescribes *ṇa* for *na* (e.g. *nayaṇa* for *nayana*), but he also gives *analao* where *na* is retained; also *ṇaro* as well as *naro; ṇhāvio* as well as *nāvio.* Further, while prescribing the rules for Paisācī dialect, Hemacandra (ibid., 8.4.306) prefers *na* for *ṇa* (*guna* for *guṇa*). Mārkaṇḍeya (*Prākṛta* 2.41-3) prescribes *ṇa* instead of *na* though the exceptions are no less.[23]

Hemacandra (8.1.23-26) has prescribed rules regarding *anusvāra,* but he mentions exceptions. Generally, in Apabhraṃsa, *anusvāra* is preferred for *anunāsika,* but as the use of Prakrits went on diminishing as living languages, we find the tendency of lengthening the short vowel with *anusvāra;* as there is a trend of using *anunāsika* or the sign of half moon (*ardhacandra* in Hindi.)

The grammarians prescribe various alternative forms for words, which again indicates that there was no uniformity in Prakrit languages. Hemacandra mentions twelve different forms of the word *bṛhaspati* (8.2.137); the Sanskrit word *iva* is rendered into *miva, piva, viva, vva va* and *via* (8.2.182); the Sanskrit root *kath* is replaced by ten substitutes in Prakrit (8.4.2) The *Vasudevahiṇḍi,* composed by

Saṅghadāsagaṇi Vācaka, contains numerous peculiar grammatical forms which go against the rules of grammar. The language of this important work is called archaic Jain Mahārāṣṭrī which is an important link between Ardhamāgadhī and Jain Mahārāṣṭrī. The language of the *Vasudevahiṇḍi* belongs to an early period when Jain Mahārāṣṭrī was forming a separate identity from Ardhamāgadhī. There are a few peculiar grammatical forms: (i) the first person singular of the present indicative ends in *aṃ* instead of *āmi* (*ahaṃ jāṇaṃ*, 174.26).[24] (ii) The first person singular optative form ends in *ijja* and *ejja* (*varamuhaṃ pāsijjaṃ*, 6, 18). (iii) The first person plural is often construed with *ahaṃ* (*ahaṃ dacchāmo*, 84.7). (iv) The first person plural of *ātmanepada* is construed with *ahaṃ*, the first person singular (*ahaṃ paḍicchāmahe*, 147, 18). (v) Until now it was taken for granted that the aorist forms have survived only in Ardhamāgadhī, but we notice them in archaic Jain Mahārāṣṭrī in the *Vasudevahiṇḍi* (*nahaṃ tubbhaṃ kuppissam*, 225.16-17; *kuppissaṃ* should not be taken here as future). (vi) Ablative singular masculine and neuter ending in *-aṃ* is a remarkable archaic form preserved here (*dukkhamaraṇaṃ*, 6, 13 instead of *dukkhamaraṇāt*). (vii) *ṇe* is used in accusative (121, 13), instrumental (233, 27) and genitive (43.3) cases. (viii) *bhe* is used in the nominative (99.26), accusative (118,4.8) and instrumental (101.4); elsewhere it is used in the genitive.[25]

Evaluating the rules of Prakrit grammar, Dinesh Chandra Sarkar observes in his *Grammar of the Prakrit Language* based mainly on Vararuci's *Prākṛtaprakāsa* that

> The earliest extant Prakrit grammar is *Prākṛtaprakāsa*. All other extant works were written when Prakrit was already a dead language. These later authors had no doubt traditions to help them; but the real authorities for their rules, so far as they added to the rules of old grammarians (many of whose works had been lost) were Prakrit works (then surviving) of authors who were long since dead. They formed their rules by an analysis of the forms contained in these works. The value of the rules of the later grammarians therefore depended largely on the manuscript material at their disposal, and it is not impossible that in some cases at least they have been misled by wrong readings in the manuscript.

According to Hemacandra (*Siddha.* 8.4.310), in Paisācī dialect *ya* in the word *hṛdaya* changes into *pa* altering it into *hitapaka*, but in the opinion of Sarkar, this seems to be a misreading.[26]

Major Dialects

Vararuci, the earliest Prakrit grammarian, deals with the four major dialects Mahārāṣṭrī, Paisācī, Māgadhī and Śaurasenī; he does not expressly mention Mahārāṣṭrī by name. Bharata in his *Nāṭyaśāstra* (XVII.48) mentions seven Prakrit dialects: Māgadhī, Āvantījā, Prācyā, Śaurasenī, Ardhamāgadhī, Vālhīkī and Dākṣinātyā. There is no mention of Maharashtri, but as Ghatge has rightly pointed out, Bharata's treatment of Prakrit in general is nothing but a brief summary of what the later grammarians have given. Here he has simply stated that seven dialects in addition to seven more were used in the dramas. Like the first nine chapters of Vararuci's *Prākṛtaprakāsa* and the first three *Pādas* of Hemacandra's *Siddhahema*, Chapter 17 of the *Nāṭyaśāstra* deals with the same language, whether it is called by the generic term Prakrit or designated by a specific name Mahārāṣṭri.[27] Then Caṇḍa in his *Prākṛtalakṣaṇa* mentions Mahārāṣṭrī as the main dialect together with Apabhraṃśa, Paisācikā, Māgadhikā, Ārṣa, and Śaurasenī. Hemacandra deals with seven Prakrit dialects where Prakrit is used as equivalent to Mahārāṣṭrī. He is followed by Trivikrama, Siṃharāja, Narasimha, Lakṣmīdhara and Appayadikṣīta. Kramadisvara mainly deals with Mahārāṣṭrī and Apabhraṃśa, as pointed out earlier. Puruṣottama, Rāmasarmā Tarkavāgīsa and Mārkaṇḍeya, all belonging to the eastern School, have identical views. They divide Prakrit into Bhāṣā, Vibhāṣā, Apabhraṃśa and Paisācikā as mentioned earlier. Rājsekhara (around AD 900) in his *Kāvyamīmāṃsā* (II, p. 6) has provided curious details about the popularity of certain languages in different parts of India.

> The Magadhas and others east of Benaras are blunt in Prakrit and good at Sanskrit, but the Gauḍas are thoroughly bad in Prakrit, the Lāṭas dislike Sanskrit but recite Prakrit poetry beautifully, the Surāṣṭras and Travaṇas mix Apabhraṃśa with Sanskrit, the Draviḍas recite musically, the Kashmirians pronunciation is as bad as their poetry is good, the Karnāṭas end up sentences with a twang, the northerners are nasal and the people of Pañcāla sweet and honey-like.

Here are some details about the dialects.

ARDHAMĀGADHĪ (LITERATURE: 500 BC-AD 600)

According to tradition, the Śvetāmbara Jain canonical literature was revealed in Ardhamāgadhī, but unfortunately we have no source on the exact nature of this dialect. It has been stated in the *Sama* (34) that the revered Mahavira preached his religion in the Ardhamāgadhī dialect and that this dialect was understood by all, Āryans and the non-Āryans, human beings, quadrupeds, animals and birds.[28] According to the *Ācā Cū* (7), having compassion on children, the aged and the illiterate people, those with the feeling of equanimity for all beings, have preached in Ardhamāgadhī which should not be disclosed to others.[29]

Hemacandra on his part gives few clues to the linguistic nature of the dialect. Moreover, it was not possible for him to provide a correct analysis of the dialect which was preached by Mahavira as far back as about the fourth century BC. In his commentary on the *Siddhahema* (8.4.287), Hemacandra quotes an old saying that the *sūtras* of the sacred canon of the Jains were written in Ardhamāgadhī (पोराणमद्धभागहभासा निपयं हवइ सुत्तं). According to him, in Ardhamāgadhī nominative singular ends in *e* as in Māgadhī, but *r* and *s* are not changed to *l* and *s* respectively as is required by the following rule (i.e. 8.4.288), nor any other phonetic changes described later. It is to be noted that Hemacandra while dealing with Prakrit dialects, has not mentioned Ardhamāgadhī, nor has he described its rules in his Prakrit grammar. While recording the rules of Māgadhī he mentions in passing one or two rules of Ardhamāgadhī. Another important point to be noted in this connection is that Haribhadrasūri, an earlier Jain writer of the eighth century, has quoted a verse in his commentary on the *Dasa* (p. 203)[30] indicating that the language of the sacred canon was called Prakrit (and not Ardhamāgadhī). The term Ardhamāgadhī is interpreted by Jain authors differently. According to the author of the *Nisi Cūr* (11.36.18), the Ardhamāgadhī dialect was either the language of half of Magadha or it comprised the eighteen types of *desībhāṣā*.[31] In the opinion of Abhayadevasūri (eleventh century), the dialect contained some characteristics of Māgadhī and some of Prakrit.[32] Hemacandra has called this dialect by the name of Ārṣa (*Siddhahema*, 8.1.3).

Ārṣa, according to Hemacandra, is the speech of the sages (*ṛṣis*); it can be compared with the Brahmanic conception of Sanskrit which is considered the language of gods (*devabhāṣā*). Hemacandra holds that in the case of Ārṣa, all the rules of grammar are subject to exceptions,[33] and elsewhere (8.2.174) he states that the limitations recorded above do not hold good for Ārṣa, and that all types of forms are permissible. Like Ardhamāgadhī, Ārṣa also does not find mention in the major six dialects discussed by Hemacandra in his grammar. Although these dialects are considered identical, Hemacandra seems to differentiate between the two in certain respects. According to him, the common feature between Ārṣa, Ardhamāgadhī and Māgadhī dialects is that the nominative singular ends in *e* of *a* stems in masculine gender, and that is all. This rule, however, is not found applicable always in the Jain canonical texts. It is applicable in the canonical texts written in prose, whereas in metrical works it ends in *o* instead of *e*. Such grammatical peculiarities can be noticed only in ancient metrical works like the *Sūtrakṛtāṅga*, the *Uttarādhyayana* and the *Dasavaikālika.*[34] As already noticed, Trivikrama excludes Ārṣa from his list of Prakrit dialects, saying that 'like desya, Ārṣa also is of an independent origin (*rūdhatvāt*) and abides mostly by its own rules (*svatantratvāt ca bhūyasā*)'.[35] Nami Sādhu commenting on Rudraṭa's *Kāvyālaṅkāra* (2.12) has stated that Ardhamāgadhī is the language of gods (*ārisavayaṇe*).[36]

As it has been stated, the Prakrit dialect changed from region to region. It was called Ardhamāgadhī or Māgadhī by the people of Magadha, Śaurasenī by the people of Sūrasena (the region of Mathura), Mahārāṣṭrī by the people of Mahārāṣṭra and so on. Being a dialect of the people, Ardhamāgadhī changed from time to time and region to region as Jain monks travelled from place to place preaching their religion. Magadha (south Bihar) was the centre of activities of Mahavira, but in course of time, due to natural calamities such as famine, the followers of Jainism migrated to the western and southern regions. Consequently, regional words and expressions became part and parcel of Jain teachings. This must have caused considerable change in the original language of the canonical text. As such, the rules framed for study by later grammarians could not be applicable to the ancient Jain canonical discourses preached by Mahavira. In course of time, a part of the canonical literature went into oblivion, and in order to ascertain the correct readings of the canonical texts, several councils of learned Jain monks were convened. The last was convened at Valabhi (Waḷā in Saurashtra) in the fifth century, about a thousand years after Mahavira's *nirvāṇa*, when a final form of the Jain canon with numerous variants was settled. But can we claim that the present canonical text really contains the original language of the teaching of Mahavira? Decidedly not. It is not even possible to ascertain the language in which the final verdict was pronounced to the text in the fifth century. Under the circumstances, Hemacandra cannot be considered an authority with regard to the grammatical rules of the existing text which was finally shaped 700 years before his time. Therefore it is not the fault of Hemacandra that he has not explained the rules of Ardhamāgadhī in his grammar to our satisfaction. It has been already pointed out that Jain authors differ from each other while explaining the meaning of 'Ardhamāgadhī'. It seems that at the time of Vararuci Ardhamāgadhī had lost its prominence as he did not recognize this dialect in his grammar.

Ardhamāgadhī in the Nāṭyaśāstra

Bharata in his *Nāṭyaśāstra* has mentioned Māgadhī, Āvantījā, Prācyā, Śaurasenī, Ardhamāgadhī, Vālhīkā and Dākṣiṇātyā as the main dialects (XVII.48) under Bhāṣā. It is said that Ardhamāgadhī should be spoken by menials, princes and leaders of bankers' guilds (*sreṣṭhi*), but it is to be noted that no extant Sanskrit drama seems to illustrate this rule. For example, Candanādasa, who acts as a *sreṣṭhi* in the *Mudrārākṣasa* of Visākhadatta, does not speak Ardhamāgadhī. In the *Karṇabhāra* ascribed to Bhāsa, Indra in the disguise of a Brāhmaṇa, speaks this dialect.[37] Keith also informs us that with the exception of Asvaghoṣa's dramas and Bhāsa's *Karṇabhāra*, Ardhamāgadhī is not used in extant Sanskrit drama.[38] Therefore it seems that the dialect of Ardhamāgadhī ceased to be employed in later Sanskrit plays, Śaurasenī taking its place. In the fourteenth century the rhetorician Visvanātha in his *Sāhityadarpaṇa* (17.50) mentions Ardhamāgadhī, speaking of the application of this dialect in a play, but it is only a copy of Bharata. Thus we see that Ardhamāgadhī remained only in name and was no more used in Sanskrit theatre. Mārkaṇḍeya, as we have seen, rejects Ardhamāgadhī as an independent dialect beside Māgadhī, Mahārāṣṭrī, Śaurasenī and others. While dealing with the characteristics of Māgadhī, he recognizes Māgadhī itself as Ardhamāgadhī, as it is not far away from Śaurasenī.[39] According to Kramadīsvara, the dialect of Ardhamāgadhī is considered the mixture of Mahārāṣṭrī and Māgadhī[40] and not an independent dialect. And Trivikrama, who follows Hemacandra in his classification of the Prakrit dialects, mentions Ārṣa (Ārdhamāgadhī) but does not like his predecessor provide us with its rules.

Thus we see that though Ardhamāgadhī formed the dialect of the Śvetāmbara Jain canonical literature supposedly based on the teachings of Mahavira, it had in course of a period of more than two thousand years, lost its real form, and the later grammarians were obliged to explain its rules without actually knowing the original text. It is significant that the Ardhamāgadhī of the Jain Canon is different from the Ardhamāgadhī dialect employed in the Sanskrit drama mentioned by Bharata Muni in his *Nāṭyaśāstra.* We have seen that Ardhamāgadhī of Jains went on changing from time to time as a result of which, in course of time, it got mixed up with other dialects such as Śaurasenī, Mahārāṣṭrī and Māgadhī and was therefore called a mixed Prakrit. It has been also known as Ardha-prakrit, Ārṣa-Prakrit or Prācīna-Prakrit.

It is noteworthy that looking to the subject-matter, the grammatical forms and the metres, a portion of canonical literature, comprising the *Ācārāṅga,* the *Sūtrakrtāṅga,* the *Uttarādhyayana,* the portions of the *Dasavaikālika,* the old *Chedasūtra,* the *Āvasyaka* and the *Ṛṣibhāṣita,* belong to the earlier period. These *sutras* contain typical words, fixed phrases, conventional descriptions and stereotype terms which can be compared with the Pali canon of Buddhist literature.[41] Making a comparative study of Pali and Ardhamāgadhī, H. Jacobi in his introduction to the *Ācārāṅga* has given a short form of grammar. R. Pischel too has noticed some old forms of Ardhamāgadhī in his *Grammatik* (Art 6).

In summary the Ardhamāgadhī dialect was ceased to be employed in the later Sanskrit dramas. Some of the Prakrit grammarians have not considered it as an independent dialect but a mixture of dialects. The rules prescribed by Bharata in his *Nāṭyaśāstra* are not strictly adhered to in the later Sanskrit dramas. The fragments of *Sārīputra-prakaraṇa* (or *Sāradvatīputraprakaraṇa*) are important in this respect as they contain some of the oldest forms of Ardhamāgadhī, Śaurasenī and Māgadhī. In his *Prakrit Languages and their Contribution to Indian Culture* S.M. Katre has pointed out: 'One of the dialects found in the fragments of Aśvaghoṣa's plays is an older phase of Ardhamāgadhī, as current in the second century AD, and is more archaic than the language of the canon.'[42]

ŚAURASENĪ (LITERATURE: AD 100-1500)

As we have seen, about the second century AD new changes were taking place in Prakrit. The Mahārāṣṭrī Prakrit was being formed in the dominions of the Sātavāhanas in the south-west. Similarly, there was a rise of Māgadhī and Śaurasenī in the work of Bhāsa and Asvaghoṣa on the one hand, and Kālidāsa on the other. As Ardhamāgadhī was the dialect of Magadha, so was Śaurasenī of Sūrasena, the region around Mathurā, or Uttara Mathurā. The region of the Midland around the Gaṅgā-Jamuna doab was very rich and a centre of trade and commerce. Mathurā is known for the Māthurī version (*vācanā*) of the Śvetāmbara Jain Canon. In about 313-300 BC, eight hundred years after Mahavira's *nirvāṇa*, a council of Jain teachers and preceptors was held here to set the canonical texts in order. The Jain inscriptions discovered here in the Kaṅkālī Ṭīlā belong to the reign of Kaniṣka and his successor proving that the Jain community flourished here in the first century AD. It is to be noted that these inscriptions bear the names of the patriarchs belonging to particular *gaṇa* (school), *kula* (family and *sākhā* (branch), coinciding with the list provided by the *Kalpasūtra* of Bhadrabāhu. The mention of a jewelled *stupa* has been made in both Śvetāmbara and Digambara texts. Mathurā had been a centre of activities of Digambara Jains too. Jambusvāmī, the last *kevalin,* is said to have achieved salvation here. Devasenasūri in his *Darsanasāra* has referred to the Mathurā *saṅgha* which is said to have been propounded in Mathurā by Rāmasena around AD 1000. As the language of the Śvetāmbara canonical literature is known as Ardhamāgadhī, so the language of the existing canonical literature of the Digambaras is known as Śaurasenī. Like Ardhamāgadhī, Śaurasenī has also originated from the Old Indo-Āryan languages and is an important phase in the development of Middle Indo-Āryan from the point of view of phonetics. The difference between Ardhamāgadhī of the Śvetāmbara canonical literature and Śaurasenī of the Digambara canonical literature is that in the former there is no uniformity of forms of the language, whereas the latter has complete uniformity. Śaurasenī unlike other Prakrits has very little influence of *desī* elements and has been greatly influenced by Sanskrit and Ardhamāgadhī. Looking to the contents, style and language, the Ardhamāgadhī text of the Śvetāmbaras speaks of more antiquity than the Śaurasenī text of the Digambaras.

Śaurasenī in Sanskrit Drama

Bharata in his *Nāṭyaśāstra* (XVII.48) includes Śaurasenī as one of the seven dialects (*bhāṣā*) but the Mahārāṣṭrī dialect is not mentioned here. Among the Prakrit dialects that are used in the prose of

Sanskrit dramas, Śaurasenī occupies a prominent place. According to the author, this dialect of the dramas should be based on the dialect spoken in the region of Sūrasena. The dialect is prescribed for the use of heroines, their lady friends, their maid-servants and generally noble ladies and middle-class people (XVII.51). We have mentioned the midland that in course of time had turned to be a centre of Āryan civilization. It is considered an important place for the origin of Sanskrit drama. In order to make their plays popular the dramatists employed local dialects to suit the social position of the speaker. And the midland dialect Śaurasenī was thought the most fit vehicle of speech for those cultured people who did not speak Sanskrit.

Śaurasenī was normally the prose Prakrit, though it appears to have been occasionally used in verse. It is more closely related to Sanskrit than Mahārāṣṭrī, especially with regard to its morphology, syntax and vocabulary. Hence it has been employed for persons of good position in the drama. Śaurasenī and other Prakrit passages in Aśvaghoṣa's work are older than the Śaurasenī and other dialects employed in later classical Sanskrit dramas. The forms of Prakrit dialects employed are decidedly older than the dialects of later Prakrit grammarians. Scholars are of the opinion that the use of Śaurasenī and other Prakrits on the stage arose at a time when Sanskrit could mostly be understood by the speakers of Prakrit.[43] This view is supported by Vararuci who considers Sanskrit as the basis of Śaurasenī (*Prākṛtaprakāsa*, 12.2).

Pracyā and Āvanti, a Variety of Śaurasenī

Of the seven major dialects only Māgadhī, Śaurasenī and Ardhamāgadhī are well known, whereas old and authentic descriptions of the rest are non-existent. Let us consider the dialects of Prācyā and Āvantī. In the *Nāṭyaśāstra* (XVII.51) Śaurasenī is ascribed to heroines and their friends and Prācyā (the eastern dialect) to *vidūṣaka* (jester). According to Pṛthvīdhara, the commentator of Śūdraka's *Mṛcchakaṭika*, the *vidūṣaka* speaks Prācyā which shows that he follows the dictate of the *Nāṭyaśāstra*. The Āvantī dialect is ascribed to *dhūrtas* (crooks) and according to Pṛthvīdhara, two police officers, Viraka and Candanaka, speak this dialect in the *Mṛcchakaṭika*. However, according to the latter's own admission, he was a man of Karnātaka and not of Ujjain. As has been pointed out earlier, no authentic account of Prācyā and Āvantī is available in

Prakrit grammars, though Mārkaṇḍeya in the 9th, 10th and the 11th *pāda* of his *Prakṛta* deals with Śaurasenī, Prācyā and Āvantī respectively. Comparative study of the dialects spoken by different characters, does not indicate significant differences between these dialects and Śaurasenī. Mārkaṇḍeya says that this dialect is marked by sentences contradicting each other, indirect speech (*chekokti*), vulgar speech (*grāmyokti*) and speech of similarity (*upamokti*).[44]

No significant difference is noticed in these characteristics of Prācyā and that of Śaurasenī spoken by the *vidūsaka*. Thus we see that Prācyā is a mere variety of Śaurasenī, though in the *Nāṭyaśāstra* both are mentioned separately. The Āvantī dialect, like Prācyā, has not been accepted as a separate *bhāṣā*. The commentator Pṛthvīdhara has mentioned Śaurasenī, Avantīja and Prācyā together as having common characteristics. Avantīja is ascribed to *dhūrtas*, or dice-players. Most of the characteristic features found in the *Prākṛta* of Mārkaṇḍeya tally with those provided by Rāmasarmā Tarkavāgīsa in his *Prākṛtakalpataru*, and Puruṣottama in his *Prākṛtānusāsana*. The rules prescribed by Mārkaṇḍeya bear closer resemblance with Rāmasarmā Tarkavāgīsa than with Puruṣottama. Following Puruṣottama's *Prākṛtānusāsana* (11.1), Mārkaṇḍeya in his *Prākṛta-sarvasva* has defined Avantijā as the admixture of Mahārāṣṭrī and Śaurasenī.[45] Mārkaṇḍeya does not admit the independent existence of Dākṣiṇātyā or Bālhikī. It is to be noted that like Prācyā and Āvantī, the authentic illustrations of Dākṣiṇātyā and Bālhikī are also absent from the works of Prakrit grammarians. The *Nāṭyaśāstra* (XVII.50-2) has prescribed Dākṣiṇātyā for the use of soldiers (*yodha*), police-officers (*nāgaraka*) and gamblers (*dīvyanta*) and there are slight traces of the dialect in the *Mṛcchakaṭika*. Bālhikī is assigned to the Khasas who belong to the north by the *Nāṭyaśāstra* but this has not yet been traced in any drama. Ṭakkī which is mentioned by Puruṣottama along with Sākārī, Cāṇḍālī and Sābarī as *vibhāṣā*, is called a mixture of Sanskrit and Śaurasenī in his *Prākṛtānusāsana* (16.1) and also by Mārkaṇḍeya in his *Prākṛta* (16.1). Puruṣottama and Mārkaṇḍeya tell us that according to Hariscandra, Ṭakkī is to be taken as an Apabhraṃśa and not a *vibhāṣā*. Thus we see that like Āvantī and Prācyā, so too Dākṣiṇātyā, Bālhīkī and Ṭakkī had no independent existence but were considered as a variety of Śaurasenī, spoken in different regions.

Vararuci, who maintains that Sanskrit is the basis of Śaurasenī, deals with the rules of this dialect in the twelfth chapter of his

Prākṛtaprakāsa; this chapter has not been commented on by Bhamaha.[46] In this work the author has provided 29 rules of Śaurasenī and in the last *sūtra* he remarks that in other respects it agrees with Mahārāṣṭrī. Hemacandra, after dealing with Ārṣa Prakrit, describes the characteristics of Śaurasenī and then deals with Māgadhī and Paisācī. In some respects Hemacandra and Vararuci differ strongly from one another. Explaining the reason, Pischel has observed that 'Hemacandra has taken into consideration also the Śaurasenī of the Digambaras, the peculiarities of which the Jains have carried over to Śaurasenī of the dramas with the result that the Śaurasenī texts of the latter have become corrupt and later writers have been misled'.

Among the Prakrit dialects that are used in the prose of Sanskrit drama, Śaurasenī occupies the first place. As employed in Aṣvaghoṣa's dramas it is older than the Śaurasenī of the other Sanskrit dramas. The grammatical and literary forms of this and other Prakrit dialects employed here are considered significant from the linguistic point of view as the transformation of the dialects that was taking place in those days can be compared with Pali and the Prakrits of the earliest inscriptions. The dialects used in the plays of Bhāsa are normally Śaurasenī and Māgadhī; the former is found in all his plays, except the *Dūtavākya* which has no Prakrit.[47] In the plays of Kālidāsa, generally, Śaurasenī is used for prose and Mahārāṣṭrī for verse. Sūdraka's *Mṛcchakaṭika* is known for its variety of Prakrit dialects. It seems the author has tried to illustrate the precepts as laid down in the *Nāṭyaśāstra.* Here Śaurasenī is assigned to the *sutradhāra,* to Naṭī, Vasantasenā, her maid-servant Madanikā, her slave Karṇapūraka, her mother, the wife of Cārudatta, his maid-servant Radanikā, bailiff of the court Sodhanaka and the *sreṣṭhī* or the guildsman.

The Prakrit grammarians indicate that one of the noted rules of Śaurasenī is the use of *da* and *dha* in lieu of *ta* and *tha* respectively. But this cannot be taken as a peculiarity of the dialect as pointed out by Jacobi and other scholars. This rule is not relevant in the elementary stages of transformation of Śaurasenī. It is not applicable in the old dialect of Śaurasenī used in the plays of Aśvaghoṣa. In the plays of Bhāsa, we have the form Sīā in lieu of Sīdā as per rules. Similarly, in ancient works of the Digambaras, we have *aisaya* in place of *adisaya.* There are several other rules prescribed by grammarians which have no uniformity of application in dramatic works and the works of Digambara Jains composed in Śaurasenī. Even in the rule of *ktvā* changing into *dūṇa* no uniformity is noticed. Hemacandra allows the

Śaurasenī forms in the absolutive in *-ttā* and *dūṇa* and such other forms which are not noticed in Śaurasenī of Sanskrit dramas. Similarly, the forms *muṇadi* and *muṇedavvo* are unknown in Śaurasenī.[48] At times we come across mutual contradictions in deciding to which dialect the characteristic of a particular word belongs. For example, Mārkaṇḍeya does not believe that the word *laṭṭhi* is Śaurasenī, whereas Hemacandra does. Coming to Rājasekhara, we notice a decline of Sanskrit drama, and he was not able to distinguish correctly his Prakrits.

MAHĀRĀṢṬRĪ (LITERATURE: AD 100-1500)

Mahārāṣṭrī is one of the important Prakrit dialects employed in the non-canonical works of the Śvetāmbaras, in Jain narrative literature, lyrical poetical works like the *Gāhāsattasaī*, Sanskrit drama and so on. The celebrated poet Daṇḍin (sixth century) in his *Kāvyādarṣa* (1, 34) has called it the best Prakrit (*prakṛṣṭaṃ prākrtaṃ*). According to him, its place of origin is Mahārāṣṭra. It is a jewel-mine of beautiful sayings and the *Setubandha* and other literary works are composed in this dialect.[49] This indicates that the Mahārāṣṭrī dialect gained such a popularity that it was identified with Prakrit in general. Vararuci in his *Prākṛtaprakāsa* has devoted nine chapters out of twelve to the discussion of general Prakrit (or the Mahārāṣṭrī dialect), and only one each to the remaining three dialects, Paisācī, Māgadhī and Śaurasenī. Another grammarian, Caṇḍa, in his *Prākrtalakṣaṇa* has dealt with general Prakrit in 99 *sūtras* in three chapters, and the remaining dialects, Apabhraṃsa, Paisācī, Māgadhī and Śaurasenī each in just in one *sūtra* in the following chapter. Hemacandra in his *Siddhahema*, Subhacandra in his *Cintāmaṇivyākaraṇa* and Srutasāgara in his *Audāryacintāmaṇi* discuss only Prakrit. Puruṣottama in his *Prākṛtanūsāsana* talks of Prakrit in general. Lakṣmīdhara following Hemcandra has treated Prakrit along with Śaurasenī, Māgadhī, Paisācī, Cūlikka Paisācī and Apabhraṃsa. He has assigned Prakrit to women and the lower classes in his commentary. The authors of the *Gāhāsattasaī* and the *Gauḍavaho* assert that their compositions are written in Prakrit, though their dialect is Mahārāṣṭrī. Rājasekhara says the dialect of his drama *Bālarāmāyaṇa* (1.10) is Prakrit. This shows that being employed in lyrical Prakrit poetry, due to its tenderness of feelings, love and charm, the Mahārāṣṭrī dialect became so esteemed and approved that it was known as Prakrit in general. Pointing out the distinguished features of Mahārāṣṭrī,

Pischel has remarked: 'No other dialect has been phonetically modified to such an extent for artificial purposes. The dropping of consonants had, in Mahārāṣṭrī so extensive as has been seen nowhere else, therefore a large number of words that were phonetically quite different, have assumed the same form: *kaa=kaca, kṛta; kai=kati, kapi, kavi, kṛti; kāa=kāka, kāca, kāya; gaā=gatā, gadā, gajā; maa=mata, mada, maya, mrga, mṛta; vaa=vacas, vayas, vrata; sua=suka, suta, sruta* and so on.'[50]

Jain Mahārāṣṭrī

Since the Ardhamāgadhī dialect contained in the existing Śvetāmbara Jain canonical literature is strongly influenced by the later south-western speech and the later texts are written in this speech, it is called Jain Mahārāṣṭrī. The prose and poetry dialect of ancient Śvetāmbara Jain scriptures, is Ardhamāgadhī, and the later works, including the commentary literature of the works and the ancient story and biographical literature, composed in Prakrit, come generally under the category of Jain Mahārāṣṭrī. It is noteworthy that the language of the *Vasudevahiṇḍi*, is called 'Archaic Jaina Mahārāṣṭrī' by L. Alsdorf. Criticizing Pischel and Jacobi, Alsdorf has pointed out that the language of the *VH* belongs to the early period when Jain Mahārāṣṭrī was forming a separate identity, different from Ardhamāgadhī. The influence of Ardhamāgadhī here is noticed in the form of the stock words, phrases and typical expressions contained in the Śvetāmbara Jain canonical literature.[51]

Pro-canonical literature of the Śvetāmbara Jains, composed in Mahārāṣṭrī (or Jain Mahārāṣṭrī) Prakrit, is very rich and available in the form of *Niryukti, Bhāṣya, Cūrṇi, Ṭīkā* and independent story literature. This covers a period from the fourth to the seventeenth century. This literature is a storehouse of popular folktales, centring around the life of common people such as farmers, manual workers, slaves, thieves, swindlers, prostitutes, traders, seafaring merchants and so on. Various Jain works composed in this dialect are available.[52]

Mahārāṣṭrī and Śaurasenī

Mahārāṣṭrī is not known to the *Nāṭyaśāstra* of Bharata. There is no evidence of the use of this dialect in the old plays of Aśvaghoṣa and Bhāsā. So too the *Mṛcchakaṭika* of Sūdraka of about the fifth century, which illustrates the dialects mentioned in the *Nāṭyaśāstra*, does not assign Mahārāṣṭrī speech to any of its characters. Most probably it was introduced in Sanskrit drama by Kālidāsa, influenced by the musical charm of lyric poetry of Hāla in the second century. It was then that Mahārāṣṭrī became important as the dialect of Sanskrit drama and of epic poetry. It was employed in lyrics to make the poetic expression effective and forceful. On account of its mellifluous sounds it was utilized as the dialect par excellence for songs by those who employed Śaurasenī or some ordinary speech. The dialect dropped intervocalic consonants, it softened surds to sonants, it reduced aspirates to *ha*, changed *ya* into *ja*, substituted *ṇa* for *na* and simplified the double consonants with compensatory lengthening, thus making the Mahārāṣṭrī lyric popular.

Mahārāṣṭrī and Śaurasenī were spoken in different regions and are hence different. But once established as literary dialects, they lost contact with the dialect spoken by the people. Under the circumstances, the grammarians tried to formulate rules of these dialects and bring them under the control of grammar. Consequently, in absence of definite rules of grammar and manifoldness of usages of the dialects, the rules applicable to one dialect began to be applied to another. Vararuci in his *Prākṛtaprakāsa* (2.2; 2.25) and Hemacandra in his *Siddhahema* (8.1.177; 8.1.187) have mentioned the common characteristics of Mahārāṣṭrī and Śaurasenī, which shows that at the time of Hemacandra a number of rules applicable to Śaurasenī were also considered applicable to Mahārāṣṭrī.[53] Yet it may be noted that the above-mentioned rules are not noticed in the unpublished manuscripts. Some modern scholars have made an attempt to follow these rules word by word but that has led to more harm than gain.

Karpūramañjarī was composed by Rājasekhara only in the Śaurasenī dialect. But Sten Konow in his critical edition of the text holds that this work was composed in two dialects of Prakrit, Śaurasenī and Mahārāṣṭrī, the former used for prose and the latter for verse. Accordingly, and in accordance with the rules laid down by grammarians, he introduced certain changes in the original text. Manmohan Ghosh, the editor of the *Karpūramañjarī* (Calcutta, 1939) does not agree with these alterations. Ghosh considers Śaurasenī as the Prakrit par excellence and what is known as Mahārāṣṭrī as its later phase, developing under the influence of the Prakrit grammarians. His argument is that Hemacandra and many others do not mention the name Mahārāṣṭrī, and the twelfth chapter of Vararuci, in which the word Mahārāṣṭrī occurs only at the end, is a spurious later interpolation. But this does not seem to be feasible, as we have seen before. Hemacandra regarded the Prakrit of Vararuci's grammar to be Mahārāṣṭrī. Ghatge has rightly pointed out that many of the rules of the first nine chapters of Vararuci, treating of Śaurasenī, are worked out by Hemacandra and others to compose their Prakrit grammars and are made to serve the purpose of Mahārāṣṭrī. P.V. Kane too does not agree with the view of M.M. Ghosh holding that no Prakrit called Mahārāṣṭrī existed before the tenth century and that Daṇḍin's praise of Mahārāṣṭrī was a patriotic exaggeration. Kane points out that Daṇḍin's native place was Kāñcī and not Mahārāṣṭra.

PAISĀCĪ

Paisācī is one of the archaic dialects of Prakrit Māgadhī and the inscriptional Prakrit, which is estimated along with Pali, Ardhā. The eastern and western grammarians differ in their accounts of this dialect. The eastern school has its own Paisācī with several dialects and forms of speech, whereas in the western school Cūlikā Paisācī is mentioned, which is of an insignificant variety. Seven different varieties of this dialect are mentioned by the eastern school, none of which agrees with any of those described by the western school.[54] Vararuci, the earliest known Prakrit grammarian of the eastern school, who refers to Prakrit, Paisācī, Māgadhī and Śaurasenī as main Prakrits, devotes the tenth chapter of his work to the treatment of Paisācī. Rudraṭa has mentioned Paisācī along with Prakrit, Sanskrit, Māgadhī, Śaurasenī and Apabhraṃśa in his *Kāvyālaṅkāra* (2.12). Nami Sadhu, commenting on the above, has called it *Paisācīka.* Hemacandra, the earliest known grammarian of the western school, deals with Paisācī in his *Siddhahena* (8.4.303-24) and the Cūlikā Paisācī (325-8) is appended to it. Trivikrama in his *Prākṛta-sabdā-nusāsana* (3.2.43) and Simharaja in his *Prākṛtarūpāvātāra* (20) have dealt with this dialect. Lakṣmīdhara in his *Ṣaḍbhāṣācandriā* has dealt with Prākṛit (Mahārāṣṭrī), Śaurasenī, Māgadhī, Paisācī, Cūlikā Paisācī and Apabhraṃsa, and according to him (verse 35), Paisācī and Cūlikā Paisācī are assigned to Rākṣasas, Pisācās and other lowly persons. He considers Pāṇḍya, Kekaya, Vāhlīka, Sahya, Nepāla, Kuntala, Sudheṣṇa, Bhoja, Gāndhāra, Naiva and Kannoujana (verses 29-30) as Pisāca countries. This list indicates that the dialect was spoken in the north-western region of India. Puruṣottama, the follower of the eastern school, has divided Prakrit into Bhāṣā, Vibhāṣā, Apabhraṃsa and Pisāca in his *Prākṛtanusāsana.* He divides Pisāca into Kaikeya-Paisācīka and Śauraseni-Paisācīka. Rāmasarmā Tarkavāgīsa of the same school has described Kaikeya, Saurasena, Pāñcāla, Gauḍa, Māgadha and Vrācada Paisācīka in his *Prākṛtakalpataru* (3.3). Then Mārkaṇḍeya in his *Prākṛta* refers to eleven types of Paisācī, Kāñcīdesiyā, Paṇḍya, Pāñcāla, Gauḍa, Mādhava, Vrācaḍa, Dākṣiṇātya, Saurasena, Kaikaya, Sābara and Drāviḍa, as held by an unknown author; but himself admits only three types, Kaikaya, Saurasena and Pāñcāla as real, because they alone were used as literary dialects.

Rājasekhara in his *Kāvyamīmāmsa,* calls Sanskrit, Prakrit, Apabhraṃśa and Pisāca the mouth, arms, buttocks and the feet of a man respectively. According to the *Dasarūpaka* (2.60) of *Dhanañjaya,* Pisāca or Māgadhī language is especially spoken by the Pisācas, people of lowly origin. The *Sarasvatīkanthābharaṇa* (57.25) forbids the use of pure Paisācī by high class people. The *Baḍḍakahā* or *Bṛhatkathā* of Guṇāḍhya is said to be the earliest work which was composed in the Paisācī dialect. Unfortunately, it is no more extant. Daṇḍin is the first author to mention the *Bṛhatkathā,* praising its literary qualities and declaring it to have been a work 'full of wonderful meaning' (*adbhutārtha*). This Paisācī dialect of the *Bṛhatkathā* is called *bhūtabhāṣā* by Daṇḍin in his *Kāvyādarṣa* (1.38). It is termed a *bhūtabhāṣita* by Vagbhaṭa in his *Vāgbhaṭālaṅkāra* (2.1). In the existing literary works the Paisācī dialect is seldom used. As we have seen, the Prakrit grammarians have noted many varieties of the dialect but we do not find it actually employed anywhere except a work that is no more extant.

Udyotanasūri (eighth century) refers to Paisācī along with Sanskrit, Prakrit, Apabhraṃśa, Māgadhī, Rākṣasī and Misrabhāṣā.[55] A century later, another Jain author, Jayasiṃhasuri, cited illustrations from Sanskrit, Prakrit, Apabhraṃśa, Paisācī, Māgadhī and other dialects in the form of questions and answers in his *Dharmopadesamālāvivaraṇa.* Then Hemacandra in his *Kumāravālacariya,* also known as the *Dvyāsrayakāvya* has cited verses in Māgadhī, Paisācī, Cūlikā Paisācī and Apabhraṃśa. According to Keith, Paisācī is practically unknown in the extant Sanskrit dramas. Since Paisācī dialect is not known in existing works and yet has been treated by Prakrit grammarians, we have to be careful regarding its rules laid down by these grammarians.

MĀGADHĪ

Māgadhī which is related to Magadha, the centre of activities of Mahavira and Buddha, is an important dialect of Middle Indo-Āryan. According to Buddhaghoṣa, the renowned Buddhist commentator, Gautama Buddha delivered his sermons in Māgadhī. Pali, which is based on Māgadhī, is called Māgadhī-Bhāṣā, though linguistically it is a midland speech, connected with Śaurasenī. The earliest forms of this dialect are noticed in the Sutanukā inscription, contemporaneous with the Asokan documents. This third-century BC inscription in the Jogimara cave on the Ramgarh hill in Sarguja State, Chotanagpur (south-west of Magadha) is called the earliest specimen of Māgadhī.[56] Since the language of this inscription has *e* for *o*, *la* for *ra*, *kha* for *ksa*, and *śa* for *sa*, it is said to be the precursor of later Māgadhī.

The Māgadhī or eastern dialect was spoken in the extreme eastern frontier of the domain of the Āryans, is regarded as a prerunner of Ardhamāgadhī in the grammatical tradition. Pointing out its special characteristics, Keith writes in *The Sanskrit Drama*,

> It substitutes *la* for *ra*, reduces all three sibilants to *sa*, and has *e* in the nominative singular in *a*. . . . But it ignores the rules of the grammarians in certain matters: hard letters are not softened (e.g. *bhoti*), nor soft consonants elided (e.g. *komudagandha*) when intervocalic. There is no tendency to cerebralise *na* and in *kālanā* the dental replaces the cerebral. Fuller forms of consonants remain in *haṅgho* (*haṅho*) and *bambhaṇa* (*bamhaṇa*). The later forms of development of consonantal conjunctions are unknown, thus for *rya* we have *jja*, not *yya*, as in *ajja*; *ccha* remains in lieu of becoming *sca*; *kṣa* becomes *kha* not *ska* or *hka*; *ṣṭa* and *ṣṭha* give *ṭṭha* not *sṭa*. In *kissa* we have an older form than *kīsa*, in *ahakaṃ* than *ahake, hake, hage.* In practically all these details we must see the earlier stage of what becomes Māgadhī in the grammarians.

As we have already seen, Bharata Muni in his *Nāṭyaśāstra* (XVII.48) has mentioned seven major Prakrit dialects for use in Sanskrit theatre. He begins with Māgadhī, followed by Āvantī, Prācyā, Śaurasenī, Ardhamāgadhī, Vālhikā and Dākṣiṇātyā. Out of these, Māgadhī, Śaurasenī and Ardhamāgadhī are well-known stage dialects but no authentic contemporary description of the others is known. Like Śaurasenī, Māgadhī too has played an important role in Sanskrit dramas. Both of them gained so much prominence that the other dialects could not compete. Like the specimen of old Ardhamāgadhī we have a specimen of old Māgadhī in the fragments of the Buddhist drama of Aśvaghoṣa. It means that the dialects of old Māgadhī and old Ardhamāgadhī are different from the dialects of Māgadhī and Ardhamāgadhī used in orthodox classical Sanskrit dramas.

'Māgadhī was not a homogeneous dialect, on the other hand, a dialectically diversified dialect: This dialect has been transmitted to us in a worse condition than Śaurasenī.' To illustrate this statement, Pischel explains the development of *kṣa* sometimes as *hka*, and sometimes as *ska*; of *ṛtha* sometimes as *sta* and sometimes as *sta*; and of *ṣka* sometimes as *ska* and sometimes as *ska*. We are not told the exact form of this dialect. Though Māgadhī is said to be the speech of Buddha and the language of the sacred texts of the Buddhist canon, it differs from Māgadhī described by the later grammarians.

According to Keith, the regular change of *ra* to *la* and the use of the form *yeva* after a long vowel as in Māgadhī and Pali show that the old Ardhamāgadhī was more akin to Māgadhī than the later Ardhamāgadhī, which came stealthily under the influence of the western dialects as shown by the tendency to change *e* of the nominative to *o*. Then, as Māgadhī was much influenced by Śaurasenī, Vararuci, in his *Prākṛtaprakāsa* (11.2) considers Śaurasenī the basis of Māgadhī (*prakṛtiḥ Śaurasenī*). Hemacandra too states *Seṣaṃ Śaurasenīvat* (*Siddhahema* 8.4.302), i.e. that the other particular rules of Māgadhī follow the rules of Śaurasenī. Mārkaṇḍeya in his *Prākṛta* has supported this view.

Besides seven Prakrit dialects, which are included under the category of *bhāṣā*, Bharata Muni has mentioned seven *vibhāṣās*, i.e. Sākārī, Ābhīrī Cāṇḍālī, Sābarī, Drāviḍī, Auḍrī and Vanaukasī, which are known as minor dialects. Out of these Sākārī, Cāṇḍālī and Sābarī are included in the dialect of Māgadhī. Puruṣottama in his *Prākṛtānusāsana* (XIII-XV) has dealt with these dialects under Māgadhī. He considers Sākārī as a secondary dialect of Māgadhī; Cāṇḍālī as its corrupt form and Sābarī a type of Māgadhī. Mārkaṇḍeya too in his *Prākṛtasarvasva* (13.1) thinks Sākārī a form of Māgadhī. He considers Cāṇḍālī a mixture of Māgadhī and Śaurasenī (14.1) and Cāṇḍālī as the origin of Sābarī (15.1). Pṛthvīdhara, the commentator of the *Mṛcchakaṭika*, explaining the prominence of palatal *sa*, has described the similar characteristics of Māgadhī, Sākārī and Cāṇḍālī dialects (मागधी तालव्य शकारवती शाकारी चांडाल्योस्ता लव्यशकारता रेफस्य च लकारता).

Regarding the use of Māgadhī, there is a difference of opinion among the grammarians of eastern and western schools. According to the *Nāṭyaśāstra* (XVII.50, 55-6), Māgadhī is ascribed to those who live in the women's apartment, diggers of underground passages, keepers of liquor shops, watchers and is used in time of danger by the hero and also by the Sakāras. According to the *Dasarupaka* (2.65), it was spoken by the Pisācas and the low classes. In Sūdraka's *Mṛcchakaṭika*, Māgadhī is assigned to the monk Saṃvāhaka (a man whose business was to rub and knead joints, but who being defeated in gambling became a *sramaṇa*), Sthāvaraka, carriage driver of Sakāra, Kumbhīlaka, servant of Vasantasenā, Vardhamānaka, servant of Cārudatta, the *bhikṣu* and little Rohasena, the son of Cārudatta. In Kālidāsa's *Abhijñānasākuntala*, Māgadhī has been ascribed to the police officers, the fisherman and Sarvadamana, the younger son of Sakuntalā. In Visākhadatta's *Mudrārāksasa*, Māgadhī is spoken by a Jain monk, by Siddhārthaka and Samiddhārthaka the Cāṇḍālas, a servant and an envoy. In the *Veṇīsaṃhara* of Bhaṭṭanārāyaṇa there are no special features regarding the use of Prakrit and Sanskrit. Here at the beginning of Act III, Māgadhī is assigned to the Rāksasa and his wife. Mārkaṇḍeya has quoted the opinion of Kohala in his *Prākṛtasarvasva* (XII.1), according to which Māgadhī is spoken by Rākṣasas, *bhiksus*, *kṣapaṇakas*, servants and others.

NOTES

1. The Indo-European Origin of English, *The Heritage Illustrated Dictionary of the English Language*, International Edition, edited by William Morris, New York, 1975, p. x.
2. P.D. Gune, *An Introduction to Comparative Philology*, edited by N.P. Gune, Poona, 1962, p. 22.
3. Gune has pointed out the following causes of changes: imitation, analogy, accent and general conditions of culture, mixture of races, conquest and mixture of dialects, ibid., pp. 34-6.
4. Hundreds of Sanskrit words have disappeared due to great upheavals in civilization and migration of people. For Sanskrit words such as वेदी, दर्वी, आसंदी, होता, पुरीडाश and many others are no more found in later ages, ibid., p. 80.
5. Suniti Kumar Chatterji, *Indo-Āryan Hindi*, Ahmedabad, 1922, p. 8.
6. Ibid., p. 28.
7. Ibid., p. 55.
8. *Siddhahema* (1.1. Commentary). The same view about the origin of Prakrit is expressed by Dhanika in the Commentary of *Dasarūpaka* (II.65), Siṃhadevagaṇi in the *Vāgbhatālaṅkāra* (II.2), Narasiṃha in *Prākrtasabdapradīpikā* (p. 1), *Lakṣmīdhara* in the *Ṣaḍbhāṣācandrikā* (I.25),

Vāsudeva in the *Prākṛtamañjarī* (IX.11), Trivikrama in the *Prākṛta-sabdānusāsana* (I.8) and Mārkaṇḍeya in the *Prākṛtsarvasva* (Introduction to the first *Pāda*) see K.C. Acharya, *Mārkaṇḍeya's Prākṛtasarvasva*, PTS, Ahmedabad, 1968, p. 39.

9. प्राकृतेति। सकल जगज्जन्तूनां व्याकरणादिमिरनाहितसंस्कार: सहजो वचनव्यापार: प्रकृति:, तत्र भवं सैव वा प्राकृतम्। . . . वा प्राक् पूर्वं कृतं प्राक्कृतं वालमहिलादिसुबोधं सकलभाषानिबंध भूतं वचनमुच्यते। मेघनिर्मुक्त जलमिवैकस्वरूपं तदेव च देशविशेषात् संस्कारकरणाच्च समासादितविशेषं सत् संस्कृताद्युतरविभेदानाप्नोति। अतएव शास्त्रकृता प्राकृतमादौ निर्दिष्टं तदनु संस्कृतादीनि। पाणिन्यादिव्याकरणोदितशब्दलक्षणेम संस्करणात् संस्कृतमुच्यते। The view is supported by R. Pischel, Grammatik der Prakrit-Sprachen; English translation, *Comparative Grammar of Prakrit Language* by Subhadra Jha, 1957, Art. 16; also K.C. Acharya, *Mārkaṇḍeya's Prākṛtusarvasva*, p. 40.
10. सयलाओ इमं वाआ विसंति एत्थ य णेंति वायाओ।
एंति समुछं चिय णेंति सयल च्चिय जलाइं॥ 93
11. *A History of Sanskrit Literature*, London, 1928, p. 26.
12. D.C. Circar, *Grammar of the Prakrit Lạnguage.*
13. R. Pischel, *Grammatik*, Art. 6.
14. Keith has provided many such Prakrit words which form as genuine Sanskrit: विच्छित्ति (from विक्षिप्ति), गोविन्द (Prakrit form) for गोपेन्द्र, भदन्त (from the phrase भद्रंते), दुरुत्तर (for दुष्तर); मारिस (for मारिष), मसिण (for मृत्स्न), रुक्ख (for रुक्ष or वृक्ष), विध्यइ (from विज्झइ), विकुर्व (from विउव्व) and so on, *A History of Sanskrit Literature*, p. 24. Besides, there are various forms and words which are pre-Vedic: ळ, कज्जइ (कर्यति), बालत्तण (बालत्त्वन), गरु (गुरु), जोत्सना (ज्योत्स्ना), विकट (विकृत), परमे व्योमन् (परमे व्योम्नि), देवेहि (देवेभि:) and many others.
15. S.K. Chatterji, *Indo-Āryan Hindi*, p. 58; *The Origin and Development of Bengali Language*, p. 82.
16. *The Vedic Age*, Vol. I, Bharatiya Itihas Samiti, 1951, p. 335.
17. Devendra Kumar Banerji, 'The Origin of Sanskrit and Prakrits', *Commemorative Essays Presented to K.B. Pathak*, 1934, p. 327.
18. Also see Sukumar Sen, *A Comparative Grammar of Middle Indo-Āryan*, 1960, p. 2; Pischel, *Grammatik*, Art. 6.
19. Murlydhar Banerji, *The Desinamamala of Hemacandra*, p. xxix.
20. For details with regard to *desi* words and the *dhātvādesas*, see Chapter 8, under '*Desīnāmamālā*'.
21. See Sukumar Sen, *A Comparative Grammar of Middle Indo-Āryan*, pp. 1-3; S.K. Chatterji, *The Origin and Development of Bengali Language*, I, Introduction, p. 16; also *A Middle Indo-Āryan Reader*, in 2 pts., edited by Suniti Kumar Chatterji and Sukumar Sen.
22. D.C. Sirkar in his *Grammar of the Prakrit Language* (p. 5) states that when a consonant is elided, Mahārāṣṭrī usually retains the inherent *a* but Ardhamāgadhī makes it *ya*. This rule is repudiated not only by modern Marathi but also by inscriptions from the Maharashtra area; e.g. *nāga*=*nāya* (Nānaghāṭa), *rājā*=*rāyā* (Nānaghāṭa, Bāsim), etc.
23. Regarding the use of *na* and *ṇa* in Old Prakrit, see Dr. K.R. Chandra's

articles in *Prakrit-vidya*, Udaipur, July-September 1989, pp. 34-8 where he emphasizes the use of *na* in lieu of *ṇa* initially; also *Prakrit-vidya*, April-June 1990, pp. 34-46. It can be noted that as Ardhamāgadhī came under the influence of Mahārāṣṭrī, *na* was converted into *ṇa*, *i* into *ti*, *ya* into *ta* and so on. Under the circumstances, the linguistic considerations alone are not sufficient to determine the date of the Jain canonical texts.

24. Figures refer to the page and the line respectively of the printed text.
25. L. Alsdorf, 'The Vasudevahiṇḍi, a Specimen of Archaic Jaina-Maharastri', *BSOS*, Vol. 8, 1936, pp. 319-33; see also, Chapter 8 below.
26. There are examples when on account of the carelessness on the part of the scribes, the words are changed beyond recognition:

    (i) In the papers left by E. Leumann, Alsdorf found that the aorist forms contained in the *Viseṣāvasyakabhāsya* were replaced by the corresponding forms of the present indicative, 'The Vasudevahiṇḍi, a Specimen of Archaic Jaina-Mahārāṣṭrī', p. 321, n. 1.
    (ii) *mā paṇatijjissaṃ* (*mā paṇakayiṣyan* is the correct reading) has been altered to *mā eṇatijjissaṃ* by the scribes; then to *moeṇa tijjissaṃ* by the editors, *Kalpsutra kī cūrni*, 94 *Jñānāñjali—Abhivādana grantha*, p. 120.
    (iii) *cahiya* (the correct reading) has been changed into *vahiya* by the scribes, *Nandī-suttaṃ and Aṇuogadārāiṃ*, p. 16.
    (iv) In the *Nandisuttaṃ* we have *besiyaṃ* (the correct reading) which has been altered to *tesiyaṃ* and then further corrupted to *terasiyaṃ*, p. 28.
    (v) In the *Anuyogadvāra* (sutra 80), we have *kāyāṇaṃ* which is the correct reading but has been changed into *kāvoyāṇaṃ*, ibid., pp. 29-30.

27. The *Gītālaṅkāra* attributed to Bharata mentions as many as 42 different dialects, out of which he enumerates only 30, K.C. Acharya, *Mārkaṇḍeya's Prākṛtasarvasva*, p. 58.
28. भगवं च णं अद्धमागहीए भासाए धम्मं आइक्खइ। सा वि य णं अद्धमागही भासा भासिज्जमाणी तेसिं सव्वसिं आयरियमणायरियाणं दुपयचउप्पय मिय पसु-पक्खि-सिरिसिवाणं अप्पप्पणो भासत्ताए परिणमइ। Also see *ovā*, 34, p. 146; *paṇṇ*, 1.37; Vāgbhaṭa *Alaṅkāratilaka* (1.1), cf. *Vibhaṅga-Aṭṭhakathā*, pp. 387f. *Māgadh-nirutti* or the *Māgadhī* idiom was the *mūla-bhāṣā* or the primary speech of all men. This view is criticized by B.C. Law, saying that it was a pure invention of the theras of Sri Lanka, *A History of Pali Literature*, p. x.
29. अम्ह इत्थिबालवुड्ढ अक्खर अयाणमाणाणं अणुकंपणत्थं सव्वसतसमदरसीहिं अद्धमागहाए भासाते सुतं उवदिट्ठं, तं च अण्णेसिं पुरतो ण पगासिज्जति।
30. बालस्त्री वृद्ध मूर्खाणां नृणां चारित्रकांक्षिणाम्।
    अनुग्रहार्थं तत्त्वज्ञैः सिद्धान्तः प्राकृतः स्मृतः ॥
    The knowers of the truth have taught the original doctrine (*Prākṛta*), having compassion on children, women, aged and illiterate ones and those who aspire for good conduct.

31. मगहद्धविसयभासानिबद्धं अद्धमागहं, अहवा अट्ठारस देसीभासाणियतं अद्धमागहं।
32. मागधभाषालक्षणं किंचित्, किंचिच्च प्राकृतभाषालक्षणं यस्यामस्ति सा अर्धमागध्याः इति व्युत्पत्या *Viyāha* 5.4; *Ovā* Com. 34.
33. आर्षे हि सर्वे विधयो विकल्प्यन्ते (8.1.3).
34. See Pischel's *Grammatik*, Art.17.
35. देश्यमार्षं च रूढत्वात्स्वतंत्रत्वाच्च भूयसा।
लक्ष्म नापेक्षते तस्य सम्प्रदायो हि बोधकः॥ *Prākṛtaśabdānuśāsana*, 7, p. 2.
The desya and the Ārṣa are not treated here as they are of independent origin, not having Sanskrit as their source, and both abide mostly by its own rules—this is recognized by tradition.
36. आरिसवयणे सिद्धं देवाणं अद्धमागहा वाणी।
37. Bharata Muni, *The Nāṭyaśāstra*, translated by M.M. Ghosh, Vol. I, 'Use of Major Dialects', p. 49.
38. *The Sanskrit Drama*, p. 336.
39. शौरसेन्या अदूरत्वादियमेवार्धमागधी (*Prākṛtasarvasva*, 12.38).
40. महाराष्ट्रीमिश्राऽर्धमागधी (*Saṃkṣiptasāra*, 8.5.98).
41. *LAI*, pp. 42ff.
42. According to Keith, the old Ardhamāgadhī, used in Aśvaghoṣa's dramas may have been the dialect of Mahavira. He writes, 'the early Jain scripture now extant is redacted in a form strongly influenced by the later south-western speech Mahārāṣṭrī, while later texts are written in what has been fairly called Jain Mahārāṣṭrī, and the Digambaras adopted under western influence what has been styled Jain Śaurasenī', *History of Sanskrit Literature*, p. 28.
43. Manmohan Ghosh, *Karpūramañjarī*, Introduction, p. 33.
44. पूर्वापरहतं क्वापि क्वचिच्छेकोक्ति सुन्दरम्।
ग्राम्यां उपमोविमभ्यां युक्तं वक्ति विदूषक॥ beginning of the 10th *pāda*, p. 122.
45. आवन्ती स्यात् महाराष्ट्री शौरसेन्योस्तु संकरात् (11.1).
46. In Cowell's edition of *Prākṛtaprakāsa*, from the *puṣpikā* of this chapter, it is presumed that originally this chapter had a commentary that has been lost. Dineshchandra Sirkar has remarked in his *Grammar of the Prakrit Language*, p. 5: 'The three supplementary chapters (i.e. X, XI and XII) were probably added to the *Prākṛtprakāsa* before the time of Hemacandra, who in his grammar treats not only of Mahārāṣṭrī, Śaurasenī, Māgadhī, Ardhamāgadhī, Paisācī, Cūlikā Paisācī, but also Apabhraṃsa.'
47. For a comparative study of Śaurasenī used in the plays of Aśvaghoṣa and Bhāṣā, see Keith, *The Sanskrit Drama*, pp. 121f.
48. See A.N. Ghatge, 'Śaurasenī Prakrit', *JUB*, May 1935; Pischel, *Grammatik*, Art. 21.
49. महाराष्ट्राश्रयां भाषां प्रकृष्टं प्राकृतं विदुः।
सागरः सूक्तिरत्नानां सेतुबन्धादियन्मयम्॥
50. *Grammatik*, Art.12.
51. See Jagdish Chandra Jain, *The Vasudeva*, Appendix VIII, pp. 691-2.

52. See Chapter 6.
53. Puruṣottama in his *Prākṛtānusāsana* (11.1) has supported this view.
54. D.C. Sirkar, op. cit., pp. 3f.
55. Pages 175, 14-15.
56. शुतनुक नाम देवदासिक्यि
    तं कमयिथ बलनशेये
    देवदिने नाम लुपदखे
    सतनुका नाम देवदासिका तां अकामयिष्ट वाराणसेयः देवदत्तो नाम रूपदक्षः,
    Annual Report, Archaeological Survey of India, 1903-4, pp. 128ff, after S.K. Chatterji, *Origin and Development of Bengali Language,* Introduction, p. 59.

2

Religious Literature in Prakrit: The Contribution of the Jain Thinkers

Magadha, situated in south of Videha and east of Kashi, on the right bank of the Gaṅgā, was a region of great intellectual and spiritual ferment in eastern India in the sixth century BC. It was called Daṇḍipura as numerous *daṇḍi* mendicants, carrying a *daṇḍa* or a staff as their religious paraphernalia, made this land their headquarters. It was a home of ascetics, recluses, mendicants and hermits, who having abandoned the worldly pleasures, roamed about from place to place preaching the norms of morality. These wandering ascetics denied the authority of the Vedas as having a superhuman origin, rejected the utility of sacrificial rites, denied the existence of an intellectual primary cause of this universe, and did not believe in hierarchy of caste.

The Jain and Buddhist texts refer to numerous classes of ascetics such as the Sramaṇas, the Sākyas, the Tāpasas, the Parivrājakas, and the Ājīvikas, upholding various views and opinions current at the time of Mahavira and Buddha.[1] The *Sūya* (I.12) mentions the four primary philosophical schools, which further divided under various categories come to 363. They include those who deny the fruits of human actions and endeavours, monists, pluralists, hedonists, eternalists, annihilationists, agnostics and those who believed in practising certain moral codes without knowing their real impact. The Buddhist texts refer to sixty-two philosophical schools, out of which the views of six celebrated religious teachers mentioned in the *Dīghanikāya* (*Brahmajālasutta*) are worthy of note. These six leading teachers, contemporaries of Buddha and Mahavira, are Pūraṇa Kassapa, Makkhali Gosāla (Maṅkhaliputra according to Jains), Pakudha Kaccāyana, Ajita Kesakambalin (of the hairy blanket which was his garment), Sañjaya Belaṭṭhiputta (of the Belaṭṭhi clan) and Nigantha Nātaputta (of the Nāta or Jñātṛ clan). Each one of them is described as the leader of a school, learned, celebrated, a Tīrthaṅkara revered by the people, experienced and long initiated. These distinguished religious teachers arose from the tribal Kṣatriya class like Mahavira and Buddha and founded their own sect. In those early days, a new type of society, distinct from that based on Brahmanic ritual, was being formed. Following the ascetic tradition, several new teachers preached self-restraint, detachment from worldly pleasures, penance and renunciation. They moved in congregation, propagating their religious and philosophical dogmas.

As Vardhamāna Mahavira was born in Vesāli, he was known as Vesāliya (Vaisālika). Vaisāli (the large city) was a capital of Licchavī *rājās.* It was a tribal settlement belonging to confederation of tribal people, collectively known as the Vajjis. The Vajjis are said to have incorporated the eight tribes of confederacy (*aṭṭhakula*), including the Licchavīs, the Jñātṛkas, the Videhas, the Tīrabhuktis and so on.[2] These tribal people were ruled by collective republic government and followed the principles of democracy. The Licchavīs and the Videhas occupied a prominent position in the tribal confederacy. The Licchavīs were known for their unity and organization. They had formed their *saṅgha* or *gaṇa,* governed by an organized corporation and not by an individual sovereign. We learn from the Buddhist canonical literature that they had their public hall or *saṃthāgāra* where meetings were held and religious and political matters discussed. As Mahavira himself was a Licchavī, there is no wonder if he had accepted the pattern of the *saṅgha* to organize the Jain community into a four-fold division. Mahavira was the son of a nobleman Siddhārtha, of Kāsava *gotra,* by his wife Tisala of Vasiṭṭha *gotra.* He retired from the worldly life at the age of thirty, and, followed by thousands of people, reached the garden Nāyasaṇḍa where the renunciation ceremony was performed with pomp and gaiety. In the Śvetāmbara tradition, for a period of thirteen months he went about with a robe and then naked. He practised severe penance for a period of twelve years and wandered naked and homeless. During the course of his visit to the country of Lāḍha (identified with Rāḍha, comprising the modern districts of Hooghly, Howrah, Bankura, Burdwan and the east portion of Midnapora), he is said to have been persecuted in various ways.

After twelve long years of severe asceticism and hard life, he attained omniscience (*kevalajñāna*) at the age of forty-two. According to the *Kalpa* (5.112-28), Mahavira passed the rainy seasons at the following places: Aṭṭhiyagāma, Campā and Piṭṭhicampā, Vesāli, and Vāṇiyagāma. Soon after Mahavira attained *Kevalajñāna*, a religious conference (*samavasaraṇa*) was convened on the northern bank of the river Ujjuvāliyā flowing near the village Jambhiyagāma, but we are told that his first teaching remained unsuccessful. Then he is said to have returned to Majjhima Pāvā whence he had arrived, and there the second conference was held. After a long discussion, eleven learned Brahmanas, who later were called the *gaṇadharas* (heads of school), were ordained by Mahavira.

Now Mahavira was called a Tīrthaṅkara and was entitled to preach his religious sermons. During his career as a Tīrthaṅkara, he roamed from place to place for eight months in the year, dwelling the remaining four months at one place during the monsoon. In this manner Mahavira established his *saṅgha*, explained the theme of his teachings, initiated men and women without distinction of caste, creed or sex, and emphasizing new social values in a fast changing society. We learn from the *Ovā Sū* (27, 107-11) that when Mahavira arrived in Campā (identified with Campānagar and Campāpura near Bhagalpur, Bihar) at the Puṇṇabhadda shrine, there arose a great uproar in the town and people set out to pay a visit to the Teacher. Some went to pay him reverence, some simply to have a glimpse of him, some to satisfy their curiosity, some to ascertain the truth, and others to hear from him what was unheard so far. People considered it a great privilege even to hear the name of such saintly persons, leave alone to approach them, pay reverence to them and to get an opportunity to listen to their sermons. A beautiful description of Kūṇika Ajātasatru's pilgrimage accompanied by his attendants to Mahavira's *samavasaraṇa* is provided here.

In this way Mahavira spent thirty years preaching his sermons, enlightening people and creating religious and moral awareness in them. During this time, he is said to have passed thirty monsoons at the following places: Vesāli and Vāṇiyagāma, Rāyagiha and Nālandā, Mithilā, Bhaddiyā (Bhadrilapura), Ālabhiyā and Paṇiyabhūmi (situated in Vajjabhumi in the country of Lāḍha according to commentary), Sāvatthī, and the last in Pāvā or Majjhima Pāvā (identified with Saṭhiyāṅv Dīha, ten miles south-east of Kusīnārā near Fazilpur).[3] His last rainy season was spent at Pāvā in the office of a Survey-Minister of King Hatthivāla, where he is said to have attained *nirvāṇa* in 527 BC. At the time of his death Mahavira is said to have preached fifty-five discourses on the results of good deeds, the same number on the results of bad deeds and thirty-six related to unasked questions (*apuṭṭhavāgaranāiṃ*). In Jain tradition, the night Mahavira attained *nirvāṇa*, the eighteen confederate kings (*gaṇarāyāṇo*) of Kashi and Kosala, the nine Mallakīs and the nine Licchavīs are said to have observed fasts and celebrated the great occasion with the lighting of lamps (*davvujjoyaṃ*).[4]

It is stated in the *Bṛh Sū* (1.50) that during his sojourn in Sāketa, Mahavira commanded his itinerant monks and nuns to frequent Aṅga-Magadha in the east, Kosambī in the south, Thūṇā in the west and Kuṇālā (Uttara Kosala) in the north, but not beyond. Thus we see that during his ascetic life Mahavira's itinerary covered roughly the region of Bihar, a part of northern-western Bengal and a part of eastern Uttar Pradesh.

The Teachings of Mahavira

The teachings of Mahavira centred around the principle of cessation of worldly activities by practising penance and self-mortification. According to him, to keep away from sins and passions, one has to devote oneself to right conduct and self-restraint and not be enticed by worldly pleasures, so that one can achieve final emancipation by putting an end to one's *karmas*. Mahavira laid down rules of maintaining strict discipline. He exhorted the *sramaṇas* saying,

> Oh long-lived *sramaṇas*, control your senses; be on alert every moment, whether sleeping or awake, standing or sitting and moving around. Do not slacken even for a moment, for, you can never be sure from which direction temptations may invade you and cause your downfall. Hence just as a turtle hides all his parts under his shell to protect himself against any trouble, you too should keep your mind under control and prevent your restless thoughts from wandering in many directions.

In the sermon of the 'Leaf of the Tree' (*duma-pattaya*) of the *Uttarā* (X.1-2) Mahavira prompts his disciple Gautama Indrabhūti to remain always alert and watchful. He says, 'As the fallow leaf of a tree falls on the ground, so when the duration of time is over, life comes to an end. As a dew-drop oscillating on the top of the blade of grass lasts for a short time so is the life of men. O Gautama, therefore be alert and watchful.' It is said that this sermon was preached by Mahavira to help Gautama attain *kevalajñāna* which enabled him to cut off love and reach perfection. Elsewhere in the Kāpilīya Section, in answer to a query of his pupil, the teacher admonishes the monks to cast off all things which fetter the soul, give up all hate, renounce the world and not kill any living being. It is stated, 'And if somebody should give the whole earth to one man, he would not have enough; as difficult is it to satisfy anybody. The more you get, the more you want; your desire increases with your means' (VII.16-17).[5]

It has been stated in the *Das* (1.1-3), 'The righteousness is the highest bliss which consists of non-injury, self-restraint and penance, and even gods bow down to the one who abides by this law.' 'As bees feel gratitude by tasting the juice of flowers without hurting them, so does a monk, being engaged in begging alms just to maintain himself.' Further, 'All living beings want to live, they do not want to die, therefore a monk refrains from their dreadful killing' (6.10). 'As long as the old age does not afflict, the ailments do not overpower and the senses remain intact, one should practise righteousness' (8.36).

The *Ācā*, which is one of the oldest texts of the Śvetāmbara canonical literature, treating of the way of life of a monk, has enunciated the cardinal doctrine of *ahimsā* in the following words: 'Everybody wants to live, life is dear to everyone. Everyone wants happiness and shuns misery. Nobody wants to be killed or injured (I.2.3.81). . . . Only one who understands his own suffering can understand the suffering of others and thus realises one's own suffering, therefore a person free from passions and the one who is restrained, never desires to live by injuring or hurting others.' It is stated in the ninth Chapter of the *Uvahāṇa-sūya* that when Mahavira travelled through the country of Lāḍha, divided into Vajjabhūmi and Subbhabhūmi, the land of the Suhmas, he had to undergo untold sufferings. This country has been described as a pathless (*duccara*) country where there were no regular routes and one had to travel a long distance before reaching a village. The land was inhabited by tribal people, known as *vajja-lāḍhas* (explained as *Mlecchas* in the *Ācā Cū*, 296), who on account of eating coarse food, are said to have been furious by nature and who set their dogs upon ascetics who dared to enter the region. They hit them with sticks, fists or lances, cut their flesh, tore their hair and ill-treated them. In the absence of clothes they covered their body with grass.[6] In this way Mahavira had to undergo insults, abuses, harassment and various kinds of physical torture, and yet he is said to have remained steadfast. In winter he is said to have meditated in the shade and in the heat of summer in the scorching sun. Often he is said to have drunk no water and fasted for months together.

Thus we see that Mahavira in order to curb passions, preached the doctrine of self-restraint so that one may not to have undergo endless suffering in the succeeding births in worldly existence. In ancient Jain tradition we come across innumerable Jain monks, who by undergoing severe penance died and are said to have achieved liberation. Some of them were thrown off from boats into the river, the entrails of some were eaten by animals, others were crushed, or, pinned to the ground like wet skin with hundreds of nails, bitten by swarm of ants, worms and insects, withered by intense cold and heat. Travelling from one place to the other was full of calamities and peril, there was a fear of being attacked by an organized band of thieves and robbers. Political disturbances in the country led to their arrest, being taken as spies. To obtain lawful alms during the long famines in the country was difficult and medical treatment was a problem in case a monk suffered from serious illness.[7]

The Authenticity of the Jain Canon

Mahavira preached his religion 2500 years ago from now and since there had been no written records about what he actually said, it is not easy to decide where and on what occasions the Master delivered a speech or uttered a sermon. From his teachings contained in the available canonical literature of the Śvetāmbaras, it is not always possible to ascertain how much of his teachings should be exactly attributed to Mahavira. We are told that the *Āgama* or *Siddhānta,* also known as *niggantha-pāvayaṇa, duvālasaṅga gaṇi-piḍaga* (*dvādasāṅga gaṇi-piṭaka*), or *Veda* (*Ācā Cū,* 5,185) was expounded by Mahavira to his chief disciples (*gaṇadharas*) as contained in the *Pūrvas* (Old Texts). Since the teachings of the Master were delivered orally, it is to be decided how much of that was retained by the disciples which they composed later in the *Sūtras.* However, it is to be noted that there had been a long tradition of his disciples who faithfully preserved in memory the teachings of the Master, as in the case of the teachings of the Buddha and those of the Vedic philosophers.

The eldest of the eleven *gaṇadharas* ordained by Mahavira was Indabhūi. The first three *gaṇadharas* are said to have been brothers and belonged to the Goyama *gotra*; they were residents of

Gobbaragāma, situated in Magadha. The fifth *gaṇadharas* Suhamma belonged to the Aggivesāyaṇa *gotra* and is said to have been a resident of Moriya Sannivesa. We are told that except Indabhūi and Suhamaa all other *gaṇadharas* died during the lifetime of Mahavira. It is said that the day when Mahavira attained *nirvāṇa*, Indabhūi had gone in a neighbouring village to preach. When he returned he found that the Master was no more. He cut asunder the bond of attachment towards him and is said to have attained omniscience the very night. He survived Mahavira for twelve years and finally attained *nirvāṇa* at Rāyagiha at the age of seventy-two. The next important *gaṇadharas* after Indabhūi (or Gautama Indrabhūti) is Suhamma (Sudharmā) who is mentioned in the Śvetāmbara Jain canon frequently. After Mahavira's *nirvāṇa* he became the head of the Jain *saṅgha* and remained in that position for a period of twenty years till he attained omniscience. He is said to have explained the Jain Canon to his disciple Jambu in the manner he had heard from the Master. Like the Śvetāmbaras the Digambaras too believe in the existence of Gautama Indrabhūti, Sudharmā and Jambu after Mahavira which shows that the schism of the Digambara and Śvetāmbara in the Jain *saṅgha* did not exist at that time. No authentic information about the life of the first three *gaṇadharas* is available. We do not hear much about the remaining ones they seem to be more or less of fictitious nature.

Redaction of the Jain Canon

In order to retain the teachings of Mahavira, his disciples memorized his speeches, conversation, dialogues, sayings, narratives and codes of conduct. They preserved the various examples, illustrations, parables, summaries and tales provided by Mahavira to make his teachings effective and powerful. A code of rules was laid down by the Master for the guidance of monks and nuns so that they could guard themselves against the temptations and allurements of the world.

Yet it is to be noted that during the course of time, the teachings of Mahavira must have suffered numerous changes and modifications as is evident from the study of canonical texts and the various conventions of the learned Jain monks like those of the *Savṅgītis* of the Buddhists held from time to time in order to set the canon right. It is stated that after about 160 years of Mahavira's *nirvāṇa* (about 367 BC), a terrible famine struck Magadha which is said to have lasted for twelve years. Candragupta Maurya was the ruler of Magadha at that time and Sthūlabhadra, the leader of the Jain *saṅgha.* The famine seriously hampered the study of the Jain monks who could hardly get sufficient alms for survival. During this period a number of monks under the leadership of Bhadrabahu migrated to the seashore (*samudda-tīre*).[8] After the famine was over, they re-assembled in Pāṭaliputra under the leadership of Sthūlabhadra. A council was convened at this time when the monks started collecting a section (*uddesa*) from one and a portion (*khaṇḍa*) from another and thus were compiled the eleven *aṅagas* of the Śvetāmbara Jain Canon. As nobody remembered the *Diṭṭhivāya*, the twelfth *Aṅga*, it was declared lost. This council of the learned Jain monks was held in Pāṭaliputra, therefore it is known as the Pāṭaliputra version (*vācanā*) which is said to be the earliest version held after about 160 years of Mahavira's *nirvāṇa.*[9]

But this was not the end. We are told that as the grasping power and the retentive capacity of the monks was diminishing day by day, the contents of the Canon could not be preserved in memory as a result the Canon of the Śvetāmbaras was reduced to a state of disorder. Hence arose the necessity of holding another convention. This time the venue of the convention was Mathura. It is stated that about 827 or 840[10] years after Mahavira's death (i.e. about AD 300 or 313), there occurred another terrible famine which also is said to have lasted for twelve years.[11] The intensity of the famine was so great that to obtain alms became extremely difficult for the monks and as a result they found themselves incapable of grasping, retaining and pondering over the canonical texts which resulted in doing great damage to them. At this time another council was convened under the leadership of Ārya Skandila in Mathura which is known as the Māthurī version of the Jain Canon. In this convention whatever could be gathered from different sources was collected and fixed in the form of the *Kālika Sruta.* According to some, however, no canon was lost during this period, but except Ārya Skandila, most of the distinguished monks versed in the *Anuyoga* (*anuyogadhara*) had lost their lives.[12]

Simultaneously, yet another attempt was made to hold a council under the presidentship of Nāgārjuna at Valabhi (Waḷā in Saurashtra) to give final shape to the Canon. This is known as the Nāgārjunī or the Valabhi version of the Jain Canon. Whatever portion of the Canon was remembered by Nāgārjuna and other monks, was reduced to writing and what was forgotten was set right after checking references.[13] This statement is corroborated by Malayagiri in his commentary on the *Joisakaraṇḍaga* where it is stated that in the time of Skandila there occurred a terrible famine which caused a great damage to the study and recapitulation of the monks. At the end of the famine the members of both the *saṅghas* met. One assembled at Valabhi and another at Mathura.[14] According to Malayagiri, the *Aṇu* and other canonical texts are based on the Māthurī *vācanā*, and the *Joisakaraṇḍaga* on the Valabhi. Unfortunately, after the redaction of the Canon in the above-mentioned councils, Ārya Skandila and Nāgārjuna could not have an opportunity to meet each other and hence the two different versions of the Canon remained unreconciled.

Later, after 980 or 993 years of Mahavira's *nirvāṇa* (AD 453 or 466) yet another council, the fourth one, was convened under the presidentship of Devardhigaṇi Kṣamāsramaṇa at Valabhi. In this council a serious attempt was made to reconcile the different readings of the Canon decided in the Māthurī and Valabhi councils. As in this council prominence was given to the Māthurī version of the Canon, the readings of the Nāgārjunī version were given a secondary place. It has been stated in Samayasundara's *Sāmācārīsataka*: 'When due to the twelve-year long famine, a majority of the monks lost their lives and a major portion of the Canon went into oblivion, Devardhigaṇi Kṣamāsramaṇa, for the benefit of those who were capable of attaining *mokṣa* (*bhavyaloka*) and were devoted to the holy scripture, directed by the Jain *saṅgha*, called a convention of the remaining monks at Valabhi. He collected the portion of the Canon from their mouth whatever remained, uninterrupted, less or more, broken or entire, put it in order according to his intellect and finally reduced it to writing (*pustakārūḍhāh kṛtāḥ*).'[15] As stated already, prominence was given to the Māthurī version in this council. Only important variants of the canonical text supplied by Nāgārjuna were recorded by Devardhigaṇi Kṣamāsramaṇa; this is indicated by the words '*vāyaṇantare puṇa*' (according to another version) or '*nāgārjunīyastu evaṃ paṭhanti*' (the followers of Nāgārjuna read in this manner).[16] Since Devardhigaṇi was a distinguished scholar of the Māthura *saṅgha*, naturally he accepted the Māthurī version of the Canon. The council at Valabhi held under his presidentship was attended by both Ārya Skandila and Nāgārjuna and other prominent scholars of the age.

According to Ārya Skandila, this council was convened 980 years after Mahavira's death, whereas in the opinion of Nāgārjuna it was after 993 years. Regarding the last Valabhi version of the Canon, it is to be noted that Devardhigaṇi neither added anything to the canonical text nor deleted anything from it. As already indicated, it contains the canonical text, only approved by Ārya Skandila and Nāgārjunasūri, the leaders of the Māthurī and Valabhi versions respectively. Devardhigaṇi only tried to reconcile the contradictory statements retained in the above-mentioned versions. He noted the important variants and got the text based on the Pāṭaliputra version of the Canon written down in the council. Thus he can be called only a redactor of the Canon and not the author. In this connection the statement of H. Jacobi is worth quoting. He writes,

> Devardhi's position relative to the sacred literature of the Jains appears therefore to us in a different light from what is generally believed to have been. He probably arranged the already existing manuscripts in a canon, taking down from the mouth of learned theologicians only such works of which manuscripts were not available. Of this canon a great many copies were taken in order to furnish every seminary with books which had become necessary by the newly introduced change in the method of religious instructions. Devardhi's edition of *siddhānta* is therefore only a redaction of the sacred books which existed before his time in nearly the same form. Any single passage in sacred text may have been introduced by the author but bulk of *siddhānta* is certainly not of his making. (*Jain Sūtras*, XXII, p. xxxix)

Thus we see that the earliest portions of the Jain Canon may quite possibly belong to the time of Mahavira and his disciples, though it is difficult to point out which particular portion was directly uttered by him. A certain portion would have been added by later writers taking account of different situations. Since so far there has not been a standard critical edition of most of the canonical texts, it is rather difficult to distinguish between old and new, authentic and unauthentic. As it is, we have to go to the second century after Mahavira's *nirvāṇa* as the earliest time when a council was held in order to set the Canon right. The latest time of the Canon can be dated to the fifth century AD and the council under the presidentship of Devardhigaṇi at Valabhi. It is also to be noted that as the commentaries on the canonical texts record a number of variants and texts that are no more extant, it appears that even the *vācanā* of Devardhigaṇi held in Valabhi has not come down to us in its original form (see Winternitz, *A History of*, II, p. 435n).

Classification of the Canon

Suyanāna or scriptural knowledge, otherwise known as *Siddhānta* or *Āgama* consists of (i) the twelve *Aṅgas,* (ii) the twelve *Upāṅgas,* (iii) the ten *Paiṇṇas,* (iv) the six *Chedasūtras,* (v) the four *Mūlasūtras* and (vi) the two individual texts.

(i) The twelve *Aṅgas:* 1 *Āyāraṅga* (*Ācārāṅga*), 2 *Sūyagaḍāṅga* (*Sūtrakṛtāṅga*), 3 *Ṭhāṇāṅga* (*Sthānāṅga*), 4 *Samavāyāṅga,* 5 *Viyāhapaṇṇatti* (*Vyākhyāprajñapti* or *Bhagavatī*), 6 *Nāyādhammakahāo* (*Jñātādharmakathāḥ*), 7 *Uvāsagadasāo* (*Upāsakadasāḥ*), 8 *Antagaḍadasāo* (*Antakṛddasāḥ*), 9 *Aṇuttarovavāiyadasāo* (*Anuttaroupapātikadasāḥ*), 10 *Paṇhavāgaraṇaiṃ* (*Prasnavyākaraṇāni*), 11 *Vivāgasuyaṃ* (*Vipākasrutam*), 12 *Diṭṭhivāya* (*Dṛṣṭivāda*).

(ii) The twelve *Upāṅgas:* 1 *Ovāiya* or *Uvavāiya* (*Aupāpatika*), 2 *Rāyapaseṇaijja* or *Rāyapaseṇaiya* (*Rājaprasnīya*), 3 *Jīvābhigama,* 4 *Paṇṇavaṇā* (*Prajbñāpanā*), 5 *Sūrapaṇṇatti* or *Sūriyapaṇṇatti* (*Sūryaprajñapti*), 6 *Jambuddīvapaṇṇatti* (*Jambudvīpaprajñapti*), 7 *Candapaṇṇatti* (*Candraprajñapti*), 8 *Niryāvaliyāo,* 9 *Kappavaḍiṃsiyāo* (*Kalpāvataṃsikāḥ*), 10 *Pupphiyāo* (*Puṣpikāḥ*), 11 *Pupphāculiyāo* (*Puṣpacūlikāḥ*), 12 *Vaṇhidas-o* (*Vṛṣṇidasāḥ*).

(iii) The ten *Paiṇṇas* (*Prakīrṇakās*): 1 *Causaraṇa* (*Catuḥsaraṇa*) by *Vīrabhadra,* 2 *Āurapaccakkhāṇa* (*Āturapratyākhyāna*), 3 *Bhattapariṇṇā* (*Bhaktaparijñā*), 4 *Saṃthāra* (*Saṃstāra*), 5 *Tandulaveyāliya* (*Tandulavaicārika*), 6 *Candāvijjhaya* (*Candravedhyaka*), 7 *Devindatthaya* (*Devendrastava*), 8 *Gaṇivijjā* (*Gaṇividyā*), 9 *Mahāpaccakkhāṇa* (*Mahāpratyākkhyāna*), 10 *Vīratthaya* (*Vīrastava*).

(iv) The six *Cheyasūttas* (*Chedasūtras*): 1 *Nisīha* (*Nisītha*), 2 *Mahānisīha* (*Mahānisītha*), 3 *Vavahāra* (*Vyavahāra*), 4 *Āyāradasāo* (*Ācāradasāh*) or *Dasāsuyakkhandha* (*Dasāsrutaskandha*), 5 *Kappa* (*Kalpa* or *Bṛhatkalpa*), 6 *Pañcakappa* (*Pañcakalpa*). Instead of the last-named work the *Jīyakappa* (*Jītakalpa*) by Jīnabhadra is also mentioned.

(v) The four *Mūlasūttas* (*Mūlasūtras*): 1 *Uttarajjhāya* (*Uttarādhyāya*) or *Uttarajjhayaṇa* (*Uttarādhyayana*), 2 *Āvassaya* (*Āvasyaka*), 3 *Dasaveyāliya* (*Dasavaikālika*), 4 *Piṇḍanijjutti* (*Piṇḍaniryukti*). [Instead of the third and the fourth *Mūlasūtras,* sometimes *Ohanijjutti* (*Oghaniryukti*) and *Pakkhiyasutta* (*Pakṣika Sūtre*) are mentioned respectively. Sometimes *Piṇḍanijjutti* and *Ohanijjutti* appear in the list of the *Chedasūtras.*]

(vi) The two Individual texts: 1 *Nandi,* 2 *Aṇuogadāra* (*Anuyoga-dvāra*).

Of all these, the *Aṅgas* seem to be the old and uniform, though there are differences in nomenclature[17] and the original contents of several of them have not been preserved or recorded in tradition. Although the twelve *Aṅgas* have been mentioned in the *Ṭha* (X.755), the *Sama* (136, pp. 99-123), the *Nandi* (45, pp. 96-108) and the *Pakkhiyasutta* (p. 70a), the contents of several of them do not correspond to the table of contents referred to in these works.[18]

The sacred literature of the Jains originally was contained in the twelve *Aṅgas*. Even the Digambaras believe in the existence of twelve *Aṅgas*, the names of which have been mentioned in their literature. Not only that, Aparājitasūri in his *Śrīvijayodayā* commentary on the *Bhag Ārā* (421, pp. 611-15) has quoted from the *Ācā*, the *Sūyaa*, the *Dasha*, the *Uttarā*, the *Nisi* and other Jain canonical works. Out of the twelve *Aṅgas*, the *Dṛṣṭivāda*, the twelfth one, has been declared lost. Thus the number of the *āgamas* according to the Śvetāmbara Jains (*mūrti-pūjakas* = idol worshippers) is 45. The *sthānakavāsīs* (non-idolatrous) and the *terāpanthis* (a sub-sect of the former; path of the thirteen) repudiate 13 out of 45 and consider the following texts as authentic: 11 *Aṅgas*, 12 *Upāṅgas*, 4 *Chedasūtras*, 4 *Mūlasūtras* and *Āvassaya*. They do not include the *Piṇḍanijjutti* and the *Ohanijjutti* among the *Mūlasūtras*. They do not believe in the *Niryuktis* and other commentaries on the *Āgamas*, composed by later writers. According to another tradition (see *Bṛahṭṭipaṇikā*, also known as *Jaingranthāvali* (Shri Jain Śvetāmbara Conference, Mumbai, vs 1965, p. 72), the number of Jain *Āgamas* is 84: 11 *Aṅgas*, 12 *Upāṅgas*, 5 *Chedasūtras* (excluding *Pañcakappa*), 5 *Mūlasūtras* (*Uttarajjhayaṇa*, *Dasaveyāliya*, *Āvassaya*, *Nandi* and *Aṇuoga*), 8 miscellaneous (*Pajjosaṇākappa* or *Kalpasūtra*, *Jīyakappa*, *Jaijīyakappa*, *Saḍḍhajīyakappa*, *Pakkhiya*, *Khamaṇā*, *Vandittu*, *Isibhāsiya*); 30 *Paiṇṇās* (*Causaraṇa*, *Āurapaccakkhāṇa*, *Bhattapariṇṇā*, *Saṃthāraga*, *Tandulaveyāliya*, *Candāvijjhaya*, *Devindatthaya*, *Gaṇivijjā*, *Mahāpaccakkhāṇa*, *Vīratthava*, *Ajīvakappa*, *Gacchāyāra*, *Maranasamāhi*, *Siddhapāhuḍa*, *Tittogāli*, *Ārādhanāpatākā*, *Dīvasāgarapaṇṇatti*, *Joisakaraṇḍaga*, *Aṅgavijjā*, *Tihipaiṇṇaya*, *Piṇḍanijjutti*, *Sārāvali*, *Pajjantārāhaṇa*, *Jīvavibhatti*, *Kavaca*, *Joṇipāhuḍa*, *Aṅgacūliyā*, *Vaṅgacūliyā*, *Vuḍḍhacausaraṇa*, *Jambupayaṇṇa*); and 12 *Nijjuttis* (*Āvassaya*, *Sūyagadaṅga*, *Pajjosaṇākappa* (*Kalpasūtra*), *Dasaveyāliya*, *Kappa* or *BṛhatKalpa*, *Piṇḍanijjutti*, *Uttarajjhayaṇa*, *Vavahāra*, *Ohanijjutti*, *Āyāraṅga*, *Dasāsuyakkhandha*, *Saṃsatta*); and the *Viseṣāvasyaka-Bhāṣya* by Jinabhadragaṇi Ksamāsramaṇa.

There is yet another classification of the Jain *Āgamas*. According to the *Nandi* (*Sū* 43 commentary, pp. 90-5), *Suyaṇāṇa* (the scriptural knowledge) is divided into *Aṅgabahira* (*Aṅgabāhya*, outside the *Aṅgas*) and *Aṅgapaviṭṭha* (*Aṅgapraviṣṭa*, contained in the *Aṅgas*). The *Aṅgabāhira* is further divided into *Āvassaya* and *Āvassaya-vairitta*. The *Āvassaya* has six subdivisions, *Sāmāiya*, *Cauvīsatthava*, *Vandaṇaya*, *Paḍikkamaṇa*, *Kāussagga*, and *Paccakkhāṇa*. *Āvassaya-vairitta* is further divided into *Kāliya* (studied with certain hours) and *Ukkāliya* (studied at all times). The *Kāliya suya* is subdivided into 31: *Uttarajjhayaṇa*, *Dasāo*, *Kappa*, *Vavahāra*, *Nisīha*, *Mahānisīha*, *Isibhāsiya*, *Jambuddīvapaṇṇatti*, *Dīvasagarapaṇṇtti*, *Candapaṇṇatti*, *Khuḍḍiyā-Vimāṇapavibhatti*, *Mahalliā-Vimāṇapavibhatti*, *Aṅgacūliyā*, *Vaggacūliyā*, *Vivāhacūliya*, *Aruṇovavāya*, *Varunovavāya*, *Garulovavāya*, *Dharaṇovavāya*, *Vesamaṇovavāya*, *Velandharovavāya*, *Devindovavāya*, *Uṭṭhaṇāsya*, *Samuṭṭhāṇasuya*, *Nāgapariyāvaniyāo*, *Niryāvaliyāo*, *Kappiyāo*, *Kappavaḍiṃsiyao*, *Pupphiyāo*, *Pupphacūliyāo*, and *Vaṇhidasāo*. The *Ukkāliya suya* is subdivided into *Dasaveyāliya*, *Kappiyākappiya*, *Cullakappasua*, *Mahākappasua*, *Uvavāia*, *Rāyapaseṇia*, *Jīvābhigama*, *Paṇṇavaṇā*, *Mahāpaṇṇavaṇā*, *Nandi*, *Aṇuogadāra*, *Deviṇdatthaya*, *Tandulaveyāliya*, *Candāvijjhaya*, *Sūrapaṇṇatti*, *Porisimaṇḍala*, *Maṇḍalapavesa*, *Vijjācaraṇavṇicchaa*, *Gaṇivijjā*, *Jhāṇavibhatti*, *Maraṇavibhattī*, *Āyavisohī*, *Vīyarāgasuha*, *Saṃlehaṇāsuya*, *Vihārakappa*, *Caraṇavihī*, *Āurapaccakkhāṇa*, and *Mahāpaccakkhāṇa*.[19]

THE PUVVAS (PŪRVAS)

Puvvagaya comprises 14 *Pūrvas*.[20] *Aṇuoga* deals with the legends of the Tīrthaṅkaras and other great personalities. It is divided into four sections, *Prathamānuyoga*, *Karaṇānuyoga*, *Dravyānuyoga* and *Caraṇānuyoga*.[21] The *Prathamānuyoga* includes *Padmapurāṇa* of Raviṣeṇa, *Harivaṃsapursāṇa* of Jinasena I, *Ādipurāṇa* of Jinasena II, *Uttarapurāṇa* of Guṇabhadra and others; the *Karaṇānuyoga* comprises *Sūryaprajñapti*, *Candraprajñapti*, *Jayadhavalā* and others; the *Dravyānuyoga* comprises *Pravacanasāra*, *Pañcāstikāya*, *Samayasāra* of Kundakunda, *Tattvārthasūtra* of Umāsvāmi, *Āptamīmāṁsā* of Samantabhadra and others; the *Caraṇānuyoga* comprises *Mūlācāra* of Vaṭṭakera, *Trivarṇācāra* of Brhmasūri, *Ratnakakaraṇḍasrāvakācāra* of Samantabhadra and others.

The *Cūliyā* (*Cūlikāḥ* or 'Addenda' or 'Supplement') is also known as *Culla-Vatthu*; whatever is not explained in *Parikamma*, *Sutta*, *Puvvagaya* and *Aṇuoga*, is explained in the *Cūliyā*. Only the first four *Pūrvas* have *Cūliyās*: the first has 4, the second 12, the third 8 and the fourth 10. Of the above-mentioned five divisions, the first two, i.e. *Parikamma* and *Sutta* had become extinct by the time of the author of the *Nandi-Cūrṇi.*

THE *DṚṢṬIVĀDA*

We have referred above to the loss of the *Dṛṣṭivāda.* It is stated that at that time Bhadrabāhu, the leader of the *saṅgha,* who had the knowledge of the 14 *Pūrvas,* had gone to practise *mahāprāṇa* meditation to Nepāla. It was decided to depute a pair of monks (*saṅghāṭaka*) to Bhadrabāhu to learn the *Dṛṣṭivāda.* But the leader of the *saṅgha* expressed his inability to teach as he was occupied in meditation. Thereupon the monks returned and reported the matter to the *saṅgha.* At this the *saṅgha* decided to depute another pair of monks with the command as to what penalty could be imposed on the person who dared to disobey their order. Ultimately Bhadrabāhu agreed to teach the *Dṛṣṭivāda.* As a result, along with a number of monks, Sthūlabhadra was deputed to Nepāla where he was given instruction in seven instalments during the day.[22] Thus in course of time, Sthūlabhadra acquired the knowledge of 10 *Pūrvas.* The remaining 4 were taught to him on the condition that he would not disclose them to anyone. Thus according to tradition, knowledge of the last 4 *Pūrvas* was lost 170 years after Mahavira's *nirvāṇa,* the year when Bhadrabāhu died.[23] Later on as Sthūlabhadra was asked not to disclose the last 4 *Pūrvas* to anyone, the knowledge of the first ten alone continued. Ārya Vajra (584 years after Mahavira's *nirvāṇa,* or 57 BC) according to Śvetāmbaras, and Dharmasena (345 years after Mahavira's *nirvāṇa,* or AD 182), according to Digambaras, were conversant with these ten *Pūrvas* (*dasapūrvins*). Then comes Ārya Rakṣita, who was conversant with the 9 *Pūrvas* and a part of the tenth, according to the Śvetāmbaras.[24]

It is to be noted that after Mahavira, the succession of Gautama Indrabhūti, Sudharmā and Jambu has been commonly accepted by both the Śvetāmbaras and the Digambaras, indicating that there was no discord till then in the Jain *saṅgha.* Jambu was the last *kevalin,* who attained omniscience in this *avasarpiṇī* era. After that the list of the *Srutakevalins,* i.e. those who did not attain omniscience during their lifetime but at the same time possesses the knowledge of complete *sruta,* or those conversant with the 14 *Pūrvas,* varies in both traditions. Prabhava, Sayyambhava, Yasobhadra, Sambhutavijaya and Bhadrabāhu are known to be five *Srutakevalins* in the Śvetāmbara tradition, whereas according to Digambaras, they were Viṣṇu, Nandimitra, Aparājita, Govardhana and Bhadrabāhu (Bhadrabāhu being common to both). All of them possessed the knowledge of the fourteen *Pūrvas*, and the twelve *Aṅgas*. Then comes the era of the *ācāryas* who possessed the knowledge of only ten *Pūrvas*; they were: Visākha, Proṣṭhila, Ksatriya, Jaya, Nāga, Siddhārtha, Dhrtisena, Vijaya, Buddhilla, Gaṅgadeva and Sudharmā. After that there was none to have possessed the knowledge of the *Pūrvas*. The following *ācāryas* knew only eleven *Aṅgas*: Nakṣatra, Jayapāla, Pāṇḍu, Dhruvasena and Kaṃsa. The following were conversant with the *Ācā*, the first *Aṅga* only: Subhadra, Yasobhadra, Yasobāhu, and Loha or Lohācārya.[25] This whole period covers 683 years from the *nirvāṇa* of Mahavira in the Śvetāmbara tradition and a thousand years after Mahavira's *nirvāṇa* in the Digambara tradition.

The *Dṛṣṭivāda*, also known as *Bhūtavāda*,[26] is said to have contained a discourse of (heretical) views. It is called an excellent sacred text (*uttama-sruta*) as it deals with the four *anuyogas*, the *dravyānuyoga*, *caraṇānuyoga*, *dharmānuyoga* and *karaṇānuyoga*. The subject explained here is with regard to the *nayas*, and we are told that various powers and superhuman qualities are accomplished by studying this text.[27] According to another tradition, it deals mainly with *dravyānuyoga*. Elsewhere, we are told that it deals mainly with the divisions and subdivisions of *nayas* such as *naigama* and others.[28] Though the contents of the *Dṛṣtivāda*, like the remaining eleven *Aṅgas*, are enumerated in the *Sama* and the *Nandi*, they are so scanty and inadequate that it is difficult to build a clear picture. It is stated that there is no subject or topic which is not contained in this text. Further, the *Dṛṣṭivāda* is equated with the pre-eminent texts such as the *Aruṇopāta*, and the *Nisītha* (the second *Cūlikā* of the *Ācā*) which are not to be studied by the dull-headed (*dummedha*) or by women, who are said to have inflated with conceit, have unsteady organs and are weak-minded.[29]

This shows that the Jains did not have uniform opinions about this text. Under the circumstances, there is no wonder that it was declared lost by both Śvetāmbaras and Digambaras. As stated earlier, according to Śvetāmbaras, it was lost from the time Bhadrabāhu, whereas the Digambaras declared that the text survived partly in the form of *Saṭkhandāgama* and *Kaṣāyaprābhṛta* which are based on the second and the fifth *Pūrvas* respectively. It is interesting that even in the Śvetāmbara tradition, a number of important canonical texts or their portions are based on the *Pūrva* literature. It has been stated in the *Das* commentary of Haribhadra that 'those who are conversant in 10 *Pūrvas* (*desapuvvī*) drew from the *Pūrvas* definitely, whereas those conversant in 14 *Pūrvas* (*caudasapuvvī*) drew from them only occasionally'.[30] According to Bhadrabāhu's *Das Nijjutti* (16-17), the 4th, 5th and the 7th sections of the *Das* are derived from the 7th, 8th, and the 6th *Pūrvas* successively, and the rest of the sections from the 9th *Pūrva*. According to the commentator Vādivetāla Sāntisūri, the second section of the *Uttarā* is based on the 8th *Pūrva*. Then the *Dasā*, the *Kalpa* (*Bṛhatkalpa*), the *Nisī*, the *Vavahāra*, the *Oha-nijjutti* and the *Nisīhiyā* (the second *Cūlikā* of *Ācā*), all are said to have been derived from the 9th *Pūrva*. Further, *Siddhapāhuḍa* is attributed to the 2nd *Pūrva*, *Nayacakra* to the 5th; the *Sayaga*, the *Pañcasaṅgaha*, the *Sattariyā*, the *Jīvasamāsa* (all *Karmagranthas*), and the *Pañcakappa*, the *Mahākappasuya* and the *Uvasaggahara* are all attributed to a certain *Pūrva*.[31] According to Saṅghadāsagaṇi Vācaka, the author of the *Vasudevacariya* (*Vasudevahiṇḍi*), his work is drawn from the *Prathamānuyoga*[32] and in the opinion of Haribhadra (commentary on the *Upadesapada*, 357), the *Bamhadattacariya* is based on the *Diṭṭhivāya*. According to the author of the *Maraṇasamāhī*, the story of an elephant he narrates (512-20) had been inherited from the *Dṛṣṭivāda*. It is to be noted that we have a similar story in the *VH* (*Bālacandālambha*, pp. 255-7), Hariṣeṇa's *BKK* (78. 138-42) and the *Merumandarapurāṇa* in Tamil.[33]

The *Aṅgas* and the *Pūrvas*

The question arises whether the twelve *Aṅgas* were composed first, or the *Pūrva* texts. As it is, the *Aṅgas* do not seem to be additions to something previously existing. We have seen that the *Pūrvas* form a constituent of the *Dṛṣṭivāda*, the twelfth *Aṅga*, and if the composition of the *Aṅgas* has taken place in order, naturally, the *Pūrvas* follow the *Aṅgas*. This view is held by Abhayadeva in his commentaries of the *Sama* and the *Nandi*. While explaining the word *Pūrva* he asserts that the *Aṅgas* were composed by Mahavira's *ganadharas* either immediately in the spirit of the preceding (*pūrva*) oral tradition, or indirectly after first (*pūrva*) having established that tradition. Anyway, he does not seem to derive the *Aṅgas* from the *Pūrvas*. This view is supported by the *Nandi* (*Sū*. 57) where the *dvādasāṅga* has been called eternal, perpetual and everlasting. It has been stated in

Bhadrabāhu's *Āva Nir* (92) that an *Arhat* (worthy of worship) preaches the meaning of an oral tradition (*pūrva*) and the *gaṇadharas* compose the preaching in the form of *Sūtras* or *Āgamas* for the benefit of the Order (*Sāsana*).[34] Yet there exists another tradition according to which the *Pūrvas* were composed first and then followed the *Aṅgas*. We have already seen how a number of canonical texts of both Śvetāmbaras and Digambaras have been derived from the *Pūrva* texts. In the explanation of the word *Pūrva* given by Abhayadeva, if the word is taken in the sense of the 'earlier texts' it can be said that the *Aṅgas* have been derived from the *Pūrvas*. But in that case the *Pūrvas* would have absorbed all the *Aṅgas*. It appears that the earlier Jain *ācāryas* were conscious of this anomaly and they do not seem to be sure whether *Pūrva* should be taken in the sense of 'earlier texts' or '*Pūrva* texts'. A question has been asked: in case everything is incorporated in the *Pūrvas* (which is a part of the *Dṛṣṭivāda*, the twelfth *Aṅga*), it was not necessary to explain the *Aṅgas* separately. The reply given is that as dull-headed persons and women are prohibited study of the *Dṛṣṭivāda*, the *Aṅga* literature has been explained for their benefit.[35] However, in the opinion of Schubring, the *Aṅgas* and the *Pūrvas* are not interdependent but go parallel to each other.

The Age of the Canon

The entire *Āgama* does not belong to one particular period. While taking into account the antiquity of the canonical literature, we have to look to the subject matter, language, grammatical forms, style and above all metre. As stated already, the Tīrthaṅkaras preached the principles which they are said to have known by themselves and the *gaṇadharas* put them in writing. Thus on the whole, the canonical literature should be as old as Mahavira himself. But as various councils were convened from time to time to put the Master's teachings in order, new material must have been added to the original. Jacobi, Leumann, Schubring and Alsdorf have contributed a good deal to ascertain the period of the canonical text. After a critical study of the Jain Canon, Schubring considers the *Āyāra*, the *Sūya*, the *Uttarā*, the old *Chedasūtras*, the *Isi* and some portions of the *Das* as the most ancient texts of the Canon as they have employed typical words, fixed phrases, conventional descriptions and stereotype terms besides old grammatical forms, the old metres such as the triṣṭubh, Jagati, Vaitālīya, *aupachandasaka* and a primitive form of Āryā;[36] they also contain expressions such as *suyaṃ me āusaṃ* (I have heard, o long-lived one) and *ti bemi* (thus I say), indicating the antiquity of the texts. Such is not the case with the later canonical texts, comprising the later grammatical forms, the common Āryā metre being replaced by *śloka* and having partly a symmetrical arrangement of subjects. This tendency is marked in most of the *Paiṇṇās* and the *Nijjuttis.*[37] It is on the basis of the metrical investigation that Jacobi places the origin of most of the ancient texts of the Śvetāmbara Jain Canon about the end of the fourth and the beginning of the third century BC. Alsdorf has drawn our attention to the importance of metre in textual studies of the canonical texts of the Jains. He observes:

> First even the oldest and the best commentaries are completely unreliable . . . ; but in countless instances they misunderstand and misinterpret perfectly clear passages and offer fanciful explanations for palpably corrupt ones. Second, many if not most, of the real textual corruptions are very old, much older in fact than all our commentaries, let alone even the oldest Mss. This is why high hopes based on the old palm leaf Mss. at last becoming accessible have been and will be largely disappointed. We are not only entitled but bound to disregard the commentaries wherever necessary or advisable and to correct the text even against them and the combined authority of all our Mss.[38]

Alsdorf points out the parallels between the *Hariesaijja,* the twelfth chapter and the *Jannaijja,* the twenty-fifth chapter of the *Uttarā* with the Buddhist *Jātaka* and the *Suttanipāta* observes that in both of the above-mentioned chapters there remain a considerable number of dark or corrupt passages. In this context Alsdorf has discussed a few readings of the text which are very important from the point of view of the textual history and criticism of the Jaina Canon.[39]

Modifications and Alterations in the Jain Canon

Whatever sermons were delivered by Mahavira, were composed in the form of the *Aṅgas* or the *Dvādasāṅga.* But after the death of Mahavira the sacred literature of the Jains became irregular and disorderly. In order to set this literature right various councils were convened as we have seen already. The main work undertaken in these councils was the recension of the twelve *Aṅgas*, and the final shape to this literature was given at Valabhi in the fifth century. Under the circumstances, it was not possible to preserve the canonical literature in its original form. We have seen that there is no uniformity of names and different titles are ascribed to one and the same canonical text. Their number also varies. Out of 45 *āgamas*, only 42 have been noted in the *Nandi* and the *Pakkhiya Sutta*. Except the existing order of the 11 *Aṅgas*, the order of the rest of the canonical texts is not noticed either in the *Nandi* or the *Pakkhiya Sutta*. Then the contents of the available *āgamas* do not correspond to the table of contents recorded in the *Sama* and the *Nandi*, as noted earlier. Our contention is supported by the commentators. In numerous places they find it difficult to explain the text and they simply refer to the old tradition. The number of the *padas* of the *Viyāha*, for example, referred to in the *Sama*, the *Nandi* and in the commentary of Abhayadeva differ from one another. The *Paṇha*, the tenth *Aṅga*, does not correspond either to the title or the table of contents recorded in the *Thā* or the *Nandi*. Similarly the *Anta* and the *Aṇuttaa* both seem to have lost their original texts as their contents do not tally with those noted in the commentary of the *Ṭhā*. Even the names and characters described here are quite different and the reason provided by the commentator Abhayadeva is the difference in the *vācanā*. Then, there seems to be no relation between the *Aṅgas* and the *Upāṅgas*; the former are composed by the *gaṇadharas*, the latter by the *sthaviras*. Both are not noted in the *Nandi* (44), some later *ācāryas* have tried to relate the *Aṅgas* and the *Upāṅgas*, though their subject-matter is quite different. The earliest known reference to the *Upāṅga* literature occurred not earlier than the twelfth century.[40] As we have noticed a portion of the *Jambu* has been restored with the assistance of the *Jīvā* and other canonical texts. The contents of the *Niryā* do not tally with the contents recorded in the *Ṭhā*. Originally, only five *upāṅgas*, the *Niryāvaliyāo*, the *Kappavadaṃsiyao*, the *Pupphiyāo*, the *Pupphacūliyāo* and the *Vaṇhidasāo*, constituted the *Upāṅga* literature.[41]

Barring the *Aṅga* literature, a number of works of the canonical texts are said to have been written by distinguished authors. For example, the *Paṇṇa*, the fourth *Upāṅga*, was written by Ārya Syāma (died AD 151); the *Dasā*, the *Kappa* and the *Vavahāra* by Bhadrabāhu, who was well-versed in the 14 *Pūrva*s (died 357 BC); the *Nisīha*, one of the most important *Chedasūtras*, by Bhadrabāhu or Visākhācārya; the *Aṇu* by Āryā Rakṣita (died AD 57); the *Nandi* by Devavācaka (died

AD 466).[42] The number of the *Paiṇṇās* is not fixed. We are told that at the time of Mahavira there were several thousands of *Paiṇṇās*, now this number is reduced to ten. The *Causaraṇa*, the *Āurapaccakkhāṇa*, the *Bhttapariṇṇā* and the *Ārādhanāpatākā*, all of them are said to have been composed by Vīrabhadragaṇi (tenth century). The last-mentioned work is said to have been based on the *Bhag Ārā* of Sivakoṭi of *Yāpanīya Saṅgha.*[43]

Besides, certain canonical texts or parts of texts have become totally extinct. We have seen how the *Dṛṣṭivāda*, the twelfth *Aṅga*, was declared lost from the time of Sthūlabhadra and how the knowledge of the *Pūrva* literature went on diminishing after the *nirvāṇa* of Mahavira. Then, the *Mahāpariṇṇā*, the seventh chapter of the first *Suyakkhandha* of the *Āyāra*, was extinct at least by the time of the commentator Sīlāṅka. The original *Paṇha* no more exists. Similarly the *Dasās*, the *Dogiddhadasā*, the *Bandhadasa*, the *Dūhadasā* and the *Saṃkhartadasā*, referred to in the *Ṭhā*, (X. 755, pp. 482 aff) are lost. The *Pañcakappa*, one of the *Chedasūtras*, is extinct, though its *Cūrṇi* and *Bhāṣya* are available. Then, a portion of the *Kālika* and the *Utkālika sruta* has gone into oblivion. The *Mahā Nī* was not available at the time of Haribhadrasūri, who restored it to best of his ability. According to the *Jain Granthāvali* (p. 16), it had undergone three *vācanās*, out of which only the *bṛhadvācanā* is available at present. In the *Vivi* (p. 147, note 2) it has been stated that the text was eaten by white ants and its pages damaged. Then, several *Niryuktis* have been lost. Govinda Vācaka's *Nijjutti* is not available, so is the case with the *Sīr Nijjutti* and the *Isi Nijjutti*, composed by Bhadrabāhu. The *Pañcamaṅgalasuyakkhandha*, originally a separate canonical work, was incorporated in a *Mūlasūtra* by Vajrasvāmin.[44] Even some of the *Nijjuttis* on the *Pañcamaṅgalasuyakkhandha* are not available. Though the *Piṇḍaṇijjutti* and the *Ohanijjutti* are included among the *Mūlasūtras*, they are only the portions of the *Das Nir* and the *Āva Nir* respectively. The *gāthās* of some of the *Niryuktis* and the *Bhāṣyas* are so mixed up that even the authors of the *Cūrṇis* found it impossible to separate them.[45]

We have referred to different recensions of the canonical text and the variant readings noted in their commentaries. Prominent commentators such as Sīlāṅka, Abhayadeva and Malayagiri have pointed out contradictory versions which were not easily intelligible. Sīlāṅka in his commentaries on the *Āyāra* and the *Sūya* have noted various readings. Those under the name of Nāgārjuna are more distinct and elaborate than readings accepted by the commentator himself. Sīlāṅka has stated in his commentary of the *Sūya* (II.2.39): 'Often we come across various readings here; there is not a single ideal reading, concurring with the commentary. Under the circumstances, we have accepted what is considered the best, therefore the readers should not get confused in case there appeared some contradiction.'[46] The commentator Abhayadeva has expressed similar views in his commentaries on the *Ṭhā*, the *Sama* and the *Paṇha.* In the commentary of the *Ṭhā* (p. 499af) he has stated:

> As the real traditions have been lost, as there has been no systematic reasoning, as one's own religious treatises and the treatises of others are not to be seen, and forgotten, as there have been a variety of readings, as the sacred books have not been written correctly, as they contain deep meaning and as the opinions differ, it is possible to make errors in explaining the subject-matter, therefore only the meaning following the sacred text should be followed by those who are endowed with discriminative power.[47]

Abhayadeva has composed this commentary with the assistance of Droṇācārya. Elsewhere in the *prastāvanā* of the *Paṇha,* he has stated: 'We are ignorant and the sacred texts are fathomless, the texts are often puzzling, therefore after giving a serious thought, one should decide the *Sūtra* and should not fully depend on my explanation.'[48]

Malayagiri in his commentary on the *Rāya* has noted a number of variants that are quite different from the ones accepted by him. Then, in his commentary of the *Jīvā,* he has alluded to the difference in *vācanā* at numerous places. Originally, this text contained twenty *pratipattis* but now has only nine.[49] Malayagiri also wrote a commentary on the *Jambu* which is no more available. The present available commentary on this *Upāṅga* composed by Sānticandra has been completed with the assistance of the readings from the *Jīvā* and other texts.[50] Siddhasena Divākara, who is highly respected among Jains, was criticized by some members of the Śvetāmbara community for his challenge to orthodoxy, for his reliance on logical arguments against strict fidelity to the canonical texts of the Śvetāmbaras article 'Siddhasena Divākara and Svāmī Samantabhadra', *Jaina Sāhitya Saṃśodhaka,* Vol. I, Pt. I, Mahavira Samvat, 2446.

A Brief Survey of the Canonical Works

The sacred books of the Jains are recognized under the title of *Āgama, Siddhānta* or *Sruta.* The twelve *Aṅgas* or *dvādasāṅga,* also known as *gaṇi-piṭaka* (basket of teachers) constitute the first and most important part of the Canon. The *dvādasāṅga* is the fundamental basis of the Jain *Siddhānta.* As this literature composed by the *gaṇadharas* is directly based on the preachings of Mahavira, it is considered the only authoritative literature of the Jains. Both sects are unanimous in calling this literature the *dvādasāṅga.* The language is Prakrit, also known as *Ārṣa* (i.e. the language of the *Ṛṣis*) or Ardhamagādhī. This literature is valuable as besides the teachings of Mahavira and his disciples, it contains social and cultural material which is very important from the point of view of making an ana-lytical study of ancient Indian history and culture. It also throws flood of light on the history and development of Indo-Āryan languages.

The *Ācārāṅga* is the first *Aṅga* which treats of the way of life (*ācāra*). It deals with rules and regulations pertaining to the conduct of monastic life, self-restraint, endurance in hardships and non-injury to living beings. The last chapter, known as *Uvahāṇasuya,* of the first *Srutaskandha,* composed in ancient Āryā metre offers a vivid description of Mahavira's early career as an ascetic. The second *Srutaskandha* is divided into four *cūlikās,* dealing with begging for alms, wandering, speech, asking for garments and alms-bowl and residence. The first *Srutaskandha* is considered more original and older.[51]

The *Sūyagaḍaṅga* (*Sūtrakrtaṅga*) which deals with the pious life of the monks, is also divided into two *Srutaskandhas.* The first comprises 16 *adhyayanas,* which are poetical compositions except for the last, known as *Gāthā,* which is in prose. The second *Srutaskandha* contains 7 sections, composed in prose and poetry. As pointed out earlier, like the *Ācā,* here also the second *Srutaskandha* has been added later only as an appendix. The language used here is archaic like the *Ācā* and the different metres employed are Anuṣṭup, Vaitālīya[52] and Indravajrā. Various similes are given to explain the sermons and to refute certain theoretical doctrines. Alsdorf remarks: 'The *Sūyagaḍaṅga* is, besides the *Āyāraṅga* the *Dasaveyāliya* and the *Uttarajjhāyā,* one of the four "senior" texts of the *Siddhānta* of the *Śvetāmbara* Jains.' He considers the 53 stanzas of this chapter of unusual interest as they have been composed in a rare metre of older form of Aryā.[53] The sixteenth chapter, entitled 'Gāthā', is devoted to Mahavira where the terms *māhaṇa, samaṇa, bhikkhu* and *nigganṭha* applied to Mahavira are explained.

The Thāṇāṅga (Sthānāṅga) and the Samavāyāṅga provide a list of dogmatic topics which can be arranged in groups. Like the *Aṅguttaranikāya* of the Buddhists, the former enumerates topics in numerical order from 1 to 10. Here we come across a table of contents of the *Dṛṣṭivāda* which is no more available. In the *Sama* also a similar numerical method of presenting the subject-matter is followed. Here we come across a table of contents of the 12 *Aṅgas* and the 14 *Pūrvas*. The *Viyāh* or the *Bhagavatī* explains various topics concerning the soul as preached by Mahavira. It contains dialogues giving vivid pictures of the activities of Mahavira and his answers to the questions to his chief disciple Goyama Indrabhūti. Numerous topics are discussed here at different places which do not seem to be interconnected. A detailed account of Maṅkhaliputta Gosāla is provided which throws light on the relationship of Mahavira and Gosāla. *The Nāyādhammakahāo* (*Jñātṛdharmakathāḥ*) contains examples (*nāya*) and religious narratives (*dhammakahā*) or the religious stories from Mahavira, who is known as *Nātaputta* (*Jñātṛputra*). It is divided into two *Srutaskandhas*, the former containing 19 subdivisions, and the latter 10. The eighth section of the first *Srutaskandha* has the story of Malli, the nineteenth Tīrthaṅkara, and a female.[54] In Section 16 the legend of Draupadī is narrated. Here we meet *veḍhas* (*veṣṭas*) in most of the narratives. The *Uvāsagadasāo* (*Upāsakadasāh*) narrates the duties of the 10 lay-adherents at the time of Mahavira. The seventh section deals with the story of Saddalaputta, a devotee of Ājīvika sect. Both Mahavira and Gosāla try to win over Saddālaputta and his wife; in the end they accept the religion preached by Mahavira. The stories are told here in a stereotyped manner.

The Antagaḍadasāo (*Antakeṛddasāh*) deals with ten pious ascetics who attained liberation. The Kṛṣṇa legend is incorporated here along with the story of Ariṣṭanemi, the twenty-second Tīrthaṅkara. The downfall of the city of Dvārakā and the death of Kṛṣṇa are narrated. *The Aṇuttarovavāiya dasāo* (*Anuttaraupapātikadasāh*) contains ten chapters on pious ascetics who attained the highest region of heaven, the Anuttara. Here the narrations are not in full, merely a skeleton is provided, the rest is to be filled with set words and phrases with the help of other canonical texts. Like the *Anta* here also the stories are of the same pattern. The severe penance practised by ascetic Dhanya is described.

The Paṇhavāgaranāiṃ (*Prasnavyākaraṇāni*) or 'Questions and Explanations', is a comparatively modern treatise, the contents of which do not correspond either to the title of the work or to the table of contents in the *Ṭhā* (10) and in the *Nandi*. It is written in prose mixed with *veḍhas*. *The Vivāgasuya* (*Vipākasruta*), also known as *Kammavivāgadasāo* in the *Ṭhā* (10), is divided into two *Srutaskandhas*, dealing with the legends on the consequences of good and evil deeds.

THE TWELVE *UPĀṄGAS*

1. The *Ovaiya* or *Uvavāiya* (*Aupapātika*) deals with the attainment of existence (*uvavāya*) in the worlds of gods and denizens of hell. It contains various descriptions such as the departure of Mahavira for the shrine of Pūrṇabhadra and the pilgrimage of King Kūṇika Ajātasatru with his entourage to pay homage to the Master. Here are given descriptions of the city of Campā, the shrine of Pūrṇabhadra, the *asoga* tree in the surrounding garden, King Kūṇiya, son of Bimbasāra, his queen Dhāriṇī and Mahavira. These descriptions are so vivid and graphic that they provided a model for a number of canonical texts. These descriptions are reproduced, indicated by the word *vaṇṇaa* (*varṇaka*, meaning description) and introduced by the word *jāva* (*yāvat*, meaning till). Very often we come across these descriptions in the canonical texts. They are ready-made descriptions which can be supplied to other works.[55] Such descriptions are given in the first two *Upāṅgas* as well as the *Kalpsūtra* (or the *Pajjosaṇākappa*, the eighth chapter of the *Dasāsuyakkhandha*). They appear in *veḍha* metre.

2. The *Rayapaseṇaijja* or *Rājapasenaiya* (*Rājaprasnīya*) is an important *Upāṅga*. Here we come across a dialogue between King Paesi and the monk Kesi which can be well compared with Pāyāsi Sutta of the *Dīghanikāya* of the Buddhist Canon. Winternitz considers this dialogue where the monk Kesi endeavours to prove the independent identity of soul of the body, a splendid and lively one.[56] The god Sūryābha ascends from his celestial *vimāna* and pays homage to Mahavira. Here we get a magnificent description of the abode of Sūryābha which is considered a model for the stūpas of Bharhut and Sanchi, Amaravati and Mathura. The Āmrasālavana sanctuary described here is also quite old.[57] The 32 dramatic performances described here are unique. The names of some musical instruments are also provided.

3. The *Jivā* deals with the fundamental principles of Jainism. It furnishes us the details of animate and inanimate objects. 4. The *Paṇṇa* (*Prajñāpanā*), also known as *the Bhagavatī*, has been ascribed

to Āryā Syāma. It is a systematic treatise of questions and answers with regard to nine *tattvas*, divided into 36 *padas*. Here we come across people divided into Āryan and non-Aryan (*Mleccha*). Twenty-five and a half Āryan countries are mentioned besides those who are Āryans by birth, family, trade, language and art and handicraft. A list of non-Āryan people is provided. 5. The *Suriyapaṇṇatti* (*Sūryaprajñapti*), 6. The *Jambuddivapaṇṇatti* (*Jambudvīpaprajñapti*), 7. The *Canda-paṇṇatti* (*Candraprajñapti*) deal with astronomy and cosmology. The fifth and the seventh *Upāṅga* deal with the description of heavens based on the sun and the moon respectively. Both the available texts seem to be completely identical. It is said that originally there must have existed another work of the title *Candapaṇṇatti*. *Jambuddiva-paṇṇatti* contains the mythological geography of Jains. The *Niryāvalī* group of five *Upāṅgas* (8-12) consist of *Niryāvaliyā* or *Kappiyā* (*Kalpikā*), *Kappavaḍiṃsayā* (*Kalpāvataṃsikā*), *Pupphiyā* (*Puṣpikā*), *Pupphacūliyā* (*Puṣpacūlikā*) and *Vaṇhidasā* (or *Andhaga-Vaṇhidasā Andhaka-Vṛṣṇidasā*). According to Winternitz, originally, these *Upāṅgas* formed one text; later on, they were counted separately to make the number of *Upāṅgas* tally with the number of *Aṅgas*. The eighth *Upāṅga* gives the lives of the ten princes of Sreṇika, the ninth one of the ten sons of the same princes, and the twelfth contains the legends of twelve princes of the Vṛṣṇi race.

THE TEN *PAIṆṆĀS (PRAKĪRṆAKAS)* OR 'SCATTERED PIECES'

The *Paiṇṇās* were composed by the *sramaṇas* in the knowledge of the preaching of Mahavira. They deal with religious matter and are written in verse.[58] The *Causaraṇa* (*Catuḥsaraṇa*) or 'Fourfold Refuge', also known as *Kusatanubandhi adhyayana*, is composed by Vīrabhadra. The first few verses prescribe the six daily duties (*ṣaḍāvasyaka*). The *Aurapaccakkhāṇa* (*Āturapratyākhyāna*) or 'The Sick One's Refusal' by Vīrabhadra, deals with various types of death. Several verses of this work are found in Vaṭṭakera's *Mulācāra*. *Bhattapariṇṇaya* (*Bhaktaparijñā*) or 'Dispensing With Food' deals with various types of death. The *Saṃthāra* (*Saṃstāra*) or 'Pallet of Straw' points out the importance of pallet of straw, upon which the sage, preparing for death, stretches himself in order to meditate. In order to illustrate his point the author has referred to sages Annikāputta, Sukosala, Cāṇakya, Gajasukumāla and others. The *Tandulaveyāliya* (*Tandulavaicārika*) is in mixed poetry and prose. It is a dialogue between Mahavira and Goyama where topics pertaining to physiology, and anatomy and the life of the embryo are discussed. A peculiar etymology of the title is given by Vijaya Vimala: 'an examination of rice grains (*tandula=taṇḍula*), characterized by the number of rice grains, to be eaten day by day, by a man who lives for a hundred years.'[59] The *Candāvijjhaya* (*Candravedhyaka*) literary means 'the apple of the eye which is to be bored through' (*candravedhyaka*). It is stated that just as a well-equipped person while shooting due to the slightest negligence on his part, can miss the mark, so too a person efficient in all respects may not be able to achieve liberation, if at the time of death he shows the slightest negligence.[60] It deals with monastic discipline, the virtues of a teacher and of a pupil in education (*niggaha*) through discipline, knowledge, practice and in dying.[61] The *Devindatthaya* (*Devendrastava*) contains a classification of masters of gods according to their groups, and residence. The *Gaṇivijjā* (*Gaṇividyā*) deals with astrology with regard to auspicious and inauspicious days, constellations, etc. The *Mahāpaccakkhāṇa* (*Mahāpratyākhyāna*) or 'The Great Refusal' deals with the rules pertaining to confession, renunciation, etc. The *Vīratthaya* (*Vīrastava*) is a hymn in praise of Mahavira whose various names have been enumerated.

THE *CHEYASUTTAS* (*CHEDASŪTRAS*) OR 'A TREATISE'

The *Cheyasuttas* (*Chedasūtras*) prescribe 'cut' or reduction in seniority. The *Chedasūtra* could collectively be called a Jain 'book of discipline' as the *Vinaya* in Buddhist literature where the rules of life for monks and nuns, and atonements and penances are prescribed. They belong to the earliest portion of the Canon. Since they lead to the purity of conduct (*caraṇa-visuddhi*) they are included in *uttama sruta* (excellent scripture). The *Chedasūtra* is called a secret of sacred teaching (*pravacanarahasya*), therefore like the Buddhist *Vinaya*, it is to be disclosed only after ascertaining the proper place, time and the person.[62] Like other parts of the canonical texts, there is no homogeneity in the classification of these *Sūtras*. Some consider *Dasā* (*Dasāsrutaskandha*) and *Kappa* (*Bṛhatkalpa*) or *Kalpa* and *Vavahāra* as one and in order to make number six, *Pañcakappa* and *Jīyakappa* are added as two separate *Sūtras*.

The *Nisīha* (*Niśītha*), also known as *Ācārapagappa* or *Nisīhajjhayaṇa*, is the first *Chedasūtra*. *Niśītha* means night or darkness or obscurity (*aprakāsa*); as it is concealed in secrecy (*aprakāsadharma=rahasyadharma*), it should not be disclosed to others.[63] According to some, the Sanskritization of the title should be *niseha* (*niṣedha*) or 'prohibition'. It is a cross form between *niseha* and *nisīhiyā* (place of study) as it contains the rules and regulations for punishment for various transgressions against the rules of daily life. This *Sūtra*, being considered as a fifth *Cūlā* of the *Ācā*, is presumed as a part of the *Ācā* and is known as *Nisīthacūlā*, the fifth Cūlā.[64] It is also known as *Pakappa* or *Ācāraprakalpa* or *Ācārakalpa*. It has been stated that this *Sūtra* was based on the *Paccakkhāṇa Puvva*[65] and was composed by those who were proficient in the knowledge of the fourteen *Pūrvas*.[66] However, according to the author of the *Pañcakalpa-Cūrṇi*, Bhadrabāhu has been mentioned as the author of the *Āyārakappa* (= *Nisīha*), *Dasākappa* and *Vavahāra*.[67] The text contains 20 *uddesakas*, each with numerous *Sūtras*. There is *Niryukti*, *Bhāsya* and *Cūrṇi* on this important work. *Nisīha* is counted among three important *Chedasūtras*, the others being *Vavahāra* and *Kappa* (*Bṛhatkalpa*).

The *Vavahāra* (*Vyavahāra*) is called *navanīta* (fresh butter) of the *Dvādasāṅga*. The *Kappa* or the *Bṛhatkalpa* and the *Vavahāra* are supplementary to each other. According to Schubring both have flowed together from different sources.[68] The former teaches the liability for punishment, whereas the latter meting out of the punishment.[69] It contains 10 *uddesakas*. Bhadrabāhu is the author; he has also composed the *Niryukti* on this *Sūtra*. A *Bhāṣya* has also been written on this work but its author is not known. The verses of *Niryukti* and *Bhāṣya* have got mixed up. Its *Cūrṇi* remains unpublished.

The *Mahānisīha* (*Mahāniśītha*) or 'the Greater Niśītha' sometimes is taken as the second or sometimes the sixth *Chedasūtra*. It is known as the essence of the sacred teaching (*Pavayaṇa-sāra*). It has many topics common with those of the *Nisīha*. Looking to its language and subject matter it appears that the real *Mahā Nī* has gone astray. This work is compared with a surpassable desire-yielding fabulous gem and is called the highest essence of the whole of the sacred teaching. Its leaves were eaten away by white ants, later it was restored due to love for the sacred teaching.[70] It was reconstructed by Haribhadrasūri according to tradition and was honoured by Siddhasena, Vrddhavādin, Devagupta, Jinadāsagaṇi and others.

Dasāo or *Āyāradasāo* or *Dasāsuyakkhandha* (*Dasāsrutaskandha*) is considered the fourth *Chedasūtra*. Some add *Dasā* with *Kappa* (*Bṛhatkalpa*) and separate *Vavahāra*, others make *Dasāo* independent and combine *Kappa* and *Vavahāra* as one. This indicates the importance of this *Sūtra*. According to Winternitz, *Dasā-Kappa-Vavahāra* are treated as one book (*srutaskandha*) in tradition and belong to the earliest portion of the Canon.[71] This work is ascribed to Bhadrabāhu by tradition. The eighth section of the *Dasāo* has long been known as *Kalpa* or the *Pajjosaṇākappa*. We are told that the *Kalpa* was recited before King Dhruvasena in order to comfort him for the loss of his son. Three different texts are united to form the *Kalpa*. Section I contains *Jiṇacariya* (the biographies of Jinas) where a lengthy account of Mahavira's birth and life is provided[72] in many *veḍhas* owing to which the text becomes a model like *Ovā* with its descriptions of Mahavira's *samavasaraṇa*, the city of Campā, and the shrine of *Pūrṇabhadra*. Then follow the biographies of the remaining twenty-three Tīrthaṅkaras in a much shorter and stereotyped manner. Section II consists of the *therāvali*, a list of immediate disciples of Mahavira and the patriarchs following them with their schools (*gaṇa*), family (*kula*) and branches (*sākhās*) which are represented in the inscriptions Kaṅkālī Ṭīlā at Mathura. Section III contains *Sāmācārī*, laying down prescriptions for monastic life during the rainy season (*pajjūsana*). This is assumed to be the oldest part of the work; the complete title of the *Kalpasūtra* is known as *Pajjosavaṇā-kappa* or the *Paryūṣaṇā-kalpa*.[74] Even today the *Kalpasūtra* is recited during the annual ceremony of public confession and forgiveness known as *saṃvatsarī* (great annual rite).

Kappa or *Bṛhatkalpa* is counted among the important *Chedasūtras*. It is syled the *Bṛhatkalpasūtra* in order to distinguish it from the *Kalpasūtra* mentioned above. Along with *Vavahāra* and *Dasā*, it forms one *Srutaskandha*. It deals with the rules and regulations for the monks and nuns and their residence, dress and alms-bowl. It contains six *uddesakas*. As stated earlier, the last *srutakevalin* Bhadrabāhu I (357 BC) was the author of the *Kappa*, the *Dasā* and the *Vavahāra*, whereas Bhadrabāhu II (sixth century AD), who was well-versed in the eightfold *Mahānimittas*, composed *Niryuktis* on the *Kappa*, the *Vavahāra* and the *Nisiha*. Saṅghadasagaṇi Ksamāsramaṇa composed *laghu Bhāṣya* on the *Kappa*, Malayagiri (twelfth century) wrote a commentary on the *Kappa* which was completed by Kṣemakīrti in 1275. There is also a *Bṛhadbhāṣya* on this work which is available to the end of the third *uddesaka*. It had also *Viseṣacūrṇi* which is unpublished. A critical edition of the *Bṛh Sū* along with *Nir*, *Bhā* and *Ṭī*, edited by Muni Punyavijayaji with a valuable introduction and published by

Atmanand Jain Sabha Bhavnagar, 1933-8 and 1942. W. Schubring had brought out an edition of this work titled '*Das Kalpasūtra, die alte Sammlung (=Collection) jinistischer Mönchsvorschriften (=Monaistic Order), Einleitung (=Introduction), Text, Anmerkungen (Notes), Übersetzung (Translation), Glossar (Glossary)*', Leipzig, 1905. The Nagari transcription of the text with Gujarati translation with a glossary of Prakrit words and Sanskrit equivalents by Jivraj Ghelabhai Doshi, was published in Ahmedabad, 1915. *Kalpa-vyavahāra-Nisītha-sūtrāṇi* (retranscription of Schubring's edition) is published by Jain Sahitya Saṃśodhaka Samiti, Puna, 1923.

The *Pañcakappa* (*Pañcakalpa*) is the same as the *Pañcakalpa-Mahābhāṣya.* As *Piṇḍa Ni* is a part of the *Das Nir,* the *Ogha Nir* of the *Āva Nir,* the *Pañcakalpa Nir* of the *Kalpa Nir,* similarly, the *Pañcakalpa Bha* is a part of the *Bṛh Bhā. Saṅghadāsagaṇi Kṣamāsramaṇa* is the author of this *Bhāṣya.* It contains 2666 *gāthās,* edited by Muni Punyavijaya, published in *Indologia Berolinensis,* V, 1977.

Jīyakappa (*Jītakalpa*) deals with ten kinds of punishment. Its authorship is attributed to Jinabhadragaṇi Kṣamāsramaṇa. Jinabhadra has also composed a *Bhāṣya* on this *Sūtra* which is simply a collection of *gāthās* from the *Bṛh Bhā,* the *Vyava Bhā,* the *Pañcakalpa Bhā,* the *Pinda Nir* and so on.[74]

THE *FOUR MŪLASŪTRAS* (THE ROOT SŪTRAS)

According to Schubring they were intended for those 'still at the beginning (*mūla*) of their spiritual career'.[75] Like the twelve *Upāṅgas,* the four *Mūlasūtras* also do not find mention in the early canonical texts. The earliest reference to the *Mūlasūtras* is found in Bhāvaprabhasūri's commentary (p. 94) on *Jainadharmavarastotra* (verse 90).[76]

The *Uttarajjhāya* (*Uttarādhyāya*) or *Uttarajjhayana* (*Uttarādhyayana*) is one of the earliest sacred writings of the Jains and one of the most valuable portions of the Jain Canon. It contains 36 chapters, a compilation of various texts, belonging to different periods. The earlier portion of this work consists of valuable poems—a series of gnomic aphorisms, parables and similes, dialogues and ballads—which belong to the ascetic poetry of ancient India. The contents of this work have their parallels with the *Dhammapada* and the *Suttanipata,* the Buddhist canonical texts. We have already referred to the *Uttarajjhāya* as one of the 'senior' texts of the Jain Canon. Alsdorf has pointed out that a chapter of the *Uttarajjhāya*, entitled *Kāvilīyaṃ* is one of the only three chapters of the whole Jain Canon (except for verse 17, which is a *sloka*) written in the old Āryā metre; the remaining oldest texts are: the *Āyāraṅga* I, 9 and the *Sūyagaḍaṅga* I, 4. Further, presenting a critical treatment of selected chapters of the *Uttarajjhāya*, he had made certain observations in another article entitled '*Uttarajjhāyā Studies*' (*IIJ* 6, 1962, pp. 110-36; *L. Alsdorf Kleine Schriften*, pp. 225-51). *Dumapattayaṃ*, the tenth chapter, is a poetical sermon put in the mouth of Mahavira. The interest of this remarkable piece of genuine ancient 'ascetic poetry' is enhanced by its form: it is one of not more than four chapters in the whole of the Jaina Canon composed in the old Vaitālīya Aupacchandasaka metre (the others are: *Sūyagaḍa* I, 2 [Vaitālīya] and *Uttarā* 15, *Das* 10 [Aupacchandasaka], the two *Sabhikkhu* chapters).[77]

Further, Alsdorf deals with the *Hariesaijja*, and *Jannaijja* chapters. He considers both interesting specimens of 'ascetic poetry'. In order to recognize and correct corruptions, he emphasizes the metre of the canonical text. The chapter *Hariesaijja* is composed in Triṣṭubh metre and while making a comparison of this chapter with that of the Buddhist *Jātaka* (497), Alsdorf has pointed out the similarity of the *gāthās* between the two.[78] Further, while discussing the corrupt text of the chapter *Jannaijja*, he has mentioned a parallel *gāthā* in the *Suttanipāta* (598).[79]

Āvassaya (*Āvasyaka*) means 'essential'; it deals with six essential daily duties: (i) *sāmāyika* (equanimity) obtained by desisting from all evil, (ii) *caturviṃsatistava* (glorification of the twenty-four Tīrthaṅkaras), (iii) *vandana* (veneration), (iv) *Pratikramaṇa* (confession), (v) *kāyotsarga* (penance through standing or sitting posture of the body), and (vi) *pratyākhyāna* (renunciation of certain pleasures). This *Sūtra* has come down to us in conjunction with the *Niryukti*. Bhadrabāhu has written *Niryukti* on this *Sūtra*; the *Niryukti* and *Bhāṣya* are printed together. Jinabhadragaṇi Kṣamāsramaṇa has written *Viseṣā* on the section of *Sāmāyika*. Jinabhadragaṇi Mahattara has written *Cūrṇi*; Haribhadra has written a '*siṣyahitā*' commentary and Malayagiri another, while Māṇikyasekharasūri has composed '*Dīpikā*' on *Niryukti*. E. Leumann has published the first three *Sūtras* of the *Āvasyaka* with German translation in *Übersicht Über die Avasyaka-Literatur* (Hamburg, 1934); K. Bruhn has published 'Āvasyaka Studies I' in *Studien zum Jainismus und Buddhismus, Gedenk schrift für Ludwig Alsdorf*, Weisbaden, 1981. *Dasaveyāliya* (*Dasavaikālika*) means 'Ten

Lectures beyond the prescribed study hours'. It contains ten lectures and two appendices (*Cūlikā*). The work is ascribed to Āryā Sayyambhava who is said to have composed it for his son Maṇaga. Some of the sayings contained in this *Sūtra* remind us of the sayings in the Buddhist *Dhammapada* and the Sāntiparva of the *Mahābhārata.* It begins with a declaration that *dharma* consists of *ahimsā* (non-injury), *saṃyana* (self-restraint), and *tapas* (austerity), and that even the gods bow down to one who abides by this law.[80] Aparājitasūri, a Yāpaniya, has written a commentary known as the *Vijayodayā* on this work. Bhadrabāhu has composed a *Niryukti,* Agastyasiṃha *Cūrṇi,* Jinadāsagaṇi Mahattara another *Cūrṇi* and Haribhadrasūri has written a '*sisyabodhinī*' commentary on this work. E. Leumann has published *Dasavaikālika-Sūtra und-Niryukti* in the *ZDMG,* 46 (1892), pp. 581-662 where he has translated the original *Sūtra* in German and edited the *Niryukti.* W. Schubring translated *Dasaveyāliya Sutta* with Introduction and notes, Ahmedabad, 1932. *Piṇḍanijjutti* (*Piṇḍaniryukti*) is a treatise on food (*piṇḍa*) eaten by a monk; composed in 671 *gāthās.* Sometimes *Ohanijjutti* (*Oghaniryukti*) is mentioned in its place, and occasionally the *Pakkhī* (*Pākṣikasūtra*). The *Piṇḍa-Nijjutti* and the *Oha-Nijjutti*[81] are ascribed to Bhadrabāhu, and are sometimes counted among the *Chedasūtras*; *Oha* conveys the sense of 'general'. In the *Oha-Nijjutti,* without going into details, general explanation of subjects and activities of monastic life is provided. The *Pakkhī* is a ritual in verse for the fortnightly confession (*pratikramaṇa*). It is recited by Jain monks during *pratikramaṇa.* It also supplies us with a list of canonical treatises.

THE INDIVIDUAL TEXTS

The *Nandi* and the *Aṇuogadāra.* These *Sūtras* are also called *Cūlikā-sūtras, Cūlikā* meaning appendix. Both these works are supposed to be appendices of the canonical text. The *Nandi* or Auspicious Introduction was composed in the fifth century by Devavācaka, pupil of Dūṣyagaṇ. It is partly in prose and partly in verse. It begins with a hymn of praise to Mahavira. It also provides us with a list of *therāvali* (elderly teachers) slightly different from the one given in the *Kalpa.* Five kinds of knowledge are described here in detail. Under *Srutajñāna,* a survey of canonical literature is provided which is of great importance. Under *mithyāsruta* (false knowledge) the non-Jain works like the *Mahābhārata, Rāmāyaṇa, Kauṭilīya Arthasāstra,*

Kāmasūtra, Vaiseṣika, Buddhasāsana, Kapila, Lokāyata, Patañjali and others are mentioned. *Aṇuoga* means investigation or exposition of knowledge from four different points of an entrance (*dvāra*). It is mostly in prose, in the form of questions and answers. The six *āvasyakas* (the essential duties) are described here. Like the *Nandi*, a list of non-Jain works, under the title of *mithyāsruta* is provided. Its authorship is attributed to Āryarakṣita, who compiled this work between AD 57 and 70.

The Exegetical Literature on the Jain Canon

Like the *Aṭṭhakathās* (*Arthakathā*) of the Buddhists, the exegetical literature on the Jain Canon is vast and extensive and without it, it is not possible to interpret the canon. As it is not possible to present a detailed survey of this literature, we are restrained to give only a brief survey.

The exegetical literature consists of (1) the *Nijjutti* (*Niryukti*), (2) the *Bhāsa* (*Bhāṣya*), (3) the *Cuṇṇi* (*Cūrṇi*) and (4) the *Ṭikā*; including the original texts, it is known as *Pañcāṅgī* (consisting of five parts). *Saṃgahaṇī* is also added to this list.[82] The *Niryukti*, the oldest explanatory literature on the Canon, is a very concise explanation in Āryā verses. *Niryuktis* were memorial verses which could be memorized by the teacher to impart interpretation of the text. Since they were composed in concise form, it was difficult to understand them without explanation, therefore they were commented upon. Only certain *āgamas* have *Niryuktis* and *Bhāṣyas*, not all of them. Others have only *Niryuktis* and *Bhāṣyas*, and not their original text; the *Piṇḍaniryukti*, the *Oghaniryukti* and the *Pañcakalpa-Bhāṣya* can be cited as examples. Originally, the *Niryuktis* were of very small size, containing a few hundred *gāthās*, but as the verses from the *Bhāṣya* got mixed up, they expanded. The following *āgamas* have been furnished with *Niryuktis*: (1) *Āvassaya*, (2) *Dasaveyāliya*, (3) *Uttarajjhayaṇa*, (4) *Āyāraṅga*, (5) *Sūyagaḍanga*, (6) *Dasāsuyakkhandham*, (7) *Kappa*, (8) *Vavahāra*, (9) *Sūriyapaṇṇatti*, and (10) *Isibhāsiya*. Of these the last two *Niryuktis* are not available.[83] The *Piṇḍanijjutti*, the *Ohanijjutti*, the *Pañcakappanijjutti* and the *Nisīhanijjutti* formed a part of the *Dasaveyāliya-nijjutti*, the *Āvassaya-N*, the *Kappa-N* and the *Āyāraṅga-N* successively. Bhadrabāhu II, who is different from Bhadrabāhu I (third century BC), the author of the *Chedasūtras*, is said to be the author of the *Niryuktis*; he belongs to the sixth century AD.

The *Bhāsa* (*Bhāṣya*) is chronologically the next stage in the development of the exegetical literature. Like the *Niryuktis* it is also composed in a concise form in Prakrit Āryā metre. The verses of the *Niryukti* and the *Bhāṣya* got so mixed up that it is difficult to separate them. *Bhāṣyas* were composed on the following ten canonical texts: (1) *Avassaya*, (2) *Dasaveyāliya*, (3) *Uttarajjhayaṇa*, (4) *Ksayaappa*, (5) *Pañcakappa*, (6) *Vavahāra*, (7) *Nisīha*, (8) *Jīyakappa*, (9) *Ohanijjutti*, and (10) *Piṇḍanijjutti*. The *Bhāṣya* on the *Pañacamaṅgalasūyakkhandha* can also be added to the list.[84] The *Bhāṣyas* can be divided into three categories: (i) the *Mūla-Bhāṣya*, (ii) the *Bhāṣya*, and (iii) the *Mahābhāṣya*. The *Āva Bhā* is most important in this respect. Out of nearly 2000[85] verses of the present *Āva Nir*, only 257 belong to the *Mūla-Bhāṣya* and it is noteworthy that they are identical with Jinabhadragaṇi Kṣamāsramaṇa's *Viseṣā Bhā*. Making a critical study of this important work, E. Leumann has stated, 'The language of this work is much more correct and its style more intelligible than of the old *Nijjutti* and their *Bhāṣya* insertions.'[86] Some *Bhāṣyas* were composed on the *Nijjutti*, others on the original *Sūtras*. Under the first category are included the *Viseṣāvasyaka-Bhāṣya* (on the *Āva Nir*) and the *Ogha-Nir-Mahābhāṣya* (on the *Ogha-Nir*); neither of them has *Laghu-Bhāṣya*. Under the second category is incorporated the *Jītakalpa-Bhā*. It contains no *Niryukti* and the *Mahābhāṣya* is composed only on the *Sūtra*. Some *Mahābhāṣyas* have been written on the *Laghu-Bhāṣyas*. The incomplete *Kalpa-Bṛhad-Bhā* and the *Nisitha* and *Vyavahāra Mahābhāṣyas* can be cited as examples; unfortunately, these *Mahābhāṣyas* are not available. Generally, the period of these *Bhāṣyas* is the fourth century AD or earlier; they contain valuable material regarding social and cultural life of the ancient days as well as the life-conduct of Jain monks and nuns of early period.

Cuṇṇi (*Cūrṇi*) is an intermediatory stage between the *Bhāṣya* and the *Ṭīkā*. Unlike *Niryukti* and *Bhāṣya*, it is written in prose, in mixed Prakrit and Sanskrit, and can be compared with hybrid Sanskrit of the Buddhist literature. The following canonical texts contain the *Cūrṇis*: (1) *Āyāraṅga*, (2) *Sūyagaḍaṅga*, (3) *Viyāhapaṇṇatti*, (4) *Jīvābhigama*, (5) *Jambuddīvapaṇṇatti*, (6) *Nisīha*, (7) *Mahānisīha*, (8) *Vavahāra*, (9) *Dasāsuyakkhandha*, (10) *Kappa*, (11) *Pañcakappa*, (12) *Ohanijjutti*, (13) *Pañcamaṅgalasuyakkhandha*, (14) *Jīyakappa*, (15) *Uttarajjhyayaṇa*, (16) *Āvassaya*, (17) *Dasaveyāliya*, (18) *Nandi*, (19) *Aṇuogadāra*, and (20) *Pakkhiya*.[87] The *Paṇṇavaṇā*, the *Piṇḍa-Niryukti*, the *Aṇuogadāra-Aṅgulapada*, the *Srāvakapratikramaṇa*, the

Ītyāpathikī and others can be added to the list. The *Nisīha-cuṇṇi* contains two *cuṇṇis*, of which only the *Nisīha-Viseṣa-Cuṇṇi* is available. Both the *cuṇṇis* of the *Kappa* (or *Bṛhatkalpa*) are available. The *Dasaveyāliya* has two *cuṇṇis*, one by Agastyasiṃha, another by an anonymous author. The former was composed 200 or 300 years before the Valabhi council held in the fifth century.[88] The author has made a reference to some old *vrtti* in his work and it is interesting that a number of *gāthās* of the existing *Dasaveyāliya Sutta* are stated to form a part of this commentary. The *Cūrṇi* is important as it records various readings of the original text. The inconsistency of the *Niryukti gāthās* is also noticed here. The *Nisiha* and the *Āva Cūrṇis* can be considered most important, as they contain material pertaining to social and cultural life as well as historical and semi-historical information of that period.

Ṭīkā is also known as *vivaraṇa, vācanā, vivṛti, vṛtti, avacūri, avacūrṇi, dīpikā, vyākhyā, vacanikā, bhaṣaṭīkā, bālāvabodha, ṭippaṇaka, ṭabbā* and so on. The *agamaic* literature was composed in Ardhamāgadhī, the dialect of Magadha and in order to explain the sacred texts, the later writers preferred to write their commentaries in Sanskrit. Among the distinguished commentators the names of Jinabhadragaṇi Kṣamāsramaṇa (sixth century); Haribhadrasūri, the son of Yākinī (eighth century); Sīlāṅkasuri (ninth century); Vādivetāla (an excellent disputer like a vampire), Sāntisūri (eleventh century), composer of the '*siṣyahitā-vṛtti*' (also known as *Pāiya-Ṭīkā*) on the *Uttarajjhayaṇa*; Nemicandrasūri (also known as Devendragani) (eleventh century, composer of the *sukhabodhā* commentary) can be mentioned. Like Haribhadra, Sāntisūri and Nemicandrasūri have also retained original Prakrit stories in their commentaries. Among other writers of the twelfth century, mention may be made of renowned Abhayadevasūri, who is known as *navāṅgī-ṭīkākāra* (commentator on nine *Aṅgas*), Droṇācārya, Maladhāri Hemacandra, a pupil of Abhayadeva and a senior contemporary of Ācārya Hemacandra, Malayagiri commentator of six *Upāṅgas*. Then we have Kṣemakīrti, who completed Malayagiri's unfinished commentary on the *Bṛh Bhā* in 1276, Sānticandra, a pupil of Hīravijaya, who completed the commentary on the *Jambu* in 1594, and many others who enriched the sacred Jain Canon by writing their valuable commentaries and explanations. Commentary literature was also written in Gujarati under various titles such as *dhabo, bālāvabodha, akṣarārth* and so on.

NOTES

1. See Jagdish Chandra Jain, *LAI*, Chapter 20.
2. Kauṭilya's *Arthasāstra* (11.1.5) refers to the Licchavika, the Vṛjika, the Mallaka, the Madraka, the Kurus, the Pañcālas and others, calling them *rājopasabdajīvinaḥ* (using the title of a king). The commentary of the *Vya Bhā* (7.459) mentions the Aṅgas, the Vaṅgas, the Magadhas, the Vajjis, the Nātas, the Lāḍhās, the Mallas, the Hastipālas, the Sārasvatas and the Kumbhakāras; see also *Bṛh Bhā* (6.6302).
3. Some identify it with Padrauna in Deoria district, U.P.
4. *Kalpa*, 5.127. According to Jinasena, people started celebrating the feast of Dīpāvali from this time, *Harivaṃsapurāṇa* (66.21).
5. Jacobi, *SBE*, Vol. 45, 34f.
6. *Parṇa-Sabaras* (the Sabaras covering their body with leaves are referred to in Varāhamihira's *Bṛh Saṃ* (14.X).
7. Jagdish Chandra Jain, *LAI*, pp. 292-7.
8. According to the Digambara tradition Karnāṭaka in the south.
9. *Āva Cū*, II, 187; also Haribhadra, *Upadesapada* and commentary, p. 89.
10. According to the school of Ārya Skandila, the council was held 827 years after Mahavira's *nirvāṇa*, whereas according to the followers of Nāgārjuna, after 840 years. This indicates that the difference of opinion about Mahavira's *nirvāṇa* is quite old.
11. The number twelve seems to be an example of the number-motif, see Jagdish Chandra Jain, *PNL*, p. 62.
12. *Nandi Cū*, p. 8.
13. *Kahāvali*, 298 after Muni Kalyanvijay, *Vīr Nirvān*, p. 110 and n. according to Hemacandra, the Jain Canon was reduced to writing in the form of books (*pustakeṣu nyastaṃ*) in the last two councils, *Yogasāstra* Commentary, 3, 206a.
14. Muni Kalyanvijay, op. cit., pp. 112-18.
15. The text of the passage is provided in H.R. Kapadia's *HCLJ*, 63, n. 1.
16. The variants of versions of the Jain canonical text supplied by Nāgārjuna have been recorded only in the *Cūrṇi* literature and not in the original texts of the canon, according to Muni Punyavijay. In his valuable paper titled 'Jain Āgamadhara aur Prakrit Vāṅmaya', read as the Chairman of the Prakrit and Jainism section of the All India Oriental Conference held in Srinagar on 14-16 October 1961 (see *Jñānāñjali*, a Commemoration Volume, Bombay, 1969), he has pointed out the variants of the Nāgārjunīya version in the following *Cūrṇi* texts (Hindi Section, pp. 31-2):
    (a) *Dasavaikālika Cūrṇi*, page 204 by an unnamed author (published).
    (b) *Ācārāṅga Cūrṇi* and the commentary of Sīlāṅka on the text (here the page numbers given are from the texts, edited by Ācārya Sāgarānandasūri). Here out of 15 references only 10 are found in

the commentary of Sīlāṅka. They are noticed only in the first *Srutaskandha* of the text.

(c) *Sūtrakṛtāṅga Cūrṇi* refers to the Nāgārjunīya version 13 times; 4 times in the first and 9 times in the second *Srutaskandha.* Sīlāṅka in his commentary refers to it at 4 places.

(d) *Uttarādhyayana Cūrṇi* refers to it at 5 places. The same thing is done by Vādivetāla Sāntisūri in his *Pāiya* Commentary.

For the variants referred to H.R. Kapadia in the *Pajjosaṇākappa* (*Sū* 147) and in the commentary of Sīlāṅka on the *Ācārāṅga* and the *Sūtrakṛtāṅga,* see *HCLJ,* p. 64 and note.

17. For example, the *Sūyagadaṅga,* the *Viyāhapaṇṇatti,* the *Paṇhavāgaraṇāim,* the *Diṭṭhivāya,* the *Nāyādhammakahāo,* the *Uvāsagadasāo,* and the *Anuttarovāvaiyadasāo* have more than one title, H.R. Kapadia, *HCLJ,* pp. 53-4; Bechardas J. Doshi, *Rāya,* Introduction, pp. 8f; *JSBI,* I, 39-42.

18. For instance, compare the number of the *padas* of the *Nāyā* and the *Viyāha;* noted in the *Nandi;* the *Paṇha* neither corresponds to the title nor to the table of contents; the *Anta,* the *Aṇu* and the *Niryā* have lost their original texts; the *Jambu* has been restored with the assistance of other canonical texts. Jagdish Chandra Jain, *LAI,* 47-8.

19. There is a different list in the *Pakkhiyasutta,* pp. 66a, 66b. The following works are added here: (i) *Sūrapaṇṇatti,* (ii) *Vaṇhiya,* (iii) *Āsīvisabhāvaṇā,* (iv) *Diṭṭhīvisabhāvanā,* (v) *Cāranabhāvanā,* (vi) *Mahāsumiṇabhāvaṇā,* (vii) *Teyaganisagga.* There is no mention here of *Dharaṇovavāya; HCLJ,* p. 25. Also see the variants given in the footnotes of *Nandisūtta,* 84, pp. 32-3, Punyavijaya, *Nandisuttaṃ* and *Anuogaddārāiṃ,* Bombay, 1968.

20. They are (i) *Uppāya,* (ii) *Aggāṇīya,* (iii) *Vīria,* (iv) *Atthinatthippavāya,* (v) *Nāṇappavāya,* (vi) *Saccappavāya,* (vii) *Āyappavāya,* (viii) *Kammappavāya,* (ix) *Paccakkhanappavāya,* (x) *Vijjaṇuppavāya,* (xi) *Avañjha,* (xii) *Pānāu,* (xiii) *Kiriāvisāla,* (xiv) *Lokabindusāra* (*Nandi, Sūtra* 57). The *Pūrvas* too have variation in names as well as in contents. In *Pravacanasāroddhāra* (*dvāra* 92), *Samayappavāya* and *Bindusāra* are substitute for *Kammappavāya* and *Lokabindusāra* respectively; in the *Nandi* (57) *Aṇuppavāya* is mentioned in place of *Vijjānuppavāya.* In the Digambara tradition, *Avañjha* is known as *Kallānavāda.* For further details regarding *Pūrvas,* see *HCLJ,* pp. 85-91.

21. The order in the Śvetāmbara tradition is as follows: (i) *Dharmakathānuyoga,* (ii) *Gaṇitanuyoga,* (iii) *Dravyānuyoga,* (iv) *Caraṇakaranānuyoga.* For further details with regard to 4 *Anuyogas* see *HCLJ,* pp. 10-12. According to Schubring, the names *Aggāṇīya, Avañjha, Kiriyāvisāla* and *Logabindusāra* are indicators of their obscurity, *The Doctrine of the Jainas,* 75. However, Yativṛṣabha, in his *Tiloyapaṇṇati* refers to *Aggāyaṇīya, Diṭṭhivada, Parikamma* and other ancient texts and their readings. In the Śvetāmbara tradition, *Caraṇakaraṇānuyoga* comprises *Kālikasruta, Dharmānuyoga Ṛṣibhāṣita, Gaṇitānuyoga, Sūryaprajñapti* and *Drvyanuyoga*

comprises the *Dṛṣṭivāda*, see *Āvasyaka-Mūlabhāṣya* (124), *Viseṣāvasyaka-Bhāṣya* (2294), *Uttarā Cū*, p. 1; also see Sīlāṅka, Commentary on *Ācā*, p. 1a; *HCLJ*, p. 11n.

22. For the period of the *vācanās*, there is a difference of opinion between Hemacandra's *Pari* (lx.68-9) and the *Titthogāliya* (736), see *HCLJ*, p. 72n.
23. *Āva Cū*, II, 187; Haribhadra, *Āva Vr*, 696-8; Haribhadra, *Upadesapada* and its commentary, p. 89.
24. *Āva Cū*, I, 404.
25. Yativṛṣabha, *Tiloyapaṇṇatti*, 4.1482-92; also Padmanandi Muni, *Jambuddīvapaṇṇattisangaha.*
26. The commentator Abhayadeva explains the title as भूता: सद्भूता: पदार्था: तेषां वादो भूतवाद: thereby indicating that the text dealt with the refutation of heretical doctrines.
27. *Nisī Bhā*, 19.6184 and *Cū*.
28. *Āva Nir*, 760
29. *Bṛh Bhā Pī*, 145; *Āva Cū*, I. 35; Bhadrabāhu, *Kappanijjutti*, 146; *Visēṣā*, V. 551f. Here quoting the pertinent excerpt in full, Ludwig Alsdorf has observed, '"The *Dṛṣṭivāda* contains everything" is a belief obviously betraying complete ignorance of the real contents of the long-last text.' He adds further, 'I know of no other passage where the universality of contents of the *Dṛṣṭivāda* is claimed so openly and so bluntly. And this bluntness and naivety is no doubt the reason why, significantly, the great Haribhadra in his *Āva Tī* omits our passage altogether'; *German Scholars on India*, I. 5.
30. Page 12b, after *HCLJ*, p. 88.
31. Ibid., pp. 88f. For the quotations and the extracts from the *Pūrvas*, see pp. 86-7.
32. सुहम्मसामिणा जंबुनामस्स पढमाणुओगे तित्थयर-चक्कवट्टि -दसार-वंसपरूवणागयं वसुदेवचरियं कहियं, p. 2, lines 3-4.
33. See *LAI*, p. 35, fn. 6.
34. Also *Nandi Cū*, 56; *Āva Nir*, 270.
35. *Āva Cū* I, 35; *Bṛh Bhā*, pp. 46, 146, *Viseṣā*, 551ff.
36. While discussing the importance of 'Itthiparinna', the fourth chapter of the first *Suyakkhandha* of the *Sūya*, composed in the old Āryā metre, Alsdorf has made certain important observations. He writes: 'The 53 stanzas of our text are of unusual interest in their form: they are composed in a metre which is as rare as it is important for their history of Indian prosody, viz., the older form of the Āryā. As is well known, the later or "common" Āryā, the most popular metre of Prakrit poetry, is characteristic of the latest stratum of the Jain Canon but completely absent from (the genuine parts of) its older layers. The old Āryā, its forerunner, is, on the contrary, restricted to only three chapters of the

very oldest Jain texts, viz., *Āyāra* 1.9, *Sūya* 1.4, and (partly) *Uttarajjhāyā* 8, and two chapters of one of the very oldest Pali texts, viz., *Suttanipāta* 8 and 14. This metre was first discovered by Jacobi in *Āyāra* 1.9 and *Sūya.* 1.4, and described in *ZDMG* 38, 595ff . . .'; 'Itthiparinna'—A Chapter of Jain Monastic Poetry, *As a Contribution to Indian Prosody*, edited by Alsdorf, *IIJ* 2, 1958, pp. 249-70, reproduced in *Ludwig Alsdorf Kleine Schriften*, pp. 193f. This article is published in Gujarati in *Shri Mahavira Jain Vidyalaya Suvarṇa Mahotsava Granth*, Bombay, 1968, pp. 237-60.

37. *The Doctrine of the Jainas*, p. 81. Schubring in his *Worte Mahaviras* (pp. 3-5) has determined the chronology of the metrical portions of the Canon as follows:
    1. The oldest stratum consists of Triṣṭubh, Jagatī, Vaitālīya, Aupachandasaka, *śloka*, and Āryā (or Gāthā of the old form).
    2. The second stratum consists of those texts in which the *śloka* predominates.
    3. The third stratum consists of those texts in which the *Veḍha* predominates.
    4. The last stratum consists of those texts in which the *Gāthā* or *Āryā* of the common form predominates.

    Also see A.C. Sen, *A Critical Introduction to the Panhavāgaraṇāiṃ*, 10.

38. *IIJ* 2, 1958, pp. 249-70; reproduced in *Ludwig Alsdorf Kleine Schriften*, pp. 225-6; also read Alsdorf's articles: 'vāntuṃ āpātuṃ' *Sunitikumar Chatterji Jubilee Volume*, Poona, 1955=*Indian Linguistics* 16, 1955, pp. 21-8; 'The Story of Citta and Sambhūta', *Felicitation Volume presented to Prof. S.K. Belvalkar*, Benaras, 1957, pp. 202-8; 'Namipavvajjā', *Indological Studies in Honor of W. Norman Brown*, New Haven, 1962, pp. 8-17; all reproduced in *Ludwig Alsdorf Kleine Schriften*, pp. 178-85; 186-92; 215-24; also see *The Āryā Stanzas of the Uttarajjhāyā*—Contributions to the Text History and Interpretation of a Canonical Jain Text, Meinz, 1966.

39. Here we take liberty to reproduce Alsdorf:

    (i) 'जे य वेय-विऊ-विप्पा, जन्नट्ठा य जे दिया, जोइसंग-विऊ जे य, जे य धम्माण पारगा (Hariesajjja 17) देवेन्द्र', commentary: 'जन्नट्ठा य' त्ति 'यज्ञार्थाश्च' यज्ञ प्रयोजना ये तत्रैव व्याप्रियन्ते 'द्विजाः' संस्कारापेक्षया द्वितीयजन्मानः ।

    This interpretation of Devendra, is unconvincing and as unsatisfactory as the metre of the *pāda* which lacks one syllable. That ancient students of the text were not insensitive to this deficiency is shown by the variant जन्नट्ठाय जिइं दिया read by Jacobi, Charpentier and old (Hyderabad) Sthānakavāsī edition: manifestly the unsuccessful emendation of a very ancient corruption; it does rectify the metre but leaves untouched the crux जन्नट्ठा and gives the second half of the *pāda* a Jaina flavour unsuited to the context. An easier way out of the metrical difficulty was found later: in both Devendra and Kamalasaṃyama (edited by Jayantavijaya, Agra, 1923) the *mūla* reads जन्नमट्ठा य ये दिया, but this is at once contradicted by the text of both commentaries quoted above; there can be no doubt that Devendra reads जन्नमट्ठा and that जन्नमट्ठा is much younger emendation than जन्नट्ठा य जिइंदिया. In the opinion of Alsdorf, the correct reading should have been जन्न-जट्ठा य जे दिया, i.e. यज्ञ-यषारश्च ये द्विजाः, 'and brahmins sacrificing sacrifices'. (pp. 248f.)

(ii) जहा चंदं गहाईया, चिट्ठंते पंजलीउडा
वंदमाणां नमंसंता, उत्तमे मणहारिणो (Jannaijja 17)
देवेन्द्र explains: यथा चन्द्रं ग्रहादिकाः 'पंजलीयड' त्ति कृत प्रांजलयः 'वन्दमानाः' स्तुवन्तः 'नमस्यन्तः' नमस्कुर्वन्तः 'उत्तम' प्रधानं 'मणोहारिणो' त्ति विनीततया चित्ताक्षेप-कारिणस्तिष्ठन्तीति संबंधः, तथैनमपि भगवन्तं देवेन्द्रप्रमुखा इत्युपस्कारः।

Jacobi accordingly translates: 'The beautiful (gods) with joined hands praise and worship the highest Lord (i.e. the Tīrthaṅkara) as the planets, and c. (praise) the moon.'

This stanza corresponds to *Suttanipāta* 598:
चन्दं यथा खयातीतं पेच्च पंजलिका जना
वन्दमाना नमस्संति, एवं लोकस्मिं गोतमं।

'As the people, when they see the moon waxing again (lit.: gone beyond waning), salute and worship here with joined hands so (they worship) Gotama in the world.' The Pali *pāda* चन्दं यथा खयातीतं can leave no doubt that we have to read जहा चंदं गहाईयं and that गहाईय is not ग्रहादिक but ग्रहालीत which, as ग्रह is primarily a name of Ketu, means 'gone beyond Ketu', i.e. reappeared after an eclipse; this makes decidedly even better sense than खयातीत.

That the last *pāda*, उत्तमं मणहारिणो, is not in order is suggested by the fact that Sāntisūri records two variant readings: उद्धत्त मणहारिणो and उद्धतुं अणगारिणो, both of which, however, do not seem to make sense. In any case मणहारिणो can hardly, as assumed by Devendra, qualify the subject; more probably we have to read मणहारिणं and to take it as an attribute of चन्दं. It looks as if the stanza, taken from different context or from the stock of 'floating' stanzas, was imperfectly adapted to its present use suggested by the preceding stanza: the praise of the *Jina* likening him to the moon reappearing after an eclipse was a particularly apt continuation of नक्खत्ताणं मुहं चन्दो, घम्माणं कासवो मुहं (16 stanzas), pp. 49-50.

(iii) धिरत्थु ते, जसो-कामी, जो तं जीविय-कारणा वन्तं इच्छसि आवेउं। सेयं ते मरणं भवे (Dasaveyāliya, 2.8).

Here while explaining the meaning of 'जसो-कामी', Alsdorf criticizes the translations rendered by Jacobi, Leumann and Schubring, and asserts that, it means only a '*kṣatriya' and not* 'famous knight' or 'with your desire of glory' or 'greedy of glory' as suggested by the above-mentioned translator successively. His contention is supported by the *Das Cū* where the word has been explained as 'जसो-कामिणो खत्तिया भण्णंति', see '*Vāntaṃ Āpātuṃ*', p. 178.

40. See *HCLJ*, pp. 29, 34.

41. *Niryā*, pp. 3-4.
42. The last two texts seem to have been included in the canonical texts much later. According to Schubring and Alsdorf, they belong to the groups of preliminary study, and they are nothing but the parts of the *Āvassaya* exegesis grown independent through amplification. They were received in the canon after the *Āva Nijjutti*, Alsdorf, *Jain Exegetical Literature and the History of the Jaina Canon*, 7f.; *Mahavira and His Teachings*, Bombay, 1977.
43. *Jñānāñjali* (*Muni Shri Punyavijayaji Commemoration Volume*, Pt. I, 'Hindi Tatha Sanskrit Lekho', p. 45.
44. *HCLJ*, 80.
45. Agastyasiṃha in his *Das Cū* records only 54 Niryuktrgathas, whereas in Haribhadra's commentary the number goes to 157, Punyavijaya Introduction *Bṛh Bhā*, Vol. VI, p. 5.
46. इह च प्रायः सूत्रादर्शेषु नानाविधानि सूचाणि हश्यन्ते न च टीका-संवाद्ये (?) कोऽ प्यस्माभिरादर्शो समुपलब्धोऽत एकमादर्शमंगीकृत्यां-स्माभिर्विवरणं कियत इति, एतदवगम्य सूत्रविसंवाददर्शनाच्चित्त-व्यामोहो न विधेयः।
47. सत्संप्रदायहीनत्वात्, सदूहस्य वियोगतः।
सर्वस्वपरशास्त्राणामदृष्टेरस्मृतेश्च मे ॥
वाचनानामनेकत्वात्, पुस्तकानामशुद्धितः।
सूत्राणामतिगांभीर्यान्मतभेदाच्च कुत्रचित् ॥
क्षुण्णांनि संभवन्तीह, केवलं सुविवेकिभिः।
सिद्धान्तानुगतो योऽर्धः, सोऽस्माद् ग्राह्यो न चेतरः ॥
48. अज्ञा वयं शास्त्रमिदं गभीरं, प्रायोऽस्य कूटानि च पुस्तकानि।
सूत्रं व्यवस्थाप्यमतो विमृश्य, व्याख्यान कल्पादित एव नैव ॥
49. इह भूयान् पुस्तकेषु वाचनाभेदो, गलितानि च सूत्राणि बहुषु पुस्तकेषु ततो यथावस्थित वाचनाभेदप्रतिपत्यर्थं गलित-सूत्रोद्धरणार्थं चैव सुगमान्यपि विव्रियन्ते, *Jīvā* commentary, 3, 376.
50. *Jambu*, 2, 117a.
51.. In the *Ācā Nir* (287), it has been stated that the second *Srutaskandha* has been composed by the *sthaviras*, which is a later addition. This view is supported by Jacobi in the Introduction (p. xli) of the *SBE* (Vol. XXII). He says: 'I am of the opinion that the first book of the *Ācārāṅga Sūtra* and that of the *Sūtrakṛtāṅga Sūtra* may be reckoned among the most ancient parts of the Siddhānta. . . . But both the *Ācārāṅga* and the *Sūtrakṛtāṅga* contain each a whole lecture in Āryā verses of a form which is decidedly older than, and probably the parent of the common Āryā. . . . On page xlvii he continues: 'The first book, then, is the oldest part of the *Ācārāṅga Sūtra*; it is probably the old *Ācārāṅga Sūtra* itself to which other treatises have been added.'
52. For discussion on the Vaitālīya metre see Jacobi's article, 'Uber die Entwicklung d. indischen Metrik in Nachvedischer Zeit' (*ZDMG*, 38, pp. 592-619). The Āryā metre of the *Ācā* is also dealt with.
53. See supra, n. 36.
54. According to the Digambara sect, Malli was a male.

55. Winternitz has pointed out something similar in the Canon of the Sarvāstivdins where the tales are narrated after one stereotyped pattern so that certain phrases and descriptions of situations occur again and again in exactly the same words, *A History of*, II, pp. 450. fn. 3; 280.
56. Ibid., p. 455.
57. V.S. Agrawala, *Ancient Indian Folk Cults*, 138.
58. Ibid., 457f.
59. Ibid., 460n.
60. उप्पीलिया सरासणगहियाउहचावनिच्छय मईओ।
विंधइ चंदगविज्झं झायंतो अप्पणो सिक्खं॥ 128
जइ य करेइ पमायं थोवंपि य अन्नचित्तदोसेणं।
तह कयसंधाणो वि य चंदगविज्झं न विंधेइ॥ 129
तम्हा चंदगविज्झस्स कारणा अप्पमाइणा निच्चं।
अविराहियगुणो अप्पा कायव्वो मुक्खमग्गंमि॥ 130
61. विणयं आयरियगुणे सीसगुणे विणयनिग्गह गुणे य।
नाणगुणे चरणगुणे मरणगुणे इत्थ वुच्छामि॥ 3
62. जम्हा एत्थ सपायच्छित्तो विधीभण्णति, जम्हा य तेण चरण-विसुद्धी करेति तम्हा तं उत्तमं सुतं।
Nisī, 19.6184 *cū*
तम्हा न कहेयव्वं आयरियेण पवयणरहस्सं।
खेत्तं कालं पुरिसं नाऊण पगासए गुज्झं॥ *Nisī Bhā* 19.6184, 6227, 6243
63. जं होति अप्पगासं, तं तु निसीहं ति लोगसंसिद्धं।
जं अप्पगासधम्मं, अण्णं पि तयं निसीधं सि॥ *Nisī Bhā* 69
64. It appears that formerly the second *Srutaskandha* of *Ācā* had five *Cūlās* (appendices instead of four; it is confirmed by the following verse in the *Āyāranijjnti* (11):
णवबंभचेरमइओ अट्ठारसपयसहस्सिओ बेओ।
हवइ य सपंचचूलो बहुबहुतरओ पयग्गेणं॥
Here 'सपंचचूलो' is explained by Sīlāṅka as 'पंचमी निशीथाध्ययनं'. . . । *HCLJ*, p. 78n.
65. आयारपकप्पो पुण पच्चक्खाणस्स तइयवत्थूओ।
आयारनामधिज्जा वीसइमा पाहुडच्छेया॥ *Ayāranijjutti* 291
66. कामे जिणपुव्वधरा, करिंसु सोधिं तहा वि खलु एण्हिं।
चोछसपुव्वणिबद्धो, गणपरियट्टी पकप्पधरो॥ *Nisī Bhā* 6674.
67. तेंण भगवता आयारकप्प-दसाकप्प-ववहारा नवमपुव्वनीसंदभूता निज्जूढा, *Pañcakalapa-Cūrṇi, NS*, p. 1. Punyavijaya, Introduction to *Bṛh Bhā*, VI, p. 3. However, according to Jinadāsagaṇi Mahattara, Visāhagaṇi was the author of the *Nisī Sū*.
68. *The Doctrine of the Jainas*, 111.
69. *A History of*, II, p. 464.
70. एत्थ य जत्थ जत्थ पयंपयेणाऽणुलग्गं सुत्तलावगं ण संपज्जइ तत्थ तत्थ सुयहरेहिं कुलिहियदोसो ण दायव्वो। किंतु जो सो एयस्स अचिंतचिंतामणिकप्पभूयस्स महानिसीहसुयक्खंधस्स पुव्वायरिसो आसि तहिं चेव खंडा खंडीए उद्देहिया एहिं हेऊहिं बहवे पण्णगा परिसडिया तहावि अच्चंत समुहत्थाइसयं ति इमं महानिसीहसुयक्खंधं कसिणपवयणस्स परमसारभूयं परं तत्तं महत्थं ति कलिऊण पवयणवच्छल्लत्तणेण quoted from the manuscript copy in possession of late Muni Punyavijaya. We are told in the *Jain Granthāvali* (p. 16) that this work had three *vācanās*: *laghu*,

madhyama and *Bṛhat,* out of which only the text one is available, *HCLJ,* 31.

71. *A History of,* II, 462.
72. The biography with descriptions in Kāvya style reminds us of the biography of the Buddha in the *Lalitavistara,* op. cit., 463.
73. In the opinion of Muni Punyavijaya a part of the ornamental description of dreams, *therāvali* (list of elderly monks) and a part of *sāmācārī* is a later addition to the text, *Introduction to Kalpa,* pp. 9-11.
74. Edited by Muni Punyavijaya with *Bhā,* Ahmedabad, vs 1994; ed. by Muni Jinavijaya with *Cū* and *Ṭī,* 1926.
75. *Worte Mahaviras,* p.1, cf., also *Orientalististische Literaturzeitung* (*OLZ*), 1924, 484 and above, II, p. 461, n. 4, after Winternitz, *A History of,* II, 466n.
76. *HCLJ,* 43 n.
77. P. 226.
78. Alsdorf, op. cit., 244.
79. Alsdorf, op. cit., 249. The *Āryā Stanzas of the Uttarajjhāyā. Contributions to the Text History and Interpretation of a Canonical Jaina Text* by the same author is also worth reading.
80. धम्मो मंगलमुक्किट्ठो अहिंसा संजमो तवो।
देवा वि तं नमंसंति जस्स धम्मे सया मणो॥ 1.1
81. Commentary by Droṇācārya, AGS, Mehsana, 1919; Muni Manavijaya, together with Droṇācārya's Com., Surat, 1957; ed. by A. Mette, 'Piṇḍesana Das Kapitel der Oha-nijjutti uber den Betterlgang, uber setzi und kommentiert', Wiesbaden, 1974.
82. According to the *Pañcakalpa-Mahābhāṣya,* the *Saṃgrahaṇīs* are said to have been composed by Āryā Kalaka, Muni Punyavijaya, *Jñānāñjali,* Hindi Section, p. 48; *Saṃgahaṇī gāthās* are found in the *Viyaha, Joga-saṃgaha, Padikkamaṇasutta* and also in the *Upāṅgas, HCLJ,* 205. For the 'Dhammillahiṇḍi-Saṃgahaṇi' and the 'Vasudevahiṇḍi-padhaṃa-saṃahaṇī', see *Vasudevahiṇḍi,* Appendix I.
83. According to Alsdorf, these two *Nijjuttis* never existed. The *Isibhāsiya* does not belong to the Canon and no commentary on this text has ever been known, and it is not even certain that our present text is identical with the one named as in the *Nijjutti* list. Regarding the other, he has quoted the commentator saying that the *Nijjutti* on the *Sūr* has been lost through the wickedness of the Kali age. However, to complete the list of ten, the *Piṇḍa* and the *Oha-Nijjutti* might have been added, or else their number should be considered eight instead of ten, 'Jaina Exegetical Literature and the History of the Jaina Canon', p. 6, *Mahavira and His Teachings,* Bombay, 1977.
84. The *Bhāṣya* containing 2666 *gāthās,* ed. by Muni Punyavijaya is published in the Roman script in *Indologia,* Berolinensis 6, 1977; also Vol. 6, 1980.

85. The number of *Āvassayanijjutti gāthās* varies from 2575 to 3550, *HCLJ*, 173. According to Haribhadrasuri, the number is 2386, whereas according Bhaṭṭāraka Jñānasāgar 1637 and according to Manikya-sekharasūri only 1615.
86. *Ubersicht*, p. 31b.
87. *HCLJ*, 190; Muni Punyavijaya, 'The Āgamadhara and Prakrit Vānmaya', *Jñānāñjali*, 48.
88. Muni Punyavijaya, Introduction to *Bṛhatkalpa*, VI.

3

The Canonical Literature of the Digambaras

As indicated earlier, the Digambaras disown 45 *Āgamas* that are accepted by the Śvetāmbaras. They believe that after Mahavira's *nirvāṇa*, gradually the scriptural knowledge went into oblivion; but they do believe in the twelve *Aṅgas*, composed by the *gaṇadharas*. According to them, the *Āgama* text is divided into *Aṅgabāhira* and *Aṅgapaviṭṭha*. The latter is divided into the following twelve *Aṅgas*: *Āyāro* (*Ācāra*), *Sūdayada* or *Suddayaḍa* (in *Gommaṭasāra*, *Jīvakāṇḍa*) or *Sūdayaḍa* (in *Aṅgapaṇṇatti*) (*Sūtrakṛta*), *Thāṇaṃ* (*Sthāna*), *Samavāyo* (*Samavāya*), *Viyāhapaṇṇatti* or *Vikkhāpaṇṇatti* (in *Gommaṭasāra Jīva*) or *Vivayāpaṇṇatti* (in *Aṅgapaṇṇatti*; *Vipākaprajñapti* in Sanskrit) (*Vyākhyāprajñapti*), *Ṇāhaddammakahā* or *Ṇāhassa Dhammakahā* (in *Gommaṭasāra Jīva*) or *Ṇāhaddammakahā* (in *Aṅgapaṇṇatti*) (*Nāthadharmakathā*), *Uvāsayajjhayaṇaṃ* (*Uvāsagadasāo* in Śvetāmbara Canon) (*Upāsakādhyayana*), *Antayaḍadasa* (*Antagaḍadasāo*) (in Śvetāmbara Canon) (*Antakṛddasā*), *Aṇuttarovavādiyadasāo* (*Anuttarovavāiyadasāo* in Śvetāmbara Canon) (*Anuttara-upāpadika-dasā*), *Paṇhavāgaraṇaṃ* (*Prasnavyākaraṇa*), *Vivāgasuttaṃ* (*Vivāgasuya* in Śvetāmbara Canon) (*Vipākasūtra*) and *Diṭṭhivādo* (*Diṭṭhivāya* in Śvetāmbara Canon) (*Dṛṣṭivāda*).[1]

The Digambaras believe in the *Dvādasāṅga* which was composed by the *gaṇadharas* and was based on the teachings of Mahavira but has gone gradually been lost (though it is available in the Śvetāmbara tradition). As we have seen earlier, even according to the Śvetāmbaras, there is no uniformity in the titles of the *Dvādasāṅga*, nor do their contents tally with the contents recorded in the Śvetāmbara canonical texts. Even the number of *pādas* do not correspond with the *pādas* noted in these texts. For instance, the number of the *pādas* of the *Viyāhapaṇṇatti*, according to the *Samavāyāṅga* is 84,000, according to the Nandi 2,88,000 and according to the commentator Abhayadeva

4,00,000. Similarly, the *Nāyā*, originally, is said to have contained 3,50,00,000 *pādas*. The total number of the *pādas* contained in the eleven recorded *Aṅgas* is 4,15,02,000, according to the *Saṭkhaṇḍāgama* (I, pp. 99-107; IX, pp. 197-203; also *Kasāyapāhuḍa*, I, pp. 93-6).[2]

The contents of these *Aṅgas* recorded in the Digambara texts differ from those recorded by the Śvetāmbaras. The *Sūtrakṛta*, for instance, deals with *jñāna, vinaya, prajñāpanā, kalpyākalpya, chedopasthāpanā* and *vyavahāra-dharma-kriyā*. The *Vyākhyāprajñapti* contained the discussion of 60,000 questions and answers with regard to the existence and non-existence of the *Jīva*. The *Nātha-dharmakathā* has stories about the teachings of the Tīrthaṅkaras and the removal of doubts on the part of the *gaṇadharas*. The *Antayaḍa* contains the stories of ten monks, Nami, Mātaṅga, Somila, Rāmaputra, Sudarsana and others, as well as stories of monks belonging to the era of other Tīrthaṅkaras. The *Anuttaradasā* contains narratives about Ṛṣidāsa, Dhanya, Sunakṣatra, Kārtika, Nanda, Nandana, Sālibhadra, Abhaya, Vāriṣeṇa, and Cilātaputra—all belonging to the era of Vardhamana Mahavira. It contains also the narration of monks belonging to the era of other Tīrthaṅkaras. The *Paṇhavāgaraṇa* contains a discussion of questions with regard to *ākṣepa, vikṣepa, hetu* and *naya*.[3]

The *Dṛṣṭivāda*, which has been declared lost, is divided into five sections: *Parikamma, Sutta, Puvvagaya, Aṇuoga* and *Cūlikā*. *Parikamma* is an 'introduction' to the study of the *Sūtras*.[4] It is divided into five parts: *Candapaṇṇatti, Sūriapaṇṇatti, Jambuddīvapaṇṇatti, Dīvasāgarapaṇṇatti* and *Viyāhapaṇṇatti*.[5] (Of these the first four are included under the *Upāṅga* and the fifth under the *Aṅga* constituent of the Śvetāmbara Canon). The *Sutta* explains the meaning of all *dravyas, paryāyas* and *nayas*.[6]

The *Puvvagaya* comprises fourteen *Pūrvas*. The titles of these texts in Digambara and Śvetāmbara traditions generally are the same, except that the *Kalyāṇavāda* is substituted by the *Avañjha* (*Avandhya*) in the latter tradition.[7] There is a variation in contents according to both. According to the Digambaras, the *Vijjāṇuvāda* deals with 700 small magical lores such as the *aṅguṣṭha* (thumb) and *prasena*[8] and 500 great magical lores such as *rohiṇī* and others. It also deals with the 8 *Mahānimittas* such as the *antarikṣa, bhauma, aṅga, svara, svapna, lakṣaṇa, vyañjana* and *chinna*. The *Kallāṇavāda* deals with the omens pertaining to the movements of the sun, the moon, the constellations and stars, and also with great auspicious occasions (*mahākalysāṇa*) such as conception and birth of the Arhatas, the Baladevas, the Vāsudevas, the Cakravartins and others. The *Pāṇānuvāda* deals with various aspects of Ayurveda and the treatment of the body (*kāyacikitsā*), *bhūtikarma* (the auspicious ceremony at the time of birth, marriage, etc.), *jāṅguli* (toxicology) and the division of inspiration (*prāṇa*) and expiration (*apāna*). The *Kiriāvisāla* deals with seventy-two *kalās*, beginning with writing (*lekha*), sixty-four arts of women, the manual crafts, the qualities and the defects of poetry, the employment of metre (*chandoviciti*) and the enjoyment of the fruits of action (*kriyā-phaloprabhoktā*). The *Lokabindusāra*, the fourteenth *Pūrva*, deals with eight kinds of *vyavahāras* (behaviour), four kinds of *bījas* (origin), *parikarma*, *rāsi*, the division of performance (*kriyā-vibhāga*) and the essence of all scriptures.[9] The *Cūlikās* are divided into five sections: *Jalagatā*, *Sthalagatā*, *Māyāgatā*, *Rūpagatā* and *Ākāsagatā*. According to the Śvetāmbaras, they are incorporated in the *Pūrvas*, whereas according to the Digambaras, they have nothing to do with this literature.

The *Aṅgabāhira* is divided into fourteen parts: *Sāmāiya*, *Cauvīsatthavo*, *Vaṇḍaṇā*, *Paḍikkamaṇa*, *Veṇaiya*, *Kidiyamma* (in the Śvetāmbara tradition they are included in the *Āvasyaka Sūtra*), *Dasaveyāliya* and *Uttarajjhayaṇa* (in the Śvetāmbara tradition they are incorporated in the *Mūlasūtras*), *Kappavavahāra*, *Kappākappiya*, *Mahākappiya*, *Puṇḍarīya*, *Mahāpuṇḍarīya* and *Nisihiya*.[10] (Of these *Kappa*, *Vavahāra* and *Nisītha* form an important part of the *Chedasūtras* of the Śvetāmbara Canon.) In the Digambara tradition this literature has also gone into oblivion like that of the *Aṅgapaviṭṭha* which incorporates the *Dvādasāṅga*.

The *Uttarajjhayaṇa* and the *Dasaveyāliya* are considered to belong to the few ancient *Sūtras* of the Jain canonical literature in contents as well as the language. They can be compared with the Buddhist *Sūtras*, the *Suttanipāta* and the *Dhammapada*.[11] It is significant that these important *Sūtras* could not be sidetracked even in the Digambara tradition. Pūjyapāda in his *Sarvārthasiddhi* (I.20) has referred to the significance of the *Dasaveyāliya* and other similar works. He writes,

> The *ārātiyā ācāryas* (who have succeeded the *gaṇadharas* and the *srutakevalins*), have composed the *Dasavaikālika* and the other *Sūtras*, showing favour to the pupils, taking into consideration their short duration of age, intellect and strength on account of wickedness of time. These works have the same authenticity as the *Sūtras* composed by the *gaṇadharas* and the *srutakevalins*. As the milk poured from the ocean of milk in an earthen pot is not different

from the milk of the ocean, so is the case with the works composed by *ārātiyās.*[12]

Vīrasena (AD 816), the author of the *Dhavalā*-commentary on the *Saṭkhaṇḍāgama,* has extensively quoted from canonical texts such as the *Ācāraṅga, Bṛhatkalpasūtra, Dasavaikālika, Anuyogadvāra, Āvasyaka-Niryukti* and others. Aparājitasūri, also known as Srīvijayācārya, who has written the *Vijayodayā* commentary on the *Bhagavatī Ārādhanā,* has also composed a commentary bearing the same title on the *Dasavaikālika.* Unfortunately, this commentary is not available. In his commentary on the *Bhag Ārā* he has cited illustrations from the *Ācāraṅga,* the *Sūtrakṛtaṅga,* the *Dasavaikālika,* the *Uttarādhyayana,* the *Nisītha* and the *Bṛhatkalpa* (421, pp. 611-15). In support of Mahavira's moving about nude, he has quoted authority from these scriptures. Regarding the statement recorded in *Bhāvanā,* the third *Cūlikā* and the twenty-fourth section of the *Ācāraṅga* that 'for twelve months Mahavira roamed about with a robe and then wandered nude' (वरिसं चीवरधारी तेण परमचेलगोजिणो), he has pointed out certain contradictions and difference of opinion.[13] Besides, the *Bhag Ārā,* a work of antiquity, has almost identical contents and even common verses with the Śvetāmbara canonical texts which indicates that in early Jainism when there was no schism of Digambara and Śvetāmbara, and both the sects drew from the common source acceptable to both.[14]

The Saurasenī Literature

We have seen how the text of the *Dṛṣṭivāda* went into oblivion from the time of Bhadrabāhu, according to the Śvetāmbara. In the view of the Digambaras none of the scriptural texts has survived in its authentic form, but they hold that a section from the *Dṛṣṭivāda,* known as *Puvvagaya* (belonging to the *Pūrva* literature), and dealing with the *karma* theory, has survived[15] in the form of the *Chakkhaṇḍāgama* (*Ṣaṭkhaṇḍāgama*)[16] and the *Kasāyapāhuḍa* (*Kaṣāyaprābhṛta*).[17] These texts are based on the second and the fifth *Pūrva* texts respectively. We are told that once Ācārya Dharasena (second century AD), who possessed the knowledge of the complete *Ācāraṅga,*[18] was occupied in meditation in the Candraguphā of Girnar in Kāṭhiyāwād. Reflecting that sacred knowledge was going into oblivion, he sent for Puṣpadanta and Bāhubali from the region of Andhra so that he could train them.[19] When they arrived at the Mount Girnar, Dharasena imparted to them the knowledge of a portion of the

Pūrvas and the *Viyāhapaṇṇatti.* Later, on the basis of their teaching, they composed the *Chakkhaṇḍāgama Sūtra* in Saurasenī.

The *Chakkhaṇḍāgama* is also known as the *Kammapāhuda, Mahākammapayaḍipāhuda, Āgamasiddhānta, Ṣaṭkhaṇḍāgama, Paramāgama, Khaṇḍasiddhānta,* or *Ṣaṭkhaṇḍasiddhānta.* The first part of Book I contains a section on *Ṣaṭprarūpaṇā,* comprising 177 *Sūtras.* They deal with the *guṇasthānas* and *mārgaṇas.* Puṣpadanta, composed part one in 177 *Sūtras* and the remaining portion covers 6,000 *Sūtras* by his colleague Bhūtabali. In this manner a major portion of the *Ṣaṭkhaṇḍāgama,* based on the *Kammapayaḍi,* the fourth *pāhuḍa,* of the fifth *vatthu* of the *Agrāyaṇī,* the second *Pūrva,* was restored.

The *Chakkhaṇḍāgama* text, as the name indicates, is divided into six parts: *Jīvaṭṭhāṇa* (*Jīvasthāna*), *Khuddābandha* (Kṣudraka-bandha), Bandha-sāmitta-vicaya (Bandha-svāmitva-vicaya), Vedanā, Vaggaṇā (Vargaṇā) and Mahābandha. Part one deals with *ṣaṭprarūpaṇā* in 177 *Sūtras.* In the beginning, obeisance is paid to five *Parameṣṭhis* (dignitaries); fourteen *gunasthānas* and fourteen *mārgaṇas* are explained. Here *samyaktvotpatti* (the origin of right faith), the third *Cūlikā* of *Jīvaṭṭhāna,* is said to have been based on the *Sūtra,* the second section of the *Dṛṣṭivāda,* and the *gati-āgati,* the ninth *Cūlikā,* on the *Viyāhapaṇṇatti.* Part one contains eight *anuyoga-dvāras* and nine *Cūlikās;* part two eleven *anuyoga-dvāras;* part three the bondage of *karma;* part four the two *anuyoga-dvāras;* part five, twenty-three kinds of *vargaṇās,* and the last part, known as *Mahābandha,*[20] deals with the four kinds of *bandhas,* i.e. *Prakṛti* (determination of the nature and type of the bondage), *sthiti* (bondage of duration), *anubhaga* (intensity of fruition) and *pradesa* (space-point). It is divided into seven parts. The *Mahābandha,* also known as *Mahādhavalā,* is much longer than the first five parts, and Vīrasena, the commentator of the first five parts of the text, did not consider it necessary to write a commentary on this portion.[21]

The Commentaries

The *Chakkhaṇḍāgama* was so popular among the Digambaras that numerous commentaries and explanations were written on this text.[22] The following commentaries can be mentioned. 1. Ācārya Kundakunda of Kundakundapura, also known as Padmanandin (second century AD), wrote his commentary *Parikarma* on the first three parts. The commentary was in Prakrit and has been referred to several times in Vīrasena's commentary. 2. Sāmakuṇḍa (third century) wrote his commentary *Paddhati* on the first five parts of the text. The language of the commentary was mixed Prakrit, Sanskrit and Kannaḍa. He also composed a commentary on the *Kasāyapāḥuḍa*. 3. Tumbulūra (fourth century) wrote *Cūḍāmaṇi* in Kannaḍa on the first five parts. He also wrote *Pañjikā* on the sixth part of the *Kasāyapāhuḍa*. 4. Samantabhadra (fifth century) wrote his Sanskrit commentary. The commentator Vīrasena has referred to Samantabhadra's *Āptamīmāṃsā* and other works and to this commentary. 5. Bappadeva wrote *Vyākhyāprajñapti* on the first five parts of the text; his commentary on the sixth was brief. He also had a commentary on the *Kasāyapāhuḍa*. These commentaries were written in Prakrit. Bappadeva has been referred to once in the *Jayadhavalā* commentary on the *Kasāyapāhuḍa*. Unfortunately, all these are not available.

The most important available commentary known is *Dhavalā*, which gained such importance that the whole of it came to be known as the *Dhavala-siddhānta*. The commentator Vīrasena was the pupil of Āryanandin, the pupil of Candrasena, and Elacarya was his teacher. He had a mastery over *siddhānta*, *chanda*, *jyotiṣa*, *vyākaraṇa* and *pramāṇa* (logic) and had acquired the status of a Bhaṭṭāraka. This commentary is based on the *Vyākhyāprajñapti* of Bappadeva, and is composed in the form of *Cūrṇi* in mixed Prakrit and Sanskrit. It was written in Vāṭagrāmapura in Śaka saṃvat 738 (AD 816). Virasena was an erudite scholar who has freely quoted the canonical texts. He has referred to the *tāla-palamba Sūtra* of the *Bṛhatkalpasūtra* in his commentary. He has also cited quotations from important works such as the *Ṣaṭkarmaprābhrta*, *Kaṣāyaprābhṛta*, the *Sanmatisūtra*,[23] *Trilokaprajñaptisūtra*, *Pañcatthipāhuḍa*[24] (*Pañcāstikāyaprābhṛta*), Gṛddhapiccha Acāryā's *Tattvārthasūtra*, *Ācāraṅga* (*Mūlācāra*), Pūjyapāda's *Sārasaṅgraha*,[25] *Tattvārthabhāṣya*, *Jīvasamāsa*, the *Chedasūtra*, the *Karmapravāda*, the *Dasakarṇīsaṅgraha* and others. A number of these works are well known, but little information is available about the *Sārasaṅgraha*, the *Dasakarnisangraha* and others. In the third book the commentator has cited examples from the *Pariyammasutta* (*Parikarmasūtra*), an ancient prose work on mathematics; this work is also not available at present.

Three-fourths of this commentary is written in Sauraseni, the remaining in Sanskrit. In the beginning, the author pays obeisance to Srutadevatā, *gaṇadharas*, Dharasena, Puṣpadanta and Bhūtabali. Mahavira first preached this scriptural knowledge to his disciple

Gautama Indrabhūti, who is said to have composed the twelve *Aṅgas* and the fourteen *Aṅgabāhya Prakīrṇakas.*[26] Then the knowledge was imparted to Lohārya or Lohācārya,[27] then to Jambusvāmi. After they attained liberation, there came Viṣṇu, Aparājita, Govardhana and Bhadrabāhu, all of them possessing the knowledge of fourteen *Pūrvas.* Then we have Visākhācārya, Proṣṭhila, Kṣatriya, Jayācārya, Nāgācārya, Siddhārthadeva, Dhṛtisena, Vijayācārya, Buddhila, Gaṅgadeva and Dharmasena, they were holders of the knowledge of eleven *Aṅgas,* ten *Pūrvas* and the partial knowledge of four *Pūrvas.* Then were born Nakṣatra, Jayapāla,[28] Paṇḍu, Dhruvasena,[29] and Kaṃsācārya, all of them possessing the knowledge of the *Aṅgas* and partial knowledge of the *Pūrvas.* Then, Subhadra, Yasobhadra, Yasobāhu,[30] and Lohācārya possessed the knowledge of *Ācārāṅga* and the partial knowledge of the remaining *Aṅgas* and the *Pūrvas.* After Lohācārya attained liberation, the responsibility of preservation of scriptural knowledge fell on the shoulders of Bhaṭṭaraka Dharasena. He possessed the partial knowledge of the *Aṅgas* and *Pūrvas.* It was he who was fortunate to relish the sweetness of the nectar-like scripture, the *Mahākammapayaḍipāhuḍa.* He imparted this important knowledge to his talented disciples, Puṣpadanta and Bhūtabali, whom he sent for from the Andhra region. They got the credit of dividing their knowledge into six parts and composed the *Cakkhaṇḍāgama.*

Contradictions in Scriptural Texts

There was no uniformity of text or contents among the manuscripts of the *Chakkhaṇḍāgama* used by Vīrasena. He has referred to numerous contradictions in his commentary, expressing his inability to overcome some of them. The question is asked why there has been a contradiction in the statements of the *Chakkhaṇḍāgama* and the *Kasayāpāhuḍa.* The reply is that since the *gaṇadharas* have composed these *Sūtras* based on the teachings of Mahavira, there should be no possibility of contradictions in the *Sūtras,* but as time passed, the traditional knowledge of the *Dvādasāṅga,* on account of short of memory and intelligence, kept diminishing. In that case, of the two opposite statements, which should we take as true? The answer is that as the author himself is not in a position to say anything, it can be decided only by those holders of the knowledge of fourteen *Pūrvas,* and since they do not exist any more, both views should have to be explained. In such cases he has advised the readers to consult Gautama Indrabhūti himself, because in his commentary he has tried to explain what was recorded in the scriptures. This means that Vīrasena, the commentator, wanted to be true to the scriptures which were supposed to be the words of Mahavira.[31] At several places the commentator has referred to different views of the *Uttarapratipatti* and the *Dakṣinapratipatti*. The latter view, according to him, is simple and traditional, known as *pavāijjanta* (*pravā-hyamāna*); the former is complicated and non-traditional, known as *apavāijjanta* (*apravāhyamāna*).[32]

Being a Digambara Jain, Vīrasena has discussed the delicate point of *strī-mukti*—whether a woman is entitled to attain liberation in this birth. Consider his style of questions and answers:

'Does the same verbal authority (*ārṣa*) maintain the liberation of a *dravya-strī* (physical woman)?'

'No, as they remain dressed in clothes, they are entitled to possess the *apratyakhyana* (aptitude for renunciation of pleasures) *gunasthāna* (stage of spiritual development), they are not in a position to have saṃyama (self-restraint).'

'But even though they are with clothes, a *dravya-strī* (physical woman) can achieve *bhāva-saṃyama* (internal self-restraint), there should not be any objection to that?'

'It is not true, they are not in a position to achieve *bhāva-saṃyama* because in that case, they cannot put on clothes, the abandonment of which is an essential characteristic of *bhāva-saṃyama*.'

'But in that case how can they be entitled to achieve fourteen *guṇasthānas*?'

'In *manuṣya-gati* (human existence) a *bhāva-strī* can attain 14 *guṇa-sthānas*, there is no objection to that.'[33]

In Book III, the commentator discusses various points of controversy. A point is raised about the total number of *mithyadṛṣṭis* the one who has perverse attitude towards truth in infinite-infinite (*anantānanta*) world. The answer is, since it is a word of God Jina, who is free from telling falsehood, it must be taken for granted.[34] At another place, the total number 5,93,58,206 of the souls 'possessing self-control with spiritual inertia' (*pramatta-saṃyata*) is questioned.

The traditional authority of God Jina is cited. Regarding the extension of the *tiryakloka* (animal region), while discussing the two contradictory views, the author's own view is stated as the final truth, though it is said to be against the traditional view preached by the preceding teachers, according to him. There has been a difference of opinion as to how many *ucchavās* (respirations) make one *muhūrta* (=48 minutes). According to some the number is 720, but in the opinion of our commentator it should be 3,773. He gives prominence to mathematics (*gaṇita*) in *dravyānuyoga*, which indicates his knowledge of the subject.[35] Book IV discusses the measurement of the world (*lokākāsa*). According to one opinion, it is of round shape, measuring seven *rāju* (a measure of 8 *hastas* or 192 inches) in diameter; its lower part like *vetrāsana* (a small oblong low couch of cane-work), the middle like a *jhallarī* (drum) and the upper like *mṛdaṅga*. But the author of the *Dhavalā* does not agree with this view. According to him, in eastern and western directions the earth goes on increasing and decreasing upwards, and in the north and south remains only 7 *rājus* all over. In his opinion, the universe is not round but square, and in two directions it appears like *vetrāsana, jhallarī* and *mṛdaṅga*. Similarly, in Jain tradition, there is no living space beyond the Svayambhuramana ocean, but Vīrasena does not agree with the view. In the ninth Book, the commentator pays homage to Jinas and designates Vardhamāna as *Buddha-ṛiṣi* and *bhaṭṭāraka*, the maker of the ford (*tīrtha*). Vardhamāna Mahavira was born in Kuṇḍalapura.[36] There has been a difference of opinion about Mahavira's age. According to some, he lived for seventy-two years, others say seventy-one years, three months and twenty-five days. The author is at a loss to express his opinion. He observes, 'the pupil of Elācārya does not wag his tongue in this connection; the reason being there are no instructions in this matter from any source; moreover, there is nothing wrong in accepting either of the views; but at the same time it is certain that both the views cannot be right'.[37]

Such contradictory statements in his opinion, should not damage the scripture. Instead, it is a sign of healthy enquiry; it should be taken as a broad concept on the part of the *ācāryas* which leads to arrive at truth. However, the idea of an omniscient (*sarvajña*), who is beyond attachment (*rāga*) and aversion (*dveṣa*), and the knower of absolute truth seems to be of late origin, according to the present writer.

THE *KASĀYAPĀHUḌA*

Like the *Chakkhaṇḍāgama*, the *Kasāyapāhuḍa* also is an important constituent of the *Dvādasāṅga*. Unlike the *Chakkhaṇḍāgama* it is composed in verse. It has been restored from the *Pejjadosapāhuḍa* (*Pejjadoṣaprābhṛta*), the third *Prābhṛta* of the tenth *Vastu* of the *Ṇāṇappavāya*, the fifth *Pūrva*. Since it is based on the *Pejjadosapāhuḍa* it is also designated by the same title (*pejja* or *preya* meaning attachment and *dosa* or *dveṣa* is aversion). *Ācārya* Guṇadhara who seems to be a contemporary of *ācārya* Dharasena, also possessed some knowledge of the *Dvādasāṅga*. As this knowledge was gradually diminishing, Bhaṭṭāraka Guṇadhara (around AD 200) thought of composing his work in 180 *gāthās*, and explained this to Ārya Mankṣu and Nāgahasti. Then Yativṛṣabha (say AD 500) studied this work from them and wrote the *Cūrṇi-Sūtras* in Prakrit, known as *Pāhuḍacuṇṇisutta*.[38]

The *Kasāyapāhuḍa*, as the name indicates, deals with transformation of passions (*kaṣāya*) into *raga* and *dveṣa* leading to the bondage of *karmas* in the form of *prakṛti*, *sthiti*, *anubhāga* and *pradesabandhas*. Like the *Chakkhaṇḍāgama* this important work also has several commentaries and explanations. We have referred to Yativṛṣabha's *Cūrṇisūtras*. Uccāraṇācārya having studied them, composed the *Uccāraṇasūtras* in Prakrit. Unfortunately, this work is not available to us. Then comes Sāmakuṇḍa who wrote his commentary *Paddhati* in mixed Prakrit, Sanskrit and Kannaḍa. Tumbulūrācārya wrote his *Cūḍāmaṇi* commentary in Kannaḍa. Then comes Bappadeva, the writer of the *Vyākhyāprajñapti* commentary. The last commentator is Vīrasena, who in AD 874 wrote his *Jayadhavalā* which was completed by his pupil Jinasena during the reign of the Rashtrakuta king Amoghavarṣa. Of these commentaries only the first and the last are available.

Ācārya Vīrasena has written a *Jayadhavalā* commentary on the *Kasāyapāhuḍa*, divided into fifteen *adhikāras*. This is as important as his *Dhavalā* on the *Chakkhaṇḍāgama*. The *Jayadhavalā* has been written on both the *Kasāyapāhuḍa*, the original text and its *cuṇṇi* by Yativṛṣabha. In his *Dhavalā* the commentator has referred to both on several occasions. Here also the commentator has recorded the differing views of scholars like Ārya Maṅkṣu and Nāgahasti. In support of simultaneity of *kevalajñāna* and *kevaladarsana*, he has cited several *gāthās* from the *Sanmatitarka* of Siddhasena.[39] Vīrasena has also referred to the *Uccāraṇāvṛtii* of Bappadevācārya. He has mentioned the difference of opinion between this work and a work of the same title written by *Uccāraṇācārya.*[40] Elsewhere he has pointed out the difference of opinions of *Uccāraṇācārya* and other commentators.[41] He has also indicated the different views held in the *Cūrṇisūtras*, Bappadeva's *Uccāraṇā*, and his own, *Uccaraṇā.*[42]

The *Tiloyapaṇṇatti* (*Trilokaprajñapti*)[43] is another important work of Yativṛṣabha, the writer of the *Curṇi-Sūtras* on the *Kasāyapāhuḍa.* It is an ancient work of karaṇānuyoga, written in Saurasenī, and deals with the description of three regions (*triloka*). This text has been referred to in the *Dhavalā* commentary of Vīrasena on several occasions. The author has referred to several works of antiquity such as the *Aggāyaṇī, Saṃgoyaṇī, Saṃgāhanī, Diṭṭhivāda, Parikamma, Mūlāyāra, Loyaviṇicchaya, Logāiṇī* and *Lokavibhāga*, along with their variants. The subject matter of the text is quite similar to the Śvetāmbara canonical works such as the *Sūriapaṇṇatti, Candapaṇṇatti* and *Jambuddīvapaṇṇatti* as well as the Digambara texts such as the *Dhavalā, Jayadhavalā* and Nemicandra's *Trilokasāra.* The text has numerous *gāthās* common with the *Lokavibhāga*, the *Mūlācāra*, the *Bhagavatī Ārādhana*, the *Pañcāstikāya*, the *Pravacanasāra*, the *Samayasāra* and so on.[44]

The text is divided into nine *mahādhikāras,* comprising *sāmānyaloka, narakaloka, bhavanavāsiloka, manuṣyaloka, tiryakloka, vyantaraloka, jyotirloka, devaloka* and *siddhaloka,* particularly dealing with geography and astronomy in 5677 verses. Between descriptions the author has employed various metres, which indicates his literary taste. In the first *mahādhikāra,* while illustrating the *kṣetra-maṅgala,* he has mentioned Pāvā, Ūrjayanta (Girnār), Campā and other places of pilgrimage. He has referred to eighteen *sreṇis* (guilds) to the commanders of elephants (*hasti*), horses (*turaga*), and chariots (*ratha*), the general (*senāpati*), foot-soldier (*padāti*), head of the mercantile guild (*sreṣṭhi*), head police officer (*daṇḍapati*), sūdra, kṣatriya, vaisya, village-head (*mahattara*), brāhmaṇa (*pravara*), the leader of the confederate rulers (*gaṇarāja*), counsellor (*mantrī*), city guard (*talavara*), adviser on religious and secular matters (*purohita*), minister (*amātya*) and prime minister (*mahāmātya*). While describing the body of Mahavira, eighteen kinds of *mahābhāṣās* (great dialects) and 700 kinds of degraded dialects (*kubhāṣā*) are alluded to.[45] Five hills of Rājagṛha are mentioned: Vipula, Ṛṣisaila, Vaibhāra, Chinna and Pāṇḍu.[46] The thickness, width and length of the three regions (*triloka*) is said to be based on a statement of the *Dṛṣṭivāda.* This chapter contains 283 *gāthās* and three sections in prose. Chapter 2 deals with the region of hell in 367 *gāthās.* Chapter 3 describes in

243 *gāthās* various halls in the palatial buildings of the Bhavanavāsī gods. They are the halls of birth, coronation, decoration, copulation and bodily treatment (*olaggasālā*). Then we have ordinary houses, interior houses, plantain-houses, picture-houses, seating-houses, music-houses (*nādagṛha*), creeper-bowers and so on. Ten desire-yielding trees (*caityvṛkṣas*) are the asvattha, saptavarṇa (sattivaṇṇa), sālmali, jambū, vetasa, kadamba, priyaṅgu, sirīsa, palāsa and rājadrumạ. The fourth chapter is the longest, containing 2691 *gāthās*, dealing with the details of human region. It deals with 63 great personalities (*salākāpuruṣa*), including Tīrthaṅkaras, Cakravartins, Baladevas, Vāsudevas, and Prativāsudevas. Here we come across the traditional dates of birth of the Tīrthaṅkaras, the rise of constellations at the time of their birth, their family, age, childhood and height, the duration of their reign, renunciation, undertaking of fasts and attainment of omniscience (*kevalajñāna*). It has been stated that the Tīrthaṅkaras Nemi, Malli, Mahavira, Vāsupūjya and Pārsva accepted asceticism while they were *kumāra* (meaning a prince or also bachelor) and the remaining Tīrthaṅkaras at the end of their reign (*rājya*). In other words, the former renounced worldly pleasures while they were princes, without any desire for a coronation ceremony, whereas the others chose to renounce enjoying their full period of reign.[47] The assembly-hall (*samavasaraṇa*) is described in great detail in more than 200 *gāthās*. The eight *maṅgala dravyas* (auspicious objects) are referred to: they are *bhṛṅgāra* (golden pitcher), *kalasa* (vessel), *darpaṇa* (mirror), *vyajana* (fan), *dhvajā* (banner), *chatra* (umbrella), *camara* (flywhisk) and *supratiṣṭha* (a kind of vessel).[48] Among yakṣas the following are mentioned: Govadana, Mahāyakṣa, Trimukha, Yakṣesvara, Tumburavas, Mātaṅga, Vijaya, Ajita, Brahma and others. Among yakṣiṇīs we have Chkresvarī, Rohiṇī, Prajñapti, Vajrasṛṅkhalā, Vajrāṅkusā, Apraticakresvarī, Puruṣadattā, Jvālāmālinī, Kūṣmāndī and others. The fifth chapter containing 321 *gāthās*, mostly in prose, deals with continents and oceans such as Jambudvīpa, Lavaṇasamudra and so on. The sixth, the seventh and the eighth chapters contain 103, 619 and 703 *gāthās* respectively. The last chapter deals with liberated souls (*siddha*). *Lokavibhāga* has been referred to in the *Tiloyapaṇṇatti* several times. Like the *Tiloyapaṇṇatti,* it deals with *karaṇānuyoga*. This work is not available; and its author is not known. Fortunately, a Sanskrit version is available and according to its author Siṃhanandi, there existed a Prakrit *Lokavibhāga* which was composed by Sarvanandi in AD 458. The Sanskrit version of this

important text contains eleven sections dealing with Jambudvīpa, Lavaṇasamudra, Mānuṣa-kṣetra, Dvīpa-samudra, Kāla, Jyotir-loka, Bhavanavāsī-loka, Adho-loka, Vyantara-loka, Svarga-loka and Mokṣa.[49]

The Works of Kundakunda

The *Pañcatthikāya-saṃgaha* (or *Pañcāstikāyasāra*);[50] *Pavayaṇasāra* (*Pravacanasāra*); *Samayasāra* are very popular among Digambaras. Kundakunda is also known as Padmanandi, Vakragrīva, Elācārya or Gṛddhapiccha. Since his name is associated with a village Koṇḍakundi[51] some four or five miles away from Guntkal railway station, he is called by the name Kundakunda. His position is unique and his name comes after only Mahavira and Gautama.[52] In his Introduction to the *Pravacanasāra* (p. 22) Dr. A.N. Upadhye, under the circumstantial evidences, has placed him in the first two centuries of Christian era.

The above-mentioned three works are technically called *Nāṭaka-traya* or *Prābhṛta-traya*. The word *saṃgraha* in the title of the work indicates that it is mainly a compilation and not a composition.[53] The text describes the five groups of existence (*pañcāstikaya*): *Jīva* (soul), *pudgala* (matter), *dharma* (principle of motion), *adharma* (principle of rest) and *ākāsa* (space). Written in Sauraseni, it is preserved in two recensions, one in the Sanskrit commentary of Amṛtacandra, consisting of 173 *gāthās* and the other of Jayasena, comprising 181 *gāthās*. The last *gāthā* refers to the *Paṁcatthikāyasaṅgahasutta*. According to Amṛtacandra, the text is divided into two *srutaskandhas*, the first containing 104 *gāthās*, the other 69. The first part deals with six *dravyas* and five *astikāyas*. Here we have the characteristics of *dravya*, its divisions, seven-fold prediction (*saptabhaṅgī*), *guṇa* (quality), *paryāya* (modifications), characteristics of *kāla* (time), of soul (*jīva*), and of the *siddhas* (liberated souls), of the bondage of *jīva* and *pudgala*, and the explanations of *dharma*, *adharma*, *ākāsa* and *kāla*. The second part deals with nine *padārthas* (categories): *Jīva*, *ajīva*, *punya*, *pāpa*, *āsrava* (influx of *karman*), *bandha* (bondage of *karman*), *saṃvara* (stoppage of influx of *karman*), *nirjarā* (partial destruction of *karman*) and *mokṣa* (release from worldly existence). Several commentaries were written on the text. Amṛtacandra wrote his *Tattvadīpikā* (also known as *Samaya-vyākhyā*). Jayasena wrote *Tātparya-vṛtti*. According to him, the original text is divided into three *adhikāras*, containing 111, 50 and 20 *gāthās* respectively. This commentary is mentioned in his commentary on *Pavayaṇasāra* and *Samayasāra*. Brhamdeva was another commentator, and Mallisena yet another, reported to have written a Sanskrit commentary on the *Pañcāstikaya* and the *Pravacanasāra*. Hemarāja Pāṇḍe, a resident of Agra, has written his Hindi *Bālāvabodha*.[54]

The *Pavayaṇasāra* (*Pravacanasāra*)[55] is another important work of Kundakunda. Winternitz has called it 'a much prized book on Jinistic dogmatics, psychology, and ethics'.[56] The text has been commented upon by Amṛtacandrasūri and Jayasena. According to the former it contains 275 *gāthās*, and according to the later, 311. There is another commentary by Prabhācandra (early fourteenth century), known as *Sarojabhāskara*. It is a 'word-for-word explanation' of the Prakrit text. Bālacandradeva in the beginning of the thirteenth century wrote his *Tātparya-vṛtti* in Kannaḍa. Malliṣeṇa is reported to have written his Sanskrit commentary on the *Pañcāstikaya* as well as the *Pravacanasāra* as already stated. Hemarāja Pāṇḍe wrote his *Bālāvabodhinī* in vs 1709 (AD 1653) when Emperor Shah-Jahan was ruling in Delhi. It had a metrical version by Vṛndāvana (born in vs 1848).[57]

The text is divided into three *srutaskandhas*, the first dealing with *cāritra*, identity of *cāritra* with soul, *suddhopayoga* (auspicious manifestation of consciousness), development of omniscience (*sarvajñatva*), coexistence of the knower and the knowledge, the separate identity and non-identity of soul and knowledge, transcendental aspect of omniscience, its state of happiness, the birth of soul in various states the subhuman, human or divine, the state of an Arhanta, and understanding of self and non-self. The second section deals with object of knowledge, substance endowed with various qualities and modifications, characterization of origination, destruction and permanence, relation between substance, quality and modification, nature of soul, nature of *jīva, ajīva, dharma, adharma, ākāsa* and *kāla*, space-point (*samaya*), characteristics of physical world (*loka*), binding of soul with *karmans* and meditation of self. The third section deals with Jain ascetic emblems, perfect non-attachment, the meaning of attachment, study of scriptures by a monk, self-discipline and self-control, the diet and touring of a monk, devotion to Arhantas, non-attachment to external and internal paraphernalia and release from worldly existence. Like the *Paṃcatthikāyasāra*, this text also has several commentaries. The oldest and the most important is that of Amṛtacandrasūri, known as *Tattvadīpikā*. He has cited quotations from the *Gommaṭasāra* (*Jīvakāṇḍa* and *Karmakāṇḍa*). Jayasena's *Tātparyavṛtii* is another important commentary. The commentator has quoted from the *Mūlācāra*, the *Siddhabhakti*, the *Pañcāstikāya*, the *Bārasa-Aṇuvekkhā*, the *Tattvārthasūtra*, the *Svayambhū-stotra* and other works.

According to the author, nudity is essential for liberation and a woman in this birth cannot be liberated from worldly existence. While explaining the external emblem (*liṅga*), he has stated that unless a monk is possessed of the form in which he was born (*yathājāta-rūpaṃ*) and pulls out his hair and moustache (*uppāḍida-kesa-maṃsugaṃ*) and is free from committing harm to living beings, he is not entitled to *mokṣa*.[58] Here nudity (*acelaṃ*) with other qualities is considered the primary virtue (*mūlaguṇa*) of an ascetic.[59] If a monk accepts a piece of clothing (*celakhaṇḍa*) and possesses a pot (*bhāyaṇaṃ*), how can he be called independent (*cattālambo*)?[60] Similarly, women are not allowed to achieve *nirvāṇa* as they are liable to infatuation (*moha*), aversion (*padosa*), fear and disgust (*duguñchā*) and there is a variety of crookedness (*cittā māyā*) in their minds.[61] Further, there is mental mobility (*citta-ssāva*), and fickleness (*sitthillaṃ*) and the periodical discharging of blood (*attavaṃ ca pakkhalaṇaṃ*) wherein grow subtle human organisms.[62] With growth of subtle organisms in the female organ of generation (*liṅgamhi*), between the breasts (*thaṇantare*), and in parts of their navel and armpit (*nāhi-kakkhapadese*), how can women be entitled to self-control (*saṃjama*)?[63]

The *Samayasāra*[64] (Essence of the Doctrine), is considered the best work of Kundakunda. It is highly respected by Digambara Jains and is popular amongst them. It is different from the usual trend of other Jain works, comparable to some extent with the non-dualist (*advaita*) trend of Vedanta philosophy. Upadhye has observed that

> Its contents, according to orthodox opinion, are too sacred to be read by householders, the reason being: one, the work deals mainly with spiritual topics such as *bheda-vijñāna* (discrimination between pure soul and other external objects); two, the discussion centering around *Suddha niscaya* point of view; three, the spiritual statement from *niscaya naya* may prove socially and ethically harmful to the householders who are absolutely lacking in spiritual discipline.[65]

The *Samayasāra* begins with the definition of *sva-samaya* and *para-samaya*. The former is realization of the self, identical with the right faith. When oneness (*ekatva*) of the self is realized there is no bondage of *karmas*. The ultimate aim of every aspirant is to realize the pure self as a knower (*jñātā*) from the *niscaya* point of view. The soul is bound with or free from *karmas*, can be viewed only from the point of view of *naya* (a particular approach of the knower); what is beyond the preview of *naya*, is the essence of the doctrine (*samayasāra*).[66] From the *niscaya* point of view, the self is unbound and untouched with *karmas*; it is from the *vyavahāra* point of view that we consider it bound and attached.[67] *Vyavahāra* (empirical viewpoint) is necessary to understand the *niscaya* point of view. It is said that as without knowing the language of a barbarian we cannot make him understand what we want to convey to him, so is the case with the *vyavahāra* point of view which is incapable of grasping reality, to understand the real point of view conveyed by *niscaya naya*. The ultimate object of the author is to impress on readers that ignorance, resulting from *karmic* association, has barred the soul from realization of truth, so every aspirant must rise above attachment and aversion and should make efforts to realize that as a matter of fact the self is absolutely pure, omniscient and completely distinct from *pudgala*.

The text contains ten *adhikāras*: the first deals with *sva-samaya*, *para-samaya*, *suddha naya*, *ātmabhāvanā* (realization of self) and *samyaktva* (right faith); the second deals with *jīva* and *ajīva*; the third with *karma* and *kartā* (doer); the fourth with *puṇya* (merit) and *pāpa* (demerit); the fifth with *āsrva* (influx of *karma*); the sixth with *saṃvara* (stoppage of influx of *karma*); the seventh with *nirjarā* (partial destruction of *karma*); the eighth with *bandha* (bondage); the ninth with *mokṣa* (liberation) and the tenth with pure perfect knowledge.

The text of the *Samayasāra* has two recensions. According to Amṛtacandra, it has 415 *gāthās* and according to Jayasena 439. Jayasena has also noted important and independent variants. Amṛtacandra's commentary is known as *Ātmakhyāti*. The collection of 263 verses of this commentary, known as *Samayasāra-kalasa*, has formed a separate work which has been commented upon by Subhacandra in Sanskrit and Jayacandra in Hindi. On these very *Kalasas*, poet Banārasīdās of Agra, a contemporary of Emperor Akbar, composed his well known *Samayasara-Naṭaka* which gained much popularity among the Jains of northern India. Amṛtacandra's commentary is very significant. He has called the original work which depicts this world as a true drama of life. He has divided the whole text into nine *aṅkas* (scenes) with a *pūrva-raṅga* (prologue) at the beginning and a *pariśiṣṭa* (conclusion) at the end. It is for this reason that all the three works of Kundakunda are termed as *nāṭaka-traya* (trilogy).

In the *Niyamasāra*[68] or essence of Disciplines three jewels, right faith, right knowledge and right conduct, are discussed in the beginning. They are to be observed necessarily (*niyamena*) and hence the work is called *Niyamasāra*. Then follows the description of six *dravyas*. Right conduct is viewed from *vyavahāra* and *niscaya* point of view. The former consists in observing five great vows, five *samitis* (carefulness) and three kinds of control (*gupti*). While describing the latter, a discussion is set forth regarding six essential duties (*āvasyakas*) such as *pratikramaṇa* (confession), *pratyākhyāna* (renunciation of certain pleasure), *ālocanā* (report of sins committed), *kāyotsarga* (penance through standing or sitting posture of the body), *sāmāyika* (equanimity) and *parama-bhakti* (intense devotion); the last one is divided into *nirvṛti* and *yoga-bhakti*.[69] These Essential Duties lead a monk to a passionless state (*vītarāga cāritra*), and therefore are called essential. Then omniscience (*sarvañatā*) is described with *vyavahāra* and *niscaya* point of view. According to the former, an omniscient knows and perceives everything, whereas according to the latter, he knows and perceives only his own self. Knowledge (*jñāna*) and perception (*darsana*) are believed to have possessed simultaneously, just as light and heat are simultaneous.[70] After the cessation of *karma* particles, the liberated soul shoots up and stops at the top of the universe (*loka*). Here (in *gāthā* 94) the *Paḍikkamaṇa sutta* has been referred to.[71] This work contains some traditional *gāthās* which are found in author's other works and also in the *Mūlācāra*.[72]

The *Niyamasāra* contains 186 *gāthās*. Padmaprabha Maladhārideva (twelfth century) has written his commentary *Tātparyavṛtti* on this work. He has divided the text into twelve *srutaskandhas* and quotes from the commentaries of the *Prabhṛtatraya* (the *Pañcāstikāya*, the *Pravacanasāra* and the *Samayasāra*) of Amṛtacandra and other works. In his introductory verses the commentator refers to the names of Siddhasena, Bhaṭṭākalaṅka, Pūjyapāda, Vīranandi, and others. *Rayaṇasāra*[73] contains 162 *gāthās*. The author deals with the duties of laymen and monks. The right faith (*samyaktva*) is called the best of the jewels (*ratnasāra*) and is the root of the tree of liberation. In the middle of the work we have a *dohā* and a dozen Apabhraṃsa verses. The name of Kundakunda is not mentioned in the colophon of the manuscript. There is repetition of ideas and their arrangement is not quite satisfactory. A.N. Upadhye is of the opinion that the work cannot be attributed to the authorship of Kundakunda.[74]

Aṭṭhapāhuḍa (*Aṣṭaprābhṛta*)[75] includes *Daṃsaṇa, Cāritta, Sutta, Bodha, Bhāva, Mokkha, Liṅga* and *Sīla-pāhuḍas.*

The dictionary meaning of the word *pāhuḍa* or *prābhṛta* is a present, a gift or an offering especially to a deity or a sovereign. Upadhye has quoted Jayasena, commentator on *Samayasāra* (pp. 555-6, *RJS* edition), wherein he has used the word in the sense of a present. He says that as a certain person, desirous to visit a king, approaches him with some most excellent present, called *prābhṛta,* similarly a person devoted to the Supreme Spirit (*paramātmā*), in order to pay a visit to him, approaches him with this scripture (*sāstraṃ*) as a gift.[76] *Pāhuḍa* or *prābhṛta* is used here in the sense of a small *prakaraṇa, adhikāra* (a section) or a tract. The *Suriyapaṇṇatti,* which forms a part of the *Upāṅga* literature, contains twenty *pāhuḍas* or section as we have seen. The *Siddhapāhuḍa* and the *Joṇipāhuḍa* form a part of the *Paiṇṇā* literature. Then we have the *Kasāyapāhuḍa* or the *Pejjadosapāhuḍa* on which Yativṛṣabha has composed the *Pāhuḍa-cuṇṇi-sutta* in Prakrit which has been noted already. Kundakunda is said to have been the author of 84 *Pāhuḍas,* but their names are not known.[77] We are not even sure whether he was the author of the eight *Pāhuḍas* which we will discuss here. It is stated, 'in the majority of the following works, the original text scarcely mentions the name of Kundakunda, at times traditionally they are attributed to Kundakunda, and sometimes the commentators say that Kundakunda is the author'.[78] However, W. Schubring in the introduction of *Bodha-prābhṛta* opines that these small tracts cannot be ascribed to Kundakunda.[79]

The *Daṃsana-pāhuḍa* deals with *daṃsaṇa* (*darsana*) or *samyak-darsana* (right faith) which is the foundation of religion[80] and leads to liberation. It forms the root of the tree of virtue. It contains 36 *gāthās.* We are told here of 34 superhuman qualities (*atisaya*) of a Tīrthaṅkara who is said to be endowed with 64 flying whisks. Like other five *Pāhuḍas,* Srutasāgara, pupil of Bhaṭṭāraka Vidyānandi, has written a commentary on this text. He calls himself an omniscient of the *kali* age (*kalikāla-sarvajña*), the sovereign poet of both languages (*ubhaya-bhāṣā-cakravartī*).[81] In his commentary the author refers to the Gopucchikas, the Svetāvasas (Śvetāmbaras), the Drāviḍas, the Yāpanīyakas and the Nippicchikas—the five Jainābhāsas (Jainas merely by appearance). He has attacked the followers of the Loṅkā *gaccha* (known as the Ḍhuṇḍhias or the Sthānakavāsīs, non-believers in idol worship) saying that they are not the true followers of Jainism and will never attain liberation.[82]

The 44 *gāthās* of the *Cāritta-pāhuḍa* deal with *cāritra* (right conduct) which is essential for attainment of *mokṣa*. Eight virtues of *samyaktva* are described. The conduct of laymen and monks is stated. *Sutta-pāhuḍa* contains 27 *gāthās*. It is stated that as a needle with a piece of *sūtra* (thread) put into it is not lost so a man possessed of knowledge of *sūtras* (the sacred lore) is not lost. Here the author has emphasized nudity (*acelakatva*) and eating in the cavity of palms (*pāṇi-pātratā*). Such monks are entitled to achieve the path of liberation, he says. To possess even the slightest degree of paraphernalia is harmful to monks. Women are not entitled to liberation, as severe asceticism such as going about nude is not allowed to them.

The *Bodha-pāhuḍa* contains 62 *gāthās*, split up into eleven *adhikāras*: they are (i) *āyadaṇa* (*āyatana*) or religious resort, (ii) *cediharaṃ* (*caityagṛhaṃ*) or holy shrine, (iii) *paḍimā* (*pratimā*) or Jain image, (iv) *Daṃsaṇa* (*Darsana*) or right faith, knowledge and conduct, (v) *Jiṇabimba* (*Jinabimba*) or the idol of Jina, (vi) *Jiṇamuddā* (*Jina-mudrā*) or appearance of Jina, (vii) *Ṇāṇa* (*jñāna*) or knowledge or enlightenment, (viii) *Deva* or divinity, (ix) *Tittha* (*Tīrtha*) or holy resort, (x) *Arahanta* (*Arhat*) or Jina, the one who is worthy of worship, (xi) *Pavvajjā* (*pravrajyā*) or renunciation. In the last *gāthā*, *ācārya* Bhadrabāhu is described as a *srutakevalī* who possessed knowledge of the twelve *Aṅgas* and the fourteen *Pūrvas*.

The *Bhāva-pāhuḍa* contains 163 *gāthās*, and is the biggest section. It deals with purity of psychic state (*pariṇāma*). Here purity of mind is emphasized, so that *bhāva-liṅga* (internal emblem or appearance) is more important than *dravya-liṅga* (external emblem or appearance). It is stated that a monk should become nude internally, then only he can be called a real monk, and nudity without purity of mind is valuable. The number of births one has undergone is so large that the milk drunk from mothers' breasts or the tears of mothers are sufficient to fill an ocean. Here the stories of Bāhaubali, Madhupiṅga, Vasiṣṭha, Bāhu, Dvipayana, Sivakumara, Bhavyasena and Sivabhūti have been narrated.

Further, it is stated that when the soul becomes free from the bondage of *karmas*, it comes to be designated as *Jñānin*, *Siva*, *Parameṣṭhin*, *Sarvajña*, *Visnu*, *Caturmukha* and *Buddha*. 'So long as old age does not overwhelm the body, the fire of disease does not inflame it and the strength of the sense organs does not deviate, one should look after doing one's own good (*ātma-hita*).'[83] *Mokkha-pāhuḍa* deals with the attainment of *mokṣa* (liberation) in 106 *gāthās*. The characteristics of *sva-dravya* and *para-dravya* are explained. The former, the internal object, is quite different from the latter; it is the real nature of the self which is pure, free from *karmas* and an embodiment of knowledge. One who aspires to attain the highest goal of life should avoid external activities related to the pleasure of sense organs, and should be introspective so that he is able to realize the higher self. The difference between the self and the higher self is similar to that of unwrought metal and pure gold. It is stated that one who sleeps in worldly conduct (*vyavahāra*) is really awake in his own performance, and one who is awake in his own performance sleeps in worldly behaviour.[84]

Liṅga-pāhuḍa has 22 *gāthās* dealing with a sinful monk even if he has accepted the emblem (*liṅga*) of a Jain monk. Such a monk sings, dances, has craving for meals, hurts living beings, shows love to women, gambles and arranges marriages and is no more a monk but a beast of burden.

Sīla-pāhuḍa deals with chastity in 40 *gāthās*. The illustration of Surattaputta (Saccaiputta or Sātyakīputra) is cited here, who, though he possessed the knowledge of ten *Pūrvas*, was born in hell, the reason being that he was eager to enjoy sensual pleasures. It is stated that knowledge, faith, austerities and conduct bring liberation only to those who lead a chaste life, the mere study of *sāstras* such as *vyākaraṇa*, *Chanda*, *Vaiseṣika*, *vyavahāra* and *Nyāya* is not enough.

Bārasa-Anuvekkhā (*Dvādasa-Anuprekṣā*),[85] said to have been composed by Kundakunda, deals with twelve contemplations or reflections in 91 *gāthās*.[86] *Anuprekṣā* or *bhāvana* is stated to be an important means of stoppage of the influx of *karmic* matter; the others are *gupti* (self-control), *samiti* (self-regulation), *dharma* (moral virtue), *parīṣaha-jaya* (conquest of afflictions) and *cāritra* (conduct). There are twelve *anupreksās*: *Adhruva* (transitory nature of things), *Asaraṇa* (one's helplessness in worldly existence), *Saṃsāra* (nature of the world is fraught with misery and suffering), *Ekatva* (the loneliness of the worldly sojourn), *Anyatva* (the transcendental nature of the self as distinct and separate from the body), *Asuci* (the impure character of the body), *Āsrava* (the conditions of the influx of *karmic* matter), *Saṃvara* (the nature of the condition of stoppage of *karmic* influx), *Nirjarā* (the nature of the condition of the dissociation of *karmic* matter from soul), *Loka* (the nature of the universe), *Dharma*[87] (the path of righteousness) and *Bodhi* (the difficulty of attainment of enlightenment).[88]

Importance is given to the treatment of these reflections by Digambaras as well as Śvetāmbaras. Maladhāri Hemacandrasūri, designated as Paṇḍita Svetāmbarācārya Bhaṭṭāraka, has composed his *Bhavabhāvanā* also known as *Vara-rayaṇa-māliyā* (*Vara-ratna-mālikā* or Excellent String of Pearls) in AD 1123. The author has dealt with the *Bhāvanās* in 531 *gāthās*, out of which 322 are devoted to only the *Saṃsāra-Bhāvanā* or *Bhava-Bhāvanā*.[89] Kundakunda's name as an author is mentioned in the last *gāthā* though it is not found in some of the Mss.[90] Some of the *gāthās* of the text are common with the eighth chapter of the *Mūlācāra*; possibly these verses are traditionally inherited.[91] Five verses (25-9) are common with Pūjyapāda's *Sarvārthasiddhi* (commentary, II.10), cited under '*uktaṃ ca*'. These verses also may be called traditional, emerging from older tradition.[92]

Dasa-Bhatti (*Dasa-Bhakti*)[93] or Eight Salutations are devotional prayers in praise of Tirthaṅkaras, Siddhas, sacred lore and so on. Most of them are in metric form, some are in prose. According to Prabhācandra, the writer of the *Kriyākalāpa* commentary on these *Bhaktis*, the Sanskrit *Bhaktis* are composed by Pūjyapāda and the Prakrit *Bhaktis* by Kundakunda. The eight *Bhaktis* written in Prakrit are *Titthayara* (*Tirthaṅkara*), *Siddha*, *Suda* (Sruta), *Cāritta* (*Cāritra*), *Aṇagāra* (Anagāra or Yogi), *Āyariya* (*Ācārya*), *Nivvāṇa* (*Nirvāṇa*) and *Pañcaparameṭṭhi* (*Pañcaparameṣṭhi*).

The text begins with *pañca-ṇamoyāra* (five-fold salutations), *maṅgala-sutta, longuttamā-sutta, saraṇa-sutta,* and *sāmāiya-sutta* in prose. The *Titthayara-Bhatti* offers salutations to the Tīrthaṅkaras in 8 *gāthās*. It can be compared with the *Logassa-sutta* of the Śvetāmbaras. It is followed by prose passages about *pratikramaṇa* and *ālocanā*. According to Prabhācandra, the *Siddha-Bhakri* contains 12 *gāthās* wherein salutations are offered to Siddhas (liberated ones). It has a concluding prose passage about *ālocanā*. In the *Suda-Bhatti* salutations are offered to *Dvādasāṅga* in 11 *gāthās* and a concluding prose passage. The *Cāritta-Bhatti*[94] contains 10 *gāthās* with at concluding prose passage, and deals with the five-fold rules of conduct. The *Aṇagāra-Bhatti* has 23 *gāthās* with the usual prose passage at the end. Here prayers are offered to saints with virtues; their supernatural powers are described. *Āyariya-Bhatti* contains 10 *gāthās*, giving a description of the ideal preceptor. The *Nivvāṇa-Bhatti*, also known as *Laghu-sāmāyika* (Velankar), *Prākṛta-Nirvāṇabhakti*, *Nivvāṇakāṇḍa* (Schubring), *Nivvuikaṇḍa* (verse 32) or *Nirvāṇakaṇḍagāthā*, contains 27 *gāthās*, dealing with the *nirvāṇa* of Tirthaṅkaras and other holy personalities, along with the places of their liberation. Information is provided about the details of time and place of Mahavira's *nirvāṇa* in a prose passage.[95] In the *Pañcaparameṭṭhi-Bhatti* salutations are offered to five dignitaries in 7 *gāthās* with the prose passage at the end.

These are eight Prakrit *Bhaktis*. In the case of the *Nandīsvara-Bhakti* and the *Sānti-Bhakti* we have only the concluding passage and not the metric form. There may have been metrical forms of these two *Bhaktis* so as to total the required ten, says A.N. Upadhye, who traces two strata in these texts, one with concluding prose passage and the other with metrical form. According to him, both cannot be by one and the same author. In his opinion, these texts might have been compiled by Kundakunda, based on the traditional heritage of Jain monks, hence this literature should be treated as antedating the division in the Jain community.[96]

The *Bhagavatī Ārādhanā* or *Mūlārādhanā*[97] is an important work of antiquity by Sivakoṭi or Sivārya. It deals with the detailed exposition of four-fold *ārādhanās* or the accomplishments of ascetics. They are *samyaktva* (right faith), *jñāna* (right knowledge), *cāritra* (right conduct) and *tapa* (penance). Its 2166 (or 2170) *gāthās* are written in Sauraseni Prakrit and divided into 40 *adhikāras*. The author has characterized himself as *pāṇi-tala-bhoji* (who accepted his food in the cavity of his palms). He is said to belong to the Yāpanīya school of Jains, which supported nudity (*acelakatva*) of the Digambaras and the liberation of women (*strī-mukti*) of the Śvetāmbaras.[98] At the end of his work the author has referred to Āryā Jinanandi, Āryā Sarva-gupta, and Ārya Mitranandi, at whose feet after studying the sacred lore and its significance, he composed this *Ārādhanā*, based on the works of the earlier preceptors.[99]

No fixed date has been assigned to this text but from the material it contains, it appears as old as the canonical texts of the Śvetāmbaras. Numerous *gāthās* contained in the text are identical with the *Paiṇṇās*, the *Āvassaya-Nijjutti* and the *Bṛhatkalpa-Bhāṣya* of the Śvetāmbaras. In this connection, in his Introduction to the *Bṛhatkathākosa*, A.N. Upadhye has observed,

It is quite possible that this work includes the missing *Ārādhanā-Niryukti*; the ideas and verses which it has in common (with dialectal and minor variations) with *Nijjuttis, Paiṇṇās, Mūlācāra,* etc., definitely suggest that this text contains matter which antedates the division of the Jain Church into Digambaras and Śvetāmbaras; and it substantially represents the traditional verses collected by the Digambara monks who did not recognise the authority of the Ardhamāgadhī Canon.[100]

Upadhye has listed legendary references in the text which 'breathe the same spirit as those of the Ardhamāgadhī Canon' and some of them are almost identical. For instance, the references to the stories related to the ascetic-heroes Avanti-Sukumāla, Cāṇakya, Cilātaputra, Jama (Java) Devarai and Sukosala can be mentioned.[101] He has also mentioned numerous *Kathākosas* which are associated with the contents of the *Bhagavatī Ārādhanā* and have developed their stories in full, drawing their material from early texts like the *Bhagavatī Ārādhanā* and others.[102] It is stated that noble ascetics never abandon their dignity (*māna*) even though they are confronted with pestilence (*asiva*), famine (*dubbhikkha*), dense forest (*kantāra*), intense fear (*āgāḍhe bhae*) and dreadful disease (*rogehiṃ abhibhūdā*).[103] The text refers to the *Āyāra* (*Ācārāṅga*) and the *Jīyakappa* (*Jītakalpa*),[104] the latter forming part of the *Chedasūtra* literature of the Śvetāmbara Canon. These *Sūtras* have been represented as exposing virtues (*guṇa-dīvaṇā*), leading to purity of self (*atta-sodhi*) and avoiding affliction (*ṇijjhanjhā=saṃklesābhāvaḥ,* com.).[105] The author of the text, while dealing with the ten *Kalpas,* refers to the first, the *ācelakya kalpa.* Here the commentator Aparājitasūri deals with Mahavira's moving about nude (*acela*) in detail. He has cited Śvetāmbara canonical texts in support of the theory of wearing clothes (*sacelakatva*). Criticizing this theory, he quotes statements from the *Uttarādhyayana, Dasavaikālika, Bṛhatkalpa* and other canonical texts of the Śvetāmbaras.[106] Further, the rules related to the disposal of the dead of Jain monks are dealt with; they are important as they indicate customs prevalent in the early history of Jainism. The last chapter, known as *Vijahaṇā* (*vihāna* meaning entirely abandoned body), deals with the disposal of the dead.[107]

The text has several important commentaries. Aparājitasūri (after AD 700), also known as Srīvijayācārya, wrote a Sanskrit commentary *Vijayodayā* or *Ārādhanā* and also a commentary of the same title on the *Dasavaikālika.* Another Sanskrit commentary is by Pandit Āsādhara (thirteenth century VS), known as the *Mūlārādhanā-darpaṇa.* The commentator has referred to a Prakrit commentary on the text which unfortunately is not available. The third commentary is the *Ārādhanā-pañjikā* of an unknown author, its manuscript available in the Bhandarkar Oriental Institute, Poona. The fourth commentary is the *Bhavarha-dipika,* also in the manuscript form. Then, Amitagati (twelfth century VS) of Mathura Sangha translated the text in verse form. Pandit Sadāsukhaji Kasliwal wrote the *Bhāṣā-vacanikā* (in 1906-8), published in Kolhapur. Besides, there were other commentaries, some are referred to in the commentaries of Aparājitasūri and Pandit Āsādhara.[108]

Mūlācāra,[109] also known as *Ācāraṅgasūtra*[110] or *Ācārasūtra,* is another important work as old as the *Bhagavatī Ārādhanā.* It is composed by Ācārya Vaṭṭakera, a resident of Beṭṭageri or Battakeri in Karnāṭaka.[111] Ācārya Vasunandi (probably of the twelfth century) has written a Sanskrit commentary, known as *Ācāravṛtti* or *Sarvārthasiddhi* on this work. The text, which belongs to about the second century AD, contains several *gāthās* common with the works of Kundakunda, *Dhavalā*-commentary, *Tiloyapaṇṇatti, Bhagavatī Ārādhanā* and *Sommaṭasāra* of the Digambaras, and *Āvasyaka-Niryukti, Piṇḍa-Niryukti, Jīvasamāsa* and *Āurapaccakkhāṇa* of the Śvetāmbaras.[112] Besides, the text contains verses common with ancient Buddhist texts indicating the common source of both ascetic religions.[113]

The *Ṣaḍavasyakādhikāra* section of the *Mūlācāra* is most important. It consists of six essential duties to be observed regularly, *Sāmāiya, Cauvīsatthava, Vandaṇaya, Paḍikkamaṇa, Paccakkhāṇa* and *Kāussagga*—this order is slightly different from that of the *Niyamasāra* of Kundakunda as noted earlier.[114] The *Mūlācāra* begins with the *maṅgala* passage, the *Pañca-ṇamokkāra-Nijjutti* in which obeisance is paid to the five dignitaries. Here the author proposes to deal with the *Āvassaya-Nijjutti* in brief, in order, as narrated by the *acaryas* in accordance with tradition.[115] Then we have the treatment of six essential duties under *Sāmāiya-Nijjutti, Cauvīsaya-Nijjutti, Vandaṇa-Nijjutti, Paḍikkamaṇa-Nijjutti, Paccakkhāṇa-Nijjutti* and *Kāusagga-Nijjutti.*[116] Towards the end, summarizing the *Ṣaṭ-Āvasyakas,* the author says that he has described the *Nijjutti* of the *Āvassaya-Nijjutti* in brief, and details may be had from the *Aṇiyoga* (meaning the *Ācārāṅga,* according to the commentator).[117] In the same *adhikāra* it is stated: 'The twenty-two Tīrthaṅkaras had preached *Sāmāyika* (desisting from harmful activities), whereas the first and the last (Ṛṣabha and Mahavira respectively) the *Chedopasthāpanā* (re-initiation after the rectification of the activities due to carelessness).' Why is the

Chedopasthāpanā prescribed by the first and the last Tīrthaṅkara? The answer is: 'The pupils at the time of the first Tīrthaṅkara were difficult to be corrected (*duvvisodhana*) as they were too simple (*ṛjusvabhāvājḥ*, Com.), whereas the pupils at the time of the last Tīrthaṅkara were difficult to be rectified (*duraṇupāla*) as they were not straight (*vakrasvabhāvāḥ*, Com.).'[118]

In the second *adhikāra* a reference is made to the killing of women like Kanakalatā, Nāgalatā, Vidyullatā and Kundalatā sportively by Mahendradatta in the city of Mithilā; he also killed men like Sāgaraka, Vallabhaka, Kuladatta and Vardhamāna. But nowhere do we come across the reference to the story of killing these persons by Mahendradatta, not known even to the commentator. He has directed us to refer to *āgama-upadeśa*.[119] This reflects on the antiquity of the text. The *Sāmācārī* section deals with the conduct of monks and nuns. The *sāmācāra* or conventional practices of monks and nuns are the same.[120] The rules regarding the residence (*vasati*) of nuns are laid down:

> They should favour one another and give protection to each another; they are prohibited to come into contact with men of impulsive nature, of corrupt morality and those who are evil-minded; they are directed to stay together in the company of two, three or more nuns; they are prohibited to visit the residence of a householder or even of a monk without any purpose. If at all it is essential to do so, they should obtain the permission of the head nun (*gaṇinī*). In case they have to go for begging alms they are directed to move in the company of three, five or seven, protecting each other and remain shielded by old nuns (*therīhiṃ*).[121]

At the end it is stated 'those monks or nuns, who observe the above-mentioned conduct laid down for them, are honoured in the world, become known, obtain happiness and attain liberation (*sijjhanti*)'.[122] The *Piṇḍa-suddhi* deals with various faults involved in accepting alms. Several *gāthās* of the *Samayasārādhikāra* can be compared with the *Dasavaikālika*, the *Uttarādhyayana*, *Bhagavatī Ārādhanā* and other early works.[123]

Kattigeyāṇuvekkhā (*Kārtikeyānuprekṣā*)[124] by Svāmī Kārtika or Kumāra (around the eighth century) is quite popular among Jains. It contains 489 *gāthās*, divided into 12 chapters, dealing with 12 *anuprekṣās* or contemplations. There is a similarity in subject matter and the style between this work and the *Bārasa-Aṇuvekkhā* of Kundakunda, excepting the order of the *anuprekṣās*. Here the *Saṃsāra* (5), the *Asuci* (7) and the *Loka* (6) get the 3rd, 6th and the 10th place respectively. The *Loka* and the *Dharma Anu* are described in detail, comprising 169 and 186 *gāthās* respectively. Bhaṭṭāraka Subhacandra has written a Sanskrit commentary on this work; completed in VS 1613 (AD 1556).

Gommaṭasāra[125] *or the Essence of the Jain doctrine for Gommaṭarāya* by Nemicandra Siddhānta-cakravartī, deals with soul (*jīva*) and *karma.* The work is also known as the *Pañcasaṃgraha* or Compendium of Five, namely *bandha* (binding of the soul to the *karman*), *badhyamāna* (that which is bound), *bandhasvāmī* (that which binds), *bandhahetu* (the cause of binding), and *bandhabheda* (the kinds of binding). This work is based on the *Ṣaṭkhaṇḍāgama* and the *Kaṣāyaprābhṛta* and their commentaries. The author Nemicandra states at the end that as a sovereign king gains victory over the six regions (ṣaṭ-*khaṇḍa*) of the earth, in the same way, by his intellect he has gained mastery over the scripture of the *Ṣaṭkhaṇḍāgama* and has put it in his treatise. It is for this reason that the author was honoured by the title of *Siddhānta-cakravartī.* Since this work is a collection of the material of earlier works, it is also known as the *Gommaṭa-saṃgraha* or *Gommaṭa-saṃgraha-sūtra.* It has been also designated as the *Prathama Siddhānta-grantha* or *Prathama Srutaskandha.* Nemicandra was a contemporary of Cāmuṇḍarāya, the Minister and the General of King Rācamalla II (AD 874-84). It was in response to Camuṇḍarāya's queries regarding Jain *siddhānta* that Nemicandra composed this work. Cāmuṇḍa-rāya was also known as Gommaṭa, and it is he who built the famous 58-feet granite statue of Bāhubali, one of the sculptural wonders of the world at Srvaṇabelagoḷa on the Vindhyagiri Hills. It is significant that this statue became known as Gommaṭa-jina or Gommaṭesvara. Cāmuṇḍarāya was not only a great devotee of Jainism but had various other titles of distinction.[126] This image is also known as *Dakkhiṇa-kukkuḍa-jina* and the author Nemicandra had wished victory to it along with the *Gommaṭa-saṃgahasutta* and the Gommaṭa-jina situated on the Gommaṭa-śikhara or the Candragiri Hills.[127]

The text is divided into *Jīva-Kāṇḍa* and *Karma-Kāṇḍa.* The former deals with the *jīva* and its classification, origin and nature. It contains 733 *gāthās* divided into 20 *Adhikāras.* It deals with topics like *Jīva-sthāna, Kṣudra-bandha, Bandha-svāmī, Vedanā-khaṇḍa* and *Vargaṇā-khaṇḍa,* stated to be the five *khaṇḍas* of the *Saṭ-Khaṇḍāgama,* also known as the *Mahākarma-Prābhṛta.*[128] The 20 *Adhikāras* discussed in the text are *Guṇasthāna, Jīvasamāsa, Paryāpti, Prāṇa, Saṃjñā,* fourteen *Mārgaṇas* and Upayoga.[129] The *Karma-Kāṇḍa* deals exhaustively with the nature of *karmas* and their relationship to the soul, in

972 *gāthās*. It contains the following 9 *Prakaraṇas*: *Prakṛti-samutkīrtana, Bandhodaya-sattva, Sattvasthāna-bhaṅga, Tricūlikā, Sthāna-samutkīrtaṇa, Pratyaya, Bhāva-cūlikā, Trikaraṇa-cūlikā* and *Karma-sthiti-racana.*[130] While discussing these *Prakaraṇas* the author pays homage to Nemi and Mahavira Tīrthaṅkaras, besides Muni Abhayanandī, who had crossed the ocean of scripture, Guru Indranandi and Ācārya Vīranandi. In the concluding *gāthās* the author has remembered Ācārya Ajitasena respectfully, offered his blessings to Gommaṭarāya, and has referred to his *Desī* or Kannaḍa commentary, *Vīr-mārtaṇḍī*, on the *Gommaṭasāra.*[131] Several commentaries were written on this important work. We have already referred to the Camuṇḍarāya's Kannaḍa commentary. Our author had read through it but it is not available to us. The *Mandaprabodhinī* was a Sanskrit commentary by Abhayacandra Siddhānta-cakravartī (who died in 1279). The *Jīvatattva-pradīpikā* by Kesavavarṇī in mixed Kannaḍa and Sanskrit was completed in 1359. Another Sanskrit commentary was written by Bhaṭṭāraka Nemicandra in 1515 in Chittor; it was based on Kesavavarṇī's commentary. Pandit Todarmal wrote the *Samyagjñāna* commentary in Hindi in 1761 in Jaipur; it was based on the above-mentioned two commentaries.

The *Trilokasāra*[132] or the Essence of the Three Worlds is like the *Gommaṭasāra* a compendium of *gāthās* from the *Ṣaṭkhaṇḍāgama* and its *Dhavalā* commentary and the *Tiloyapannatti.*[133] The author Nemicandra calls himself a pupil of Abhayanandi (अभयणंदि वच्छेण). This was written for enlightenment of his pupil Camuṇḍāraya. It contains 1018 *gāthās* wherein details about the Universe are treated under six sections: *loka-sāmānya, bhavana-loka, vyantara-loka, jyotirloka, vaimānika-loka* and *naraka-tiryaka-loka.* Mādhvacandra Traividya, a prominent pupil of Nemicandra, has written a commentary on this work. Some of his *gāthās* have been incorporated in the original text. *Labdhisāra*[134] (or the Essence of Attainment) is another composition of Nemicandra. While the *Gommaṭasāra* deals with the nature of *jīva* and *karma*, this work deals with the ways leading to Perfection. It is an appendix to the *Gommaṭasāra* and is based on the *Jaya-Dhavalā* commentary of the *Kasāyapāhuḍa.* Out of the 8 *karmas*, there is a powerful *mohanīya karma* (delusion), also known as *mithyātva karma* (vision-deluding). One must try to get rid of this *karma* for which one has to practise five *labdhis* (attainments). The *karaṇa-labdhi* is most significant, leading to the attainment of *samyaktva* (right perception) after release from *mithyātva.* It contains three *Adhikāras*, dealing with *darsana-labdhi, cāritra-labdhi* and *kṣāyika-cāritra.* Kesavavarṇī has composed a Sanskrit commentary on this text up to the *cāritra-labdhi* section only. Pandit Todarmal has written a Hindi commentary based on it. The *Kṣapaṇāsāra* (or The Essence of Annihilation) deals with the annihilation of four *kaṣāyas*: *krodha* (anger), *māna* (pride), *māyā* (falsehood) and *lobha* (greed). It contains 649 *gāthās* of which 261 are shared by the *Kṣapaṇāsāra.* Actually, this text has been incorporated in the *Labdhisāra.* As stated, this work deals with *Kṣāyika-cāritra,* the third *Adhikāra* referred to above. Mādhvacandra has written a commentary on this work; Pandit Todarmal's *Bhāṣā-ṭīkā* is based on this commentary. The *Davvasaṃgaha*[135] or *Dravyasaṃgraha* (or The Compendium of Substances) also is said to be the work of Nemicandra. In 58 *gāthās* it deals with six *dravyas* and *karma,* its causes, conditions and release.

The *Jambuddivapaṇṇatti-saṃgaha*[136] (*Jambudvīpaprajnapti-saṅgraha*) by Padmanandi Muni, like the *Loyavibhāga,* the *Tiloyapaṇṇatti* and the *Trilokasāra,* belongs to the *Karaṇānuyoga* category. Under the *Upāṅga* literature of the Śvetāmbaras we have already dealt with the canonical texts, the *Sūriyapannatti,* the *Jambuddīvapannatti,* the *Candapannatti* and the *Dīvasāgarapannatti* (under *Prakirṇakas*). These treatises deal with cosmology and astronomy. As people were curious to know what is behind the universe and what are the heavenly bodies, numerous works were composed by the Digambaras as well as the Śvetāmbaras on the subject.

At the end of this work the author Paumaṇandi (Padmanandi) tells us that it was his teacher Vijayaguru from whom he acquired the knowledge of *āgama* and later composed this work for Nandiguru, who was pupil of Sakalacandra, the pupil of Māghanandi. He has praised the knowledge and the austerities of his teachers and extolled himself employing various adjectives.[137] The treatise was written at Bārā, a town situated in the region of Pāriyatta (Pāriyātra),[138] in Sauraseni, and contains 2389 *gāthās,* divided into 13 *uddesas,* the last being the *Pramāṇa-pariccheda.* It deals with the seven *varṣas* or continents, the river Saila, Bhogabhūmi (realms of enjoyment), Mount Meru, Mandara-jinabhavana (Jain shrines at Mount Mandara), Devauttarakuru, Kaccha-vijaya (the presiding deity of the Kaccha region), eastern Videha, western Videha, Lavaṇa ocean, Dvipa-sāgara (island and ocean), Adho-loka (lower world), Madhya-loka (middle world), Ūrdhva-loka (upper world), Siddha-loka (the permanent abode of the liberated souls) and Jyotirloka (the stellar region). Here we come across a hierarchical list of teachers after Mahavira. They are Gautama, Lohārya (Sudharmā) and Jambu, the three *gaṇadharas.* Then we have Nandi,[139] Nandimitra, Aparājita, Govardhana and Bhadrabāhu, all equipped with the knowledge of fourteen *Pūrvas* and twelve *Aṅgas.* Then are listed *Visākhācārya,* Proṣṭhila, Kṣatriya, Jaya, Nāga, Siddhartha, Dhṛtiṣena, Vijaya, Buddhila, Gaṅgadeva and Dharmasena, all possessing the knowledge of ten *Pūrvas.* Next we have Nakṣatra, Yasaḥpāla, Pāṇḍu, Dhruvasena and Kaṃsa, all possessing the knowledge of eleven *Aṅgas.* Last come Subhadra, Yasobhadra, Yasobāhu and Loha (Lohācarya), equipped with the knowledge of only *Ācārāṅga.* Since the *Jambuddīvapaṇṇatti* and the *Tiloyapaṇṇatti* both belong to the *Karaṇānuyoga* category, the subject matter is similar and many of their *gāthās* are identical. The former also contains *gāthās* which are noticed in the *Mūlācāra* and the *Trilokasāra;* some of them may be traditional. The date assigned to this work is the latter part of the eleventh century vs. The *Dhammarasāyana* (*Dharmarasāyana*)[140] (or A Gist of Righteousness) contains 193 *gāthās* where the gist of *dharma* is explained. Its author seems to be Padmanandi.[141]

Siddhantasāra[142] is a small treatise, containing 79 *gāthās* wherein the essence of *siddhānta* is explained. The author Jinacandra belongs to the fifteenth century. Bhaṭṭāraka Jñānabhūṣana who belonged to the *Mūla-saṅgha, Sarasvatī-gaccha* and the *Balātkāra-gaṇa,* has composed a *Bhāṣya* on this work. Jñānabhūṣaṇa is also the author of the *Tattvajñānataraṅgiṇī* which was completed in vs 1560 (AD 1503).[143]

The *Kallānāloyaṇā* was composed by Ajitabrahma or Ajita Brahmacārī in the sixteenth century and the teacher's name is Devendrakīrti. It contains 54 *gāthās.* We are told that at the instance of Bhaṭṭāraka Vidyānandi the author completed his *Hanumānacaritra* in Bhṛgukaccha (Broach).

The *Aṅgapaṇṇatti* deals with the *prajñaptis* of twelve *Aṅgas* and fourteen *Pūrvas.* Subhacandra, who was a pupil's pupil of Jñānabhūṣaṇa, the author of the *Siddhāntasāra-Bhāṣya.* Like Jñānabhūṣaṇa the author is designated as *trividha-vidyadhara* (possessing the knowledge of three kinds of learning, *sabda, yukti* and *paramāgama*) and *ṣaṭ-bhāṣā-cakravartī* (the sovereign king of six languages). He is said to have defeated the disputants of Gauḍa, Kaliṅga, Karnāṭaka, Gurjara, Mālawa and other regions and propagated Jainism.

The *Tattvānusāsanādi-saṃgraha*[144] (Collection of Tatvānusāsana and other works) contains the *Tattvasāra*, the *Jñānasara*, the *Srutaskandha* and the *Ḍhaḍhasīgāthā*. The first is a small treatise of Muni Devasana written for the advancement of *dharma* and the enlightenment of those who are destined to attain liberation (*bhavya-jana*). It deals with the essence of reals (*tattva*) in 74 *gāthās*. In the end of his work, the author has stated about himself: 'After attending the teacher Devasena, the patron of monks, I have composed the *Tattvasāra*. Whosoever, possessing right faith, ponders over it, attains eternal happiness.'[145] Meditation is considered most important: without it one is not able to destroy his *karmas*.[146] The *Jñāasāra* (or The Essence of Knowledge) was composed by Muni Padmasiṃha in VS 1086 (AD 1029). It is a small work containing 63 *gāthās*, dealing with a *yogi*, *guru* (teacher) and *dhyāna* (meditation). The *Srutaskandha* by Brahmacārī Hemacandra was composed in a Jain temple, located in Kuṇḍanagara park of Tailaṅga. The author was pupil of Rāmanandi Saiddhāntika. It is a small treatise of 94 *gāthās*, dealing with scriptural knowledge (*srutajñāna*) and divided into *Aṅgabāhya* and *Aṅgapraviṣṭa*. It is stated that Mahavira attained *nirvāṇa* when there were still four years minus three and half months[147] left to the fourth era. After a hundred years of Mahavira's *nirvāṇa* no Srutakevalī was ever born. Ācārya Bhadrabāhu was efficient in the knowledge of *Aṣṭāṅga-nimitta* and Dharasena possessed the knowledge of the *Kamma-payaḍi* section of the *Agrāyaṇī Pūrva*.

The fourth section, the *Ḍhāḍhasīgāthā* by Ḍhāḍhasī Muni, contains 38 *gāthās*. The author belongs to the Kāṣṭha Saṅgha. Srutasāgarasūri (sixteenth century) has quoted a *gāthā* from this work in his *Ṣaṭpāhuḍa*-commentary.[148] Here the adherents of the Māthura-saṅgha are called *niḥpiccha* (without the whisk broom).

The *Bhāvasaṃgrahādi*[149] (Collection of Bhāvasaṃgraha and other Works) contains the *Bhavasaṃgraha*, the *Bhāva-tribhaṅgī* and the *Āsrava-tribhaṅgī*. The *Bhāvasaṃgraha* was composed by Devasena, who is different from Devasenagaṇi, the author of the *Darsanasāra*.[150] He belongs to the twelfth or thirteenth century of the Vikram era. The text contains 701 *gāthās*, some quoted from the *Darsanasāra*. Practising austerities and restraint of sense organs is rudimentary for purity; external purity such as bathing is secondary. The *guṇa-sthānas* are explained.

Bhāva-tribhaṅgī is by Srutamuni who belongs to the Mūla-saṅgha, Desīya-gaṇa, Pustaka or Sarasvatī-gaccha and Iṅgalesvara-sākhā. He was a pupil of Bālacandra. This work, also known as *Bhāvasaṃgraha*, is often considered the sixth chapter of Nemicandra *Tribhaṇgisāra.* Another work, the *Paramāgamasāra,* was composed in VS 1398= AD 1341).[151] The text contains 116 *gāthās,* dealing with the *aupasamika* (the state produced by suppression of the *karma*), *kṣāyika* of *karma* (the state produced by annihilation), *kṣayopasamika* (suppression-cum-annihilation), *audayika* (consequence of unhindered realization of *karma*) and *pāriṇāmika* (the essential state). It had a Sanskrit commentary.

The *Āsrava-tribhaṅgī* is another work of Srutamuni. He has described *mithyātva* (lack of insight), *avirati* (non-restraint), *kaṣāya* (passion) and *yoga* (activities) in 62 *gāthās.* The author has written a Kannaḍa commentary on this work, which in turn has been rendered into Lāṭī by Somadeva.[152] Most of the *gāthās* of the text are taken from the *Gommaṭasāra.*[153]

The *Tribhaṅgīsāra* of Nemicandra in manuscript form is catalogued in the Catalogue of the Jaina Manuscripts at Strasbourg (Sr. 125). It is with Sanskrit *chāyā,* and the Sanskrit commentary and a *Vacanikā* (*Tabā*) which is incomplete. It consists of the following four parts, the *Āsrava-tribhaṅgī* (1-59 *gāthās*), the *Bandha-tribhaṅgī* (60-99), the *Udaya-tribhaṅgī* (100-73), and the *Udirana-tribhaṅgī* (174-203).

Velankar calls the third and fourth parts *Udayodīraṇa-tribhaṅgī* and *Satta-tribhaṅgī* respectively. The first and second are often ascribed to Srutamuni and Madhavacandra respectively.[154]

The *Prāyascitta-saṃgraha*[155] (Collection of the *Prāyascitta* and other Works) contains the *Cheda-piṇḍa* and the *Chedasāstra.* The *Cheda-piṇḍa* is by Indranandī Yogīndra who belonged to the first part of the fourteenth century of Vikrama Era. We have already dealt with the *Chedasūtras. Cheda* means cutting off, or deprivation. A monk or a nun who violates the vows must atone for the sins committed and be re-established in the correct behaviour. It has been called as the destroyer of dirt (*mala-haraṇa*), annihilator of sins (*pāpa-nāsana*), purity, meritorious deed, sacred or holy. The text contains 362 *gāthās* wherein the rules of repentance (*vrata*), self-regulation (*samiti*), primary virtues (*mūla-guṇa*), sub-virtues (*uttara-guṇa*), austerities (*tapa*) and community (*gaṇa*) have been laid down.

The *Chedasāstra,* also known as the *Chedanavati* (ninety *chedas* or reductions), contains 90 *gāthās* wherein rules are prescribed for violating vows, self-regulation, and so on. There is a small commentary on this work. Unfortunately nothing is known about the author and the commentator. The *Darsanasāra*[156] was written by Devasenagaṇi in the Pārsvanātha temple in the city of Dhārā in AD 933 and contains 51 *gāthās* in which the origins of the Buddhists, the Śvetāmbaras, the Viparītas (the Brahmanic system) and the Vainayikas and the Drāviḍa, Yāpanīya, Kāṣṭhā, Māthura and Bhillaka *saṅghas* are described. The treatise is said to be based on the verses of the earlier teachers,[157] but does not seem to be very authentic. Marici,[158] the grandson of Ṛṣabha, the first Tīrthaṅkara, is said to be the originator of various religious faiths and systems. During the time of Pārsvanātha, *muni* Buddhakīrti, pupil of Pihitāsrava, is said to have been the founder of the Buddhist religion.[159] It is stated that in Buddhist religion there is no harm in eating meat and drinking wine. The Śvetāmbara sect came into being at Vallabhi in Saurashtra 136 years after the death of King Vikramaditya (AD 79).[160]

We are told that Jinacandra who was lax in his conduct, a pupil of *ācārya* Sānti, pupil of Bhadrabāhugaṇi, is responsible for founding this sect. The followers of this sect believe in *strī-mukti* (liberation of women) and partaking of food by omniscient beings (*kevali-bhukti*). Maskarī Pūrana[161] is mentioned as a pupil of certain *gaṇī* of Pārsvanātha. Then we come across the origin of five *saṅghas*, Drāviḍa, Yāpanīya, Kāṣṭhā, Māthura and Bhillaka; they are said to be *Jainābhāsa* (Jains in appearance only).[162]

It is stated that Vajranandi, pupil of Pūjyapāda, equipped with the knowledge of the *Prābhṛtas*, founded the *Drāviḍa-saṅgha* in Mathura (Madura), 526 years after Vikrama's death (i.e. AD 469). The well-known *ācārya*, Vādirāja (eleventh century) belonged to this *saṅgha*; he was an *ācārya* of the *Nandigaṇa* and the Aruṅgala-*anvaya*. According to the author of the *Darsanasāra*, the followers of this *saṅgha* used to maintain their livelihood by marshy land (*kaccha*), cultivating land (*khetta*), temple (*vasadi*) and trade (*vāṇijja*); cold water for bath, and thus they acquired sinful deeds.[163] They did not believe that they used a seed was a living being and did not discriminate between *prāsuka* (living) and *aprāsuka* (non-living). Vajranandi is said to have composed works related to *Prāyascitta*. The *Yāpanīya*, also known as *Āpulīya* or *Gopya-saṅgha* is said to have been founded by a Śvetāmbara monk Kalasa, 205 years after Vikrama's death (i.e. AD 148)[164] in the city of Kalyaṇa. Kumārasena is said to have founded the *Kāṣṭhā-saṅgha*[165] 753 years after Vikrama's death (AD 696) in Nanditaṭa, but to have fallen from asceticism. In order to protect tiny living beings, he carried a whiskbroom, at hard brush of chowrie, instead of a soft peacock-feather (*piñchī*). He is said to have travelled to the country of Bāgaḍa (identified with the region around Sāgavāḍā) and preached his religion. His followers preached liberation to women, adventurous exploits (*vīra-caryā*) were prescribed for *kṣullaka*-monks, and eating after sunset was prohibited. The sacred scriptures related to the precepts about *prāyascitta* were composed by the author. The Kāṣṭhā-*saṅgha* contains four main divisions: the Nanditaṭa, the Māthura, the Bāgaḍa and the Lāḍa-Bāgaḍa. Kumārasena belonged to the Nanditaṭa and was the founder of the Nanditaṭa-*gaccha*; Rāmasena of Māthura founded the Māthura-*gaccha*; then from Bāgaḍa we have the Bāgaḍa-*gaccha* and from Lāḍa-Bāgaḍa the Lāḍa-Bāgaḍa-*gaccha*. Two hundred years later Rāmasena is said to have founded the Māthura-*saṅgha* in Mathura. As the followers of this *saṅgha* did not carry the whiskbroom, they were also designated *nihpicchika*. According to some, Māthura-*saṅgha* is an offshoot of the Kāṣṭhā-*saṅgha*. Amitagati (eleventh century) belonged to this *saṅgha*. A little later was founded the Bhillak-*saṅgha* by Muni Vīracandra at Puṣkala, situated in the Vindhya mountains. It is stated that Vīracandra has his own *gaccha* and his performance of *pratikramaṇ* and other religious activities were quite different from others. This *saṅgha* is not mentioned anywhere else.

Nayacakra[166] is another work of Devasena. Sometimes it is also called *Laghu-Nayacakra*. It contains 87 *gāthās* dealing with the *nayas* (viewpoint), the *Dravyārthika* (substantial viewpoint) and the *Paryāy-ārthika* (viewpoint) and their subdivisions. Upādhyāya Yasovijaya (died in AD 1686) in his *Dravya-guṇa-paryāya-rāsa* (in Gujarati) and Bhojasāgara in his *Drvyānuyoga tarkaṇsā* (in Sanskrit) have referred to Devasena's *Nayacakra*. Bhojasāgara states that the *nayas*, the *upanayas* and the *mūla-nayas* (elementary *nayas*) are described here as Devasena has done in his *Nayacakra*. He adds that the work belongs to the Digambara sect, nevertheless the subject is based on the *āgamic* literature preached by the omniscient being, and is therefore beyond doubt.[167] According to the author, the knowledge of *naya* is very important to understand a particular subject. He says, 'As a man cannot quench his thirst without water so one cannot achieve happiness without righteousness. Similarly, an ignorant man, deprived of *naya* is unable to ascertain the knowledge of an object.'[168]

Ārādhanāsāra[169] (or the Essence of *Ārādhanā* or accomplishment), is another work of Devasena. It contains 115 *gāthās*. After developing the right view (*samyaktva*) one is able to gain the right vision of an object, which is called the essence of *ārādhanā*. It has been explained from the *niscaya* and the *vyavahāra* point of view. Here we come across the narratives of Sivabhūti, Sukumāla, Kosala, Gurudatta, the Pāṇḍavas, Gajasukumāra, Srīdatta and Suvarṇabhadra, who were able to accomplish their goal after undergoing various adversities. The mind (*manas*) is compared with a king; after he dies, his army of sense-organs also dies. Those who are not able to control their mind (like a camel), have, with the assistance of knowledge (with a nose-string), to roam about in this worldly existence. In order to root out the tree of mind, one must cut off its branches in the form of attachment and aversion, and thereafter never water the tree of mind with delusion (*moha*). It is stated that as a pinch of salt associated with water gets diluted in water so is the case with mind, associated with meditation, gets submerged into it.[170] Ratnakīrti, pupil of Kṣemakīrti of Kāṣṭhā-*saṅgha*, has written a commentary on this work wherein quotations are cited from Subhacandra *Jñānārṇava* and Kundakunda's *Samayasasāra*. Pandit Āsādhara is said to have written a commentary which is not available.

The *Davvasahāvapayāsa*[171] (*Dravyasvabhāvaprakāsa*), also known as the *Bṛhatnayacakṛa* by Māilladhavala, contains 423 *gāthās* wherein *dravya* (substance), *guṇa* (quality), *paryāya* (modifications) and *darsana* (perception), *jñāna* (knowledge) and *cāritra* (conduct) are discussed. It is a compendium of *gāthās* and incorporates all of the *Nayacakra*. The author has paid obeisance to Guru Devasena, who was able to annihilate the demon of wrong view (*durnaya*) by his *syādvāda-naya* (the right viewpoint of 'assertion of possibility or non-possibility'). His *Nayacakra* is said to have been preached by *Srutakevalin* and is compared with the *cakra* of Viṣṇu. Nothing much is known about the author.

Upāsakadhyayana or *Srāvakācāra* or *Vasunandi-sravakacara*[172] is by Vasunandi. There are several authors bearing this name, one said to belong to the end of the eleventh or the beginning of the twelfth century of the Vikrama Era. The text, which has a Sanskrit *chāyā*, contains 546 *gāthās*, dealing with the layman's discipline. In the beginning, the characteristics of right faith (*samyagdarsana*) are explained. Evil passions (*vyasana*) and twelve vows (*vratas*) are described. The special *vratas*, the *Pañcamī*, *Rohiṇī*, *Asvinī*, *Saukhya-sampatti*, *Nandīsvara-paṅkti* and *Vimāna-paṅkti*, are mentioned. Pandita Āsādhara has referred to Vasunandi in the commentary of his *Sāgāra-dharmāmṛta* with consideration and has cited verses from his *Sravakācāra*. Some of its verses are identical with the *Bhāva-saṃgraha*. *Jīva-tattva-pradīpa* with Sanskrit commentary is by Kesavārya, a pupil of Abhayacandra. The manuscript is preserved in Strasbourg. According to Leumann, Kanakanandi, pupil of Indrabhuti, composed the *Prakṛti-sattvasthāna* in 41 *gāthās* with a commentary, which forms a part of the *Jīvatattva-pradīpikā* by Kesavārya.[173] This statement is confirmed by a *Karmakāṇḍa-gāthā* (396) which says that having listened to the whole *siddhānta* (doctrine) from the teacher Indranandi, Kanakanandi has explained the *Sattaṭṭhāṇa* (*Sattva-sthāna*).[174] This work is incorporated in the *Gommaṭasāra* (*Karmakāṇḍa, Sattvasthānādhikara*) by Nemicandra Siddhānta-cakravarti.

NOTES

1. See *Ṣaṭkhaṇḍāgama*, I, p. 99; Pūjyapāda, *Sarvārthasiddhi*, 1.20; Akalaṅka, *Rājavārtika*, 1.20; Nemicandra, *Gommaṭasāra, Jīvakāṇḍa*, pp. 134f.
2. For modifications and interpolations in the Śvetāmbara Jain canonical texts see supra, Chapter 2.
3. Akalaṅka, *Rājavārtika*, 1.20.
4. As it is necessary to know fundamental operations such as addition, subtraction, etc., before one can solve arithmetic problems, so it is necessary to study *parikamma* before one takes up the study of *Sutta, Puvvagaya*, etc. *Nandi Cū*, 55, after *HCLJ*, p. 83n.
5. Regarding the subdivisions of the *Parikamma* in the Śvetāmbara Canon see *Nandi Cū*, pp. 55-61; *HCLJ*, pp. 83-96.
6. *Nandi Cū*, 56.
7. See Chapter 2.
8. A kind of jugglery referred to in the *Bṛh Saṃ, MW*, under '*prasena*'.
9. *Rājavārtika*, 1.20, pp. 52-3.
10. *Ṣaṭkhaṇḍāgama*, I, p. 96; also Pūjyapāda, *Sarvārthasiddhi* (1.20); Akalaṅka, *Rājavārtika*, 1.20; Nemicandra, *Gommaṭasāra, Jīvakāṇḍa*, pp. 134f. For their contents see *Ṣaṭkhaṇḍāgama*, I, pp. 96-8; IX, pp. 188-91.
11. See supra, 2, pp. 78f, 97-9.
12. आरातीयैः पुनराचार्यैः कालदोषात्संक्षिप्तायुर्मतिबलशिष्यानुग्रहार्थं दशवैकालिकाद्युपनिबद्धं तत्प्रमाणमर्थतस्तदेवेदमिति क्षीरार्णवजलं घटगृहीतमिव।
13. See *LAI*, 2nd edn., p. 12n.
14. In this connection the following observation of A.N. Upadhye is worth quoting. 'On account of almost identical contents dealing with monastic life, common verses showing minor changes of verbal and dialectical nature, and similar method of exposition and presentation, the conclusion appears to be inevitable that texts like the *Bhagavaī Ārādhanā, Mūlācāra, Nijjuttis* (like *Āvasyaka, Piṇḍa*, etc.) and *Paiṇṇas* (like the *Maraṇasamāhi, Bhattaparinnā*, etc.) in some portion at least, go back to the common source that was once acceptable as authoritative both by the Digambaras and Śvetāmbaras'. Introduction to BKK, p. 34. For

identical *gāthās* in the *Mūlācāra* of Vaṭṭakera and the *Āvasyaka-Niryukti* see Pandit Sukhlal's *Pañcapratikramaṇa Sūtra*, pp. 53f.

15. L. Alsdorf does not agree with the view that these two Digambara texts are based on the lost *Dṛṣṭivāda*. For discussion see *LAI*, revd. edn., 37f.
16. Ed. Hiralal Jain, with text and the *Dhavalā* Commentary (in Prakrit mixed Sanskrit), with its Hindi translation in 16 volumes; it contains the first 5 parts, Amaraoti, 1940-58. The sixth part, known as the *Mahābandha*, is edited and translated into Hindi in 7 parts by Sumerchand Diwakar and Pandit Phoolchandra Siddhantashastri, Kashi, 1947-58; Hiralal Jain and A.N. Upadhye, Vol. I, Solapur, 1973 (this is the reprint of the *Ṣaṭkhaṇḍāgama* edition of the first five parts.), Vol. II, 1976.
17. Ed. Pandit Hiralal Jain, with *Cūrni-sūtras* and translated into Hindi, Calcutta, 1955. Ed. Pandit Phoolchandra Siddhantashastri, Pandit Mahendrakumar Jain and Pandit Kailashchandra Siddhantashastri with *Jayadhavalā* Com. and Hindi translation in 15 volumes, Mathura, 1944-75.
18. According to the *Nandi the Dhavalā* and the *Jayadhavalā*, he had acquired the knowledge of all the *Aṅgas* and a part of *Pūrva* literature from tradition.
19. तेण वि सोरट्ठ-विसय-गिरिनयर-पट्टण-चंदगुहाठिएण अट्ठंग-महानिमित्त-पारएण गंथ-वोच्छेदो होहिदि त्ति जाद-भयेण पवयण-वच्छलेण दक्खिणावहाइरियाणं महिमाए मिलियाणं लेहो पेसिदो। लेह-ट्ठिय-धरसेण-वयण-मवधारिय तेहिं वि आइरिएहिं बे साहू गहण-धारण-समत्था धवलामल-बहुविह-विणय-विहूसियंगा सील-माला-हरा गुरु-पेसणासण-तित्ता देस-कुल-जाइ-सुद्धा सयल-कला-पारया तिक्खुत्ता बुच्छियाइरिया अंध-विसय-वेण्णायणादो पेसिदा, *Dhavalā*, I.1.1.
20. Ed. Pandit Phoolchandra Siddhantashastri, with original text and Hindi translation in 7 parts, Varanasi, 1947-58.
21. For detailed study see Pandit Kailashchandra Siddhantashastri, *Jain Sahitya ka Itihas*, I, Chapter I, Sections 2 and 3; Chapter II, Sections 1-3.
22. See Indranandin, *Srutāvatāra*; *Ṣaṭkhaṇḍāgama*, I, Introduction, pp. 46-53; Pandit Kailashchandra Siddhantashastri, *Jain Sahitya ka Itihas*, I, pp. 263-92.
23. The following *gāthā* has been quoted:
    उप्पज्जंति वियंति य भावा णियमेण पज्जवणयस्स।
    दत्वट्ठियस्स सत्वं सदा अणुप्पण्णमविणट्ठं॥ Book 9, p. 244.
24. Book 4, pp. 315-17.
25. Book 9, pp. 165-7.
26. In Book IX, p. 129, it is said that Gautama Indrabhūti has composed them.
27. Also known as Sudharmācārya in the *Jayadhavalā* Commentary and Indranandin's *Srutāvatāra*.
28. Yasahpāla in the *Jambuddīvapaṇṇattisaṃgaha*.
29. Abhayabhadra in the *Srutāvatāra*.
30. *Jahabāhu* in the *Jayadhavalā* and *Jayabāhu* in the *Srutāvatāra*.

31. Book I, pp. 221-2.
32. . . . एसा दक्खिण पडिवत्ती। दक्खिणं उज्जुवं आइरिय-परंपरा-गदमिदि एगट्ठो। . . . एसा उत्तरपडिवत्ती। उत्तरमणुज्जवं आइरिय-परंपराए णागदमिदि एयट्ठो, Book V, p. 3.
33. अस्मादेवार्षाद् द्रव्यस्त्रीणां निर्वृतिः सिद्धयेत् इति चेत्, न। सवास-सत्वादप्रत्याख्यानगुणस्थितानां संयमानुपपत्तेः। भावसंयमस्तासां सवाससामप्य विरुद्धं इतिचेत्, न। तासां भावसंयमोऽस्ति भावसंयमाबिनाभाविवस्त्राद्युपादानान्यथानुपपत्तेः। कथं पुनस्तासु चतुर्दशगुणस्थानानीति चेत्, न। भावस्त्रीविशिष्टमनुष्यगतौ तत्सत्त्वाविरोधात्, Book I, p. 333. For different interpretation of this passage, see Pandit Kailashchandra Siddhantashastri, *Jain Sahitya ka Itihas*, p. 220.
34. असच्चकारणुम्मुक्कजिणवयणकमलविणिग्गयत्तादो।
35. See Avadhesh Narayan Singh's articles 'Mathematics of Dhavalā' in the Introduction to Book IV.
36. Kuṇḍapura in the Śvetāmbara Canon.
37. Book IX, pp. 125f.
38. Ed. Pandit Hiralal Jain, Calcutta, 1955.
39. Book I, pp. 356f.
40. *Kasāyapāhuḍa,* II, pp. 420f.
41. Ibid., III, pp. 213-14, 532.
42. Ibid., p. 398.
43. Ed. A.N. Upadhye and Hiralal Jain, in 2 parts, Solapur, 1943 and 1951.
44. In Introduction, Dr. Hiralal Jain has presented a comparison of the subject matter, etc., of the text with the *Bṛhatkṣetrasamāsa* and the *Bṛhatsaṅgrahaṇī* of Jinabhadragaṇi Kṣamāsramaṇa and the *Pravacanasāroddhāra* of Nemicandra.
45. The *Dhavalā* Commentary refers to 18 dialects: 3 spoken in Kuru, 3 in Lāḍha, 3 in Marahaṭṭa, 3 in Mālava, 3 in Gauḍa and 3 Magadha. Seven hundred degraded dialects spoken are Kīra, Pārasīka, Siṃhala, Babbara and other regions, Book XIII, pp. 221f.
46. 1.64-5; also see Jinasena's *Harivaṃsapurāṇa* (3.53-5); *Suttanipata-Aṭṭhakathā*, 2, p. 382; *Mahābhārata,* 2, 21, 2.
47. In the Śvetāmbara texts they are designated as '*kumāra-pravrajita*', '*kumārasiṃha*' or '*gṛhastha-pravrajita*'. It seems the word '*kumāra*' in the *Āvasyaka Niryukti* (221-2) may be the cause of controversy about the marriage of Mahavira; see Premi, ibid., pp. 100-1, also Dalasukh Malavnia's article 'Tīrthāṅkara Mahavira', *JOIB,* XXIV, September-December 1974. Regarding marriage of Mahavira, we meet both the traditions in the Śvetāmbara texts: (a) he is depicted as married in the *Ācārаṅga* (II.15.15) and the *Kalpasūtra* (5.112), and (b) unmarried in the *Samavāvāyaṅga* (19), the *Sthānāṅga* (471), the *Āvasyaka Niryukti* (221-2) and Vimalasūri's *Paumacariya* (57-8). In the Digambara tradition, he is generally depicted as unmarried but Jinasena's *Harivaṃsāpurāṇa* clearly mentions about his '*vivāha-maṅgala*' meaning marriage ceremony.
48. Elsewhere, in the *Ovāiya* (31, p. 68) the following eight auspicious objects are referred to: *svastika, srīvatsa, nandyāvarta, vardhamāna*

(powder-flask), *bhadrāsana* (throne), *kalasa, darpaṇa* and *matsya-yuga* (a pair of fish). For other auspicious objects, see *LAI*, pp. 273f.

49. See Nathuram Premi, *Jain Sahitya*, 'Lokavibhāga aur Tiloyapaṇṇatti', pp. 1f, 1956.

50. V. Pavolini has edited only the text under the title *Pañcatthikāya-saṃgahasuttaṃ* in *Geornale della Societa Asiatica Italiana* (*GSAI*), 14, pp. 1-40, 1901; Aṃrtacandrasuri's *Tattvadīpikā*, in Sanskrit, and Pāṇḍe Hemarāja's *Bālāvabodha*; based on the latter is Pannalal Bakliwal's Hindi translation, Bombay, 1904; edited a second time with the addition of the Sanskrit commentary of Jayasena, Bombay, 1914; edited with an English translation by A. Chakravarti with Introduction, *SBJ*, Arrah, 1920; edited with a Hindi rendering of Jayasena's Sanskrit commentary by Brahmachari Shitalprasad, Surat; Pandit Kailashchandra Siddhantashastri, *Kundakunda-prābhṛtasaṃgraha*, Solapur, 1960; Gujarati translation with Amṛtacandra's Com., Digambara Svādhyāya Mandir, vs 2014.

51. Upadhye, ibid., Introduction, p. 23 fn. In Indranandi's *Srutāvatāra*, it is called *Kuṇḍakundapura.*

52. मंगलं भगवान् वीरो मंगलं गौतमो गणी।
मंगलं कुन्दकुन्दाद्यो जैन धर्मोऽस्तु मंगलम्॥

53. Upadhye has observed: 'The author might have put together traditional verses when trying to discuss a topic in a connected manner. . . . Some *gāthās* (64 etc.) are called *Siddhānta-sūtrāṇi* by Amṛtacandra', ibid., p. 44.

54. A.N. Upadhye's Introduction to *Pravacanasāra* (pp. 110-11).

55. Edited in *RJS*, vs 1969; with Brhmacārī Shitalprasada's Hindi translation of Jayasena's commentary in 3 vols., vs 2450-2; A.N. Upadhye with Amṛtacandra's and Jayasena's Sanskrit Commentaries and Hemarāja Pāṇḍe's *Bālāvabodhinī* (vs 1709), with text, English translation and Introduction, *RJS*, 1935; 2nd edn., 1964; Faddegon's English translation of the text and Amṛtacandra's Sanskrit Commentary, edited by F.W. Thomas, Cambridge, 1935.

56. *A History of*, II, p. 576.

57. A.N. Upadhye's Introduction to *Pravacanasāra*, pp. 97-111. Though Upadhye tried his best to edit the text critically he thinks that since the present edition simply represents a readable manuscript, and can hardly be called critical. He says that the present text represents to a great extent the text preserved by Jayasena in his Sanskrit commentary, accompanied by a table of various readings drawn from two independent MSS, p. 111.

58. जधजादरूवजादं उप्पाडिद-केस-मंसुगं सुद्धं।
रहिदे हिंसादीदो अप्पडिकम्मं हवदि लिंगं॥ III.5

59. III.8.

60. गेण्हदि व चेलखंडं भायणमत्थि त्ति भणिदमिह सुत्ते।
जदि सो चत्तालंबो हवदि कहं वा अणारंभो॥
quoted in Amṛtacandra's commentary, III.3.
61. संति धुवं पयदाणं मोहपदोसा भयं दुगुंध्छा य।
चित्ते चित्ता माया तम्हा तासिं ण णिव्वाणं॥ ibid., 9.
62. चित्तस्सावो तासिं सित्थिल्लं अत्तवं च पक्खलणं।
विज्जदि सहसा तासु अ उप्पादो सुहस-मणुआणं॥ ibid., 11.
63. लिंगम्हि य इत्थीणं थणंतरे णाहि-कक्ख-पदेसेसु।
भणिदो सुहुमुप्पादो तासिं कह संजमो होदि॥ ibid., 12.
64. With Sanskrit commentaries of Amṛtacandra and Jayasena in *SJG*, Banaras, 1914; with these two Sanskrit commentaries and a Hindi commentary by Jayacandra, *RJS*, Bombay, 1919; text with Sanskrit *chāyā*, with English translation and commentary by J.L. Jaini, *SBJ*, Lucknow, 1930; A. Chakravarti, with text and English translation of *Samayasāra-kalaśa* (which is Amṛtacandra's Sanskrit commentary, known as *Ātmakhyati.* It is treated as an independent work on which a Sanskrit commentary, titled *Paramādhyātma-taraṅgiṇi* is written by Subhacandra; pub. by SJG, No. 15, Calcutta), Murtidevi *Granthamālā*, 1950; Kailashchandra Siddhantashastri, *Kundakunda-prabhṛta-saṃgraha*, *JJG*, Solapur, 1960; Jayacandra's Hindi commentary (which closely follows Amṛtacandra) published from Kolhapur, Bombay, etc. Br. Shitalprasada's Hindi commentary, following Jayasena's commentary, Surat; Himmatlal Jethalal Shah, trans., in Gujarati verses, Jain Atithi Sevasamiti, Songarh, 1940.
65. Upadhye, ibid., p. 47.
66. कम्मं बद्धमबद्धं जीवं एवं तु जाण णय-पक्खं।
पक्खादिक्कंतो पुण भण्णदि जो सो समयसारो॥
67. जीवे कम्मं बद्धं पुट्ठं चेदि ववहार-णय-भणिदं।
सुद्ध-णयस्स दु जीवे अबद्ध-पुट्ठं हवदि कम्मं॥
68. Published by JGRK, Bombay, 1916, accompanied by Padmaprabha Maladhārideva's Sanskrit commentary and a Hindi translation of the same by Br. Shitalprasad; ed. by Ugrasen, with English translation, *SBJ*, Arrah, 1931; Himmatlal Jethalal Shah with Gujarati translation, Jain Svadhyya Mandir Trust, Songarh.
69. The order and the names in the Mūlācāra (1.22) are different: *samadā* (*samatā*), *thava* (*stava*), *vandaṇa* (*vandana*), *paḍikkamaṇa* (*pratikramaṇa*), *paccakkhāṇa* (*pratyākhyāna*) and *visagga* (*kāyotsarga*).
70. Siddhasena in his *Sanmatitarka* (II.3ff) holds a similar view.
71. पडिक्कमण-णामधेये सुत्ते जहा वण्णिदं पडिक्कमणं, Upadhye, p. 42n.
72. Ibid., p. 42.
73. Published with *Aṣṭa-pāhuḍa* in the *MDJG*, Vol. 17, vs 1977; Kṣullaka Jñānasāgaraji, Delhi, 1964; Kapilbhai T. Kotadia, in Gujarati script, Himmatnagar, 1967.
74. Ibid., p. 39.

75. *Ṣaṭprābhṛtādi-saṃgraha,* edited by Pannalal Soni, it has also included *Liṅgapāhuḍa, Sīlapāhuḍa,* and *Rayaṇasāra* and *Bārasa-Aṇuvekkhā.* The first six *Pāhuḍas* are with the Sanskrit commentary of *Srutasāgara* and the rest with only Sanskrit *chāyā, MDJG,* Vol. 17, vs 1977.
76. यथा कोऽपि देवदत्तः राज-दर्शनार्थम् किंचित् सारभूतं वस्तु राज्ञे दधति तत् प्राभृतं भण्यते। तथा परमात्माराधक-पुरुषस्य निर्दोष-परमात्म-राज-दर्शनार्थम् इदमपि शास्त्रम् प्राभृतम्, ibid., p. 24.
77. Upadhye has enumerated 43 *Pāhuḍas* attributed to Kundakunda—ibid., 25n.
78. Ibid., p. 25.
79. See his 'Kundakunda echt und unecht' (Kundakunda genuine and not genuine), *ZDMG,* 107, 1957, pp. 557-74, also containing the edition of the *Bodhaprābhṛta,* pp. 561ff, after *CJMS,* p. 124, Sr. 62 n.
80. दंसणमूलो धम्मो उवइट्ठो जिणवरेहिं सिस्साणं।
    तं सोऊण सकण्णे दंसणहीणो ण वंदिव्वो॥ २॥
81. The titles are कलिकाल-सर्वज्ञ, कलिकाल-गौतम, उभय-भाषा-कवि-चक्रवर्ती, व्याकरण-कमल-मार्तण्ड, तार्किक-शिरोमणि, परमागम-प्रवीण, नव-नवति-महा-महा-वादि-विजेता, etc., Premi, *Jain Sahitya,* p. 371.
82. For details see Premi, *Jain Sahitya,* pp. 371-4. Loṅikā Sāha (AD 1451) was the founder of the Sthankavāsī sect. He was a devout Gujarati layman, a scribe by profession. He gained access to the sacred text and was shocked to compare the discipline they demanded with the lax monkish behaviour which he saw around him, P.S. Jaini, *The Jain Path,* p. 309.
83. उत्थरइ जा ण जरओ रोयग्गी जा ण डहइ देहउडिं।
    इंदियबलं न वियलइ ताव तुमं कुणहि अप्पहियं॥
    compare with जरा जाव न पीलेइ वाही जाव न वड्ढइ।
    जाविंदिया न हायंति ताव घम्मं समाचरे॥ *Dasaveyāliya,* Ch. 7.
84. जो सुत्तो ववहारे सो जोई जग्गए सकज्जम्मि।
    जो जग्गदि ववहारे सो सुत्तो अप्पणे कज्जे॥
    ष्द्ध. जागरह नरा! णिच्चं जागरमाणस्स वड्ढते बुद्धी।
    जो सुवति ण सो धन्नो, जो जग्गति सो सया धन्नो॥
    Samaṇasuttaṃ, Apramādasūtra 168.
85. Ed. Pandit Manoharlal Gupta and Nathuram Premi, Bombay, 1910; in the *Kundakunda-prābhṛta-saṃgraha* (edited by Pt. Kailashchandra Siddhantashastri, 1960), the *BA* is published with a Hindi translation on pp. 136-53; *Srimat-Kundakundācārya-viracita Bārasa-aṇuvekkhā,* Sivānā (Rajasthan), 1963, it contains the Prakrit *gāthās* with Sanskrit *chāyā,* Hindi metrical and prose translation, and a Gujarati translation (Jinaratnasuri Jain Jñānamandira); Chandrabhal Tripathi and Bansidhara Bhatta, 'The Bārasa Aṇuvekkhā of Kundakunda', *Mahāvīra and His Teachings,* Bhagavan Mahavira—2500th Mahotsava Samiti, Bombay, 1977.
86. The number of *gāthās* varies in different manuscripts; the Kannaḍa MS of Kolhapur omits 7 verses and the Strasbourg MS omits 4, Chandrabhal Tripathi and Bansidhar Bhatt, p. 22.

87. उत्तमगुण in *Bhavabhāvanā.*
88. अद्धुवमसरणमेगत्तमण्णसंसारलोगमसुचित्तं।
    आसवसंवरणिज्जरघम्मं बोहिं च चिंतेज्जो॥ *Maṅgala* 2.
89. See Chapter VI, pp. 244-5. Among other works dealing with the twelve *Anuprekṣās* are *Bhagavatī Ārādhanā, Maranasamāhi Paiṇṇā, Bārasa Aṇuvekkhā* of Kumāra or Kārtikeya, besides several other works in Sanskrit and Apabhraṃsa. See Upadhye's Introduction to *Pravacana-sāra,* p. 39n.
90. Ibid., p. 40.
91. Ibid.
92. For other common or parallel *gāthās* in the *Bhagavatī Ārādhanā,* the *Maraṇasamāhi, Mokṣa-pāhuḍa, Kallāṇāloyaṇā,* the *Darsana-pr. (Daṃsaṇa-pāhuḍa),* the *Gommaṭasāra (Jīva)* and *Trilokasāra,* see Chandrabhal Tripathi and Bansidhar Bhatt, Table, pp. 25-31.
93. Ed. Pandit Jinadasa Parsvanatha with Marathi translation, Mahavira Press, Agra, vs 1993; the *Iriyāvahiyā* is also incorporated. The *Kriya-kalāpa* Com. also has incorporated the Dasa-Bhatti. Doshi Sakharam Nemacanda, Solapur, 1921, with Prabhācandra's Sanskrit commentary. Also incorporated in Pandit Kailashchandra Siddhanta-shastri's *Kundakundaprābhṛtasaṃgraha.*
94. See *CJMS,* Sr. 65, p. 126f.
95. See Upadhye, p. 28.
96. Upadhye, ibid.
97. *ADJG,* vs 1989; with commentaries of Aparājita and Āsādhara, Solapur, 1935; with Aparājita's commentary, Karanja, 1935; K. Oetjens, *Sivārya's Mūlārādhanā,* Hamburg, 1976; Kailashchandra Siddhantashastri, in 2 Pts., Solapur, 1978.
98. Premi, *Jain Sahitya,* pp. 56-73.
99. अज्ज-जिणणंदि-गणि सव्वगुत्त-गणि अज्जमित्तणंदीणं।
    अवगमिय पादमूले सम्मं सुत्तं च अत्थं च॥ 2559॥
    पुव्वायरिय-णिबद्धा उवजीवित्ता इमा ससत्तीए।
    आराधणा सिवज्जेण पाणि-दल-भोइणा रइदा॥ 2560॥
100. Page 54.
101. Ibid.
102. See Section 4 (iv) '*Kathākosas* Associated with the *Bhagavatī Ārādhanā*', pp. 58ff; and 5 '*Bhagavatī Ārādhanā* and Dependent *Kathānakas*', pp. 73-80.
103. For hardships undergone by Jain *sramaṇas* under these and such other conditions, narrated in the *Chedasūtra* of the Śvetāmbaras, see Jagdish Chandra Jain, *LAI,* pp. 292-9.
104. *Gāthā* 132, 411. Sometimes it is considered a constituent of the Śvetāmbara *Chedasūtras.* It deals with ten kinds of *prāyascitta* (atonement), it is composed by the well known Jinabhadragaṇi Kṣamāsramaṇa; also referred to in the *Mūlācāra* (5.190).

105. आयार-जीदकप्प-गुण-दीवणा, अत्त-सोधिणिज्झंझा ॥ 4 ॥

106. See commentary on *gāthā* (423), pp. 320-7.

107. Also see *Āva Nir* (94-130), *Bṛh Sū* (4.29) and *Bhā* (4.5497-5565), *Vya Bhā* (7.442-6), *Āva Cū* (pp. 102-9). The *Āva Nir.* and *Āva Cū* treat the subject under the title *pariṭṭhavaniyā* (*pratiṣṭhāpanikā*=placing of the dead) and the *Bṛh Bhā* under *visumbhaṇa* (*visvagbhavana*=separation of soul from body); also see Jagdish Chandra Jain's 'Disposal of the Dead in the *Bhagavatī Ārā*', *JOIB*, Vol. 38, Nos. 1-2, September-December 1988, Baroda; also his *Studies in Early Jainism*, Navranga, Delhi, 1991.

108. See Premi, *Jain Sahitya*, pp. 78-86.

109. With Vasunandi's Sanskrit Com. in 2 Pts., *MDJG*, vs 1977 and 1980; with Hindi translation and an alphabetical index of *gāthās*, *ADJG*, Bombay, 1919; K. Okud, *Eine Digambara-Dogmatik*, Wiesbaden, 1975; R.P. Jain, *Piṇḍasuddhi: Das Sechste Kapitel von vaṭṭakeras Mūlācāra und der adhākamma-āhschnitt der Piṇḍa-nijjutti*, New Delhi, 1983; Phoolchand Jain 'Premi', *Mūlācāra kā Samīkṣātmaka Adhyayana*, with *Prastāvanā* of Jagdish Chandra Jain, Varanasi, 1987.

110. In *Ṣaṭkhaṇḍāgama*, *Dhavalā*, IV, p. 316, a *gāthā* from the *Mūlācāra* (*Ācāraṅga*) has been quoted.

111. See Premi, pp. 548f.

112. Sukhlalji Sanghavi in his *Pañcapratikramaṇa Sūtra* has provided a list of *Mūlācāra's gāthās*, common with the *Āvasyaka-Niryukti*; A.M. Ghatge in the *IHQ* (1935) has compared the *gāthās* of *Mūlācāra* and the *Dasavaikālika-Niryukti*; also Phoolchand Jain 'Premi', ibid., pp. 14-29.

113. See Jagdish Chandra Jain, *Prastāvanā to Mūlācāra ka Samīkṣātmaka Adhyayana*, pp. 24f.

114. Supra, p. 121.

115. आवासय-णिज्जुत्ती वोच्छामि जहाकमं समासेण।
आयरिय-परंपराए जहागदा आणुपुव्वीए॥ 7.2

116. In the *Āvassaya-Nijjutti* of Bhadrabāhu, the number of *gāthās* in these Sections are 139, 100, 62, 189, 51, 90 and 172 respectively. Here the order is slightly different: *Pacchakkhāṇa* precedes *Kāussagga*. For difference in the order of the *Āvasyakas* in Kundkunda's *Niyamasāra*, see supra, p. 121.

117. णिज्जुत्ती णिज्जुत्ती एसा कहिदा मए समासेण।
अह वित्थार-पसंगोऽणियोगदो होदि णादव्वो॥ 7.192

118. बावीसं तित्थयरा सामायिय-संजमं उवदिसंति॥
छेदुवठावणियं पुण भयवं उसहो य वीरो य॥ 7.36
आदीए दुव्वि सोधण णिहणे तह सुट्ठु दुरणुपाले य।
पुरिमा य पच्छिमा वि हु कप्पाकप्पं न जाणंति॥ 7.38
Here the first *gāthā* is recorded in Bhadrabāhu's *Āvassaya-Nijjutti*. Also compare with the *Uttarā* (23-6):

पुरिमा उज्जु-जडा उ बंक-जडा य पच्छिमा।
मज्झिमा उज्जुपन्नाउ तेण धम्मे दुहाकए॥

119. See II.86-7 Com.
120. एसो अज्जाणंपि अ सामाचारो जहक्खिओ पुव्वं।
सव्वम्हि अहोरत्ते विभासिदव्वो जधाजोग्गं॥ 4.187
121. Read 188, 191, 192, 194, compare with *Bṛ Bhā* 3.4106, also see *LAI*, pp. 219-21 under Female Ascetics.
122. एवंविधाणचरियं चरंति जे साधवो य अज्जाओ।
ते जगपुज्जं कित्तिं सुहं च लद्धूण सिज्झंति॥ 4.196
The meaning of the *gāthā* is very clear. But Phoolchandra Jain 'Premi' has tried to twist it according to his wishes supporting 'non-liberation of women'. In his opinion (p. 418), it has not been stated by the author of the *Mūlācāra* that women can attain liberation in this very birth (इसमें यह कथन नहीं है कि इसी भव से मोक्ष प्राप्त करेंगे, p. 418 of his edition). The present author, in his *Prastāvanā* of this edition, had specifically noted that 'unlike Kundakunda, Vaṭṭakera had been a supporter of "*stri-mukti*",' but unfortunately that particular portion of the *Prastāvanā* has been deleted without consulting the author. In this connection the author had a correspondence with the Chief Editor of the *Parsvanātha Vidyasrama Granthamālā* but unfortunately there had been no response. Late Pandit Nathuram Premi has also mentioned the above *gāthā* of Vaṭṭakera in support of '*strī-mukti*' in his *Jain Sahitya aur Itihasa* (p. 552). This reference from Vaṭṭakera is significant to prove that as he was not against '*strī-mukti*', and has cited the scriptures of the Digambara and the Śvetāmbara traditions at that early period, he is earlier than Kundakunda. Even E. Leumann, a pioneer German scholar of Jainism, in his studies of the *Āvasyaka* literature, holds that Kundakunda is posterior to Vaṭṭakera. Leumann has edited the seventh chapter (*Ṣaḍavasyaka Adhikāra*) of the *Mūlācāra* from the MS. and has described the work an 'excellent one'. See his monumental incomplete work *Übersicht über die Āvasyaka Literature* (pp. 15b, 58); also *CJMS*, Sr. 77, p. 138.
123. Compare 10.121-2 *gāthās* with *Das* (4.6-7); 10.102 with *Ḍas* (8.54-6); 10.49 with *Bhag Ārā* (7) and so on.
124. Published by Gandhi Natharang with *Bhāshā-tīkā* of Pandit Jayachanda, Bombay, 1904; Patni Digambar Jain Granthamala with Mahendrakumar Jain Patni's Hindi translation; Ed. A.N. Upadhye, with a valuable Introduction, and Subhacandra's Sanskrit commentary, *RJS*, 1960; also Sulabha Jain Granthamala, 1921.
125. With Abhayacandra's Com. on Jīva-Kāṇḍa and Keshavavarni's Com. on Karma-Kāṇḍa, Gandhi Haribhai Devakaraṇa Granthamala, Calcutta, 1921; Jīva-Kāṇḍa with *mūla* and Hindi translation by Pandit Khubchand Jain, *RJS*, 1959; Karma-Kaṇḍa with *mūla* and Pandit

Manoharlal's Hindi translation, *RJS*, 1928; J.L. Jani's English translation, *SBJ*, 1927 (translation of 1-397 *gāthās* only); Pandit Todarmal's Hindi commentary based on the above-mentioned two Sanskrit *Ṭīkas*, completed in 1761 in Jaipur, pub. Bharatiya Jain Siddhanta Prakashini Samstha, Calcutta. The above-mentioned Hindi translations are based on this Com. One Dilaram had prepared a Persian version of Karma-Kāṇḍa (Catalogue, Oxford, 1864). This information was provided to me during my tenure in Santiniketan in 1933 by late Professor Ziauddin of Persian Dept. of Vidyabhavana.

126. They are समर-धुरंधर, वीर-मार्त्तण्ड, रण-रंग-सिंह, वैरिकुल-काल-दण्ड, असहाय-पराक्रम, प्रतिपक्ष-राक्षस, भुज-विक्रम, समर-परशुराम, सत्य-युधिष्ठिर et al., Premi, ibid., p. 267.
127. गोम्मट-संगह-सुत्तं गोम्मट-सिहरुवरि गोम्मट-जिणो य।
गोम्मटराय-विणिम्मिय-दक्खिण-कुक्कुड-जिणो जयउ ॥ 968
128. Supra, p. 104.
129. गुण-जीवा पज्जत्ती पाणा सण्णा य मग्गणाओ य।
उवओगो वि य कमसो वीसं तु परूवणा भणिदा ॥ 2 ॥
130. It is not unnatural that the details of karmic matter (*karma-prakṛti*) with regard to the nature and process of *karmas*, their classification, bondage with soul, their influx, fruition, annihilation, etc., may appear monotonous, particularly to a foreign scholar. In this connection the observation of Maurice Winternitz will be interesting. He writes, 'On the whole it (*Gommaṭasāra*) is nothing but dry-as-dust, purely scientific enumerations, descriptions and calculations. Only rarely do we light upon a simile, such as the Verse 202. . . .'
131. गोम्मटसुत्त-ल्लिहणे गोम्मटरायेण जा कया देसी।
सो राओ चिरकालं णामेण य वीरमत्तंडो ॥ 972
132. Gandhi Natharang, Bombay, 1911; *MJG*, 1919.
133. See Introduction to *Ṭiloyapaṇṇatti.*
134. With Manoharlal's Hindi translation, *RJS*, 1916; with Kesavavarṇī's Sanskrit Com. and Todarmal's Hindi-*Tīkā*, Bharatiya Jain Prakashini Samstha, Calcutta.
135. With a commentary by Brahmadeva, ed. with Introduction, Translation, Notes and an original commentary in English by S.C. Ghoshal, *SBJ*, Arrah, 1917.
136. Ed. A.N. Upadhye and Hiralal Jain, *JJG*, Solapur, 1958. Here in the Introduction an important article regarding Mathematics of *Tiloyapaṇṇatti* is added.
137. गुण-गण-कलित, त्रि-दंड-रहित, त्रि-शल्य-शुद्ध, त्रि-गारव-रहित, सिद्धांत-गत-पार, तप-नियम-योग-युक्त, ज्ञान-दर्शन-चरित्र-उद्युक्त, आरम्भ-करण-रहित, Premi, p. 264.
138. Premi, p. 259.
139. The same tradition is preserved in the *Tiloyapaṇṇatti*, Guṇabhadra's *Uttara-purāṇa*, Brahmacāri Hemacandra's *Srutaskandha* and Indranandi's *Srutāvatāra*, the *Harivaṃsapurāṇa*, the Prakrit *Paṭṭāvali* (patriarchal list of teachers) of the Nandi-saṅgha Balātkāra-gaṇa-Sarasvatī-gaccha and the *Paṭṭāvali* of Sena-gaṇa and the Kāṣṭha-

saṅgha, here Viṣṇu is mentioned in place of Nandi, Premi, p. 262.

140. Published along with the *Siddhāntasāra*, *Kallāṇāloyaṇā*, *Nijātmāṣṭaka* and the *Aṅgapaṇṇatti* in the *Siddhāntasārādi-saṃgraha*, *MJG*, vs 1979.
141. See Premi, p. 261.
142. See n. 140 above.
143. Premi, ibid., p. 382.
144. Published by *MDJ*, vs 1977.
145. सोऊण तच्चसारं रइयं मुणिणाह देवसेणेण।
जो सद्दिट्ठी भावइ सो पावइ सासयं सोक्खं॥
146. चलण-रहिओ मणुस्सो जह बंछइ मेरू-सिहरमारुहिउं।
तह झाणेण विहीणो इच्छइ कम्मक्खयं साहू॥
147. The Royal Asiatic Society of Bombay has a MS of this work with Sanskrit commentary. But no information is available either about the author or the work.
148. Premi, ibid., p. 313n.
149. Published in *MDJ*, vs 1978.
150. See Kailashchandra Siddhantashastri, *Jain Sahitya ka Itihas*, I, p. 429.
151. Jugalkishor Mukhtar, *Jain Grantha Prasasti-saṃgraha*, 1954, Intro. 94-5; *PJVS*, 110-11 (No. 54), *CJMS* (Sr. 128, p. 189).
152. Kailashchandra Siddhantashastri, ibid., p. 461.
153. Jugalkishor Mukhtar, *PJVS*, pp. 111-12 (No. 55). Sarsawa, 1950; *CJMS* (Sr. 125, p. 186).
154. See *CJMS*, Sr. 125, pp. 185-6.
155. Published by *MDJG*, vs 1978.
156. Ed. Nathuram Premi, *JGRK*, Bombay, vs 1974; A.N. Upadhye has edited the text critically with several MSS, *ABORI*, 15 (1934).
157. पुव्वाइरिम कयाइं गाहाइं संचिऊण एयत्थ।
158. According to tradition, he was reborn as Mahavira, *Viseṣā Bhā* 1781-1812; *Ādipurāṇa*, 18.61-5; *TSPI*, VI. 1-52, after P.S. Jaini, *The Jain Path*, p. 32.
159. Amitagati of Māthurā Saṅgha in his *Dharmaparīkṣā* (6) has pointed out Maudilayāna? (Maudgalyāyana), belonging to the succession of Pārśvanātha's pupils, as the founder of Buddhism. Premi, '*Darsanasāra-vivecanā*' (*Jain Hitaishi*, 13, 13, 5-6, pp. 262-75).
160. In the Śvetāmbara tradition the period of the origin of the Boḍiyas (Digambaras) is almost the same.
161. In Buddhist literature Makkhali Gosālā and Pūraṇa Kassapa were two adherent leaders.
162. The study of various Jain *saṅghas*, *gaṇas* and *gacchas* would be quite interesting for the social development in the history of Jain community. Unfortunately, this aspect of Jainism remains unstudied so far. As far as the Digambara sect is concerned, we have more than 500 Sravaṇabeḷgoḷ inscriptions which refer to numerous traditions of teachers with their *saṅghas*, *gaṇas* and *gacchas*. From the Siddharabasti inscription we learn that 683 years after Mahavira, Arhadbali divided

the Mūlasaṅgha into four branches: Sena, Nandi, Deva and Siṃha. Ācārya Kundakunda is said to have belonged to the Mūla-saṅgha. Here we have Mūla-saṅgha, Nandi-saṅgha, Namilūra-saṅgha, Mayūra-saṅgha, Kiṭṭūra-saṅgha, Kollatūra-saṅgha, Nandi-gaṇa, Desī-gaṇa, Dramila (Tamila)-gaṇa, Kāṇūra-gaṇa, Pustaka or Sarasvatī-gaccha, Vakra-gaccha, Tagarila-gaccha, Maṇḍitaṭa-gaccha. Iṅgulesvarabali and Panasogebali Hiralal Jain, *Bharatiya Samskriti men Jain Dharma ka Yogadana*, pp. 32-3.

Guṇaratnasūri (circa 1400) in his commentary on Haribhadra's *Ṣaḍdarsana-samuccaya* (IV.1) refers to the four *saṅghas* of the Digambaras: Kāṣṭhā, Mūla, Māthura and Gopya. They go about nude and receive offerings in their palms (*pāṇi-pātra*=hand-bowl)—these are their main symbols. The adherents of the Kāṣṭhā-saṅgha use chowrie brush instead of a *rajoharaṇa* (whiskbroom); the adherents of Mūla and Gopya *saṅghas* use the peacock-feather, while the followers of the Māthurā *saṅgha* do not carry any kind of whiskbroom. The monks of the first three *saṅghas*, while offering their blessings to their devotees, utter '*dharma-vṛddhi*' (may your righteousness enhance), they do not believe in the liberation of women and according to them, an omniscient being does not eat (*kevali-bhukti*). The Gopyas, also known as Yāpanīyas, offer their blessings by uttering '*dharma-lābha*' (may you be profited in righteousness); they believe in liberation of women and affirm partaking of food by an omniscient being.

We have already referred to Ācārya Srutasāgara, commentator of Kundakunda's *Darsanaprābhṛta.* He belonged to the Mūla-saṅgha, Sarasvatī-gaccha and the Balātkāra-gaṇa. Talking about the Yāpanīyas in his commentary, he has stated that like mules (*vesarā*), they believe in both (Digambara), worship three jewels (*ratna-traya*), recite the Kalpa, believe in emancipation of women in that very birth, and admit partaking of food by omniscient being; they declared emancipation even to those who followed the non-Jain faith (*para-sāsane mokṣaḥ*) and are permitted to attain emancipation even without initiation into monkhood (*sagranthāṇaṃ mokṣaḥ*). Also see Premi; *Darsana-sāra-vivecanā* and its Appendix, *Jain Hitaishi,* Pt. XIII, 5-6 and 9-10; Upadhye, *Yāpanīya-saṅgha: A Jaina Sect, JUB,* I, Pt. VI, 1933.

163. कच्छं खेत्तं वसदिं वाणिज्जं करिऊण जीवंतो।
ण्हंतो सीयलनीरे पावं पउरं स संजेदि ॥ 27 ॥

164. कल्लाणे वरणयरे दुण्णिसए पंच-उत्तरे जादे।
जावणिय-संघभावो सिरि-कलसादो हु सेवडदो ॥ 29 ॥

The origin of the Sevadas (Śvetāmbaras), according to the author, is after 136 years of Vikrama's death (i.e. AD 79):

छत्तीसे वरिससए विक्कमरायस्स मरणपत्तस्स।
सोरट्ठे वलहीए उप्पण्णो सेवडो संघो ॥ 1 ॥

Thus we see that the Yāpanīyas came into being only after 69 years of the Śvetāmbara or the Digambara-Śvetāmbara schism. In other works all the three Jain sects more or less are contemporary; also see Premi, ibid., p. 56 and n.

165. The town Kāṣṭhā situates on the bank of the Jamuna river in the north of Delhi, Premi, ibid., p. 276n.

166. Incorporated in the *Nayacakra-saṃgraha, MDJG*, 1920.

167. The author in this work has literally translated the portion with regard to *naya* from the *Nayacakra*, Premi, ibid., p. 171.

168. धम्मविहीणो सोक्खं तण्हा-छेयं जलेण जह रहिदो।
तह तह बंधइ मूढो णय-राहिओ दव्व-णिच्छित्ती॥

169. With Ratnakīrti's Commentary published in *MDJG*, vs 1973; the text with Hindi translation pub. Shri Shantisagara Jain Siddhanta Prakashini Samstha, vs 2484.

170. Compare with Kaṇhapa's *Dohākosa* (32):
जिम लोण विलिज्जइ पाणिएहिं तमि घरिणि लइ चित्त।
समरस जाई तक्खणे जइ पुणु ते समणित्त॥

171. Published under the title 'Nayacakrasaṃgraha', *MDJG*, 1920.

172. Ed. Pandit Hiralal Jain, *Murtidevi Granthamala*, Kashi, 1952.

173. See *CJMS*, Sr. 127, pp. 187-8; also Pandit Jugalkishor Mukhtar, *PJVS*, Intr., pp. 72-4; A.N. Upadhye, 'Jīva-tattva-pradipika—Its Author and Date', *Indian Culture*, VII, No. 1.

174. वरइंदणंदि-गुरुणो पासे सोऊण सयल-सिद्धंतं।
सिरि-कणयणंदि-गुरुणा सत्तट्ठाणं समुद्दिट्ठं॥
Reference from Premi, ibid., p. 271n.

4

Post-canonical Literature of the Śvetāmbaras

KARMA-SIDDHĀNTA LITERATURE

Karma means actions. It is any religious act or rite such as sacrifice or oblation, especially one originating in the hope of future reward, in Brahmanic terminology. The doings of the past birth are responsible for what one has to face in the present life, and this is called the *karma-vipaka* theory. For the ripening of action, good or bad, performed in a previous life, one has to bear the consequences in this life. The result of the former act done previously is inevitable. The bonds of action lead to transmigration or repeated worldly existence as a result of action, known as *karma-bandha* in Indian philosophy. This doctrine of *karma* was universally accepted by Indian philosophy. The logic was simple: as you sow so shall you reap. A farmer cuts or harvests grain, he obtains a return or reward as a result of his efforts. In accordance with this theory, because of his good or bad deeds a living creature would be reborn in any species 'particularly suited to and measured by the action, from the vilest insect to a god'. In Hindu mythology even Indra was subject to his *karma* as a result of which he fell from the world of gods and was reborn as an earthworm. Here there is truth and justice, norms of law are observed and there is no distinction of caste, creed or class as everyone is given his due share. There cannot be a better review of the *karma* doctrine than the following: 'The *karma* could grow and ripen like a seed planted in the previous season, or mature like a debt, while it never failed to pay in exact proportion. It can be seen how this would appeal to peasant and trader, even to the Śūdra who might thus aspire to be reborn a king.'[1]

According to the Jain doctrine of *karma*, every being in this vast universe is guided by his or her own *karma*, and the heavenly bodies and the gods are no exception to this rule. In fact, every event in the life of an individual is due to good or bad deeds done in the previous life. According to Jain philosophy, *karma* is not just a deed or action. It is essentially material, an aggregate of particles of very fine matter not perceptible to the senses; it is not some sort of quasi-physical or psychological elements as held by other systems of Indian philosophy. The question arose as to how the particles of material *karma* get attached to the soul which is non-physical and non-material in nature. The reply is that as particles of dust get attached to a piece of cloth, or the light of the sun is obscured by dust, fog or a patch of cloud, so is the case with the unity of *karma* particles with the soul. The highest goal in Jainism is to get rid of *karmas* and stop their influx into the soul.

There is a vast Digambara and the Śvetāmbara literature on *karma-siddhānta* that discusses the doctrine of *karma* in its various aspects so that it becomes difficult to comprehend the minute details and at times it appears monotonous. Its technical terminology, derived from the old canonical scripture, is said to have been preached by Mahavira himself. The doctrine of *karma* is considered so important that in Jain narrative literature we often come across discourses on religion and morality wherein emphasis is laid on the *karma* theory—rebirths of men and women of the narrative are nothing but the result of their good or bad deeds. The implication of such an intricate complex study in minute detail on the part of Jain writers needs to be scrutinized in the socio-cultural background.

As we have seen, according to the Digambaras, a section of the *Dṛṣṭivāda* known as *Puvvagaya* (*Pūrvagata*) deals with the doctrine of *karma*. In Jain tradition the eighth *Purva* known as the *Karmapravāda* must have dealt with the *karma-siddhānta* with all its minutest details, but unfortunately is no more extant. Digambaras also believe that their *Chakkhaṇḍāgama* and *Kasāyapāhuḍa* form part and parcel of the lost *Dṛṣṭivāda*. According to them, the *Chakkhaṇḍāgama*, also known as *Mahākammapayaḍipāhuḍa*, has derived its contents from the *Kammapayaḍi* which is the fourth *Pāhuḍa* of the fifth *Vastu* of the *Agrāyaṇī-pūrva* as we have seen earlier. Similarly, the *Kasāyapāhuḍa* is said to have been derived from the *Pejjadosapāhuḍa*, the third *Pāhuḍa* of the tenth *Vastu* of the *Jñānapravadapūrva*. These two important works with their extensive commentaries deal fully with the *karma-siddhānta*.

The *Pañcasaṃgraha*[2] of the Digambaras can be added to this list. It is a collection of the works of earlier teachers. It contains the five *adhikāras*: Jīvasamāsa, Prakṛtisamutkīrtana, Karmastava, Sataka and Sattari or Saptatikā. The first section deals with 20 *prarūpaṇas* in 206 *gāthās*. The treatment of *guṇasthānas* and *mārgaṇas* by Virasena in his *Dhavalā* commentary on the *Ṣaṭprarūpaṇāsutra* of the *Jīvasthāna* section of the *Chakkhaṇḍāgama* is based on this part of the text. The second section has treated the nature of eight *karmas*. Several of its *gāthās* are identical with the *Dhavalā* and the *Gommaṭasāra*. Section 3 has 77 *gāthās* of which 53 are identical with the *Karmastava* or the *Bandhodayasattvayukta*, the second of the *Prācīna Karmagrantha* of the Śvetāmbara. Here bondage (*bandha*), realization (*udaya*), the process of premature realization (*udīraṇā*) and existing in potential (*satva*) are explained. Section 4 has 422 *gāthās*, and it is stated that some of these have been borrowed from the *Dṛṣṭivāda*.[3] In the end, in *gāthā* 103 it is said that the treatment of *banda-samasa* is based on the eighth *Pūrva* of the *Karmapravāda*. Here is incorporated the *Sataka*, or the *Bandhaśataka*, the fifth *Prācīna Karmagrantha* of the Śvetāmbaras. In the beginning of the *Sattari* or *Saptatikā* the author has referred to the *Dṛṣṭivāda*, the flow of which has been incorporated in this work.[4] Here the sixth *Prācīna Karmagrantha*, also designated under the same title, has been included. Ācārya Amitagati (vs 1073= AD 1016) and Pandit Āśādhara (thirteenth century) have mentioned this work. Amitagati is also an author of the same title of the work in Sanskrit. According to Pandit Kailashchandra Siddhānta-shastri, the *Pañcasaṃgraha* text was written in the eighth century of the Vikrama Era.[5]

Among other important Digambara tracts on *karma-siddhānta* we have already dealt with Nemicandra Siddhānta-cakravarti's *Gommaṭasara* (*Jīvakāṇḍa* and *Karmakāṇḍa*), *Labdhisāra* and *Kṣapaṇāsāra*.

KARMA-SIDDHĀNTA LITERATURE OF THE ŚVETĀMBARAS

Śvetāmbara literature on *karma-siddhānta* is vast. The doctrine of *karma* is explained in great detail with the help of *Curṇi*, *Bhāṣya*, *Ṭikā*, *Avacūri*, *Ṭippaṇaka*, *Ṭabā* and so on. It is significant that there is no doctrinal difference between the Digambaras and the Śvetāmbaras with regard to the subject; even the titles and the *gāthās* of several works are identical. According to both traditions the treatises are based on the teachings of the earlier *ācāryas*.

The *Kammapayaḍi* (*Karmaprakṛti*)[6] by Ācārya Śivaśarman (fifth century VS) is an important work on *karma-siddhānta*, containing 475 *gāthās* which are said to be based on the *Agrāyaṇī-pūrva*. Here the author has dealt with the various processes the karmic matter undergoes due to various conditions of activities. These infinite variations are due to manifold processes of energy, known as *karaṇas*. *Karaṇas* are classified into eight types: (i) *bandhana*, the condition of energy responsible for bondage, (ii) *saṃkramaṇa*, the condition of the energy responsible for transformation, (iii) *udvartanā*, the condition of the energy responsible for increased realization, (iv) *apavartanā*, the condition of the energy responsible for decreased realization, (v) *udīraṇā*, the condition of the energy responsible for premature realization, (vi) *upaśamanā*, the condition of the energy responsible for subsiding *karmas* from rising to fruition, (vii) *nidhatti* or the energy that is capable of making the *karmas* incapable of all processes (*karaṇa*) other than *udvartanā* and *apavartanā*, and (viii) *nikācanā* or the energy that renders *karmas* incapable of all processes. To these eight types of *karaṇas* can be added *sattā* or the endurance of the *karmas* for a certain period of time and *udaya* or coming into effect of the *karmas*. All these states of *karmas* have been described elaborately in the text.[7]

There are several commentaries on the treatise. The well known Malayagiri and Upādhyāya Yaśovijaya (who died in AD 1686) wrote their commentaries on this work. It has also a *Cūrṇi*, its author is unknown. The commentators have referred to this *Cūrṇi*.

Sayaga (*Śataka*)[8] or *Bandhaśataka* is said to be another tract by Śivaśarman. This important text has 3 *Bhāṣyas*, of which 2 are *Laghu* and 1 is *Bṛhat*. The authors of the *Laghu-Bhāṣyas* are not known, the *Bṛhad-Bhāṣya* is authored by Cakreśvarasūri in VS 1179 or AD 1122. The author of the *Cūrṇi* is not known. Some of the *gāthās* of the *Laghu-Cūrṇi* are identical with the *Bhagavatī Ārādhanā*, the *Pañcasaṃgraha*, the *Gommaṭasāra* and the *Dravyasaṃgraha*.[9] The *Bṛhccūrṇi* is not available. The commentaries are by Maladhāri Hemacandra and Udayaprabhasūri in the beginning of the twelfth century, and by Guṇaratnasūri. *Pañcasaṃgaha* (*Pañcasaṃgraha*)[10] or Epitome of Five, by Śvetāmbaraācārya Candrarṣi Mahattara is an important exposition on the doctrine of *karma*. It contains 963 *gāthās* which are divided into five sections, *Sayaga* (*Sataka*), *Sittari* (*Saptatikā*), *Kasāyapāhuḍa* (*Kaṣāyaprābhṛta*), *Chakkamma* (*Ṣaṭkarma*) and *Kammapayaḍi* (*Karmaprakṛti*)[11] which means the work has been compiled from existing literature, or five *dvāras*, viz., *yogopayoga-mārgaṇā*, *bandhaka*, *bandhavya*, *bandhahetu* and *bandhavidhi*, hence it is called *Panca-saṃgraha*[12] (Collection of Five). The author has written his own commentary on this work. Muni Punyavijayaji has placed him in the ninth or tenth century of Vikrama Era. Malayagiri has written another commentary. Except the *Kasāyapāhuḍa*, Malayagiri has cited the remaining four books as authority, of which the *Ṣaṭkarma* is said to be not available, even though Malayagiri in his commentary has quoted from this work.[13] It seems there was a vast literature on *karma* which was beyond the reach of the writers and therefore they were unable to explain certain important points regarding the subject; certain traditions were lost; and texts like the *Kammapayaḍipāhuḍa* had gone extinct.[14]

THE *KARMAGRANTHAS*

The *Karmagranthas*[15] are classified into two, the old and the new. The old ones are written by different authors; they form the basis of the new *Karmagranthas* written by Devendrasūri.

The old *Karmagranthas* are five: *Kammavivāga* (*Karmavipāka*), *Kammatthava* (*Karmastava*), *Bandhasāmitta* (*Bandhasvāmitva*), *Saḍasīi* (*Saḍaśīti*), *Sayaga* (*Śataka*), and *Sittari* (*Saptatikā*). These works are important as here the doctrine of *karma* which is very intricate and has got a unique place in Jain religion, is explained with all its details.

The *Karmavipāka* of Gargarṣi, said to have belonged to the tenth century of Vikrama Era, deals with the retribution of *karma*. It has several commentaries: *vṛtti* by Paramānandasūri, *ṭippana* by Udayaprabhasūri and *vyākhyā* by some unknown author. All of them are said to date two or three centuries later.

The author of the *Karmastava*, also known as *Bandhodayasatva-yuktastava*, is not known. Several commentaries and explanations are written on this work. It has two *Bhāṣyas* and two *Ṭikās*; one *Tīkā* by Govindācārya, the *Ṭippana* by Udayaprabhasūri.

The author of the *Bandhasvāmitva* is not known. Haribhadrasūri, a pupil of Devasūri, has written a commentary on this work in 1172 vs. The *Ṣaḍaśīti*, also known as *Āgamika-vastu-vicāra-sāra-prakaraṇa* is authored by Jinavallabhagaṇi, a pupil of the renowned Jineśvarasūri, in the twelfth century of Vikrama Era. It has also several commentaries to its credit. It has two *Bhāṣyas*, their authors unknown. Among commentators, Haribhadrasūri and Malayagiri are prominent.

Śataka by Śivaśarman. We have already dealt with this *Karmagrantha*.

Saptatikā, the sixth *Karmagrantha*, contains 70 *gāthās*. Unfortunately, its author is not known. According to some, Candrarṣi Mahattara was its author but Muni Punyavijaya does not agree with this view. Jinabhadragaṇi Kṣamāśramaṇa in his *Viśeṣaṇavatī* has made a reference to this work as *Sayarī* (*Sittari*),[16] therefore the author of the *Saptatikā* must have existed before AD 588. As this treatise is quite old, several commentaries were written on it. Abhayadevasūri has written a *Bhāṣya*; there is a *Cūrṇi*[17] by an unknown author; Candrarṣi Mahattara has written *Prākṛta-vṛtti*; Malayagiri has written a *Ṭīkā*. Merutuṅgasūri's *Bhāṣya-vṛtti*, Rāmadeva's *Ṭippana* and Guṇaratnasūri's *Avacūri* are also known.[18] The *Saptatikā* has dealt with the topics like *bandha, udaya, Prakṛtisthāna, uttara-prakṛtis* of *Jñānāvaraṇīya* (knowledge-obscuring) and other *karmas*, bondage of *karma* and other stages and *udīraṇā, guṇasthāna, Prakṛtibandha*, etc., of eight *karmas.*

THE *NAVYA* OR NEW *KARMAGRANTHAS*

Devendrasūri of Tapāgaccha, a pupil of Jagaccandrasūri, was a learned scholar of the thirteenth century. Besides composing the *Five Navya Karmagranthas* with his commentary, he is also the author of the *Sudaṃsaṇācariya*, the *Bhāṣyas* on *Deva, guru* and *pratyākhyāna-vandana*, the *Siddha-pañcāśikā-sūtra-vṛtti*, the *Śrāddha-dina-kṛtya-vṛtti*, the *Vandāru-vṛtti* and others.[19] Devendrasūri based his writings on the *Five Prācīna Karmagranthas*, composed by different authors, wrote the *Five Navya Karmagranthas* bearing the same title, viz., the *Karma-vipāka*, the *Karma-stava*, the *Bandhasvāmitva*, the *Ṣaḍaśīti* and the *Śataka.*[20]

The *Karma-vipāka* deals with the eight *karmas*, their divisions and subdivisions and their retribution, in 60 *gāthās.*

The *Karma-stava* deals with the four stages of *karma* such as *bandha* (bondage), *udaya* (arising), *udīraṇā* (process of premature realization) and *sattā* (existence) in 34 *gāthās.* The characteristics of *guṇasthana* (stages of purification) are explained.

The *Bandhasvāmitva* has treated the bondage of *karma* with the soul from the point of view of *mārgaṇā* and *guṇasthāna* in 24 *gāthās.*

The *Ṣaḍaśīti* is so called as it contains 86 *gāthās.* Here we have a detailed explanation of *jīva-sthāna, mārgaṇā-sthāna, guṇa-sthāna, bhāva* and *saṃkhyā.* It is also known as the *Sūkṣmārtha-vicāra.*

The last *Navya Karmagrantha*, the *Śataka*, deals with the nature of *karma-prakṛtis* (*karmic* matter bound with the soul) in detail in 100 *gāthās.*

As stated earlier, Devendrasūri has written his own commentary on all five *Karmagranthas*, but unfortunately, his commentary on the *Bandhasvāmitva*, the third, is not extant. On this some other *ācārya* has written an *Avacūri*. Among other authors Guṇaratnasūri and Muniśekharasūri have written an *Avacūri* on all five books. Other commentaries, besides Hindi and Gujarati explanations on the texts, were composed from time to time.[21]

General Works of Importance

The *Viśeṣāvaśyaka-Bhāṣya*[22] by Jinabhadragaṇi Kṣamāśramaṇa who died in AD 540, is a very important text for the comprehensive study of Jainism. Though it is a *Bhāṣya* on the *Āvaśyaka Sūtra*, it is honoured being considered a constituent of 84 *āgamas*. The *Viśeṣāvaśyaka-Bhāṣya*, or *Viśeṣāvaśyaka-Mahābhāṣya*, is a commentary only on the first *Āvaśyaka* out of six, of the *Āvaśyaka-Sūtra*, therefore it is also called the *Sāmāyika-Bhāṣya*. Leumann made a critical study of the manuscripts of this comprehensive work more than eighty years ago, and published his thought-provoking *Übersicht über die Āvaśyaka-Literatur* (1934) in German. He referred to its two recensions, one preserved in Maladhāri Hemacandra's *Śiṣyahitā* commentary, containing 3603 *gāthās*,[23] the other with 4360 *gāthās*. The *Niryukti* and the *Bhāṣya gāthās* have been intermixed as pointed out earlier.

Leumann surveyed only the first three divisions of the *Āvaśyaka-Sūtra*, i.e. *sāmāyika*, *caturviṃśati-stava* and *vandana*. He had realized the significance of *Āvaśyaka*-literature in the Jain system of thought. He noted that the language of the *Viśeṣāvaśyaka-Bhāṣya* is much more correct and its style more intelligible than that of the old *Nijjuttis* and their *Bhāṣya* insertions. He remarked, 'Jinabhadra has done away with that old slovenliness.' According to him, 'Our text has not only inspired the later writers to while composing their works but it has also influenced the latest version of the *Āvaśyaka-Niryukti* as well as Haribhadra's and Malayagiri's commentaries.' Out of 2000 *gāthās* of the *Āvaśyaka-Niryukti*, only 257 belong to the *Mūla-bhāṣya* and are identical with the *Viśeṣāvaśyaka-Bhāṣya*, which shows that they must have been inserted from the latter into the former.[24]

Jinabhadragaṇi has written his commentary on the portion till the assertion up to the sixth *gaṇadhara*, and this was then completed by Koṭṭārya (or Koṭyārya) Vādigaṇi Mahattara. Among other commentators Koṭyācārya and Maladhāri Hemacandra can be mentioned. Jinabhadragaṇi has also composed the *Jītakalpasūtra*,

Jītakalpa-sūtra-Bhāṣya, Bṛhatsaṃgrahaṇī, Bṛhatkṣetrasamāsa, Viśeṣaṇavatī, and *Anuyogadvāra-Aṅgulapada-cūrṇi.* As pointed out earlier, this text is considered an ocean of information on Jain *Siddhānta.* It deals with five types of knowledge: *matijñāna* (sensuous knowledge), *śrutajñāna* (scriptural knowledge), *avadhijñāna* (visual intuition), *manaḥparyaya-jñāna* (intuition of mental modes) and *kevalajñāna* (perfect intuition) in detail. We have elaborate description of *nikṣepa* (a method of investigation to which any word or concept can be subjected by applying different viewpoints), *naya* (a particular standpoint) and *pramāṇa* (knowledge of a thing in itself). The *gaṇadharavāda* (the account of eleven *gaṇadharas*) is described in detail.[25] Eight *ninhvas* (denial or disowning) and five *parameṣṭhis* (supreme beings) are dealt with. In the *Siddha-namaskāra-vyākhyā, samudghāta* (extension of the soul to the limits of the inhabited universe—*lokākāśa*), the state of *śaileśī* (steady like the mountain Meru), *ananta sukha* (infinite bliss), *avagāhanā* (extension), etc., are explained. The author, the great upholder of the *āgamic* view, believes the occurrence of *kevala-jñāna* and *kevaladarśana* in succession and not simultaneously.[26] It is stated that when a liberated soul is free from all activities whatsoever, it moves upward to the summit of the universe due to an inherent tendency, as a bottle-gourd (*alābu*) shoots up to the surface of the water from the river bed, or the seed of a castor-oil plant speeds up after it becomes ripe, or the flame of fire moves upward, or the flight of an arrow moves upward.

Pravacanasāroddhāra[27] by Nemicandrasūri is an equally important work dealing with various topics on Jainism. It can be called an encyclopaedic work. It deals with *vandana* (veneration), *pratikraman* (confession), *pratyākhyāna* (renunciation of certain pleasures), *kāyotsarga* (penance through standing or sitting posture), *mahāvrata* (great vows), *parīṣaha-jaya* (victory over afflictions) and other aspects of ascetic conduct. Then we have the symbols of God Jina, their attending *yakṣas* and *yakṣṇīs,* the colour of their body, duration of time, their emancipation, *prātihārya* (miracles), *atiśaya* (miraculous events related to their life) and many other things. The characteristics of *Jinakalpa* and *Sthavirakalpa* are described. The author deals with five types of *caitya* (shrine), five types of *pustaka* (book),[28] five types of *daṇḍa* (staff),[29] five types of *tṛṇa* (grass), five types of *carma* (skin), five types of *dūṣya*[30] (high variety of cloth), and five types of *avagraha*[31] (cloths allowed to be used by nuns) and the types of *sthaṇḍila* (a piece of open ground free from tiny living beings).[32] This extensive work contains 1599 *gāthās* divided into 276 *dvāras*. Siddhasenasūri wrote a commentary, *Tattvajñānavikāsinī*, on it in vs 1248 or 1278. The commentator has cited several quotations. He has mentioned the *Paumappaha-cariya*, the *Sāmācārī* and the *Stuti* as his own compositions. Udayaprabha, a pupil of Raviprabha, wrote the *Viṣamapada* commentary on this work. There were other *Ṭīkās* whose authors are unnamed. Padmamandiragaṇī wrote the *Bālāvabodha*.[33]

Vicārasāra-prakaraṇa[34] by Pradyumnasūri is yet another exhaustive exposition of a variety of topics concerning Jainism. The author lived in vs 1325. Māṇikyasāgara has composed a Sanskrit *chāyā* of this work. It contains 900 *gāthās*, dealing with *karma-bhūmi* (realms of action), *bhogabhūmi* (realms of enjoyment), *anārya deśa* (non-Aryan countries), capitals of Ārya *janapadas*, previous births of Tīrthaṅkaras, their parents, dreams, birth, consecration, constellation, symbols, colour, *samavaśaraṇa* (assembly hall), *gaṇadharas* (heads of school), twenty-two *parīṣahas*, purity of *vasati* (dwelling place), characteristics of *pātra* (bowl), staff, types of *vinaya* (discipline), *saṃstārakavidhi* (ritual arrangement for death-bed), *rātri-jāgaraṇa* (night-watching), eight great miracles (*aṣṭa mahā-prātihārya*), *vīra-tapā* (heroic penance), ten *āścaryas* (wonders), the eras of Kalki, the Nandas, the Sakas, and Vikrama, ten *ninhavas*, the origin of the Digambara sect, types of *caityas*, 84 lakh births, the types of *siddhas* (liberated souls) and numerous other topics of importance. There are certain topics which are common with the *Pravacanasāroddhāra* mentioned above.[35]

Works on Siddhānta

Jīvasamāsa[36] was composed by early *ācāryas* who possessed the knowledge of the *Pūrvas*. Like the *Jyotiṣkaraṇḍa* this work is also composed in accordance with the Valabhī version of the Jain canon. In 286 *gāthās* it deals with *nikṣepa*, *anuyoga-dvāra*, knowledge of *jīvasamāsas* by way of 14 *mārganas*, 14 *guṇasthanas*, types of earth-bodied and other living beings (*pṛthvīkāya ādi*),[37] types of *dharmaastikāya* (principle of motion) and other inanimate substances, divisions of time (*kāla*) from *samaya* (the smallest unit of time) to *palyopama* (innumerable number of years), types of *nayas* (viewpoint) and *samudghāta* and so on. Maladhāri Hemacandra's commentary on this work dates to about vs 1164 (AD 1107). The commentator has referred to other commentaries. Sīlāṅka is said to be one of the commentators.

Viśeaṣaṇavati[38] is another important work by Jinabhadragaṇi Kṣamāśramaṇa. It deals with *jīva* and *ajīva* and such matters in 286 *gāthās*. The author has supported the view of the alternate succession of *jñāna* and *darśana* and rejects their simultaneity. The text refers to the *Vasudevacarica* (*Vasudevahiṇḍi*) of Saṅghadāsagaṇi Vācaka.

The *Siddhāntaviyāragāhā*[39] contains 180 Prakrit verses with Sanskrit explanation. The first verse is from the *Uttarādhyayana*, the remaining from the other *āgamas*. The *Anāi-vīsiyā* (*Anādi-viṃsikā*) or *Viṃśati-viṃśika*[40] by Yākinīsūnu Haribhadra holds that the world is eternal (*anādi*) and is not created by superhuman agency. In each *adhikāra* there are 20 *gāthāsa* which deal with eternity, family conduct (*kula-nīti*), worldly custom (*lokadharma*), last wandering (*caramāvarta*), seed (*bīja*), righteousness, charity, worship, duties of a layman, duties of a monk, self-introspection (*ālaocanā*), expiation (*prāyaścitta*), activity (*yoga*), perfect *Sārdhaśataka*,[41] also known as *Sūkṣam-ārthavicārasāra* by Jinavallabhasūri of Kharatara *gaccha*, a pupil of Abhayadevasūri, the *navāṅga-vṛtti-kāra* (died in vs 1167). It deals with the *karma-siddhānta* in 110 *gāthās*. It has several commentaries and explanations. It contains a *Bhāṣya* of an unknown author; Municandrasūri's *cūrṇi* in vs 1170; Sīlabhadra's pupil Dhaneśvara-sūri's *vṛtti* in vs 1171; Haribhadra's *vṛtti* in vs 1172 and Cakreśvara's *vṛtti*. Jinavallabhasūri's pupils Rāmadevagaṇi and Maheśvarasūri have written *ṭīkās*; there is another *Ṭīkā* by an unknown author and there is a *vṛtti-tippaṇa* also.[42]

Bhāṣārahasya-prakaraṇa[43] by Upādhyāya Yaśovijaya deals with *bhāṣā* (language) in 101 *gāthās*. Dealing with *drvya-bhāṣā* (external language) and *bhāva-bhāṣā* (internal language), the author has explained ten kinds of truth: *janapada, sammata, sthāpanā, nāma, rūpa, pratītya, vyavahāra, bhāva, yoga* and *aupamya*.

Ābhavva-ṇābhavva-viyāra (*Ābhavya-nābhavya-vicāra*)[44] deals with the *abhāvya* (acceptable) and *anābhāvya* (not acceptable), for instance, the kinds of location, accessories, pupils that should be received or rejected. The author is not known.

Āvassaya-sarūva (*Āvaśyaka-svarūpa*),[45] also known as *Āvaśyaka-saptati* or *Pākṣika-saptati*, by Municandrasūri, deals with essential duties (*āvaśyaka-kriyā*). The text is based on the *Mahānisītha*, the *Kalpa*, the *Vyavahāra* and other canonical works. The author was a pupil of Yaśobhadrasūri. He was made an *ācārya* by Nemicandrasūri, the author of the *Sukhabodhā* commentary on the *Uttarādhyayana*.

He died in vs 1178. Among his other works the following can be noted: *Aṅgulasattari*[46] with *svopajña-ṭīkā*; *Vanaspati-saptatikā*; *Gāhākosa*[47] (*Gāthākośa*), also known as *Rasāula* or *Rasāulagāhākosa*; *Hiovaeasakulaya*[48] (*Hitopadeśakulaka*); *Aṇusāsaṇāṃkusakulaya*[49] (*Anuśāsanāṃkusakuḷaya*), also known as *Dhammovaesapañcavīsiyā*; *Kālasayaga*;[50] *Uvaesāmayakulaya*[51] (*Upadeśāmṛtakulaka*); *Jīvovaesa-pañcāsiyā* (*Jīvopadeśa-pañcāśikā*).[52]

Philosophy

Sammaipayaraṇa[53] (*Sanmatiprakaraṇa*), also known as *Sammai-sutta* or *Sanmatitarka* by Siddhasena Divākara (fifth century vs) is a very important work dealing with Jain philosophy and logic. Here we have a treatment of *nayavāda* and *anekantavāda*. As already mentioned, Vīrasena, the author of the *Dhavalā-Ṭīkā* on the *Ṣatkhaṇḍāgama* has referred to this work and has cited quotations. Some of its *gāthās* have been incorporated by Haribhadrasūri in his *Upadeśapada*. It contains three *kāṇḍas*. The first deals with *nayas*, their divisions and the limit of *anekānta* in 54 *gāthās*; the second deals with *jñāna* and *darśana* in 43 *gāthās*, and the last with *utpāda*, *vyaya* and *dhravya* and *jñeya* (the objects to be known). Here the author has given a new interpretation to the philosophy of *anekāntavāda*. As in this philosophy all other non-Jain philosophical systems are viewed as partially true, it is termed as a concord (*samūha*) of these systems; it is called essence or nectar (*amayasāra*).[54] Elsewhere, he has paid obeisance to *anekāntavāda*, the only teacher (*guru*) of the whole world as no usual current practice (*loka-vyavahāra*) is possible without it.[55] Several commentaries were written on this important work. Pradymnasūri's pupil Abhayadevasūri's commentary, the *Vādamahārṇava* or the *Tattva-bodha-vidhāyinī*, is well known and discusses Jain philosophy and logic in detail. Then Sanmati, a Digambara Jain, has composed a *Vivaraṇa*. Ācārya Mallavadi, the author of the *Dvādaśāra-naya-cakra* has also written a Sanskrit commentary which is not available.

Dhammasaṃgahaṇī (*Dharmasaṃgrahani*)[56] is a philosophical work by Haribhadrasūri in 1396 *gāthās*. The first part deals with the examination of *puruṣavādi-mata* (creatorship of god), *anādi-nidhanatva* (eternity), *amūrtatva* (formlessness), *pariṇāmitva* (changeableness), and *jñāyakatva* (knowledgeability); the second part discusses *kartṛtva*, (agency), *bhoktṛtva* (possession) and the validity of omniscience (*sarvajña-siddhi*).

Pavayaṇa-parikkhā (*Pravacana-parīksā*), also known as *Kupakṣa-kauśika-sahasra-kiraṇa* (The Sun for the Owls of the Heretical Doctrine) or *Kumati-kuddāla* (Spade for bad Intellect) by Dharmasāgara Upādhyāya of Tapāgaccha is a refutation of various sects written in VS 1629 with a commentary in Sanskrit. The author was a pupil of Ānandavimalasūri and was offered the status of a *gaṇi* sometime before VS 1606. He has tried to prove that the Tapāgaccha is the best and only valid *gaccha*, all others are false. In 1617 there occurred a violent dispute between the followers of the Tapāgaccha and the Kharataragaccha whether Abhayadevasūri belonged to the Kharataragaccha. When the discussion reached its height Vijayadānasūri, the leader of the Tapāgaccha, is said to have brought the discussion to the end by immersing the treatise in water. The author felt apologetic in the presence of the community. The treatise is divided into two parts, dealing with the characteristic of *tīrthas* (holy places), refutation of Digambaras, their view on going nude, exclusion of women from liberation, refutation of Kharatara-gaccha, the Āñcalika-gaccha, sārdha-paurṇimīkaya-mata, āgamika-mata, lumpāka-mata, kaṭuka-mata, bījāyata-mata and the refutation of Pāśacandra-mata. Among other works of the author, the following can be mentioned:

1 *Kayaṭṭhiitthaya* (*Kāyasthitistava*),[57] 2 *Sarvajña-śataka*, 3 *Iriyāvahiya-viyāra-chattīsiyā*,[58] 4 *Lokanālikā*,[59] 5 *Tapāgaccha-paṭṭāvali-sūtra*,[60] 6 *Uṭṭhiyamaya-ussutta* (*Auṣṭrika-mata-utsūtra*), 7 *Guru-parivāḍī*, 8 *Tatta-taraṅgiṇī*,[61] 9 *Pajjusaṇa-dasa-sayaga*[62] (*Paryūṣaṇa-daśa-śataka*), 10 *Ussutta-khaṇḍana* (*Utsūtra-khaṇḍana*).[63] *Juttipaboha-nāḍaya* (*Yuktiprabodha-nāṭaka*)[64] by Meghavijaya Mahopādhyāya (eighteenth century) is another work on the subject. The author has composed an auto-commentary on this work. It contains 25 *gāthās*, criticizing the Vārāṇasīya (Banārasīdāsa) sect of the Digambaras which came into existence in (AD 1623). Rūpacanda, Caturbhuja, Bhagavatīdāsa, Kumārapāla and Dharmadāsa, the associates of Banārasīdāsa, also find a mention here. The author has mentioned eighty-four major differences between the Digambara and the Śvetāmbara sects.

YOGA

Jains also have contributed to the field of *Yoga*. Patanjali's *Yogadarśana* in 195 *Sūtras* has an important commentary by Vyāsa. Upādhyāya Yaśovijaya has written a commentary on twenty-seven *Sūtras* of

Yagodarśana which is based on Vyāsa's *Bhāṣya.* Besides, Jain authors have written a number of independent works on *Yoga.*

The *Jogavihāṇavīsiyā* or *Jogavīsiyā* (*Yogaviṃśikā*)[65] is by Haribhadrasūri. His *Vīsa-vīsiyā* (*Viṃśati-viṃśikā*) is divided into 20 sections, each containing 20 *gāthās.* The *Joga-vihāṇa-vīsiyā* is the seventeenth section, and deals with *yoga. Yoga* is defined as the state of mind which leads to emancipation. Its five types are mentioned: *sthāna* (position), *ūrṇa* (word), *artha* (meaning), *ālambana* (support) and *anālambana* (without support), and *nirvikalpa cinmātra-samādhi.* The first two come under *karmayoga* and the last three under *jñānayoga.* The definition of '*tīrtha*' is provided. Upādhyāya Yaśovijaya has written a commentary on this work in Sanskrit. He has stated that only the proper conduct of monks, nuns, laymen and laywomen can be called a '*tīrtha*'. *Ṣaḍośaka*[66] or *Ṣoḍaśaka-prakaraṇa* or *Ṣoḍaśaka-sūtra* by Haribhadrasūri, is written in Sanskrit. It contains 16 chapters, having 16 verses each. Two chapters deal with *yoga* practices leading to eternal bliss, incorporating self-consciousness. Yaśobhadrasūri has written a *vivaraṇa* and Yaśovijaya Upādhyāya a *Dīpikā* on this treatise.

Yoganirṇaya by Haribhadra is referred to in the *Yogadṛṣṭisamuccaya* (verse 1) and its auto-commentary, but is not available.[67] *Yogaśataka*[68] by Haribhadrasūri contains 101 *gāthās* dealing with *niścaya-yoga, vyavahāra-yoga,* the master of *yoga,* his characteristics and the state of *yoga* in the form of meditation and so on. Muni Punyavijayaji has edited this work with Sanskrit *prastāvanā* wherein he has compared the subject matter of this work with the *Brahmasiddhānta-samuccaya* of the same author.

The *Jhāṇajjhayaṇa*[69] or *Jhāṇasaya* (*Dhyānādhyayana* or *Dhyānaśataka*) contains 105 *gāthās.* According to some, its author is Jinabhadragaṇi Kṣamāśramaṇa, but since it is a part of the *Āvaśyaka-Niryukti* (after Pratikramaṇa-Niryukti), Bhadrabāhu II is considered by some its author.[70] Haribhadrasūri has written a commentary on this work, who has called this treatise of great significance (महार्थत्वात्) and different from other works(शास्त्रान्तरत्वात्).[71] It deals with *dhyāna* (meditation) and its various forms.

On the Conduct of Laymen (*Śrāvakācāra*)

Jain authors have written studies in Prakrit regarding the conduct of laymen. Amongst them, the explanatory literature composed on the *Mūla Āvaśyaka-sūtra* plays an important role.

Sāvaya-pannatti[72] (*Srvāka-prajñapti*) describes the conduct of lay adherents in 405 *gāthās*. According to some, this treatise is written by Umāsvāti, the author of the *Praśamarati*, but from the commentary of Abhayadevasūri on Haribhdrasūri's *Pañcāsaga* and from the reference of the *Drvyasaptati* of Lāvaṇyasūri, we learn that the author is Haribhadrasūri.[73] Here the author deals with the etymological meaning of *śrāvaka, samyaktva* (right faith), eight types of *karman*, nine *tattvas* ('reals'), and twelve vows of a *śrāvaka* and *sāmācārī* (the conduct of a monk). Haribhadrasūri himself has written a commentary on this work.

Sāvaya-dhamma-vihi[74] (*Śrāvaka-dharma-vidhi*) by Haribhadrasūri, contains 120 *gāthās*. Mānadevasūri has composed a commentary on this treatise.

Darisaṇa-suddhi (*Darśana-śuddhi*, or *Darisaṇa-sattari* (*Darśana-saptati*) or *Samyaktva-saptati*[75] by Haribhadrasūri, contains 70 *gāthās* dealing with *samyaktva* (right faith), divided into twelve *adhikāras*. It has several commentaries. Guṇaśekharasūri's pupil Saṅghatilakasūri wrote a *vivaraṇa*, known as *Tattvakaumidī* in VS 1422; Guṇanidhānasūri's pupil has composed an *Avacūri*; another *Avacūri* is by an unknown author. Munisundarasūri's pupil Śivamaṇḍanagaṇi has composed a *Ṭīkā* and the *Bālāvabodha* is written by Śānticandra's pupil Ratnacandragaṇi in VS 1676.

Sammatta-payaraṇa (*Samyaktva-prakarana*) or *Daṃsaṇa-suddhi* (*Darśana-śuddhi*)[76] by Candraprabhasūri, deals with the purity of *samyaktva*. The author himself has written a *Bṛhad-vṛtti* on this. Dharmaghoṣasūri's pupil Vimalagaṇi has written a *Ṭīkā* (AD 1127). Then Dharmaghoṣasuri, a pupil of Devabhadra has written a *vṛtti*; another *vṛtti*, known as *Ratnamahodadhi*, was composed by Cakreśvara and completed by his pupil's pupil Tilakasūri a hundred years later. There is another *vṛtti* by an unknown author and a *Ṭīkā*.

Jīvānusāsana (*Jīvānuśāsana*)[77]: Devacandrasūri, a pupil of Vīracandra, has composed this work in VS 1162. It contains 323 *gāthās*, divided into 38 *adhikāras*. It deals with various topics such as instalment of the Jina image, paying obeisance to *deva*, *guru* and *pratyākhyāna*, fortnightly *pratikramaṇa*, *saṅgha* (community), neglect of knowledge, non-abandonment of the words of *gaccha* and *guru*, the right of the sacred texts, laymen to study *māsakalpa*, service to a layman, characteristics of a *mithyādṛṣṭi*, the meaning of *asaṃyata*, and so on. The author's commentary was edited by Nemicandrasūri.

Duvālasa-kulaya (*Dvadāsa-kulaka*)[78] by Abhayadevasūri's pupil Jinavallabhasūri who belonged to the Kharatara *gaccha* and died in

AD 1110 contains 232 *gāthās* in different metres. Jinapālagaṇi has written a *vivaraṇa* in VS 1293; there is another *vivaraṇa* also.

Paccakkhāṇa-sarūva (*Pratyākhyāna-svarūpa*)[79] is composed by Yaśodevasūri, a pupil of Candrasūri, pupil of Vīragaṇi, in AD 1185. The author himself has written a commentary; there is another commentary by an unknown author. This treatise is based on the commentaries of the *Āvaśyaka*, the *Pañcāsāka* and the *Pañcavastuka*. It contains 329 *gāthās* dealing with *pratyākhyāna* in its various aspects.

Paccakkhāṇa-bhāsa (*Pratyākhyāna-bhāṣya*)[80] by Devendrasūri, the author of the *Ceiya-vandaṇa-bhāsa*, contains 48 *gāthās*, divided into 9 *dvāras*. It deals with various aspects of *pratyākhyāna*: ten kinds of *pratyākhyāna*, four precepts of *pratyākhyāna*, four types of food, its purity, its fruit and so on. It contains an *Avacūrṇi* by Somasundarasūri.

Ceiya-vandaṇa-bhāsa[81] (*Caitya-vandaṇa-bhāṣya*), also styled as *Deva-vandaṇa-bhāṣya*, by Devendrasūri, teacher of Dharmaghoṣasūri, deals with the rules and regulations pertaining to the salutation to the Tīrthaṅkaras. It has 900 *gāthās*. It contains an *Avacūrṇi* by Jñānasāgara and a *Vārtika* by Jñānavimalasūri with a Gujarati explanation. The work is based on several *Vṛttis*, *Bhāṣyas* and *Cūrṇis*.

Ceiya-vandaṇa-kulaya[82] (*Caitya-vandaṇa-kulaka*) by Jinadattasūri, grandpupil of Abhayadevasūri, deals with a salutation to *caitya* or *deva*. Jinakuśalasuri, pupil of Jinacandrasūri, has written a *vṛtti*.

Vandaṇaya-bhāsa[83] (*Vandanaka-bhāṣya*) by Devendrasūri deals with threefold salutation to the preceptor. The *Bhāṣya* contains several explanations: *Avacūrṇi* by Somadevasūri, together with a small Sanskrit commentary (drawn from the *Āvaśyaka-ṭīkā*); *Vṛtti* (drawn from the *Āvaśyaka-ṭīkā*); *Vārtika* by Jñānavimalsūri, with Gujarati explanation; *Bālāvabodha* with Gujarati explanation.

Saḍḍhadiṇakicca[84] (*Śrāddhadinakṛtya*) by Devendrasūri, pupil of Jagaccandrasūri, contains 344 *gāthās*; it deals with the daily functions of the Jain laity. It has several commentaries including one by the author. It contains an *Avacūrṇi*; another *Avacūrṇi* is by an unknown author. Rāmacandragaṇi's pupil Ānandavallabha has written *Bālāvabodha* in VS 1882.

Saḍḍhavihi (*Śrāddhavidhi*)[85] by Somasundarasūri's pupil Ratnaśekharasūri, is another work that deals with the duties of lay believers in 17 *gāthās*. The author has written his own commentary, *Vidhikaumudī*, in AD 1449. It contains various stories. The following works are listed in the *DCGCM*, Vol. XVIII, Pt. 1:

Ajjhappa-maya-parikkhā (*Adhyātma-mata-parīkṣā*) or the Examination of the Opinion of the Supreme Spirit, by Upādhyāya Yaśovijaya, pupil of Nyāyavijaya with explanation in Sanskrit. The views of the Digambaras are challenged here.

Aṇiccayā-kulaga (*Anityatā-kulaka*) or Exposition of Transitoriness of Worldly Objects. The author is not mentioned. It is referred to in the *Jain Granthāvali.*

Āgama-Aṭṭhuttariā[86] (*Āgamaṣṭottarikā*) by Abhayadevasūri. The importance of *samyaktva* (right faith) is pointed out in 114 *gāthās.*

Āgamika-vastu-vicāra-sāra-pagaraṇa[87] also known as *Ṣaḍasītika* (see *Ṣaḍdasītika*). It is an exposition of the doctrine of *karma* and soul regarding its grade of existence.

Appa-sikkhā (*Ātma-śikṣā*) or Spiritual Advice with regard to the Soul by Sakalacandra, pupil of Vijayadānasūri. In the index of Jain Authors and Works (p. 495) to *BBRAS* (Vols. III-IV) a work known as *Ātmasikṣā* is noted. In the *JRK* (p. 26) *Srutāsvāda* is mentioned as another name of the work.

Appahiya-kula (*Ātma-hita-kulaka*) or the Advice to *ātma-hita* (well-being to oneself) by Ratnasūri, pupil of Dharmasūri.

Appāṇusāsaṇa (*Atmanuśāsana*) or Advice to the Soul by Nemicandra Bhaṇḍārika.

Appāvaboha-kulaya (*Ātmāvabodha-kulaka*) or An Appeal to the Spiritual Power by Jayaśekhara, pupil of Mahendraprabhasūri. It contains 43 *gāthās*; noted in the *JRK* as the *Ātma-bodha-kulaka.*

Āloyaṇā-vīsiyā[88] (*Ālocanā-viṃśikā*) by Yākinī-sūnu Haribhadrasūri. It deals with *ālocanā* or confession of sins in 20 *gāthās.*

Rayaṇattaya-kulak[89] (*Ratnatraya-kulaka*) deals with the *ratnatraya* (three jewels) in 31 *gāthās.*

Visaya-ṇindā-kulaya (*Viṣaya-nindā-kulaya*) or the Condemnation of Worldly Pleasures in 25 *gāthās.*

Sammattupāya-vihi[90] (*Samyaktvotpāda-vidhi*) or the Rules of Production of *samyaktva* in 29 *gāthās.*

Sāmaṇṇa-guṇovaesa-kulaya[91] (*Sāmānya-guṇopadeśa-kulaya*) or preaching of common virtues in 25 *gāthās.*

We have also the following works:

Dhammarayaṇa-pagaraṇa[92] (*Dharma-ratna-prakaraṇa*) by Sāntisūri (twelfth century) with his self-composed *vṛtti.* The characteristics of laymen are explained. Six types of *śīla* (conduct) and seven types of monks (*bhava-sādhu*) are mentioned.

Dhamma-vihi-payaraṇa[93] (*Dharma-vidhi-prakaraṇa*) by Srīprabhasūri pupil of Sarvadevasūri of Candra kula (around AD 1200), contains 50 *gāthās*, dealing with eight *dvāras* of righteousness: its examination, achievement, qualities, the cause of its destruction, the teacher who bestows righteousness, the one who is capable of acquiring it, its types and its fruit. Various narratives are provided to explain or to illustrate these points. Besides the author's own commentary, the author's pupil's pupil Udayasiṃhasūri wrote a *vṛtti* in VS 1256 in Candrāvatī. In his *praśasti* the commentator has referred to the loss of the author's commentary. Jayasiṃhasūri has written yet another commentary.[94]

Sāvayadhammatanta[95] (*Srāvaka-dharmatantra*), also known as *Śrāvaka-dharma-prakaraṇa*, deals with the duties of a layman in 120 *gāthās*. It is composed by Haribhadrasūri. Manadevasūri has written a commentary.

Paryusaṇa-daśa-śataka[96] by Dharmasāgara Upādhyāya, contains 110 *gāthās*; with his own *vṛtti*.

Airyāpathikī-ṣaṭtriṃśikā[97] by Dharmasāgara Upādhyāya, contains 36 *gāthās*; with his own commentary.

Deva-vandanādi-bhāṣya-traya[98] by Devendrasūri, contains three *Bhāṣyas* on *Deva-vandana*, *guru-vandana* and *pratyākhyāna-vandana*. Somasundarasūri has written an *Avacūri*.

Saṃboha-sattari (*Saṃboha-saptati*). According to some it was composed by Haribhadrasūri. No manuscript is available.[99]

Saṃboha-sattari[100] (*Saṃbodha-saptatikā*) by Ratnaśekharasūri, the author of the *Sirivālakahā*. He was a pupil of Vajrasenasūri, pupil of Jayaśekharasūri; he belongs to the fourteenth century. The work is based on the *gāthās* collected from ancient works such as the *Niśitha-cūrṇi* and others. The author deals with various topics: the characteristics of *deva*, *guru*, *kuguru*, *dharma*, difficulty in acquiring right faith, virtues of a teacher, equanimity of mind, compassion for living-beings, prominence of sacred literature of Jains, community (*saṅgha*), worship, *gaccha*, 11 *pratimās* of a *śrvāka* and so on. There are several commentaries. One is by Amarakīrtisūri, pupil of Mānakīrtigaṇi; another by Guṇavinaya, pupil of Jayasoma, written in AD 1594. Equanimity of mind (*Samatā-bhāva*) is characterized as follows: Whether one belongs to the Śvetāmbara or Digambara fold, whether one is a Buddhist or otherwise, one is capable of attaining *mokṣa* only if he has developed the realization of equanimity of mind.[101]

The *Dhamma-parikkhā* (*Dharma-parīkṣā*)[102] by Upādhyāya Yaśovijaya deals with the characteristics of *dharma*, criticism of religious systems outside the purview of one's own faith, virtues of a preacher of sacred *sūtras*, discussion on the omniscient being, a virtuous teacher, eulogy of spiritual meditation and so on.

Pauṣadha-prakaraṇa,[103] also known as *Pausadha-ṣaṭtriṃśikā*, by Jayasomagaṇi (AD 1588), contains 36 *gāthās*. The author has written his own commentary. There was a religious discussion in the court of Akbar when the author is said to have defeated the disputants in the assembly. *Vairagya-śataka*[104] was written by some early *ācārya*. Guṇavinayagaṇi (seventeenth century) has written a *vṛtti*. *Vairāgya* (indifference to worldly objects) is treated in a forceful manner.

Vairāgya-rasāyana-prakaraṇa[105] by Lakṣmīlābhagaṇi, deals with *vairāgya* in 102 *gāthās*.

Indiya-parājaya-sayaga[106] (*Indriya-parājayā-śataka*) contains advice to control the senses. The author is not known. Guṇavinaya has written a commentary in AD 1607.

Vyavahāra-śuddhi-prakāśa[107] by Ratnaśekharasūri, deals with seven means of earning livelihood, training to be imparted to one's son, illustrations with regard to debt, guidance on foreign travel, purity in dealings, collection of one hundred stanzas about fools (*mūrkha-śataka*), characteristics of a man who does good to others, the nature of the senses, and other useful things in worldly life.

Paripāṭī-caturdaśakaṃ[108] by Unādhyāya Vinayavijaya deals with 14 ways of offering salutations to various holy places: the Aṣṭāpada, the Sammetaśikhara, the Śatruñjaya, Nandīśvara-dvīpa-caitya, the wandering Jinas, the twenty holy places (*jāta-tīrtha*), the holy places in the region of Bharata and Airāvata, and so on.

Among other treatises mention may be made of the *Jīva-dayā-payaraṇa*, the *Nāṇā-citta-payaraṇa*, the *Micchatta-mahaṇa-kulaya* and the *Daṃsaṇa-kulaya*.

Prakaraṇas or Systematic Scientific Treatises

The *Prakaraṇas* are small treatises which can be easily committed to memory. These treatises were helpful in the preaching of sermons. Besides, those who knew them could comprehend the canonical literature without much difficulty. Jain authors have composed numerous such *Prakaraṇas* in Prakrit dealing with a variety of topics.

Muni Caturvijayaji Maharaj has published a number of such treatises in the *Ātmānanda Grantha-ratnamālā*.

Jīva-viyāra-pagaraṇa[109] (*Jīva-vicāra-prakaraṇa*) or Investigation to Living Beings by Sāntisūri (who according to Winternitz, died in AD 1039)[110] in 51 *gāthās* discusses *jīvas* or living beings. They are divided into liberated souls (*siddha*) and those who are still in the cycle of rebirths; subdivisions are discussed. It has various commentaries: (i) Pāṭhaka Ratnākara has written a Sanskrit *vṛtti* based on a Prakrit *vṛtti*, in AD 1553. The former has been published; the latter is not available. (ii) Samayasundara has written another *vṛtti* (AD 1841). (iii) Īśvarācārya has written a commentary known as *Artha-dīpikā*. (iv) Kṣamākalyāṇa has written a commentary in VS 1850. (v) An unknown author has written an *Avacūri*, known as *Pradīpikā*. A. Guerinot has published a French translation of this work in Extract from *Journal Asiatic* (March-April 1902), and Jayant P. Thakur, an English translation.[111] *Navatatta-payaraṇa* (*Navatattva-prakaraṇa*)[112] or a Treatise on the Nine *Tattvas* or fundamental truths by Devagupta of Ūkesś *gaccha*; his earlier name being Jinacandragaṇi. The *tattvas* are *jīva, ajīva, puṇya, pāpa, āsrava, sāṃvara, bandha, nirjarā* and *mokṣa*. It consists of 53 *gāthās* on which the well known Abhayadevasūri wrote a *Bhāṣya* around AD 1063 and Yasodeva, a *vṛtti* in the twelfth century. Dharmavijaya wrote *Sumaṅgala Ṭīkā*.

Navatatta-payaraṇa (*Navatattva-prakaraṇa*) is another work of the same title. Its author is not known. Here we have the characteristics of nine *Tattvas*. It has several commentaries: by Kulamaṇḍana (died AD 1398), Sādhuratna, Māṇikyaśekhara, Paramānandasūri, Samayasundara (AD 1641), Ratnacandra (AD 1740), and others.[113]

Nava-paya-payaraṇa (*Nava-pada-prakaraṇa*)[114] is another tract by Devaguptasūri. It contains 137 *gāthās* describing *mithyātva, samyktva*, twelve *vratas* of a lay adherent and *sallekhanā* (ritual death by fasting). The author wrote his own commentary known as *Śrāvakānandī* or *Śrāvakānanda-kāriṇī* in AD 1016. Yaśodevasūri, Devendra, Kulacandra and others also have commented.[115]

Vicāra-chattīsiyā[116] (*Vicāra-ṣaṭtriṃśikā*) is also known as the *Daṇḍaka-prakaraṇa* or the *Laghu-saṃgrahaṇī*. It has been composed by Dhavalacandra's pupil Gajasāra in 44 *gāthās* wherein 24 *daṇḍakas* are dealt with in 24 *dvāras*. The author has written (AD 1522) an *Avacūrṇi* wherein it is styled as the *Vicāra-ṣaṭtriṃśikā-sūtra*. Udayacandra's pupil Rūpacandra has written a *vṛtti* in 1618 wherein it is styled as the *Laghu-saṃgrahaṇī*.[117]

Jambūdīva-saṃgahaṇī[118] (*Jambūdvīpa-saṃgrahaṇī*) by Haribhadrasūri of *Bṛhad-gaccha.* The author deals with the Jambūdvīpa region in 29 *gāthās.* The whole work is divided into ten *dvāras*: *khaṇḍa, yojana, kṣetra, parvata, kūṭa, tīrtha, śreṇī, vijaya, draha* and *nadī.* It contains 3 commentaries, of which two are by unknown authors, and the third is by Prabhānandasūri of Kṛṣṇa *gaccha,* composed in 1333. It is also styled as the *Kṣetra-saṃgrahaṇī*[119] or *Kṣetradi-saṃgrahaṇī.*

Saṃgahaṇī (*Saṃgrahaṇī*) or *Bṛhatsaṃgrahaṇī* by well known Jinabhadragaṇi Kṣamāśramaṇa, the author of the *Viśeṣāvaśyaka-Bhāṣya.* The author has called it the *Saṃgahaṇī* and later to distinguish it from other works, the *Bṛhat-Saṃgrahaṇī.* It contains 367 *gāthās,* out of which according to the commentator Malayagiri, a few are interpolated, some are by other authors, and some from the *Sūrapaṇṇatti.* It deals with cosmology, geography, and four kinds of *gatis,* hellish, celestial, human and animal. Several commentaries are written by Malayagiri, Śīlabhadra, Jinavallabha and others.[120]

Saṃkhitta-saṃgahaṇī (*Saṃkṣipta-Saṃgrahaṇī*) or *Saṃgahaṇī-rayaṇa* (*Saṃgrahaṇī-ratna*)[121] by Srīcandrasūri, pupil of Maladhāri Hemacandra, who also composed the *Munisuvvaya-carita* (vs 1193), the *Kṣetrasamāsa* and the *Pratyākhyāna-kalpākalpa-vicāra,* also known as the *Laghupravacanasāroddhāra-prakaraṇa.* It contains 273 *gāthās* dealing with *śarīra* and other topics in 24 *dvāras.* It is based on Jinabhadragaṇi's *saṃgrahaṇī,* and is also called *Laghu-saṃgrahaṇī.* Sricandrasūri's pupil Devabhadrasūri has written a commentary known as the *Saṃgrahaṇī-vṛtti* which contains quotations from the *Sūrapaṇṇatti.* The commentator has also referred to the *Anuyogadvāra-Cūrṇi* and a *Ṭīkā* by Haribhadra. Dharmānandagaṇi and Cāritramuni both have written a separate *Avacūri* on this work.[122]

Samayakhitta-samāsa[123] (*Samayakṣetra-samāsa*) or *Khetta-samāsa* (*Kṣetra-samāsa*) or *Bṛhat-Kṣetra-samāsa* by Jinabhadragaṇi Kṣamāśramaṇa contains 637 or 655 *gāthās,* dealing with the time (*samaya*) of two and a half continents. It consists of 5 *adhikāras* wherein we are told about half the portions of Jambūdvīpa, Lavaṇasamudra, Dhātakīkhaṇḍa, Kālodadhi and Puṣkaravaradvīpa. It has several commentaries, three being by unknown authors. Among others are Haribhadrasūri (vs 1185), Siddhasūri (1192), Malayagiri (1200), Vijayasiṃha (1215), Devabhadra (1233), Devānanda (1455) and Ānandasūri; Malaygiri's is the largest.[124]

Laghu-kṣetrasamāsa[125] or *Kṣetrasamāsa* or *Narakhitta-payaraṇa* (*Narakṣetra-prakaraṇa*) by Ratnasekharaśūri, pupil of Vajrasenasūri and *paṭṭa-dhara* of Hematilakasūri, is based on Jinabhadragaṇi's *Samayakhitta-samāsa* or *Bṛhat-kṣetra-samāsa.* It contains 264 *gāthās,* dealing with a description of two and a half continents. Besides the author's own commentary, it has several other explanations in the form of *Avacūri* and *Bālāvabodha.*[126]

Navya-bṛhat-kṣetra-samāsa by Somatilakasūri, contains 489 *gāthās.* Guṇaratna and others have written commentaries.

Śrīcandrīya-sangrahaṇī by Śrīcandrasūri, contains 313 *gāthās.* Maladhāri Devabhadra has written a *vṛtti.*

Samayasāra-prakaraṇa[127] by Devānanda. It contains an anonymous Sanskrit commentary. It has ten chapters dealing with *jīva, ajīva, āsrava, bandha, saṃvara, nirjarā, moksa, samyak-jñāna* and *darśana, samyak-cāritra* and the consequences of worship (*ārādhanā*) and injury (*virādhanā*).

Pañcāsaga-payaraṇa[128] (*Pañcāśaka-prakaraṇa*) by Haribhadrasūri is also known as '*Śrāvakadharma*'. It contains 19 parts, each called *prakaraṇa* or *pañcāśaka,* and each containing fifty verses. Abhyadevasūri has written a *vṛtti* in vs 1124. Yaśodevasūri, a pupil of Candrasūri has written a *Cūrṇi* in vs 1172 on the first *Pañcāśaka. Sattari-saya-ṭhāṇa-payaraṇa*[129] (*Saptati-śata-sthāna-prakaraṇa*) by Somatilakasūri, pupil of Somaprabhasūri, pupil of Dharmaghoṣasūri of Tapāgaccha. He was born in vs 1355 (AD 1298) and died at the age of 69. It contains 170 *prakaraṇas,* dealing with the lives of the twenty-four Tīrthaṅkaras. Devavijaya wrote a commentary in vs 1370. The following *Prakaraṇas* can be mentioned:

Ikkavīsa-ṭhāṇa-pagaraṇa[130] (*Ekaviṃśati-sthāna-prakaraṇa*) by Siddhasena, designated 'Sādhāraṇa'. He was a pupil of Yaśodevasūri, a descendant of Bappabhaṭṭisūri. The author also composed the *Vilāsavaikahā,* an Apabhraṃśa work in vs 1123. It contains 64 *gāthās,*[131] also known as *Catuḥṣaṣṭi.*

Uvaesa-rahassa-pagaraṇa[132] (*Upadeśa-rahasya-prakaraṇa*) by Upādhyāya Yaśovijayagaṇi. He has written his own commentary. It contains 203 *gāthās.*

Kāla-sattari-pagaraṇa (*Kāla-saptati-prakaraṇa*) by Dharmaghoṣa.

Kūpadṛṣṭānta-viśadīkaraṇa-prakaraṇa[133] by Upādhyāya Yaśovijaya.

Kṣullaka-bhavāvali-prakaraṇa by Dharmaśekharagaṇi.

Guṇasthāna-kramāroha-prakaraṇa,[134] or *Guṇasthānaka* or *Guṇasthāna-ratna-rāśi* by Ratnaśekharasūri, dating to vs 1447. It deals with 24 *guṇasthānas.* The author has written his own commentary. He is also an author of the *Kṣetrasamāsa* and the *Sirivālakahā.* Vimalasūri and Jayaśekharasūri also wrote bearing the same title separately.

Guru-guṇa-ṣaṭtriṃśika by Vajrasena.

Devendranarendra-prakaraṇa[135] by Haribhadra.

Dharmaratna-prakaraṇa[136] by Sāntisūri. Devendra has written a commentary.

Bandha-ṣaṭka-triṃśikā by Dharmaghoṣasūri.

Bandha-hetūdaya-tribhaṅgī by Harṣakulagaṇi, written in the sixteenth century vs.

It contains 65 *gāthās*. Vānaraṣi has written a commentary in vs 1602.

Bandhodaya-sattā by Vijayamalagaṇi, in the beginning of the seventeenth century vs. It contains 24 *gāthās*; there is a self-composed *Avacūri*.

Maṇḍala-prakaraṇa by Vinayakuśala.

Lokanalikā[137] by Dharmaghoṣa, pupil of Devendrasūri. It has an anonymous Gujarati *Tabo*.

Vanaspati-sattari (*Vanaspati-saptatikā*) by Municandra, the author of the *Aṅgula-sattari* and other works. It deals with vegetables (*vanaspati*) in 70 *gāthās*. It is not printed. It contains two commentaries, one by the author himself, the other by Guṇadevasūri of Nāgendra *gaccha*; an *Avacūri* by an unknown author.[138]

Vicāra-pañcāśikā by Vijayamala.

Vicāra-sattari by Mahendrasūri.

Samavasaraṇa-prakaraṇa by Dharmaghoṣasūri.

Siddha-daṇḍikā by Devendrasūri (died vs 1327); also an author of the *Five Karmagranthas* (with commentary), *Śrāddhadinakṛtya-vṛtti, Siddha-pañcāśakā-vṛtti, Sudarśanā-caritra, Vandāru-vṛtti* and others.

Sūkṣmārtha-sattari-prakaraṇa by Cakreśvarasūri.

The following *Prakaraṇas* can be noted:

Aṅgula-sattari (*Aṅgula saptati*)[139] by Municandrasūri, a pupil of Yaśobhadra. He was a teacher of Ajitadevasūri and the desputant Devasūri. He died in vs 1178. It contains 70 *gāthās*; an author of 31 treatise. It has an auto-commentary; also an *Avacūri* by an unknown author.[140]

We must list also the following:

Annāyauñcha-prakaraṇa.

Karma-saṃvedya-bhsṅga-prakaraṇa by Devacandra (beginning of the seventeenth century vs).

Kālacakra-vicāra-prakaraṇa.

Gāṅgeya-prakaraṇa.

Jīvājīvābhigama-saṃgahaṇī by an unknown author. It contains 223 *gāthās*; in manuscript.

Triṣaṣṭi-śalākā-pañcāśika-prakaraṇa.

Dehasthiti-prakaraṇa.

Nigoda-ṣaṭtriṃśikā-prakaraṇa.

Paramāṇu-vicāra-ṣaṭ-triṃśikā.

Pudgala-parāvarta-svarūpa-prakaraṇa.

Pudgala-bhaṅga-prakaraṇa.

Pudgala-ṣaṭ-triṃśikā-prakaraṇa.

Paṇṇavaṇā-taiya-paya-saṃgahiṇī (*Prajñāpanā-tṛtīya-pada-saṃgrahaṇī*)[141] by Abhayadevasūri; contains 133 *gāthās*. Taking into consideration the '*alpa-bahutva*', the third *pada* of the *Paṇṇavaṇā*, the author has dealt with '*alpa-bahutva*' of *jīvas* in 27 *dvāras*. An *Avacūrṇi* by Kulamaṇḍanasūri is VS 1471 in date.

Bandhodaya-prakaraṇa.

Bhūyaskārādi-vicāra-prakaraṇa by Lakṣmīvijaya (seventeenth century VS).

Yonistva-prakaraṇa.

Labdhi-stava-prakaraṇa.

Lokāntika-stava-prakaraṇa.

Śrāvaka-vrata-bhaṅga-prakaraṇa.

Chaṭṭhāṇa-payaraṇa (*Ṣaṭ-sthāna-prakaraṇa*)[142] by Jineśvarasūri, teacher of Abhayadevasūri; also known as the *Śrāvaka-vaktavyatā.* It contains 104 *gāthās*, dealing with six *sthānakas*. It has several commentaries. Abhayadevasūri has written a *Bhāṣya*; Upādhyāya Jinapāla, pupil of Jinapatisūri, a *vṛtti* in VS 1262; Śāntisūri of Thārāpada *gaccha* another *vṛtti*; another by an unknown author.[143]

Samyaktva-pañca-viṃśatikā-prakaraṇa.[144]

Sāmācārī or Rules for Ascetics

As seen earlier, the *sāmācārī* probably is the oldest nucleus of the *Kalpasūtra*, the eighth chapter of the *Dasāsuyakkhanda*. Several works were written on this subject in Prakrit.[145]

Āyāravihi, also known as *Sāmācārī-prakaraṇa*[146] by an unknown author, deals with rituals pertaining to 21 items, including *samyaktva* (right faith), *vrata* (vow), pratimā (stage of renunciation for a layman), *tapa* (austerities), *pravrajyā* (renunciation), *yoga-vidhi* (practice of *yoga*) and so on.

Sāmācārī-saṃgraha by Nareśvara, also known as *Sūrivallabha-sāmācārī.* It contains 10 *paricchedas.* The concluding text which is in Sanskrit, is called *Laghu-śānti-stava* or *Śānti-stava* and is ascribed to Mānadevasūri.[147]

Sāmāyārī (*Sāmācārī*) by Jinadattasūri with 30 *gāthās.* It is cited in the *Sāmācārī-śataka;* also known as *Praśnottara-śataka* (in Sanskrit) by Somasundaragaṇi (published in Jinadattasūri, Jñānabhaṇḍāra, 1939).

Sāmāyārī (*Sāmācārī*) by Jinapatisūri, Jinadattasūri's grand pupil. It contains 79 *gāthās;* cited in the *Sāmācārī-śataka* (pp. 139ā-141ā).

Paḍikkamaṇa-sāmācārī (*Pratikramaṇa-sāmācārī*) by Jinavallabhagaṇi in 40 *gāthās;* cited in the above-mentioned *Sāmācārī-śataka* (pp. 137a-138a).

Sāmācārī[148] by Tialakācārya, deals with the conduct of ascetics including *yoga, tapasyā, keśa-loca* (practice of pulling out one's hair), *upasthāpanā* (a kind of initiation), *vasati* (dwelling-place) and so on.

Subodha-sāmācārī[149] by Śrīcandrasūri, pupil of Dhaneśvarasūri.

Jai-sāmācārī (*Yati-sāmācārī*) or *Yatidinacaryā*[150] by Bhāvadevasūri, who completed the *Pārśvanāthacaritra* in vs 1412. It contains 154 *gāthās* dealing with the daily duties of an ascetic right from getting up in the morning till *saṃthāraga* (preparation of pallet of straw upon which the sage, sick unto death, stretches himself in order to meditate). Matisāgarasūri has written an *Avacūri.*

Pañcasutta or *Pañcasūtraka*[151] by an earlier author; consists of five *Sūtras*: the first *Sūtra* deals with four refuges (*śaraṇa*) and the approval of meritorious deeds; the second with abandonment of an evil friend, taking company of a friend of virtue; the third with the manner of accepting initiation; the fourth with the observance of eight *pravacana-mātṛkā* (consisting of three *guptis* or restrains and five *samitis* or rules of conduct); and the fifth *Sūtra* deals with *mokṣa* or liberation. It has several commentaries, one by Haribhadra, another by Jñānasāgarasūri and still another by Śivatilaka, pupil of Lakṣamīsāgarasūri. Śivatilaka's *vṛtti* is based on that of Jñānasāgara, and the latter on Haribhadra's. Municandrasūri has written an *Avacūri;* another *Avacūri* is by an unknown author.

Pañca-niyaṇṭhī (*Pañca-nirgranthī*) is said to have been composed by Haribhadrasūri.[152] From its title it appears that it describes the nature of five *nirgranthas*: the *pulāka, bakuśa, kuśīla, nirgrantha* and *snātaka,* all having to do with laxity in conduct.

Pañca-niyaṇṭhi[153] (*Pañca-nirgranthi*), also known as *Pañca-nirgranthī-vicāra-saṃgrahaṇī* by Abhayadevasūri. It contains 107 *gāthās* and is based on the twenty-fifth Śataka of the *Viyāhapaṇṇatti.* It treats with the five types of *nirgranthas. Āhārovahisejjāviyāra*[154] (Āhāropadhiśayyā-vicāra) by an unknown author, deals with the exposition of food, accessories and bedding of Jain monks.

Saṃthāraga-porisī-sutta[155] (*Saṃstāraka-pauruṣī-sūtra*). Its author is not known. It deals with what a Jain monk ought to do before going to bed. It contains 14 *gāthās* with explanation in Gujarati.

Pañcavatthuga[156] (*Pañcavastuka*) by Haribhadrasūri, contains 1714 *gāthās,* divided into five *Adhikāras*: the mode of renunciation, daily duties, the act of obtaining the permission of the elders and *sallekhanā* (ritual death by fasting). The author has written his own commentary. Upādhyāya Yaśovijaya's *Mārga-viśuddhi* is based on this treatise.

Samboha-payaraṇa[157] (*Sambodha-prakaraṇa*), also known as *Tatta-payāsaga* (*Tattva-prakāsaka*) is another work of Haribhadrasūri. It contains 1590 *gāthās,* divided into 12 *Adhikāras,* dealing with *deva, guru, samyaktva, śrāvaka, vrata, leśyā* (karmic stain), *dhyāna* (meditation), *ālocanā* (confession) and so on. Ratnaśekharasūri has cited several *gāthās* of this work in his *Samboha-sattari.*[158]

Gurutattva-viniścaya[159] by Upādhyāya Yaśovijaya with his self-composed *vṛtti.* It contains 4 *ulāsas,* dealing with the importance of *guru,* explanation of five *vyavahāras, agama, śruta, ājñā, dhāraṇā* and *jīta,* bad teachers such as *pārśvastha* and others, entering into another *gaccha,* norms of the *sādhu* community, characteristics of five *nirgranthas* and so on.

Yatilakṣana-samuccaya[160] is another composition of Yaśovijaya. It deals with the conduct of ascetics in 227 *gāthās.*

Vidhi or Ritualistic Works

Vihi-maggappavā[161] (*Vidhi-mārgaprapā*) was composed in AD 1306 at Kosala (Ayodhya), by Jinaprabhasūri an influential Jain teacher who wielded lot of influence on Mahmud Tughlaq. It contains the *sāmācārī,* the methods of performing religious ceremonies by Jain clergy and the laity, specially pertaining to the followers of the Kharatara *gaccha* (*viddhi-mārga* is another name of Kharatara *gaccha*). This ritualistic work is divided into 41 *dvāras,* dealing with *samyaktva-vrata-āropaṇa-vidhi, parigraha-parimāṇa-vidhi, sāmāyika-āropaṇa-vidhi, upadhāna-nikṣepaṇa-vidhi, mālāropaṇa-vidhi, Uvahāṇa-paiṭṭhā-pañcāsaya* (*Upadhāna-pratiṣṭhā-pañcāśaka*), *pauṣadha-vidhi, pratikramaṇa-vidhi, tapa-vidhi, pravrajyā-vidhi, upasthapanā-vidhi, mahāpāriṣṭhāpanikā-vidhi, prāyaścitta-vidhi, tīrthayātrā-vidhi, aṅgavidyā-siddhi-vidhi* and so on.

In this work several treatises written by other authors have been incorporated either fully or partially. For instance, in the *Upadhāna-vidhi*, the seventh *dvāra*, Manadevasūri's *Uvahāṇa-vihi-prakaraṇa*, comprising 54 *gāthās*, has been incorporated. This *Prakaraṇa* is said to have been based on the *Mahānisīhasutta*. In the *Uvahāṇa-paiṭṭhā-pañcāsaya*, the ninth *dvāra*, the *Uvahāṇa-paiṭṭhā-pañcāsaya-prakaraṇa*, comprising 51 *gāthās*, is incorporated; in the *Nandi-racanā-vidhi*, the fifteenth *dvāra*, the *Arihāṇādi-thotta* comprising 36 *gāthās*, is incorporated; the *Yoga-vidhi*, the twenty-fourth *dvāra*, incorporates the fourth chapter of the *Uttarādhyayanasūtra*, comprising 13 *gāthās*; the *Pratiṣṭhā-vidhi*, the thirty-fifth *dvāra*, incorporated the *dhayā-ropaṇa-vihi-payaraṇa* (*dhvajā-ropaṇa-vidhi-prakaraṇa*), comprising 50 *gāthās* from the *Kahārayaṇa-kosa* as well as the *Pratiṣṭhā-kāvya-saṃgraha* of Candrasūri. The *Yoga-nikṣepaṇa-vidhi*, the twenty-third *dvāra*, refers to the *Kālika* and the *Utkālika* division of the Āgamic literature. The *Yoga-vidhi*, the twenty-fourth *dvāra*, described the contents of the canonical literature. The *Pratiṣṭhā-vidhi*, the thirty-fifth *dvāra*, and the *Mudrā-vidhi*, the thirty-seventh *dvāra*, are both in Sanskrit.

Jinavallabhasūri has also composed the *Posaha-vihi-payaraṇa* (its summary is given in 15 *gāthās* in the *Vihi-magga-ppavā*), *Dāna-vihi*, *Pratyākhyān-vicāraṇā*, and *Nandi-vidhi*.[162]

Tīrthas (Holy Places)

Vividha-tīrtha-kalpa[163] or *Kalpa-pradīpa* is another important work of Jinaprabhasūri. As Hīravijayasūri was greatly honoured in the court of Akbar so was Jinaprabhasūri in the court of Tuglak Muhammad Shah. The latter had widely travelled for pilgrimage to Jain holy places and the result was his composition of the *Vividha-tīrtha-kalpa*, AD 1332. It gives a description of Jain pilgrimages together with the names of their founders, the kings and rulers who restored them and the dates of the years. Though the work contains legends mixed with facts, nevertheless it has some historical significance. It is based on the earlier sources and narrates events belonging to the author's own period. It is written partly in Sanskrit and partly in Jain Maharashtri.

It contains about 62 *kalpas*, describing 37 or 38 places of pilgrimage.[164] The *Aṇahilla-vāḍaya-kalpa* refers to the ministers Vastupāla and Tejapāla who were responsible for constructing the magnificent Dilwara Jain temples at Ābu. The *Ahicchatā-nagarī-kalpa* mentions numerous great medicines growing in the region. The *Mathurāpurī-*

kalpa refers to god-made *stūpa*, adorned with festoons and enclosed with three bands. Some called it the *stūpa* of Svayambhūdeva (Lord Śiva), some of Nārāyaṇa (as an *ananta-śāyī*), whilst Buddhists claimed it to be a *Buddha-aṇḍa*. It was a centre of heretical ascetics and was known for the pilgrimage of the Bhaṇḍīra garden. We are told that in vs 826 Bappabhaṭṭasūri restored this place of pilgrimage and installed the idol of Vīra Jina. The well known Jinabhadragaṇi Kṣamāśramaṇa, having worshipped the divine *stūpa*, restored the manuscript of the *Mahānisīha* which was damaged by white-ants. The *Apāpāpurī-kalpa* records the 42 places where Mahavira passed his *cāturmāsa* (four months of rainy season). In the end he arrived at the toll-house of King Hastipāla where he attained *nirvāṇa*. In the *Kavaḍḍiya-jakkha-kalpa* the origin of the Kāpardika *yakṣa* is mentioned. The city of Śrāvasti was known by the name of Maheṭhi.[165] The *Vārāṇasī-nagarī-kalpa* has referred to the *Maṇikarṇikā-ghāṭa*, the *Deva-vārāṇasī* where existed the Viśvanātha temple, the *Rājadhānī-vārāṇasī*, the dwelling place of Yavanas, the *Madana-vārāṇasī* (identified with modern Madanpurā) and the *Vijaya-vārāṇasī*.

Settuñja-kappa (*Śatruñjaya-kalpa*),[166] by Dharmaghoṣasūri, contains 40 *gāthās*. Muni Sundaragaṇi's pupil Śubhaśīlagaṇi has written an elaborate commentary on this work which is full of narrative. This commentary is also designated as the *Śatruñjaya-bṛhatkalpa*, the *Śatruñjaya-kalpakathā*, the *Śatruñjaya-kalpakośa*, the *Śatruñjaya-kathākośa* or the *Kathākośa*. The commentary was written in vs 1518. The commentator has written another *Kathākośā*, known as the *Bharateśvara-bāhubali-vṛtti*).

Ujjayanta-kalpa[167] is said to have been composed by Pādaliptasūri; it is quoted from the *Vijjāpāhuḍa*. Ujjayanta is another name for Girnar mountain.

Girinära-kalpa[168] by Dharmaghoṣasūri contains 32 *gāthās*. It is based on the above-mentioned work of Pādaliptasūri, according to the author.

Tīrthamālā-prakaraṇa[169] by Mahendraprabhasūri or Mahendrasūri; also known as *Pratimāstuti*, contains 111 *gāthās*. Numerous Jain sacred places are mentioned here.

Paṭṭāvalis or List of Teachers

There are numerous *Paṭṭāvalis*[170] and *Therāvalis*, genealogical lists of teachers and heads of schools, some of which are very important for the chronological data. In these *Paṭṭāvalis*, frequently the same name occurs several times and it is not easy to distinguish one teacher from another of the same title. The medieval Śvetāmbara community was divided into a number of groups. The two major groups in north-west India being the Kharataragaccha, mainly centred in Rajasthan, dating to the eleventh century and the Tapāgaccha, centred in Rajasthan and Gujarat, dating to the thirteenth. Relationships between these various groups were not always peaceful and intense competition broke out between the rival monks by way of public debates, seeking royal patronage and public support. The monks belonging to these groups considered themselves the standard bearers of a tradition which had been corrupted by their opponents. The whole atmosphere was marked by strident competition. Acuity or sharpness in philosophical argument was regarded by the authors of the *Payṭṭāvalis* as a necessary gift of the monk who managed to defeat one from the rival group in public debate.[171]

The Kharataragacchabṛhadgurvāvali provides an account of Kharatara, head monk Jinapatisūri, who entered into a debate with a Digambara monk. The author Jinapāla has provided details of the Kharataragaccha. The text is edited by Muni Jinavijaya, *SJS*, 1956 and analysed by Mahāmahopadhyāya Vinayasāgara under the title *Kharataragaccha kā Itihāsa* in Hindi, Ajmer, 1959; see *CJMS*, Sr. 239, p. 301. Professor Dr. Phyllis Granoff of McMaster University in Hamilton, Ontario is preparing a study of the *Kharatara-gaccha-bṛhadgurvāvali* where she is going to discuss its particular conventions and patterns and compare them with those found in the *Prabandhas*, 'The Biographies of Siddhasena', *Journal of Indian Philosophy* 17: 329-84, 1989.

The *Kharataragacchapaṭṭāvali* provides a list of teachers of the Kharataragaccha. Śrī Jineśvarasuri held the sixty-first *paṭṭa*, whose date of birth recorded as VS 1524 (AD 1467).

The *Paṭṭāvalisamuccaya* is in two parts. It is a collection of the Tapāgaccha. It is edited by Muni Darśanavijaya, Śrī Cāritra Smāraka Granthamālā, 1933. The articles in the *paṭṭāvalis* include Johannes Klatt 'Extracts from the Historical Records of the Jains', *Indian Antiquary*, Vol. II, 1882, pp. 245-56, Dasaratha Sarma, 'Gleanings from the Kharataragacchapaṭṭāvali', *IHQ*, Vol. 26, 1950, pp. 224-31; Dasaratha Sarma, 'Kharataragacchapaṭṭāvali compiled by Jinapāla', *IHQ*, Vol. 11, 1935, pp. 779-81.

Munisundara's *Gurvāvali*,[172] also known as the *Bṛhatta-pāgacchagurvāvali* or the *Tridaśataraṅgiṇī*. The *mūla* with its *svopajña* commentary was composed at Ahmedabad in AD 1591 by Dharmasāgaragaṇi under the patronage of Hīravijayasūri. The work is based on older works such as Munisundara's *Tridaśataraṅgiṇī, Dussamāsaṅghastotra, Jīrṇa, Paṭṭāvali,*[173] *Aṅcalagacchīya, Bṛhatpaṭṭāvali.*[174]

Cāhamāna-vaṃśāvali comprises the genealogy of King Cāhamāna (or Cāhumāna or Cauhana).[175]

Paṭṭana-rāja-paṭṭāvali[176] provides the *paṭṭāvali* of King Paṭṭana (Pāṭan). Other *Paṭṭāvalis* comprises: *Balātkāra-gaṇa-paṭṭāvali*[177] (in Sanskrit) with 35 verses, *Paṭṭāvali-parāga-saṃgraha,*[178] *Mūlasaṃgha ki Paṭṭāvali,*[179] *Nandisaṃgha-gurvāvali,*[180] and *Five Digambara Paṭṭāvalis.*[181]

Prabandhas or Semi-historical Accounts

The *prabandhas* are semi-historical accounts which are composed with regard to some historical event, pertaining to an administrator, a learned scholar, a monk, a layman or a pilgrimage. Their main object was to propagate religion and to entertain by way of illustrations and examples. Since they are collections of more or less anecdotes, they should not be taken as biographies or history. At the same time they cannot be entirely rejected as historical sources, but they can be used only with extreme caution.[182] These *prabandhas* were written mostly in the region of Gujarat and Malwa. Though they are generally written in Sanskrit, they are intermixed with the uses of Prakrit and the old regional dialect. The difference between the *paṭṭāvalis* or the *gurvāvalis* and the *prabandhas* is that the former are related with the deeds of a particular group of monks who belong to a specific *gaccha* or lineage, whereas the *prabandhas* praise the deeds of monks from various groups. Here we have the following *prabandhas.*

Prabandhāvali[183] by Jinabhadra pupil of Udayaprabhasūri, contains 40 prose *prabandhas,* mostly concerned with the personages of Gujarat, Rajasthan, Malwa and Vārāṇasī. It was written at the initiation of Jaitrasiṃha, son of minister Vastupala in his lifetime in VS 1290 (AD 1233). It has provided the biographical accounts of Mānatuṅga, Pādalipta, Haribhadra, Abhayadeva, Siddharsi and Devācārya. *Prabhāvakacarita,*[184] also known as *Pūrvarṣicarita* by Prabhacandra. Here we have a biographical account of twenty-two Jain teachers, poets and authors, including Pādalipta, Siddhasena, Mallavādi, Haribhadrasūri and Bappabhaṭṭi also Vīrasūri, Śāntisūri, Mahendrasūri, Sūrācārya, Abayadeva, Vīradeva and Hemacandrasūri, contemporary of Cālikya rulers, which is important for the history of

Gujarat. The work was revised by Pradyumnasūri in AD 1277.

Prabandhacintāmaṇi[185] by Merutuṅga was completed in AD 1306. The work is divided into 5 *Prakāśas*, comprising 11 *prabandhas*. They contain the life-story of Vikramāditya, and Sātavāhana, a brief history of Cālukyas, of Muñirāja, the relation between Bhoja and Bhīma, King Siddharāja, King Kumārapāla and his conversion to Jain religion, the activities of Vastupāla and the Tejapāla brothers. The author was a pupil of Candraprabha of Nagendra-*gaccha*; among his other works can be mentioned the *Vicārasreṇī* or *Sthavirāvali* and the *Mahāpuruṣacarita*.

Prabandhakośa,[186] is also known as *Caturviṃśati-prabandha* by Rājaśekharasūri. It contains *prabandhas*[187] or life-stories of twenty-four persons: ten Jain teachers, including Hemacandra; four poets: Śrīharṣa, Harihara, Amaracandra and the Digambara Madanakīrti; seven kings, and three others. This important work is based on earlier *prabandhas*. The author belongs to the Praśnavāhana *kula*, Koṭika *gaṇa*; he was a descendant of Maladhāri Abhayadevasūri of the Madhyama *śākhā* of Harṣpurīya *gaccha*, and was a pupil of Tilakasūri. He composed this work in VS 1405 (AD 1348) in the Mahaṇasiṃha's *vasati* of Delhi. Among other works of the author are the *Antarkathāsaṃgraha*, *Syādvādakalikā*, *Syādvādādipikā*, *Ratnāvatārapañjikā*, *Nyāyakandalīpañjikā* and *Ṣaḍdarśana-samuccaya*.

Among other *caritas* and *prabandhas*, we have *Prabhāvakacarita* (written in AD 1277 by Prabhācandra, *Bappabhaṭṭiprabandha*, *Mallavādiprabandha*, *Siddhasenaprabandha*, *Vastupālaprabandha* and so on.

NOTES

1. D.D. Kosambi, *Indian History*, p. 168, Bombay, 1975.
2. With Sumatikīrti's Sanskrit Commentary and with Hiralal's *Bhāṣā-Ṭīkā*, BJP, 1960; Sanskrit *Pañcasaṃgraha* by Ḍaḍḍha, son of Lakṣamaṇa with Prakrit *Cūrṇi* is also published.
3. वोच्छं कदिवइ गाहाओ दिट्ठिवादाओ, after Hiralal Jain.
4. वोच्छं संखेषेण निस्संदं दिहिवाददी Ibid., *Bhartiya Saṃskriti*, p. 50.
5. *Jain Sahitya ka Itihas*, 1, 325-51.
6. With Malayagiri's Commentary, *DLJP*, Bombay, 1912; with Malayagiri's and Yaśovijaya's Commentaries, *JDPS*, Bhavnagar, 1917; Malayagiri's and Yaśovijaya's Commentaries, ed. Padmavijayagaṇi, Ahmedabad, 1934; with *Cūrṇi* and Malayagiri's and Yaśovijaya's Com., Muktabai Jñāna-mandira, Dabhoi, 1937; with Original text, Sanskrit *chāyā*, and Gujarati

trans by Pandit Chandulal Nanchandra, Rajnagar, 1938; also Helmuth von Glasenapp, *The Doctrine of Karma in Jaina Philosophy*, Bombay, 1942; *JRK* has referred to eight works under the title.

7. For details see *JSBI*, IV, pp. 114-21.
8. Jain Atmananda Sabha, Bhavnagar, 1940, along with this is published Devendrasūri's *Śataka*, the 5th *Navya Karmagrantha* with its self-composed com.; Virasamaja Grantha-Ratnamala, Ahmedabad, 1922-3.
9. See Pandit Kailashchandra Siddhantashastri, *Jain Sahitya ka Itihas*, I, pp. 316-17.
10. With author's self-composed commentary, Jain Atmanand Sabha, 1927; with Malayagiri's Com. in 4 parts, Hiralal Hamsraj, Jamnagar, 1909 and onwards; with original text, Jain Atmanand Sabha, Bhavnagar, 1919; with self-composed com. and Malayagiri's Com., Muktabai Jñānamandir, Dabhoi, Pt. I, 1938, Pt. II, 1937; with original text, Sanskrit *chāyā* and with Gujarati trans. of the text and Malayagiri's Com., in 2 parts, Ahmedabad, Pt. I, 1935, Pt. II with *āmukha* of Muni Punyavijaya, 1941 (reproduced in the *Jñānānjali*, pp. 138-44); also Glasenapp, pp. xiii-xiv.
11. This information is given in Malayagiri's Com. on the *Pañcasaṃgraha* (*gāthā* 1).
12. These have been several works of the same title. We have already dealt with the *Pañcasaṃgraha* popular with the Digambaras; Amṛtacandra *ācārya* also is said to have written a work of the same title in Sanskrit. Pandit Kailashchandra Siddhantashastri has discussed the difference of opinion of the author with Digambara writers, 354-6.
13. ये पुन: सत्कर्माभिध-ग्रन्थकारादयस्ते क्षपकक्षीणमोहान् व्यत्रिरिच्य शेषाणामेव निद्राद्विकस्यो दयमिच्छन्ति। तथा च तद् ग्रन्थ:—'निछादुगस्स उदओ, खीण (ग) खवगे परिच्चज्जा'. . . . Dabhoi, ed., p. 116 after Muni Punyavijaya, *Āmukha* to *Pañcasaṃgraha*, Pt. II (Jain Karmasāhitya and 'Pañcasaṃgraha', *Jñānāñjali*, p. 142n).
14. . . ."ताते अणुओगो वोच्छिन्नो तो तं अजाणंतो आयरिओ जाणंतस्स नमोक्कारं करेति।"- कर्मप्रकृतिपूर्ण-उपशमनाकरणे॥
"अकरणकृतोपशमनाया नामधेय द्वयम्, तद्यथा-अकरणोपरशमना, अनुदीर्णशमना च। तस्याश्च सम्प्रत्यनुयोगो व्यवच्छिन्न:"। -मलयगिरि-टीका।
(b) "तत्र या करणरहिता तस्या व्याख्या नास्ति, तद्वेतृणामभावात्।" पंचसंग्रहे स्वोपज्ञ-टीका।
(c) ". . . ते च कर्मप्रकृतिप्राभृतादयो ग्रन्था न सम्प्रति वर्तन्ते इति लेशतोऽपि दर्शयितुं न शक्यन्ते. . . ." Malayagiri's Com. on *Saptatikā* (53), p. 241, ibid., *Jñānāñjali*, p. 139n.
15. The first four *Karmagranthas* (सकाश्चचार: प्राचीना: कर्मग्रन्था:) with Sanskrit Com. ed. by Muni Caturvijaya with his learned *Prastāvanā*, Jain Atmanand Sabha, vs 1972; the *Fifth Karmagrantha*, Virasamaja Grantharatnamala, Ahmedabad, 1922 and 1923; the *Sixth Karmagrantha*, *JDPS*, Bhavnagar, 1919; the *Fifth and the Sixth Karmagranthas*, ed. Muni Caturvijaya with *Prastāvanā* of Pt. I and Muni Punyavijaya's *Prastāvanā* under the title '*Karmagranthonu Sampādana*' (reproduced in the *Jñānāñjali*, pp. 145-57), Jain Atmanand Sabha Bhavnagar, 1940. This volume also contains a very important comparative study of Digambara and Śvetāmbara

works regarding *karma-siddhānt* (षट्कर्मग्रन्थान्तर्गत-विषय-तुल्यता-निदेशकानां दिगम्वरीयशास्त्र-मध्यवर्तिनां स्थलानां निर्देश:)

16. See *Gāthā* 90-1, etc., Muni Punyavijaya, *Prastāvanā* to the *Fifth and the Sixth Karmagrantha, Jñānāñjali*, p. 148, n. 3.
17. There is a mention of the *Kasāyapāhuḍa* in this *Cūrṇi*, Pandit Kailashchandra Siddhantashastri, p. 368.
18. See *JSBI*, IV, pp. 127-8.
19. Muni Caturvijaya in the *Prastāvanā* of the *Fifth Karmagrantha* has dealt with Devendrasūri and his *Five Navya Karmagranthas*.
20. The *First*, the *Second* and the *Fourth Karmagranthas* with auto-commentary by Devendrasūri and the *Third Karmagrantha* by other *ācāryas* along with *Avacūri*, ed. Munis Caturvijaya and Punyavijaya, *JDPS*, Bhavnagar, vs 1966-8; Muktikamala Jain Mohanamala, Baroda, vs 2447; Jain Atmanand Sabha, Bhavnagar, 1934; with auto-commentary the *Fifth Karmagrantha* and along with Candrarṣi Mahattara's *Saptatikā* Com., *JDPS*, Bhavnagar, 1919; ed. Munis Caturvijaya and Punyavijaya, Jain Atmanand Sabha, Bhavnagar, 1940. In this edition a comparative list of *gāthās* of the *Sixth Karmagranthas* and the works of the Digambaras regarding the *karma-siddhānta* is provided; also see Helmuth von Glasenapp, *The Doctrine of Karma*, Bombay, 1942; also H.R. Kapadia, *Karmasiddhānta-sambandhī Sāhitya*, Surat, 1965, Chapter 7, pp. 75-86.
21. *JSBI*, IV, pp. 132f.
22. Maladhāri Hemacandra, *Bṛhad-vṛtti*, *YJG*, Banaras, vs 2427-41; Gujarati trans., *AGS*, 1924-7; Index of *gāthās* and the subject matter, *AGS*, 1923; with Koṭyācārya's Com., *ṚKSS*, Ratlam, 1936-7 (in 2 pts.), here the number of the *Niryukti* and *Bhāṣya gāthās* combined is 4346 (4354); with *svopajña* Com., Pandit Dalsukh Malavania, Pts. I and II; Pt. III edited by Pandit Bechardas J. Doshi, *LDS*, Ahmedabad, 1966, 1968 (the number of *gāthās* is 4329). For a detailed account of the text see *JSBI*, III, pp. 138-201. The late Muni Punyavijaya was kind enough to show me a palm-leaf manuscript of the text, obtained from the Jaisalmer Bhandar.
23. The five sections are as follows: I: 1-1548, II: 1549-2024, III: 2025-2609, IV: 2610-2804, V: 2805-3603.
24. L. Alsdorf in 'Jain Exegetical Literature and the History of the Jaina Canon' has observed that the *Viśeṣāvaśyaka-Bh.* is a mere versification of the prose tradition represented by the *Āvaśyaka-Cūrṇi*, p. 5, *Mahavira and His Teachings*, Bombay, 1977.
25. Gujarati trans. by Pandit Dalsukh Malvania, Gujarat Vidyasabha, Ahmedabad, 1952. For English trans. see Śramaṇa Bhagavān Mahāvīra, ed. Muni Ratnaprabhavijaya; trans. Prof. Dhirubhai P. Thakar, Jain Grantha Prakashak Sabha, Ahmedabad, 1942; Shri Jain Siddhanta Society, Ahmedabad, 1950; also E.A. Solomon, *Gaṇadharavāda*, Prakrit text ed. and trans., Ahmedabad, 1966.

26. The *āgamas* admit the impossibility of the simultaneous occurrence of *jñāna* and *darśana*. For the views of Siddhasena Divākar, Akalaṅka, Vidyānandi, Haribhadra and Yaśovijaya, see Nathmal Tatia, *Studies in Jaina Philosophy*, pp. 70-80.
27. With Siddhasenasūri's *Tattvaprakasinī Vṛtti* by *DLJP*, in 2 pts., 1922 and 1926. Pt. 2 contains *upodghāta* in the beginning and various indexes at the end. Pt. I contains 771 *gāthās* divided into 103 *dvāras* and Pt. II the remaining *gāthās* and the *dvāras*.
28. They are mentioned as गंडि, कच्छवी मुट्ठी, संपुरफलक, and छेदपाटी in *Bṛh Bhā*, 3.3822, *LIA*, p. 231n.
29. See *Bṛh Bhā* (3.4097): दंडक, विदंडक, यष्टि, वियष्टि and नालिका.
30. See *Bṛh. Bhā* (3.3823): कोयव, पावारग, दाढिआलि, पूरिका and विरालिका, also see *LIA*, p. 176.
31. *Uggahaṇantiga (uggaha is yoni-dvāra), paṭṭa, addhoruga (urukārdha), calanikā* and *abbhintara-niyaṃsiṇī* are mentioned in *Bṛh Bhā* (3.4082-91 and Com.), also *LAI*, pp. 179f.
32. For contents in detail see *JSBI*, IV, pp. 175-8.
33. See Ibid., p. 179.
34. *AGS*, Bhavnagar, 1923.
35. For the list of such similar contents see the *upodghāta* of the second part of *Pravacanasāroddhāra*.
36. With Maladhāri Hemacandra's Com., *AGS*, Bhavnagar, 1927.
37. See *gāthās* 30, 36, 65 et al.; such types are not to be traced in available *āgamas*, *JSBI*, IV, p. 165.
38. *ṚKŚS*, Ratlam, 1927.
39. H.R. Kapadia, Govt. Collection of MSS, *BORI*, Vol. VII, Pt. IV, p. 158.
40. *ṚKŚS*, 1927; with original text and Sanskrit *chāyā*, trans. by Prof. K.V. Abhyankara, Ahmedabad, 1932.
41. With Dhaneśvarasūri's Com., *JDPS*, Bhavnagar, 1915.
42. See *JSBI*, IV, p. 191.
43. Jain Grantha Prakashaka Sabha, Rajnagar (Ahmedabad), vs 1917.
44. Kapadia, Cat. *BORI*, Vol. XVIII, Pt. 1, p. 252.
45. Ibid., pp. 271ff; *JSBI*, IV, pp. 183, 187, 191, 195, 224, 225.
46. Published, see Kapadia's *Paiyabhāsāo*, p. 162.
47. See *JRK*, p. 104.
48. Published in *Prakaraṇasamuccaya*, 25-8.
49. Ibid., 30-1.
50. See *Jain Granthavali*, p. 208.
51. In *Prakaraṇa-samuccaya*, pp. 38-40.
52. Ibid., pp. 22-5.
53. With Abhayadevasūri's Com., ed. Pandit Sukhalal and Pandit Bechardas, Puratattvamandira, Ahmedabad, vs 1980, 1982, 1984, 1985 and 1987; with Gujarati trans., *vivecana* and *prastāvanā*, Punjabhai Jain Granthamala, 1932; with English trans. and Introduction, Shvetambara Education Board, 1939; Pandit Dalsukh Malvania, *SJS*, 1939.

54. अछं मिच्छादंसण-समूह-मइअस्स अमयसारस्स।
जिण-वयणस्स भगवओ संविग्ग-सुहाइ-मग्गस्स॥ 3.69
55. जेण विणा लोगस्सवि ववहारो सव्वहा न निव्वडइ।
तस्स भुवणेक्कगुरूणो णमो अणेगंतवायस्स॥ 3.68
56. *DLJP* in 2 parts, 1916 and 1918.
57. See Chapter 5.
58. It contains 36 verses dealing with ritualism as to when the *Iriyāvahiya Sūtra* should be recited, *AGS*, 1927.
59. Atmananda Granthamala, Bhavnagar, vs 1968; included in *Prakaraṇa-ratnākara*, Pt. 2, pp. 720-36.
60. With a Sanskrit Com., ed. Darśanavijaya, under *Paṭṭāvali-samuccaya*, Pt. 1, Viramgam, 1933, pp. 41-77; Panyāsa Kalyanvijaya, Bhavnagar, 1940. This work was written in Ahmedabad in vs 1648 (AD 1591) under the patronage of Hiravijayasūri and others.
61. With a Sanskrit Com., written in AD 1615.
62. With a Sanskrit Com., written in AD 1628.
63. Written under the instruction of the teacher Jinadattasūri. It deals with various topics such as exclusion of women from worship of Jina, forbidding a woman to dance in a Jain temple, *māsa-kalpa-vihāra* (consideration of dwelling at one place for a month), *mālāropaṇa* (placing of garland), *paṭala-adhikāra*, propitiating Cāmuṇḍā and adoration of *pañcanadī* and so on.
64. Published by *ṚKŚS*, Ratlam, 1927.
65. Shri Jain Grantha Prakashaka Sabha, Rajnagar (Ahmedabad), vs 1997, along with *Bhāṣā-rahasya-prakaraṇa.*
66. *DLJP*, 1911.
67. See *JSBI*, IV, pp. 229f.
68. Indukalā H. Jhaveri, with Gujarati trans., explanation and Introduction, with six appendices, Gujarat Vidyasabha, Ahmedabad; edited by Punyavijaya, with self-composed com. together with the *Bṛahmasiddhānta-samuccaya, LDS*, 1965. It also contains the Sanskrit *Prastāvanā* by the editor, English introduction by Jhaveri, K.K. Dixit's English translation, and eight appendices.
69. Published with the *Āvassaya-Nijjutti* and the *Śiṣyahitā Ṭīkā* of Haribhadrasūri in 4 parts, *AGS*, Bombay, 1916-17; in the *Pūrvabhāga* (pp. 582a-611a) of the *Āvassaya-Nijjutti*, after 1271 *gāthās*, we come across these 105 *gāthās*; with the commentary of Haribhadrasūri and the *Ṭippaṇaka* of Maladhārī Hemacandra, Vinaya-bhakti-sundara-carana-granthamālā, vs 1997.
70. See *JSBI*, IV, pp. 250f.
71. Ibid.
72. Ed. K.P. Modi with Sanskrit *chāyā*, *Jñānaprasāraka-maṇḍala*, Bombay, vs 1961.
73. See *JSBI*, IV, p. 271.

74. Atmanand Jain Sabha, Bhavnagar, 1924.
75. With *Tattvakaumidī* published in *DLJP*, 1913.
76. See *JSBI*, IV, pp. 219f.
77. With self-composed com. published in *Hemacandracarya Granthavali*, Patan, vs 1984.
78. With Jinapāla's *Ṭīkā* in Jinadattasūri Prachina Pustakoddhara Fund, Bombay, 1934.
79. *ṚKŚS*, Ratlam, 1927.
80. Kapadia, *DCGCM*, Vol. VII, Pt. IV, p. 99; *JSBI*, IV, p. 281.
81. Several editions are published: Bhimsi Manek in the *Pratikramaṇasūtra* (pp. 384-431) with Gujarati trans.; *Bālāvabodha* in the *Caitya-vandana-bhāṣya-traya* (pp. 1-105) by Venichand Surchand, Mehsana, 1906; *JDPS*, Bhavnagar, vs 1977; along with the *Saṅghācāravidhi* by *ṚKŚS*, 1938.
82. With text and com. and Upādhyāya Labhi (Labdhi)gaṇi Sūri's *Tippaṇikā* on this com., Shri Jinadattasūri Prachina Pustakoddhara Fund, 1920.
83. With Gujarati *Bālāvabodha* by Bhimsimha Manek in his edition of *Shri Pratikra-maṇusūtra* (pp. 431-66), AD 1888; with Gujarati explanation by Venichand Surchand, Mehsana, 1906. The edition is styled as *Shri Caityavandanādi-bhāṣya-trayaṃ* on pp. 106-9; *JDPS*, Bhavnagar, vs 1969.
84. With Gujarati *Bālāvabodha* of Ānandavallabha, 1876.
85. With auto-commentary by Jain Atmanand Sabha, Bhavnagar, vs 1974; with text and Gujarati translation of *Vividhakaumudī Ṭīkā* by *DLJP*, 1952.
86. Balubhai Khushal Bhai, Ahmedabad (year not given).
87. Published with Mallagirisūri's Sanskrit Com., Jain Atmanand Sabha, vs 1972.
88. *ṚKŚS*, Ratlam, 1927.
89. Published in the *Prakaraṇasamuccaya* (pp. 41-3).
90. Ibid., pp. 34-6.
91. *Prakaraṇasamuccaya* (pp. 31-3).
92. Jain Grantha Prakashak Sabha, Ahmedabad, vs 1953.
93. Hamsvijayaji Free Library, Ahmedabad, 1924 (with Udayasiṃha's *vṛtti* and Sanskrit *chāyā*).
94. *JSBI*, IV, p. 205.
95. With Mānadevasūri's Com. under the title '*Shri Śrāvaka-dharma-vidhi-prakaraṇa*', Kesharbai Jain Jñānamandira, 1940.
96. *ṚKŚS*, Surat, 1936.
97. *DLJP*, 1912.
98. Atmanand Jain Sabha, Bhavnagar, vs 1969.
99. *JSBI*, IV, p. 220.
100. With Amarakīrtiśūri's Com., Hiralal Hamsraj, 1911 (contains 76 *gāthās*);

with Guṇavinaya's Com., Jain Atmanand Sabha, vs 1972.

101. सेयंबरो य आसंबरो य बुद्धो व अहव अन्नो वा।
समभाव-भावियप्पा लहेय मुक्खं न संदेहो॥

102. Hemacandrācārya Sabha, Ahmedabad, 1922. Yet another work under the same title is written by Jinamaṇḍanagaṇi, the author of the *Kumārapāla-prabandha* (in vs 1492).

103. Jinadattasūri Prachina Pustakoddhara Fund, Surat, 1933.

104. *DLJP*, 1941.

105. Ibid.

106. With com. by Guṇavinaya, published with Gujarati exposition in the *Prakaraṇaratnākara* (Vol. IV, pp. 1-21) by Bhimsi Manek, Bombay, 1912.

107. Harshasūri Jain Granthamala, Bhavnagar, vs 2006.

108. *JDPS*, Bhavnagar, vs 1984.

109. Incorporated in *Shri Pratikramaṇasūtra* by Bhimsiṃha Manek, 1888, with Sanskrit rendering and Gujarati trans. in *Pañcapratikramaṇasūtrāṇi*, pp. 423-31; Shri Jain Shreyaskara Mandala, Mehsana, 1915.

110. H.R. Kapadia does not agree, *JSBI*, IV, p. 166.

111. Ibid., pp. 166f.

112. With Abhayadevasūri's *Bhāṣya*, Atmanand Jain Sabha, vs 1969; with Dharmavijaya's *Ṭīkā*, Muktikamala Jain Mohanamala, Bhavnagar, 1934.

113. See *JSBI*, IV, p. 182.

114. With auto-commentary, *DLJP*, 1926; with Yaśodeva's *Vivaraṇa*, 1927.

115. See *JSBI*, IV, pp. 275f.

116. Under the title of *Daṇḍaka-prakaraṇa*, with Gujarati explanation, etc., Granthaprakashaka Sabha, 1935; the latter part contains *Svopajña Avacūrṇi* and Rupacandra's Sanskrit *vṛtti*.

117. See *JSBI*, IV, p. 174.

118. With Prabhānandasūri's *vṛtti*, *JDPS*, Bhavnagar, 1915.

119. *JSBI*, IV, p. 171.

120. Under the title '*Bṛhat-saṃgrahiṇī*' with Malayagiri's *vivṛti*, Atmanand Jain Sabha, Bhavnagar, vs 1973; *Shri Bṛhat-saṃgrahaṇī* along with Malayagiri's *vivṛti* and its Gujarati trans., *JDPS*, vs 1991.

121. With Devabhadrasūri's Commentary, *DLJP*, 1915 (contains only 273 *gāthās*); with Sanskrit *chāyā* and with Muni Yaśovijaya's Gujarati explanation, etc., Muktikamala Jain Mohanamala, 1939 (contains 349 *gāthās*).

122. See *JSBI*, IV, p. 173.

123. With Malayagiri's *Ṭīkā*, under the title '*Bṛhatkṣetrasamāsa*', *JDPS*, Bhavnagar, vs 1977. *The New Catalogus Catalogorumm*, Vol. V (by V. Raghavan), pp. 158-60 has mentioned as many as 23 works with the same or a similar title, *CJMS*, Sr. 133, p. 192.

124. *JSBI*, IV, p. 169.

125. With auto-commentary in Atmanand Jain Sabha, vs 1972; with Gujarati explanation, Muktikamala Jain Mohanamala, vs 1990.
126. *JSBI*, IV, p. 170.
127. Atmanand Jain Sabha, Bhavnagar, vs 1971; with Gujarati trans. in *Prakaranaratṇa-saṃgraha*, Pt. 3, *JDPS*, Bhavnagar, vs 1998.
128. With Abhayadevasūri's *vṛtti*, *JDPS*, 1912; with Yaśodevasūri's *Cūrṇi* with five appendices, *DLJP*, 1952.
129. With Devavijaya's Com., *AGS*, vs 1975; with Ṛddhisagarasūri's *chāyā* and Gujarati trans., Buddhisāgarasūri Jain Jñānamandira, Bijapur, vs 1990.
130. Published by Muni Caturvijaya (pupil of 'Dakṣiṇa-vihārī' Amaravijaya), Sinor: Khimcand Phulcand, 1924, Kapadia, *DCGCM*, 18.1, p. 469; *CJMS*, Sr. 148, pp. 207f.
131. The different MSS contain different number of *gāthās*, *CJMS*, op. cit.
132. Kapadia, *DCGCM*, p. 465.
133. *JDPS*, Rajnagar (Ahmedabad), vs 1997.
134. With auto-commentary, *DLJP*, 1916; with text and Gujarati explanation, Sarabhai Jaisinghbhai, vs 2013; with trans. of auto-commentary, *JDPS*, vs 1989; with Hindi explanation, Shri Atma-Tilak Grantha Society, vs 1975.
135. Jain Grantha Prakashaka Sabha, Ahmedabad, vs 2010.
136. Published by Atmanand Jain Granthamala, Bhavnagar, vs 1970.
137. Shri Jain Atmanand Granthamala, vs 1968; also in the *Prakaraṇa-ratnākara*, Pt. 2, pp. 720-36.
138. See *JSBI*, IV, p. 187.
139. With Gujarati trans., Mahavir Jain Sabha, Khambat, 1918.
140. See *JSBI*, IV, p. 183.
141. With *Avacūri*, Jain Atmananda Sabha, Bhavnagar, vs 1974.
142. With Jinapāla's Com., Jinadattasūri Prachina Pustakoddhara Fund, Surat, 1933.
143. *JSBI*, IV, pp. 183-4.
144. See *Jain Granthavali*, Shri Jain Shvetambara Conference, Mumbai, pp. 155-7.
145. See *Jain Granthavali*, pp. 155-7.
146. Published as *Sāmācārī-prakaraṇa* (*Yogaviśeṣa-vākya-yutaṃ*), *AGS*, 1919.
147. Often published for instance in *Ṣaḍavaśyaka-sūtrāṇi*, *ṚKŚS*, Ratlam, vs 1992, pp. 20-2, *CJMS*, Sr. 59, p. 119.
148. Dahyabhai Mokamchand, Ahmedabad, vs 1990.
149. *DLJP*, 1924.
150. With Matisāgarasūri's *Vyākhyā*, *ṚKŚS*, Ratlam, 1936, also *JSBI*, IV, p. 287.
151. With Gujarati trans. Jain Atmananda Sabha, vs 1970; with Gujarati explanation based on Haribhadra's Com. by Bhanuvijaya Muni, Vijayadāna-sārīśvara Granthamala, vs 2007; A.N. Upadhye with

Introduction in English, Kolhapur, 1934; see *JSBI*, IV, pp. 268-9; *CJMS*, Sr. 147, pp. 206-7.

152. See *JSBI*, Vol. IV, p. 269.
153. With an unknown author's *Avacūri*, Jain Atmanand Sabha, vs 1974.
154. *DCGCM*, XVIII, 1952, p. 280.
155. Ibid., VII, 4, p. 151.
156. With *svopajña Ṭīkā*, *DLJP*, 1932.
157. *JDPS*, 1916.
158. *JSBI*, IV, p. 220.
159. Atmananda Jain Sabha, Bhavnagar, 1925.
160. *JDPS*, Bhavnagar, vs 1965.
161. Ed. Muni Jinavijaya, *NP*, Bombay, 1941.
162. See Jain Granthavali, pp. 148-54.
163. Ed. Muni Jinavijaya, *SJS*, 1934.
164. For the alphabetical list of these places, see *JSBI*, IV, pp. 322-3.
165. It is Sahitamahakā in the *Aṅgavijjā*; identified with Sahet-Mahet, situated on the bank of Rapti.
166. *JSBI*, IV, p. 319.
167. Ibid.
168. With Gujarati translation, published in Appendix 2 of the '*Bhaktāmarastotrani Pādapūrtirūpakāvyasaṃgraha* (Pt. 1), 1926, ibid., p. 320.
169. Bhimsi Maneka, incorporated in the *Vidhi-pakṣa-pratikramaṇa*, *JSBI*, IV, p. 324.
170. Edited or extracted by J. Klatt, *Ind. Ant.* 11, 245ff; 293f; 23, 169ff; Hoernle, *Ind. Ant.*, 19, 233f; 20, 341ff; 21, 57ff (it also contained the Digambara Paṭṭāvali).
171. See Phyllis Granoff, 'The Biographies of Siddhasena', *Journal of Indian Philosophy*, 17: 329-84, 1989; Muni Uttam Kamal Jain, *Jaina Sects and Schools*, Delhi, Concept Publishing Company, 1978.
172. *YJG*, Varanasi, *Vīr Saṃ.* 2437.
173. See *CJMS*, Sr. 237, p. 300. Published, Pannyāsa Kalyanvijayaji, Bhavnagar, 1940.
174. Jamnagar, *Vīr Saṃ.* 2455.
175. Ibid., 240. p. 302.
176. Ibid., Sr. 241, pp. 302f.
177. Ibid., Sr. 242, p. 303.
178. Ibid, Sr. 234, p. 295.
179. By K.C. Kaslival, *CJMS*, Sr. 242, p. 304.
180. Registered by J. Mukhtar, *PJVS*, Intr., pp. 115-16, *CJMS*, op. cit.
181. Ed. Hoernle, *Ind. Ant.*, 20, 1891, *CJMS*, op. cit. See Guérinot, *Essai de Bibliographie Jaina*, Paris (1906), pp. 379-82, Nos. 661-2. For Padmanandin in verses 34-5, see Johrapurkar, *Bhaṭṭāraka Sampradāya*, Solapur (1958), pp. 95-6 ff.
182. See G. Bühler, *Life of Hemacandra*, pp. 3f.

183. Incorporated in the *Purātana-prabandha-saṅgrah*, ed. Muni Jinavijaya, *SJS*, 1936.
184. Ed. Pandit Harinanda Sharma, *NSP*, Bombay, 1909; Muni Jinavijaya, *SJS*, 1940.
185. Ed. Rāmcandra Dīnānātha, Bombay, 1888; translated into English by C.H. Tawney, Bibl. Ind. 1901; Muni Jinavijaya, *SJS*, 1933. Merutuṅga is not reliable even in passages where he is apparently stating exact dates, Winternitz, *A History*, II, p. 520n.
186. Ed. Jinavijaya, *SJS*, 1935; edited and translated in Gujarati by H.R. Kapadia; Bombay Forbes Guj. Sabha Granthamala (12, 1932) and 18, 1934 respectively.
187. They are: 1 भद्रबाहु-बराह-प्रबन्ध, 2 आर्य-नन्दिक प्रबन्ध, 3 जीवदेव-सूरि-प्रबन्ध, 4 आर्य खपटाचार्य, 5 पादलिप्त, 6 वृद्धवादिसिद्धसेन-सूरि, 7 मल्लवादिसूरि, 8 हरिभद्र सूरि, 9 वप्पयहिसूरि, 10 हेमचन्द्रसूरि, 11 हर्षकवि, 12 हरिहरकवि, 13 अमरचन्द्रकवि, 14 मदनकीर्तिकवि, 15 सातवाहन, 16 वंकचूल, 17 विकुमादित्य, 18 नागार्जुन, 19 वत्सराज-उदयन, 20 लक्ष्मणसेन-कुमारसेन, 21 मदनवर्गा, 22 रत्नश्रावक, 23 अभदश्रावक, 24 वस्तुपाल-तेजपाल.

5

Poetic Composition in Prakrit

Poetic composition has an important place in Prakrit literature. As we have seen, Prakrit poetic literature was generally confined to religious sermons, narrative tales and biographies of great men, but in course of time numerous fascinating poetic compositions were brought out in this language.

According to Daṇḍin (AD 660-89), one of the reputed rhetoricians representing the early school of poetics, every poem necessarily consists of a body (*śarīra*) and embellishments (*alaṃkāra*). By the body of poem is understood the set of words put in a sentence (*padāvalī*) so as to convey the desired sense (*iṣṭārha-vyavacchinnā*).[1] This set of words may consist of verse, prose or both. In his *Kāvyādarśa* Daṇḍin is more preoccupied with the *alaṃkāra* than the body of poetry. He defines *alaṃkāras* as attributes that lend glitter to poetry.[2] They are divided into *arthālaṃkāra* (embellishments of meaning) and *śabdālaṃkāra* (embellishments of sound). The former comprises natural description, the simile (*upamā*) and the metaphor (*rūpaka*). The latter is restrained to a figure of speech depending on its pleasingness on sounds or words such as the *yamaka* and *anuprāsa*, etc.

Further, enumerating various kinds of verse, Daṇḍin deals with *sargabandha* (a poem or composition divided into sections or chapters) or *Mahākāvya*, which should consist of descriptions of the town, sea, mountain, seasons, rising of the moon and the sun, sports in pleasure-gardens or in tanks, banquets, love-scenes, feasts, marriages and the birth of a son. The epic should be embellished and elaborate; it should be permeated with *rasa* (sentiment), along with its corresponding *bhāva* (emotion). It should consist of numerous *sargas* (cantos), not too long, composed in sonorous verses.[3]

Bhāmaha (AD 700-50), another reputed rhetorician, refuting the idea that one can become a poet only through mastery of rhetoric, lays emphasis on poetic genius (*pratibhā*).[4] He compares an *a-kavi* (who is not a poet), though he possesses the knowledge of sciences, with a beggar who shows generosity, with a coward who exhibits bravery and a man of no-letters (*ajñāna*) who displays proficiency in art.[5] He holds that as there is no charm without grace and no night without moon, so there is no skill in speech without poetic gift.[6] However, he considers both words (*ṣabda*) and meaning (*artha*) essential for poetry; both losing their identity to become one.[7]

Vāmana (*c* 800) considers style (*rīti*) the soul of poetry.[8] Since according to him, style is the soul of poetry and *śabda* and *artha* are just its body, he differs from Daṇḍin and Bhāmaha. In his *Kāvyālaṃkāra* (with his own commentary) he deals with aesthetics and the rules of prosody and grammar. Vāmana gives a list of qualities expected from a poet: he must have worldly knowledge, understand what is possible or not; be a master of grammar and know the lexicon and the correct meaning of the word; he must study metrics; must be expert in the arts of singing, dancing and painting; he must study the *Kāmaśāstra* (the Science of Love) so that he is aware of the usage of love.[9]

LYRIC POETRY (*MUKTAKA*)

Muktaka or lyric poetry differs from *prabandha-kāvya* or narrative poetry.[10] In the latter the episodes are knit together in an continuous manner, carrying the narrative further. Such is not the case with the lyric poetry. *Muktaka* means detached, separate or independent. It is a detached *śloka*, the meaning of which is complete in itself.[11] The name of Ānandavardhana (AD 850-75), the author of the *Dhvānyāloka* and its commentary, is of great significance here. He has propounded the doctrine of *dhvani* or suggested meaning in rhetorics. While defining *kāvya*, he says that poetry is the best in which the implied or suggested sense of a passage (*pratiyamāna*) is more striking than the expressed sense (*vācya*); or where the expressed sense is subordinate to the suggested sense (*vyaṅgya*).[12] The *vācya* sense in the form of figures of speech is well-known; the *pratīyamāna* is like personal charm of beautiful ladies, which is different from the body and limbs. The latter is not understood by those who merely know grammar and lexicon but only by those who know the essence of poetry (see *Dhvanyāloka*, I.3-4,) To elaborate, the author has submitted: 'in the refined society of cultured people it is a settled practice that one does not speak out what lies in one's inmost heart in a straightforward manner, instead, one should convey it in the form of a suggestion'.[13] Here we find the conception of lyric poetry is based on the principle of *dhvani.* A *muktaka* is a highly poetic composition, conveying a complete idea or situation in its most salient details, not connected with the preceding or following stanzas. It is confined to one metre, sparks vitality and is capable of causing astonishment. It is a small composition, in a few select words, creating a profound impression on the mind of the reader, who is expected to appreciate poetry. Ānandavardhana has stated: a good poetical composition is endowed with two-fold meanings: the spoken one, what is expressed by words and decorated with *alaṃkāra,* and the unspoken one, which is not expressed but inferred by the reader. The latter which is called *dhvani* is the real soul of poetry according to him. Emotion (*bhāva*) and sentiment (*rasa*) belong to the unspoken poetical composition. The *alaṃkāras* and other poetical figures become so much more impressive that they allow the implied meaning only to be hinted at or guessed 'in the same way as the bodice covers the breast and thereby lends it greater charm'.[14] Later Kuntaka (AD 950-1000) proposed the doctrine of *vakrokti* (indirect mode of expression) which has been much influenced by the theory of *dhvani,* though he denies the independent existence of *dhvani* or *vyaṅgya* as the soul of poetry. The principles of *vakrokti* or figurative speech based on witty turnings are laid by Kuntaka in his *Vakroktijīvita* are based on the *Dhvanyāloka* of Ānandavardhana. According to him, it is a striking mode of speech differing from and transcending the ordinary everyday mode of speaking about a thing; it is speech that charms by the skill of the poet (*vaidagdhya-bhaṇiti*).[15] In the opinion of Kuntaka, *vakrokti* is the soul of poetry, it breathes life into poetry and without it *kāvya* or poetry cannot exist. He emphasizes on the poet's necessary fancy and imagination or poet's own genius which he calls *kavi-vyāpara.*[16] Kuntaka gives prominence to the aesthetic pleasure that a man of taste (*sahṛdaya*) enjoys from poetry.

Muktaka poetry is divided into four categories by Daṇḍin in his *Kāvyaprakāśa* (1.13): *muktaka* (single verse), *kulaka* (groups of five verses), *kośa* (unconnected verses by different authors) and *saṅghāta* (verses similar by one author).[17]

PRAKRIT LYRIC POETRY

The *Gāhāsattaśaī* and the *Vajjālagga* in Prakrit, the *Amaruśataka,* the *Āryāsaptaśatī* and the *Bhartṛhariśataka* in Sanskrit and the *Bihārīsatasaī,* the *Nītiśataka* and the *Bhāvapañcāśikā* in Hindi can be cited as examples of lyric poetry.

According to Winternitz, 'the oldest love-songs were not composed in Sanskrit but in the vernacular languages, and it is on this account that the major portion of the Indian lyric poetry belongs to Prakrit literature'.[18] The simple Āryā metre, also known as *Gāthā*, a special metre employed in Prakrit lyric poetry for melodious songs, according to H. Jacobi, appears to have primarily belonged to Prakrit poetry and only later to have been taken into Sanskrit.[19]

Since Prakrit had been a dialect of the masses, it was supposed to have a better emotional appeal than Sanskrit. Ratnadeva, the commentator (commentary in AD 1336) of *Vajjālagga*, a well-known Prakrit anthology by Jayavallabha, has stated in his introductory remarks: 'Although the author is well-versed in Sanskrit, knowing that the people in general are erotic minded, he has written the present anthology of Prakrit verses.'[20] According to Jayavallabha, Prakrit verses have varied emotional appeal.[21] Moreover, as Prakrit is a dialect spoken by common people, it surpasses Sanskrit; it is within their reach.[22] The Prakrit poetry has been described as 'charming, full of melodious words, dear to the heart of young ladies and characterized with erotic sentiments. . . .' '. . . if that is true, who would like to read Sanskrit?' asks the author.[23] Comparing Prakrit lyric poetry with nectar, he has asserted that if one does not know how to read and listen to Prakrit poetry, he should feel ashamed of talking love.[24] The author has compared Prakrit poetry with the heart of woman; both are subtle and mystical, they cannot be appreciated by those who are devoid of literary taste (or devoid of emotional excitement) just as wealth cannot be procured by those who are devoid of meritorious deeds.[25]

As already noted, the great rhetorician Daṇḍin has declared Prakrit (Mahārāṣṭrī) the most elegant dialect with a jewel-mine of beautiful sayings.[26] It is to be specifically noted that the well-known authors of rhetorics, in order to illustrate the examples of *guṇa, doṣa, alaṃkāra, bhāva, rasa, vyañjanā, rati, nāyikā* and so on in their works, do not draw from Sanskrit poetic, but prefer citing Prakrit verses from well-known works like the *Gāhāsattasaī*, the *Setubandha*, the *Vajjālagga* and others.[27] Some of the Prakrit works were composed by these very rhetoricians.[28] Ānandavardhana, the propounder of the *dhvani* theory, selects for the *Dhvanyāloka* examples of suggested meaning, irony, etc., from the *Gāhāsattasaī* and other Sanskrit works only. Abhinavagupta, the author of the *Locana*, an elaborate commentary on the *Dhvanyāloka*, quotes numerous Prakrit verses from these works also. Ānandavardhana, writing about *muktaka* poetry in his commentary on the *Dhvanyāloka* (II.7, p. 142; also see Abhinavagupta's commentary) has also quoted lyrical verses from the *Amaruśataka* of Amaru, the most famous Indian lyric poet, with the remark that each of these stanzas convey so much sentiment that it appears like a great independent work in miniature. And it need not to be stated that this well-known work of Amaru has been greatly influenced by Prakrit lyrical poetry. Govardhana (eleventh century), a court poet of Lakṣamaṇasena of Bengal and contemporary of Jayadeva, is of the opinion that only Prakrit compositions can be expressive of poetical sentiments. In his *Āryāsaptaśatī* which takes as its model the Prakrit *Gāhāsattasaī* of Hāla, he has stated: 'He has for the first time carried over to Sanskrit by force the type of poetry that usually found elegant expression in Prakrit, in the same manner as Balarāma raised up into the sky the river Yamunā, of which the water was suitable for a lower plain.'[29] Then we come to King Bhojarāja (eleventh century) of Dhārā, who holds that there is only one sentiment, namely the erotic, which is dominant in poetry. His *Sarasvatīkaṇṭhābharaṇa* is a compilatory work of great dimension. It is divided into five chapters. Here he deals with 24 *śabdālaṃkāras*, 24 *arthālṃakāras*, 24 varieties of *śabdopamā* and 24 varieties of *arthopamā, rasas, bhāvas,* the nature of heroes and heroines and so on. His other important work is the *Śṛṅgāraprakāśa* which is a voluminous treatise, larger than any other work on Sanskrit poetics. It refers to the female author Vikaṭanitambā along with the Śākalya, Vāguri and others. Though generally he speaks of eight *rasas*, he lays special emphasis on *śṛṅgāra*, as already stated. In order to illustrate the examples of *guṇa, doṣa, rasa, vyañjanā, alaṃkāra*, etc., he has quoted 1650 verses from the *Gāhāsattasaī*, the *Rāvaṇavaho*, the *Gaṇḍavaho* (or *Setūbandha*), the *Harivijaya*, the *Mārīcavadha*, the *Rāvaṇavijaya* and other Prakrit compositions; 350 Prakrit verses have been quoted in the *Sarasvatīkaṇṭhābharaṇa* alone.

As stated due to its tenderness, grace, elegance, love and charm the Mahārāṣṭrī Prakrit was considered best for Prakrit lyrical poetry. Another advantage of composing poetry in this dialect was that it could be modified phonetically, i.e. the consonants could be dropped and the remaining letters could assume delicate forms, more suitable for poetical—musical—purposes.

GĀHĀSATTASAĪ

Gāhāsattasaī (*Gāthāsaptaśatī*), also known as *Gāhākosa*, is a collection of 700 Prakrit erotic verses par excellence. It appears that at that time, Prakrit rather than Sanskrit was the language of poetry in the south. This work has undergone various recensions and it is said that 430 stanzas are common to all the recensions. Compositions of eminent poets were added from time to time to this great work of Prakrit anthology until the eighth century, and in about the ninth century, it was known as the *Gāhāsattasaī* instead of *Kośa*.[30] As stated by Sushilkumar De in his *Treatment of Love in Sanskrit Literature* (p. 25): 'It is almost impossible to give an adequate idea of the extraordinary variety and elegance of the 700 poems collected together by Hāla, the majority of which are erotic in theme. They consist of isolated stanzas without any inner connection but each of itself has a finished form and a charm of its own.' This work contains the best selected lyrical poems, independent, unconnected with each other, full of meaning, abounding in suggestive or figurative speech (*vyañjanā*) rather than in *lakṣaṇā* (indicative or secondary significance of the word) and *abhidhā* (expressed meaning of the word's denotation), with depth of emotional feelings. It is not a small wonder that Prakrit poetic composition had reached such a peak in about the first or the second century AD.

Sātavāhana (Śālivāhana) which was a dynastic title derived from the name of an earlier king and used by many subsequent rulers in that family or Hāla (a shortened Prakrit form of Sātavāhana), who had been ruling at Pratiṣṭhāna in the first or second century AD, is known as the compiler of the *Gāhāsattasaī*. According to the *Sarasvatīkaṇṭhābharaṇa* (2.15) of Bhoja, as King Vikramāditya was an advocate of Sanskrit so was King Sātavāhana or Śālivāhana of Prakrit. Supporting this view in his *Kāvyamīmāṃsā* (10, p. 50) poet Rājaśekhara has stated that the king used to have conversations with the queens of his inner apartment only in Prakrit.[31] Bāṇabhatta, Udyotanasūri, Govardhana, Rudraṭa, Mammaṭa, Vāgbhaṭa, Viśvanātha and others have offered profound appreciation for this Prakrit anthology. Bāṇabhaṭṭa in his *Harṣacarita* (verse 14) has stated, 'Sātavāhana (Hāla) with his beautiful songs composed in 101 faultless metres has built up an imperishable charming store as (a king, an inexhaustible treasure, not collected from villages—*agrāmya*) with diamonds (of unadulterated purity)'.[32] Here Bāṇabhaṭṭa has called Sātavāhana a compiler of jewels of pithy sayings (*subhāṣita-ratna*). However, it appears that Sātavāhana was not merely a compiler, but a poetically gifted redactor, who made an excellent selection of the stanzas with dexterity and skill, including several of his own. It has been stated: 'out of a crore of embellished stanzas, Hāla, the friend of poets, has made the collection of 700 beautiful verses (provided with *alaṃkāras*)'.[33]

Since *Gāhāsattasaī* is a compilation, we find in it the names of several poets, men and women. Among male poets, we have Rairāa (Ratirāja), Miaṅga (Mṛgāṅka), Hāla, Pavarasena (Pravarasena), Kesava (Keśava), Guṇāḍhya, Aṇiruddha (Aniruddha), Maaranda (Makaraṇda), Kumārila, Candasāmi (Candrasvāmin), Avantivamma (Avantivarman), Hariuḍḍha[34] (Harivṛddha), Nandiuḍḍh (Nandivṛddha), Poṭṭisa,[35] Candahatthi (Candrahastin), Pālita (Pādalipta),[36] Vallaha (Vallabha), Māhavaseṇa (Mādhavasena), Īsāṇa (Īśāna), Mattagainda (Mattagajendra), Visamaseṇa (Viṣamasena), Bhoja, Siridhamma (Śrīdharma), Naravāhaṇa (Naravāhana), Dāmoara (Dāmodara), Mallaseṇa (Mallasena), Tiloaṇa (Trilocana)[37] and so on. Among female poets, mention is made of Revā, Sasippahā (Śaśiprabhā), Rohā, Girisutā, Guṇamugdhā and others.

Sushilkumar De has referred to Vikaṭanitambā[38] along with Vijjā or Vijjakā[39] and Śilābhaṭṭārikā.[40] He has also quoted verses from Bhāvakadevī, Mārulā and Indulekhā in his *Treatment of Love in Sanskrit Literature.*[41]

The popularity of the love songs of this anthology is revealed by the fact that it had at least six versions and eighteen commentaries. Jain authors also have commented on this work. Mathuranatha Shastri's commentary titled *Vyaṅgyasarvaṅkaṣā* is well known; here in the introduction, the commentator has compared the verses of the *Gāhāsattasaī* with the *dohās* of *Bihārī Satasaī.* In this anthology of Prakrit love-lyrics the feelings that are most tender and sensuous are frankly expressed in female voice. Here we come across young passionate women, who are one's own (*svakīyā*) or another's (*anyā*); they are 'damsels', who are not yet married, who are bashful and arrived at the age of puberty they are fond of festivals and similar occasion of amusement and some are a disgrace to their family and destitute of modesty. The women are either chaste, virtuous and faithful or else unrestrained (*svairiṇī*), faithless mistresses and courtesans. They talk about landscapes, rain, clouds, peacock dancing, water springs, the Vindhya mountain, the Sahyādri, the Narmadā and the Golā (Godāvarī), which indicates the locality of the composition of most of the verses. The anthology is a rich collection of maxims and popular sayings and throws good deal of light on popular customs and conventions of contemporary society. On the whole the poems centre on separation and parting, about grievances and resentment and above all supreme love—all depicted in a poetic and artistic manner.

It is said that after Kālidāsa there is hardly any poet who is esteemed by Indian poeticians as Amaru. Like the stanzas of the *Gāhāsattasaī* the lyric stanzas of the *Amaruśataka* are called 'miniature paintings' from amorous life. Such depiction of the theme of love in one hundred verses is not an easy task. The common feature of the *Sattasaī* and the *Amaruśataka* is that every individual stanza is a solitary self-standing complete poem, depicting some phase of emotion. It is no wonder if this composition of poet Amaru has been influenced by the immortal work of Hāla.

Hāla's *Gāhāsattasaī*, Amaru's *Amaruśataka* and Govardhana's *Āryāsaptasātī* are the most important lyrical works, depicting tender and delicate sentiments of love in Prakrit and Sanskrit. These works have exercised considerable influence on later poets. In this connection the name of the seventeenth-century Hindi poet Biharilal is worth mentioning. He has composed his *Bihārī Satasaī* in 700 stanzas in Braj dialect. Many of his stanzas are based on the *Gāhāsattasaī* of Hāla.[42] Admiring his poetic skill, George Grierson has stated: 'His verses show the charm and elegance of language, on account of which Kalidasa would have envied him.'[43]

The *Gāhāsattasaī* or *Gāhākosa* has undergone several editions in India and foreign countries. A. Weber had published its 370 verses and in *E. Über das Saptaśatakaṃ des Hāla*, Leipzig, 1870. He also published the complete text in 1881 from Leipzig; he translated them into German. Metrical translation was made by H. Brunhofer in *Über den Geist der Indischen Lyrik*, Leipzig, 1882, and G. Meyer in *Essays und Studien*, Strassburg, 1885. Adolf Wilbrand first published 32 stanzas in the *Neuen Freien Presse*, Vienna, 1899, and later 62 stanzas in *Westermanns Illustrierten Monatschriften*, 1900.[44] Among Indian editions are those of Durgaprasad and Kashinath Pandurang Parab, with the commentary of Gangadhar Bhatt, *KM* 21, Bombay, 1889, 2nd edn., 1911, 3rd edn., Bombay 1933; Mathuranath Shastri with his *Sarvaṅkaṣā* commentary in Sanskrit; Jagdishlal Shastri, the *Śatakas* IV-VII with *Hāritāmrapītāmbara*'s commentary, Lahore, 1942; Joglekar, text with elaborate introduction and Marathi translation, Poona,

1956; edited by A.N. Upadhye, *ABORI*, Poona, Vol. 11, No. 4, June 1962, pp. 385-402; M.V. Patwardhan, *Hāla's Gāhākosa*, Pt. I, Prakrit Text Society, 1980; Pt. II, Delhi, 1988.

It is not easy to render these lyrical stanzas, which abound in intense emotion within very restricted limits, into English. A.B. Keith has drawn our attention to this fact, saying, 'the effect on the mind is that of a perfect whole in which the parts coalesce by inner necessity, and the impression thus created on the mind cannot be produced in an analytical speech like English, in which it is necessary to convey the same content not in a single sentence but in a series of loosely connected predications'.[45]

Here we give a few selected *gāthās* (stanzas) where a sentiment is expressed in a few words, pregnant with ideas, saturated with intense emotion.

No suffering is called worse than the separation of lover and beloved, when for instance the lover goes away. A woman whose husband has gone far away from home, suffers from mental distress, generated by love, is known as *proṣita-patikā* in Sanskrit literature.[46] A lover's state of mind, when he is making preparations to go abroad, is depicted in the following manner: 'He is staring at the four directions, he has started breathing fast, yawning, singing, crying, losing consciousness, falling down and laughing.' Seeing this state of mind of his, somebody questioned, 'O traveler, what use is there of undertaking your journey when you feel so upset even now?'[47] And what about the beloved? Her friends are trying to console her asking her to stop weeping. But her reply is 'O dear friend, only today, do not stop me from weeping. After his departure, tomorrow morning, if I do not die, I shall weep no more.'[48] The heroine tried to reach her husband by writing a letter, but she was unable to hold the pen even to write the word '*svasti*' (used in expressing one's approbation in the beginning of letters), let alone write the letter. The heroine is narrating her state of mind to a friend, saying: 'The writing pen, being held in wavering perspired hand, stumbled, O dear friend, I was unable to write even the word "*svasti*", how could I write the whole letter!'[49]

Ultimately, when all her hopes were beguiled, giving her expression of her feeling of anguish on account of love, the maiden 'begs of the moon to touch her with the same rays she has touched her lover travelling in a distant land'.[50]

Somehow the time passes. It is time for her husband to return.

'But what shall I do? How shall I behave?' she ponders. 'Shall I show my anger?' and 'Will he try to pacify me?' She does not know how to receive him. 'When he actually arrived, it was an occasion of rejoicing, yet she hesitated to adorn herself with festal dress as she never wanted to embitter the grief of the neighbouring lady whose husband was still on journey.'[51]

Some more illustrations follow.

A lady is talking to a guest: 'O guest! since you are suffering from night-blindness (*ratti-andhaa=rātri-andhaka*), mark properly during daylight that my mother-in-law sleeps here; by negligence you may not fall on our cot.'[52] Here the lady is warning the guest not to come near her bed as her mother-in-law would be sleeping fast nearby, but actually she is inviting him to come to her bed in the night.

Elsewhere, prominence is given to the suggested meaning (*dhvani*) and not to the expressed one. A lady is addressing a holy man suggesting him: 'you can now roam about fearlessly as an arrogant lion dwelling in a bower near the bank of the Godāvarī, has mauled the dog'.[53] A lady had a place of assignment in a flowery grove. But a religious man used to visit that place and disturb the solitude of the grove. The lady in order to frighten the holy man fabricates a cook-and-bull story that a lion was seen roaming about in the adjoining region. Here a suggestion is made by introduction of a lion so that the holy man keeps away from that path. It is an example of suggestion of fear through implication.

VAJJĀLAGGA

Like *Gāhāsattasaī*, the *Vajjālagga*[54] or *Javallahaṃ* is another important anthology compiled by Jayavallabha, a Śvetāmbara Jain of unknown date. It is a rich collection of stanzas composed in Āryā metre in Mahārāṣṭrī Prakrit. Originally, it seems, it had 700 stanzas as in the *Sattasaī*, though the number in the existing edition goes up to 795.[55] Its stanzas, like those of the *Sattasaī* are scattered in the works of the authors on rhetorics and are inserted in Sanskrit drama as well.[56] The chapters (*vajjā*) are arranged according to their subject-matter, hence the name *Vajjālagga*. The author's idea was to compile the sayings of famous poets, whose names unfortunately are not known to us. There are stanzas concerning three ends of life, conduct (*dharma*), practical wisdom (*artha*) and love (*kāma*); only one-third of the verses fall to conduct and practical wisdom, the remaining two-thirds are erotic. The work has been divided into 95 *prakaraṇas*, dealing with poetry, the virtuous man, the wicked man, destiny, poverty, elephant, lion, bumble bee, dalliance, love, a female whose husband has gone abroad, faithful wife, faithless wife, astrologer, writer, physician, religious man, mechanic, prostitute, miner, old age, mare's fire or fire of the lower region (*baḍavānala*) and so on. It has a Sanskrit rendering (*chāya*) by Ratnadeva (AD 1326).

We have already mentioned how the author of the *Vajjālagga* was fond of Prakrit poetry. He has compared it with nectar and in his opinion one unable to read and listen to this beautiful poetry will be deprived of knowing love. Here we are tempted to quote a few illustrations from this work: It is night time, the husband is trying to reconcile her beloved, 'O dear, be pacified, give up your indignation, give me pleasure; it is dawn and the cock is crowing!'[57]

Tonight is going to be the last night of love; tomorrow morning the husband will be going away leaving his beloved alone. The beloved is addressing the Night: 'O goddess Night, my hard-hearted husband will be going away in the morning, please be extended so that never comes the dawn.'[58]

But the husband had to depart. The beloved was losing her senses. After regaining her consciousness, she inquired: 'Has he left?' 'Yes' came the reply. 'When did he leave?' 'Today'. 'How many days passed?'. 'One'. Hearing this, once again she fell into a swoon.[59]

So the poor lady was left alone, brooding over all the time, tortured by love. In the meantime, she comes across a traveller; she hurries up, stretches out her arms and addresses him: 'O traveller, kindly do not tread upon this path, otherwise the foot-prints of my dear will be scratched and spoiled.'[60]

The woman longing for her husband becomes a *kāpālikā* (a Śaiva female ascetic).'On account of the pang of separation she kept her hand on her forehead (or carrying a human skull for begging alms) and was lying on the sick-bed (or carrying a staff with a skull at the top).'[61]

Bhoja in his *Sarasvatīkaṇṭhābharaṇa* (3.73) has quoted the following verse as an illustration of *anyonya-alaṃkāra* (where one and the same action describes the mutual cause of two things) and *pratīyamāna-alaṃkāra* (where the unspoken meaning is indicated by suggestive expression): 'As the traveller continues to drink water, served by the maiden in-charge of the water shed, with his eyes raised, and lengthens out the process of drinking with the fingers of his hands separated from one another, the water-serving maiden makes the slender stream still slenderer so that the water-serving process may be prolonged.'[62]

A certain woman's husband died while he was abroad but the poor woman was ignorant of his death. Thinking he was alive and would return soon, she would scare the crow away every day. The idea is expressed in the following verse: 'The housewife ignorant of her husband's death, binding her braid of hair neatly, scared the crow away (the crowing of a crow is an auspicious sign indicating the arrival of somebody home) every day, saying to the crow, "get away, my consort is coming soon"—this causes the village people to be moved to tears.'[63]

Here is an illustration of 'poetic fancy' (*utprekṣā*): A certain woman at the departure of her husband, is not able to restrain her tears. People ask her, 'Why are you weeping? It is an inauspicious sign.' She replies, 'I am not weeping, nor am I showing anything inauspicious; on the contrary, I wish him all prosperity and good luck. The reason for my tears is that my eyes feel irritated by the smoke of fire of separation.'[64]

At another place, a woman is requesting a hunter (lover) to stop discharging arrows (of love). She says, 'O hunter, only one arrow will do, why are you ready with another one? Oh wretched one, don't you see that there is only one soul oscillating in the bodies of both of us?'[65]

EPIC POETRY

We have already mentioned the *sargabandha* (chapter-construction), which is a poem or composition divided into sections or chapters, especially a *Mahākāvya* or great poem.[66] Like lyrical poetry epic poetry was also composed in Prakrit. The *Setubandha*, the *Gauḍavaho* and the *Līlāvatī* can particularly be mentioned in this connection.

Setubandha

As pointed out the poet Daṇḍin found Mahārāṣṭrī the most elegant form of Prakrit, and considers *Setubandha*,[67] an ocean of wise sayings, an example of this dialect. The *Setubandha* (Construction of a Bridge), also known as *Rāvaṇavadha* or *Daśamukhavadha*, was composed by Pravarasena,[68] patronized by Kashmir King Pravarasena II in the second half of the sixth century. Bāṇabhaṭṭa has referred to this important work. It contains 15 cantos (*āśvāsa*), describing the expedition of Rāma to rescue Sītā, beginning with the march of the monkey-army up to the death of Rāvaṇa.

During this period of ornate court poetry, there seems to be a close relation between Sanskrit and Prakrit poetry. Like *Gauḍavaho* of Vākpatirāja, which we will shortly discuss, the *Setubandha* also followed the artificial literary tradition of Sanskrit poetry. Both these works have been strongly influenced by patterns followed by Sanskrit poets like Bhavabhūti and others. Both have been composed in thoroughly high-flown artificial language and are full of far-fetched metaphors, puns, alliterations and long compounds extending to entire lines. The use of Sanskrit metres such as Skandhakam, Galitaka, Anuṣṭup and others in *Setubandha* also indicates the influence of Sanskrit poetry.

It is noteworthy that in spite of artificial and affected style and language of *Setubandha*, Daṇḍin in his *Kāvyādarśa* has referred to this work as an example of Mahārāṣṭrī, the most elegant Prakrit dialect. Pischel has mentioned the *Rāvaṇavaho* (*Setubandha*) along with the *Gauḍavaho* and Hāla's *Sattasaī* as most important sources of our knowledge of Mahārāṣṭrī as they furnish excellent word indices (*Grammatik*, Art.15). The *Setubandha* has exercised great influence on literary style in contemporary Prakrit, Sanskrit and Apabhraṃśa literature. Later, works like the *Gauḍavaho, Kaṃsavaho, Śisupālavadha* and others were composed on the same pattern. Several commentaries were written on this work.

The work is based on the *Yuddha-kāṇḍa* (Battle-Section) of the *Vālmīki-Rāmāyaṇa*. Grieved with the pangs of separation from Sītā, Rāma proceeds to Laṅkā. But he could not get ahead due to the sea on his way. The monkey-army constructs a bridge to join the Indian peninsula and Ceylon. A severe fight ensues in which Rāvaṇa, Kumbhakarṇa and others are killed. Rāma rescues Sītā and returns to Ayodhya where his coronation ceremony takes place. Here we have a poetic description of autumn, moon-rise, dawn, mountain, sea-beach, sun-rise, construction of the bridge by monkeys, the city of Laṅkā, pleasure-gardens, Sītā's falling into a swoon, the battle, and the killing of Rāvaṇa. Here we give a few extracts.

About the discourse of poetry (*kathālāpa*) it is said that it enriches knowledge, helps in achievement of good qualities, and one gives us an opportunity to listen to the life of virtuous people—in this way there is nothing left in poetry which does not attract the heart.[69]

The melancholic state of mind of Rāma, separated from Sītā, is depicted: 'The wind is blowing touching the *kadamba* flowers, the surface of the sky is covered with dark clouds, the thundering of clouds can be heard, but there does not seem any enthusiasm (in the life of Rāma).'[70]

Here is an example of *sahokti alaṃkāra* where two simultaneous things are indicated at one and the same time. 'The sea is witnessed holding a mass of water like a courageous man, retaining mountains with their wings (according to tradition, formerly, mountains possessed wings which are clipped by Indra, hence is known as *Parvatāri,* i.e. the enemy of mountains) like a *timiṅgala* fish (a large fabulous fish), having tidal waves like the stream of river and possessing precious stones like hundreds of great virtues.'[71]

Poetic skill is evident in the passage in which Rāma warns the ocean: 'Bellowing, now the ocean stirs the submarine fire, Like a lion that roars and shakes his mane, With anger, after he is aroused from deep slumber, Having been pierced through by an arrow.'[72]

Or else, the monkeys in order to reach the island of Laṅkā are constructing a bridge: 'The monkeys are holding the mountains on their arms, the mountains are supporting the trees and the trees are upholding a mass of cloud roving in the sky; it is not exactly known whether the army of monkeys is engaged in constructing the bridge or measuring the surface of the sky.'[73]

'Learning of the sudden arrival of their husband, women feel their hair thrilled with emotion, are excited with bashfulness, move their bangles up and down, stretch their garments properly and pretend to gossip with their female friends.'[74]

Bhoja in his *Sarasvatīkaṇṭhābharaṇa,*[75] and Hemacandra in his *Kāvyānuśasana,*[76] and Mammata in his *Kāvyaprakāśa* have quoted numerous stanzas which indicate the popularity of this great Prakrit epic.

Gauḍavaho

Gauḍavaho (Slaying of Gauda-ruler),[77] as we have seen, has been composed in artificial Prakrit poetry by Vappairāa or Vākpatirāja (about AD 750) on the pattern of Sanskrit poetry. It is one of the earliest historical epics, though really speaking, it is a panegyric, eulogising Yaśovarman, the King of Kannauja. *Gauḍavaho* was written in Mahārāṣṭrī Prakrit in Āryā metre in 1209 verses. The poet is the chief narrator, addressing the entire poem to his beloved at her explicit request. It does not show any division but contains only groups of verses according to the topic. It has been divided into *kulakas* instead of *sargas*, the longest *kulaka* containing 150 verses and the shortest only 5. This work is important from the point of view of the study of Prakrit dialect. As it is composed on the pattern of Sanskrit poetry, a few *deśī* words have been incorporated. The author has embellished it by employing various *alaṃkāras* such as *utprekṣā*, *upamā* and *vakrokti*.

It seems that the work is incomplete or if complete not available in original. It should have contained the slaying of the King of Gauḍa (Magadha) which has been described only in two verses. It contains a wholly incomplete account of the military expedition of King Yaśovarman. At the outset he offers homage to deities Brahmā, Hari, Vāmana, Kṛṣṇa, Gaurī, Sarasvatī, Candra, Sūrya, Gaṇapati, Lakṣamī, Gaṅgā and others. Among meritorious poets, he mentions Bhavabhūti,[78] Bhāsa, Jvalanamitra, Kāntideva, Kālidāsa (Raghukāra), Subandhu and Haricandra. Glorifying the Prakrit dialect he says: 'It points out to a new meaning, it is rich and melodious on account of its tenderness. All other dialects are amalgamated in it and are originated from it just like all waters enter into an ocean and are later generated from it. By reading Prakrit poetry we acquire a special kind of delight, our eyes bloom and are closed for a moment and our heart expands out of joy.' Then begins the exploits of King Yaśovarman.

After the rainy season is over he proceeds to a victory-march. Here we come across the description of autumn and winter. Arriving at the Vindhya mountain he offers homage to the goddess Vindhyavāsinī. We meet a lovely description of the goddess' temple. The description of summer and the rainy season is recorded. A fight ensues between King Yaśovarman and the ruler of Gauḍa in which the latter is killed. King Yaśovarman, on his return to his native land Kannauja, passes through Vaṅga (Bengal), the mountain Malaya, the land of Pārasīkas, Koṅkaṇa, the country of Maru, Śrīkaṇṭha, Kurukṣetra, Ayodhyā, the mountain Mahendra and then turns to the north. Here the author finds an opportunity to show his poetic skill, inserting pictures of landscapes, mountains, rivers, ponds, trees and scenes from rural life, interwoven with a large number of mythical narratives. The author is not very fond of the play of words and puns, but we come across long compounds in the composition.

Eulogising his patron King Yaśovarman, the poet writes: 'See the contradiction between liquor (*mdirā*) and affluence (*laksamī*); if you drink much you feel intoxicated, if it is in small quantity, it will not affect you; but in the case of affluence it is just the opposite; a man in possession of small quantity of money gets intoxicated, whereas it is not the case with a man of affluence.'[79] Here is another example of suggested meaning: 'If any virtuous man can have access to the royal court, it means entry is open even to an ordinary person; or there can be any other reason for his entry, but at least never his virtues.'[80]

The *Mahu-Maha-Viaa=Madhu-Matha-Vijaya=The Conquest of Viṣṇu* is another important work of Vākpatiraja which has been unfortunately lost. He has referred to it in his *Gauḍavaho*; it is earlier and superior to *Gauḍavaho*.[81] Abhinavagupta has cited a verse from this work in his *Locana*, a commentary on the *Dhvanyāloka* (III.15, p. 152).[82] Hemacandra in his *Alaṃkāracūḍāmaṇi*, commentary on the *Kavyānusāśana* (*śloka* 151, p. 81) has cited the same verse.[83] This work was composed in *Gāthā* metre.

HARIVIJAYA

The *Harivijaya* by Sarvasena is no more available at present but it was known to earlier scholars. Ānandavardhana (AD 850-75) was the earliest writer to have mentioned this work in his *Dhvanyāloka*. He has cited verse from the Harivijaya to illustrate पदप्रकाशध्वनि (suggestive sense ilustrating the wrod) (3, p. 127). Elsewhere he has cited another verse from this wrok as an illustration of अर्थशक्ति-उद्रव-ध्वनि (suggestive sense produced by अर्थशक्ति), generated by कवि-प्रौढोक्ति (poet's bold expression).[84] Further, the author of the *Dhvanyāloka*, comparing Sarvasena with Kālidāsa, points out that Sarvasena deviates for the sake of *rasa* from the original. He writes:

इतिवृत्तवशायत्तां कथञ्चिद्रसानुगुणां स्थितिं त्यक्त्वा पुनः उत्प्रेक्ष्यापि अभीष्टरसोचितकथोन्नयो विधेयः- यथा कालिदासप्रबंधेषु यथा च सर्वसेनविरचिते हरिविजये[85]

Kuntaka (about 950-1000) has equated Sarvasena with Kālidāsa as a poet of graceful genius—dominated with his delicate (*sukumāra*) style.[86] Vādijaṅghāla, the commentator of Daṇḍin's *Kāvyādarśa* (I.34) has referred to this work being composed in Mahārāṣṭrī Prakrit. Bhojadeva has quoted numerous verses from *Harivijaya* in his *Sarasvatīkaṇṭhābharaṇa* and the *Śṛṅgāraprakāśa*. As we shall see below, the four verses of the former are cited from the *Harivijaya*. The *Śṛṅgāraprakāśa* contains numerous references to the *Harivijaya* of Sarvasena and numerous verses have been cited from this work;

sometimes they may be of anonymous nature.[87] As we shall see below this contains a reference to the *Harivijaya*, the *Rāvaṇavijaya* and the *Setubandha*, and is composed in *āśvāsakas* in *Skandhaka* metre. It is stated that as the poem of Āḍhyarāja is marked by the word of *dhairya* in the last verse of each section, and as the poem (*Setubandha*) of Pravarasena is marked by the word *anurāga*, similarly the poem (*Harivijaya*) of Sarvasena is marked by the word *utsāha* in the last verse of each *āśvāsa.*[88] In the same section Bhoja has referred to this work as containing various descriptions: it excels in the description of the city (*nagara*), mountain (*śaila*), season (*ṛtu*), hero (*nāyaka*), his vehicle (*vāhana*) and a drinking party (*madhupāna*).[89] Bhoja has mentioned three types of messengers: निसृष्टार्थ, परिमितार्थ and शासनहर. The messenger Satyaka in the *Harivijaya*, and Vāsudeva in the Udyogaparva of the *Mahābhārata* are cited examples of the *nisṛṣṭārtha* (to which the management of an affair is entrusted).[90] Then Viṣṇu (Kṛṣṇa) is cited as an example who in order to fulfil her beloved's desire (*abhimātartha-siddhi*), that is to remove Satyabhāmā's anger, brought *pārijāta* tree for her.[91] The work is further mentioned as an example of submission (*uparati*) of the enemy.[92]

Hemacandra too has made a reference to the *Harivijaya* of Sarvasena. He mentions it along with the *Rāvaṇavijaya*, the *Setubandha*, the *Śiśupālavadha*, the *Kirātārjunīya* and other works in his commentaries, i.e. the *Alaṃkāracūḍāmaṇi* and the *Viveka* on the *Kāvyānuśāsana*. He points out an error on the part of Sarvasena, saying that the author has presented a disproportionately lengthy description of the sea in alliterative verses and that he has done in a situation of *vipralambha rasa.*[93] But as Raghavan has pointed out, Bhoja does not agree with Hemacandra's criticism of Sarvasena. Raghavan says: From what Kuntaka says of Hemacandra, we cannot take Sarvasena to have erred in the manner described by Hemacandra. It is likely that the alliterative description of the ocean in it is an interpolation.[94] There is also a reference to Sarvasena, the author of *Harivijaya*, as a king in the *Avantisundarī.*[95]

Sarvasena composed this epic in the first half of the fourth century on the model of the *Setubandha*. The epic contains long compounds and figures of speech as in the *Setubandha*. The main episode of the work is as follows:

Hari is the hero; Ruppiṇī (Rukmiṇī) his chief queen; Saccabhāmā (Satyabhāmā) the rival heroine. Once Hari offered a garland of *pārijāta* flowers to Rukmiṇī, which aroused the jealousy of Satyabhāmā. In order to pacify her, Hari prostrates at her feet, which causes her eyes to fill with tears out of joy. Hari promises to get her the *pārijāta* tree. He sends his envoy to Indra in order to procure that celestial tree. A fight is ensued between Hari and Indra in which the latter surrenders and Hari returns with the *pārijāta* tree. Hari plants this tree in the garden near Satyabhāmā's residence and thus her wrath is pacified. She feels that Hari's love towards her is a thousand time more than towards Rukmiṇī.

Besides, this being an epic, we come across descriptions of the city, mountain, sunset, hero, his vehicle, his envoy, his march for battle and his conquests, as noted earlier.

MĀRĪCAVADHA

Unfortunately nothing is known about this Prakrit poetical work except that Bhoja cites a verse from it as an example of *vastūpakṣepa.*[96] This verse is also quoted in his *Sarasvatikaṇṭhābharaṇa.* A *Mārīcavadha* of *rāga-kāvya*-type of *uparūpaka* is cited by Abhinavagupta in his *Abhinavabhāratī* (GOS edition, I, pp. 183, 184).[97] Hemacandra too refers to the *Mārīcavadha* along with the *Rāghavavijaya* in his *Kāvyānuśāsana,* pointing out that the former is sung in *Ḍhakka* (or *Ḍakka*) *rāga,* and the latter in the *grāma-rāga* called *Kakubha.*

RĀVAṆAVIJAYA

The is another important Prakrit poetical work which has been equated with the *Harivijaya* and the *Setubandha,* composed only in one metre called *āśvāsakabandha.*[98] A verse from the introductory portion of this work, the praise of a poet (*kavi-praśaṃsā*), has been cited by Bhoja in his *Śṛṅgāraprakāśa* (II.ii, p. 473).[99] Elsewhere in the same work, it is referred to as containing *nāyaka-varṇana* and *vāhana-varṇana.*[100]

VISAMABĀṆALĪLĀ

This work by Ānandavardhana, like the *Mahu-maha-viaa* of Vākpatirāja, the *Harivijaya* of Sarvasena and the *Rāvaṇavijaya* is no more extant. It deals with the subject of love on the model of the *Sattasaī,* and is also designated as the *Ānandakathā.*[101] Hemacandra has mentioned it along with the *Mahu-maha-viaa* in his *Kāvyānuśāsana* where in the *Alaṃkāracūḍāmaṇi* he has cited a verse from it.[102]

Ānandavardhana in his *Dhvanyāloka* has cited a verse from this work of his own where the cupid is said to have conquered the three worlds and defeats the *asuras.*[103] Ānandavardhana has cited yet another verse which seems to be a popular saying.[104] Another reference from the *Dhvanyāloka* indicates that the work contained the speeches of a youth to cupid (or of a pupil to his teacher).[105] There is another reference from this unknown work in the *Dhvanyāloka* where the speech of good poets is described as knowing no limit and compared with the sport of good ladies.[106] Elsewhere it is pointed out that amorous sports are so forceful that it is difficult to resist them.[107] Hemacandra has referred to a yet another verse of this work in the Viveka of the *Kāvyānuśasana.*[108]

The *Kuvalyāśvacarita* or *The Story or Adventures of Kuvalayāśva*: It appears that there existed more than one title of this work. According to the Purāṇas, Madālasā was the daughter of the Gandharva Viśvavasu. She was carried off by the Daitya Pātālaketu and subsequently made the wife of Kuvalayāśva.[109] Bhoja has referred to the *Madālasopākhyāna* of the *Mārkaṇḍeya Purāṇa* where the intense love of Kuvalayāśva and Madālasā is depicted[110] in his *Śṛṅgāraprakāśa* along with the *Kumārasambhava,* the *Jānakīharaṇa* and the *Subhadrāharaṇa* for the description of a *nāyikā* (heroine).[111] This work was also known to Hemacandra. Later Kavirāja Viśvanātha, the author of the *Sāhitya-darpaṇa,* composed a poem of the same title in Prakrit which he has referred to as saying '*yathā mama*':

यथा मम कुवलयाश्वचरिते प्राकृतकाव्ये: णवरिअ तं जुअजुअलं अण्णोण्णं णिहिदसजलमंथरदिट्ठिं।
आलेक्खआपिअं विअ खणमेत्थं तत्थ संठिअं मुअसण्णं॥ *Sāhityadarpaṇa,* III.148

Lilāvaī (*Līlāvatī*)[112] is another important poetic work by Koūhala (Kutūhala) written at the request of his wife in the *Marahaṭṭa-desī-bhāsā* using very few *desī* words.[113] At the end of the text, addressing his readers, the author observes: 'This has not been written for the virtuous or the wicked people, the former will trace only merits and the latter only flaws; it is meant for the common reader, who avoiding the two extremes, would appreciate the true worth of my poetry.'[114] Finally, addressing his beloved, he ends his work saying: 'One who reads or listens to this poem daily, does not suffer from the pang of separation from her lover.'[115] The *Lilāvatī* was composed in 1800 verses in *anuṣṭup* metre. It is a continuous poem without sections, narrated not by the hero but by others. The predominant sentiment is love. The hero is king Hāla Sātavāhana of Pratiṣṭhāna, the reputed compiler of the *Gāhāsattasaī*. He was a friend and patron of Nāgārjuna who was skilled in alchemy (*rasa-siddha*), of Pālita (Pādalipta?), Kumārila (probably not Bhaṭṭakumārila, the well-known Mīmāṃsaka philosopher of AD 700) and Poṭṭisa. The Līlāvatī story is of the divine and human type (*divya-mānuṣa*). The theme is the marriage of king Sātavāhana with Līlāvatī, the daughter of king Śilāmegha of Siṃhala. Sātavāhana deputes his commander-in-chief to the island of Siṃhala.

The poet was acquainted with the works of Kālidāsa, Subandhu, Bāṇabhaṭṭa and others and he has borrowed from Bhāravi and Māgha. Memorable maxims (*subhāṣita*) occur all through the work. In between the story, we read about the arts of painting, music, dance, and a variety of tales. The Rāṣṭrakūṭas and Solaṅkīs are mentioned. Saurāṣṭra was known for its good breed of dogs. Composed in the eighth century, in an ornate literary style, the work is in lucid Prakrit dialect. It has a Sanskrit commentary, known as *Līlāvatī-kathā-vṛtti*, by an unknown author, probably a Śvetāmbara Jain of Gujarat between AD 1172 and 1404.[116]

Hemacandra in order to illustrate the rules of Prakrit grammar, has cited verses from the *Līlāvaī* in his Prakrit Grammar.

Here are a few verses from the work to illustrate the style:

Once in an autumnal moonlit night, when the poet and his beloved were seated comfortably on the terrace of the palace, the beloved requested him to narrate a novel story, pleasing to women for the evening entertainment: 'The night is extremely fascinating, the autumn is bright and clean, besides you are by my side and the company of people is excellent; I feel, there is nothing wanting.'[117]

The poet describes the intense love between the sun and the day: 'One and only one accomplishment of love between the sun and the day is always to be admired, that throughout their life, one is never seen separated from the other.'[118]

By the time the king marched with his army, it was sunset. It was dark all over and the moon appeared in the sky, creating an occasion for amorous sports. Then came the dawn. 'When a creeping plant (identified with night) is uprooted by an elephant (identified with morning), the birds (the moon) fly away and the white flowers (stars) drop down from the plant; so the night is pulled out when it is dawn, the moon sets and the stars vanish.'[119]

'The deer-marked moon is falling from the sky as a crystal white wine-glass is dropped from the hand of a damsel (identical with night) after drinking the wine (identical with moonlight).'[120]

KUMĀRAVĀLA-CARIYA (*KUMĀRAPĀLA-CARITA*)

Kumārapāla-carita,[121] also known as *Dvyāśraya-kāvya* (having a twofold connection) is a grammatico-poetic work, illustrating the grammatical treatise *Siddhahema-śabdānusāśana* by Hemacandra. It is called *Dvyāśraya* as it is composed partly in Sanskrit, containing 7 chapters divided into 20 cantos, and partly in Prakrit, containing an eighth chapter divided into 8 cantos. The first 20 cantos, a part of which (16-20) deals with king Kumārapāla and the rest with his predecessors, is important for the history of the Cālukyas of Gujarat. In this section the rules of Sanskrit grammar have been illustrated side by side. The second section of 8 cantos, written in Prakrit, deals entirely with Kumārapāla, excepting the last two cantos containing no historical matter but moral and religious teachings. Thus the alternative title *Dvyāśraya* refers to the twofold medium, the description of the life of Kumārapāla as well as the illustration of the rules of Sanskrit and Prakrit grammars composed by the author himself.

As a great epic the *Kumārapāla-carita* provides the description of activities of Kumārapāla: the description of Aṇahillanagara where the king rules, his waking up by bards, performance of daily duties, physical exercise, worshipping in Jain temple, sports, seasons, water sports, the rise of the moon, the conquest of various countries and battles. The last two chapters deal with moral and religious teachings delivered for the enlightenment of the king. Here we come across the illustrations of Māgadhī, Paiśācī, Cūlikā Paiśācī and Apabhraṃśā dialects.

The Sanskrit portion of the *Kumārapālacarita* has been commented upon by Abhayatilakagaṇi whereas Pūrṇakalaśagaṇi is the commentator of the Prakrit *Kumārapālacarita*.[122] It appears that on the model of the *Rāvaṇavadha*, commonly designated as the *Bhaṭṭikāvya* of poet Bhaṭṭi, which illustrates a few grammatical rules in accordance with Pāṇinī's *Aṣṭādhyāyī*, Hemacandra was inspired to illustrate the rules of his grammatical treatise the *Siddhahemaśabdānuśāsana*.[123] Hemacandra, also known as *Kalikālasarvajña* (Omniscient of the Kali Age), was a versatile author of his age. There is practically no subject on which he has not written. Besides being a historian and a grammarian in two languages, he has also contributed in the field of lexicon, metrics, rhetoric, philosophy, logic and poetry. Here is an illustration as to how the singular and plural forms of nominative case of the word '*yuṣmad*' have been incorporated in a verse:

'O friend, though (*taṃ, tuṃ, tuvaṃ, tuha, tumaṃ*—Prakrit forms of nominative singular) bringest the *kadamba* flowers; O friends, you (*bhe, tubbhe, tumhoyhe, tumhe, tujha*—Prakrit forms of nominative plural) arrange for a seat.'[124]

Biographical Literature

There is a vast biographical literature in Prakrit by Jain writers. It consists of popular epic themes such as the legends of Rāma and Kṛṣṇa besides the lives of 63 *Śalākāpuruṣas* or 'Excellent Men' (i.e. 24 Tīrthaṅkaras, 12 Cakravartins, 9 Vāsudevas, 9 Baladevas and 9 Prativāsudevas), a large number of legendary heroes, ascetic heroes, eminent Jain *ācāryas*, patriarchs, renowned saints, outstanding writers, royal patrons, merchant-princes and many others who served the cause of the religion in different ages.

The Prakrit epic *Paumacariya*[125] by Vimalasūri (fourth century according to Jacobi), seems to be the earliest record of the Jain Rāmāyaṇa. According to the author, he composed this work, *Rāghava-carita* (also as *Rāmadeva-carita* or *Rāmāravinda-carita*) 530 years after Mahavira, based on the *Pūrva* literature, in Prakrit in Āryā metre. It consists of 118 *uddesas* or *parvans*, containing 8651 *gāthās*. In the opinion of the author, the *Rāmāyaṇa* of Vālmīki contains contradictory and unbelievable statements and hence is not trustworthy. To illustrate his point the author asks how Rāvaṇa, of noble descent, and other demons (*rākṣasas*) are said to have eaten meat. How could Rāvaṇa's brother Kumbhakarṇa, in spite of all the disturbances, sleep for half a year and after his awakening, devour elephants and buffaloes? And how could Indra, though he rules over gods and men, be said to have been made captive by Rāvaṇa and brought to the city of Laṅka? All this is as good as to affirm that a lion is overcome by a gazelle or an elephant by a dog.

The text is divided into seven sections: the position of the universe, the origin of the clan, marching for the battle, the battle, the birth of Lava and Kuśa, nirvāṇa and the numerous rebirths. In the first 24 *uddesas* along with the lives of the Tīrthaṅkaras we read about the origin of the Ikṣvāku and Candra clans. It has been stated that the 'race of monkeys' in reality is a race of *Vidyādharas*. In the same way, the *rākṣasas* are not man-eating demons but belong to the race of *Vidyādharas*. Rāvaṇa's mother had hung around his neck a wonderous ring of pearls in which Rāvaṇa's face was reflected nine times, hence he was called Daśamukha (the man with ten faces). Then we read the main story of the *Rāmāyaṇa.* King Daśaratha is presented with sons by his three queens. Aparajitā (according to Haribhadra's *Upadeśapada,* it is Kauśalyā) gives birth to Padma (Rāma), Sumitrā to Lakṣamaṇa and Kaikeyī to Bharata and Śatrughna. Here begins the main story: kidnapping of Sītā by Rāvaṇa, deputing of Hanumana to Laṅkā, the fight with Rāvaṇa leading to his defeat, bringing home of Sītā, the consecration of Rāma, discontent of the people, banishment of Sītā, lamentation of Padma, the birth of Kuśa and Lava and ultimately the attainment of *nirvāṇa* by Padma.

The author of the *Paumacariya* differs from Vālmīki in several respects: Sītā is born in a natural way by Videhā, the queen of king Janaka, and not out of the earth. Similarly, Sītā is betrothed to Padma by Janaka as the former had aided him in the fight against the *Mlecchas.* Daśaratha wishes to become a monk and entrusts Padma with the responsibility of governing the country. Here Bharata too desires to relinquish the world but is persuaded by Kaikeyī and Padma not to do so but take over the reins of the government.

The theme of the *Mahābhārata* also occupies an important place with the Jains. Here we have the popular epic themes such as the Kṛṣṇa legend, and the legend of Draupadī and the five Pāṇḍavas. The race of Harivaṃśa has been noted by Jain authors. The *Vasudevahiṇḍi* which contains a biography of Vasudeva, father of Kṛṣṇa Vāsudeva, records the history of the Harivaṃśa (*Harivaṃsa-kulassa-uppatti*) in the twenty-fourth *Lambha,* known as the *Paumāvatīlambha.* The *Paumacariya* of Vimalasūri also has given an account of this race in its twenty-first *uddeśa.* It is noteworthy that in the *Thānāṅga Sutta* the origin of the Harivaṃsa race has been counted among ten wonders (*dasa accheragā*).[126]

According to H. Jacobi, the formation of the Jaina *Harivaṃsapurāṇa* goes back to the third century BC, though the whole mythology of Kṛṣṇa legend was given final shape in the beginning of the Christian era. He has stated that since out of 63 Great Men, 27 (i.e. 9 Baladevas, 9 Vāsudevas and 9 Prativāsudevas) are multiplications of the Kṛṣṇa legend, it seems that the adaptation of the latter motivated the Jainas to build up their world history. 'But most probably Jainas have canonised Kṛṣṇa when they spread and settled in the original area of the Kṛṣṇa legend,' he adds.[127] It is to be noted that in the Jain tradition Nemi or Ariṣṭanemi, who is considered as the twenty-second Tīrthaṅkara, was a cousin of Kṛṣṇa Vāsudeva. He has been mentioned in the Śvetāmbara Jain canonical literature, in the *Nāyādhammakahāo,* the *Antagaḍa,* the *Vaṇhidasāo* and the

Uttarajjhayaṇa. It has been said that before Ariṣṭanemi joined the ascetic order, there ensued a battle (*bāhu-juddha*) between him and his cousin Kṛṣṇa. We are given to understand that being defeated in the battle, Kṛṣṇa got jealous of his cousin lest he might encroach on his kingdom.[128] Further, Devendragaṇi, the commentator of the *Uttarajjhayaṇa* has recorded a legend of the destruction of the city of Dvārakā by the sage Dvīpāyana, who was provoked by Śamba and other Yādāva princes while in a drunken state of mind.[129] We also come across here the descent of the Gaṅga river and the destruction of the sixty thousand sons of Sagara Cakravartin.[130] As we have seen earlier, Maladhāri Rājaśekharasūri in his *Bhāvabhāvanā* has devoted a major portion of his work to the life of Ariṣṭanemi, including the origin of the Harivaṃśa lineage, Daśāra kings, the birth of Kaṃsa, the account of Vāsudeva, his wives, the marriage of Devakī with Vāsudeva, the birth of Kṛṣṇa and so on. The name of Rājīmatī, also known as Rājul in later Jain texts, is very popular among Jain writers. The *Raha-nemīya* chapter of the *Uttarajjhayaṇa* provides an interesting account of the virtuous lady Rājīmatī, who following the footsteps of her would-be husband Ariṣṭanemi, abandoned worldly pleasures and joined the order of nuns. Once it so happened that Ariṣṭanemi's elder brother, the ascetic Rathanemi, had previously taken refuge in a cave on the same mountain where Rājimatī was practising penance. When Rathanemi saw his sister-in-law in her nude beauty, he was seized by passion and he made advances towards her. Rājīmatī resisted and baffled her brother-in-law's attempt by offering him a drink in which she vomitted in his presence. The Rājīmatī episode has such popularity among Jains that numerous stories, dramas and *caumāsas* were composed on this theme.

Regarding the *Harivaṃśa*, various works in Prakrit, Sanskrit and Apabhraṃśa were composed by Jain authors. *Harivaṃsacariya* was composed in Prakrit, and has been praised along with the poet Harivarṣa (Harivarisa) and Vimala (the author of the *Paumacariya*) by Udyotanasūri in his *Kuvalayamālā.* The well-known Jinasena I of the Punnāṭa *Saṅgha,* different from Jinasena II, the author of the *Ādipurāṇa,* composed his *Harivaṃśapurāṇa,* also known as *Harivaṃśacarita* in Sanskrit in the eighth century. Then Svayambhū (AD 677 to 783) wrote *Harivaṃsapurāṇa,* also known as *Riṭṭhaṇemicariu,* and the poet Dhavala (eleventh century) the *Harivaṃsacariu,* both in Apabhraṃśa.

Like the biography of Rāma the biography of Kṛṣṇa also was

written by Jain authors. One such work under the title of *Kaṇhacariya*[131] was composed by Devendrasūri of Tapāgaccha in the later fourteenth century. This work has been taken from the commentary of the *Śrāddhadinakṛtya*; the biography of Neminātha (*Nemināthacarita*) has been also incorporated here. Details of Kṛṣṇa's life are provided. According to Jain tradition, Kṛṣṇa was to be born as a hellish being after his death, but in future he is destined to be a Tīrthaṅkara, Amama by name. His elder brother Baladeva is going to achieve liberation during his life as a Tīrthaṅkara.

The *Kahāvali* by Bhadreśvara (twelfth century), the teacher of the well-known Abhayadevasūri, is an important Prakrit work which deals with not only the 63 Great Men but also provides an account of eminent teachers from Kālakācārya to Haribhadrasūri. The *Caüppannamahāpurisacariya*[132] was composed in AD 868 by Śīlāṅkacārya, also known as Śīlācārya, a pupil of Mānadevasūri. The accounts of Draupadī, Sitā and others are provided here. We are told in the *Nāyādhammakahāo* that the five Pāṇḍavas obtained the permission of Draupadī before entering the ascetic order. Here we come across an account of Draupadī—her previous births, her birth in the house of King Drupada, her *svayaṃvara* marriage, marriage with the five Pāṇḍavas, the birth of Paṇḍusena and her joining the order of the nuns. Several works under the title of the *Draupadīcarita* and the *Pāṇḍavacacarita* were composed by Jain authors. The *Sītācarita* was composed by Bhuvanatuṅgasūri in 465 stanzas in Prakrit; there were other works which are still unpublished.

Then there are numerous biographies in Prakrit of individual Tīrthaṅkaras, Cakravartins, Baladevas (including Rāma), Vāsudevas (including Kṛṣṇa), Prativāsudevas (including Rāvaṇa) and numerous eminent Jain *ācāryas* and authors, who contributed a good deal in spreading the tenets of Jainism far and wide. This biographical literature was composed not only in Prakrit but also in Sanskrit, Apabhraṃśa, Kannaḍa and Tamil.[133] Jinasena, Guṇabhadra and Hemacandra composed the biographies of Great Men in Sanskrit; Svayambhu, Puṣpadanta and Dhavala in Apabhraṃśa and Cāmuṇḍarāya in Kannaḍa.

Besides there are some other important Prakrit works on biographical literature composed by Jain writers. Jambu or Jambusvāmin, one of the ancient Jain teachers, is very popular among Jain writers. We are told that after the death of Mahavira, Sudharma became the head of the Jain *saṅgha* and is said to have narrated the Jain Canon to his disciple Jambu in the manner he had learned from his Master. Jambu is said to have been the last *kevalin*; after him the doors of liberation are said to have closed. Jambu was so popular with Jains that numerous works in Prakrit, Sanskrit, Apabhraṃśa and regional languages were composed by Jain writers. It is said that more than one hundred works were composed on the life history of Jambu. Guṇapāla Muni, a pupil or pupil's pupil of Vīrabhadrasūri, has composed the *Jambucariya*[134] in the eleventh century or earlier. This work contains 16 *uddeśas*. Sakalakīrti, a pupil of Bhuvanakīrti (in VS 1520) and Upādhyāya Padmasundara Nāgauri (VS 1626-39) wrote their works of the same title '*Jambūcariya*'. Ācārya Jinavijaya, under the instruction of Vijayadayāsūri, composed the *Jambusvāmicarita* (in VS 1785). Rajamalla composed his *Jambusvāmicarita* in Sanskrit (in VS 1632).[135]

There is also *Surasundarīcariya*[136] by Dhaneśvara, pupil of renowned Jinésvarasūri, written in VS 1095; the *Rayaṇacūḍācariya*[137] by the well-known Nemicandrasūri (also known as Devendragaṇi), the author of the *Sukhabodhā* commentary on the *Uttarādhyayana*, the *Ākhyānamaṇikośa* and the *Mahāvīracariya*. It contains a palm-leaf MS written just after twenty years after its composition. It is recorded in the collection of Jaisalmer Durg Jain Bhandar; contains 2385 *gāthās*. K. Kasliwal, *Prākṛta-Vidyā*, July-Dec. 1990 (in VS 1141); the *Pāsanāhacariya*[138] and the *Mahaviracariya*[139] both by Devabhadrācārya (also known as Guṇacandragaṇi) in VS 1139; he is also the author of the *Kahārayaṇakosa* as we have noted earlier. Then, *Supāsanāhacariya*[140] was composed by Lakṣamaṇagaṇi, a pupil of Hemacandrasūri, in VS 1199 (AD 1142) at the time of King Kumārapāla's coronation. *Sudaṃsaṇācariya*,[141] also known as *Śakunikāvihāra* (it gives an account of Śakunikāvihāra, a Jain shrine dedicated to Munisuvratanātha in 16 chapters, containing 4502 *gāthās*) was composed by Devendrasūri, pupil of Jagaccandrasūri of Tapāgaccha; he died in VS 1327 (AD 1270). *Jayantīcarita*,[142] also known as *Jayantīprakaraṇa*, *Siddhajayantīcaritra*, *Jayantīpraśnottarasaṃgraha* or *Praśnottarasaṃgraha*, is based on the second *uddeśaka* of the twelfth *Śataka* of the Bhagavatī. It gives an account of virtuous Jayantī, daughter of king Sahasrānīka of Kauśāmbī, sister of Śatānīka and the father's sister of Udayana. The questions asked by her to Mahavira have been recorded here. This work was written by Mānatuṅgasūri with Malayaprabhasūri's commentary in VS 1260. The *Kummāputtacariya*[143] was composed by Jinamāṇikya, pupil of Hemavimala or by Anantahaṃsa, pupil of Jinamāṇikya in AD 1513. Kummāputta is considered as one of the

Pratyakabuddhas in Jain tradition. The *Ṛṣibhāṣita* contains Kummāputta's account along with other *Pratyakabuddhas* such as Nārada, Aṅgarisi (Aṅgirasa), Valkalacīrin, Maṅkhaliputta, Jaṇṇavakka (Yājñavalkya) and others. Kummāputta is also mentioned as a *sthavira* in Buddhist literature.[144] The *Maṇipaticarita*[145] was composed by Haribhadrasūri, pupil's pupil of Mānadeva of the Bṛhadgaccha and pupil of Upādhyāya Jinapati, in VS 1172 (AD 1115). Various biographies of the monk Maṇipati were composed in Sanskrit by Jain writers.

Letters in Prakrit

Letter writing in Prakrit shows the popularity of the language. See the following love-letter, contained in the collection in the Pande Luṇkaran Shastra Bhandar (with the courtesy of Dr. Kasturchand Kasliwal). The letter is addressed by a lover to his wife.

कुसल अम्हाण वरं अणवरयं तुम्ह गुणलियंतस्स।
पट्ठाविय नियकुसलं जिम अम्हं होई संतोसो॥ 1॥
सो दिवसो सा राई सो य पएसो गुणाण आवासो।
सुहगुरु तुह मुहकमलं दीसई जत्थेव सुहजणणं॥ 2॥
किं अब्भुज्जो देसो किं वा मसि नत्थि तिहुयणे सयले।
किं अम्हेहिं न कज्जं जं लेहो न पेसिओ तुम्हे॥ 3॥
जइ भुज्जो होइ मही उयहि मसी लेहिणि य वणराई।
लिहइ सुराहिवणाहो तुम्ह गुणा ण याणंति॥ 4॥
जह हंसो सरइ सरं पड्डुल कुसुमाइं महुअरो सरइ।
चंदण-वणं च नागो तह अम्ह मणं तुमं सरइ॥ 5॥
जह भद्दवए मासे भमरा समरंति अंब-कुसुमाइं।
तह भयवं मह हिययं सुमरइ तुम्हाण मुहकमलं॥ 6॥
जह वच्छ सरइ सुरहिं वसंतमासं च कोइला सरइ।
विज्झो सरइ गइंदं तह अम्ह मणं तुमं सरइ॥ 7॥
जह सो नीलकलाओ पावस कालम्मि पंजरे छूढो।
संभरइ वणे रमिउं तह अम्ह मणं तुमं सरइ॥ 8॥
जह सरइ सीय रामो रुप्पिणि कण्हो नलो य दमयंती।
गोरी सरइ रुद्दं तह अम्ह मणं तुमं सरइ॥ 9॥[146]

Religious Lyrics

The tradition of composing hymns in praise of divinities is old in Indian literature. Those in adoration of Indra, Varuṇa, Agni, Uṣas and other divinities were popular. The *Atharvaveda* contains a well-known magnificent hymn, known as *Pṛthivī-sūkta* in which Mother

Earth is extolled as the supporter and preserver of everything earthly, and entreated for happiness and blessing and protection from all evil. It can be called a national hymn. Later a number of hymns were dedicated to Sūrya, Viṣṇu, Kṛṣṇa, Rāma, Śiva, Durgā, Caṇḍī, Gaṅgā and others.[147]

Although according to Jains, God is free from passion and desire and therefore incapable of granting boon or conferring curse, ancient Jain authors have composed numerous *stotras* and *stutis* in praise of their divinities in Prakrit, Sanskrit, Apabhraṃśa and regional dialects. Besides, a large number of hymns have been composed in praise of Mahavira and other Tīrthaṅkaras as well as ancient Jain teachers. The *Cauvīsatthaya* (*Caturviṃśatistva* (Glorification of 24 Tīrthaṅkaras) is one of the six Essential Duties; this being the second as we have seen. The *Cauvīsatthaya* corresponds to one of the 14 divisions of the *Aṅgabāhya* literature in the Digambara tradition. The most ancient reference to the hymn in praise of Mahavira is in the sixth chapter, entitled '*Mahāvīratthava* or *Vīratthui* of the *Sūyagaḍaṅga*. Here Mahavira is praised as *Nāta-suta* (the son of Jñātṛkas), wise (*kheyaṇṇa=kṣetrajna*), competent (*kusala*), quick witted (*āsupaṇṇa=āśuprajña*), possessing infinite knowledge (*aṇantaṇāṇī=anantajñānī*), possessing infinite insight (*aṇantadaṃsi=anantadarśī*), possessing knowledge of all (*savvadaṃsī=sarvadarśī*). He is also praised as *Kāsava* (Kāśyapa, his family name), *anuttara* (unique), the leader of the Jinas (*Jiṇāṇaṃ netā*) and the Thousand-Eyed (*sahassanetā=sahasranetra*) like Indra.

Mahavira is praised by means of various similes. He is the *Śālmalī* tree (silk-cotton tree) providing shelter to birds, thunder (*thaṇiya=stanita*) the loudest of sounds, the Moon (most glorious among heavenly bodies), and sandalwood (most pleasant of aromas). He has been also compared with the Svayambhūramaṇa, the best among oceans, the Dharaṇendra, most excellent among Nāgas, and the Rasa-vaijayanti (the juice of sugarcane, the best of all juices). Then he is called the Erāvata among elephants, the lion (*mṛgendra*) among beasts, the Gaṅgā among rivers, the eagle Veṇudeva among birds, so too Nāyaputta among those who preach *nirvāṇa*. Further, 'as Vīsasena (Viṣvaksena) or Vāsudeva is the most celebrated among warriors, the lotus among flowers and Dantavakra among Kṣatriyas so is Vardhamāna among sages'. 'As *abhaya-dāna* (affording protection) is the best among gifts, as the finest speech is that which causes no distress and as chastity is the highest of austerities, so is Samaṇa Nāyaputta supreme in the world (*loguttama*).'[148]

In the *Ovāiya* (*Aupapātika*) king Śreṇika Bimbasāra, after listening to the news of venerable Mahavira's arrival in Campā, rushes to pay his obeisance.

I bow to those who are self-enlightened (*sayaṃ-saṃbuddha*), the supreme among humans, the lion, the 'scent-elephant' (*gandha-hatthi*), and the white lotus among men, and very superior among people, the Lord of the world, the Benefactor of the people, the light of the world, giving assurance of safety, the Giver of sights, the Guide, affording refuge, Instiller of *bodhi* (perfect knowledge), the Giver of *Dhamma* (Law), the preacher of Law, the leader of the *Dhamma* (the Order), the charioteer of the Order-vehicle, the Sovereign King of the four-fold Order; those who are like an island, give shelter, the refuge, those who are force, support, possessors of undiminished knowledge and insight, whose condition of obscuration is ended; those who have crossed the ocean of the world, those who help those who want to cross it, those who are enlightened and help those who want to be enlightened, those who are emancipated and help others to obtain emancipation; those who are all-knowing, those who are all-seeing, those who are doers of good, are immovable, disease-free, endless, imperishable, painless, and non-returning to the cycle of births and deaths, they have reached the destination of the Siddha-state.[149]

Elsewhere, in the *Rāyapaṇiyasutta* we come across the description of the heavenly god Sūryābha, who eulogised the idol of God Jina with splendour, reciting verses containing 108 metres. Almost a similar description is provided in the *Jīvābhigama* when the heavenly god Vijaya recites praises in honour of the idols of Jina.

The *Uvasaggahara-Thotta* contains only five verses, and is extremely popular among Jains. It is a hymn in adoration of Pārśvanātha, ascribed to Bhadrabāhu II, the author of the Niryukti literature. It is also known as *Upasargahara-stava-stavana, Upasarga-haraṇa-stotra, Uvasaggaharaṃ, Uvasaggahara-tthaya-thotta, Pārśvajinalaghu-stavana-stava, Pārśvanātha-stavana-stotra* and so on. It is usually included in *Navasmaraṇa* and occupies the second position after *Navakāra mantra.* This hymn is said to contain the *Viṣadhara-sphuliṅga-mantra, Oṃ namiūṇa pāsa visahara vasaha jiṇa phuliṅga,* which has been called the *Pārśva-mantra* by W. Schubring in his *Jñānamuktāvali* (New Delhi, 1959, pp. 214, 217).[150] This *Stotra* has been furnished with 9 commentaries[151] and has undergone several editions,[152] which indicates its popularity.

The *Ajiya-Santi-Thava,* also called *Ajiya-Santi-tthaya, Ajiya-Santi-thava, Ajita-Śānti, Ajita-Śānti-stotra-stava* and so on, contains a beautiful poem in 39 or 40 different metres.[153] It is ascribed to Nandiṣeṇa who lived before than the ninth century according to Winternitz. The hymn is recited in praise of Ajita the second and Śānti, the sixteenth Tīrthaṅkara, together. As the legend goes, both of them spent their rainy season at the Śatruñjaya mountain. This *stotra* is considered the destroyer of calamities. It is said that one who recites it or listens to it, never suffers from disease.[154] The author was known for his magical powers to which a reference is made by Somadharmagaṇi in his *Upadeśasaptatikā*. He is said to have received a boon from goddess Padmāvatī to become the favourite of kings in vs 1332. He had visited the court of Mahmudshah, the successor of Alauddin. He also had assisted Malliṣeṇasūri in composing his well known *Syādvādamañjarī*. This work seems to have been quite popular. According to the *Jinaratnakośa* it was the subject of six commentaries. Jinaprabha himself wrote the *Bodha-dīpika* commentary which he styles *vivṛti* and *ṭīkā*, composed in vs 1365. Govindācārya wrote its *vivṛti* and explained it in Sanskrit. It had also an *avacūri*, but the author is not known. Out of 40 Prakrit verses 39 are explained. The author of its *avacūrṇi* is also unknown. It contains 38 Prakrit verses with a small commentary in Sanskrit. Then Harṣakīrti, pupil of Candrakīrtisūri, wrote a *vivaraṇa* explaining the text in Sanskrit.[155] The text has undergone several editions.[156]

Laghu-Ajita-Santi-Thava or Ajita-Śānti-Laghu-Stavana, also known as *Ullāsi-kama-thaya* (*Ullāsi-krama-Stotra*), is ascribed to Jinavallabhasūri (died AD 1110). The Tīrthaṅkaras Ajita and Śānti have been glorified here. It contains 17 *gāthās* with a commentary *Ullāsikrama* by Dharmatilaka Muni.[157]

Ṛṣabhapañcāśikā is a Prakrit poem in 50 stanzas composed by Dhanapāla, probably the same who composed the Prakrit *Kośa Pāiyalacchī* (in 972) and the *Tilaka-mañjarī*. It contains 7 commentaries,[158] including the commentary of the author, which has been published several times. The hymn contains beautiful metaphors: life is an ocean on which Ṛṣabha is the boat, or a forest full of robbers, namely the passions, against which one can find protection only with Ṛṣabha, or a night of false belief, in which Ṛṣabha rises like the sun. The world is to him a chess-board with human chess-men or a stage from which all the actors make their exit at the end.[159] Dhanapāla was the author of *Vīrathui* (*Vīrastuti*) also.[160]

The *Kayaṭṭhii-Tthaya* (*Kayasthiti-Stava*) is ascribed to Dharmaghosa;[161] contains 24 verses,[162] and has an anonymous Sanskrit *Avacūri*.[163]

The *Isimaṇḍala-thotta* (*Ṛṣimaṇḍala-Stotra*) is a hymn in praise of Jain teachers Jambusvāmin, Śayyambhava, Bhadrabāhu and others. Its author is Dharmaghoṣasūri, different from the author of the *Kāyaṭṭhii-tthaya.* Padmamandira has written a commentary on this treatise in AD 1496.[164] Subhavardhana, Harṣanandana, Bhuvanatuṅga, etc., are mentioned as other commentators.

Among other hymns in Prakrit, mention may be made of the *Namiūṇa Pārśvanāth* or *Bhayahara*[165] of Mānatuṅga, *Pāsajina-thava* of Dharmavardhana, *Santināha-thava* of Jinapadma, *Sattarisaya-thotta* and *Mahāvīra-thava*[166] of Nannasūri, *Namukkāra-phala-pagaraṇa* of Jinacandrasūri, *Pañcanamaskāra-stavana* and *Pañcanamaskāra-phala* of Mānatuṅga, and *Parameṣṭhi-namaskāra-stava* (or *Mantrarāja-guṇakalpa-mahodadhi*) by Jīnakirtisūri.[167] The *Jain Granthāvali* has referred to Devendrasuri's *Cattāriaṭṭhadasa-thava,*[168] *Samyaktva-svarūpa-stava, Gaṇadhara-stavana, Caturviṃśati-jina-stavana, Jinarāja-stava, Nemicaritra-stava, Parameṣṭhi-stava, Puṇḍarīka-stava, Vīracaritra-stava, Vīra-stavana, Śāśvatajina-stava, Saptaviṃśati-jina-stotra, Siddhacakra-stavana,* etc.

The *RORI Jodhpur Collection* of Mss. Pt. I, 1963; 1964 records the following:

1. *Tijaya-pahutta-stotra* with *Ṭīkā* by Mānadevasūri; composed in the nineteenth century VS; its first *gāthā* begins with '*tijaya-pahutta-payāsaya*'.

2. *Nava-smaraṇāni,* containing nine *stotras*: (i) in Sanskrit (ii) *Ajiya-santi-thava* by Nandiseṇasūri (iii) *Jayai-navanalina-kuvalaya-stava* by Pādaliptasūri (iv) *Uvasaggahara-thotta* by Bhadrabāhu (v) *Namiūṇa Bhayahara-stotra* by Mānatuṅgasūri (vi) in Sanskrit (vii) *Śakra-stotra* (viii) *Laghu-Ajita-santi-thava* by Vīragaṇi (ix) in Sanskrit.

3. *Pārśvanātha-stotra* with *ṭīkā* by Jinaprabhasūri (nineteenth century VS). It begins with '*dosāvahāra-dakkho nālīyāyara-viyāsago*'.

4. *Mahāvīra-stavaṃ* by Abhayadevasūri, begins with '*jaijjā samaṇe bhayavaṃ*'.

5. *Mahāvīra-stavaṃ* by Pādaliptasūri, begins with '*jayaī navanalina-kuvalaya*'.

6. *Upadhāna-stavana* (seventeenth century VS), begins with '*asura-sura-khayara-mahiyaṃ*'.

7. *Jayatihuyaṇa* by Abhayadevasūri, written for Jorāvarmal-Sultānmal Patvā of Rajasthan by Śankaradās Muni, pupil of Ramacandra. It contains an *Avacūri*; also *Bālāvabodha.*

8. *Ādinātha-stava* with *Bālāvabodha* by Vijayatilaka (seventeenth century VS).

9. *Sapta-smaraṇāni* in Sanskrit and Prakrit (seventeenth century VS), contains the following *stotras*: (i) *Namiūṇa stotraṃ*, (ii) *Laghu-śānti-thava*, (iii) *Tijaya-pahutta-stotra*, (iv) *Bṛhat-śānti-stotra*, (v) *Ajita-śānti-thava*, (vi) *Bhaktāmara-stotra*, (vii) *Kalyāṇamandira-stotra*.

The *Jinaratnakośa* adds:

Tīrthamālā-stavana, in praise and description of the holy places of Jains; also known as *Pratimā-stuti*. It is composed by Municandrasūri, it has a commentary by Mahendrasiṃhasūri of Añcala *gaccha*; contains 111 or 112 *gāthās*.

Pārśvanātha-stotra composed by Somasundarasūri of the Tapā-*gaccha*. It is written in different languages.

Ṣaḍbhāṣā-garbhita-stavana is recorded in the *Catalogue of Mss in the Panjab Jain Bhandar*, composed by Jinakīrti in Sanskrit, Prakrit, Magadhi, Paisaci and Gujarati.

Jain Stotra-saṃdoha is a collection of Jain *stotras* in two volumes, published by Sarabhai Navab with a learned introduction discussing the dates and authors of the *stotras*, Ahmedabad, 1932, 1936. The hymns were also written in several other languages, each stanza in a different dialect. *Ṣaḍbhāṣānirmita-Pārśvajinastavana* by Dharma-vardhana (about 1200) and *Ṣaḍbhāṣāvibhūṣita-Śāntinātha-stavana* by Jinapadma (AD 1325-44) were written in six languages: Sanskrit, Mahārāṣṭrī, Māgadhī, Śaurasenī, Paiśācī and Apabhraṃśa.[169]

Poetic hymns composed in Apabhraṃśa include the *Jayatihuyaṇa* by celebrated commentator Abhayadeva, *Aṇatthami-paddhaḍi* by Raīdhū, *Daśalakṣaṇa-jayamālā* by the same author, *Dharma-Jayamālā* (anonymous), *Pañcakalyāṇiky-ekādaśī-stavana* (anonymous) *Daśa-lakṣaṇa-samuccaya-jayamālā* by Raīdhū; *Padmāvatī-stuti* (addressed to the deity Padmāvatī) partly written in Kannaḍa; *Tīrtha-jayamālā* by Sumati-sāgara and *Sarovara Pāṇī sialā* by Sevaka in Gujarati; *Brahmadīpa-rāsa* by Bhīmsena, *Jogī-rāsa* by Jinadāsa, *Mālī-rāsa* by the same author, *Neminātha-lāvaṇī* by Caturakuśala in Rajasthani; *Maṅgalagīta* by Rūpacanda and *Ekadanta-mantra* in Hindi; *Ratnākarādhīśvara-sapādaśataka* by Ratnākara in Kannada.[170]

Several collections of Jain *Stottras* have been published: *Kāvyamālā*, Pts. I and VII; ed. Muni Caturvijaya, *Jainstotra-saṃdoha*, Pts. I and II; ed. Muni Caturvijaya, *Jainstotra-samuccaya*, Pts. I and II; *Jainstotra-saṃgraha* in *YJG*, Nos. 7 and 9, 1906; *Stutisaṃgraha* with *Avacūri*, Bombay, *NSP*, 1912; *Jainstotra-ratnākara*, I and II, Yashovijaya-Jain-

Sanskrit Pathshala, Mehsana, Bombay, *NSP*, 1913 and 1914; *Pañcapratikramaṇāadi-sūtrāṇi* in Sanskrit, Prakrit and Gujarati, Ahmedabad, 1915; ed. H.R. Kapadia, *Jain Stotras* with commentaries, illustrations and *mantras, AGS, Mahāprābhāvika Navasmaraṇa; Siddhāntasārādi-saṃgraha, MDJG*, Bombay; *JRK*, pp. 145, 453; Dr. Charlotte Krause, *Ancient Jain Hymns*, Sindhia Oriental Series, No. 2, Ujjain, 1952; *Jain Hymns*, Shri Yasobhārati Jain Prakashan, Bombay, 1975; also see M.A. Dhaky, ibid.

GNOMIC POETRY

Gnomic poetry is pithy and contains aphorisms in verse, embodying some moral sentiment or precept. We come across various expressions with regard to *subhāṣitas* (good eloquent speech) in Sanskrit literature, i.e. *Sūkti-ratñavali, sūkti-ratnakośa, sūkti-ratna-saṃdoha, sūkti-ratnākara, sūkti-rasāsvāda-jāta-romāñca-kañcuka* (having as it were armour consisting of bristling or thrilling hair produced by the taste of flavour of delightful words).[171]

Indian writers have always taken delight in the expression of pithy observations on life and morals. In the words of Winternitz, 'They have not more wonderfully succeeded in anything as in the art of giving brief and accurate expression to an idea in two lines.'[172] Most of these expressions are composed in Sanskrit *ślokas* or Prakrit *gāthās* providing an accurate picture of life ornamented with intelligent similes and metaphors. These pithy sayings are often based on extensive personal experience and are related to worldly wisdom and virtue. There is hardly any sphere of life which is not touched by them and they are often remembered by heart by common people. Indian writers had a fancy for inserting such epigramatic stanzas in their writings. We find them in the *Ṛgveda*, the *Aitareya Brāhmaṇa*, the *Upaniṣadas*, the *Mahābhārata*, the *Dhammapada*, the *Suttanipāta*, the *Uttarādhyayana*, prose novels, and Sanskrit drama.

The Sāvitrī-episode in the *Mahābhārata* can be noted. Princess Sāvitrī goes in search of her husband, she remains steadfast to her choice, practises asceticism and offers sacrifices. She pleads for the life of her husband and is able to impress the god of death by her knowledge of wise sayings. This beautiful song in praise of the 'faithful wife' is narrated by the seer Markaṇḍeya to Yudhiṣṭhira in order to comfort him regarding the fate of Draupadī. The Buddhist *Dhammapada* and the Jain *Uttarādhyayana* are important from the point of view of valuable poems in the form of a series of aphorisms, parables and similes, dialogues and ballads which belong to the 'ascetic poetry' of ancient India. It is stated in the Nāgavagga (Elephant Section) of the *Dhammapada*:

As the elephant in battle bears the arrows at him hurled,
I must bear men's bitter tongues, for very evil is the world.[173]
Good are well-tamed mules, and good are Saindhava (coming from Sindhu) steeds of lineage famed;
Good indeed the mighty tusker; best of all the man self-tamed.[174]
Better is the lonely life, for fools companions cannot be.
Live alone and do no evil, live alone with scanty needs,
Lonely, as the mighty tusker in the forest lonely feeds.[175]

In the *Uttarā* we come across numerous sayings concerning self-control, renunciation of worldly pleasures, penance and mortification, virtuous and disciplined life and so on. The question is asked: 'By what acts can I escape a sorrowful lot in this unstable internal *saṃsāra* which is full of misery?'[176] The answer is: 'Severing your former connections, place your affection on nothing; a monk who loves not even those who love him, will be freed from sin and hatred.'[177]

In the Sermon of the 'Leaf of the Tree' (*Dumapattaya*) Mahavira exhorts his disciple Gautama Indrabhūti to remain always alert and watchful. 'As the yellow leaf of a tree falls to the ground, so when the duration of time is over life comes to an end. As a dew-drop is oscillating on the top of the blade of grass lasts for a short time, so is the life of men. O Gautama, therefore be ever alert and watchful.'[178]

Besides conventional moral lessons, we have also sayings with regard to worldly wisdom and guidance (*artha* and *nīti*). Read in the *Uttarā-Nir* in the Māgadhikā metre: 'The time has passed since the rise of the sun, the crows seated on the pillar of the sanctuary have started cawing, the sun-light has wrapped the walls, yet O friend, this happy jolly fellow has not yet awakened!'[179]

Here is another pithy saying with regard to moral behaviour: 'You are keen about noticing the smallest defect just like a *rāi* seed among others, whereas you are unable to see your own even though it is as big as a *bel* fruit (wood-apple tree, its leaves are employed in the ceremonial of the worship of Siva).'[180]

Further, 'Where does not the fire burn? When does not shine the moon? Where do the virtuous people, endowed with auspicious marks, not attract the attention of people? The fire does not burn in water; the moon does not shine when it is wrapped in clouds;

distinguished learned people do not attract others in the assembly of fools.'[181]

Numerous stanzas have been recorded on various aspects of human conduct and behaviour.

'Whatever is to be done tomorrow, do it today itself before cruel-hearted death is seen approaching! Therefore one should perform religious duties without showing negligence even for a moment; every moment is full of obstacles, do not wait for the latter part of the day.'[182]

'The blind man falls in the well, the deaf does not listen to the preachings of the holy man. It is a wonder that a man though seeing and listening, falls to the region of hell.'[183]

'So long as old age does not overpower, disease in the form of fire does not consume the body and the vigour of the senses does not drop, devote your time in what is beneficial to yourself (*ātmahita*).'[184]

'A self-restrained person in the company of wicked people, is watched with suspicion just as a Brahmana, though drinking milk in a tavern, is taken to be drinking wine.'[185]

'The approaching beloved, youth, wealth, royal splendour and the moonlight during the monsoon—they must be enjoyed quickly without delay.'[186]

'There is no one in the whole world who does not feel tormented by the heat of summer. The only exception is the donkey who bears it voluntarily.'[187]

'A husbandsman with one wife, who may not be virtuous, is far better than a virtuous sovereign king with numerous wives.'[188]

'Crows, cowards, women and domestic cocks, if they stay at one place for long, they perish.'[189]

Maheśvarasūri, in his *Naṇapañcamī-kahā*: 'Whatever a cow-dung-insect may do—it may fly high in the air, it may be bumble and is may manifest its black colour, but it can never attain the conduct of a bumble-bee.'[190]

Devendragaṇi, in his *Ākhyānamaṇikośa*, with the commentary of Āmradevasūri: 'It is only for a day or so that one's father-in-law's house looks like a heaven, but later it burns with the fire of humiliation from all over.'[191]

Sumatisūri in his *Jinadattākhyāna*: 'One who affords to dwell in a village of sugarcane, dons white garments, affords to eat rice with milk and has a beloved wife, why should he care about the royal kingdom?'[192]

'What is religion? Compassion on living beings. What is happiness?

Healthy body. What is affection? Amiability. What is prudence? Discrimination between good and bad.'[193]

'Whose reputation brilliant like the autumnal moon, does not illumine the world, is just like an abandoned bull who is simply occupied in feeding itself.'[194]

'One who finds fault with an innocent person, ultimately the same fault recoils on him just as the dust flung on the moon comes back on the same person.'[195]

'Let rank, beauty and learning—all of them—go down in a cavern, let wealth alone enhance so that all other virtues becomes manifest.'[196]

'The physician without reason, the learned man without distinctive characteristics and religion without objective—all are the greatest mockery in the world.'[197]

'One should care for what is beneficial to oneself; and in case it is possible, one should also care for others. If there is a choice between one's own welfare and the welfare of others, priority should be given to one's own welfare.'[198]

'The donkey, the bull, the horse, the gambler, the learned man and the children cannot be brate one another and at the same time cannot live without one another.'[199]

ANTHOLOGIES

We find a very large number of gnomic and lyric stanzas in anthologies. We have already mentioned the *Vajjālagga*,[200] a Prakrit anthology by Jayavallabha. Peterson has referred to *Gāthākośa* by Municandrasūri (died AD 1122).[201] The *Gāthāsahasrī* by Samayasundaragaṇi is a more comprehensive anthology, with one thousand stanzas compiled from earlier works by Haribhadra, Devendra and others. It is partly in Sanskrit and partly in Prakrit and compiled in VS 1686 (AD 1629). Besides citations from the Mahāniśītha, the *Vyavahāra-Bhāṣya* and the *Puṣpamālā*-commentary, the author has also cited from the *Mahābhārata*, the *Manusmrti* and the like. An aphorism by Devendra: 'You cannot tread two paths at once, You cannot sew with a needle with two points; You cannot enjoy both at the same time, the pleasure of the senses and release in the beyond.'[202]

Among other Prakrit anthologies mention may be made of *Bhavavairagya-śataka* (a collection of hundred verses on the vanity of existence),[203] Jineśvarasūri's (AD 1115) *Gāthākośa*, Lakṣamaṇa's

Gāthākośa. Then we have *Rasālaya*, Municandra's *Rasāula*, *Vidyālaya*, *Sāhityaśloka*, *Subhāṣita* and others.[204]

Jain authors also composed anthologies in Sanskrit. In this connection, mention may be made of Amitagati's *Subhāṣita-ratna-saṃdoha* (AD 994)[205] and *Dharmaparīkṣā*. The former contains 32 chapters, each of which treats of a special subject, written in a unified metre. The *Dharmaparīkṣā*[206] or Examination of Religion deals with a large number of popular anecdotes, including those drawn from the *Mahābhārata* and the *Rāmāyaṇa*. Among other Sanskrit works, we may list Hemacandra's *Yogaśāstra*, Somaprabha's *Śṛṅgāra-vairāgya-taraṅgiṇī*,[207] Ramacandra's *Subhāṣitakośa*, Kīrtivijaya's *Subhāṣitagrantha*, Munideva Ācārya's *Subhāṣitaratnakośa*, Sakalakīrti's *Subhāṣitaratnāvali* or *Subhāṣitāvali*, Tilakaprabhasūri's *Subhāṣitāvali*, Jñānasāgara's *Subhāṣitasattriṃśikā*, Yaśasvīgaṇi's *Subhāṣitaṣaṭtriṃśika*, Dharmakumāra's *Subhāṣitasamudra*, and Śubhacandra's *Subhāṣitārṇava*.

NOTES

1. तैः शरीरं च काव्यानामलंकाराश्च दर्शिताः।
   शरीरं तावदिष्टार्थव्यवच्छिन्ना पदावली॥ *Kāvyādarśa*, 1.10.
2. काव्यशोभाकरान् धर्मान् अलंकारान् प्रचक्षते।
   ते चाद्यापि विकल्प्यन्ते कस्तान् कार्त्स्न्येन वक्ष्यति॥ ibid., 2.1.
3. नगरार्णवशैलर्तुचन्द्रार्कोदयवर्णनैः॥
   उद्यानसलिलक्रीडामधुपानरतोत्सवैः।
   विप्रलंभैर्विवाहैश्च कुमारोदयवर्णनैः॥
   अलंकृतमसंक्षिप्तम् रसभावनिरन्तरम्।
   सर्गैरनतिविस्तीर्णैः श्रव्यवृत्तैः सुसन्धिभिः॥ 1.16-18
4. *Pratibhā* (genius) means 'that mental faculty which presents ever fresh flashes or coruscations of ideas (with *unmeṣa*) or "ever fresh delineations or pictures of the matters to be described" (with ullekha)'. P.V. Kane, The *Sāhitya-darpaṇa of Viśvanātha*, Pt. II, p. 335. It is said that *vyutpatti* (culture) and *abhyāsa* (practice) polish, brighten and sharpen *pratibhā*. In order to point out the genius of a poet, the author of *Dhvanyāloka* (p. 222; also *Śṛṅgara P.*, Josyer edn. 7, p. 240) has quoted the following verse from an unknown source:

   अपारे काव्यसंसारे कविरेव प्रजापतिः।
   यथास्मै रोचते विश्वं तथेदं परिवर्तते॥
   श्रृंगारी चेत्कविः काव्ये जातं रसमयं जगत्।
   स एव वीतरागश्चेन्नीरसं सर्वमेव तत्॥

'. . . The poet is a creator in the boundless world of poetry; his universe appears to assume that form which he is pleased to give to it; whatever *rasa* (either love or pathos or heroism) he puts into his poem the world becomes immersed therein and if he himself becomes devoid of *rasa* then all follow suit' (translation after P.V. Kane, *Sahityā-darpaṇa* 338); also see Vāmana's *Kāvyālaṃkāra vṛtti* (3.1.11-20) and Rājaśekhara's *Kāvyamīmāṃsā* (X); A.B. Keith, *A History of Sanskrit Literature*, pp. 338ff.

5. अधनस्येव दातृत्वं क्लीवस्येवास्त्रकौशलम्।
अज्ञानस्येव प्रगल्भत्वं अकवेः शास्त्र वेदनम्॥ *Kāvyālaṃkāra*, 1.3f.
6. विनयेन विना का श्रीः का निशा शशिना विना।
रहिता सत्कवित्वेन कीदृशी वाग्विदग्धता॥ Ibid., 1.4
7. शब्दार्थौ सहितौ काव्यम्, Ibid., 1.16.
8. रीतिरात्मा काव्यस्य, *Kāvyālaṃkāra-vṛtti* 1, 2.6.
9. See *Kāvyālaṃkāra sūtra-vṛtti*, 3.1.10; A.B. Keith, *A History of Sanskrit Literature*, 340.
10. Rājaśekhara in his *Kāvyamīmāṃsā* (9) has spoken of two categories of poetry, *Prabandha-kāvya* and *Muktaka* (स पुनर्द्विधा मुक्तक-प्रबन्ध-विषयत्वेन), p. 46.
11. मुक्तकं श्लोक एवैकश्चमत्कारक्षमः सताम्, Daṇḍin, *Kāvyādarśa*, 1.13 Commentary (quoted from the *Agnipurāṇa*).
12. प्रसिद्धिश्चेयमस्त्येव विदग्धविद्वत्परिषत्सु यदभिमतं वस्तु व्यंग्यत्वेन प्रकाश्यते न साक्षाच्छाब्दवाच्यत्वेन, *Dhvanyāloka*, IV.5, p. 239.
13. प्रतीयमानं पुनरन्यदेव वस्त्वस्ति वाणीषु महाकवीनाम्।
यत्तत् प्रसिद्धावयवातिरिक्तं विभाति लावण्यमिवाङ्गनासु॥ 1.4
Kuntaka has quoted this verse in the commentary on *Vakroktijivita* (1.88); also *Śṛṅgāra P.* 6, p. 221.
14. *Dhvanyāloka*, p. 24.
15. शब्दो विवक्षितार्थैक वाचकोऽन्येषु सत्स्वपि।
अर्थः सहृदयाह्लादकारी स्वस्पन्दसुन्दरः॥
उभावेतावलंकार्यौ तयोः पुनरलंकृतिः।
वक्रोकिरेव वैदग्ध्यभंगी भणितिरुच्यते॥ 1.10-11
वक्रोक्तिः प्रसिद्धाभिधान-व्यतिरेकिणी विचित्रैवाभिधा। . . .
वैदग्ध्यं कविकर्म कौशलं तस्य भंगी विच्छित्तिः Commentary. Poet Mammaṭa has defined it in his *Kāvyaprakāśa* (9. *Sūtra* 103, *Śloka* 78) as follows:
यदुक्तमन्यथावाक्यमन्यथान्येन योज्यते।
श्लेषेण काक्वा वा ज्ञेया सा वक्रोक्तिस्तथा द्विधा॥
16. See *Vakroktijivita* (1.18ff).
17. According to Ānandavardhan's *Dhvanyāloka* (III.7, Commentary, p. 141), they are: मुक्तक, सन्दानितक, विशेषक, कलापक, कुलक and पर्यायबन्ध. Hemacandra in his *Kāvyānuśāsana* (8.10-13, pp. 465f) enumerates them as follows: मुक्तक, सन्दानितक, विशेषक, कलापक, कुलक, पर्याय, कोश, संघात and संहिता.
18. *Sanskrit Literature*, III, Pt. I, p. 122.
19. *ZDMG*, 40, 1886, 336ff, after Winternitz, op. cit., 123n.
20. तथा च श्रृंगारिणं जनमवलोक्य आत्मना संस्कृतपारंगतोऽपि प्राकृतगाथासंग्रहमिमं चकार, Commentary on 1.1.

21. अन्नन्नरागरसियं (Com. on 1.29).
22. संस्कृतादपि प्राकृतमतिरिच्यते।
आबालगोपालप्रसिद्धत्वात् सुगमत्वाच्च तस्य
23. ललिए महुरक्खरए जुवईजणवल्लहे ससिंगारे।
संते पाइयकव्वे को सक्कइ सक्कयं पढिउं ॥ 29 ॥
24. अमयं पाइय कव्वं पढिउं सोउं च जे न जाणंति।
कामस्स तत्ततत्तिं कुणंति ते कह न लज्जंति ॥ 2 ॥
25. एयं चिय नवरि फुडं हिययं गाहाण महिलियाणं च।
अणरसिएहि न लब्भइ दविणं च विहीणपुण्णेहिं ॥ 11 ॥
26. See supra, p. 34.
27. An alphabetical list of such verses is published in the *Prākṛtapuṣkariṇī* by this author with Introduction and Hindi translation, 1961.
28. Kavirāja Viśvanātha in his *Sāhityadarpaṇa* has referred to *Kuvalayāśvacarita* as a Prakrit poetic composition, see infra, p. 233.
29. वाणी प्राकृतसमुचितरसा, बलेनैव संस्कृतं नीता।
निम्नानुरूपनीरा, कलिन्दकन्येव गगनतलम् ॥ 52 ॥ Granthārambha-Vrajyā
30. See V.V. Mirashi, 'The Original Name of Gāthāsaptaśatī'; 13th All India Oriental Conference, Nagpur, 1946.
31. श्रूयते च कुन्तलेषु सातवाहनो नाम राजा, तेन प्राकृतभाषात्मकमन्तःपुर एवेति समानं पूर्वेण।
It is also noteworthy that the inscriptions and coin legends of the Āndhra kings are in Prakrit.
32. After Winternitz, *Sanskrit Literature*, III, Pt. I, 129.
33. सत्तसत्ताइं कइ-वच्छलेण कोडिअ मज्झआरम्मि।
हालेण विरइआइं सालंकाराणं गाहाणं ॥ 3 ॥
A. Weber in *Indische Studien*, 16, 202ff has given a list of *alaṃkāras* employed in the *Sattasaī*.
34. Referred to in Rājaśekhara's *Karpūramañjarī* (I, p. 10) and Bhoja's *Sarasvatikaṇṭhābharaṇa* (I, 133, p. 80). Namisādhu has quoted a *gāthā* from Haribuḍḍha mentioning his eight anuprāsa varieties (*vṛtti*):
तथा ह्यष्टौ हरिणोक्ताः, यथा-
महुरं फासं कोमलमोज्जस्सिं निट्ठुरं च ललियं च।
गंभीरं सामण्णं च अद्धाट्ठभणिति उ नायच्चा (व्वा)
after Raghavan's *Bhoja's Śṛṅgāra P.*, p. 835.
35. He has been referred to in the *Karpūramañjarī* (I, p. 10). 3 *gāthās* from Hala's *Gāhākosa* (I.89, III.33 and V.3) are attributed to Poṭṭisa; *NSP*, Bombay, 1911, *Gāthānukramaṇikā*, pp. 5, 10, 12; A.N. Upadhye, Introduction to *Līlāvatī*, p. 51, fn. 4.
36. He seems to be a well-known Jain poet, author of the *Taraṅgavaikahā* which is no longer available. He might have participated in shaping the *Sattasaī* of Hāla, A.N. Upadhye, ibid., p. 51 and fn 1. According to Pischel (*Grammatik*, Art.13) he is credited with the authorship of ten verses in this anthology. Prabhācandra in his *Prabhāvakacarita* (revised in AD 1277 by Pradyumnasūri) has provided an account of Pādalipta; also see *Purātana-prabandha-saṃgraha*.

37. The *Prākrta-paiṅgalam* (I.64) refers to the poets Śarabha, Śeṣa and Śaśadhara.
38. कान्ते तल्पमुपागते विगलिता नीवी स्वयं बन्धनात्।
वासश्च श्लथमेखलागुणधृतं किंचिन्नितम्बे स्थितम्॥
एतावत् सखि वेद्मि केवलमहं तस्याङ्गसङ्गं पुनः।
कोऽसौ काऽस्मि रतं च किं कथमिति स्वल्पाऽपि मे न स्मृतिः॥
'When the beloved came to the couch, the knot of my garment dissolved of its own accord, and checked for a while by my loosened girdle, it slipped on my hips. All this I remember clearly: but at his intimate touch, dear friend, I swear if I have the faintest recollection of myself or of him or what he did to me.' (Translated by S. Dey.)
This verse seems to be quite popular with ancient Sanskrit poets. It is quoted in Jalhaṇa's *suktimuktāvali* (p. 299) where it is attributed to some unknown poet (*Kasyāpi*). It has been quoted in the *Daśarūpaka* (2.19) as cited in Bhoja's *Śṛṅgāra P.* (19, p. 968).
Rājaśekhara's *Kāvyamīmāṃsā* (1934, p. 223), has attributed it to the *Amaruśataka* (101) while Dey has attributed to Vikaṭanitambā.
There are two more verses of the same author recorded in the *Sūktimuktāvali*, pp. 209 and 273.
Bhoja too has quoted her verses anonymously. Rājaśekhara has another verse of her in which he extols her poetry as sweeter than the words of one's beloved. The verse is as follows:
के वैकटनितम्बानां गिरां गुम्फेन रंजिताः।
निन्दन्ति निजकान्तानां न मौग्ध्य-मधुरं वचः॥
The same verse is quoted by Bhoja in his *Śṛṅgāraprakāśa* (XXII, p. 809) to illustrate a variety of public love, *prakāśānurāga,* called *punarbhū-viṣayānurāga.*
At yet another place (XXIX, p. 970), Bhoja, in order to illustrate an aspect of *dautya-karma* (the function of a messenger), quotes the following verse. It is put in the mouth of Vikaṭanitambā's female messenger:
पृष्टः काले वदनि स माषं तद्विपरीतं सस्यहिरण्यं।
लुम्पति चोष्ट्रे रं वा षं वा तस्मै दत्ता विकटनितम्बा॥
The same verse with explanatory remarks and slightly differently is quoted by Namisādhu in his commentary on Rudraṭa's *Kāvyālaṃkāra* (p. 73, *KM* edition).
यथा विकटनितम्बाया. पतिमनुकुर्वाणा सखी प्राहः-
काले माषं सस्ये मासं, ददति शकाशं यश्च सकाशं।
उष्ट्रे लुम्पति रं वा षं वा, तस्मै दत्ता विकटनितम्बा॥
The female messenger who goes between the woman poet and her husband pities the fate of the woman who is a master of Sanskrit and has been given away (*dattā*) to an illiterate fellow who cannot pronounce three *cerebrals* together (i.e. *ṣa* as in *māṣa* and *māsa*; *śa* as in *śakāśaṃ* and *sakāśaṃ*; *ra* and *ṣa* as in *uṣṭra*) in a conjunct consonant and will

change a cerebral into a dental and a dental into a palatal (Raghavan, *Bhoja's Śṛṅgara P.*, 834). Bhojadeva also refers to Vikaṭanitambā in his *Sarasvatīkaṇṭhābharaṇa.* The following *śloka* has been cited in three different ways (pp. 139, 617, 625, etc., *NSP*, Bombay, 1925):

किं द्वारि दैवहतके सहकारकेण
संवर्धितेन विष-पादप एष पापः।
अस्मिन्मनागपि विकास-विकार-भाजि
भीमा भवन्ति मदनज्वर-संनिपाताः (2, 35)

also quoted in the *Śṛṅgāra P.* (II, p. 58; XI, p. 449; XXII, p. 800).
The following verse is assigned to Vikaṭanitambā in the *Sāhityadarpaṇa* (III, 169, p. 178).

अन्यासु तावदुपमर्दसहासु भृङ्ग! लोलं विनोदय मनः सुमनोलतासु।
मुग्धामजातरजसं कलिकामकाले व्यर्थं कदर्थयसि किं नवमल्लिकायाः॥

39. A verse from Vijjā, Vijjakā, Vijjākā, Vijjikā or Vidyā is quoted in the *Sūktimuktāvali* (p. 299). At another place the poet has made a reference to poet Daṇḍin (p. 47). 29 verses that are ascribed to her are composed in very fine language, dealing with various topics such as love, seasons and damsels, see 'Sanskrit Poetesses', Part A by Dr. J.B. Chaudhury and English translation by Dr. Roma Chaudhury, pp. xxxviii-xlv, after P.V. Kane, *The Sāhityadarpaṇa of Viśvanātha* with Exhaustive Notes, 3rd edn., 1951, p. 121.

Bhoja in his *Sarasvatīkaṇṭhābharaṇa* cites the following verse under the name of Vijjikā or Vijjākā, also known as Mārulā (*aparaṃ mārulā iti nāma*). It refers to poet Daṇḍin:

नीलोत्पलदलश्यामां विज्जकां मामजानता।
वृथैव दण्डिना प्रोक्तं सर्वशुक्ला सरस्वती॥

The same verse is noticed in the *Subhāṣitāvali.* (इत्यपि पद्यं सुभाषितावलौ प्राप्यते।) Also see fn under Mammaṭa's *Kāvyaprakāśa* (IV.61) Another verse:

उन्नमय्य सकचग्रहमास्यं चुंबति प्रियतमे हठवृत्त्या।
हुं हुं मुञ्च ममेति च मन्दं जल्पितं जयति मानवतीनाम्॥

This is also noticed in the *Subhāṣitāvali* I, 123, p. 74; V, 85, p. 517. Still another verse:

विलासमसृणोल्लासन्मुसललोलदोष्कन्दली
परस्परपरिस्खलद्वलयनिस्वनोद्दन्तुराः।
हरन्ति कलहुंकृति प्रसभकंपितोरः स्थल-
त्रुटद्गमक संकुलाः कलमकण्डिनीगीतयः॥

also in the *Subhāṣitāvali,* V, 87, p. 517.

In his *Śṛṅgāraprakāśa* (II, p. 47) Bhoja cites a verse of Rājaśekhara about Vijayāṅkā or Vijayā. He says, there are two kinds of persons. There are men who talk incorrect Sanskrit like the sages, who speak 'यर्वाणः तर्वाणः' (वैयाकरणोऽप्यवज्ञया कदाचिदवैयाकरणवद् ब्रूते; श्रूयते हि-यर्वाण-स्तर्वाणा नाम साक्षात्कृतधर्माण ऋषयो बभूवुः। ते हि अन्तर्वेद्यामेव न म्लेच्छितव्यं, अतोऽन्यत्रावज्ञया इति यद्वानस्तद्वान इति वक्तव्ये यर्वाणस्तर्वाणः इत्यूचुः) and there are women who are masters of Sanskrit and speak like men (अवैयाकरणोऽव्ययं वैयाकरणवद् ब्रूते, योषिदपि कदाचित् आश्रित-प्रागल्भ्यात् पुंवद्वक्ति).

In illustration of the latter, the following verse is cited:
सरस्वतीव कर्णाटी विजयाङ्का जयत्यसौ।
या वैदर्भगिरां भूमिः कालिदासादनन्तरम्॥
Then Rājaśekhara in his *Kāvyamīmāṃsā* (XII, p. 67, edn. 1934) has cited the following verse under the name of Vijjākā:
धन्यास्तु याः कथयथ प्रियसङ्गमेऽपि
विस्रब्धचाटुशतकानि रतान्तरेषु।
नीवीं प्रति प्रणिहितश्च करः प्रियेण
सख्यः शपामि यदि किञ्चिदपि स्मरामि॥ p. 223, Explanatory Notes.
Also cited in Mammaṭa's *Kāvyaprakāśa* (IV.61) with the remark: विज्जिकाया पद्यमिदं शाङ्गधर-पद्धतौ स्पष्टम् also cited in the *Sāhityadarpaṇa,* III, 60, p. 116.
The *Sāhityadarpaṇa* (IV, 8, p. 250) cites another verse assigned to Vijjākā:
दृष्टिं त्वं प्रणिधायिनि! क्षणमिहाप्यस्मद्गृहे दास्यसि
प्रायेणास्य शिशोः पिता न विरसाः कौपीरपः पास्यति।
एकाकिन्यपि यामि सत्वरमितः स्रोतस्तमालाकुलं
नीरन्ध्रास्तनुमालिखन्तु जरठच्छेदा नलाग्रन्थयः॥
(The commentator Shivdatta Kaviratna remarks:
पद्यमिदं कस्याश्चन कुलटायाः।)

40. Śilābhaṭṭārikā was another well-known poet. Her three verses are cited in the *Sūktimuktāvali* (pp. 145, 166 and 301). Mammaṭa in his *Kāvyaprakāśa* (I, p. 17) has cited the following verse under the name of Śilābhattārikā:
यः कौमारहरः स एव हि वरस्ता एव चैत्रक्षपास्ते चोन्मीलित-मालती-सुरभयः प्रौढाः कदम्बानिलाः।
सा चैवास्मि तथापि तत्र सुरत-व्यापार-लीला-विधौ रेवा-रोधसि-वेतसी-तरु-तले चेतः समुत्कण्ठते॥
commentary: शिलामहारिकायाः पद्यमिदमिति शार्ङ्गधर-पद्धतौ स्पष्टम्। Note: शिलानाम्नी महारिका स्वामिनी इत्यर्थः। काश्मीरदेशस्था शिलाख्या गौरी-विकटनितम्बा-सूरीका-विज्जिकादिवत् काचन कवयित्री तस्याः also cited in the *Sāhityadarpaṇa,* I, 2.
She is praised by Rājaśekhara, as cited in the *Sūktimuktāvali* (p. 47), along with Vikaṭanitambā, Vijayāṅkā, Prabhudevī and Subhadrā (*Kāvyamīmāṃsā,* X, p. 53nn and p. 200).

41. The verses of Bhāvadevī, Mārulā and Indulekhā are cited by Sushilkumar Dey in his *Treatment of Love* (p. 48). A verse from Mārulā has been quoted in the *Sūktimuktāvali* (p. 140). As we have noticed earlier, Bhojadeva in his *Śṛṅgāraprakāśa* identifies her with Vijjikā. The poetess Indulekhā too was quite popular. Her five verses have been cited in the *Sūktimuktāvali* (p. 167). Dey has rendered one of her following verses into English:
Some say 'it drops into the ocean'; others believe 'it mixes and becomes one with fire', while still others think, 'it goes to another world'. But how can I believe all this? For I see with my own eyes that every evening the sun with its fierce heat comes and hides itself in the heart of the maiden whose lover has gone abroad.
The following verse of Subhadrā is cited in the *Sūktimuktāvali* (p. 47).

She was known for her dexterity of expression:
पार्थस्य मनसि स्थानं लेभे लघु सुभद्रया।
कवीनां च वचोवृत्ति-चातुर्येण सुभद्रया॥ *Kāvyamīmāṃsā,* p. 200, notes
See also Raghavan, 'Sanskrit and Prakrit Poetesses', *Quarterly Journal of the Mythic Society,* Banglore, Vol. XXV, Nos. 1-3; J.B. Chaudhuri, 'Sanskrit Poetesses Vijjā and Morikā', *IHQ,* Calcutta, Vol. XVI, pp. 543-60.
Among other women writers, mention may be made of (i) Rāmabhadrāmbā of Tanjore, who wrote a poem entitled *Raghunāthābhyudaya* to celebrate the greatness of her lover Ragunātha Nāyaka of Tanjore (early seventeenth century), (ii) Tirumalāmbā, the writer of *Varadāmbikā-pariṇaya,* a highly artificial *Campū,* describing the romance of love and the wedding of Varadāmbikā with her own husband or lover Acyutarāya, king of Vijayanagara, (iii) A queen of Vīrakampana or Kamparāya composed the *Madhurā-vijaya* or *Vīrakamparāya-carita.* See S.N. Das Gupta, *A History of Sanskrit Lit. Classical Period,* 1947, pp. 417f.

42. See *Prākṛta puṣkariṇī,* footnotes on pp. 8, 9, 14, 19, 20, 29, 31, 35; also Mathuranath Shastri's Introduction to *Gāthāsaptaśatī.* On the same pattern, Sūryamalla, a poet of ḍiṅgala, has composed *Vīrasatasaī;* in Gujarati, Dayārām and Dalpatrām have composed *Satasaiyā* and *Dalapatsatasai* respectively. These Prakrit lyrics have also influenced Apabhraṃśa poetry as found in Hemacandra's Prakrit Grammar, see *Prākṛtapuskariṇī,* p. 74 fn; Winternitz, *Sanskrit Literature,* III, Pt. I, 132. The *Bihārī-satasai* gained such popularity that a Sanskrit commentary *śrutābodha* was composed on it by Nāvhāvyāsa, the son of Vyāsaśukadeva: इतिश्री महमेवाडाज्ञाति-व्यासशुकदेवसूनुना नाहाव्यासेन बिहारीदास-सतसैया-टिप्पणं श्रुतबोधाख्यं सम्पूर्णम्, *A Catalogue of Sanskrit and Prakrit Mss in the Raj OIJ Collection,* Pt. I, Appendix I, p. 108.
43. *JRAS,* 1894, p. 110 after Winternitz, ibid., p. 153.
44. Winternitz, *Sanskrit Literature,* III, Pt. I, p. 123 fn.
45. *History of Sanskrit Literature,* p. 178.
46. नानाकार्यवशाद्यस्या दूरदेशं गत: पति:।
सा मनोभवदु:खार्ता भवेत् प्रोषितभर्तृका॥ *Sāhityadarpaṇa,* III.84.
47. आलोअन्त दिसाओ ससंत जंभंत गंत रोअंत।
मुज्झंत पडंत हसंत पहिअ! किं ते पउत्थेण॥ *Gāhāsattasaī,* 3.36.
48. अज्जवि ताव एक्कं मा मं वारेहि पिअसहि! रूअंतिम्।
कल्लि उण तम्मि गए जइ ण मरिस्सं ण रोइस्सं॥ Ibid., 5.2.
49. वेविरसिण्णकरंगुलि परिग्गहक्खलिअ लेहणीमग्गे।
सोत्थि च्चिय ण समप्पइ पिअसहि! लेहम्मि किं लिहियो॥ *Gāhāsattasaī,* 3.44.
50. अमयमय-गयणसेहर-रयणीमुहतिलय-चन्द! दे छिवसु।
छित्तो जेहिं छिपिओ ममंपि तेहिं चिय करेहिं॥ Ibid., 1.16.
51. साहीणे वि पिअअमे पत्ते वि खणे ण मंडिओ अप्पा।
दुक्खिअपउत्थवइअं सअज्झिअं संठवंतीए॥ Ibid., 1.39.
52. अत्ता एत्थ णिमज्जइ, एत्थ अहं दिअसअं पलोएहि।
मा पहिअ रत्ति-अंधअ! सेज्जाए महँणिमज्जहिसि॥ *Gāhāsattasaī,* 7.67; it is cited as an

illustration of *abhinaya* and *niyama ulaṃkāra*, quoted in *Kāvyānuśāsana* (p. 53), *Sāhityadarpaṇa* (p. 17) and *Kāvyaprakāśa* (5, 136). महँण=आवयोः

53. भम धम्मिय! वीसत्थो सो सुणओ अज्ज मारिओ तेण।
गोलाणइकच्छ कुडंगवासिना दरियसीहेण॥ *Gāhāsattasaī*, 2.75; quoted in *Kāvyādarśa*, p. 47, 13; *Sāhityadarpaṇa*, p. 242; *Dhvanyāloka*, p. 16; *Kāvyaprakaśa*, 5, 138; *Rasagaṅgādhara*, 1, p. 15.
54. Julius Labor, Calcutta, 1914, 1923 and 1944; M.V. Patwardhan, Ahmedabad, 1969.
55. The two available recensions have 692 and 652 stanzas respectively, Winternitz, ibid., p. 195, fn. 2.
56. Even *gāthās* from Hemacandra and Abdurrahamān's *Sandeśarāsaka* are quoted here; for common *gāthās* from Hāla's *Sattasaī*, see Introduction to *Vajjālagga* by Patwardhan, pp. 26-9.
57. ए दइए ! मह पसिज्जसु माणं मोत्तूणं कुणसु परिओसं।
कयसेहरेण सुम्मइ आलावो झत्ति गोसम्मि॥
58. कल्लं किर खरहिअओ, पविसिहिइ पिओ त्ति सुव्वइ जणेण।
तह वड्ढ भअवइ निसे! जइ से कल्लं न होइ॥
(also quoted in Bhoja's *Sarasvatikaṇṭhābharana*, 20, 89) Compare with
सजन सकारे जायेंगे नैन मरेंगे रोइ।
या विधि ऐसी कीजिये फजर कबहुं ना होहि॥ *Bihāri Satasai.*
59. 'कइआ गओ पिओ', 'अज्ज पुत्ति', 'अज्जेण कइ दिणा होंति'।
'एक्को' एद्दहमेते भणिए मोहं गआ बाला॥379॥
(also quoted in *Śṛṅgāraprakāśa* (23.71) and *Sarasvati:* (5.254).
60. इय पंथ मा वच्चसु गयवइ भणियं भुयं पसारेवि।
पंथिय! पियपायमुद्दां, मइलिज्जइ तुज्झ गमणेण॥
61. हत्थट्ठियं कबालं न मुयइ नूणं खणं पि खट्टंगं।
सा तुह विरहे बालय! बाला कावालिणी जाया॥
62. उद्धच्छो पिअइ जलं जह जह विरलंगुली चिरं पहिओ।
पावावलिआ वि तह तह धारं तणुअंपि तणुएइ॥445॥
63. अमुणियपियमरणाए वायसमुड्डाविरीइ घरिणीए।
रोवाविज्जइ गामो अणुदियहं बद्धवेणीए॥460॥
64. न मए रुण्णं न कयं अमंगलं होंतु सयलसिद्धीओ।
विरहग्गिधूमकडुयाइयाइं पयलंति नयणाइं॥370॥
65. एक्केण वि सरउ सरेण वाह! किं वीएण गहिएण।
एक्कं वि वसइ जीयं हयास! दोण्हं पि य सरीरं॥277॥
66. Traditionally this title is applied to the following six distinguished poems: *Raghuvaṃśa, Kumārasaṃbhava* and *Meghadūta* by Kālidāsa, *Śisupālavadha* by Māgha, *Kirātārjunīya* by Bhāravi and *Naiśadhacarita* by Śrīharṣa.
67. A. Hoefer brought this work to light in 1846; Paul Goldschmidt published *Specimen des Setubandha* in 1873 with a Word-Index; with a German translation in Srassburg, 1880. On the basis of this Śivadatta and K.P. Parab brought out a Bombay edition with the commentary of Rāmadāsa, *KM* 47, 1895. It is noteworthy that this work was popular up to the reign of Akbar. Rāmadāsa wrote his commentary in 1596 under

orders of Akbar, and Akbar's son Jahangir authorized a Sanskrit translation, Winternitz, *Sanskrit Literature,* III, Pt. I, p. 79, fn. 1.

68. One Pavaraseṇa (Pravarasena) is also mentioned in Hāla's *Gāhāsattasaī,* as one of the most excellent poets of Prakrit. He seems to be different from the author of our *Setubandha.*
69. परिवड्ढइ विन्नाणं, संभाविज्जइ जसो विढप्पंति गुणा।
    सुव्वइ सुपुरिसचरिइं, कित्तं जेण न हरंति कहालावा॥ 1.10
70. गमिआ कदंबवाआ, दिट्ठं मेहंधआरिअं गअणअलं।
    सहिओ गज्जिअसद्दो, तह वि हु से णत्थि जीविए आसंगो॥ 1.15
71. धीरं व जलसमूहं, तिमिणिवहं विअ सपक्खपव्वअलोअम्।
    णइसोत्तेव तरंगे, रअणाइं व गुरुअगुणसआइं वहन्तम्॥ 2.14
72. णवरिअ सरणिभिण्णो, बलआमुहविहुअकेसर सदुग्धाओ।
    उद्धाविओ रसन्तो, विसत्थपसुत्त केसरिव्व समुद्दो॥ 5.34 (translation after Winternitz, *Sanskrit Literature,* III, Pt. I, p. 79.
73. धरिआ भुएहि सेला सेलेहिं दुमा दुमेहि घणसंघाआ।
    ण वि णज्जइ किं पवआ, सेउं बंधंति ओमिणेंति णहअलम्॥ 7.58
74. अलअं छिवइ विलक्खो, पडिसारेइ वलअं जमेइ णिअत्थम्।
    मोहं आलवइ सहिं दइआलोअणडिओ विलासिणीक-सत्थो॥
75. Cited about 28 stanzas, *Prākṛtapuṣkarṇī.*
76. Cited about 5 stanzas, ibid.
77. With Haripāla's commentary published by Shankar Pandurang Pandit. Bombay Sanskrit Series 34, 1887; Ed. Shankar Pandurang Pandit and Narayan Bapuji Utgikar, BOI, Poona, 1927; Narhar Govind Suru, Prakrit Text Society, 1969.
78. Vākpatirāj was a disciple of famous dramatist Bhavabhūti; both lived in the court of Yaśovarman, the earliest king of Kannauj, in the seventh century.
79. पेच्छह विवरीयमिमं बहुया मइरा मएइ ण हु थोवा।
    लच्छी उण थोवा जह मएइ ण तहा इर बहुया॥ 860
80. पत्थिवधरेसु गुणिणो वि णाम जइ केवि सावयासव्व।
    जण सामण्णं तं ताण किंपि अण्णं चिय निमित्तं॥ 876
81. महुमह-विअअ-पउत्ता वाआ कह णाम मउलउ इमम्मि।
    पढम-कुसुमाहि तलिणं पच्छा-कुसुमं वणलआण॥ V. 69
82. The verse लीलादाढ, etc. (see the following footnote) is misprinted in the text. For its Sanskrit *chāyā* see *Bālapriyā* commentary on *Dhvanyāloka* by Pandit Shri Mahadevashastri, Chaukhamba Sanskrit Series, 1940, p. 346.
83. लीलादाढग्गुवूढसयलमहिमंडलस्स चिय अज्ज।
    कीस मुणालाहरण पि तुज्झ गरुआइ अंगम्मि॥
    It is addressed to god Viṣṇu: one who had raised the whole earth on his large tooth sportively assuming the form of a boar, now why does he feel even the decoration of a lotus-fibre heavy on his body.
84. चूअंकुरावअंसं छण-पसर-महग्घ-मणहर-सुरामोअं।
    अपणामिअं पि गहिअं कुसुम-सरेण महुमास लच्छीए मुहं॥
    Dhvanyāloka, III, p. 127; *Kāvyānuśāsana,* pp. 79, 74.

The god of love held down by force the bent face of the spendour of Spring who looks pretty with ear-ornaments of a cluster of mango blossom, and at the time of the spring festival appears splendid and lovely and is replete with fragrance.

कवि प्रौढोक्ति is explained by Mammaṭa in his *Kāvyaprakāśa* (IV, *sutrā* 54, *śloka* 39f) as follows

अर्धशक्त्युद्भवोऽप्यर्थो व्यंजकः संभवी स्वतः ॥ 39

प्रौढोक्तिमात्रात्सिद्धो वा कवेः तेनोम्भितस्य वा।

स्वतः संभवी न केवलं भणितिमात्रनिष्पन्नो यावद्बहिरप्यौचित्येन संभाव्यमानः । कविना प्रतिभामात्रेण बहिरसन्नपि निर्मितः . . . (i.e. which does not exist in reality but is created by poet's genius).

85. The Commentator Abhinavagupta has explained it: हरिविजये कान्तानुनयनांगत्वेन पारिजातहरणादि निरूपितमितिहासेषु अदृष्टमपि, ibid., p. 148; *Dhvanyāloka*, 3, p. 148, after V. Raghavan, *Bhoja's Śṛṅgāra P.*, p. 824.

86. एवं सहजसौकुमार्यसुमगानि कालिदास-सर्वसेनादीनां काव्यानि दृश्यन्ते। *Vadroktijīvita* (1.52 commentary).

87. In 'The Harivijaya and Sarvasena', V.M. Kulkarni observes: 'We are a little more fortunate to have at least twenty-two verses which we can definitely ascribe to *Harivijaya* on the strength of their contents and/or on the basis of clear references by Ānandavardhana and Bhoja. There are many more verses in *Śṛṅgāraprakāśa* and quite a few in *Sarasvatīkaṇṭhābharaṇa* which are in Mahārāstri Prakrit and are composed in the *Skandhaka* metre. As they are not found in *Setubandha*, they may have been drawn from *Rāvaṇavijaya* or *Harivijaya*, most probably from *Harivijaya*, the model of *Setubandha*.' *Studies in Sanskrit Sāhitya-Śāstra*, Patan, 1986, pp. 162-79.

88. तेष्वभिप्रायाङ्कता यथा-धैर्यमाढ्यराजस्य उत्साहः सर्वसेनस्य अनुरागः प्रवरसेनस्येति, I, 11, p. 474.

89. नगरवर्णनं यथा सेतुबन्ध-हरिविजय...शैलवर्णनं यथा किरातार्जुनीय-शिशुपालवध-सेतुबन्ध-हरिविजयादौ-...तत्रर्तुवर्णनेन शरद्-वसन्त-ग्रीष्म-वर्षादि वर्णनानि सेतुबन्ध-हरिविजय ...आदौ ...नायक-वर्णनं यथा हरिविजय ...आदौ ...वाहनवर्णनं यथा हर्षचरित-कादम्बरी-हरिविजय ...आदौ ...मधुपानं द्विधा, गोष्ठीगृहे वासभवने च। तत्राद्यं यथा हरिविजये शिशुपालवधे च।। I, 11, pp. 475, 476; also *Kāvyānuśāsana*, pp. 458f.

90. तत्र निसृष्टार्थो यथा, उघोरापर्वणि वासुदेवः, हरिविजये वा सत्यकः, Ibid., p. 475; also *Kāvyānuśāsana* (सत्यकिः सात्यकिः or सत्यकः), p. 458.

91. अभिमतार्थसिद्धये यथा विष्णोः पारिजातहरणाय हरिविजये, Ibid., also *Kāvyānuśāsana*, p. 458.

92. तत्रारि-विजयो द्विधा, शत्रुच्छेदेन तदुपरत्याश्च। स पूर्वो यथा रावणवधादौ; द्वितीयो यथा हरिविजयादौ, Ibid., p. 476; also *Kāvyānuśasana*, p. 459.

93. अंगस्य अप्रधानस्य अतिविस्तरेण वर्णनं यथा-

तथा हरिविजये-ईर्ष्यानुकुपित सत्यभामानुनयन-प्रवृत्तस्य हरेः

पारिजात-हरण-व्यापारेण उपक्रान्त-विप्रलम्भस्य वर्णन-प्रस्तावे

गलितक-निबन्ध-रसिकतया कविना समुद्र-वर्णनं अन्तरा गडुस्थानीयं विस्तृतं, *Kavyānuśāsana*, p. 171.

94. Raghavan, ibid., p. 825.

95. राजा श्री सर्वसेने (न) . . . विजयं हरे: । *Śloka* 12 at the beginning (Trivandrum Sanskrit Series edn., p. 172), after Raghavan, *Bhoja's Śṛṅgāra Prakāśa,* p. 825.
96. मअ-वह-णिमित्त-णिग्गअ-मइन्द-सुण्णं गुहं णिएऊण।
लद्धावसरो गहिऊण मोत्तिआइं गओ वाहो॥ *Śṛṅgāraprakāśa,* II.11, p. 472.
A hunter who had gone to kill a lion, found the cave empty and getting an opportunity, picked up some pearls and returned home.
97. न काव्यार्थविपर्यास वशेन रागभावादिविपर्यासो नाट्य एव। तथाहि राघव-विजयस्य हि ठक्करागेणैव विचित्रवर्णनीयत्वेऽपि निर्वाह: मारीचवधस्य ककुभग्रामरागेणैव। अत एव रागकाव्यानीत्युच्यन्त एतानि after Raghavan, ibid., pp. 550, 822f. The *Rāghava-vijaya* is throughout sung only in *Ṭhakka-rāga* and the *Nārīcivadha* in the *grāma-rāga* called *Kukubha.* Both these works are called *Rāga-kāvyas.* The *Rāga-kāvya* is a musical composition covering a complete story, i.e. a whole Kāvya in the shape of songs.
98. ननु चाश्वासकबन्धेषु तत्समाप्तावपि न च्छन्दोभेद उपलभ्यते। तथाहि रावणविजय-हरिविजय-सेतुबन्धेष्वादि-तत्समाप्ति पर्यन्तमेकमेव च्छन्दो भवति। *Śṛṅgāra Prakāśa,* I.11, p. 473; also *Kāvyānuśāsana,* pp. 461f.
99. सअलं चेव णिबंधं दोहिं पएहिं कलुसं पसण्णं च ठिअं।
जाणंति कईण कई सुद्धसहावेहि लोअणेहि व हिअअं॥ ibid., p. 823. Given in the form of correct text in the *Kāvyānuśāsana* commentary, p. 456.
100. नायकवर्णनं यथा हरिविजय-हर (रावण) विजय-जानकीहरण-रघुवंशादौ। ...वाहन-वर्णनं यथा हर्षचरित-कादम्बरी-हरिविजय-रावणविजयादौ। हस्त्यश्व गरुत्मत्-पुष्पकादि वर्णनादि ...*Śṛṅgaraprakaśa,* II. 11, p. 475 also *Kāvyānuśasana,* p. 458. It appears that this work began with the praise of good poets, providing descriptions of towns, sunsets, heros, horses, elephants and other things, required for a *Mahākāvya.*
101. See his *Devīśataka* (V.104), *KM,* Pt. IX, p. 30, A.M. Ghatge, Mahārāṣṭrī Language and Literature, *JUB,* Vol. IV, May, 1936, Pt. 6, p. 64.
102. See supra, p. 226.
103. तं ताण सिरिसहोअर-रयणाहरणम्मि हिअअमिक्करसं।
बिंबाहरे पिआणं निवेसियं कुसुमबाणेण॥ *Dhvanyāloka* (II, p. 111; IV, p. 24); *Kāvyānuśāsana,* A, p. 74, *śloka* 70.
104. ताला जायंति गुणा जाला ते सहिअ एहिं घिप्पंति।
रविकिरणाणुग्गहिआइं हुंति कमलाइं कमलाइं॥
Also *Dhvanyāloka,* II.1, p. 62; also Rājānaka Ruyyaka, *Alaṃkārasarvasva,* p. 23; *Kāvyaprakāśa,* 7, 315; *Kāvyānuśāsana, A,* pp. 209, 235.
105. स्मरं प्रति यौवनोक्ति: (गुरुं प्रति शिष्योक्ति:):
हुमि अवहत्थिअ-रेहो णिंरकुसो अह विवेक-रहिओ वि।
सिविणे वि तुमम्मि पुणो पत्तिहि मत्तिं न पुप्फुसिमि॥ *Dhvanyā* (III.15, *Bālapriyā* Com., p. 346; *Kāvyaprakāśa,* VII. 320; *Kāvyānuśāsana,* p. 82, *śloka* 152 *(viveka).*
106. ण अ ताण घडइ ओही ण ते दीसंति कहवि पुणरुत्ता।
जे विब्भमा पिआणं अत्था वा सुकइ-वाणीणम्॥ *Dhvanyā* IV, p. 241.
It appears that it contained the speeches of cupid and this companions, A.M. Ghatge, ibid., p. 64. *Dhvanyā* IV, p. 241.
107. जे परिहरिउं तीरइ मणअं पि ण सुंदरत्तणगुणेण।
अह णवरं जस्स दोसो पडिपक्खेहिं पि पडिवण्णो॥ *Kāvyaprakāśa* VII.216.

108. तो ताण हअच्छाअं णिच्चल-लोअण-सिहं पउत्थपआवं।
आलेक्ख पईवाणं व णिअअं पइइ-चडुलत्तणं पि विअलिअं॥
Sarasvatīkanṭhābharaṇa (IV, 56; V, 24); *Kāvyānuśāsana*, p. 145, *śloka* 170; also *Setubandha*, 2.45).
109. MW.
110. Raghavan, ibid., p. 797.
111. नायिका वर्णनं यथा कुवलयाश्वचरित, etc. The same in the *Kāvyānuśāsana*, p. 458.
112. Ed. with Introduction etc. by A.N. Upadhye, *SJS*, 2nd edn., 1966.
113. पविरल-देसि-सुलक्खं, 41
114. सुयण-खलेहि अलं चिय गुण-दोसे जे णियंति किं तेहिं।
गुण-दोस-रया जाणंति मज्झिमा कव्व-परमत्थं॥ 1332
115. दीहच्छि कहा एसा अणुदियहं जे पढंति णिसुणंति।
ताणं पिय-विरह-दुक्खं ण होइ कइया वि तणुअंगि॥ 1333
116. Dr. A.N. Upadhye. *Līlāvatī*, Introduction, p. 80.
117. अइ-रमणीया रमणी सरओ विमलो तुमं च साहीणो।
अणुकूल-परियणाए मण्णे तं णत्थि जं णत्थि॥ 32
118. एक्कं चिय सलहिज्जइ दिणेस-दियहाण णेह-णिव्वहणं।
आजम्म एक्कमेक्केहिं जेहिं विरहो च्चिय ण दिट्ठो॥ 222
This *gāthā* is found also in the *Vjjālagga*, 65.
119. पच्चूस-गय-वरुम्मूलियाए उड्डीण-ससि-बिहंगाए।
धवलाइं गलंति णिसा-लयाए णक्खत्त-कुसुमाइं॥ 1091
Hemacandra has cited this verse in his *Chandonuśāsana*, p. 1a, Bombay, 1912, after A.N. Upadhye, *Līlāvatī*; Notes, p. 379.
120. पाउं जुण्हा-मइरं जामिणि-विलयाए फलिह-चसओ व।
मुक्को णहाहि णिवडइ णिलीण-मय-महयरो चंदो॥ 1092
121. Ed. S.P. Pandit, Bombay Sanskrit Series, 1900 with the commentary of Pūrṇakalaśagaṇi; P.L. Vaidya, Bhandarkar Oriental Institute, Poona, 1936; Satyapal Narang, New Delhi, 1972.
122. According to P. Peterson, there had been an author's own commentary on this work. G. Bühler has referred to *Dvyāśraya-kośa-vṛtti* which seems to be a commentary on the *Dvyāśrayakāvya*, Satyapal Narang, Hemacandra's *Dvyāśrayakāvya*, p. 12.
123. Similar is the case with Kṛṣṇalīlāśuka's *Siricindhakavva* (*Śrīcinhakāvya*, also known as *Govindābhiṣeka*; its first canto has been edited by A.N. Upadhye (*Bhāratīya Vidyā*, 3.1) where the author has given illustrations to explain the grammatical rules contained in Vararuci's *Prākṛtaprakāśa* and Trivikrama's *Prākṛtavyākaraṇa*.
124. तं तुं तुवं तुह तुमं आणेह नीवकुसुमाइं।
भे तुब्भे तुम्होय्हे तुय्हे तुज्झासणं देह॥
125. H. Jacobi, Bhavnagar, 1914; Muni Punyavijaya, with Hindi translation by S.M. Vora, *PTS*, 1962, 1968. It has an old palm-leaf MS written in vs 1198 in the collection of Jaisalmar Jain Bhandar, K. Kasliwal, *Prakrit-vidya*, July-Dec. 1990.

126. उवसग्ग-गब्भहरण, इत्थी-तित्थं अभाविया परिसा।
कण्हस्स अवरकंका, उत्तरणं चंदसूराणं॥
हरिवंस-कुलुप्पत्ती, चमरुप्पातो य अट्ठसयसिद्धा।
अस्संजतेसु पूआ, दसवि अणंतेण कालेण॥
127. *The Vasudeva,* pp. 26f; *ZDMG,* 42, 1888, p. 494.
128. Devendragaṇi, *Uttarajjhayaṇa* Com., 22, pp. 278ff.
129. Ibid., pp. 36a-44.
130. Ibid., 233a-236.
131. *RKŚS,* Ratlam, 1930.
132. Ed. Amritalal Bhojak, *PTS,* 1961; with an introduction of Klaus Bruhn, Hamburg, 1954.
133. For a list of manuscripts on the subject see the following works:

(a) *Jain Granthāvali,* Shri Shvetambara Jain Conference, Bombay, vs 1965. Here are mentioned: Vardhamānasūri's *Ādināhacariya,* Somaprabha's (pupil of Vijayasiṃha) *Sumatināhacariya,* Devasūri's *Paumappahacariya,* Yaśodeva's *Candappahasāmicariya,* Ajitasiṃha's *Sejjaṃsanāhacariya,* Candraprabha's *Vāsupujjasāmicariya,* Nemicandra's *Anantanāhacariya* (vs 1213), Devacandra's (teacher of Hemacandra) *Santināhacariya,* Jineśvara's *Mallināhacariya* (vs 1175), Śrīcandra's *Muṇisuvvayasāmicariya,* containing 10994 (Śricandra, pupil of Maladhāri Hemacandra completed it in vs 1193). Its MS prepared five years later (in 1198) at the instance of the author is contained in the collection of the Jaisalmer Bhandar, K. Kasliwal, *Prakrit-Vidyā,* July-Dec. 1990. Ratnaprabhasūri's (pupil of Vādidevasūri) *Nemināhacariya* (in vs 1233) and so on (pp. 238-45). Then the following works have been recorded: *Atimuktakacarita, Isidattācariya* (by Gunapāla Muni; ninth-tenth century), *Devakīcariya, Rohiṇīcariya, Manoramācariya* (by Vardhamānasūri in vs 1140), *Paumāvaicariya, Haribalacariya, Vairasāmicariya, Nāgadattacariya, Bharahacariya* and many others (pp. 220-37).

(b) The *Jinaratnakośa* records the following:
Anjañāsundarīcarita by Guṇasamṛddhimahattarā, pupil of Jinacandrasūri. It contains 503 *gāthās* and was composed in Jaiselmere in vs 1400.
Damayantīcarita contains 20 chapters, each having 105 *gāthās.* The MS is preserved in the Bhandar of Lodhi Posala Sanghavi Pada Patan. (It is a very valuable collection of about 500 palm-leaf MSS.)
Devakī-suta-carita. It is the same as *Sukosala-carita,* containing 97 *gāthās.* It is mentioned in Peterson's collection, I A, p. 95.
Pṛthvīcandra-carita by Śāntisūri, pupil of Nemicandra, pupil of Sarvadevasūri of Bṛhadgaccha. The treatise contains about 7500 verses, composed in vs 1161. *Malayasundarī-carita* by an unknown author, consists of 1296 *gāthās.*

Mahāpuruṣa-carita by Śīlācārya, pupil of Mānadevasūri. It was composed in vs 925 and describes the lives of the *śalākā-puruṣas.*

The RORI Jodhpur Collection, Pt. II (A), 1964, p. 312 records *Javarājarṣi-carita* in Prakrit, composed in the nineteenth century vs.

Bhuvanatuṅgasūri's *Rāma-Lakṣmaṇa-caritra*; *Hariṣeṇacaritra*, *Jayacakrīcarita*, *Śālibhadracaritra*, *Ārdrakakumāracaritra*, *Gāṅgeyabhaṅga-prakaraṇa* (by Padmavijaya vs 1878; published by Ātmavīra Granthamālā, 1917; by Śrīvijaya with his own *Avacūri*, published by Jain Atmananda Sabha, Bhavnagar), *Prabhāvatī-dṛṣṭānta*, *Siddhasena-carita*, *Mallavādikathā*, *Bappabhaṭṭicarita* and many others.

(c) *Jain Sahitya ka Brhad Itihasa* (Pt. VI, ed. by Gulabchandra Chaudhari) mentions the following: *Śaṇakkumāracariya* by Śrīcanda-sūri (vs 1214), *Nalacarita* (the seventeenth Kāmadeva), *Vijaya-candracarita*, also known as *Haricandrakathā* (the fifteenth Kāmadeva) by Candraprabha Mahattara (in vs 1127), *Pratyekabuddhacarita* by Tilakasūri (in vs 1261) and others.

(d) *The Catalogue of Patan Grantha Bhandar* (Gaikwad Oriental Series), Pt. I has recorded: *Sagaracakrīcarita*, *Vasudevacarita* (the twentieth Kāmadeva) and others.

134. *SJS*, Bombay, 1959. There has a MS in the collection of Jaisalmer Durg Shastra-Bhandar, K. Kasliwal, *Prakrit Vidyā*, July-Dec. 1990.
135. Ed. Jagdish Chandra Jain, *MJS*, Bombay, vs 1993. For a list of Prakrit and Sanskrit works see *JSBI*, 6, pp. 154ff.
136. Ed. Muniraj Shri Rājvijaya, Jain Vividh Sahitya Shastramala, Benaras, 1916.
137. Panyāsa Māṇivijaya Gaṇivara Granthamālā, Ahmedabad, 1942.
138. Ahmedabad, 1945; Gujarati translation, Jain Atmanand Sabhā, Bhavnagar, vs 2005.
139. *DLGP*, 1929; Gujarati trans. Jain Atmanand Sabhā, Bhavnagar, vs 1914. It has a MS written in vs 1240 in the collection of the Jaisalmer Shastra-Bhandara, K. Kasliwal, op. cit.
140. Jain Vividha Sahityamālā, Banaras, 1918.
141. Atmavallabha Grantha Series, Valād (Ahmedabad), 1932.
142. Panyāsa Maṇivijaya Granthamālā, Leench (Mehsana), vs 2006.
143. Jain Vividhashastra Sāhityamālā, No. 131, Varanasi, 1919; P.L. Vaidya, Poona, K.V. Abhyankara, Ahmedabad, 1931; A.T. Upādhyāya, Belgaum, 1936.
144. See *Theragāthā* (4).
145. Hemacandra Granthamālā, Hiralal Hansraj, Jamnagar, vs 1978; R. Williams, Two Prakrit Versions of the *Maṇipati-carita* with English translation, London, 1959.
146. *Prākṛtā-vidyā*, July-Dec. 1990.
147. The *Caṇḍiśataka* by Bāṇabhaṭṭa, the *Sūryaśataka* by Mayūra, the *Yamunāṣṭaka* by Vallabhācārya, the *Gaṅgālaharī* by Jagannātha and others can be mentioned. Pandit Jagannātha, a lyrical poet, composed the *Gaṅgālaharī* in praise of the Gaṅgā. He is said to have married a

Muslim girl for which he was excommunicated. One day, seated with his wife on the bank of the Gaṅgā, he began to pray the holy river. With the completion of each stanza the river continued to rise and when he recited the 52nd stanza the river reached him and his consort and washed off their sin. Both were drowned in the river and were never seen again. Among the Buddhist *stotras*, the *Catuḥ-Śataka Stotra* (the Hymn of Four Hundred Verses) and the *Śatapañcāśikā Stotra* (the Hymns of One Hundred and Fifty Verses) by most famous Mātṛceṭa, *Catuḥstava* (Collection of Four Hymns in Tibetan translation) by Nāgārjuna, *Suprabhāta Stotra* (Morning Hymn in praise of Buddha) and *Aṣṭa-Mahāśrīcaitya-Stotra* (Hymn in Praise of Eight Great Shrines) by King Harṣavardhana, *Lokeśvara-Śataka* by Vajradatta, the *Sragdharā-Stotra* (*sragdharā* meaning the female wearer of the wreath, an epithet of goddess Tārā; also name of the metre in which the poem is written) or *Ārya-Tārā-Sragdharā-Stotra* by Sarvajñamitra and others can be noted.

148. Also M.A. Dhaky, 'The Jina Image of the Nirgrantha and Hymnic Imagery', *The Śāstric Traditions in Indian Art*, 2 vols., pp. 99f, edited by Dallapiccola, Anna Liber, Stuttgart, 1989.

149. Ibid., p. 101.

150. *CJMS*, p. 323. Serial No. 262.

151. *JRK*, p. 54.

152. Ed. H. Jacobi, *Kalpasūtra*, 1881, Introduction and English translation; along with *Saptasmraṇa*, published with the commentaries of Jinaprabhasūri, Siddhacandragaṇi and Harṣakīrti, *DLJP*, Bombay, 1933; H.R. Kapadia, *Uvasaggaharā-thotta ek Adhyayana*, Mohanlalji Granth, Bombay, 1964, Sec. D, pp. 24-43.

153. The following metres are employed: अपरान्तिका (34), आलिंगणय (5), किसलयमाला (19), कुसुमलया (15), खित्तय (24-5), खिज्जिअअ (खिद्यतक-17), गाहा (1-2: 35-40), चित्तक्खरा (27), चित्तलेहा (13), दीबय (26), नंदिअय (नन्दितक-29), नारायअ (14, 28, 31), भासुरय (20), भुयंगपरिंगिय (16), मागहिया (4:6), रयणमाला (23), रासानंदिय (12), रासालुद्धअ (10), ललियअ (18:32), वाणवासिया (33), विज्जुविलसिय (21), वेड्ढअ (वेधृक-9; 11; 22), सिलोग (3), संगयय (7), सुमुह (20), सोवाणय (8) For details see infra pp. 342f; also Sushil Vijaya, *Shri Ajitashantistavana anetanā chhando, Jain Sahitya Prakash*, Vol. 5, No. 12.

154. जो पढइ जो य निसुणइ उभओ कालं पि अजियसंतिथयं।
न वि हुंति तस्स रोगा पुव्वुप्पन्ना विणा संति॥ 39॥
In this connection read Phyllis Granoph, 'The Power of Hymns and the Miracle at the Liṅga: The Jain Version', *Journal of Indian Philosophy* 17:329-84, 1989. Here, besides the famous hymn, the *Bhaktāmarastotra*, she refers to the story of Bappabhaṭṭisūri, Abhayadevasūri, Bhadrabāhu, Aryanandila (his composition of *Vairoṭhyāstava*, a hymn to the Snake Goddess Vairoṭhyā to free people from any threat from snakes), Jinaprabhasūri (he is said to have written 700 hymns and to have made

a vow that he would never eat without first reciting a new hymn to the Goddess Padmāvatī), Mānadeva (who recites a hymn in honour of Śāntinātha in order to avert the plague), Munisundarasūri, Samantabhadra and Siddhsena (pp. 362-5).

155. H.R. Kapadia, *DCGCM, BORI*, Vol. XVII, Pt. I, 1935, pp. 10f, 23-5, 28f.
156. Schubring, *Zeitschrift für Indologie und Iranistik*, Leiptzig, II, pp. 178-203; Bhavnagar, vs 1982; Muni Vīrvijaya, Ahmedabad, vs 1992. Bechardas Doshi has published this hymn in his *Prakrit Nārgopadeśikā, Pahali*, Appendix 6, pp. 361-6 where the names of metres are given.
157. See *JRK* for similar works.
158. Ibid., p. 58.
159. Winternitz, ibid., pp. 553-4.
160. Both published in the *ZDMG*, Vol. 33; *KM*, Pt. 7, Bombay, 1980; *Ṛṣabhapañcāśikā* along with *Avacūri*, and *Virathui*, published by *DLJP*, Bombay, 1933.
161. There have been a number of Jain writers of this name. One Dharmaghoṣa, pupil of Devendra (died in AD 1270) was the author of the *Yamakastuti*, and probably also of the *Catuviṃśatijinasturi* (see Winternitz, ibid., 557); he was also author of the *Lokanālikāprakaraṇa*. Another Dharmaghoṣa was the author of *Isimaṇḍala thotta* (see below). According to Dharmasāgara's Gurvāvali, *Kāyaṭṭhii-tthaya* is a work of Dharmaghoṣasūri (died vs 1357). However, this work has been ascribed to Kulamaṇḍana by Schubring and others, but Kulamaṇḍana, on the other hand, is recorded to have composed an *Avacūri* on this work, see *CJMS*, p. 325, Serial 264.
162. *JRK*.
163. *CJMS*, p. 324, Serial No. 264.
164. Ed. Yashovijaya Maharaj, Baroda, vs 2012.
165. Jinaprabhasūri wrote a commentary on this work in AD 1309, Winternitz, ibid., p. 556, fn. 2.
166. Here the same words occur three times over with a different meaning each time, Winternitz, ibid., p. 558.
167. Published in *SJS*, Bombay.
168. *DLJP*, 1933.
169. Winternitz, ibid., 558.
170. See *CJMS*, pp. 346-55.
171. See *MW*, under '*Subhāṣita*' (1) The *Kavīndra-vacana-samuccaya* is supposed to be the earliest known anthology which is incomplete and anonymous, published from a unique manuscript in Nepalese characters of about the twelfth century AD (F.W. Thomas, *Bibliothica Indica*, Calcutta, 1912). (2) *Subhāṣita-ratnāvali* of Kashmīraka Vallabhaḍeva (P. Peterson & Durgaprasad, *BSS*, 1886). (3) *Sadūkti-karṇāmṛta* by Śrīdharadāsa, composed in AD 1206. (4) *Subhāsita-muktāvali* or *Sūkti-muktāvali* by Jalhaṇa, edited by Ember

Krishnamacharya, Baroda, 1938. See S.N. Das Gupta, *A History of Sanskrit Literature Classical Period*, 1947, pp. 412-14. For further list, see Satyaprakash, *Jainism: A Select Bibliography*, 1984.

172. *A History of*, III, Pt. I, p. 168.

173. अहं नागो व संगामे चापितो पतितं सरं।
अतिवाक्यं तितिक्खिस्सं दुस्सीलो हि बहुज्जनो॥ 320॥

174. वरं अस्सतरा दंता अजानीया च सिन्धवा।
कुंजरा च महानागा अत्तदंतो ततो वरं॥ 322॥ Translation by F.L. Woodward, Winternitz, *Sanskrit Literature* II, pp. 81, 82.

175. एकस्स चरितं सेय्यो नत्थि बाले सहायता
एको चरे न च पापानि कयिरा
अप्पोस्सुक्को मातंग रञ्ञे व नागो॥ 330॥ Ibid.

176. अधुवे असासयम्मी, संसारम्मी दुक्खपउराए।
किं नाम होज्ज तं कम्मयं, जेणाहं दोग्गइं न गच्छेज्जा॥ VIII.1

177. विजहित्तु पुव्वसंजोयं, ण सिणेहं कहिं चि कुव्वेज्जा।
असिणेह सिणेहकरेहिं, दोस-पओसेहिं मुच्चए भिक्खू॥ VIII.2

178. दुमपत्तए पंडुयए जहा, निवडइ राइगणाण अच्चए।
एवं मणुयाण जीवियं समयं गोयम! मा पमायए॥
कुसग्गे जह ओस बिंदुए, थोवं चिट्ठइ लंबमाणए।
एवं मणुयाण जीवियं, समयं गोयम! मा पमायए॥ X.1-2

179. अइरूग्गयए य सूरिए, चेइय थूभगए य वायसे।
भित्ती गयए व आयवे, सहि! सुहिओ हु जणो न बुज्झइ॥ *Uttarā. Nir.*

180. राईसरिसवमित्ताणि परछिद्दाणि पाससि।
अप्पणो बिल्वमित्ताणि पासंतोऽवि न पाससि॥ Ibid., 140.

181. कत्थ व न जलइ अग्गी, कत्थ व चंदो न पायडो होइ।
कत्थ वरलक्खणधरा, न पायडा होंति सप्पुरिसा॥
उदए न जलइ अग्गी, अब्भच्छिन्नो न दीसइ चंदो।
मुक्खेसु महाभागा, विज्जापुरिसो न मायंति॥ *Bṛh Bhā, Uddeśa* 1.

182. जं कल्लं कायत्वं, णरेण अज्जेव तं वरं काउं।
मच्चू अकलुणहिअओ, न हु दीसइ आवयंतो वि॥ Ibid., *Uddeśa* 3.

183. अंधो णिवडइ कूवे बहिरो ण सुणेदि साधु उवदेसं।
पेच्छंतो णिसुणंतो णिरए जं पडइ तं चोज्जं॥ *Tiloyapaṇṇatti*, IV.622.

184. उत्थरइ जा ण जरओ रोयग्गी जा ण डहइ देहउडिं।
इंदियबलं न वियलइ ताव तुमं कुणहि अप्पहियं॥ Kundakunda, *Aṣṭapāhuḍa, Bhāvapāhuḍa* 131, Compare with जरा जाव न पीलेइ वाही जाव न वड्ढइ।
जाविंदिया न हायंति ताव धम्मं समाचरे॥ *Das.* Chapter 7.

185. दुज्जण संसग्गीए संकिज्जदि संजदो वि दोसेण।
पाणागारे दुद्धं, पियंतओ बंभणो चेव॥ *Bhag Ārā.*

186. सयमागया पिया जोव्वणं च अत्थो य राय-लच्छी य।
वास-समये य जोण्हा पंच वि तुरमाण-भोज्जाइं॥ *Vasudevahiṇḍi.*

187. सो णत्थि कोइ जीवो जयम्मि सयलम्मि जो ण गिम्हेण।
संताविओ जहिच्छं एक्कं चिय रासहं मोत्तुं॥ *Kuvalayamālā*, 418, p. 276.

188. वरि हलिओ वि हु भत्ता अनन्नभज्जो गुणेहि रहिओ वि।
मा सगुणो बहुभज्जो जइ राया चक्कवहट्टी वि॥ *Nāṇapancamikahā*, 1.39

189. कागा कापुरिसा वि य इत्थीओ तह य गामकुक्कडया।
एगट्ठाणे वि ठिया मरणं पावेंति अइबहुहा॥ op. cit., 10.452.
190. उप्पयउ गयणमग्गे रुंजउ कसिणत्तणं पयासेउ।
तह वि गोब्बरईडो न पायए भमरचरियाइं॥ 183,8
191. दो तिन्नि वासराइं सासुरयं होइ सग्गसारिच्छं।
पच्छा परिभव-दावानलेण सब्बत्थ पज्जलइ॥
192. उच्छुगामे वासो सेयं वत्थं सगोरसा साली।
इट्ठा य जस्स भज्जा पिययम! किं तस्स रज्जेण? 49, p. 47.
193. को धम्मो? जीवदया, किं सोक्खं? अरोग्गया उ जीवस्स।
को णेहो? सब्भावो, किं पंडिच्चं परिच्छेओ॥ *Uvaesapada.*
194. सारय-ससंक-धवला, कित्ती भुवणं न जस्स धवलेइ।
नियपोट्ट-भरण-वावड-रिट्ठ-सरिच्छेण किं तेण?॥ *Dharmopadeśamālā-vivaraṇa.*
195. सुद्धसहावम्मि जणे जो दोसं देइ पडइ तस्सेव।
गुंडिज्जइ नणु सो च्चिय, जो धूलिं खिवइ चंदस्स॥ ibid.
196. जाई रुवं विज्जा तिन्निवि निवडंतु कंदरे विवरे।
अत्थो च्चिय परिवड्ढउ, जेण गुणा पायडा होंति॥ *BHBH*, p. 534.
197. तक्कविहूणो विज्जो, लक्खणहीणो य पंडिओ लोए।
भावविहूणो धम्मो तिण्णिवि गरूइ विडंबणया॥ *Sudaṃsaṇācariya.*
198. अप्पहियं कायव्वं जइ सक्कइ परहियं च कायव्वं।
अप्पहिय परहियाणं अप्पहियं चेय कायव्वं॥ *Vajjālagga*, 83.
199. रासहवसहतुरंगा, जूआरा पंडिया डिंया।
न सहंति इक्क इक्कं इक्केण विणा ण चिट्ठंति॥ *Rambhāmañjarī*, I, 40.
200. In *JRK* (pp. 340, 236) also known as *Padyālaya*, *Vajrālaya*, etc.
201. Edited and translated by L.P. Tessitori in *Giornale della societa Asiatica Italiana*, 22, 179-211; 24, 405ff, Winternitz, ibid., p. 575.
202. Winternitz, ibid., 574.
203. Winternitz, ibid., p. 575.
204. *Jain Granthāvali*, p. 341.
205. Edited in *KM*, 82; edited and translated by R. Schmidt and J. Hertel in *ZDMG*, 59, 1905, and 61, 1907.
206. Jain Siddhanta Prakashini, Calcutta, 1908; Hindi translation, *JGRK*, Bombay, 1908; N. Mironow, *Die Dharmaparīkṣā* des Amitagati, Leipzig, 1903.
207. *NSP*, Bombay, 1942. For other works on Sanskrit anthologies see Winternitz, *A History of*, III, Pt. I, pp. 196-200; Keith, ibid., pp. 227-36.

6

Narrative Literature in Mahārāṣṭrī

We have seen that Daṇḍin regarded Mahārāṣṭrī Prakrit as the language par excellence. Numerous poetic works have been composed in this dialect which we have discussed in the previous chapter. This popular dialect was so flexible that besides poetry, Jains also wrote a vast narrative literature in it. As we have seen, the Śvetāmbara Jain canonical literature was composed in Ardhamāgadhī, the dialect spoken in Magadha. Although the disciples of Mahavira tried to preserve his teachings in their original form it was not possible to do so. First, the dialect went on changing from time to time; it also was modified when it travelled from one region to another. Then the canonical texts were finally restored about a thousand years after Mahavira, at Valabhi in Gujarat. Certainly, during this long period, the canonical texts must have undergone considerable change and modification in presentation of subject matter and particularly language.

In course of time, slowly and gradually the Ardhamāgadhī dialect was replaced by a more popular dialect, Mahārāṣṭrī. The origin and development of Mahārāṣṭrī (or Jain Mahārāṣṭrī as it called by Jacobi and other western scholars) and its relation to other Prakrit dialects is an interesting topic of study for a student of linguistics. Unfortunately, reliable manuscripts are not available; besides, the scribes have incorporated changes in places while copying the manuscript. As a result the later grammarians also could not do justice to the subject while laying down the rules of the dialect. Obviously, it was not possible for Hemacandra to explain the rules of the dialect which was spoken at the time of Mahavira. However, we find that the language of the Śvetāmbara canonical literature is different from that of the commentary literature of the canonical texts as well as the later narrative literature written independently by Jains.

In this connection the *Vasudevahiṇḍi*, an important Jain text written in archaic Jain Mahārāṣṭrī by Saṅghadāsagaṇi Vācaka, different from Saṅghadāsagaṇi Kṣamāśramaṇa of the *Bṛh Bhā*, is worth mentioning. Unfortunately, we know very little about the author—his date, his origins or other works. The *Vasudevahiṇḍi* (*VH*) (Wandering of Vasudeva), also known as *Vasudevacariya* (Biography of Vasudeva) deals with the wanderings (*hiṇḍi*) of Vasudeva, the father of Kṛṣṇa Vāsudeva. The author of the *VH* states, 'I am going to narrate the *Vasudevacariya*, a compilation (*saṃgaha*) which has been handed down through a succession of teachers.' According to him, Sudharma Svāmī had narrated story to his disciple Jambu as told in the *Prathamānuyoga*, describing the life of the Tīrthaṅkaras, the Cakravartin and the rulers of the Dasāra clan.[1] The *VH* seems to have been a popular text among the Śvetāmbara Jains. Jinabhadragaṇi Kṣamāśramaṇa has referred to the *Vasudevacariya* in his *Viśeṣaṇavatī* (AD 610). Jinadāsagaṇi Mahattara has quoted the text in his *Āvaśyaka-Cūrṇi* (600-50), saying *jahā Vasudevahiṇḍīe*, while recording the biography of Ṛṣabha, the first Tīrthaṅkara,[2] the story of Pasannacanda and Vakkalacīrin, and the story of Dhammillahiṇḍi. A comparative study of the texts of the fourth *lambha*, the Nīlajasālambha of the *VH* (beginning with the biography of Usabhasāmin until the account of Vairaseṇa, pp. 157-78, 14) with that of the *Āvaśyaka-Cūrṇi* (pp. 128-30) is worth making.[3] Dharmasenagaṇi Mahattara in the beginning of his work claims to have completed the unfinished portion of the *VH*, and this shows that he was well-acquainted with the work of Saṅghadāsagaṇi. Further, Vādivetāla Śāntisūri (died AD 1040) in his *Pāiya-ṭīkā* commentary on the *Uttarādhyayana* narrates verbatim the story of Agadaḍatta as told in the *VH*.[4]

The *VH* is divided into six *adhikāras*: (i) *Kahuppatti* (*Kathotpatti*), (ii) *Peḍhiyā* (*Pīṭhikā*), (iii) *Muha* (*Mukha*), (iv) *Paḍimuha* (*Pratimukha*), (v) *Sarīra* (*Śarīra*), and (vi) *Uvasaṃhāra* (*Upasaṃhāra*). The first section (2-26) deals with religious stories, ending with a reference to the origin of the *Vasudevacariya*. Section two (77-104) contains a part of the Kṛṣṇa legend where the story of the princes Pajjuṇṇa (Pradyumna) and Samba (Śamba) is narrated. This section is important as here Śamba's love for a courtesan's daughter Suhiraṇyā is portrayed. It can be well compared with prince Naravāhanadatta's love for Madanamañjukā in the *BKŚS* (*Bṛhatkathāślokasaṃgraha*) of Budhasvāmin.[5] The *Muha* (105-9) contains the boyish pranks of the princes Śamba and Subhānu. The *Paḍimuha* (110-13) narrates the wanderings of Vasudeva, who proposes to tell the long tale of his wanderings to his grandson Pajjuṇṇa. Section five, known as the Sarīra (114-370), is most important as it narrates the wanderings of the hero Vasudeva. This section contains 28 *lambhas* bearing the names of 26 heroines whom the hero married during the course of his wanderings. This section should have ended with the Rohiṇī-*lambha* (p. 366) though in the printed text it ends with the incomplete Devakī-*lambha.* It seems to be doubtful whether this *lambha* formed a part of the original text. In this section right in the middle of the story, between the eighteenth Piyaṅgusundarī-*lambha*, and the twenty first *lambha*, the Ketumatī-*lambha*, two important *lambhas*, are missing.[6] Since the *VH* is incomplete, it contains no *Uvasaṃhāra*, therefore no union of the hero Vasudeva with the heroine Somasiri is described here as in the Kashmiri versions, the *Kathāsaritsāgara* (=*KSS*) of Somedeva and the *Bṛhatkathāmañjarī* (=*BKM*) of Kṣemendra.

The text of the *VH* has been edited with utmost care with the help of twelve manuscripts, including the palm-leaf manuscripts by Munis Caturvijaya and Punyavijaya, published by Shri Jain Atmanand Sabha, Bhavnagar (1930-1), but unfortunately, the text is corrupt and badly mutilated. The Piyaṅgusundarī-*lambha* (No. 18) and the Ketumatī-*lambha* (No. 21) seem to be the most corrupt *lambhas* and it is interesting that it is between them two important *lambhas* are missing from the text. According to the editors, the missing portion altogether is about 22 per cent, or little less than one-fourth of the text. In other words, according to their estimate, the whole text contains 11,000 *ślokas*, of which about 500 are missing. Besides, some external material that is out of context has been incorporated in the text. It contains inconsistencies and there are points that cannot be explained; at places poetry is mingled with prose and the author has referred to certain variants (*pāḍho*), which indicates that there may have been more than one version of the text.

However, the *VH* remains an important Prakrit text for the study of history and development of Jain story literature, development of Jain Harivaṃśa tradition, evolution of Jain Mahārāṣṭrī different from Ardhamāgadhī dialect of the canonical text, preservation of the lost *Baḍḍakahā* of celebrated Guṇāḍhya in a different version, and above all maintaining the cultural and social material of the relevant period which is hardly available elsewhere. 'The Vasudevahiṇḍi, a Specimen of Archaic Jains Mahārāṣṭrī', Ludwig Alsdorf has pointed out:

The scope and plan of the *Vasudevahiṇḍi* has no parallel in the older non-canonical Jaina literature. The style is far from being concise or dry; it presents us with a vivid, characteristic and highly interesting picture of a living language. The tale is frequently embellished with flowery descriptions so dear to Indian poets, and some of them are—at least partially—in the old *veḍha*metre, hitherto unknown to occur outside the canon—an unmistakable sign of great antiquity.[7]

Richard Pischel in his *Grammatik Der Prakrit Sprachen* (=Grammatik) and H. Jacobi in his *Ausgewählte Erzählungen in Mahārāṣṭrī* have discussed various aspects of Prakrit language and thereby have rendered a great service in the field of Prakrit languages. However, in their time few publications of Prakrit literature were available, therefore they had to draw their conclusions from manuscripts. There have been grammatical forms given by Prakrit grammarians but these could not be traced from literary evidence. There have been also forms recorded from other Prakrit dialects, but the same forms found in the Jain Mahārāṣṭrī could not be traced by Pischel. Besides, there are certain grammatical forms that go against the observations made by Pischel. Alsdorf, after making an elaborate study of the *Vasudevahiṇḍi*'s grammatical forms and expressions in his above-mentioned article, has observed that in the light of the study of *VH*'s grammar,[8] the views of Pischel and Jacobi need to be modified. He writes:

The *VH* has presented us a picture of Jaina Mahārāṣṭrī materially different from that which is familiar to us from Pischel *Prakrit Grammar* and Jacobi's *Ausgewählte Erzählungen in Mahārāṣṭrī.* Its main features are: first, an even much closer affinity to Ardhamāgadhī than that prevailing ordinary Jaina Mahārāṣṭrī and Ardhamāgadhī (cf. Pischel's *Prakrit Grammar,* 20)—we are markedly near the time when Jaina Mahārāṣṭrī came first into being as an individual dialect, distinct from Ardhamāgadhī. Secondly, a great number of archaisms and other interesting peculiarities which not only in themselves are valuable additions to our knowledge, but also help to elucidate many a dark point of Prakrit grammar and linguistic study. Ultimately the great problems of the origin and true character of Ardhamāgadhī and Jaina Mahārāṣṭrī, of their development, and their relations to each other as well as to the other Prakrit dialects, the Pali, etc., are raised anew and demand new answers.[9]

Majjhimakhaṇḍa Vasudevahiṇḍi-Madhyama Khaṇḍa, Pt. I (1 to 18 *Lambhas*), ed. H.C. Bhayani and R.M. Shah, *LDS,* Ahmedabad, 1987 (*The Middle Part*), also styled as the Second Part (*Dvītīya Khaṇḍa*) of the *VH* by the editors of the *Vasudevahiṇḍi* (p. 308, footnote), is equally important. As stated earlier, the *VH* is an incomplete distorted version of the *Bṛhatkathā* and is supplemented by Dharmasenagaṇi in his *Majjhimakhaṇḍa* (*MKH*). In the introduction, the author states that as Vasudeva, the hero, married a hundred girls during the course of his wandering for a hundred years, the *VH* should have contained 100 *lambhas*. Yet he asserts that the existing text of the *VH* contains only 29 *lambhas*, and that the remaining 71 *lambhas* have been left out as they contained lengthy descriptions of the tale. Therefore Dharmasenagaṇi claims to present the entire missing part of the *VH* through his composition of the *Majjhimakhaṇḍa*. Instead of commencing at the end of the *VH*, he commences at the nineteenth and the twentieth *lambhas*, the two missing *lambhas* between the *Piyaṅgusundarī-lambha* and the *Ketumatī-lambha*. Thus the first *lambha* of the *MKH* is the *Pabhāvatī-lambha* which deals with the conquest of Prabhāvatī provides many interesting details which are not available even in the *KSS* and the *BKM*, the two Kashmiṛian versions of the *BK*. It is noteworthy that the tale of Prabhāvatī in the *VH* seems to be incomplete and told very briefly, though the text contains the *Pabhāvatī-lambha* (22) and certain points are introduced in brief in the beginning of the *Ketumatī-lambha* (21). The story of Prabhāvatī is so sketchy in the *VH* that the episode remains fully unexplained.

It is difficult to say whether the original *VH* contained 100 *lambhas* and the author has retained only 29, the rest being left out considering them as lengthy. But one thing is certain: the author of the *MKH* has rendered a great service by completing the incomplete account of Prabhāvatī which forms an important part of the Vasudeva story. Another important point regarding the *MKH* is that as the incomplete *VH* has no conclusion (*upasaṃhāra*), no union of the hero with the heroine could have been narrated. But in the *MKH* the hero Vasudeva pardons Mānasavega, the abductor of his beloved Somasiri, even though the latter was intensely keen to take revenge on the former; then Mānasavega carries both Vasudeva and Somasiri to the city of Mahāpura where a tumultuous reception is given to them.[10]

Part II (19-36 *Lambhas*) of the *MKH* remains unpublished. The whole manuscript[11] is in four volumes, containing 71 *lambhas*. Volume one was collated by the late Muni Punyavijaya, providing variants from several manuscripts. It contains the *Pabhāvatī-lambha*, the first *lambha* of the composition. The second volume contains 2 to 44 *lambhas* (pp. 86-276).[12] The third *khaṇḍa*, also known as *Uttarārdha*, contains two volumes, with 45-56[13] and 57-71[14] *lambhas* respectively. At the end there is an *upasaṃhāra* where the union of Vasudeva with Somasiri is described.

The style of the *MKH* is very vivid, lively and fluent; it is highly interesting, providing flowery descriptions, romantic scenes and dramatic touches with witty dialogues. Like the *VH*, it does not contain moral lessons within the main story. The whole account is written in the first person which indicates its antiquity, and like the *VH* it is also related to the lost *Bṛhatkathā* of Guṇāḍhya. It seems that this Mahārāṣṭri composition belongs to the fourth or fifth century, but according to the editors of the *Vasudevahiṇḍi Madhyamakhaṇḍa*, it is about AD 700.

It was natural that Jain authors imparted religious instructions leading to renunciation from worldly pleasures, but at the same time they had to make these instructions full of delight and lively so that their purpose was served. Therefore they had to employ the technique of disguising their teaching in the form of love stories. The author of the *MKH* affirms that generally people take delight in listening to love stories such as those of Nahusa, Nala, Dhundhumāra, Nihasa, Purūrava, Mānadhātā, Rāma, Rāvaṇa, Janamejaya, Rāma, Kaurava, Paṇḍusuta, Naravāhanadatta and others so that no desire is left in them to listen to religious stories. Therefore he proposes: 'As a physician administers his own nectar-like medicine to an unwilling patient under the pretext of what the patient desires, so should a virtuous story be told under the pretext of love story.'[15] But the question remains how exactly happiness is acquired by listening to erotic tales. The reply is 'by practising good conduct'. It has been stated: 'The happiness of a cakravartin, the happiness of humans, and even the extraordinary happiness of liberation is not difficult at all for those who have well practised penance.'[16]

Here we reproduce an episode from the *Pabhāvatī-lambha.* Prabhāvatī was carrying Vasudeva through the air to his beloved Somasiri, who was taken captive by Mānasavega and kept in his pleasure-garden in the city of Suvarṇapurī. On his way, while being carried through the air, fascinated by her superb beauty and excited by her delicate touch,

I (Vasudeva) thought for a moment to get united with her and enjoy pleasure! I was being carried by her through the sky which was shining with bright rays of the moon. After observing her way of looking at me and her replies to my questions, her amazement, amorous absorption and her laugh, biting of her lip, giving a sigh, showing gestures, and the whole range of her movements, I began to reflect: 'Has this strange-hearted Prabhāvatī fallen in love with me? Why is she revealing such passionate gestures? Or is she trying to create an infatuation on my side?' I thought that the lust for love could not be satisfied while travelling in the air. So I told her: 'in order to quench my thirst I would like to have some water.' She brought me down to a water pond. There was a thicket of trees where was seated Prabhāvatī under the shade of a lovely *saptaparṇa* tree. She looked like the goddess of fortune seated on the spotless lotus, as beautiful as a sylvan deity descended in person. I stood still looking at the bright autumnal moon in the sky. Seeing me standing motionless, she asked me, 'O prince, what are you thinking of?'

'I am thinking of love,' I answered.

'Is there any reason why?'

'I do not think without reason. There is reason: The moon is free from clouds, spotless, and pure with pleasing rays and cool; The water is fragrant with lotuses—These are two reasons for love.'[17]

I continued: 'So, O lady with thighs like the trunk of an elephant, this bank is beautiful with the rays of the autumnal moon, lovely with fragrant flowers, giving delight to lovers and worthy of enjoying pleasures. If you have some desire, why not fulfil it here?'

Prabhāvatī, a smile on her face, replied, 'At the moment I have no other desire than to carry out the mission of my friend (Somasiri).'

'Do you know me?' I asked.

'Yes, you are Vasudeva, the moon in the sky of the Hari line.'

'I did not ask that.'

'Then what are you asking?'

'Do you know that I am longing for a divine, delicious taste of you?'

Hearing this, Prabhāvatī's lotus-like eyes and face lit up like a lake beautiful with blossoming lotuses. She replied, 'O prince, I have never heard such pleasing words in my life. Any young lady who even has presented sexual enjoyment with you is lucky and has fulfilled the object of her life, not to speak of her who is requested by the most prominent person in the whole world.'

'Enough of this fooling about,' I said. 'O fair lady! Tell me honestly whether you love me or not?'

'I have never heard such unpleasant words as those contained in the end of your sentence', she replied.

'If that is so, then come, get on this bed of flowers and propitiate the god of love (जइ एवं ततो आगच्छ इहं कुसुम-सत्थरे, माणिज्जउ भगवं रतिपती).'

'O prince!' she cried, 'You know I am a maiden, my parents are living, and it is not proper for me to behave in this manner without first getting married.'

'But then why did you tell me how unpleasant it was to hear the words "you don't love me"?'

'Whatever I said was a joke', she replied. 'Do you really think all that was true? It was all fun; I don't love you.'
I told her, 'O lady of jasmine-like teeth, if it is true, then swear by your virtuous deeds that you don't love me.'
'I swear that I do not love you', she answered.
'Swear by your magic art!'
'Yes, I do.'
'Then swear by me that you don't love me!'
At this Prabhāvatī frowned and said angrily, 'Does the judge esteem the truth so much that he must impose such conditions? Or tell me who am I to you that I should swear by you!' After saying this she turned her face aside and stayed there in feigned anger.
Reading her mind, I said lightly, 'Swear by your beloved!'
Hearing this, she turned away her face slightly like a lotus bent beneath the wind, and an expression of bashfulness accompanied by sighing, shivering and whispering were visible on her; then she closed her eyes for a moment. I knew that she was afflicted with love.
Knowing me under the influence of a strong passion, and thinking of her future, Prabhāvatī restrained me saying: 'O prince, O prince, don't make haste! Listen to me O master, you are looking for delight and satisfaction!' She kept talking to me in this manner and with great difficulty I resisted the force of my passion. I felt as if my life had fallen in danger and had been lost in vain.[18]

Further, after meeting Somasiri and defeating Mānasavega in the court of the *Vidyādharas,* Vasudeva was carried to the world of the Nāgas where he was most delighted to see the beautiful Prabhāvatī who looked like a divine damsel. He held her in her arms and making her sit on his lap, inquired about the mountain they had come to. She brought delicious food from the desire-yielding food-tree. A bed was prepared of various flowers and leaves. Vasudeva was ready for sport. As an elephant in rut crushes the lotus flower blossomed in the spring, so Vasudeva humiliated Prabhāvatī's pride. She bent her face with bashfulness! She was shivering at the time of the first intercourse, her body horripilated with delight. With great joy and excitement she came to my bed. Then Vasudeva enjoyed sexual pleasure with her like Indra with his wife Śacī.[19]

It is noteworthy that the story of Prabhāvatī narrated in the *MKH* is unique. It is lucidly presented in a realistic and romantic manner with explicit details. The contents of this *lambha* might have been the contents of the missing *lambha* in the *VH.* This account is corroborated by Jinasena's (I) *JHP* (30), a later Sanskrit work of the eighth century.[20] The story of Prabhāvatī is also narrated in the *TSP* (8.2.560-88) of Hemacandra and the *BHBH* (2099-2105) of the same period. These Jain versions of the Prabhāvatī story minimize both erotic and violent scenes, whereas the story narrated in the *MKH* is more explicit and colourful. At places it is more akin to the *KSS* of Somadeva and the *BKM* of Kṣemendra[21] both of the eleventh century. Take for instance the part about Dharaṇa or Dharaṇendra's image installed in the court room of the *Vidyādharas*. The fight ensues between the two *Vidyādhara* armies, some on the side of Vasudeva and others on the side of Mānasavega; Dharaṇa, the king of the Nāgas, breaks out of his own image, carries Vasudeva in the air and arrives at the top of the golden mountain. Vasudeva feels as if he has ascended the Cullahimavanta mountain. Later he desires to visit the Siddhāyatana mountain and pay homage to the Jain shrines there. In the *KSS*, in a similar context, Śiva, assuming the terrific form, carries Naravāhanadatta the hero to the top of the mountain called Ṛṣyamūka.[22]

Here we have some common verses.

A complaint was lodged by Mānasavega against Vasudeva that he had no authority to enter his harem without permission and live illegally with Somasiri. The court was presided by king Vāuvega (Vāyupatha in the *KSS* and the *BKM*). Replying to the charges of Mānasavega and asserting the sanctity of the court, Vasudeva remarked: 'There is no court without elderly people; They are not elderly who are not virtuous; There is no virtue without truth, and there can be no truth which is full of deceit.'[23]

The *Taraṅgavaīkahā* (*Taraṅgavatīkathā*) by Pālita (Pādalipta) or Śrīpālita, named as one of the renowned poets by Hāla, whose verses have been incorporated in the *Gāhāsattasaī*. According to Pischel, he is credited with ten verses in this anthology. He might have participated in the formation of the anthology. *Taraṅgavaīkahā* contains a romantic story of a beautiful nun Taraṅgavatī ('having waves'). Taraṅgavatī is said to have been a disciple of Candanabālā, the first well known female disciple of Mahavira. Pādalipta seems to be the first writer of independent stories in Prakrit after canonical literature. This important work seems to be quite popular among Jains. The *Anuyoga-dvāra* (*Sūtra* 130) mentions Pādalipta as an author of the *Taraṅgavaī* (*Taraṅgavaikkāra*). It is also referred to in the *Viśeṣāvaśyaka-Bhāṣya* of Jinabhadragaṇi Kṣamāśramaṇa (sixth century); in the *Niśītha-Bhāṣya* among extraordinary (*lokottara*) love stories together with he *Malayavatī* and the *Magadhasenā*; and in the *Daśavaikālika-Cūrṇi* Udyotanasūri (eighth century) in his *KVLM* has respectfully referred to Pādalipta as the beauty of Sātavāhana's court, who has composed the *Taraṅgavatī*, Looking like the Gaṅgā, charming with a pair of *cakravāka* birds, giving delight to the beautiful royal swans. Dhanapāla (tenth century) in his *Tilakamañjarī* is full of praise for *Taraṅgavatī*, as endowed with pleasing and deep words (*pada* or route) and associated with a pair of *cakravāka* birds, which purifies speech like the sacred Gaṅgā. Lakṣamaṇagaṇi (twelfth century) in his *Supāsanāhacariya* has admired this work. Prabhācandra in his *Prabhāvakacarita*, quoting an old *Gāthā*, has remarked: 'How is it that the head of the God of Death has not broken off while taking away Pālitta, from whose mouth the river rolling with waves has come out.'[24] According to Prabhācandra, Pādalipta's father's name was Phulla and Pratimā was his mother. He was initiated in his childhood and during his ascetic career, he visited Mathura, Pāṭaliputra, Lāṭa, Śaurāṣṭra, Śatruñjaya and other places. Unfortunately, this important work is no more available. E. Leumann has ascribed it to the second or third century.

Taraṅgalolā or Saṅkhitta-Taraṅgavaī[25] by Nemicandra or his pupil Jasa, is a digest of the *Taraṅgavaī-kahā*. It is composed in 1642 Prakrit stanzas, a continuous narration without any sections. According to the author,

> the original work of Pādalipta had a plenty of *Deśī* words. It was charming and detailed and was composed sometime in *kulakas* (a collection of three, four or five stanzas where the government of verb and noun is carried throughout), sometimes in *yugalas* (a pair of verses) and in *ṣaṭkas* (*chakkalāiṃ*, a collection of six verses). Bearing at difficult text this story was neither told, nor narrated, nor inquired into by people. Being difficult to comprehend, it could be understood only by those who were learned; it was not of much use to a common man. Here I have abridged the verses composed by Pādalipta in *Deśī* words so that this important work may not go into oblivion.[26]

When we compare this work with Udyotanasūri's *KVLM* we notice a lot of similarity between the two. The motifs of *jāti-smaraṇa* (re-collection of previous birth), inviolability of the consequences of *karma* and renunciation of worldly pleasures are common features in both. The *gandharva* marriage, the Śabara chief's looting of a caravan and retiring to his residence, and the offerings to Goddess Katyāyanī are common.[27]

As in the *VH* and the *MKH*, the whole episode is narrated in the first person. The nun Taraṅgavatī, who was the charming daughter of a rich merchant of Kauśāmbī, narrates her life-story to a rich woman of Rājagṛha where she had gone to beg. She succeeded in tracing the husband of her previous life. She established contact with him through a female friend. They wanted to marry but Taraṅgavatī's parents would not agree as the bridegroom was always travelling and had no house of his own.[28] Thereupon they escaped secretly in a boat and married according to *gandharva* rites. They were captured by robbers and were to be sacrificed to the goddess Kātyāyanī. Taraṅgavatī started crying bitterly. Thereupon the robber-chief took pity on them and released them. They returned to Kauśāmbī where with the consent of Taraṅgavatī's parents they got married. Later they encountered a Jain monk who initiated them to the order of monks.

In this episode of Taraṅgavatī we find mention of various important references with regard to social and cultural study: The country of Magadha was known for narration of stories (*gāthā* 14); it is of no use to trace the origin of an excellent woman (*mahilā-ratna*); a river and a monk—they are pure by themselves (76); a *sapta-parṇa* (seven-leaved) tree is 'manifested, projected and radiant; it emanates fragrance in all four quarters and is eminently fragrant like the smell of an intoxicating beverage of an excellent elephant in rut'.[29] The *Pupphajoṇi-sattha* (*Puṣpayoni-śāstra*)[30] and the *Gandhajutti-sattha*[31] are mentioned. Hunters and physicians have been described. The temple of the deity of hunters was endowed with peacock feathers and moistened with fresh blood. The hunters used to tie wild flowers to their tufts (vendo?), they fastened shoes to their feet and carried the bow, fitted with fire-producing piece of wood (*araṇi*) to its back. We come across the temple of Kātyāyanī. After the monsoon was over, the husband and wife made an offering to the deity (990) in which two *mahāpaśus* (two human beings)[32] were sacrificed. There was a common belief that by favour of the deity, work was accomplished, victory achieved, wealth acquired and there prevailed all happiness.[33] *Sītāgṛha* was a public place where the feasts and festivals were held; where the knaves gathered as spectators and the stories were narrated. It was a four-faced place, supported on four pillars; travellers used to rest here; it was a meeting place of householders and a house of magical charms (*mohana-gṛha*) for village people and servants. *Saindhava* horses are described. We are told that during the monsoon (*vāsāāla=varṣākāla*) Mahavira sojourned here in a village known as Vāsāliya. People used to pay homage to the banyan tree, going around it thrice. A hunter is advised not to kill a dog, a hero, a leader of a herd, a young one of an elephant,[34] or a cow-elephant. Characteristics of a *bhadra* elephant are mentioned. There was an abundance of farmers (*kāsaga-jaṇa*) in the *janapada* of Kāśī. It was a centre of rich merchants, each one of them capable of buying and selling goods worth one crore. Sīhaguhā-*palli*, situated in the Vindhya forest, was a centre of activity of valiant robbers. They used to employ various methods to attack people. Once they captured a young couple and took them to their chief, but as the chief was afraid of the deity Kātyāyanī, he refused to make the woman his wife. A lofty banyan tree was situated in front of the theatre-hall of a temple: it was flanked with banners and flags, furnished with umbrellas, flowers and garlands; it was equipped with a brush of yak-tail, smeared with sandalwood paste and encircled by a thicket of trees. Amongst the narratives we come across various maxims or epigrams. There are several words and expressions which can be compared with the *VH*[35] which reflects on the antiquity of this work. A saying has been cited from the *Atthasattha* indicating the existence of a Prakrit *Arthaśāstra*, which is no more extant.[36]

The *Samarāiccakahā* (*Samarādityakathā*; the Story of Samarāditya) is a religious novel (*dharmakathā*) which narrates the nine births (*bhavas*) of King Samarāditya of Ujjain and the counter-hero Agniśarmā. The main story is based on the idea of penitential action or remunerative hankering (*nidāna*) which is developed by ascetic Agniśarmā to take revenge on the king Guṇasena. The king used to mock at the ugliness of his priest's son Agniśarma which made him take to asceticism in desperation. Guṇasena invited the ascetic to dine with him several times, but every time as the king was preoccupied, the ascetic returned without being entertained. The ascetic Agniśarmā thought that the king still held enmity against him. Thereupon he developed a strong desire to take revenge on the king and said to himself that if his asceticism was of any use, let him be born as his enemy in succeeding births. Thus in intense anger, deceit and avarice he was born as an enemy of Guṇasena in a series of nine births. Thus the whole story is based on the principle of retribution. Haribhadra, the author, has remarked, 'Really speaking, we ourselves are responsible for the consequences of the *karmas* performed in previous births, others are just instrumental causes while being disposed towards us rightly or wrongly.'[37] The main story has several interlinking stories, also emphasizing the evil consequences of vices, leading to the diversity of transformation of *karmas*, diversion of mind, intensity of passion and ultimately renunciation of sensual pleasures and taking to ascetic life and attain *mokṣa*.

Haribhadrasūri, son of Yākinī Mahattarā (Yākinī-sūnu), the author of the *Samarāicca-kahā*,[38] also known as *Samaramiyaṅkākahā* referred to by Udyotanasūri, was a versatile writer of the eighth century. He was born at Citrakūṭa (Chitore, in Rajasthan) in the family of a Brahman and was well-versed in the Brahmanic lore. Haribhadra was one of the pioneers of Jain learning and his name is mentioned along with Pādalipta and Bappabhaṭṭi. He has written tracts on various branches of Jainism, including philosophy and Yoga. He has also written a commentary on the *Nyāyapraveśa*, a Buddhist work of renowned Diṅnāga. Haribhadra has written both in Sanskrit and Prakrit, in prose and poetry. He seems to be the first Jain *ācārya* to have written commentaries on the Jain canonical literature in Sanskrit. From his *Lokatattvanirṇaya* (Investigation of the True Nature of the World) we learn that Haribhadra was not biased towards any particular religious or philosophical view, including that of Mahavira himself. He declared that he would like to accept whichever doctrine was true; not biased in favour of Mahavira, he felt no hatred for Kapila or any other philosopher.[39] Udyotanasūri refers to Haribhadra as his *guru* in Jain scripture (*sāstra-guru*) and the science of reasoning (*yukti-śāstra*). He mentions his *Samarā*[40] specifically, as we have seen. Siddharṣi (beginning of the tenth century) has mentioned Haribhadra's name with great respect in his *Upamitibhavaprapañcā Kathā*. He calls him a teacher who awakened in him the knowledge of *dharma* (*dharmabodhakara*). Siddharṣi has derived great inspiration from his writings and his *Samarā* has served a model for him.

The *Samarā* is composed in Mahārāṣṭrī, though here and there we also come across the peculiarities of Śaurasenī. The style is simple and lucid; in between there are descriptions, with long compounds, employing questions and answers (*praśnottara-paddhati*)[41] and the *gūḍhacaturthapāda-goṣṭhi* (wherein an assembly a verse is recited in which the fourth foot is missing and it has to be supplied).[42] There are other popular artifices which were the delight of the assembly, employed by the author. There is another verbal artifice which was employed both in verse[43] and prose passages[44] by him. Here each line or phrase opens with a word repeated from the end of the preceding one. This artifice is called *sṛṅkhalā*, a kind of *yamaka* by H. Jacobi, the oldest instance of which he has traced to the fifteenth *adhyayana* of the first *Śrutaskandha* of the *Sūtrakṛtāṅga.*[45] There is scarcely any variety of metres in this work. The common metre employed is Āryā (*gāthā* in Prakrit); Vipulā is a variant. Haribhadra has also used *duvaikhaṇḍaṃ* which is the same as *dvipadī* of Hemacandra.[46]

As the *Samarā* was read aloud before an assembly, its style had to be simple, flowing and delightful. It seems to be general practice in olden days that a considerable number of the members of the Jain community were able to understand Prakrit and easy Sanskrit.[47] This important composition is helpful for a social and cultural study of the medieval period of Rajasthan and Gujarat. Pradyumnasūri, who is esteemed to be a known critic and who has edited several works of various contemporary Jain writers, completed the *Samraditya-saṃkṣepa* in AD 1268 in Sanskrit. It is a digest of Haribhadra's Prakrit work.

This work contains numerous interesting stories, parables and fairy tales, some of them are important from the point of view of universal literature. The parable of the Honey-Drop (*mahu-bindu-diṭṭhanta=madhu-bindu-dṛṣṭānta*) is a genuine production of ancient Indian ascetic poetry. A certain person who was travelling in a forest, was attacked by a band of robbers. Wandering here and there, he was overtaken by an elephant. In order to escape from him, he ran fast and caught hold of an overhanging branch of a banyan tree and swung down into the well. At the bottom of the well there was a huge serpent with open jaws. In the four corners of the well there were four snakes who were trying to sting him. Then there were two rats, one black and the other white, gnawing at the root of the thin branch which was held by him. On the top of the tree there was a big beehive, swarming with bees. They were flying to the body of the man to bite him. In the meantime, the tree was being shaken by a mad elephant, as a result the honey-drops from the shattered hive fell on the man's lips which he relished excessively. The moral of the story is: the worldly man wanders about in a world abounding in birth, old age, disease and death. In the world a man is always overpowered with the fear of death. The banyan tree is the abode of salvation where there is no fear of death. The well is human life, the four serpents are four passions (*kaṣāya*), the tree is life which is being gnawed constantly by the two rats in the form of bright half and the dark half of the month. The bees are various kinds of diseases and the honey-drops the sensual pleasures which are difficult to abandon. Therefore a man in difficulty should desist from enjoying worldly pleasures.[48]

Further, we are told of another episode which causes a man to renounce the world and accept asceticism. A snake devours a frog, but is itself devoured by a sea-eagle and in its turn the sea-eagle by a boa constictor.[49] At another place a metaphor of roads (*mārga*) is employed. A caravan-leader made a declaration that whosoever wanted to accompany him for a trip, he would lead him to the destination provided he followed his instructions. After hearing his declaration many tradesmen approached him. The caravan-leader instructed them as follows: 'There are two roads, one is crooked, another is straight. The crooked one is easy but it takes longer time to reach the destination, whereas the straight road is more troublesome but it takes shorter time.' He advised them to follow the straight road. While travelling by it they would come across numerous obstacles such as wild animals, trees, bamboo-bowers, various kinds of fruits, high mountains and so on, but they should not stop in the middle of the journey, neither should they try to rest under the shade of the trees; they would be provided with simple tasteless food, but they should not worry about, they should carry on with their journey without mental agony. Then only would they be able to reach their destination, the city of salvation (*nirvṛti-pura*) where they will be free from all kinds of suffering and would enjoy perfect peace and happiness. Here the caravan-leader stands comparison with God Jina, his declaration with religious story, leading to the city of salvation with crossing the jungle which is abounding in wild beasts, poisonous trees, thick bamboo-bowers, etc., with worldly passions, attachment, aversion and so on.[50]

Further we come across the motif of the dough cock. According to the custom, in order to avert evil, a fowl had to be sacrificed at the altar of the family deity, the Caṇḍī. But a Jain king refused to follow the custom. Under the circumstances, he had a cock made of dough (*piṭṭhamaya kukkuḍa*) which was beheaded in front of the deity and he performed the ritual of eating the 'meat' of the rooster.[51] There are descriptions of the sea-voyage. Traders used to undertake long journeys to foreign lands. They filled their vessels with saleable commodities, offered charity to the poor, paid homage to the sea-deity and made offerings to the vessel. They raised flags on the mast, observed omens and boarded the ship with the fellow passengers, and then with the beating of drums, and laudation of panegyrists, set forth on a voyage. There was terrible cyclones and storms blowing on the way, causing a shipwreck, when the ship passengers had to encounter many difficulties. They travelled as far as China and the Suvarṇadvīpa (Burma).[52]

To glance at a woman is strictly prohibited. It has been stated, 'It is better to embellish one's eye with hot iron rods than to look at the charm of their body. It is better to swallow poison than to enjoy sensual pleasures. It is better to cut off one's tongue than to tell a lie.'[53]

The *Dhuttakkhāṇa* (*Dhūrtākhyāna*)[54] is another important Prakrit work of Haribhadra. It is unique in the history of Indian narrative literature—in an amusing style, the author ridicules the exaggerated mythological legends narrated in the *Mahābhārata* and the *Rāmāyaṇa.* Haribhadra was a man of literary genius. By employing his imaginative power he has composed this satirical masterpiece in a simple and lucid language which shows that the Mahārāṣṭrī Prakrit had developed to a great extent at his time. It contains about 480 *gāthās* divided into five *ākhyānas.*

Once upon a time, in a park of Ujjayinī five rogues (*dhūrtas*) assembled together. It was raining continuously and it was difficult to arrange for food. They were Mūlaśrī,[55] Kaṇḍarīka, Elāṣāḍha, Śaśa[56] and a female Khaṇḍapāṇā. All were expert in the art of roguery and each had five hundred rogues as pupils. Mūladeva proposed that let every one narrate one's experiences and the one who did not believe them, should arrange for food for all, and that one who confirmed them pointing out parallels from the *Mahābhārata,* the *Rāmāyaṇa* and the Purāṇas, would be considered as the leader of all. This idea was approved by all of them.

(1) First Mūlaśrī narrated his experience: In order to hold the Gaṅgā on my head, I went to my master's house. I was proceeding towards my destination carrying an umbrella and a gourd-kettle in my hand when a wild elephant rushed after me. I was so frightened that seeing no other alternative, I entered the gourd-kettle. The elephant also followed me. It went on running after me for six months. Then I escaped through the spout. The elephant also tried to escape but its tail-end was caught in the spout. On my way I crossed the Gaṅgā and took the stream on my head which I continued holding for six months. Then I returned to Ujjayanī and here I am in front of you.

(2) Then Kaṇḍarīka started his story: Once I was turned out of my house by my parents. Wandering about I arrived at a village, where I saw a *yakṣa* temple under a banyan tree. I went to pay homage to the deity. In the meantime there was an attack of robbers. Being scared,

the entire village, all men and animals entered a cucumber (*cibbhaḍa*). The robbers returned to their place. The cucumber was swallowed by a goat, the goat in turn was gulped by a boa, who was picked up by a crane. The crane flew and perched on a banyan tree with one of its legs dangling down. Thinking that a branch of the tree, a mahout tied his elephant's leg to it. The crane started flying and the elephant was pulled up. Seeing this there was a noise in the king's military camp. At this time some skilled archers shot the crane down. The crane's body was vivisected and there came out the boa, the goat, the cucumber and then the whole village and the animals. I retunred home and here I am in front of you.

(3) Then Elāṣāḍha narrated his experience: I had an intense desire since childhood to acquire money. I went to a mountain and brought elixir (*rasa*), employing which I earned lot of wealth. Once some robbers entered my house, a battle ensued and I killed many of them with my bow and arrow. Those who were left alive beheaded me, cut me into pieces, threw me on the shrubs and robbed my house. The next day at the time of sunrise people saw me eating the fruits of the shrub. Thinking that I was alive, they joined up the parts of my body. Here I am in front of you.

(4) Now it was turn of Śaśa. He started narrating his experience: I had a sesamum field near my village. Once during autumn when I went to the field, an elephant pursued me. I climbed the sesamum tree. The elephant rushed round the tree showering the seeds. As a result the seeds were crushed under his feet and a stream of oil started flowing. The elephant got stuck in the mud and died. I got down from the tree. I ate lot of sesamum cakes and drank ten pots of oil. I prepared a bag from elephant's skin and filled it with oil. I put this bag on the branch of a tree outside the village. I asked my son to fetch the bag. He was not able to see the bag so he pulled the whole tree and brought it. After finishing the story, he added, 'Now whoever does not believe my story better be prepared to feed all of us.'

(5) Last of all, Khaṇḍapāṇā narrated her experience as follows: I was very beautiful in my youth. Once upon a time, having bathed after menstruation, I was sleeping in a bower, when the wind, wonderstruck looking at my beauty, enjoyed pleasures with me. Immediately I gave birth to a son. He went away without permission. She added, 'If my story is false, then you arrange for a feast for all of us; if true, no woman in this world should be without a son.'

Then she narrated another amazing story which proved that all of them were her servants who had run away from her house and whom she was looking for. She continued: 'I am daughter of a royal washerman. Once accompanied by my father I went to the river with a cartload of clothes to be washed. After washing clothes I spread them in the sun to dry. There occurred a storm which blew off all my clothes. I got scared and changed myself into a lizard and entered the garden and became a mango tree. One day I heard the royal announcement saying that the washerman should not get scared, he should return home, he will not be punished. Hearing this I changed myself into my original form. The cartload of clothes had been eaten by dogs and vultures.' She asked her friends whether they believed her. She added that she could prove that she was more intelligent than all of them. The friends became indignant at this and asked her to prove it. She continued, 'When my clothes blew off by the storm, I started in search of them. All my servants ran away and I have been looking for them. After carrying out a search at many places I have come here. I notice that you are donning my clothes and you are my servants.' She added, 'If this is true, you return my clothes, and if not you provide food for all of us.' Hearing this all the rogues were struck dumb, they saluted her and provided food for all, declaring her to be their leader.

It is stated that whatever narrations were told by Mūlaśrī (Mūladeva), Kaṇḍarīka, Elāṣāḍha, Śaśa and Khaṇḍapānā successively, were confirmed by their predecessors, producing the evidence from the *Mahābhārata*, the *Rāmāyaṇa* and the Purāṇas.

The *Kuvalayamālā*[57] is a unique *Campū* in Prakrit, composed by Udyotanasūri, known as Dākṣiṇya-cihna, in Jābālipura (Jalore, in south of Jodhpur) in AD 779. From the author's biographical *praśasti* (in 27 verses) we learn that he composed his work with Hrī-devī in his heart and that he received lessons in *Siddhānta* from Ācārya Vīrabhadra and training in *yukti-śāstra* from Haribhadrasūri; Tattvācārya was Udyotanasūri's teacher. Udyotanasūri has referred to a number of *kathās* and their authors in Sanskrit, Prakrit and Apabhraṃśa, such as Pālittaya (Pādalipta) and his *Taraṅgavaī*, Sālāhaṇa (Sātavāhana), also known as Hāla and his *Kośa*, Chappaṇaya,[58] Guṇāḍhya (who is called Brahmā, a lotus being his seat) and his *Baḍḍakahā* (*Bṛhatkathā*), Vyāsa and his *Bhārata*, Vālmīki and his *Rāmāyaṇa*, Bāṇa and his *Kādambarī*, Vimalāṅka (Vimala; the author of the *Paumacariya*) whose Prakrit language is called *sarasa* like nectar, the royal saint Devagupta and his *Supurisacariya*, Harivarisa (Harivarṣa) the author of the *Harivaṃsuppatti, Sulocanā* a well-narrated *dharmakathā*, the royal saint Pabhañjaṇa (Prabhañjana) and his *Jasaharacariya* (*Yaśodharacarita*), Jaḍiya (=Jaṭila) and his *Varāṅga-carita*, Raviṣeṇa and his *Padma-carita*, and lastly Virahāṅka (=Haribhadrasūri), the author of the *Samaramiyaṅkā Kahā* (*Samaramitārkā Kathā= Samarāiccakahā*) who was the teacher of the author himself. The mention of these learned *ācāryas* and scholars indicates that the author of the *KVLM* was directly or indirectly influenced by their writings.

The *KVLM* has been composed in Prakrit with *marahaṭṭhayadesī* descriptive pattern; it is almost a pure *sakala-kathā* in which are introduced *tāpasa, Jina* and *sārthavāha*;[59] here are introduced various characters speaking Sanskrit, Apabhraṃśa and Paiśācī. It is an important work composed in literary Prakrit style. Primarilya *dharma-kathā* (religious narrative), it has become *saṃkīrṇa-kathā* (mixed narrative) as incidentally it includes topics connected with *artha* and *kāma*. The author has divided the *dharma-kathā* into four categories: (i) *akkhevaṇī* (*ākṣepiṇī*), pleasant or catching, (ii) *vikkhevaṇī* (*vikṣepiṇī*), unpleasant or distracting, (iii) *saṃvega-jaṇaṇī*, leading to knowledge or enlightening, (iv) *ṇivveya-jaṇaṇī* (*nirveda-jananī*), leading to detachment or renunciation. The *dharma-kathā* has been compared to a newly-wedded bride in form of beauty and charm: both are decorated with ornaments (an ornament of the sense or the sound), charming (pretty), possessed of beautiful steps (portion of a verse), endowed with delicate and pleasant conversation (dialogues) and both give pleasure.[60] The author has stated that though the *dharma-kathā* is associated with *kāma-kathā* (love story), it is not without purpose as it leads to religious gain in the form of an *ākṣepiṇī* story, as stated above.[61]

Udyotanasūri is a master of Prakrit expression. His *KVLM* is a type of elaborate composition in which the same subject is contained through alterations in prose and poetry in the style of a *Campū*. It has *varṇaka* type of descriptions which can be compared with the style of the *VH*. The author has employed various *alaṃkāras* such as *upamā, rūpaka* and *utprekṣā* and varieties of metres such as *dvipadī, gīti, duvalaya, cakkalaya, tiyalaya, daṇḍaka*[62] and so on. In order to make his work interesting, he has also used *prāsnottara* (questions and answers),[63] *prahelikā* (riddles), *antimakkharāo* (*antimā-kṣarikā*[64]), *bindumati*[65] and so on. The author has introduced interesting scenes of towns, seasons, battlefield, wedding ceremony and natural beauty.

The work is not divided into *adhyāyas, prakaraṇas* or *kaṇḍikās*. The story begins with the presentation of the biography through a number of rebirths of five souls: 1 Caṇḍasoma (in the following birth reborn as a lion; in the third birth as Svayambhūdeva), 2 Mānabhaṭṭa (Kuvalayacandra; Maṇirathakumāra), 3 Māyāditya (Kuvalayamālā; Mahārathakumāra), 4 Lobhadeva (Sāgaradatta; Vajragupta), 5 Mohadatta (Pṛthvīsāra; Kāmagajendra). Since anger, vanity, deceit, greed and infatuation have been called the main causes of wandering in the endless world which is full of misery and unhappiness, it is significant that the characters Caṇḍasoma, Mānabhaṭṭa, Māyāditya, Lobhadeva and Mohadatta are represented by anger, vanity, deceit, greed and infatuation respectively. Interesting biographical narratives are provided of these characters where various catching parables and illustrations are employed to enlighten laymen. Out of the above-mentioned five characters Kuvalayacandra and Kuvalayamālā represent the hero and the heroine respectively.

The hero Kuvalayacandra, who was born as the son of King Dṛḍhavarman, the ruler of Vinītā, sets out in search of Kuvalayamālā, the daughter of King Vijayasena of Vijayāpurī. After reaching the capital Vijayā of Vijayāpurī, Kuvalayacandra learnt from the people that the princess Kuvalayamālā was very beautiful, and that she had hung in public an incomplete verse, with the announcement that she would marry the one who completed it. The princess was known for her hatred of men (*puruṣa-dveṣiṇī*), whom she would never like to see. The prince recited the completed verse to the satisfaction of Kuvalayamālā, who garlanded him and chose him as her bridegroom. Both exchanged affectionate messages and love letters and learnt more and more about each other. The wedding was celebrated with great pomp and gaiety. In course of time, Kuvalayacandra, accompanied by his beloved Kuvalayamālā returned to Vinītā (Ayodhya) where both of them received a huge reception. Kuvalayacandra was crowned heir-apparent. King Dṛḍhavarman accepted *dīkṣā.* In course of time Kuvalayamālā gave birth to a son who was named Pṛthvīsāra. We are told that during the age of Mahavira, Kuvalayacandra was born as Maṇirathakumāra and Kuvalayamālā as Mahārathakumāra. Both renounced the world and after practising severe penance attained *nirvāṇa.*

Udyotanasūri was a talented author who had a keen observation of things around him and gifted with pictorial memory. He has incorporated socio-cultural glimpses, including art, architecture, culture, commerce, prevailing customs, magical lores, feasts and festivities and so on in his composition. The narrative is also important from the point of view of study in the Middle Indo-Āryan prevalent in the eighth century.

Vinītā, the capital city of Madhyadeśa, has been described. Here the names of shops according to articles displayed in them are given. Many commodities were sold. (1) कुंकुम-कप्पूर-अगरु-मयण-अभिवास-पड़वास; (2) एला-लवंग-कक्कोलय; (3) मुत्ताहल-सुवण्ण-रंयण; (4) णेत्त-जुयल; (5) वसण; (6) विडाओ (a kind of salt); (7) संख-वलय-काय-मणिय; (8) सर-सरासण; (9) संख-चमर-घंटा; (10) विविह-ओसहीओ; (11) सिणेह-णिरंतर-बहु-खज्ज-पेज्ज; (12) हलिद्दी; (13) सुरा-महु-मासाओ। (7, 26-9; 8, 1-5)

We come across a graphic description of an orphanage (*Anāthamaṇḍapa*), situated in the city of Mathura. There dwelt people who were disabled, suffering from various diseases; some were poor, or helpless, blind, lame, or hump-backed. They were discussing which sin may be washed out and at what place. One of them remarked, 'the sin of leprosy could be washed out at Vārāṇasī', another mentioned the name of the Sun Temple at Mūlasthāna (modern Multan in Pakistan), another, the Mahākāla Temple at Ujjainī, someone mentioned the Akṣayavaṭa at Prayāga, others said the confluence of the Gaṅgā with the sea, and others suggested that paying homage to the deity Bhairava Bhaṭṭāraka can wash out the sin.

The city of Vārāṇasī, situated in the *janapada* of Kashi, has been described. It was a centre of learning where there was a provision for teaching *Cāṇakya-śāstra* of Kauṭilya. There was a saying that if one did not succeed in earning anywhere, he could go to Vārāṇasī to earn money by gambling, committing theft, pick-pocketing and employing other deceitful means.

Māyāditya wants to undergo expiation for betraying his friend for which he would like to commit suicide by entering into a burning fire. But a chief *mahāmahattara*, who was in charge of all the *draṅgas* or defence posts (*jeṭṭha-mahāmahattara sayala-draṅga-sāmi*), adviced him to enter the sacred water of the Gaṅgā. He was of the opinion that it was gold that was purified by fire and not the person who committed treachery to a friend. Such a man is not purified even by practising the vows of a *kāpālika*, he remarked. He can be purified only by the river Gaṅgā whose spotless bright water falls on the matted hair of fair-bodied Śiva, riding on a bull. The same idea is put in the mouth of *grāma-mahattara* in the mid-Indian colloquial dialect as follows:

एत्थ सुज्झति किर सुवण्णं पि। वइसाणर-मुह-गतउं।
कउं प्रावु मित्तस्स वंचण। कावालिय-वत-धरणे।
एउ एउ सुज्झेज्ज णहि॥
तथा-
धवल-वाहण-धवल-देइस्स सिरे भ्रमिति जा विमल-जला धबलुज्जल सा भडारी।
यति गंग प्रावेसि तुहुं मित्र-द्रोज्झु तो णाम सुज्झति। (63, 22-6).

The *KVLM* provides an interesting account of traders and merchants of the time who travelled to distant countries. There is a description of a *sārthavāha* carrying a trading expedition from Takṣaśilā in the north to Śūrpāraka in the west. Lobhadeva was told by his father that there was plenty of wealth which would last for generations so he need not go abroad to earn more money. But his son would not listen to his father's advice. He reached Śūrpāraka where he sold horses and earned an enormous amount of wealth. There was a local traders' association (*vāṇiyameli*) there, the members of which gave a reception to merchants from different parts of the country. They spoke different dialects (*deśabhāṣā*) in their territories and could be distinguished from their temperament, habits and build of the body. The trading merchants coming from outside narrated their experiences to the members of the association. In the course of conversation it was disclosed that *neema*-leaves could fetch precious stones from Ratnadvīpa. Learning this, Lobhadeva made up his mind to make a trip to the island. Accompanied by his associates, Lobhadeva reached the island and in course of time, while he was returning with his ship loaded with exchange-commodities, there occurred a terrible storm in the sea and his ship was smashed to pieces. It was with great difficulty that Lobhadeva with the help of a plank was able to reach the seashore (65-79; 152-3).

Elsewhere the *Kāmaśāstra* is referred to for choice of a girl (*Kaṇṇā-saṃvaraṇa*). If she is pre-eminent in charm, beauty, playful gestures, dance, knowledge, intelligence, fortune and various arts, she should be conciliated by means of appeasement, isolation and offering presents. In case it is not possible to subdue her in this manner, she should be married by demonstrating heroism, or employing deceitful means or force or various kinds of fraud. Later on, the girl married in this manner, with the fear of disgrace to the family, would automatically be offered to the person by her family.

The lore of mining (*khanyavāda*) is revealed. It has been stated, 'If there is a tree other than the tree of milky juice, one is sure to have some small or big amount of wealth hidden below.' A royal parrot is mentioned, who was expert in all arts, including reading, dancing, shooting (*viśākhila*) and knowledge of characteristics of horses, elephants, cocks, men and women. *Samudra-śāstra* or *Sāmudrika* is referred to. Various kinds of magic lore (*vidyās*) are mentioned; they were presented to Nami and Vinami by Dharaṇendra, who was favoured by revered Ṛṣabha, the first Tīrthaṅkara of Jains. The details of accomplishment of Śābarī *vidyā* are provided. Here we are provided the information of educational institutions and residential schools (*maṭha*). Students from various countries such as Lāṭa, Karṇāṭaka, Mālava, Kaṇṇaujja, Golla, Maharashtra, Saurashtra, Ḍhakka, Śrīkaṇṭha and Sindha, used to assemble here to study. Various branches of learning are mentioned, including archery, waving of sword and shield (*pharakheḍḍa*), drawing and painting, music, dramatic performance and so on. The conversation and irresponsible gossip of students is recorded, which throws light on the contemporary Middle Indo-Aryan dialect. The painted scroll illustrating the *saṃsāra-cakra*, the wheel of all the three worlds of hell, human life and gods, is introduced. Agriculturists (*haliyauttā*) are engaged in ploughing field; people are suffering from various kinds of diseases; they are lying on their cots, they are meeting their death, there is a mourning by wife, friends and servants, coffins (*śava-śayana*) are borne by relatives and the body being cremated on the funeral pyre, the devoted wife crying and weeping for the departed lover, and many other interesting scenes are depicted. Then follows the motif of 'Chain of Destruction' where one animal is shown killing another. A fight is on between a lion and an elephant (as depicted in Kailāśa temple at Ellora), a tiger and a wild bull, a serpent is swallowed by a large monster and a small fish by a large fish and so on. This motif has been depicted to instigate a man to follow religion.

We are told about two merchants who made a loss in business and took to agriculture. They invested all the money they had in farming but it so happened that there was no rain and the field did not produce a crop. The merchants tried other professions but did not succeed. They made a foreign trip in order to earn money but there was a shipwreck and it was with great difficulty they reached the island with the help of a plank. They also tried *dhātuvāda*, the art of making artificial gold, but there also they failed miserably. Depressed, both determined to fall from a mountain peak. At this time when they were actually to fall down from the mountain, a heavenly voice was heard, saying 'poverty is our renunciation'. Immediately a monk appeared before them and explained the spiritual interpretation of agriculture (*kisikamma*), tending cattle (*govālaṇa*), seafaring (*jāṇavatteṇa-gamaṇa*), mining (*rohaṇa khaṇaṇa*), carrying merchandise (*thorakamma-karaṇaṃ*), begging (*bhikkhā*), gambling (*jūyaṃ*), alchemy (*dhātuvāda*), fighting (*jujjhiyaṃ*), wrestling (*mallattaṇaṃ*), miraculous eye-paint (*añjaṇajutti*) and so on. The monk explained the real meaning of agriculture as follows: 'One who sows the seed in the field cultivated by a plough of mind, is bound to reap a good harvest.'[66] On seafaring he remarked, 'If you are a seafaring merchant, you should fill in your ship with the jewels of virtue, and after crossing the world-like ocean, reach the island of salvation.'[67] The merchants questioned the monk to kindly explain, so that in the following rebirths they might not suffer from poverty. The monk replied: 'If after being ordained into asceticism, you practise severe penance, then you will never come across poverty in life.'[68]

The *Kahāṇayakosa* (*or Kathākoṣa-prakaraṇa*)[69] is a treatise on the treasury of tales, composed by Jineśvarasūri, renowned author of the Śvetāmbara sect. He has been referred to as *yuga-puruṣa* (the Man of his Age). High tributes are paid to him by Dhaneśvara, the author of the *Surasundarī-cariya*, Abhayadevasūri, the well known commentator of nine *Aṅgas* (navāṅgīkāra), Jinacandrasūri, the author of the *Saṃvegaraṅgaśālā*, Vardhamānasūri, the author of the *Ādinātha-carita* and Guṇacandragaṇi, the author of the *Mahāvīracariya*—all of them happened to be his pupils or pupils' pupils. Somatilakasūri has admired the resoluteness and sincerity of purpose of Jineśvarasūri, comparing him with the devotees of Śiva, who out of intense devotion, make openings in their shoulders, specifically made for the purpose of filling them with oil and go on walking with lighted oil lamps on their shoulders.[70] Besides being a learned scholar, Jineśvarasūri had been a man of radical outlook. Aṇahillapura in Gujarat in those days, was a centre of activities of the *caitya-vāsī* sect. Followers of the sect were also known as Jatī or Śrīpūjya; they were called *caitya-vasī* as they made Jain temples their home. In his *Sambodha-prakaraṇa* Haribhadrasūri (eighth century) has called them depraved, dwelling in *maṭhas*, offering *pūjā* to the deity, eating offerings made to the divinity, encouraging construction of Jain temples, wearing variegated perfumed clothes, performing dance before women, dined two or three times a day and eating betel and cloves. They also performed magical incantations causing a man to quit his occupation, they prescribed amulets to do away with evil spirit and were keen about making their disciples grow in number.[71]

Jineśvarasūri was born a Brāhmaṇa in Vārāṇasī. He visited Dhāra, the capital city of Malwa and was initiated to the Jain ascetic order along with his brother. He travelled far and wide and made Gujarat, Malwa and Rajasthan the main centres of his activities. Jineśvarasūri was well-versed in Prakrit, Sanskrit and Apabhraṃśa languages. *Kathakośa-prakaraṇa,* which is perhaps the last work of the author, was completed in VS 1108 (AD 1051) in the village called Ḍiṇḍāūṇā in Malwa. It contains 30 Prakrit *gāthās,* explained in Sanskrit, with illustrative stories in Prakrit in prose and poetry. The author has written a Prakrit commentary on these verses, and in all there are 36 main stories and 4 or 5 subsidiary stories. Most of the stories are traditional, coming from early Jain sources, though some have been composed by the author himself for the benefit of the *bhavyas* (those who are capable of attaining *mokṣa*). These stories are composed in Prakrit prose, interspersed with stray verses in Sanskrit, Prakrit and Apabhraṃsa. The author has called his composition a *dharma-kathā* which ultimately leads to the attainment of *mokṣa.* The narratives are written in simple lucid style without employing long compounds, unnecessary verbosity or ornamental language.

The other main works of the author are: (i) *Līlāvatīkathā* or *Nivvāṇalīlāvaīkahā* probably the longest in Prakrit prose. It was written on the pattern of the *KVLM* of Udyotanasūri in Āśāpalli (Asaval, a suburb of Ahmedabad) between VS 1082 and 1095 (AD 1025 and 1038). It contained charming words and was ornamented with *śleṣa* and other *alaṃkāras.* Unfortunately, only a summary of this important work in Sanskrit verses is available in manuscript in Jaisalmer Bhandar. We are told that Jinaratnasūri wrote it in 1284 in Jābālipattana (Jalore). The original was divided into 21 *utsāhas.* It has been referred to in the *Surasundarīcariya* as a popular work, pleasing to all, like a courtesan decorated with finery and ornaments. (ii) *Chhaṭṭhāṇapayaraṇa*[72] (*Ṣaṭsthānaprakaraṇa,* also known as *Śrāvaka-vaktavyatā praharaṇa*). It has been stated here that a *śrāvaka* (a layman) who is expert in love making, should always try to please his wife. Here are mentioned various kinds of dresses worn by religious people,[73] pole-dancers and singers[74] and by prostitutes.[75] (iii) *Pañca-liṅgiprakaraṇa:*[76] Here the study of the *Cāṇakya,* the *Pañcatantra,* the *Kāmandaka* and such other works is prohibited; a monk is asked to refrain from the practice of astrology (the *Arghakāṇḍa*),[77] giving medical treatment to a person, an elephant or a horse, application of *dhātuvāda* (alchemy), practice of *dhanurveda* (archery) and so on.[78] (iv) Commentary on Haribhadrasūri's *Aṣṭaka-prakaraṇa.* (v) *Caityavandana-vivaraṇa* (commentary on the *Caityavandana*), and others.

Jineśvarasūri in his *dharmakathā* has narrated stories related to *jina-pūjā, sādhu-sevā, dāna-phala, jina-śāsana-prabhāvanā, dharmotsāha* and such other topics, leading to the highest end of life. As the author was well-read and had a wide outlook, he has dealt with various aspects of social and cultural matters of his time. He has mentioned people saying: 'In Gujarat there is nothing which is true, there is nothing which is sacred, no woman is devoted to her husband; in the country of Gurjara, there is one mother and more than one father.'[79] Further, 'Though the body of women of Gujarat is worn out due to old age, they still attract people; their bodices are tied fast and they are able to seduce the world.'[80] The *śabara-vidyā* is mentioned; when this magic lore was accepted or offered to some one, the *vidyādharas* used to assemble in front of the statue of Tīrthaṅkara Ṛṣabhadeva and have a feast (*Śukamithunaka-kathānaka,* p. 2). Sanskrit verses are quoted from the *Garuḍaśāstra.* The practice of bringing a snake-bitten man to life is mentioned. The practice of burning a wife at the pyre of her husband is referred to (*Nāgadatta-kathānaka*). *Jinadatta-kathānaka* has given a few details with regard to shooting of an arrow (*sandhānaṭṭhāṇa*) while standing in a particular posture; different postures *sātaka, risikanna, bharaha* and *chanda* are referred to.[81] The *Śūrasena-kathānaka* refers to the goddess Kātyāyanī, before whom people, in order to have a son, used to offer their flesh. Prakrit verses are quoted here from *Āyurveda.* The *Siṃhakumāra-kathānaka* is important as it provides details with regard to *gandharva-kalā* (the science of music). It contains an interesting story of a married woman, who in the absence of her husband abroad, eloped with a prince. The Sālibhadra-*kathānaka* narrates the story of a wealthy merchant Śālibhadra, so well known in Jain literature. Merchants dealing in costly blankets are referred to. The characteristics of prostitutes (*vesitthi*) are mentioned in the *Kṛtapuṇya* and the *Mūladeva-kathānaka.* Prakrit verses regarding the nature of prostitutes are quoted. The story of the city of Dvārakā's destruction is told in the *Hariṇa-kathānaka.* There is a reference to a dispute between Jain and Buddhist monks in the *Subhadrā-kathānaka.* Śreṇika

Bimbasāra has been called a great patron of Jainism in the *Śreṇika-kathānaka.* From the *Datta-kathānaka* it appears that the dissension between the Digambara and the Śvetāmbara monks was on increase. The word *ḍoḍḍa* was used for Brāhmaṇas and (*Kauśika-vaṇik-kathānaka*) and *kirāḍa* for traders (*Dhanadeva-kathānaka,* p. 121). The *Dhavala-kathānaka* tells us about the conduct of *caityavāsī* monks. It has been stated that the Śvetāmbara canonical literature was not written down in the form of books.[82] The *Sundarīdatta-kathānaka* has referred to the *Joṇipāhuḍa,* an important Prakrit work on the science of prognostication. It has been stated that it should be consulted only for the sake of the *saṅgha* and not for personal gain.[83] The author has also referred to training in *Gāndharva, Nāṭya, Saṅgīta, Kāmaśāstra, Arthasāstra,*[84] *Aśvasikṣā* and so on.

Akkhāṇamaṇikosa (*Ākhyānamaṇikośa*)[85] is another important treasury of jewels of tales. Its author is Nemicandrasūri, also known as Devendragaṇi, a renowned commentator of *Sukhabodhā* on the Uttarā. Nemicandrasūri belongs to the last quarter of the eleventh century and the beginning of the twelfth. He belongs to the *Vaḍḍa* (*Bṛhad*) *gaccha* and was a pupil of Āmradeva Upādhyāya. Nemicandrasūri was a prolific writer with a lucid style. His important works are: (i) *Ātmabodhakulaka,* also known as *Dharmopadeśakulaka* in 22 *gāthās,* (ii) *Sukhabodhā* Commentary on the *Uttarā* (completed in 1072), (iii) *Rayaṇacūḍācariya* or *Ratnacūḍākathā,*[86] (iv) *Pāsanāhacariya*[87] (completed in 1111 in Broach, (v) *Mahāvīracariya*[88] (completed in 1082).

The *Ākhyānamaṇi-kośa* comes under the category of *aupadeśika-kathā-sāhitya* (didactic narrative literature) which contains 52 Prakrit *gāthās* in Āryā metre, dividing the subject into 41 *adhikāras.* In these narratives only the name of the hero or heroine is indicated in the text. Most of these stories are found in early Jain narrative literature. The author has classified them according to their subject matter. Of 146 *ākhyānakas,* 19 are incorporated in other *ākhyānakas,* therefore only 127 are contained in the commentary composed by Āmradevasūri.

Āmradevasuri, the pupil of Jinacandrasūri and the fellow-student of Nemicandrasūri, composed his *vṛtii* on the *Ākhyāmaṇi-kośa* in VS 1190 (AD 1133) in the city of Dhavalakkapura (Dholka in Gujarat) during the reign of Siddharāja Jayasiṃha. The commentary was written at the instance of Nemicandrasūri within a period of about nine months, just 60 years after the composition of the original work.

We find that the commentator Āmradeva was an erudite scholar and a poet of high order. He was well-versed in the science of rhetoric and has used a variety of *alaṃkāras* and metres successfully. He had a great command over poetic acrobatics which is evidenced by his employment of *goṣṭhis* (assemblies) such as *Paṇḍita-goṣṭhi, vidvat-goṣṭhi* and *praśnottara-goṣṭhi.* The author has also provided us with beautiful descriptions of cities like Ujjainī, Rājagṛha, Kashi and other places. Mahākāla *caccara* (a public place) in Ujjainī is mentioned where the sick and poor could stay and pious people gave them pieces of fine *chapāti* (*maṇḍa-khaṇḍāiṃ*). The city of Ujjainī seems to have been a cultural capital of north India in those days. We come across various descriptions of seasons, forests, mountains, camps, caravans, kings and queens, amusements and sports, and feasts and festivals. Being a didactic story, it deals with *dāna, tapa, bhāvanā, brahmacarya,* obeisance to *sādhus,* practice of *vinaya, sāmāyika,* protection of living beings, propagation of Jain faith, teachings of Jain Canon, consequences of *rāga, dveṣa, krodha,* control over senses, and so on. The *Śīla-māhātmya-varṇana-adhikāra* deals with the accounts of Davadantī (Damayantī), Sītā, Rohiṇī and Subhadrā; the *Jina-bimba-darśana-phalādhikāra* with the accounts of Śayyambhava and Ārdrakakumāra; the *Sāmāyika-phala-varṇana-adhikāra* with the account of Samprati, an influential ruler, who helped spreading the teachings of Jainism; the *Svādhyāya-adhikāra* is about King Yava; the *Rāja-haṃsa-ākhyāna* which forms a part of *Niyama-vidhāna-phalādhikāra* provides an account of Mahākāla *caccara*; the *Vinaya-phala-varṇana-adhikāra* describes Citrapriya and Vanavāsi *yakṣas*; the *Pravacanonnati-adhikāra* is about great *ācāryas* like Viṣṇukumāra, Vajrasvāmin, Siddhasena, Mallavādin, Samita and Ārya Khapuṭa; the *Siddhasena-ākhyāna* refers to the Kuḍaṅgesaradeva monastery in Avanti; the *vyasana-śata-janaka-yuvati-avśsvāsa-varṇana-adhikāra* provides the accounts of Nūpura-paṇḍitā, Dattakaduhitā and Bhāvaṭṭikā;[89] the *rāgādi-anartha-paramparā-varṇana-adhikāra* accounts of Vaṇik-patnī, Nāvika-nandā, Caṇḍabhadrā, Citra-sambhūta, Māyāditya, Lobhanandi and Nakulavāṇijya.[90]

The original text by Nemicandrasūri and the *vṛtti* by Āmradevasūri are in Prakrit verse. The commentator seems to be well-versed in Prakrit, Sanskrit and Apabhraṃśa. Some *ākhyānas* are composed in prose while some in verses. The first half of each verse of the *Kulānanda-ākhyāna* in *Adhikāra* 40, is composed in Sanskrit, while the latter half is in Prakrit. Some *ākhyānas* have been composed in Apabhraṃśa, but in between we also come across Sanskrit verses.

The learned commentator has quoted numerous Prakrit and Sanskrit verses. He has quoted the *Candanāryā-ākhyāna* and the *Kambala-śabala-ākhyāna* verbatim from the *Mahāvīracariya* of Nemicandra-sūri. Similarly, in order to know the details of the *Bakulākhyāna*, the commentator has made a reference to the *Rayaṇacūḍācariya* of the same author. Elsewhere the commentator has referred to earlier authentic works such as the *Bhagavatī*, the *Uttarādhyayana*, the *Āvaśyaka-vivaraṇa*, the *Niśītha*, the *Upadeśamālā*, the *Nayacakra*, the *Ślokavārtika*, and so on. The *Kukkuṭa-ākhyāna*, containing the narrative of a cock and a cat, is a popular tale incorporated in the work.

The commentary on the *Ākhyānamaṇi-kośa* is rich with *subhāṣitas*, *sūktis*[91] and proverbs. The following *subhāṣitas* can be noted: 'If you are unable to practise *dharma* in greater quantity, do it step by step; see the big rivers, transformed into a big ocean, are filled drop by drop.'[92]

In between the narrations we also come across other proverbs. 'If your wrist is furnished with a bracelet, why do you need a mirror?'[93] 'How can a pumpkin be contained in the mouth of a she-goat.'[94] Besides providing material for social and cultural study this treasury of tales is important from the point of view of study and development of Middle Indo-Aryan languages. It gives numerous *deśī* words which cannot be traced even in Hemacandra's Deśīnāmalālā. These words are recorded by the editor in an Appendix III (pp. 393-7).[95] Another Appendix provides us the names of the *nirgrantha* Jain monks belonging to the *Mātaṅgas* (*Mātaṅga-jātīya-nirgrantha*) caste.[96] Another Appendix mentions the names of *Yakṣas*.

In the *Prabhākara-Ākhyāna*, the emphasis is laid on earning money. 'Grammar can not satisfy the appetite, the flavour of poetry cannot quench the thirst, the meter cannot elevate the family, thus all artistic skills are worth nothing, therefore be devoted only to earn wealth.'[97] *Kahārayaṇa-kosa* (*Kathāratna-kośa*)[98] is another important Treasury of Jewels of Stories by well known Devabhadrasūri (his previous name before being installed as an *ācārya*, was Guṇa-candragaṇi). Devabhadrasūri was a pupil of Sumativācaka, and he was inspired to compose this at the instance of Prasannacandrasūri, pupil of Abhyacandrasūri. The *Kahārayaṇa-kosa* was composed in Bharuyakaccha (*Bharuch*) in VS 1158. Among his other work are the *Mahāvīra-cariya* (composed in VS 1139), the *Pāsanāhacariya* (VS 1168), *Pramāṇa-prakāśa*, *Anantanātha-stotra*, *Stambhanaka-Pārśvanātha*, *Vītarāgastava* and so on.

This work contains 50 narratives in Prakrit which are divided into

(i) *Dharmādhikārī-sāmānya-guṇa-varṇana* (description of ordinary qualities of a claimant of righteousness) and (ii) *Dharmādhikārī-viśeṣa-guṇa-varṇana* (description of the extraordinary qualities of a claimant of righteousness); the former contains 33 and the latter 17 narratives. The narratives are composed in ornate Prakrit prose and verses; Sanskrit and Apabhraṃśa are also used which indicates author's control over these languages. The narratives are didactic, emphasizing the importance of righteousness, nobleness and virtue in life. While pointing out favourable characteristics of a monk or a layman, the author has remarked: 'A good monk or a good layman is he who is devoted to his vows' and that without being a good layman, one cannot be a good monk. One who is able to practise *aṇuvratas* (lesser *vratas*), can well practise the *mahāvratas* (greater *vratas*). And to be a good layman, one is supposed to possess both ordinary and extraordinary virtues.

Here we have an excellent collection of narratives rarely found elsewhere. There are poetic descriptions of parks, seasons, night, battlefield, cemetery, royal palace and so on, which makes the narration fascinating. In between the narratives are mentioned a variety of topics such as honouring a guest, omens about sneezing, the characteristics of royalty, fortune-telling by interpreting marks on the body (*sāmudrika*), testing of jewels (*ratnaparīkṣā*), lore of mining (*khanyavidyā*), disease of elephants, and so on. The *Garuḍopapāta*,[99] said to be a division of the *Kālika Śruta* which is no more extant, is mentioned here. We are told that the secret of sacred teaching (*pravacana-rahasya*) is not to be disclosed to a common man. It is stated that as water contained in a water-jar of unbaked clay, destroys the container, in the same way, the secret of teaching destroys the person of weak foundation.[100]

The *Nāgadatta-kathānaka* refers to the family-deity (*kula-devata*); its statue was made of wood, it was placed on the Kaliñjara mountain. Nāgadatta remained without food for five days and spent time propitiating the deity. In order to annihilate the snake poison, eight Nāgakulas (*aṣṭa Nāgakulas*) were propitiated.[101] This spell was acquired by uttering a magical formula 1008 times in a burial ground. The *Śaṅkha-kathānaka* mentions a fortune-teller (*naimittika*), Jogānanda by name. A mountain festival (*parvata-maha*) is mentioned when people sang *carcarī*, *pragīta* and other songs. We are told of a mendicant, Kālasena, who was able to subjugate a *yaṣsa* called Liṅglakṣa and had acquired the *paiśācika* lore (*vidyā*). The *Dhana-*

sādhukathānaka refers to the country of Vairāgara (Vajrākara). Jogī Divākara was expert in the lore of mining. By uttering magical formulae and propitiating the deity, he could discover the treasure trove under the earth. He had acquired this lore from a great saint (*mahāmuni*) who was engaged in meditation on the Śrīparvata mountain. Goddess Kātyāyinī was considered donor of all wealth. The science of testing jewels (*maṇi-śāstra*) and that of fortune-telling (*Sāmudrika-śāstra*) are mentioned; some verses are quoted from the latter. A great disease (*mahāvyādhi*) led to the death of elephants. On such occasions people used to propitiate special deities, hundred thousand oblations were offered to gods, homage was paid to the *navagrahas* (nine planets) and the priests were occupied in averting the evil (*śāani-karma*). The *Vijaya-kathānaka* describes details regarding the ceremony of raising the flag (*dhvajāropaṇa*) on a *caitya* (temple). A piece of bamboo, not eaten by insects and containing movable joints, was brought. Then after giving the statue a bath, removing the evil demons[102] (*bhu-śuddhi*) from all the four quarters and invoking the guardians of the quarters, the bamboo was anointed with fragrant substances, flowers were placed on it, incense was burnt and a white flag was fixed on it. We are told that in Kāmarūpa (Assam) there lived a Siddha puruṣa, who was efficient in *ākṛṣṭi* (attracting an absent person), *dṛṣṭimohana* (creating illusion before eyes), *vaśīkaraṇa* (overcoming by charms) and *uccāṭana* (ruining an adversary) and was accomplished in Yoga. The *Padmaśreṣṭhi-kathānaka* has asserted the conception of *mukti* expounded by various philosophers. The followers of Vedic religion held that salvation lies in slaughter of goats in a sacrificial ceremony, the Buddhist emphasize on *karuṇā* (compassion), the Śaivites give prominence to *dīkṣā* (initiation), the *snātakas* (one who has performed ablutions) give prominence to bathing, the followers of Kapila consider *tattvajñāna* (knowledge of truth) as a means of salvation, and according to Jains, the *ratnatraya* (three jewels, i.e. *samyak darśana, samyak jñāna* and *samyak cāritra*) is the way to salvation. A certain Jogandhara (Yogandhara=reciter of a magical formula) had specialized in *vāma-mārga* (the left-hand doctrines of the Tantras where the worship of the *Śahti* or Female Energy personified as the wife of Lord Śiva). He used to conjure up the corpse by charms (*mṛtaka-sādhana*). People worshipped the goddess dwelling in the banyan tree, also known as Kaṭapūtanā, Ḍākinī (a female goblin) who was fond of a corpse. The *Śrīgupta-kathānaka* refers to Kuśalasiddhi, who was skilled in magical formulas.

The *Sujaya-rājarṣi-kathānaka* refers to a Kāpālika *muni*, who used to travel to different countries, was expert in various languages and accomplished in magical charms; he was known as Jñānakaraṇḍaka. Having gone to the Vindhya mountain, he went to the dwelling place of a Yakṣa (*Yakṣa-bhavana*); got four goats from a nearby cow-house, gave them a bath, sprinkled them with sandalwood paste and then killed them. In order to propitiate goddess Caṇḍikā people were given bath, were made to put on white clothes and sacrificed. We come across seafaring merchants who met serious difficulties from water animals such as Timiṅgala[103] (a large fabulous fish), etc., which hopped into the vessel. The passengers in order to frighten the animals, used to beat drums loudly and kindle fires.

The *Dharmadeva-kathānaka* refers to the countries of Siṃhala and Kerala. The *Sudatta-kathānaka* provides a graphic description of a household quarrel between mother-in-law, daughter-in-law and sister-in-law. The *Rajaputra-kathānaka* gives a description of combating of great wrestlers. The temple of Mukunda is referred to in the *Dhanapāla* and the *Bālacandra-kathānaka*. Wanton women allured orphan young girls and in order to use them as prostitutes, trained them in the art of dance and music. The second section of *Dharmādhikarī-viśeṣa-guṇa-varṇana* contains stories regarding 12 *vratas*. Camels were used as a means of transport by traders. There were *praśnottara goṣṭhis* where verses containing questions and answers were recited in the assembly of learned people.[104] The *Prabhācandra-kathānaka* is composed in Apabhraṃśa.

The *Kumāravāla-paḍiboha* (*Kumārapāla-pratibodha*), or Awakening of the Religion of the Jina in Kumārapāla, also known as *Jinadharma-pratibodha or Hemakumāra-carita*[105] was composed by Somaprabhasūri in 1184, only 11 years after the death of Kumārapāla. He was born in Porwāḍ Vaishya family and was a pupil of Vijayasiṃhasūri of *Bṛhad gaccha*. He was a young contemporary of Ācārya Hemacandra and Kumārapāla, an illustrious Cālukya king.

The *Kumāravāla-paḍiboha* is a didactic poem which contains a collection of 54 tales in verses and prose, meant for enlightenment of King Kumārapāla. A major part of these tales is narrated in Prakrit in simple lucid and unsophisticated style. The composition is interspersed with beautiful sayings in Sanskrit and Apabhraṃśa. Some stories in the last chapter are composed in Sanskrit and some portion in Apabhraṃśa. Most of the stories narrated here occur in earlier Jain literature.

The work consists of the five *Prastāvas* in which Hemacandra, who is made the speaker, is supposed to have converted king Kumārapāla. The *Prastāvanā* (Introduction) begins with the description of Aṇahillapura Pāṭaṇa, the Cālukya king Kumārapāla and his desire to know *dharma*, and introduction of Hemacandra to the king. The *Prastāva* I deals with stories related to avoidance of killing, gambling, adultery, going after harlots (*veśyā-gamana*), drinking and theft. Regarding the vice of gambling the story of Nala is told. He has been condemned for deserting Damayantī, his wife, in a forest. It is stated: 'There cannot be a single person more cruel, inhuman and cowardly than Nala, who went away deserting the highly virtuous woman Damayantī at night.'[106]

Further, on the occasion of the *Svayaṃvara* when Damayantī is introduced to the dignatories present, their habits and disposition are narrated. The princess was not willing to take the ruler of Kashi as her husband as the residents of Kashi were said to have been clever in practising fraud (*para-vañcaṇa-vasaṇiṇo*). She also did not choose the ruler of Koṅkaṇa as the residents of Koṅkaṇa were supposed to get irritated for no reason whatever (*akāraṇa-kovaṇā*). The story of King Pradyota of Ujjainī is cited as an example of adultery (*paradāra-gamana*=courting with another's wife).[107] In order to illustrate the evil of drinking, is narrated the story of *Dvārikā-dahana* (the Burning of Dvārakā).[108] In between the story are inserted pithy sayings. Here is an Apabhraṃśa couplet: 'Humble your heart like a dried pepper, have control over your sense-organs. One should extend one's feet according to one's mantle.'[109]

The *Prastāva* II deals with the worship of gods and teachers. In the *Dīpaśikhā* story, the accomplisher of a magic lore goes to a burning ground and slays a girl. In the story of *guru-sevā* (service to the teacher) King Pradesī's story is narrated. Here are introduced simple and interesting sayings in Sanskrit and Apabhraṃśa verses. We have also the story of king Samprati. King Kumārapāla, accompanied by his teacher Hemacandra, pays a visit to Śatruñjaya, Girnār and other holy places. The *Prastāva* III narrates the stories of Candanabālā, Dhanya, Kurucandra, Kṛtrapuṇya and sovereign king Bharata; these stories have been narrated in the earlier Jain works. Among virtuous women we come across Śīlavatī, Mṛgāvatī, Tārā, Jayasundarī and Rukmiṇī. The story of Śīlavatī is interesting as it contains several motifs which can be traced in world literature. Śīlavatī, daughter of a wealthy merchant, offered a garland of flowers to her husband who was to set out for a long journey, asserting that as long as she remained chaste the flowers of the garland would never wither.[110] She is supposed to understand the language of birds and animals and performs all kinds of seemingly absurd actions and gives seemingly absurd answers. She surprised her father-in-law by comprehending the notes of a she-jackal and a crow. Here we come across an impressive dialogue between Śīlavatī and the father-in-law, pointing out the intelligence of the former.[111] In the story of Tārā we meet a Brāhmaṇa who in order to sell his daughter puts her on his head—a common motif in Indian literature.[112] Here is a pithy saying: 'Is it possible to hold the manes of a lion, the shanks of a virtuous woman, a warrior who has taken refuge, and the head-jewel of a venomous snake?'[113]

There is a story of loyal Jayasundarī, who feels sad at the debauched character of a rich merchant, the minister, the priest and the king of the town; she manoeuvres to put all of them in a box and hand it over to the five judges.

The *Prastāva* IV contains the stories related to the 12 vows (*vratas*) of a Jain layman. The stories of Makaradhvaja and that of Purandara are narrated in Sanskrit. The *Prastāva* V is in Apabhraṃśa. Ludwig Alsdorf has made a study of this chapter under the title *Der Kumārapāla-pratibodha, ein Beitrag zur Kenntnis des Apabhraṃśa und Erählungsliteratur der Jainas* as we have seen. In this Section we have two long narratives in Apabhraṃśa. We have a conversation between Soul, Mind and Sense in the form of allegory (*rūpaka*) in 105 stanzas. Here the king *Ātman* (Soul) appears with his consort *Buddhi* (Insight), his minister *Manas* (Mind) and his five court officials, the Five Sense-organs. A discussion takes place between *Manas* and the Five Senses about the origin of suffering. The *Ātman* takes the lead. The Mind holds ignorance (*ajñāna*) responsible for suffering, the *Ātman* the *Manas*, and the *Manas* holds five *Indriyas* (Senses) responsible for suffering. The continuous course of thoughts (*citta-vṛtti*) has to be controlled to attain happiness. In the end, the *Ātman*, in order to make life fruitful, preaches compassion towards all beings and observances of vows. Another long story in Apabhraṃśa is that of Sthūlabhadra in 106 stanzas. Sthūlabhadra takes a vow to stay in the house of courtesan Kośā, without violating his vow of chastity which he fulfils successfully.

Among other important works of Somaprabha are (i) the *Śatārthī-kāvya* (in which a single verse is explained in a hundred different ways; composed between 1177 and 1179), (ii) the *Śṛṅgāra-vairāgya-taraṅgiṇī*, (iii) *Sindūra-prakara*, also known as *Sūkti-muktāvali* (necklace of good sayings; composed in AD 1199); it is very popular among Jains. It is written on the pattern of Bhartṛhari's *Nītiśataka*; ed. in the *Kāvyamālā*, Pt. VII, pp. 35-51; translated into Italian by Pavolini in 1898; (iv) *Sumaiāaha-cariya* (in Prakrit; manuscript available in the Patan Jain Bhandar).

Besides the following works can be noted: the *Mūlaśuddhiprakaraṇa* by Pradyumnasūri (tenth century AD), also known as *Sthānaka-prakaraṇa*; *Ṇaṇapañcamīkaha* by Maheśvarasūri (before AD 1052); *Kālikāyariyakahāṇaya* by Devacandrasūri, Maladhāri Hemacandra, Bhadreśvarasūri, Dharmaghoṣasūri, Bhāvadevasūri, Dharmaprabha-sūri and others; *Nammayāsundarīkahā* by Mahendrasūri (twelfth century); *Malayasundarīkahā* by an unknown author (earlier than the fourteenth century AD; translated into German by J. Hertel in *Indische Mörchen*, pp. 185-268); *Jinadattākhyāna* by Sumatisūri (date unknown); *Bhuvanasundarīkahā* by Vijayasiṃhasūri (tenth century); *Sirivālakahā* by Ratnaśekharasūri (fourteenth century); *Rayaṇa-seharīkahā* by Jinaharṣagaṇi (late fifteenth century); *Mahīvālakahā* by Vīradevagaṇi (late thirteenth century) and so on.

The *Jinaratnakośa* records the following works in manuscript:

Candralekhā-kathā containing 286 *gāthās.*

Jayasundarī-kathā, mentioned in the Jain Granthavali, p. 252.

Dvadaśa-katha contains about 1400 *gathas*; mentioned in the Patan Catalogue, I, p. 35.

Pādalipta-kathā, manuscript referred to in the Patan Catalogue, I, pp. 194-5, dated VS 1291.

Puṣpavatī-kathā contains 643 *gāthās* in 55 folios; dated VS 1191.

Bappabhaṭṭi-kathā having 685 *gāthās*; MS. in the Patan Jain Bhandar.

Rohiṇī-kathā by Rūpavijaya, containing 134 *gāthās.*

Sarvāṅgasundarī-kathā noted in the *Bṛhaṭṭippaṇikā*, No. 342.

Hāsya-kathā preserved in the *Raj OIJ Collection*, VI, No. 1432.

Hutāśanī-kathā by Puṇyarājagaṇi; Bühler Collection, II, No. 394.

The Catalogue of the Palm-leaf MSS in the Big Bhandar of Jesalmere, p. 17 records *Vilāsavaī-kahā* by Sādhāraṇa. It contains 206 leaves, composed in VS 1225 in Aṇahillapura during the reign of King Kumārapāla.

The *Raj OIJ Collection*, I, 1963, p. 248 records *Susaḍhakathā* with *Stavaka*; composed in VS 1808, Kāntivijaya being the commentator.

Among *Kathākośas* or Treasury of Tales the following works can be added: *Kathākośa* or *Bharateśvara-bāhubali-vṛtti* by Śubhaśīlagaṇi (fifteenth century); *Kathāsamāsa* or *Upadeśamālā-kathāsamāsa* by Jinabhadra Muni (twelfth century); *Kathānakakośa* or *Dhammakkhāṇayakosa*, Sanskrit commentary by Vinayacandra; *Pāiyakahāsaṅgaha* by an unknown pupil of Paumacandasūri (around 1200) and many others.

DIDACTIC LITERATURE

As Jainism is based on the principle of renunciation (*vairāgya*), cessation of worldly objects and tranquillity of mind (*upaśama*), Jain authors were interested in composing didactic or instructive literature, known as *aupadeśika sāhitya.* This literature abounds in religious instructions or sermons and has little of the story element.[114] This literature comes under the category of *Uvaesamālā* (*Upadeśamālā* or the Garland of Instructions). In order to fulfil this object, numerous treatises in Prakrit, Sanskrit and Apabhraṃśa were composed by Jain authors such as *Uvaesamālā* (*Upadeśamālā*), *Uvaesapada* (*Upadeśapada*), *Dhammovaesa-mālā-vivaraṇa* (*Dharmopadeśa-mālā-vivaraṇa*), *Uvaesamālā* (also known as *Pupphamālā*), *Uvaesarasāyaṇa* (*Upadeśa-rasāyana*), *Uvaesacintamaṇi* (*Upadeśacintāmaṇi*), *Uvaesarayaṇā-yara* (*Upadeśasaratnākara*), *Uvaesakandali* (*Upadeśakandali*), *Uvaesataraṅgiṇī* (*Upadeśataraṅgiṇī*), *Sīlovaesamālā* (*Śīlopadesamālā*) and so on.[115]

Uvaesamālā (*Upadeśamālā*) *or Garland of Instructions*[116] (or *Uvaesamālā-pagaraṇa* (*Upadeśamālā-prakaraṇa*), like a garland of flowers, is a garland of preachings of God Jina. It produces the feeling of renunciation towards worldly objects, mental tranquillity, welfare and good fortune. It has been stated, 'As a mouse has nothing to do with wealth, as a crow has nothing to do with a golden necklace, similarly a person consumed with infatuation has nothing to do with the *Uvaesamālā*.'[117]

Further, after listening to this treatise, 'if one does not strive towards righteousness and the feeling of renunciation is not produced in one's mind, that man is sure to wander in this world till eternity'.[118]

'One who reads, listens to and preserves it in his heart, will apprehend his own good and will attain happiness.'[119]

Uvaesamālā, a didactic poem, contains 542[120] Prakrit verses, comprising 70 narratives dealing with moral instructions, pertaining to abandonment of five sins, avoidance of evil company, attachment to sensual pleasure, four passions, equanimity of mind, discipline, right faith and so on. These narratives are told by way of numerous edifying episodes and legends of men and women who were able to control sensual pleasures and attain happiness. These narratives written in simple unsophisticated Mahārāṣṭrī dialect are intercalated with religious and moral sayings leading to enlightenment.

In Jain tradition, Dharmadāsagaṇi, the author of the *Uvaesamālā*, is said to be a contemporary of Mahavira, but from the contents and the language of the work, he seems to belong to the fourth or fifth century AD. At the same time it is to be noted that a number of narratives told here belong to a period of antiquity. According to A.N. Upadhye, the work looks like a compilation, and some verses may go back to an earlier stratum of Jain literature corresponding to *Ṇijjuttis* and the *Paiṇṇās*.[121] Schubring has traced a number of stanzas of this work to the *Mahā Nī*.[122]

This work is a rich mine of religious tales and legends. Very often, only the names of heroes and heroines are referred to in the text, the full stories are supplied by commentators. Numerous commentaries were written on this work which indicates the popularity of the work. (1) The first commentary was written in VS 913 (AD 858) in Jain Mahārāṣṭrī by Jayasiṃhasūri, pupil of Kṛṣṇamuni; (2) The well-known Siddharṣi, the author of *Upamitibhavaprapañcā Kathā*, wrote *Heyopādeyā* in Sanskrit in VS 962 (AD 905), this is considered to be the most important commentary; (3) *Doghaṭṭi*[123] is another important commentary written by Ratnaprabhasūri, pupil of Devasūri, author of the Ratnāvatārikā, in Sanskrit in VS 1238 (AD 1181); (4) Vardhamānasūri has written *Bṛhad-Vṛtti*; here the author has added more stories to the commentary of Siddharṣi; its manuscript written in VS 1298 (AD 1241) is available; (5) Udayaprabhasūri, pupil of Vijayasena, teacher of Malliṣenasūri, has composed *Kaṇikā* in VS 1299 (AD 1242); (6) Udayadharma in VS 1605 (AD 1548) has explained the 51st *gāthā*, beginning with *Dosasayamūlajālaṃ* in one hundred different ways.[124]

The work is divided into 4 *Viśrāmas*; divided into 2 *Khaṇḍas*. The first *Khaṇḍa* continues till some portion of the third *Viśrāma*, then we have the second *Khaṇḍa* till the end of the fourth *Viśrāma*. This deals with the life-story of Raṇasiṃha, Candanabālā, Bharata, Mṛgāvatī, Jambūsvāmin, Makaradāḍhā Veśyā, Lohārgalā Gaṇikā, Cilātiputra, Ḍhaṃḍhaṇa Muni, Vajrasvāmin, Avantisukumāla, Kālikācārya,

Vāratraka Muni, Sahasramalla, Satyakī, Annikāputra, Maṅgu Ācārya, Śelakācārya, Dardura *deva* and so on.

Further, to illustrate what is good and evil company, the examples of *giriśuka* (mountain parrot) and *puṣpaśuka* (flower parrot) are cited. It is said that a mountain parrot was caught by a *Mleccha* and brought up in a mountain-village. Once a king riding his horse happened to be there from Vasantapura. A thief also was passing that way. Encouraging the thief, the mountain parrot started chirping 'run and catch hold of this man'. Followed by the thief, the king ran to a hermitage for safety. The flower parrot was brought up in the hermitage. It encouraged the hermit boy to welcome the guest who was looking tired. Here we are told the difference between good and bad company.[125]

A popular tale of a bird is incorporated who was trying to take out a piece of flesh from inside the mouth of a sleeping tiger. Seeing this incident a Brāhmaṇa cried, 'Look at the great daring of the bird.' All such tales and legends woven together are meant to lead to peace and tranquillity of mind, fortune and happiness and ultimately to the permanent bliss which is *nirvāṇa.* In the same context emphasis is laid on avoidance of *rāga* (attachment) and *dveṣa* (aversion). It has been stated, 'If one is free from *rāga* and *dveṣa,* how could he be affected by suffering and how could he feel bewildered at the gain of happiness, and who would not be able to attain *mokṣa*?'[126]

Emphasizing the knot of deceitfulness (*kapaṭa-granthi*) the author writes: 'A man well understands and realises the suffering produced out of birth, old age and death, yet he does not detract himself from sensual pleasures! Oh! how the knot of deceitfulness is tied up so fast!'[127]

Uvaesapaya[128] (*Uvadeśapada: The Steps in Teaching*) is a didactic work by Haribhadrasūri, composed on the pattern of Dharmadāsagaṇi's *Uvaesamālā.* This treasury of religious tales is written in Mahārāṣṭrī Prakrit. It is meant for the enlightenment of slow-witted simple people. It contains 1039 *gāthās* in Āryā meter. The learned author has incorporated Prakrit verses from earlier works such as the *Uttarā Nir,* the *Nandi,* the *Sanmati-prakaraṇa* of Siddhasena and so on. Several commentaries were written on this important work. Municandrasūri, the teacher of Vādidevasūri, the well known author of the *Syādvādaratnākara,* wrote his *Sukhasaṃbodhinī* in (AD 1117). This is written in Prakrit and Sanskrit prose and verse, enriched with numerous pithy and crisp sayings; some of which are in Apabhraṃśa which indicates that the commentator had a mastery over Prakrit, Sanskrit and Apabhraṃśa. The commentary was composed in Aṇahillapura. It appears from the third verse of the commentary that the work contained still another important commentary which is not known to us. Vardhamānasūri wrote another commentary in vs 1055.

Numerous popular interesting tales, explaining the teachings of Mahavira, are incorporated in this composition. We also come across witty tales and anecdotes, eloquent speeches, witty sayings, didactic verses, riddles and questions and answers. It begins with the assertion that to achieve human birth is most difficult. The statement is illustrated by citing various similes as *collaka* (food),[129] *pāsa* (dice-play), *dhānya* (corn), *dyūta* (gambling), *ratna* (jewels), *svapna* (dream), *cakra* (a circle), *carma* (skin), *juga* (axle) and *paramāṇu* (atom).[130] Explaining the simile of corn, it is stated that as it is most difficult to separate a handful of mustard seeds from a huge heap of corn so is the attainment of human birth from innumerable births of this mundane world. Four kinds of intellect (*buddhi*) are explained: *autpattikī*, *vainayikī*, *karmajā* and *Pāriṇāmikī*, with illustrations. Under the category of *Bharata-śilā*, the story of Rohaka, an acrobat's son, is narrated; he unravelled various riddles and as a result the king impressed by his sharp intellect, appointed him his prime minister.[131]

Besides, various other interesting riddles are told here. A dialogue between two ascetics is noted. One asked the other, 'can you tell me the number of crows living on the river bank'? He replied, 'Sixty thousand'. 'How do you know the exact number?' the first one inquired. 'You can count them; if you find less, they must have flown to some other place; if more, they must have come and joined them from outside he retorted.'[132] A story of Mūladeva, a crest-jewel of rogues, and his friend Kaṇḍarīka is recorded.[133] Dealing with the Vainayikī intellect, the commentator has mentioned 18 types of script.[134] Here we come across a slightly different version regarding the banishment of Sītā in the Rāmāyaṇa. It has been stated that after dwelling in a forest for fourteen years, when Rāma, Lakṣamaṇa and Sītā returned to Ayodhyā, some people raised objection with regard to the chastity of Sītā as she had stayed at Rāvaṇa's palace in Laṅkā. One day, making use of this opportunity, a co-wife of Sītā asked her to draw a painting of Rāvaṇa. But as Sītā had a glance of his feet only and not the upper part of his body, she was able to draw only his feet. Thereupon showing the painting to Rāma, the crooked co-wife pointed out, 'See, my Lord, she still feels infatuated with Rāvaṇa.'[135]

Further, we have the narrations of Vajrasvāmin, the sage Kūlavālaka, who caused the destruction of the city of Vaiśāli, Ārya Mahāgiri and Ārya Suhastin, the origin of Daśārṇapura, also known as Eḍakākṣa-pura, Avantisukumāla, and a great disputant Govindavācaka and the Sovereign King Brahmadatta. In Part II, in order to illustrate the *vratas*, the examples of Sudarśana *Setha*, Somā and others are cited. The story of a merchant known as Jhuṇṭana is told, where righteousness is preached by way of an allegory of an animal, Jhuṇṭaṇaka.[136] Consider the following questions and answers:

'What is righteousness? Compassion on living beings. What is happiness? Freedom from disease. What is love? Uprightness. What is learning? Discrimination between right and wrong.'[137]

'What is unsteady? The progress of work. What is to be achieved? Appreciation of merits. What is to be conducted easily? A good man. What is to be conducted with difficulty? A wicked man.'[138]

The story of Śaṅkhakalāvatī is narrated as an illustration of righteous practice (*dharmācaraṇa*). Here we come across a miserable account of a good man whose family members had nothing to eat due to extreme poverty. With great difficulty he was able to procure a little sugar, coarse meal, fried barley (*sattu*), a little *ghee* and milk, but unfortunately, the pot containing sugar and coarse meal turned upside down. The fried barley got mixed up with sugar-candy powder and the pot containing *ghee* fell on the ground and the milk which was thickened by heating, spilled all over and slipped from the hand.[139]

Dharmopadeśamālā-Vivaraṇa[140] has been composed in Prakrit verses in Āryā meter, by Jayasiṃhasūri a pupil of Kṛṣṇa Muni in VS 915 (AD 858). He has followed the footsteps of Dharmadāsagaṇi, the author of the *Dharmopadeśamālā*. Several expositions have been written on this work and the present one is the oldest.[141] Jayasiṃhasūri, instead of introducing didactic teachings, has preferred to tell didactic stories. It contains 156 narratives told in 98 *gāthās*, whereas the *Upadeśamālā* comprises only 70 narratives in 540 *gāthās*. The *Vivaraṇa* was written in the temple of Nagore during the reign of the well known king Bhojadeva. Here the verses are explained in Sanskrit but the stories are in Jain Mahārāṣṭrī.[142] At the end of each story the author has paid veneration to the goddess of learning (*Śrutadevatā*). It is stated that one who having given a proper thought to this work, reads it in the assembly, would be able to comprehend bondage and freedom from *karmas*.

Jayasiṃhasūri was a prolific writer of Prakrit prose. As he has used various forms of poetic expression, he can be compared with Bāṇa. He has employed, *Praśnottara*[143] of which numerous alternatives or varieties are known, arising out of grammatical or dialectal and other variations. Here the answer of two, three or four questions is given in a line of a stanza (*pada*). It has various categories: consisting of a similar meaning, different meanings, mixed meaning, *ālāpaka* (statement of the question in an arithmetical or algebraic sum); consisting of different gender, case-termination, tense (*kāla*), syntax (*kāraka*) and number; written in Sanskrit, Prakrit, Apabhraṃśa, Paiśācī, Māgadhī, Rākṣasī, Miśra languages; *madhya-uttara* (containing the answer in the middle), *bahiḥ-uttara* (containing the answer outside), *ekālāpa* (sounding as one answer but expressing more than one), and *gata-pratyāgata* (coming back again of the answer after it had gone away).[144] Besides, *gūḍha-uttara* and *paṭṭhaṭṭha* (*spṛṣṭārtha*) are mentioned by Udyotanasūri in his *KVLM.*[145] The former, consisting of a concealed answer, is an important variety of *praśnottara.* In *spṛṣṭārha,* the answer given to a question is clear, it is not hidden.

The following is cited as an illustration of *praśnottara*: 'Viṣṇu having gone to sleep in time, the nights were darkened with clouds, O large-eyed one, I am not telling a lie, you have faith in the first letter of each *pada.*'[146] This message was sent by a merchant's son of Mathura to the queen of the city. The queen immediately sent the following reply: 'In this world there is no happiness at all, it is shrouded with evil; the duration of life is limited, therefore put your mind in righteousness.'[147]

Besides numerous copious descriptions of cities, mountains, forests, gardens, sunrise, sunset, sea-voyage, wedding ceremony, heroism, love and pity the author has introduced various other literary forms such as *prema-patrikā* (love-letters), *pāda-pūrti* (filling out the measure of a verse), *vakrokti* (indirect mode of expression), *vyājokti* (dissimulating statement), *śleṣokti* (with double meaning), *guḍhokti* (with a hidden meaning), *anyokti* (with a different sense), *chekokti* (insinuation) and so on.

Generally the narratives are based on the earlier texts, yet the style of their narration is different. The stories are related to charity (*dāna*), virtue (*śīla*), austerities (*tapas*), reverence to teachers (*guru-vinaya*), excess of blemishes (*doṣa-bāhulya*), self-denial (*ātma-damana*), good company (*satpuruṣa-saṅga*), performing one's duty (*kartavya-karaṇa*), negation of anger (*kopa-niṣedha*), compassion (*anukampā*), devotion (*bhakti*), enlightenment (*bodha*), honey-drop (*madhu-bindu*), steadiness in righteousness (*dharma-sthairya*), absence of covetousness and (*niḥspṛhatā*), forgiveness (*kṣānti*) and so on. In these narratives are incorporated the accounts of great personalities like those of Bharata Cakravartin, Metārya, Āṣāḍhasūri, Śreyāṃsa, Kṛtapuṇya, Śālibhadra, Mūladeva, Āryarakṣita, Nandiṣeṇa, Pratyekabuddha, Brahmadatta, Tripṛṣṭha Vāsudeva, Cāṇakya, Nāgila, Subandhu, Keśī-gaṇadhara, Āryā Candanā, Subhadrā, Sulasā and so on.

It appears that Pāṭaliputra (modern Patna) was a centre of arts in those days. In the story of *Dvija-tanaya* it is stated that in order to get training in *yuvatī-carita* (the conduct of young women) people used to visit this city. Various marriage customs have been mentioned: in the country of Lāṭa, maternal uncle's daughter was allowed to be married to her cousin; the younger brother of a husband (*devara*) was allowed to marry his elder brother's widow. It seems there also existed a custom of marrying the step-mother (*sapatnī*) as well as one's own sister (*sahodarā*).[148]

Dealing with the fruit of chastity (*śīla-phala*), the author, while giving a glorious account of virtuous Rājīmatī, condemns women in general; but at the same time has favoured to remain in a household life before retiring from the worldly pleasures. When Ṇemī (Ariṣṭanemi) was bent upon renouncing the world, he was told by Kṛṣṇa: 'O prince, even Ṛṣabha and other Tīrthaṅkaras relinquished the worldly pleasures only after being married (*dāra-saṅgaha*), having enjoyed worldly life, having raised children, having fulfilled the desire of those who were humble, having looked after his subjects, and yet they attained *nirvāṇa.*'[149]

The story of *Nūpura-paṇḍitā* (Anklet-Wise;) which is important from the point of view of universal literature, is quite popular among Jains.[150] It is to be noted that Malayagiri in his commentary on the *Piṇḍa-Niryukti* (*gāthā* 181) regarding the story, has referred to the *DSMV* which reflects on the popularity of the work. It is not wanting in pithy sayings. A man who has not acquired fame, is compared with a bull who somehow fills his belly roaming about here and there.[151] Further, a saying is quoted about women: 'They please others but are never pleased themselves; they capture the heart of others but never give their own heart, fifty-six intellects of others are equal to two of their own.'[152]

The author seems to be conversant with various popular sciences such as music, dance, painting, drama, astrology, medicine and so on. There are numerous Sanskrit and Prakrit quotations which are cited in between the stories; they are arranged in Appendix I, at the end of the work. The work is important for the study and development of New Indo-Aryan languages.

Uvaesamālā-pagaraṇa (*Upadeśamālā Prakaraṇa*) (*Garland of Instructions*) or *Puṣpamālā*[153] (*Garland of Flowers*) is another important work of Maladhāri Hemacandra with his own commentary on it. Here religious and moral instructions are noted for the guidance of laymen and monks. Maladhāri (bearing filth or dirt) Hemacandra was a renowned Jain scholar of the twelfth century, who is mentioned with great respect. He was a senior contemporary of *Kalikāla-sarvjña* Hemacandra and was known as Paṇḍita Śvetāmbarācārya Bhaṭṭāraka, learned pupil of Abhayadeva, pupil of Jayasiṃhasūri. He was not only a religious preacher but also a poet with a command on ornate style and poetic grace. He was a prolific writer, well-versed in Prakrit, Sanskrit and Apabhraṃśa. The contribution of Maladhāri Hemacandra in the field of didactic literature is so great that he comes next to only Dharmadāsagaṇi.

Maldhāri Hemacandra is an author of several other important works: he has written the *Bhavabhāvanā* with his self-composed *Vṛtti*; *Vivaraṇa* on the *Viśeṣāvaśyaka-Bhāṣya* of Jinabhadragaṇi Kṣamaśramaṇa; *Vyākhyā* on the *Anuyogadvāra-Sūtra*; *Ṭippaṇa* on the *Āvaśyaka-Vṛtti* of Haribhadrasūri; the *Vivaraṇa* on the *Jīvasamāsa*; the *Vivaraṇa* on the *Śataka* and others. Mostly Rajasthan was the centre of his activities where he composed a number of his works.

The author has stated about his work: 'It has been composed by employing excellent words (*suvaṇṇa* or colourful) of extraordinary quality (*guṇa* or chord), picked up from the garden of sayings of God Jina (*jiṇavayaṇa*). Thus the *Upadeśamālā* is woven like a garland of flowers.'[154] According to him, 'One who reads it with sincere heart, meets with fortune, accomplishment and final emancipation.'[155]

The work comprises 500 *gāthās* in Mahārāṣṭrī Prakrit, divided into 20 *Adhikāras*: *Abhaya-pradāna*, *Jñāna*, *Dāna*, *Śīla*, *Tapa*, *Bhāvanā*, *Samyaktva-śuddhi*, *Cāritra-śuddhi*, *Indriya-jaya*, *Kaṣāya-nigraha*, *Gurukula-vāsa*, *Doṣa-vikaṭanā*, *Virāga*, *Vinaya*, *Vaiyāvṛtya*, *Svādhyāya-rati*, *Anāyatana-tyāga*, *Para-parivāda-nivṛtti*, *Dharma-sthiratā*, and *Parijñāna*. In each of these sections numerous traditional religious and popular stories are told in an elaborate style with illustrations and examples explaining the tenets of Jainism. Numerous characters are borrowed from the *Upamiti-bhava-prapañcā-kathā* (narrative in which the manifoldness of existence is presented in Parables), a well known

Sanskrit allegorical novel by Siddharṣi. The passions (*kaṣaya*) are described as 'inward' companions of the 'wandering soul' leading to trouble. Anger is compared with a conflagration (*krodha-dava*), pride with the mountain (*māna-giri*), deceit with a female snake (*māyā-bhujaṅgī*), and avarice with the demon (*lobha-piśāca*). Moha or infatuation is moving with its troops (*moha-sainya*) so we have to be very careful. He is joined by his two sons, one is 'lion-passion' (*rāga-kesarī*), the other being 'elephant-aversion' (*dveṣa-gajendra*). The 'infatuation-king' is accompanied by the god of love as his governor (*madana-māṇḍalika*), he is equipped with the weapons of love (*smara-astra*) and falsehood is his vassal (*viparyāsa-sāmanta*). The 'wandering soul' (*saṃsārī jīva*) is compared with a king deprived of enlightenment (*bodha*): lot of harm is done to him by the company of 'infatuation'. Consciousness is revived in him by whispering *mantras* in his ears; the army of the virtue of good conduct (*cāritra-dharma*) makes 'infatuation' and other thieves flee. Sometimes it happens that obstacles are created by ignorance (*ajñāna*) as a result the 'wandering soul' gets stuck, therefore ultimately 'infatuation' and others have to be rooted out.[156]

The section Granting Fearlessness (*Abhaya-pradāna*) begins with the ten illustrations cited to prove the rarity of acquiring human life. *Ahiṃsā* or non-violence is called the best of religion. The autumn and the summer seasons are described. In granting fearlessness, an illustration of prince Vajrāyudha is provided. A dove was pursued by a hawk, the former seeking shelter, which was granted. Soon after the hawk flew there and demanded his prey as he was hungry. The prince offered to give his own flesh instead. A weighing scale was brought and the prince started weighing the dove with his flesh. The prince cut off his flesh put it on the scale but it could not balance the weight of the dove. Ultimately, the compassionate prince threw his whole body. Thereupon the dove assumed his real form of a celestial being and praised the prince and disappeared.[157] In the section of knowledge (*jñāna*) the life history of the prince Purandara is narrated. We come across the description of winter. The accomplishment of magic lore (*vidyā*) is mentioned. The act of robbery (*ṭhaga-vidyā*) is referred to. It is stated: 'whether one possesses intelligence or not, in order to attain right knowledge, in no circumstances, one should give up making efforts'.[158]

In the section of *Śīla* the stories of Ratisundarī, Ṛddhisundarī, Buddhisundarī and Gunasundarī are narrated.[159] Haribhadrasuri's

Upadeśapada has been recommended for the details. The story of Sītā is narrated in the *Śīlamāhātmya*. The section on *Bhāvanā* is divided into 14 categories. Under the category of *aparigraha* (not longing for possession), wealth is called the source of all kinds of evil.[160] It is stated, 'If a monk having obtained the teaching of *nirgranthas*, in some form or the other, is in possession of wealth, although apparently he appears to be unattached (*nirgrantha*), he tarnishes the Jain teaching.'[161] It is stated that though the Brāhmaṇas maintain the caste system, numerous sages are said to have taken their birth from different sources: the sage Acala is born from female elephant, Kesakambala from female owl, Agastya from the *agasti*-flower, Kauśika from *kuśa*-bed, Kaṭhina from an earthen vessel (*kaṭhina*), Gautama from a clump of reeds (*śara-gulma*), Droṇācārya from a water pitcher (*kalaśa*), Taittirīya from a partridge (*tittiri*); Reṇukā gave birth to Rāma, a female deer (*mṛgī*) to Ṛṣiśṛṅga in a forest, Kaivartī to Vyāsa, Śūdrikā to Kakṣivanta, Cāṇḍālī to Visvāmitra, Urvaśī to Vasiṣṭha—all of them, though not born in the *dvijāti* family, are known as the best of *dvijas*.[162]

Bhavabhāvanā[163] (Contemplation of the Nature of the World), also known as *Vararayaṇamāliyā* (Excellent String of Pearls) is another important work of didactic literature by Maladhari Hemacandra in Meḍatā and Chhatrapalli with self-composed *vṛtti*. The work comprises 531 *gāthās*, containing the account of 12 *bhāvanas* (reflections). Pointing out the importance of this work, the author has stated: 'One who reads the Sūtras, listens to their meaning and contemplates constantly over them, develops the feeling of disgust towards worldly objects and ultimately attains the highest end of life. He is neither affected by pleasure and joy, nor disturbed by adverse misfortune or discontentment, purified in his mind by reading it, he remains as if impregnated by ambrosia.'[164]

The *Upadeśamālā* and the *Bhavabhāvanā* both pertain to didactic teaching, the main difference between the two being that the former deals with charity, virtue, penance, right faith and so on, whereas the latter emphasizes on the disgusting nature of worldly objects leading to the development of a feeling of righteousness, attainment of right faith and thereby achievement of liberation which is free from pleasure and pain. Here the emphasis is laid on renunciation so that one may work hard to do good to others, befitting a man of resolution.[165]

The author deals with the twelve-fold reflections (*bhāvanā*): *anitya* (impermanence), *aśaraṇa* (helplessness), *ekatva* (loneliness), *anyatva* (distinctiveness), *bhava* or *saṃsāra* (nature of worldly existence), *aśuci* (impurity), *loka* (nature of the universe), *āsrava* (inflow of karmic matter), *saṃvara* (stoppage of karmic flow), *nirjarā* (dissociation of the karmic matter from soul), *uttamaguṇa* (contemplation in the excellent virtues) and *bodhi* (difficulty in attaining enlightenment). Numerous illustrations are provided to explain these *bhāvanās*. It has been stated that this work containing 12 *bhāvanās* should be read in twelve days, one *bhāvanā* per day. Out of these, the fifth, the *Bhavabhāvanā* or the *saṃsārabhāvanā* is given prominence and described in detail, comprising a large number of *gāthās*, whereas the rest of the *bhāvanās* are mentioned only incidentally or briefly.[166] The text is in Mahārāṣṭrī Prakrit with its exposition in Sanskrit. The self-composed commentary narrates numerous religious and moral stories and tales which are considered essential for the development of renunciation towards sensual pleasure. It is interspersed with Sanskrit and Apabhraṃśa prose and poetry. The major part of the work narrates the life history of Nemi (Ariṣṭanemi) which includes the origin of the Harivaṃśa, Daśārha kings, the birth of Kaṃsa, the account of Vasudeva, comprising the story of Cārudatta, Yājñavalkya-Sulasā-pippalāda, anārya *Veda*, birth of Anādhṛṣṭi, wives of Vasudeva and so on.[167] The region of Siṇavalli is referred to, which was visited by Kṛṣṇa in order to slay Jarāsandha. It is located in western India after traversing 45 *yojanas* in the east-northern direction of the city of Dvārakā.[168]

We are told that a certain Sarasvatī, daughter of a caravan leader, used to study various arts from a Brāhmaṇa teacher. After completing her education she married to a merchant's son Devadatta, who was her class-mate. The character of Bhui, the mother-in-law has been depicted. She quarrelled with her daughter-in-law, insulted the saints and monks and was never took interest in doing religious deeds. Emphasis is laid on earning money. What is the use of leading the life of a pauper? For him all the four quarters look deserted, therefore one should make efforts to earn money so that one may possess virtues which were absent in him. It is said: 'Let caste, beauty and learning disappear in the hollow of a cavern, but let there be increase in wealth so that the virtues become perceptible.'[169] Further, it is stated: 'If one has sufficient wealth, one can do business, if one has little wealth, one can take the profession of agriculture; if there is no wealth, one can join service, and after all, if one has self-confidence one can do anything by firm resolution.'[170] The pithy sayings (*subhaśitas*) are enlisted in Appendix 5 at the end.

The following works can be added: 1 *Sīlovaesamālā* by Jayakīrti, pupil of Jayasiṃhasūri; Somatilakasūri has written a commentary (AD 1337); 2 *Saṃvegaraṅgasālā* by Jinacandrasūri (eleventh century); 3 *Vivegamañjarī* and 4 *Upadésakandali* by Āsada (twelfth century) son of Kaṭukarāja of the Bhillamāla family; 5 *Uvaesarayaṇāyara* by Munisundarasūri (fourteenth century); 6 *Vaddhamāṇadesanā* by Śubhavardhanagaṇi (fifteenth century); 7 *Upadesaprakaraṇa* (by unknown author); 8 *Dhammavihi* by Śrīprabhasūri; 9 *Darisaṇasuddhi* or *Darisaṇasattari* by Haribhadrasūri; 10 *Sammattapayaraṇa* by Candraprabhasūri; 11 *Dāṇasīlatavabhāvaṇākulaya* by Devendrasūri of Tapāgaccha (thirteenth century); 12 *Sambohapayaraṇa* or *Tattapayāsaga* by Haribhadrasūri; 13 *Hiovaesakulaya*; and 14 *Uvaesakulaya* both by Municandrasūri (see *JSBI*, IV, pp. 193-226). The *Jain Granthavali* (pp. 168-94) adds *Antaraṅgaprabodha, Antaraṅgasandhi, Gautamabhāṣita, Daśadṛṣṭāntagītā* (by Somavimala), *Nāribodhaṃ, Hitācaraṇa, Hitopadeśāmṛta* (in 207 leaves).

The Descriptive Catalogue of MSS, Government MSS (*DCGCM*), *BORI*, Poona, 1952, VIII, Pt. I, edited by H.R. Kapadia adds (pp. 302-478) the following works: 1 *Uvaesacintāmaṇi* (*Upadeśacintāmaṇi*) by Jayasehara (Jayaśekhara) Suri, pupil of Mahendrasūri of Aṅcala *gaccha* (AD 1379), published with self-composed commentary and Gujarati translation Hiralal Hansraj, Jamnagar in 4 parts, vs 1977, 1979, 1980 and 1980. 2 *Uvaeasamaṇimālā-kulaya* (*Upadeśamaṇimālā-kulaka*) by Jineśvarasūri. 3 *Uvaesarayaṇamālā* (*Upadeśaratnamālā*) by Padmajineśvarasūri. 4 *Uvaesarasāyaṇa* (*Upadeśarasāyana*) with *vṛtti* by Jinadattasūri of Kharatara *gaccha*, pupil of Jinavallabhaṣūri, pupil of Abhayadevasūri. It contains another commentary by Jinapāla, pupil of Jinapatisūri. 5 *Uvaesarahassapagaraṇa* (*Upadeśarahasya-prakaraṇa*) by Nyāyaviśārada Yaśovijayagaṇi with commentary, Mansukh Bhai Bhagubhai, vs 1967. 6 *Uvaesāmayapañcavīsisyā* (*Upadeśāmṛta-pañcaviṃśatikā*), author not mentioned, published in *Prakaraṇa-samuccaya*, pp. 28-30. 7 *Ikkavīsathāṇa-pagaraṇa* (*Ekaviṃśati-sthāna-prakaraṇa*) by Siddhasenasūri, pupil of Yaśodevasūri, a descendant of Bappabhaṭṭasūri, published with a Sanskrit commentary *Bodhadīpikā* by Caturvijaya. 8 *Eguṇatisabhāvanā* (*Ekonatriṃśadbhāvanā*), author not mentioned; referred to as *Appabohakulaya* (*Ātmabodhakulaka*) in Peterson Report, V, p. 111.

The *Jinaratnakośa* adds the following:

Upadeśamālā-kathā-samāsa composed by Jinabhadra Muni, pupil of Śālibhadra in vs 1204.

Upadeśaratna-kośa by Padmajineśvarasūri in 26 *gāthās*.

The *Raj OIJ Collection*, Pt. II (A), 1964, has recorded the following: *Aupadeśika-kathā-saṃgraha* in Prakrit and Sanskrit (eighteenth century vs) contains the following *kathās*: (i) *Tridaṇḍī-kathā*, (ii) *Śreṇikarāja-kathā*, (iii) *Aṭṭaṇamalla-kathā*, (iv) *Rajaka-kathā*, (v) *Saṃyati-kathā*, (vi) *Dhīriṇī Pramukhādevī-kathā*, (vii) *Niṣpuṇya-kathā*, (viii) *Kūṇika-kathā*, (ix) *Datta-kathā*, (x) *Vasurāja-kathā*.

Aupadeśika-padyāni composed in vs 1760.

Bhava-vairāgya-śataka (seventeenth century).

SUPPLEMENT[171]

(A) *A Summary of the Contents of the MKH (2 to 18 Lambhas)*

The third *lambha*, the *Mehamālā-lambha*, deals with the acquisition of the *Mahārrajñpti* magical spell, acquired by remaining standing for 7 days in chest-deep water. The *Isidattā-kahā-lambha* refers to a miraculous herb. If by tearing open the left thigh of a woman, this herb is thrust, she is transformed into a male. Similarly, if it is thrust inside the right thigh of a man, he is transformed into a female.[172] It also refers to the *Osovaṇī*, the Tālugghāḍaṇī, the *Thambaṇī* and the *Vimokkhaṇī* spells, the last two, we are told, were accomplished with difficulty. The *Aṇilajasā-lambha* refers to the *Mahārohiṇī* spell which was preached by Satya (*saccovadiṭṭhā*), who was known as incarnation of truth. We come across a golden image of the goddess *Śaṅkuka-vidyā*. It was large (*mahāpramāṇā*) with a terrible appearance; it had a stern look, its eyebrows were moving constantly, its lower lip was quivering and its lustre like the radiance of the sun was emerging from its teeth, the flame of fire was emanating from its mouth, it was giving out a frightful loud laugh, its eyes looked violent with excitement and its sight was most disagreeable. It has been stated that this magic spell could be accomplished by assuming the terrible (*rudra*), dreadful (*bhairava*) forms having a spear in hand (*śūla-pāṇi*).[173] A victim was to be sacrificed to the goddess. Vāyuratha ordered that Vasudeva be offered to the goddess. The goddess was given a bath and the victim was washed by its bath-water. First, the victim was confined in a pit in an underground cell, guarded by armed soldiers where he had to remain without food or drink. Then the victim (*mahāpasu*)[174] was brought before the goddess for a blood-sacrifice (*rudhira-bali-kajje*). At the order of Vāyuratha, an ugly looking terrible Vidyādhara raised his sword to sever Vasudeva's head. At this time there was a violent trembling in the statue and it rushed towards Vāyuratha emitting flames of fierce rage from its mouth. It threatened Vāyuratha, proclaiming, 'O you are dead!' and then left its jewelled pedestal. The frightened Vāyuratha fell to its feet, asking for shelter (*saraṇaṃ*). Then the statue caught hold of Vasudeva, flew in the air quickly and brought him to a mountain-peak.[175]

SĪMAṆAGA AND HIRIMANTA IDENTIFIED?

It is to be noted that in the *VH* Sīmaṇaga and Hirimanta (Hrīmat) are two separate mountains known for accomplishing magical spells. The former was situated on the confluence of five rivers (*pañca-nadī-saṃgame*).[176] The mountain was visited by Vasudeva with his beloved Vagavatī, who had lost her magic powers while protecting her husband against the attack of Śūrpaṇakhī and consequently had became an earth-dweller.[177] The mountain was also known for the shrine of revered Ṛṣabha and it was here that Acala, one of the Baladevas, attained *kevala*.[178] The mountain was also visited by Amiyatejas, the lord of the *vidyādharas*.[179] Hirimanta is mentioned another holy mountain associated with Dharaṇa. The statue of Dharaṇendra was installed here along with the statue of revered Saṃjayanta and Amiyatejasa had arrived here in order to accomplish the Mahājvālā spell.[180] However the author of the *MKH* considers the Sīmaṇaga and the Hirimanta one and the same. He has stated that on the top of this mountain a shrine of Ṇābheya (Ṛṣabha) was constructed by Dharaṇa, the king of the Nāgas.

Since this shrine was constructed by Dharaṇa, it was called Dharaṇudbheda.[181] It was constructed at the time when Dharaṇa was bestowing *vidyās* to Nami and Vinami, the first *vidyādhara* kings of Bharata, who had been serving the first Tīrthaṅkara standing before his statue. After bestowing the *vidyās* Dharaṇa had laid down the law that any one who attacked a person living on this mountain, even his own enemy, would perish along with his family. It has been also stated that formerly there was another temple on this mountain which was constructed by Tiviṭṭhu's son Śrīvijaya to commemorate Acala's attainment of *kevalajñāna*. Yet another shrine was constructed here by Amiyatejas, the lord of the *vidyādharas*.[182] Elsewhere we are told that in the vicinity of the Hirimanta mountain, situated in the southern region of Bharata, a festival (*jattā*) was celebrated to commemorate the Jain shrines (*jiṇāyataṇa*). Here in front of the statues of Saṃjayanta and Dharaṇa, the *vidyādharas* of both the regions stood in their groups (*nikāya*), accompanied by their wives and children and chanting their magic arts.[183]

It seems there had been some controversial views regarding the identity of Sīmaṇaga and Hirimanta mountains. These have been mentioned by Jinasena and Hemacandra in the *JHP* and the *TSP* respectively. Jinasena has tried to interpret the word Hrīmat as possessed of bashfulness (*hrī*). According to him, as the *vidyādharas* being ashamed at their behaviour towards the monk Saṃjayanta, were seated with bent heads, thus this mountain was known as Hrīmat. It is a large mountain covered with forest. It is significant to note that here in the context of Nīlajasā, what is called Hrīmat in the *TSP* (V. 58-9) is termed as Veyaḍḍha (Vaitāḍhya) in the *VH* (182, 12; also *The Vasudeva*, p. 329n). The same mountain is identified with Śrīmanta in Hariṣeṇa's *BKK*.[184]

The *Indaseṇā-lambha* mentions Vesālī as the capital city of the Vajjī *janapada*; it was an abode of Licchavī Kṣatriyas. The city of Vesālī has been compared with the city of Indra (*daṇuya-nagarī-sarisaṃ*). People were fond of horse-races. A race was organized between two horses, named Mahā-soṇa and Culla-soṇa, and the former won the contest. Then, a race was arranged between a cow-elephant, Kesiṇiyā, and the chariot-yoked Culla-soṇa horse. The cow-elephant belonged to the best species and since she walked fast, she won the race.

The *Lakkhaṇā-lambha* refers to *Hiṇḍolaya-juddha* (rocking battle). A fight ensued between the ruler of Kosalā city and the Licchavis of Vesālī. The Licchavīs routed the enemy in the battle and reached the city of Kosalā. It is stated that prosperity dwells in human effort (*purisakāre siri vasai*) (a similar statement in the *VH*, made by merchant Cārudatta when he set out for a trip to earn money (180).[185]

The *Lalidavegā-lambha* raises a discussion whether a girl whose family origin is unknown should be accepted in marriage or not. It is argued that if acceptance of such a girl is considered not permissible, then how could Śambhu have accepted Pārvatī as his spouse? In the same way, though the origin of a clove-flower is not known, it is enjoyed by eminent people and is also offered to a deity. 'Those who know the specific colour and the quality of a jewel, only can admire it and not the cowherds whose mind is suspicious.'[186]

THE TWO MISSING LAMBHAS IN THE VH

The *Kanakavatī-lambha* is the longest *Lambha*, containing 216-58 pages. Before dealing with contents of this *Lambha*, let us make a comparative study of the number of *Lambhas* contained in the *VH* of Saṅghadāsagaṇi, in the *JHP* of Jinasena, in the *TSP* of Hemacandra, in the *BHBH* of Maladhāri Rājaśekharasūri,[187] and in the *MKH* of Dharmasenagaṇi. While presenting a comparative and critical study of the *VH* and the lost *BK* of Gunāḍhya, after examining the *VH* text, we have arrived at the conclusion that in spite of its being well edited by an eminent scholar like Muni Punyavijaya, it has remained very corrupt; certain *Lambhas* are missing here, it contains some material out of context and there is lack of uniformity in the *Lambhas*. Certain *Lambhas* are very short, without sufficient information of the heroine, whereas some contain the story of two heroines in one.

Regarding the two missing *Lambhas* in the *VH* the present author contributed an article entitled 'The Missing Lambhas in the Vasudevahiṇḍi and the Story of Pabhāvatī' in the *IIJ* 17 (1975, pp. 41-56). But this article provides only the additional information about Prabhāvatī, based on the first *Lambha* of the *MKH*, which is poorly supplied by the author of the *VH*. However, nothing has been indicated here about the two missing *Lambhas* of the *VH* text. As it has been pointed out under the caption 'A Comparative List of the Wives of Vasudeva' in Appendix V, pp. 678-81 of *The Vasudeva* the names of Vasudeva's wives are missing in the nineteenth and the twentieth *Lambhas* in the *VH* as well as in the *JHP* of Jinasena and the *BHBH* of Maladhāri Rājaśekharasūri; they are available only in the *TSP* as *Sukosalā* and *Kanakavatī* respectively. Interestingly, the same *Lambhas* are also available in the *MKH* under the title *Sukosalā-lambha* and the *Kaṇagavaī-lambha*. It may not be surprising if these two *Lambhas* are the same missing *Lambhas* in the *VH* which might have been restored by the author of the *MKH*. Out of these two, the *Kaṇagavaī-lambha* seems to be more important as it is the longest *Lambha* in the *MKH* as well as in the *TSP*. In the *TSP* it forms Chapter III of the *Parvan* VIII, comprising 1077 verses (pp. 79-148, Vol. V, English translation by H.M. Johnson), which amounts to more than double the number of the second chapter of the same book. Another important thing to be noted is that out of 1077 verses, more than three-fourths deal with the pre-birth story of Kanakavatī in the form of the Nala and Damayanti story. And it is not without significance that in the *MKH*, out of 42 pages of the *Kaṇagavaī-lambha*, 25 pages are devoted to the previous birth of Kanakavatī born as Davadantī, the wife of Nala.

Regarding other *Lambhas* of the *MKH*, the *Pabhāvatī-lambha* is common to all the Jain versions, as indicated above. It receives special attention at the hands of the author of the *MKH*, who begins his work with the *Pabhavatī-lambha* and narrates the story of Prabhāvatī in a lucid charming manner which has been poorly told in the incomplete *VH* text.[188] Vasudeva's wife Avantisundarī is not mentioned in the *VH* but occurs in all the remaining Jain versions; the *MKH* contains the *Avantīvaddhaṇā-lambha*. Further, the *MKH* has recorded the *Indaseṇā-lambha* as we have seen earlier, though it is not available in either of the above-mentioned Jain versions. However, Indasena's story is told under the *Ketumatī-lambha* in the *VH* and the *JHP*. Both refer to Indaseṇā (Indrasenā) but there seems to be a slight disagreement between the two versions. According to the former, she was daughter of Jarāsandha, the ruler of Magadha, by his queen Kālindaseṇā, who was given to King Jiyasattu in marriage. Here the hero Vasudeva simply cures Indaseṇā and never marries her. He marries Ketumatī, who is called the real sister of King Jiyasattu (pp. 348f, under 'Indaseṇā-sambandho'; *The Vasudeva*, pp. 507n, 510, 511, 513). In the *JHP* (30.42-56) Ketumati is called the daughter of Jarāsandha (whereas in the *VH*, Indaseṇā is Jarāsandha's daughter; Jinasena seems to have confused with the names here). Here Vasudeva cures Ketumatī (and not Indaseṇā). In the *TSP* (VIII.2.578-88) Indraseṇā of *VH* is called Nandiseṇā, daughter of Jarāsandha and wife of Jitaśatru. As in the *VH* here also Vasudeva marries Ketumatī; so is the case with the *BHBH*.

In this *Lambha* a royal palace is described with seven apartments (*kaccha*). The details of *svayaṃvara* marriage of Kanakavatī are narrated. King Nala was fond of gambling and had perfect skill in this art (*akkha-hidaya=akṣa-hṛdaya*). He had also acquired mastery over the art of cooking (*poraga*). He was expert in cooking dishes by the rays of the sun (*ādicca-pāga*). The king also acquired proficiency in driving a chariot (*ratha-sārathi*).[189]

Emphasizing the importance of wealth, it is stated: 'Only those who possess wealth, have people, those who have wealth, have numerous friends; the one without wealth is as good as a menial or a servant.'[190]

The *Sāgaradattā-lambha* refers to Mānibhadda (Maṇibhadra), the lord of Yakṣas. Accimāliṇī was a female Yakṣiṇī. *Savvosahī* is mentioned as a necklace which was supposed to be an antedote to all diseases and sorrows. The city of Maṇivaddhaṇa was situated in the Kirāta *janapada*; it was ruled by King Mahāsīha. There was a well here which was guarded by people. It contained alchemic fluid which transformed base metals into gold, hence this area was known as Suvarṇadvīpa (the island of gold). We are told that as in the customary Kirāta way Sāgaradattā became wife of Vasudeva without undergoing any wedding ceremony.[191] The *Malayasenā-lambha* refers to the Draviḍa *janapada* with Nāgapura as its capital; it was ruled by the king Sumuha. The Kurataka Draviḍas are mentioned. There was a royal sandalwood forest (*candana-vana*) which contained a very big fragrant sandalwood tree, called *gośīrṣa*. It was declared a gift to Vasudeva from the Yakṣiṇī Arcimāliṇī.

(B) *The Union of the Hero and the Heroine*

As pointed out earlier, the text of the *VH* is incomplete, it has no *upsaṃhāra*, hence the union of Vasudeva with the heroine Somasiri does not take place. This is supplemented by the *MKH* (Uttarārdha, manuscript, pp. 290-300), a partial English version of which has been given in *The Vasudeva* (Introduction, pp. 142-9). A partial summary of the same is presented here, based on the remaining portion of still unpublished manuscript:

Once when I (Vasudeva) was sleeping happily with my wife Muktāvali, I woke up all of a sudden. With my half-closed eyes I saw Nīlayaśā, my beloved. I got up from the side of Muktāvali; Nilayaśā bowed to my feet. I embraced her, placed her on my lap and kissed her, saying, 'O dear, welcome to you.' Then I asked her, 'At this odd hour you have come here all alone!' She replied: 'Terribly afflicted by the fire of your separation, she (Priyaṅgusundarī) has given up hope for life, she is constantly crying and bemoaning and is feeling extremely exhausted, hoping somehow that you would return soon some day. Thus she is passing a very very difficult time as if deprived of her life. And you have forsaken her from a distance like the fourteenth day of the dark half of the month.' Though she is alive, she witnesses you in her dream, crying, 'O *Āryaputra*! why have you forsaken me, an unfortunate one?' She folds her hands together and offers you salutation, saying, 'kindly you give me a call, O where have you gone away. Then she wakes up and finds no one in front of her.'

This is the purpose of my coming here. I (Nilayaśā) told her to get up and I promised to get you back. She (Priyangusundarī) told me that without you she was determined to die.

After hearing this account of my beloved, I requested Nilayaśā to carry me thither.

Thereupon Nilayaśā was very happy and carrying me in her arms flew in the air.

After going a little further, I said, 'I am feeling thirsty and would like to quench my thirst'. She carried me down on the river bank surrounded by flower creepers. Anxiously waiting for enjoyment of pleasure, I took her hand and entered the creeper house. Nilayaśā retorted, 'The work is done, I offer salutation to you, you would not be able to see Priyaṅgusundarī.' Uttering these words, I took her out from the bed of excellent flowers and placed her on a slab of rock. Then after playing jokes and making merry for some time, she placed me on her shoulders and flew in the air. In a little while we arrived at Śrāvasti, we saw the dwelling house of Priyaṅgusundarī from a distance. We ourselves remained invisible and saw her in the company of Kaumudikā. Her cheeks were emaciated due to the grief of my separation, she was passing time without sleep and was locking out waiting for the arrival of Nilayaśā. At this time Nilayaśā, as if dwelling in my heart, told me, 'Let us overhear the confidential conversation between Priyaṅgusundarī and Kaumudikā from here.' Kaumudikā was talking: 'Oh! how happily was fondeled our mistress by the Noble one! No one could ever imagine that she had to undergo such a lot of suffering.'

Replying to a question, Priyaṅgusundarī said, 'In case the Noble one does not turn up with Nīlayaśā, I will give up my life.'

Nilayaśā told me, 'My dear, you stay here, I shall go ahead and tell her: "look, your husband has not come, now you do whatever you like". Let me see how she reacts.' I (Vasudeva) remarked, 'Do not play jokes with her. She is very anxious to meet her husband and is full of hopes. She might give up life after hearing what you are going to tell her. Therefore you just show me to her a little.'

Hearing this, Nilayaśā brought me down from the air in front of her house. She told Priyaṅgusundarī, 'Here I have come, take him.' Thereafter as soon as she glanced at me, without any tenderness, without showing any courteous conduct, she held me by my neck. Her pretty arms looked beautiful with armlets and her forehead was brightened with splendour of jewels.

I sat down on a seat offered by Kaumudikā. I looked at her for long while she was shedding tears and was talking at random. She was aggravated with intense sorrow and I found that having a glance at me she fell into a swoon.

I told Kaumudikā to get some water quickly as my beloved had fainted. Immediately water was brought in a golden jar and she was sprinkled with a water stream. I told her, 'O lady, here I am your follower.' She proposed, 'As long as we remain together you remain invisible.' I consented to the proposal. I was brought under the influence of magic art of Prabhāvatī; she made me invisible.

Next day, at the time of sunrise, having sighted Somasiri, decorated with all kinds of ornaments and finery, Māṇasavega reflected, 'Certainly, that wicked earth-dweller has arrived here, otherwise how could she look overjoyed like a winged elephant. Someone must have arranged for his secret entry in my pleasure-garden. Today itself I will send him to the dwelling place of god of Death.'

In the meantime, Māṇasavega commanded his *vidyāharas* to put me in bondage quickly as according to him I was hiding in terror of him. Not tolerating these words, laughing excitedly with anger, I pointed out my sword and shield to him, saying, 'O wicked *vidyādhara*, I am not hiding out of your fear. I am not approachable to your *vidyādharas*. I can single-handedly destroy your pride.' Then he remained looking at me for quite some time. He asked his *vidyādharas*, 'Look, this earth-dweller is worthy of punishment.' I retorted, 'It is of no use talking all this, you are bold only in words.' Hearing this Mānasavega was all the more annoyed and was ready to grab me. But the relatives of Vegavatī (the mother of Mānasavega) came to my side and prevented him saying, 'Why should he be killed? He has not committed any crime against you!'

'On the contrary,' I retorted, 'he has abducted my wife.'

Mānasavega replied, 'I do not know you!'

Just then a heavenly voice was heard saying, 'Like the powerful Mandaradeva in the *vidyādhara* world you will be killed. In a terrible battle you will be struck down with my foot.'

Hearing this Mānasavega was alarmed. At this time his mother approached him, saying, 'O child, listen: pacify yourself, let him go free, otherwise you will have a difficult time. You do whatever you think proper!' Then she approached me and said, 'O child, what have you to say about Mānasavega's filing a law-suit?'

I replied, 'O queen, this mean fellow has filed a lawsuit already and has lost. Now I don't want it to be repeated anymore.'

Hearing this Mānasavega was frightened and asked Aṅgāraka, Hepphaga and others to come immediately so that I could be sent to the city of god of Death soon. At this time the queen again fell to my feet, begging me to allow him to file another suit.

I consented. 'But if he loses again, what should be done to him?' I asked.

'You do whatever you think proper', she replied.

I said, 'All the *vidyādharas* are on his side, let me put up a case before them.'

Balasīha, the *vidyādhara*-lord, was appointed mediator.

Mānasavega left with his retinue. Accompanied by Somasiri and Prabhāvatī I travelled through the air with the approval of the *vidyādharas* who were moving in the air. A great tumult was heard due to the movement of the *vidyādharas*, who were never to be seen before.

In a moment we arrived at our destination. Balasīha welcomed me. He saluted me and offered his own seat to me. He asked me to be seated. Seeing me seated there, Mānasavega asked Balasīha, 'Why are you giving my place to this earth-dweller'? I retorted, 'You know, all *vidyādharas* offer salutation to me with great respect.' Mānasavega inquired if Balasīha was showing him respect because he was related to him. Balasīha replied, 'Yes, the daughter of Piṅgalagandhāra by his queen Amitaprabhā is my sister's daughter. Besides, all the *vidyādharas* are under his subjugation.' Mānasavega said, 'Had I known that he is related to you, I would have not come here but would have gone somewhere else.' Balasīha replied, 'You don't worry about it that you are filing a lawsuit here. I am a mediator, no injustice would be done. I am going to name the person who may have committed injustice.'

Then Mānasavega began to plead, 'O King, listen: He has violated my harem and has taken my sister without being offered to him.'

I replied, 'I have never seen his harem. On the other hand, he abducted my wife from the human world. When afflicted with grief I was crying and lamenting due to her separation, his sister assumed the form of my wife and appeared before me and I accepted her. What he says is not true. He himself is exposed thereby.' I continued, 'Please listen: my wife who was abducted by him, was reluctant to yield to his wishes; hearing the divine warning, he kept her in his pleasure-garden. Thus he has already insulted me. He has been taken to Vāyuvega and other *vidyādhara*-lords, but he could not be pacified by their words.' Balasīha, who was seated, accompanied by a group of *Vidyādharas,* spoke to Mānasavega thus: 'Your case regarding your sister does not stand. We protect all by our magic power. And what your have pleaded with regard to the violation of your harem, is proved false by what he has stated. Now you yourself are guilty since you have abducted the wife of an innocent person.'

Mānasavega replied, 'Please listen: Once I had gone to see the beautiful royal palace in the city of Mahāpura. When I got down there on the uppermost floor, I heard the voice of a woman, saying, "O *vidyādhara* take this girl away". I replied, "O Queen, I shall have her once she has attained youth." Then I returned to my city. Later I abducted her since she was already given to me and not because she was his wife. So how can she be his wife who has been abducted by me?'

I retorted, 'How can he say that she was given to him?'

The witnesses remarked, 'When the queen was saying, "O *vidyādhara,* take away my girl" she did not notice that you were there.' Then throbbing with violence Mānasavega replied, 'Well, I remained there hiding and she could have seen me.'

The witnesses remarked, 'A woman or a girl given in this way cannot be authorised to be abducted. Or a girl can never be won by the maxim of the crow and the palm-fruit (*kāka-tālīya nyāya*) (after the manner of the crow and the palm-fruit, denoting an unexpected and sudden fall of palm-fruit on the head of the crow just at the moment of its alighting and killing).'

Hearing this, Mānasavega flew into the air well-equipped with his army and ready with arms and weapons. By invoking his magic art he created particles of fire in the sky. The sky was covered with beats and strokes. He wanted to kill me. Then my powerful *yakṣa* invoked the flames of fire. At this time the King Piṅgalagandhāra appeared equipped with his army and confronted with Mānasavega who had lost the case filed against me. I felt courageous and having transformed my body (*veuvvida-balo=vikurvita-balo*) with the help of the *pannatti* magic art given to me by Prabhāvatī, I was ready for a confrontation. At this time king Sīha also approached equipped with the group of his warriors.

I also defending myself, got ready with my forces for fighting in the air. I was ready with arms and weapons, with marching horses, elephants, chariots and warriors, who were looking bright with shining adornments of gold, silver, jewels etc. They were emitting a loud noise and had covered the whole sky. At this time I was offered congratulations by the *vidyādhara*-lords and by my friends who had come there along with the King Piṅgalagandhāra.

A great battle ensued between the two armies, involving numerous *vidyādharas* who were fighting on my side. The *vidyādhara*-kings were well-equipped with excellent magic arts and the sky was filled with great tumult.

After some time I told the *vidyādhara*-kings who were fighting on my side: 'It is of no use to kill innocent people in the battle so I should not fight. You be a witness.' Then somehow I stopped my warriors from fighting further. In order to control the enemy forces, I attacked the enemy headquarters along with my friends.

Now remembering the cause of her suffering and my promise given to her, Somasiri told me, 'O Noble one, you catch hold of Mānasavega so that I can drink the blood gushing out from his head.' I replied, 'My dear, I will do that.'

Then putting on my armour and equipped with arms and weapons, I started my attack. With the assistance of the *pannatti* magic art I created various kinds of forces and the agitating elephants, chariots and vehicles; they overpowered the enemy forces like the fire in a forest. Unable to counter the strength of my army the enemy warriors all fled in terror. I thought of fulfilling the promise made to Somasiri. At this time Mānasavega started fleeing quickly. I ran after him and caught him by his hair. I held him like a bull and while the *vidyādharas* were praising my valour, I brought him to Somasiri. I made him sit down on the ground with his heart trembling, caught him by his hair and ready with a sword in my right hand and was ready to chop off his head. I told Somasiri, 'The head will now fall before you and be ready to drink his blood.'

Suddenly, Mānasavega's mother accompanied by his queens, making all sorts of noise, descended from the sky. She fell to my feet begging for the safety of her son. I restrained myself and with a compassionate heart did not strike Mānasavega. I bowed to Aṅgāravatī, saying, 'Although he made several attempts on my life and I am powerful enough to hit back, but because of your words and respect for Vegavatī I have pardoned him so that he may not repeat what he had done to me.'

Aṅgāravatī without feeling irritated, fell to my feet once again. I showed my great respect for her.

The assembly of *vidyādharas* praised me saying, 'You have achieved everything. Though you have not acquired any magic art, still you were able to overthrow the pride of the *vidyādharas* there you have achieved the status of a *vissa-rūvin* (=*viśva-rūpin*; appearing in various forms), *vissa-varinda* (=*viśva-varendra*; chief of the world),or *vissa-kammaṃ* (=*viśva-karman*; divine creative architect).' They were all delighted and wished me uninterrupted royal splendour. Saying this, they fell to my and Somasiri's feet. She raised her hand over them expressing joy.

Then in the presence of all *vidyādhara*-kings, having my permission, Mānasavega took us along with Balasīha with great honour to his own city. He made us enter his palace with greatest respect and honour. He arranged for the *vidyādhara* camps and looked after them. He honoured each one of them and fell to my feet.

Thus our enmity was pacified and we became great friends. I sent away the *vidyādhara*-kings and my friends to their respective places. We passed our time in warm friendship, enjoying food, drink, clothes, ornaments, songs, dances, dramas and musical instruments. Thus our friendship grew more and more.

Vegavatī felt extremely happy. She remarked, 'I could have never thought even in dreams that such a friendship could ever exist between the Noble One and my brother. Oh, how lucky I am that this great unfulfilled desire has been fulfilled!' In this manner, enjoying exclusive pleasures with Somasiri and Prabhāvatī and being highly honoured by Mānasavega, I did not know how the time passed. One day Somasiri fell to my feet and said, 'O Noble One, I do not know how time passes in your delightful company! But it is long since that I have seen my parents. Could you kindly take me to Mahāpura?'

I assented. Thereupon Mānasavega with the assistance of his magic art created various kinds of jewels, gems, golden ornaments, clothes, sandalwood and divine flowers. They were given as gifts to us by him. Then amidst the praises and proclamation and shouts of victory by great *vidyādharas*, through the air, we were taken by Mānasavega to the city of Mahāpura. The people were surprisingly overjoyed by my arrival with my beloved Somasiri. Though it was not the time, the festival of full moon day was declared in the city. A celebration in honour of the Siddhayātana-*pūjā* was declared. The ruler of the city, accompanied by his queens, performed the *pūjā*. The monks were honoured. The king distributed wealth to the people. All were delighted. 'No injury' (*amāghāta*) was declared to all living beings. Mānasavega was honoured. The king offered him various gifts. We sent him with honour and he went back to his city.

Thus honoured by the king, I passed my time in the company of my beloved.

NOTES

1. However, according to Dharmasenagaṇi Mahattara, the author of the unpublished *Majjhimakhaṇḍa* (1, 4; now Pt. I published in 1987, pp. 2, 18-19), the *Vasudevacariya* had come down from the *Dṛṣṭivada* and is based on the *Gaṇḍikānuoga* dealing with the history of the Arhata, the Cakravartins, the Balabhadras and the Vāsudevas.
2. Haribhadrasūri, referring to 8 births of Ṛṣabha, quotes the *VH* in his *vṛtti* on the *Āvaśyaka-Sūtra* (I, p. 145a); also Malayagiri's *vṛtti* on the work (p. 218).
3. For similarities and dissimilarities in the texts see author's *The Vasudevahindi—An Authentic Jain Version of the Bṛhatkathā* (*The Vasudeva*), pp. 12-13 and note.
4. See Alsdorf, 'A New Version of Agaḍadatta Story', *N. Indian Ant,* Vol. I, No. 5, August 1838, pp. 281ff.
5. See *The Vasudeva,* pp. 163-84 for comparison.
6. See 'The Missing Lambhas in the Vasudevahiṇḍi and the Story of Pabhāvatī', *IIJ,* 17 (1975) 41-6, pp. 41-56; *The Vasudeva,* Introduction, pp. 91-141.
7. *BSOS,* 8 (1936), pp. 320f.
8. It has been divided under the following heads:

   (i) *Changes in Verbal Forms* (until now it was taken for granted that the aorist forms have survived in Ardhamāgadhī only, but from the *VH* we learn that they occur in archaic Jaina Mahārāṣṭrī as well).
   (ii) *Declension of Nouns* (according to Pischel, a dative singular in *-āya* is limited to Ardhamāgadhī and Māgadhī verses, but it is also found in the *VH* in dative. According to Pischel, in instrumental, genitive, and locative singular of the feminine, *āa* is admitted only for Māgadhī, and *īa* and *ūa* only in verses where the metre demands a short vowel; but *āya* and *īya* (or *īa*) are also found in the *VH.* Ablative singular and neuter ending in *-aṃ* is a remarkable archaic form preserved in the *VN*; it is also found in the Pali *Dhammapada.*
   (iii) *Pronominal Forms* (according to Pischel, accusative singular *me* is restricted to Ardhamāgadhī, and *te* to Ardhamāgadhī, Śaurasenī and Māgadhī, but it is noted in the *VH.* According to Pischel, *mai* occurs in Śaurasenī only in locative singular, but we have it in the *VH.* Similarly, according to Pischel, *ne* is used in accusative in Māgadhī and Ardhamāgadhī; it is used in instrumental and genitive only in Ardhamāgadhī; *bhe* is used in nominative, accusative and instrumental only in Ardhamāgadhī; the same is used in genitive in Ardhamāgadhī and Jain Mahārāṣṭrī; but these forms occur in the *VH.*
   (iv) There are numerous other forms and words, etc., which occur in the *VH,* but they are either completely wanting in Pischel's *Prakrit Grammar* or attributed by Pischel to Ardhamāgadhī only (for the list of words see p. 332).

(v) Some peculiar words of Prakrit: *pattamitto* (=*prāptmātra*), *aggahatthe* (*āgrahārthe*), *bhati* (*bhṛti*), *suṇadha* (*suṇaha*), *parikkesa* (*parikleśa*), *gato* (*gajaḥ*), *kaṇḍaka* (*kaṇṭaka*), *vātiga-jaṇa* (*vādi-jana*), *diyādi* (*dvijāti*), *aulaṃ* (*atulaṃ*), *mohaṃ* (*moghaṃ*), *chhittesu* (*kṣetreṣu*), *vattaṃ* (*vyaktaṃ*) and so on.

In this regard, see K.R. Chandra in Seminar of Prakrit Studies, Ahmedabad (1973); All Indian Oriental Conference, Kurukshetra (1974); All India Oriental Conference, Dharwad (1976); also articles in the *Sambodhi* (Vol. 4, Nos. 3-4; Vol. 6, Nos. 3-4); *Vidyā* (Aug. 1976-Jan. 1977; Aug. 1979, etc.) and *Tulasī Prajñā* (April-June 1976).

9. Ibiḍ, pp. 332f.
10. Mānasavega is not to be allowed to be slain as in the Kashmiri versions.
11. The manuscript in the possession of the L.D. Institute of Indology, Ahmedabad, a photocopy of which was kindly allowed to be taken to the Department of Indology, University of Kiel (West Germany) in 1970 for the study of the author.
12. They are as follows: 2-9 *Aṭṭhakaṇṇagā-lambho*, 10 *Mehamālā-lambho*, 11-32 *Bāvīsa-kaṇṇā-lambho*, 33 *Isidattā-lambho*, 34 *Aṇilajasā-lambho*, 35 *Veruliyamālā-lambho*, 36 *Indaseṇā-lambho*, 37 *Lakkhaṇā-lambho*, 38 *Sukosalā-lambho*, 39 *Lalidavegā-lambho*, 40 *Cittalehā-lambho*, 41 *Harikantā-lambho*, 42 *Kaṇagamai-lambho*, 43 *Sāgaradattā-lambho*, 44 *Malayaseṇā-lambho*.
13. 45 *Avantivaddhaṇā-lambho*, 46 *Tārāpati-lambho*, 47 *Accharā-lambho*, 48 *Candalehā-lambho*, 49 *Sasippabhā-lambho*, 50 *Līlāpati-lambho*, 51 *Goridattā-lambho*, 52 *Pabhañjaṇavegā-lambho*, 53-6 *Caukaṇṇā-lambho*.
14. 57-61 *Pañcakaṇṇā-lambho*, 62 *Uvvasī-lambho*, 63-6 *Caukaṇṇā-lambho*, 67 *Mayūraseṇā-lambho*, 68 *Sasilehā-lambho*, 69 *Rayaṇapadī-lambho*, 70 *Muttāvali-lambho*, 71 *Vimalappahā-lambho*. Compare the names of the heroines in the *KSS*. They are: Madanamañjukā, Ratnaprabhā, Alaṃkāravatī, Lalitalocanā, Karpūrikā, Śaktiyaśas, Bhagīrathayaśas, sister of Ruciradeva, Vegavatī, Ajinavatī, Gandharvadattā, Prabhāvatī, Ātmanikā, Vāyuvegayaśas, her four female friends headed by Kālikā, Sulocanā, the five heavenly nymphs (*Pañca-lambaka*), of whom Mandaradevī is the chief, 108.97-112; 107, 95-110; also see the *BKM* (*Mahābhiṣeka-lambaka*, 17). Here the *Aṭṭhakaṇṇā-lambho* (2-9), and the *Caukaṇṇā-lambho* (52-56) of the *MKH* can be compared with the *Caturdārikā-lambaka* (5) and the *Pañca-lambaka* (14) of the *KSS*.
15. . . . सिंगारकहाववएसेण धम्मं चेव परिकहेमि, 1.3 (published text 1.2).
16. . . . कामकहारत्तहितओ य जणो पुच्छति : किह तेण एरिसा भोगा समासादिता ?
भण्णइय-सुचरितवसेण। अवि य-
चक्किसुह-मणुस्ससुहं मोक्खसुहमणुत्तरं च जं भणियं।
जे सुचरिय-सामण्णा न दुल्लहं दुल्लहं तेसिं॥ Ibid.
17. ततोहं मयण-वस-गतो तीए अभिगमणोवायंऽ[चिंतयं]तो उम्मुहो सरदपसन्नं ससिं अवलोगयंतो निच्छ लच्छो चिरं ठितो। तओ महं पभावति भणति :

कुमार! किं चिंतयसि?
मया भणिता-सुतणु, कामं चिंतयामि।
तीए भणितं-किमेयं अणिमित्ते कामचिंतणं?
मया भणिया-नाहं अणिमित्तं चिंतयामि। अत्थि णिमित्तं, जहा—गय-जलदं गय-मलयं, सुहकिरण-विसुद्ध-सीयलो चंद्रो।
सकमलं सुरभि च जलं, बिण्णि णिमित्ताइं कामस्स॥ (published text), pp. 47, 10.

18. . . . पवण-बलवसुन्नामित-कोकणद-मंडल-निभं वदणं तीए ईसि पणामितं। आढत्ता य मे सलज्जा सणियं मधुगरस्स व पवणाणामिता नलिणीमुह-पंकयं पणामेदुं। तासु अचलिय-किसलिय-लोल-पल्लव-समाउलाहिं व दुम-लताहिं चतुर-लोल-कोमलंगुलि-विरइयाहिं भुम(ज)लताहिं मम भुया-जुवलयं पवेलंबिता माघवीलता इव कुसुमितासोगसालेसु। समालग्गा पवर-पणामिताधर धरणि भुज रयगा (?) सिक्कार-ससि-सकल-मधुरभणित-वेविय-मम्मं ति भणित-ललित-निव्वावियच्छि-जुयला ग(ख)णमेत्तं। मदण-परायणा नाऊणं। ततो ममं तिव्वसंजात-मदण-रागस्स भाविय-दिण-पडिसाहित-हिदया ममं निवारयंती ममं भणति—कुमार! कुमार! मा ताव तुरध! सामि! जं भणामि वो पयत्थं, उदिक्खध मधुं तत्ति। तत्तो तीए एवं बहुप्पगारं भणंतीए मया किह किह वि अतिरेग-गतोऽपि सवेगो इव विधारितो मदणवेगो, संसय-गतमिव जीवितं आसुरेण कहं चि संधारिओ अप्पा, तीय विसंवादित-मेत्तेण मया विछायंतं पिव नियजीवियं लक्खियं मे। Manuscript 1, 83f (published text, 49, 2-13). English translation from *The Vasudeva*, pp. 97-130 (revised by Margaret Walter).
19. MSS, 1.121f (1, 67ff). Here follow the details of amorous dalliance and enjoyment of sexual pleasures.
20. See *The Vasudeva*, pp. 130-3.
21. Ibid., pp. 133-8.
22. Also read comparative footnotes in *The Vasudeva*, pp. 97-141.
23. न सभा वुड्ढविहूणा, वुड्ढा वि ण ते होंति अधम्मिट्ठा।
धम्मो न सच्चरहिओ, न य सच्चं होइ छल जुत्तं॥ 1, p. 113 (pub. text, 65, 1-2) Compare with a similar verse in *The KSS*:
सा सभा यत्र सभ्योऽस्ति, स सभ्यो धर्ममाह यः।
स धर्मो यत्र सत्यं, स्यात्तत्सत्यं यत्र न च्छलम्॥ (106.168)
in the *BKM*:
विभाति ये सदा न्यायैः सभा भाति च सज्जनैः।
ते धर्मेण प्रकाशन्ते, न सोऽस्तीह किमुच्यते॥ 13.5.130
also *Hitopadeśa*, Vigraha, verse 63, p. 76.
न सा सभा यत्र न सन्तिवृद्धाः, वृद्धा न ते ये न वदन्ति धर्मम्।
धर्मः स नो यत्र न सत्यमस्ति सत्यं न तद्यच्छलमभ्युपैति॥
Kale edn., Delhi, 1976.
24. सीसं कहवि न फुट्टं, जमस्स पालित्तयं हरंतस्स।
जस्स मुहनिज्झराओ तरंगलोलानई वूढा॥ 5, p. 39.
25. E. Leumann, *Die Nonne* (*The Nun*) translated from MSS into German, *Zeitschrift für Buddhismus*, III München, 1921, pp. 193ff, 272ff. Narsiṃha Bhai Patel has rendered it into Gujarati which is published in the *Jain Sahitya Samshodhaka*, II.2, Poona, 1924. This translation has been separately published in the form of a book by Babalchand Keshavlal Modi, Ahmedabad, 1924. Prakrit text published in the *Shri-Nemivijñāna-Granthamālā*, No. 9, edited by Kastūrvijayagaṇi, vs 2000. Edited and translated into Gujarati by H.C. Bhayani, Ahmedabad, 1979.

26. पालित्तएण रइया वित्थरओ तह य देसि-वयणेहिं।
नामेण तरंगवई कहा विचित्ता य विउला य॥
कत्थइ कुलयाइं मणोरमाइं अण्णत्थ गुविल-जुयलाइं।
अण्णत्थ छक्कलाइं दुप्परिअल्लाइं इयराणं॥
न या सा कोई सुणेइ नो पुण पुच्छेइ नेव य कहेई।
विउसाण नवर जोगा इयरजणो तीए किं कुणउ॥
तो उच्चेऊणं गाहाओ पालितएण रइआओ।
देसि-पयाइं मोत्तुं संखित्तयरी कया एसा॥
इयराण हियट्ठाए मा होही सव्वहा वि वोच्छेओ।
एयं विचिंतिऊणं, खामेऊण य तयं सूरिं॥ 5-9
27. See A.N. Upadhye, *The Kuvalayamālā*, Introduction, Notes, etc., pp. 86f.
28. कम्मं जस्स पवासो [वासो] य जस्स नियए घरे नत्थि।
कह तस्स सव्व-देसातिहिस्स दाहामि हं धूयं॥ 647
29. तत्थुग्घाडिय-निग्गय-पहाविओ दस दिसाओ पूरेंतो।
गयवर-मय-गंधो विव गंधो सो सत्तिवण्णाणं॥ (144)
Compare the description of the tree in the *MKH*:
परमसस्सिरी यादवो राया इव तस्स वणंतरस्स पविकसित कुसुममालंकारभासरे विरयितपरिकम्मो इव पढम जोव्वणो वरो पप्फुल्जमल्जियाण (व) वधूय-गाढोवगूढ पविराइतो, पवणबलचालिएसु वि विइवेसु सकुसुमेसु अवहसति विय मम दुमहरो उवणिमंतेति। (pub. text, p. 47, 1-4), 1, p. 80.
30. Dealing with the budding of flowers (152).
31. Dealing with the preparations of blending fragrant substances; also mentioned in the *VH*, 51, 3.
32. Also referred to in the *VH* (147, 9).
33. कम्मे सिद्धी, विजओ रणम्मि, अत्थो य सव्व-सोक्खं च।
कच्चाइणि-प्पसाया, अम्हं होहि त्ति न मुयामो॥ 10॥
34. *Hasti-pillaya*; *sūara-pillaya* in the *VH*.
35. Compare the following words and expressions employed here: *pāsaṇio* (95), *oyāiyā laddhiyā, pahāya-pasāhiya-jimio* (133) with those of the *VH*, pp. 101, 10; 30, 4, etc.
36. तो भणति अत्थसत्थंमि वण्णियं सुयणु सत्थयारेहिं।
दूती परिभव-दूती न होइ कज्जस्स सिद्धिकरी॥ 853
A secret is disclosed if it reaches to a female messenger. We read in the *VH* (45, 25f) the following quotation:
अत्थसत्थे य भणियं-
'विसेसेण मायाए सत्थेण य हंतव्वो अप्पाणं विवड्ढमाणो सत्तु'— the flourishing enemy should be killed by some special device or weapon.
About *Arthaśāstra* in other Jain works, see *PNL*, pp. 138f.
37. सव्वो पुव्वकयाणं कम्माणं पावए फलविवागं।
अवराहेसु गुणेसु निमित्तमत्तं परो होइ॥ *Samarā*, 2, p. 131.
38. Hermann Jacobi with Introduction, Asiatic Society of Bengal, Calcutta, 1926; Pandit Bhagvandas with Sanskrit *chāyā* in 2 parts, Ahmedabad, 1938 and 1942; Nemichandra Shastri, *Haribhadra ke Prakrit Katha Sahitya ka Ālochanātamaka Parishelan*, Vaishali Prakrit Jain Saṃsthān, 1965; Kavi Padmavijaya, Gujarati Rāsa in 9 parts, vs 1839-42; Kasturmal

Banthiya, Hindi translation, Jinadattasūri Sevāsaṅgha, Madras-Bombay, vs 2021; Hemasāgarasūri, Gujarati translation, *Ānandahemagranthamālā* (31-3), Bombay, 1966.

39. पक्षपातो न मे वीरे न द्वेषः कपिलादिषु।
युक्तिमद्वचनं यस्य तस्य कार्यः परिग्रहः॥
40. *KVLM*, p. 4, line 2.
41. For 3 *praśnottaras*, see pp. 8, 610f.
42. For 3 *gūḍhacaturthapādas*, see pp. 8, 617f.
43. See 2, 79, 1-10; 6, 449, 9-19; 7, 498, 19-499, 6.
44. See 3, 137, 6-9; 4, 213, 8-11; 6, 423, 19-424, 8.
45. Jacobi, Introduction to *Samaraiccakahā*, xxii.
46. Ibid., xxiiif.
47. Ibid., xxv.
48. Chapter 2, 110, 17-114, 10; for other references see *PNL*, pp. 194f; Winternitz, *Some Problems of India Literature*, 'Some Ascetic Literature in Ancient India', pp. 28-30.
49. Chapter 2, 121, 10-122, 12. This motif of the 'Chain of Destruction' is depicted in a painted scroll of the *KVLM* (188, 33-189, 17; 140, 8-22; also in the sculpture of Vasaveshvara Jain temple, *PNL*, p. 109; Emeneau's article 'Studies in Folk-tales in India', III, *JAOS*, 67.
50. Chapter 5, 391, 10-395, 6; the same episode is narrated in the *Āva Cū*, pp. 509-11.
51. Chapter 4, 248, 3-249, 10; for other references see *PNL*, pp. 57-8.
52. See Chapters 4, 202, 6-20 and 6; also *PNL*, pp. 74-6 for motifs pertaining to journey.
53. वारियं खु समये इत्थियादंसणं। भणियं च तत्थ-अवि य अंजियव्वाइं तत्तलोहसलायाए अच्छीणि, न दट्ठव्वा य अंगपच्चंगसंठाणेण इत्थिया, अवि य भक्खियव्वा विसं, न सेवियव्वं विसया, छिन्दियव्वा जीहा, न जंपियव्वमलियं ति। Chapter 7, 543.
54. Edited by A.N. Upadhye, with Saṅghatilaka's Sanskrit version and Old-Gujarati prose; with an elaborate critical Essay, *SJS* (No. 19), Bombay, 1944. The *Dhuttakkhāṇa* is mentioned in the *Niśitha-Viśeṣa-Bhāsya* and its *Cūrṇi* (294-6). For a comparative study of both see A.N. Upadhye 'Dhūrtākhyana in the Niśitha-Cūrṇi', *Vijayavallabhasūri Smāraka Grantha*, Bombay, 1956, pp. 143-51. Saṅghatilakācārya has composed *Dhūrtākhyāna* in Sanskrit, Jain Grantha Prakashaka Sabha, Rajnagar, 1945.
55. Mūlaśrī or Mūladeva is considered the arch-thief of Hindu fiction. M. Bloomfield has identified Mūladeva with Karṇīsuta, Goṇikāputraka, Goṇiputraka or Goṇikasuta. He was also known as Mūlaśrī, Mūlabhadra or Kalāṅkura. He is supposed to have written a manual on thieving, entitled *Steyaśāstra* or *Steyasutra*, *The Ocean of Story*, Vol. II, pp. 183f, Note on Stealing. Kṣemendra (eleventh century) in his *Kalāvilāsa* has depicted Mūladeva as excessively deceitful, expert in all kinds of arts, and a crest-jewel of rogues. In ancient India, as young people used to go to courtesans to learn the art of erotics, similarly they used to visit

Mūladeva for learning the art of knavery. He is said to have been surrounded by pupils whom he used to train in the art of fraud (*dambha*). Mūladeva also is been mentioned as having the knowledge of all kinds of hypocrisy, he was of deceitful nature and very shrewd; also see Kṣemendra's *BKM*, under Viṣamaśīla-prakaraṇa (p. 432); Daṇḍin's *Daśakumāracarita* (2); *Vetālapañcaviṃśatikā* (Story 13). The adventures of Mūladeva have been quite popular with Jain writers; see *Āva Cū* (p. 549); Haribhadra, *Upadeśapada*, Commentary of Vādidevasūri (*gāthā* 92, p. 64); Devendragaṇi's Com. on *Uttarā* (3, 59a, 63a, etc.); Jayasiṃhasuri's *DSMV*; Jineśvarasūri's *Kathākośa-prakaraṇa*; Devendragaṇi's *Ākhyānamaṇi-kośa;* Somaprabha's *Kumāravālapaḍiboha;* A.N. Upadhye, *Dhūrtākhyāna: A Critical Study,* p. 23 and note; Author's *'Dhūrta-śiromaṇi Mūladeva aur Dhūtravidyā'* (Hindi), *Ājkal,* Delhi, September 1970; and *'Prachina Jain Sahitya men Chaurakarma'* (Hindi), *Kalpanā,* Hyderabad, June, 1956.

56. Śaśa is referred to as a friend of Mūladeva in the *Caturbhāṇī,* edited by and translated by Motichandra and Vasudevasharan Agrawala, Hindi Granth Ratnakar Karyalaya, Bombay, 1960.
57. Edited by A.N. Upadhye in *SJS* (45 and 46) in two volumes, 1959 and 1970, with an exhaustive Introduction and Notes; A Cultural Note by V.S. Agrawala, Foreword by L. Alsdorf; Pt. II containing *Kuvalayamālā-Kathā,* a stylistic Digest in Sanskrit by Ratnaprabhasūri; Premasuman Jain, *Kuvalayamālā kā Sāṃskritik Adhyayana,* Vaishali, 1975.
58. A groups of poets according to A.N. Upadhye, Introduction to *Kuvalayamālā,* p. 76.
59. पाइय-भासा रइया मरहट्ठय-देसि-वण्णय-णिबद्धा।
सुद्धा सयल-कह च्चिय तावस-जिण-सत्थ-बाहिल्ला ॥ 4,11
60. सालंकारा सुहया ललिय-पया मउय-मंजु-संलावा।
सहिया ण देइ हरिसं उव्वूढा णववहू चेव ॥ 4, 18
61. . . . धम्मकहा समाढत्ता। तेण किंचि काम-सत्थ-संबंद्धं पि भण्णिहिइ। तं च मा णिरत्थयं ति गणेज्जा। किंतु धम्म-पडिवत्ति-कारणं अक्खेवणि त्ति काऊण बहुमयं। 5, 11-13.
62. See A.N. Upadhye, Introduction to *Kuvalayamālā,* pp. 84-6.
63. For details, see below, pp. 328f.
64. It is also called *pratimālā.* It is an exercise analogous to capping verses, reciting verse for verse as a trial of memory or skill, *MW,* 1976.
65. According to the author of *KVLM,* its last syllable also should have been a letter of the alphabet. Peterson, however, gives an illustration which has *bindus* in the first and the last syllables, A.N. Upadhye, Notes on *Kuvalayamālā,* p. 147.
66. मण-णंगलेण पूए, सुपत्त-खेत्तम्मि वाविए बीए।
सयसाहं होइ फलं, एस विही करिसणे होइ ॥
67. कुण देह जाणवत्तं, गुणरयणाणं भरेसु विमलाणं।
भव-जलहिं तरिऊण मोक्खद्दीवं च पावेह ॥ 192, 33

68. जइ कुणह तवं विउलं दिक्खं घेत्तूण गरुय-वेरग्गा।
ताहो पुणो ण पेच्छह दारिद्द अण्णजम्मे वि॥ 193, 30.
69. Ed. Ācārya Jinavijaya Muni, with an elaborate Hindi Introduction, *SJS*, 1949.
70. See Muni Jinavijaya, Introduction to *Kathākoṣa-prakaraṇa*, p. 33.
71. Nathuram Premi, *Jain Sahitya*, 1956, pp. 478ff.
72. Published with Jinapāla's commentary, Jinadattasūri Prachina Pustakoddhara Fund, Surat, 1933.
73. संतलयं परिहाणं झलंबचोडाइयं च मज्झिमयं।
सुसिलिद्वमुत्तरीयं धम्मं लच्छिं जसं कुणइ॥ 2, 16
(संतलयं=thigh; सांतल in Hindi; चोडाइयं=wide; चौड़ा in Hindi)
74. लंखस्स व परिहाणं गसइ व देहं तहंगिया गाढा।
सिखेढो टमरेण वेसो एसो सिडिंगाणं॥ 2, 19
(लंख=pole-dancer); अंगिया=आंगी in Hindi (Choli); टमर=केशसमूह=lock of hair; सिडिंग from सिट्=to despise
75. असिलिट्ठु नीविबंधो चूडा संफुसइ पायनहरेहं।
जंघद्धं उग्घाडं परिहाणं हवइ वेसाणं॥ 2, 20
सिहिणाणं मग्गदेसो उग्घाडो नाहिमंडलं तह य।
पासा य अद्धपिहिया कंचुओ सहइ वेसाणं॥ 2, 21
(असिलिट्ठु-अश्लिष्ट=loose; चूडा=वेणी=braid of hair; पायनहरेहं-पादनखरेखां=the line of the nails of foot; सिहिणाणं-स्तनानां=of breasts; पासा=पार्श्वभागा:=the sides) quoted on page 51, notes 1-3, Hindi Introduction.
76. Published with Jinapati's *Vivaraṇa*, Surat, 1919.
77. It was consulted by business people to ascertain profits and loss with regard to their purchased commodity, *Niśī Cū*, 13, p. 400; see infra, Chapter 9, p. 512.
78. Muni Jinavijaya, Hindi Introduction, *Kathākoṣa-prakaraṇa*, p. 56.
79. सत्यं नास्ति शुचिर्नास्ति नास्ति नारी पतिव्रता।
तत्र गुर्जरके देशे एकमाता बहुपिता॥
80. जराजर्जरमप्यंगं विभात्यो गुर्जरस्त्रियः।
दृढकंचुकसंदाना मोहयंति महीमपि॥
Jineśvarasūri-carita-varṇana in the *Gaṇadhara-sārddha-śataka-prakaraṇa parisiṣṭa* by Jinadattasūri, p. 6.
81. आलोढ-पच्चालीढ-सीहासण-मंडलावत्तेसु सातको नाओ। पच्चालीढ-गरुडासण-विनायक पय-मंडूकासण-वाराह-उभयवाराह-हणुमंत-आहेसर-नद्धारंभेसु वा रिसिकन्नो नाओ। एएसु चेव चलिए धणुए भरहो नाओ। विण्हुपए छंदो नाओ। जंघपए भरहो नाओ। एएसु पयट्ठाणेसु एयाइं संघाण ट्ठाणाइं भवंति, p. 24
82. न अज्जवि पुत्थगाणि होंति त्ति, p. 134
This reference seems to have been made with regard to the writing of the canonical literature in book form by Ācārya Devardhigaṇi Kṣamāśramaṇa in the fifth century.
83. जिणभासिय-पुव्वगए जोणीपाहुडसुए समुछिट्ठं। एयंपि संघकज्जे कायव्वं धीरपुरिसेहिं॥ p. 172
84. Compare चाओ भोगो धम्मो. सिज्झइ अत्थेण सो जहा होइा। p. 172
85. Edited by Muni Punyavijaya, with the *vṛtti* of Āmradevasūri, Introduction of U.P. Shah with 8 Appendices, *PTS*, No. 5, Varanasi, 1962.

86. *Pannyāsa Maṇivijaya Gaṇivara Granthamālā,* Ahmedabad, 1942.
87. Ahmedabad, 1945; its Gujarati translation by Atmanand Jain Sabha, vs 2005.
88. *DLJP Uddhar Granthamala,* Bombay, 1929; Gujarati translation by Atmanand Jain Sabha, vs 1994.
89. A part of it can be compared with a story in the *Arabian Nights.*
90. For *naiilaya* or *naiila,* see U.P. Shah, Introduction to *Ākhāyamaṇikośa,* pp. 26f. There was a superstitious belief that money stored in the hide of *nakulaka* (ichenuman) remains imperishable.
91. See Appendix, No. VII, pp. 401-12 for *subhāṣitas,* and Appendix No. VIII, pp. 413-15 for *sūktis.*
92. थेवं थेवं धम्मं, करेह जइ ता बहुं न सक्केह।
   पेच्छह महानईओ, बिंदूहिं समुद्दभूयाओ ॥ 177, 40
93. हत्थकंकणाणं किं कज्जं दप्पणेणऽहवा। 116, 52
94. किं छालीए मुहे कुंभडे माइ? For other proverbs, see Introduction, p. 30.
95. Note some of the *deśī* words: *daddara* (*dādar* in Gujarati; staircase), *jaddara* Śālibhadrasūri (twelfth century) in his *Bāhubalirāsa* has used *cādara*; *Cādara* in Persian; *bharavasa* (*bharosā* in Hindi, faith); *ḍhayara* (*piśāca,* goblin); *vārako* (*vāḍako* in Gujarati); *Ṭoppariā* (*ṭopali* in Hindi); *ṭoparuṅ* (*koparuṅ* in Gujarati, *khoparā* in Hindi, coconut); *kaccoliā* (a bowl-like half of the hard coconut skin), *tellaṭilla* and so on.
96. They are चित्त (चित्र), मेयज्ज (मेतार्य), संभूइ (संभूत), हरिकेसि (हरिकेश), हरिएसबल (हरिकेशबज)
97. वुभुक्षितैर्व्याकरणं न भुज्पते, पिपासितैः काव्यरसो न पीयते।
   न च्छन्दसा केनचिदुद्धृतं कुलं, हिरण्यमेवार्जय निष्फलाः कलाः
   This verse is quoted in Kṣhemendra's *Aucityavicāracarcā* (*KM,* Prathama Gucchaka, p. 150) from Māgha's *Siśupālavadha,* but it has not been traced.
98. Edited by Muni Punyavijaya, Atmanand Jain Granthamala, 1944.
99. It is mentioned under *Kālika Śruta* in the Nandi. It is said that by reciting this scripture, Lord Garuḍa become visible, *Ṭhā* (10); *PSM.*
100. आमे घडे निहित्तं जहा जलं तं घडं विणासेइ।
   इय सिद्धंतरहस्सं अप्पाहारं विणासेइ ॥
101. Hariṣeṇa in his *BKK* (10.89-97) has provided details: The eight Nāgakulas consist of अनन्त, वासुकि, ककार, तक्षिक, पद्म, महापद्म, कुकिक and शंखपाल। The physian Dhanvantarī prepared a pan with live coals and filled it with heated charcoal of *khadira* wood. Then he asked all the Nāgas to appear before him, saying, let the one who has bitten the person remain inside and all others exit the *maṇḍala* (circle). Hearing this Kulika remained in the *maṇḍala* and all the rest went out. Kulika was told either to swallow the poison back or enter into fire. Kulika preferred the latter course.
102. See *MW.*
103. At Bharhut in the second century BC was depicted a Timiṅgala fish, making an attack on a ship; the fish is shown devouring the passengers falling down in the sea, Motichandra, *Sārthavāha,* Figure No. 9.

104. Here is an illustration:
Question: के मणहरं पि पुरिसं लहुइंति ?
विणासई य को जीवं ?
उल्लसिय-पहाजालो, को वा नंदेइ घुयकुलं ?
Answer: दोसागरो (दोषाकरः=दोसा; गर; दोसागर)
(i) What detracts a charming man? His faults. (दोसा)
(ii) What destroys life? Poison. (गर)
(iii) What delight the owls? The moon (दोसागर) with its brilliant splendour (since it produces night).

105. Edited by Muniraj Jinavijaya, Introduction in English, *Prastāvanā* in Sanskrit, with Appendices, *GOS* (No. 14), Baroda, 1920; Gujarati Translation, Jain Atmanand Sabha, Bhavnagar, vs 1983; Ludwig Alsdorf, *Der Kumārapāla-pratibodha, ein Beitrag zur Kenntnis des Apabhraṃśa und der Erzählungesliteratur der Jainas*, Hamburg, 1928.

106. निट्ठुरु निक्किवु काउरिसु, एकु जि नलु न हु भंति।
मुक्कमहासई जेण वणि, निसि सुत्ती दमयंति॥

107. We come across the story in the *Āva Cū* II, pp. 159-63.

108. Also in the *Uttarā* Commentary by Nemicandrasūri, pp. 36a-44.

109. हियडा लंकुडि मिरिय जिम्व, इंदिय-पसरु निवारि।
जित्तिउ पुज्जइ पंगुरणु, तित्तिउ पाउ पसारि॥
compare with the Hindi couplet:
तेते पांव पसारिये जेती लांवी सौर।

110. In the *KSS* (2.5) Śiva bestowed Guhasena and Devasmitā a red lotus with a warning that infidelity on the part of either would cause the other's flowers to wither. A woman of the Bhūiya tribe was put to the same test, *PNL*, Motif of Chastity, p. 49.

111. See op. cit., p. 73, undcr Ovcrhcaring Motif; p. 78, under Riddles.

112. For example of Putting Grass on one's Head, indicating that one is willing to sell oneself to slavery, op. cit., p. 61.

113. सीहह केसर सइहि उरू सरणागओ सुहडस्स।
मणिमत्थइ आसीविसह किं घिप्पइ अमुयस्स॥ p. 241
cf. (i) केहरकेस भुजंगमण सरणाई सुहडाहं।
सती-पयोहर कृपणधन पड़सी-हाथ मुवाहं॥
Kanhaiyalal Sahal, *Rājasthani Kahāvaten*, p. 296.
(ii) किवणाणं धणं णाआणं फणमणी के सराइं सीहाणं।
कुलवालिआणं थणआ कत्तो छिप्पति अमुआणं॥
Kāvyaprakaśa, 10, 457.

114 Keith has observed, 'The tale which is aimed directly at edification rather than amusement is specially richly preserved in Jain literature; the Jains were very fond of stories, but they demanded a moral, and hence their writers often led to spoil good stories such as the legends of Vikramāditya by seeking to make the participants rather tedious exponents of Jainism', *A History of Sanskrit Literature*, p. 293.

115. For other important works on the subject, see *JSBI*, Vol. 4, pp. 193-226,

under '*Dharmopadeśa*'; H.R. Kapadia, *DCGCM,* XVIII, Pt. I, *BORI,* Poona, 1952, pp. 302-478.

116. Edited by L.P. Tessitori in *Giornala della Societa Asiatica Italiaṇa* (*GSAI*), 25, 1912; *JDPS,* Bhavnagar, 1915; *Shri Śrutajñāna Amidhārā,* pp. 122-50, Bombay, 1926; with commentary of Rāmavijayagaṇi, Hiralal Hamsaraj, Jamnagar, 1934; with commentary of Siddharṣi, Hiralal Hamsaraj, Jamnagar, 1939; with commentary of Ratnaprabhasūri (*Doghaṭṭī Ṭīkā*), Shri Anand Hema Jain Granthamala, Bombay, 1958.

117. किं मूसगाण अत्थेण ? कि वा कागाण कणगमालाए।
मोहमलखवलिआणं क कज्जुवएसमालाए॥ 529

118. सोऊण पगरणमिणं धम्मे जाओ न उज्जमो जस्स।
न य जणिय वेरग्गं, जाणिज्ज अणंतसंसारी॥ 534

119. उवएसमालमेयं, जो पढइ सुणइ कुणइ वा हियए।
सो जाणइ अप्पहियं, नाऊण सुहं समायरई॥ 536

120. About three verses are interpolative.

121. Introduction to *Bṛhatkathākośa,* p. 33.

122. *Das Mahānisīha-Sutta,* pp. 51ff, after Winternitz, *Sanskrit Literature,* Vol. II, p. 560, n. 4.

123. According to some, since the word '*ghaṭāghaṭī*' occurs in the first *gāthā* of the *Uvaesamālā,* this commentary is known as *Doghaṭṭī;* it is also known as *Viśeṣavṛtti, JSBI,* Vol. IV, p. 194, n. 1.

124. For other Sanskrit commentaries see H.R. Kapadia, 'Dharmadāsagaṇi-kṛta Uvaesamala ane enā prakāshano tathā Vivaraṇo' in Gujarati in *Ātmānandprakāsha,* after *JSBI,* Vol. IV, p. 194, n. 2; H.R. Kapadia, *DCGCM,* XVIII, Pt. I, Poona, 1952, pp. 361-414.

125. *Gāthā* 227; compare the story of the two parrots in Hariṣeṇa's *BKK* (33.27-34). Here the following verses are found quoted in the *Karpūrakathā* (No. 15):
माताऽप्येका पिताऽप्येको मम तस्य च पक्षिण:।
अहं मुनिभिरानीत: स चानीतो गवाशनै:॥ 37
गवाशनानां वचनं श्रृणोति अहं च राजन् मुनिपुंगवानां।
प्रत्यक्षमेतद्भवताऽपि दृष्टं संसर्गजा दोषगुणा: भवन्ति॥ 38

126. को दुक्खं पाविज्जा ? कस्स व सुक्खेहि विम्हओ हुज्जा ?
को व लभिज्ज मुक्खं, रागद्दोसा जइ न हुज्जा ? 129

127. जाणिज्जइ चिंतिज्जइ, जम्मजरामरणसंभवं दुक्खं।
न य विसयेसु विरज्जई, अहो सुबद्धो कवडगंठी॥ 204

128. With the *Sukhasaṃbodhinī* commentary of Municandrasūri, published in Muktikamal-Jain-Mohanamālā, Baroda, in two parts, 1923 and 1925; published up to 27 *gāthās,* along with *Sukhasaṃbodhinī* and Gujarati translation by Jain Vidyaprasaraka Varga, Palitana, 1909. The text along with seven other works, viz., *Pañcāśaka, Dharmasaṃgrahaṇi, Upadeśamālā, Jīvasamāsa, Karmaprakṛti, Pañcasaṃgaha* and *Jyotiṣkaraṇḍaka* is published by RKŚS under the title पंचाभकारी in 1928.

129. It is a specified dish. Śrīcandra (eleventh century) in his *Kathākośa*

(36a) in Apabhraṃśa, has explained the term as follows: महाकल्याणोपपेतं पूर्वं चक्रवर्तिगृहे भुक्त्वा पश्चात् समस्तान्तःपुरसामन्तचक्रग्राम-पुरनगरखेटकर्वट-पत्तनादिषु-गृहे-गृहे-दान-सन्मान-प्रीतिपूर्वकं यद्भुज्यते तच्चोलकमिति भण्यते, A.N. Upadhye, *BKK*, Notes on Story No. 35.

130. 4-15, pp. 3-32. Also see *Āva Nir* (833-6); *Āva Cū* (446-51); Śāntyācārya, *Uttarā* Commentary, 3, 160, pp. 145-50; *Bhag Āra*, 430; Hariṣeṇa, *BKK*, 35-44; A.N. Upadhye, Introduction, pp. 74, 381.
Read चोल्लग पासग धन्ने, जूए रयणे-य सुमिणचक्के य।
चम्म जुए परमाणू, दस दिट्ठन्ता मणुयलंभे॥ *Uttarā* Com. 3.

131. See *gāthās* 52-120, pp. 48-91; also *Āva Nir*, 932-45; *Āva Cū*, pp. 544-68; *Nandi Sūtra*, 58-71 with commentary of Malayagiri; Jayasiṃhasūri, *DSMV*, pp. 120-40. See also Jagdish Chandra Jain, *PNL*, under the Motif of 'How to break a Hidebound Contract', pp. 78-80. The verses recorded in the *Āva Nir* and the *Nandi* are identical and occur in the same order. The following are the illustrations recorded for all the four intellect: (i) *Autpattikī*: 1 *Bharata-śilā*, 2 *Paṇita*, 3 *vṛkṣa*, 4 *Khuḍḍaka* (*Aṅguliyaka*), 5 *Paṭa*, 6 *Saraṭa*, 7 *Kāka*, 8 *Uccāra*, 9 *Gaja*, 10 *Ghayaṇa* (*Bhāṇḍa*), 11 *Gola*, 12 *Stambha*, 13 *Kṣullaka* (śiṣya), 14 *Mārga*, 15 *Strī*, 16 *Pati*, 17 *Putra*, 18 *Madhusiktha*, 19 *Mudrikā*, 20 *Aṅka*, 21 *Ṇaṇaka* (*Mudrā*), 22 *Bhikṣu*, 23 *Ceṭaka*, 24 *Sikṣā*, 25 *Arthaśāstra*, 26 *Icchā*, 27 *Śatasahasra*. (ii) *Vainayikī*: 1 *Nimitta*, 2 *Arthaśāstra*, 3 *Lekha*, 4 *Gaṇita*, 5 *Kūpa*, 6 *Aśva*, 7 *Gardabha*, 8 *Lakṣaṇa*, 9 *Granthi*, 10 *Agada*, 11 *Rathika-Gaṇika*, 12 *Śītā Śāṭikā Dīrgha-tṛṇa-apasavya-kroñcaka*, 13 *Nivvodaya* (*Ṇivrodaka*), 14 *Goṇa-ghoṭaka-patanaṃ vṛkṣāt*. (iii) *Karmajā*: 1 *Hairaṇyika* (*Suvarṇakāra*), 2 *Karṣaka*, 3 *Kolika* (*tantuvāya*), 4 *Ḍoya* (*Ḍoyo* in Gujarati), 5 *Mauktika*, 6 *Ghṛta*, 7 *Plavaka*, 8 *Tuṇṇāga* (*Tunnavāya*), 9 *Vardhakī*, 10 *Pūpika*, 11 *Ghaṭa*, 12 *Citrakāra*. (iv) *Pāriṇāmikī*: 1 *Abhaya*, 2 *Śreṣṭhi*, 3 *Kumāra*, 4 *Devī*, 5 *Uditodita* (name of a king), 6 *Nandiseṇa*, 7 *Dhanadatta*, 8 *Śrāvaka*, 9 *Amātya*, 10 *Kṣapaka*, 11 *Amātyaputra*, 12 *Cāṇakya*, 13 *Sthūla-bhadra*, 14 *Nāsikya-sundarī Nanda*, 15 *Vajrasvāmin*, 16 *Caraṇāhanana*, 17 *Āmalaka*, 18 *Maṇi*, 19 *Sarpa*, 20 *Khaḍga*, 21 *Stūpa*, and 22 *Indra*.

132. *Gāthā* 85, p. 61.

133. *Gāthā* 92, p. 64. Compare with *Āva Cū*, p. 549; Hemavijaya, *Kathāratnākara*, Mitraviṣaye Kathā, No. 11; *Śukasaptati*, No. 4.

134. They are Haṃsalipi, Bhūta, Yakṣī, Rākṣasī, Uḍḍī, Yavanī, Phuḍukkī, Kīḍī, Daviḍī, Sindhaviyā, Mālaviṇī, Naṭī, Nāgarī, Lāṭī, Pārasī, Animittā, Cāṇakyī and Mūladevī.

135. A similar story is recorded in Bhadreśvarasūri's (twelfth century) *Kahāvali* where it is stated that when Sītā got pregnant and saw in her dream that she was going to give birth to two valorous sons, her co-wives were jealous and to accuse her they asked her to draw Rāvaṇa, *JSBI*, VI, p. 70.

136. *Gāthā* 551, p. 272a. It is an animal of fluffy hair out of which costly

blankets are made; it is said that it survives by the heat of the human body.

137. को धम्मो ? जीवदया, किं सोक्खमरोग्गया उ जीवस्स।
को णेहो ? सब्भावो, किं पंडिच्चं ? परिच्छेओ ॥

138. किं विसमं ? कज्जगती, किं लद्धव्वं ? जणो गुणग्गाही।
किं सुहगेज्झं ? सुयणो, किं दुग्गेज्झं ? खलो लोओ ॥
The *gāthā* is also quoted in the *Kāvyānuśāsana*, p. 395, *Kāvyaprakāśa*, 10.529 and *Sāhityadarpaṇa*, p. 815 with slight changes.

139. अह सो सक्करचुन्नमज्झिगयपुन्नु विलोहई।
खंडुम्मी सियसत्तु कुंडिघयबाहु पलोहई ॥
वाउज्जायं कढियदुद्धि लहसि हत्थह पडियं।
जं दइवि सज्जणकुडुंब एरिस निम्मबियं ॥

140. Edited by Pandit Lalchand Bhagvandas Gandhi with Introduction in Gujarati, *SJS*, Bombay, 1949.

141. Jayasiṃhasūri has also written a detailed explanation (*vakkhāṇa*), see *Praśasti*, pp. 229, 230. Besides, Vijayasiṃhasūri, the chief disciple (*paṭṭadhara*) of Maladhāri Hemacandra, wrote an explanation in Sanskrit in vs 1191; Munidevasūri, the disciple of Madanacandrasūri, wrote a *Vivṛti* (Commentary) in vs 1325, *JSBI*, Vol. IV, p. 19. The palm-leaf MSS of both are available in the Patan Jain Bhandar.

142. The Marahaṭṭaya Bhāsā has been compared with a lady (*kāminī*) and a forest (*aṭavī*):
सललियपयसंचारा, पवडियमयणा सुवण्णरयणेल्ला।
मरहट्ठयभासा कामिणीय अडवी य रेहंति ॥ p. 4.

143. The *Praśnottara* style is defined in the *Sarasvatīkaṇṭhābharaṇa* (2, 148) as follows:
यस्तु पर्यनुयोगस्य, निर्भेदः क्रियते बुधैः।
विदग्ध गोष्ठ्यां वाक्यैर्वा, तद्धि प्रश्नोत्तरं बिदुः ॥

144. For details see Hemacandra's *Kāvyänuśāsana* and its commentary, V.4, pp. 315-23.

145. Page 174, 22.

146. काले प्रसुप्तस्य जनार्दनस्य, मेघांधकारासु च शर्वरीषु।
मिथ्या न भाषामि विशालनेत्रे, ते प्रत्यया ये प्रथमाक्षरेषु ॥ p. 33
Here by joining the first letter of each *pada*, we have कामेमि ते 'I love you.'

147. Compare the illustration of *praśnottara* provided in Haribhadrasūri's *Samarā* (8, 744):
किं देंति कामणीओ ? के हरपणया ? कुणंति किं भुयगा ?
कं च मऊएहिं ससी धवलेइ ? णहंगणाभोयं ॥
What do the loving women permit? Nail-marks (*nakha*).
Who bows down before God Śīva? His attendants (*gaṇa*).
Whom does the moon whiten with its rays? The premises of the sky.
(1 णहंगणाभोयं-णह (नख), 2 गण, 3 भोय (भोग), 4 णहंगण (नभांगन).
It is to be noted that Hemacandra in his *Kāvyānuśasana* commentary holds that *praśnottara*, *prahelikā*, etc., do not come under the rubric of poetical composition, V.4, p. 323.

148. (a) Cousin-marriage was allowed in Lāṭa and Dakṣiṇāpatha and prohibited in Uttarāpatha, *Āva Cū,* II.81. Jāmāli, the cousin of Mahavira, is said to have married Mahavira's daughter, Priyadarśanā. Baudhāyana too refers to this type of marriage. Kumārila Bhaṭṭa casts an aspersion on a Dākṣiṇātya, who is overjoyed to get the daughter of his maternal uncle, Chakaldar, H.C., *Social Life in Ancient India—Studies in Vātsyāyana's Kāmasūtra,* p. 133.

(b) The marriage with one's step-mother was allowed among certain Brāhmaṇas (*vipra*) in the country of Golla, *Āva-Cū,* II.81; also *KSS,* VII, pp. 116f, also see Jagdishchandra Jain, *PNL,* under the Motif of 'Mother-Son Incest', p. 53.

(c) Sister marriage was prevalent in the country of Golla, *Āva-Cū,* ibid. In Jain tradition, Ṛṣabha, the first Tīrthaṅkara, is said to have married his twin sisters, Sumaṅgalā and Sunandā, the former giving birth to Bharata and the latter to Bāhubali. However, according to Digambara tradition, he married Yaśastī and Sunandā, the two sisters of Kaccha and Mahākaccha. Sister marriage was customary among the Śākyas and also among the Santhalas, the Egyptians, Greeks and others, see Jain, *PNL,* pp. 51f.

149. भणिओ णेमी: कुमार! उसभाइणो वि तित्थयरा काऊण दारसंगहं, भोत्तूण भोगे, जणिऊण तणए, पूरिऊण पणइणो, पालेऊण पुहइं, सव्वहा णिविण्ण-कामभोगा पच्छिम-वयम्मि पव्वइया; तहा वि संपत्ता णिव्वाणं।

150. The story is told in the *Śuka-saptati* (15); also *Das Cū,* pp. 89-91. The oldest form of this story goes to the fifth century. For further details see *PNL,* under the Motif of Chastity or Act of Truth, p. 50 and n. 2.

151. सारय-ससंक-धवला, कित्ती भुवणं न जस्स धवलेइ।
नियपोट्ट-भरण-वावड-रिट्ठ-सरिच्छेण किं तेण॥ p. 105

152. रज्जावेंति न रज्जंति, लेंति हिययाइं न उण अप्पेंति।
छप्पण्णय-बुद्धीओ, जुवईओ दो वि सरिसाओ॥
द्विज-तनय कथा, p. 148.

153. Jain Shreyakar Mandal, 1911; *RKŚS,* Indore, 1936.

154. जिणवयण-काणणाओ चिणिऊण सुवन्नमसरिस-गुणड्ढे।
उवसममालमेयं रएमि वरकुसुममालं व॥ 2, p. 4

155. किं फलम्? कल्लाण-सिद्धि-संसिद्धि-कारणं सुद्धहिययाणं। 502

156. Read *Purandara-carita* in the *Jñāna-dāna-vidhi,* pp. 70-138.

157. The same story occurs in the *VH, Ketumatī-lambha,* 21, pp. 33.5-338, 4; also the author's 'Some Old Tales and Episodes in the Vasudeva-hiṇḍi' (pp. 170-1), *ABORI,* Vol. 60, 1979.

158. मेहा होज्ज न होज्ज व लोए जीवाण कम्मवसगाणं।
उज्जोओ पुण तहवि हु नाणंमि सया न मोत्तव्वो॥ *gāthā* 28, p. 138.

159. Page 194.

160. अत्थं सव्वाणत्थं, 160.

161. जइ वहसि कहवि अत्थं, निग्गंथं पवयणं पवन्नोऽवि।
निग्गंथत्ते तो सासणस्स मइलणत्तणं कुणसि॥ 159

162. उक्तं च श्रुतौ :
हस्तिन्यामचलो जातः उलूक्यां केशकंबलः।

अगस्त्योगऽस्तिपुष्पाच्च कौशिकः कुशस्य (सं)स्तरात्॥
कठिनात् कठिनो जातः शरगुल्माच्च गौतमः।
द्रोणाचार्यस्तु कलशात् तित्तिरेस्तित्तिरी मुतः॥
रेणुकाऽजनयद्रामं ऋषिश्रृंगं वने मृगी।
कैवर्ती जनयेद् व्यासं कक्षीवन्तं, च शूद्रिका॥
विश्वामित्रं च चांडाली वशिष्ठं चैव उर्वशी।
विप्रजाति-कुलाभावेऽप्यते तावद् द्विजोत्तमाः॥
Cāritra śuddhidvāra under Bhāvanādvāra, p. 367.

163. *RKŚS*, Ratlam, vs 1992 in two parts.

164. जो पढइ सुत्तओ सुणइ अत्थओ भावए य अणुसमयं।
सो भवनिव्वेयगओ पडिवज्जइ परमपयमग्गं॥
न य वहिज्जइ हरिसेहिं नेय विसमावईविसाएहिं।
भावियचित्तो एयाए चिट्ठए अमयसित्तोव्व॥ 526-7.

165. धीरपुरिसाणुचिन्ने परोवयारंमि जइयव्वं। Introduction

166. Page 269: प्रसंगतः संक्षेपेण शेषा अपि.

167. This account can be compared with the account of the *VH*, see author's *The Vasudeva.*

168. Siṇavalli also finds mention in the *Āva Cū* (I, p. 553; II, p. 34). However, the present author has identified this place with Sanāwan or Sināwan in Muzaffargarh in Pakistan, see *LAI*, p. 413. There might have been two locations bearing the same name, one in Panjab, the other in Kathiawad.

169. जाई रूवं विज्जा तिन्निवि निवडंतु कंदरे विवरे।
अत्थोच्चिय परिवड्डउ जेण गुणा पायडा होंति॥ V, *Kauśāmbī vipra-kathā*, 8, p. 534.

170. धणमत्थि त्ति वणिज्जं, किंचिवि अत्थि त्ति करिसणं कुणइ।
सेवा सयलाभावे, साहसमवि अप्पणो भावे॥ op. cit., 20, p. 535.

171. The *Vasudevahiṇḍī Madhyama Khaṇḍa*, Pt. I, edited by H.C. Bhayani and R.M. Shah, 1987.

172. Compare a similar story in the *VH* in the *Puṇḍā-lambha* (X) (215, 7-8; *The Vasudeva*, p. 394); it is stated by Cittavegā that after cutting her thigh some medicine was thrust into it and she looked like a prince.

173. Eight magic art groups (*vijjānikāya*) have been mentioned in the *Majjhimakhaṇḍa* (I.27) as follows: विज्जाहराणं अट्ठविज्जा-णिकाया भवंति। तं जहा-गोरीयका 1, मणुपव्वका 2, गंधारका 3, माणवीयका 4, केसितपुव्वगा 5, भूमितुंडगा 6, मूजगिरिया 7, संकुगाय 8. एयाणं च एक्केक्कस्स अट्ठट्ठभेदा, एवं चउसट्ठिभेदा मुणेयव्वा। ते य पढमेल्लुग-कंडे णिरूवित्ता। तेसिंच पत्तेयं पत्तेयं सचिंधेसु रूवेसु विज्जाणं पुरच्चरण-विही कीरति। तत्थ गोरीणं कट्ठमोणेणं, मणूण परिव्वायण-रूवेणं, गंधारीणं लालायर-रूवेणं, उत्तम-य(र)रूवेण वा, माणवीणं पयति-माणुस-रुवेणं, केसियाणं पइण्ण-जडाईण धारि-रूवेणं, भूमितुंडगाणं उड्डु-रूवेणं, मूजविरियाणं सबर-किरात-चंडाल-पुलिंद-रूवेणं, संकुगाणं रुछ-भेख-सूजयाणि-रूवेणं। I, 27

174. Also occurs in *VH*, 147, 9; *The Vasudeva*, Appendix III, 671.

175. A similar incident has been narrated in the *Pabhāvatī-lambha* (I, 67f.; *The Vasudeva*, pp. 127f.) in the *MKH* when Dharaṇendra, the king of the Nāgas, broke out of his own image, held Vasudeva in his arms, flew up and arrived in northern Bharata.

176. 264, 25; *The Vasudeva*, p. 458.
177. 250, 13-23, *The Vasudeva*, pp. 450f.
178. 319, 6-10; also *MKH*, p. 156.
179. 319, 15-17.
180. 318, 14-18.
181. 155: It has been stated: एस सीमणगो णाम महा-महिधरो हिरिमंतो च्चिय भण्णति। एदं च से सिहरतले महंतं जिणायदणं णाभेंयस्स भगवदो धरणेण णागराइणा णिम्मविदं धरणुब्भेदं तित्थ भण्णति।
182. Pages 155-6.
183. Page 34.
184. Also see *The Vasudeva*, 31-3; author's 'The Role of Dharaṇendra in Jain Mythology', *AIOC*, Jaipur, 1982, pp. 394-5.
185. 145, 23-5: न सक्का अपरिच्चिएणं गिहं दट्ठुं, उच्छाहे सिरी वसति, दरिद्दो य मयसमो, सयण-परिभूओ य धीजीवियं जीवइ, सेयं चिट्ठिउं ति; also *The Vasudeva*, pp. 278f.
186. जे च्चिय जाणंतिणरा, वण्ण-विसेसं गुणं च रयणस्स।
ते च्चिय पूयंति तयं, ण उ ससंकितं जहागोवा॥ p. 184.
187. *The Vasudeva*, pp. 678-81.
188. See *The Vasudeva*, pp. 95-149.
189. This *Lambha* can be compared with Vasudeva's marriage with Kanakavatī in the *TSP* (Vol. V, Book VIII, Chapter III, pp. 79-148): (i) Vasudeva's embassy for Kubera (pp. 86-93), (ii) Seven apartments of King Hariścandra's palace (87-8), (iii) Loss of Nala's kingdom (107-10), (iv) Damayantī deserted by Nala (114), (v) Adventures of Damayantī after being deserted (115-27), (vi) Damayantī followed the instructions supplied by Nala after deserting her (115), (vii) the sun-cooked food prepared by Nala (139), (viii) Skill in driving chariot by Nala (142.43) and so on.
190. जस्स धणं तस्स जणो, जस्सऽत्थो तस्स बंधवा वहवे।
धण-रहितो हि मणुस्सो, होति समो दास-पेसाणं॥, p. 236
191. किरायाणं एस आयारो, अभिप्पाओ चेव वियाहो त्ति।

7

Prakrit in Sanskrit Drama

The common word for drama in Sanskrit is *nāṭaka*, derived from the Prakrit root *naṭ* (Sanskrit root *nṛt*) to dance, which indicates that dance was at the root of dramatic performance. *Nṛtya* is dancing, whereas *nāṭya* is mimicry or mimic representation of actions and conduct of people which is rich in various emotions and depicts different situations.[1] In the Vedic ritual texts various ceremonies are described which can be designated as a type of drama. Later on the dramatic performances with Indra's flag festival (*indradhvaja*) were celebrated at the close of the rainy season. It has been stated that when the gods under the leadership of Indra approached the Creator Brahmā, the Grand Father was pleased to create the Fifth Veda—the *Nāṭyaveda*—also known as the *Gandharvaveda.* It was proposed that the first drama should be staged on the occasion of the flag ceremony (*dhvajamaha*) to celebrate the defeat of the demons by the gods in honour of Indra.[2] Brahmā explained: 'This art has been created by me related to actions of good, bad and indifferent, and will give courage, amusement as well as counsel to them all.'[3] Further, 'This teaches duty to those who go against duty, love to those who are eager for its fulfilment and it chastises those who are ill-bred or unruly, promotes self-restraint in those who are disciplined, gives courage to cowards, energy to heroic persons, enlightens men of poor intellects and gives wisdom to the learned.'[4] Then, 'It will also give relief to unlucky persons who are afflicted with sorrow and grief or (over)-work, and will be conducive of duty as well as to fame, longlife, intellect and general good, and will educate people.'[5] We are told that there is no learning, no craft, no science, no fine art, no *Yoga* and no ascetic discipline that will not be witnessed in the *Nāṭyaveda.*[6]

A drama begins with the *Nandi,* the introductory prayer. Immediately follows *Prastāvanā,* the prologue or interlude. The *Sūtradhāra* or stage-manager appears and starts talking with an actress supposed to be his wife, and says a few words in praise of the author.

One peculiar characteristic of the Indian drama is that it has a great amount of variation of language. This indicates a development on the basis of popular models. The theatre is associated with music, song and dance. The *lāsya* dance especially, accompanied with instrumental music and singing, which is supposed to be invented by Pārvatī, is a delicate dance representing the emotions of love. According to Bharata, it consists of ten divisions or *aṅgas* (*daśarūpaka*). This dance is opposed to the *tāṇḍava* dance which is boisterous and said to be the dance of Śiva and his votaries. Both formed an invariable part of the Sanskrit drama. Variation in Sanskrit theatre is not only in the form of verse and prose, but the characters speak different dialects according to the custom. For example, Sanskrit is spoken only by members of higher classes, though according to Bharata, no Sanskrit should be spoken by a superior class of person in case he is intoxicated with wealth or overwhelmed with poverty.[7] Prakrit is assigned to persons in disguise (*vyājaliṅga-praviṣṭānāṃ*),[8] *śramaṇas* (Jain monks),[9] *tapasvins* (ascetics), *bhikṣus* (religious mendicants) and *cakracaras* (ascetics who go begging with a swing suspended on strings (*sikkaka*).[10]

Similarly Prakrit is assigned to children, persons possessed of spirits of lower order, women in feminine character,[11] persons of low birth, lunatics and phallus worshippers (*saliṅga*).[12] Sanskrit has been assigned to itinerant recluses (*parivrajaka*) and sages (*muni*), Buddhists (*Śākya*), pure *śrotriyas* (conversant with the *Vedas*) and others who have received instruction (in the Vedas) and dress according to their position (*liṅgastha*).[13]

A play is a story of life, a succession of events in real life, depicting the actions and conduct of people with force, vividness and emotional touches. Prakrit played an important role in making Sanskrit theatre realistic. Pischel, agreeing with Senart, has pointed out that all Prakrits go back to popular dialects at their source and all their essential elements originally developed from living speech. We have seen that the Jain teachers preached in Prakrit with a compassionate view towards children, women, the aged and the ignorant people who were desirous of practising good conduct. Under the circumstances, the introduction of Prakrit was desired suitable to make Sanskrit drama lively. Generally speaking, the assignment of Sanskrit and Prakrit languages to particular characters was meant to reflect the conditions of real life. But unfortunately, as the Prakrit dialects were no longer spoken, definite rules could not be prescribed for their use. Sometimes we notice different rules applicable for prose and verse. In the *Mṛcchakaṭika* of Śūdraka, the courtesan Vasantasenā speaks Prakrit as a rule but uses Sanskrit in verse. As a courtesan had to deal with all sorts of people, her house being a meeting place of different kind of social culture, she could express herself both in Sanskrit as well as in Prakrit. In Bhāsa's *Pañcarātra*, Arjuna in the guise of Bṛhannalā wants to narrate the battle scene in Prakrit, but King Virāṭa interrupts him, saying 'it is an important matter, speak Sanskrit' and he starts his narration accordingly.

Prakrit Dialects of the *Nāṭyaśāstra*

Seven major dialects have been mentioned by Bharata in his *Nāṭyaśāstra*. The most important Prakrit dialects that occur in our dramas are Mahārāṣṭrī, Śaurasenī, Māgadhī, Paiśācī and Apabhraṃśa. Vararuci has mentioned only four main Prakrit dialects.

It is to be noted that first of all these dialects had ceased to be spoken languages since long; we find them in existing Prakrit literature, including Sanskrit dramas but they are different from the originally spoken dialects. Even Māgadhī, Śaurasenī and Mahārāṣṭrī did not really remain spoken dialects of those particular parts of the country. What we have are not actually living dialects but standardized artificial literary forms of Prakrit, just like Sanskrit. These forms were elevated from popular dialects and were polished for literary use. Even with regard to the Prakrit of the Ashokan inscriptions it cannot be said definitely that it was a spoken dialect of any part of the country.

Regarding Prācyā, Bālhīkā and Dākṣiṇātyā, we do not come across any old and authentic descriptions. Though the rules of speech of these dialects have been laid down in the *Natyaśāstra*, they do not seem to have uniformity and exactness. Instead they seem to be confusing. We have already discussed Śaurasenī, Prācyā, Āvantī, Māgadhī, Ardhamāgadhī, Dākṣiṇatyā and Vālhīkī in Chapter One.

Bharata in his *Nāṭyaśāstra* (XVII) mentions four types of language:

(a) *Atibhāṣā* (superhuman language, prescribed for gods), (b) *ārya-bhāṣā* (noble languages, prescribed for kings),[14] (c) *jātibhāṣā* (common language, prescribed for use on the stage), (d) *yonyatarī* (language of birds and animals). The *jātibhāṣā* contains words of barbarian (*mleccha*) origin and is spoken in Bhāratavarṣa only (XVII.25-9).

Further, languages are divided into *bhāṣā* and *vibhāṣā*. The seven languages, Māgadhī, Āvantījā, Prācyā, Śaurasenī, Ardhamāgadhī, Bālhīkā and Dākṣiṇātyā, as stated above, are included under *bhāṣā*, whereas the less important speeches, Śākāra, Ābhīra, Cāṇḍāla, Śabara, Draviḍa, Oḍra and the lowly speech of the foresters (*vanecara*)[15] under *vibhāṣā*.

It is to be noted that neither the *Nāṭyaśāstra* of Bharata nor any other grammarian has provided clarification of *bhāṣā* and *vibhāṣā*.[16] According to the commentator Pṛthvīdharā, the latter is a dialect spoken by low characters विविध भाषा हीनप्रयोजनत्वात् हीन:.[16] According to Keith, the *vibhāṣās* seem to be modified forms of the more normal Prakrits as stereotyped for the use by certain characters in drama.[17] However, no old or authentic specimen of the *vibhāṣās* is available to us.

Mārkaṇḍeya has divided Prakrit into four categories: *Bhāṣā*, *Vibhāṣā*, *Apabhraṃśa* and *Paiśācika*. As we have seen, *vibhāṣā* is first mentioned in the *Nāṭyaśāstra*. Then we come to Puruṣottama (eleventh century) who in his *Prākṛtānuśāsana* describes the rules of Śākārī, Cāṇḍālī, Śābarī and Ṭakkadeśī. Rāmaśarmā Tarkavāgīśa also has discussed *vibhāṣā* in his *Prākṛta-kalpataru* (*stavaka* III). He has discussed only a few forms of Ābhīrikā. He includes Śākārī, Oḍrī and Drāviḍī under Apabhraṃśa, but that is not so when they are used in a drama. Although Rāmaśarmā has mentioned and discussed these *vibhāṣās* we do not have a clear exposition until we come to Mārkaṇḍeya. He too thinks Śākārī is a form of Māgadhī and calls it a language of Śakāra in Sanskrit drama. Like Rāmaśarmā, he derives Cāṇḍālī from Māgadhī and Śaurasenī. Puruṣottama calls it a corrupt form of Māgadhī (*māgadhī-vikṛtaḥ*). Śābarī is derived by Mārkaṇḍeya from Cāṇḍālī and according to him, at times it also owes to Śaurasenī, Māgadhī and Śākārī. Puruṣottama prefers to call it a dialect of Māgadhī (*māgadhī-viśeṣaḥ*). He mostly disagrees with the rules laid down by Puruṣottama and Rāmaśarmā. Oḍrī, according to Mārkaṇḍeya, is the dialect which comes off by adding local words of the Oḍra (Orissa) country and of Śaurasenī, etc., to Śābarī alone.[18] As stated, he excludes Oḍrī from the list of *vibhāṣās*, as according to him its peculiarities are to be found in Śābarī itself which in turn imitates the language of the Oḍra country.[19] Ābhīrī, according to

Mārkaṇḍeya, is exactly like Śābarī with the exception that in gerund form *ktvā* is replaced by *ia* and *ua*; for example, the form *gatvā* changes into *gaścia* or *gadua* (15.10). Puruṣottama does not accept Ābhīrī. In the *Nāṭyaśāstra* (XVIII.54) Ābhīrī or Śābarī is assigned to those who live in places where elephants, horses, goats, sheep, camels or cows are kept. Mārkaṇḍeya records Ṭakkī or Ḍhakkī along with Śākārī, Cāṇḍālī and Śābarī among the dialects of Apabhraṃśa. According to both Puruṣottama and Mārkaṇḍeya, it was spoken in the country of Ṭakka. It is a mixture of Sanskrit and Śaurasenī (Puruṣottama, 16.1; Rāmaśarmā, 2.3.28; Mārkaṇḍeya 16.1) which was used by gamblers, knaves and merchants.[20] Like Rāmaśarmā, Mārkaṇḍeya also identifies it with Drāviḍī.[21] Both Puruṣottama and Mārkaṇḍeya have quoted Hariścandra, an ancient grammarian, who considers this dialect as Apabhraṃśa and not a *vibhāṣā*.[22] According to the commentator Pṛthvīdhara, this was not a *vibhāṣā*. In his opinion, this speech is characterized by prevalence of *la* and by the use of the two sibilants, namely the dental *sa* and palatal *śa*. That means as in Māgadhī so in Ṭakkī also *ra* is replaced by *la* and *śa* by *sa*. Like Śākārī, Śābarī and Cāṇḍālī, Ṭakki also is considered as derived from Māgadhī. In the *Mṛcchakaṭika*, Māthura the keeper of the house of gambling and his fellow-players speak Ḍhakkī. However, like those of Śākārī and Cāṇḍālī, we do not come across the characteristics of Ṭakkī also. Pṛthvīdhara in his commentary has mentioned the same characteristics of Māgadhī, Śākārī and Cāṇḍālī which shows that the last two are allied with Māgadhī. The illustrations of Ṭakkī cited by grammarians are so scanty that it is difficult to ascertain its nature.

Certain Conventions in Sanskrit Drama

Sanskrit drama is the highest product of Indian literary skill. Generally, plots are derived from the epics. Numerous interesting dramas with legendary themes and comedies of court life, plays about middle class life, and those of semi-historical interest, plays pertaining to allegorical themes, and erotic and farcical theatre are documented.

Nāṭaka (drama) which is considered most beautiful among different types of poetry (काव्येषु नाटकं रम्यम्) follows certain conventions laid down by rhetoricians. *Rasa-niṣpatti* or generation of sentiment (*rasa*) in the mind of the audience is considered the most important in a poetical performance. It is stated in the *Nāṭyaśāstra* that no poetic meaning can be conveyed without sentiment. Just as different species leave behind different kinds of tastes—sweet, sour, bitter—so also the emotions (*bhāva*) represented on the stage arouse in the mind of the audience certain sentiments.[23] These are generated through love (*śṛṅgāra*), humour (*hāsya*), pity (*karuṇā*), terror (*raudra*), heroism (*vīra*), fear (*bhayānaka*), and astonishment (*adbhuta*). Keith has observed, 'They were idealist in outlook, capable of large generalization, but regardless of accuracy in detail, and to create a realistic drama was wholly incompatible with their temperament. The accurate delineation of facts or character was to them nothing; they aimed at the creation in the mind of the audience of sentiment, and what was necessary for this end was all that was attempted.'[24] He considers the Indian dramatic art aristocratic. He writes:

> This art was essentially aristocratic; the drama was never popular in the sense in which the Greek drama possessed that quality. From an early period in Indian history we find the distinction of class reflected in a distinction of language; culture was reserved largely for the two higher castes, the Brahmin and the Kṣatriya or ruling class. It was in this rarified atmosphere that the Sanskrit drama came into being, and it was probably to literati of high cultivation that its creation from the hints present in religion and in the epic was due.[25]

Another convention followed by dramatists was the *nāyaka* or hero as a lover of arts, belonging to a noble family, normally a king whose public burdens were confined to others, and whose business was to secure union with a new favourite by overcoming obstacles such as the jealousy of his queens. A hero should always be self-controlled (*dhīra*), a characteristic not universally found in heroines. He should be light-hearted (*lalita*), calm (*śānta*), exalted (*udātta*) and vehement (*uddhata*).[26] He always achieves victory and never faces death. As a result there is no tradition of true tragedy in Sanskrit drama. Tragedy is forbidden. In the long run the hero and the heroine are united in perfect happiness. Thus the subject of Sanskrit drama is drawn from tradition. The hero should be a king, royal sage, or god, who may appear in human form; the dominant sentiment must be heroic or erotic, and the sentiment of wonder is well suited for unravelling of a plot or story. The subject is often chosen from an ancient legend which is generally not dramatic. In the words of Keith, dramatists 'do no seek realism, but are content to reproduce a stereotyped scheme of love, jealousy, parting, and reunion, a sequence well calculated to evoke the sentiment of love in the mind of the audience'.[27]

Aśvaghoṣa, the First Dramatist

The credit of the discovery of Aśvaghoṣa as a dramatist goes to H. Lüders who in the year 1911,[28] found among the fragments of palm-leaf manuscripts from Turfan, pieces of three leaves written in the Central Asian script and containing a fragment of Aśvaghoṣa's drama. Fortunately, the colophon of the last ninth act has been preserved and it records that the text was the *Śāriputraprakaraṇa* of Aśvaghoṣa, son of Suvarṇākṣī.

Aśvaghoṣa (first century AD) was a Buddhist and is known for his *Buddhacarita.* As Keith has pointed out his play has close correspondence with the classical type as laid down in Bharata *Nāṭyaśāstra*: it is a piece of *Prakaraṇa* with nine acts. It is also known as *Śāradvatīputraprakaraṇa* and deals with the events which led to the conversion of Śāriputra and Maudgalyāyana by Buddha in his *saṅgha.* The *Śāriputraprakaraṇa* has also fragments of two other dramas for whose authorship no evidence is available and it is only on palaeographical grounds that they can be assigned to the age of Kaniṣka and therefore not far from the time of Aśvaghoṣa. The first contains a scene from an allegorical drama where enter the figures of *Buddhi* (Intelligence), *Dhṛti* (Patience) and *Kīrti* (Fame) who extol the Buddha. All speak Sanskrit, but from the available fragments it is not possible to give information on the general trend of the drama. The other drama gives some more matter. In addition to Buddha, Śāriputra and Maudgalyāyana there appear an ascetic, a Brāhmaṇa, a harlot named Magadhavatī and a *vidūṣaka* named Komudagandha. Although all three plays are available only in fragments, they are valuable from the point of view of the history and development of Sanskrit drama. They show that in the first century AD a play was divided into acts, an important role was assigned to the *vidūṣaka,* prose and verse could be interchanged, verse was composed in metres of classical Sanskrit poetry, and there was alteration between Sanskrit and Prakrit. As Lüders has pointed out, the Prakrit dialects employed in these fragments represent an older form as compared with one that is found in the classical Sanskrit drama.[29]

The Language of the Drama

Aśvaghoṣa used three dialects, Śaurasenī, Māgadhī and Ardha-māgadhī, in his drama which contains much older forms of these dialects. Keith has observed in this connection: 'The stage reached by the Prakrits of Aśvaghoṣa shows clearly how late are the Prakrits of the orthodox classical drama, and reminds us how much more closely akin to Sanskrit must have been the Prakrit of the drama of the time of, or shortly after, Patañjali.'[30] He has distinguished three different forms of Prakrit in Aśvaghoṣa's drama, the first spoken by the Duṣṭa, the second by the mysterious Gobaṃ (an obscure character of lower rank), and the third by the harlot and Vidūṣaka. Regarding the Duṣṭa's speech, he has pointed out that it is similar to the Māgadhī of the Prakrit grammarians in three important points: (i) it substitutes ल for र, (ii) reduces all three sibilants to श, and (iii) has ए in the nominative singular of masculine nouns ending in अ. Further, he says, it ignores the rules of the grammarians in the following respects: (i) hard letters are not softened (e.g. भोति), (ii) nor soft consonants elided (e.g. कोमुदगंध) when intervocalic, (iii) no tendency to cerebralize न, (iv) and in कालना the dental replaces the cerebral. Then, the fuller forms of consonants remain in हंघो (हंहो) and बंभण (बंहण). The later forms of development consonantal combination are unknown; thus for र्य we have ज्ज, not य्य, as in अज्ज; च्छ remains in lieu of becoming श्च; क्ष becomes क्ख, not स्क or ह्क; ष्ट and ष्ठ give ट्ठ, not स्ट. In किश्श we have an older form than कीश, in अहकम् than अहके, हके, हगे. 'In practically all these details', writes Keith, 'we must see an earlier stage of what becomes Māgadhī in the grammarians'. He continues, 'With it may be compared the metrical inscription of the Jogīmārā cave on the Rāmgarh Hill which belongs to the period of Aśoka.'

Coming to the second form of Prakrit, spoken by Gobaṃ, Keith writes, 'it agrees with this Old Māgadhī in having ल for र and ए in the nominative singular, but it reduces all sibilants to स. It thus shows a certain similarity to the Ardhamāgadhī of grammarians, but that dialect often keeps र though it frequently alters it to ल; for instance it has र for the कलेति of this Prakrit and the Old Māgadhī.' Further, 'Other points of similarity are the retention of the dental for cerebral in वन्न: the lengthening of the vowel before the suffix क (वन्नीकाहि); the accusative plural neuter in पुप्फा; and the infinitive भुंजितए (भुंजित्तए).' 'There are points of difference, but they are probably all cases of earlier forms. Thus, as in Old Māgadhī, we have no softening or loss of intervocalic consonants; न is not cerebralized, but even introduced in पलिनत: ळ appears in lieu of ल; the instrumental in आहि has no nasal; the nominative of वत् stems appears as in वा, as against वम् or वन्ते; in the infinite we find no doubling of the consonant in तये. The fact, however, of the regular change of र to ल and the use of the form येव after a long vowel as in Māgadhī and Pali show that the Old

Ardhamāgadhī was more akin to Māgadhī than the later Ardhamāgadhī, which came steadily under the influence of the Western dialects as shown by the tendency to change ए of the nominative to ओ.' He concludes, 'There are strong points of similarity between the Old Ardhamāgadhī and the language of Aśoka's pillar inscriptions. They agree as regards the use of ल, स, and ए, the dentals in पलिनत and वन्नीकाहि, येव after long vowels, and the long vowel before the suffix क. They disagree in the nominative and accusative plural neuter of अ stems, which have आनि in the inscriptions as against आ, but that is of no great importance, as these are doublets. The infinite, however, is in तवे, which can not be equated with तये; Ardhamāgadhī त्तए may be from either.'[31]

Keith has pointed out some Sanskrit words such as आर्थ for अर्थ, तुष्णीं for तूष्णीं, क्रिमि for कृमि, प्रतीगृहीत for प्रतिग्रहीत, प्रद्वेषम् for प्रदोषम् and so on, which are consider by him as examples of Prakritism. He says that आर्थ has a precise parallel in the nearly contemporaneous dialect of Mathura; तुष्णीं is frequent in Buddhist Sanskrit as well as etymologically correct; क्रिमि is found also in the *Buddhacarita*; प्रतीगृहीत has many Sanskrit parallels; प्रद्वेषम in the metre requires प्रदोषम which shows Buddhist influence.[32]

Thus we see that the Prakrit used by Aśvaghoṣa is important from the point of view of the history and development of Middle Indo-Aryan. The Ardhamāgadhī dialect used here is quite different from the Ardhamāgadhī of the Jain Canon. As has been pointed out, the Old Ardhamāgadhī used there was different from the later Ardhamāgadhī, it was akin to Māgadhī. Making a comparison between the Old Ardhamāgadhī and the Aśokan inscriptions, Keith has called the former the descendant of Ardhamāgadhī of Mahavira and probably also of Buddha, whose speech was clearly not akin to the Māgadhī of the grammarians, though it is called Māgadhī in the sacred texts.[33] Similarly the Śaurasenī dialect used by Aśvaghoṣa is much older than Śaurasenī of the Prakrit grammarians. These Prakrits with their archaic features have been placed on the same plane of change as Pali and the dialects of older inscriptions by Keith.

Dramas of Bhāsa

If Aśvaghoṣa was the oldest known dramatist, Bhāsa was the first poet, of the third century. Aśvaghoṣa was a Buddhist whereas Bhāsa was a Brāhmaṇa and a devotee of Viṣṇu. Kālidāsa, Bāṇa and Rājaśekhara have praised him and he was a favourite of Vākpati. Nothing was known about Bhāsa in Europe until 1910; it was only in 1912 that T. Gaṇapati Śāstrī first published a series of thirteen dramas attributed to the poet in the Trivandrum Sanskrit Series. His dramas are *Pañcarātra* and the one-act plays *Dūtavākya, Madhyamavyāyoga, Dūtaghaṭotkaca, Karṇabhāra* and *Urubhaṅga*; perhaps these are the earliest works of the author. Then we have the *Bālacarita, Pratimānāṭaka, Abhiṣekanāṭaka, Svapnavāsavadattā, Pratijñāyaugandharāyaṇa, Avimāraka* and *Cārudatta.*[34] The plots of these plays are derived either from the *Mahābhārata* or the *Rāmāyaṇa* or the *Bṛhatkathā* of Guṇāḍhya. The *Pañcarātra* (Within Five Days) is so called as Duryodhana agrees to surrender half of his empire to the Pāṇḍavas in case news is received from them within five days. The play has three acts and more than one hero. The *Dūtavākya* (The Message), a one-act play, is again from the *Mahābhārata,* and a free dramatization of the episode of Kṛṣṇa presenting himself as an envoy of the Pāṇḍavas. The theme of the *Madhyamavyāyoga* (The Middle) is based on Bhīma as the middle among the five sons of Pāṇḍu. Here we have the tale of love between Bhīma and the demon Hiḍimbā, out of which was born Ghaṭotkaca. The *Dūtaghaṭotkaca* (The Drama of Ghaṭotkaca as Messenger), another one-act play, is classed as a *vyāyoga* (a heroic exploit from which the sentiment of love is excluded). As the *Mahābhārata* does not actually refer to Ghaṭotkaca as a messenger, this episode is the creation of the poet Bhāsa himself. The *Karṇabhāra* (The Drama of Karṇa's Armour) is a dramatization of an episode of the *Mahābhārata* where Indra appears in the guise of a Brāhmaṇa-beggar and asks Karṇa for his armour and earring. Of these five-one-act plays the *Urubhaṅga* (The Drama of the Fracture of the Thigh) is most important. It shows the dramatic skill of the poet who dramatizes the plot of the *Mahābhārata* with a superior skill in a forceful language. Here in the fight between Bhīma and Duryodhana, the thigh of the latter breaks and he falls in agony. The battlefield and the fight with the mace are described in a poetic style. Duryodhana with his broken ribs appears on the stage, which is against the rules of Indian dramaturgy.

The *Bālacarita* (The Exploit of Boy Kṛṣṇa) is the oldest available drama connected with the Kṛṣṇa legend. It is an extraordinary dramatic composition related to the sensation of heroism (*vīrarasa*). Here is described death and the horrible scenes of slaughter on the stage against the injunction laid down by Indian dramaturgy. The play contains five acts. The *Pratimānāṭaka* (The Drama of the Portrait) reproduces in its seven acts the contents of the main narratives of the

Rāmāyaṇa in an independent manner. Here half mad with grief King Daśaratha appears on the stage, speaks incoherently and ultimately succumbs to death. The *Abhiṣekanāṭaka* (The Drama of Coronation of Rāma) containing six acts, deals with the coronation of Rāma. In the *Pratimānāṭaka* Rāma appears as a human hero, but in the present play as God Viṣṇu or Nārāyaṇa. Here Bhāsa does not follow the epic in many details. There is no mention of the construction of the bridge up to Laṅkā, but Varuṇa being frightened by the threat of Rāma, divides himself into two to enable Rāma and his army to walk over the bridge and reach Laṅkā in a moment. The poet has used simple language, creating a dramatic effect. We come across beautiful descriptions of the ocean, sun-set, and so on. All these dramas are based on elements from the epics where there is neither a *vidūṣaka* nor comic scenes and where Sanskrit holds a dominant position. The *Svapnavāsavadattā* (The Drama of Vāsavadattā who meets her Husband in a Dream) is quite different from these. It comes under the *Prakaraṇas* of Bhāsa which is considered most prominent and a masterpiece. The source of the plot of this drama is not the epics but the *Bṛhatkathā* of Guṇāḍhya. Vākpati (eighth century AD) in his *Gauḍavaho* (800) calls him a friend of fire (*jalaṇamitte*) and Rājaśekhara (AD 900) places him among the classical poets and records a verse praising the *Svapnavāsavadattā.* He writes, 'The critics cast on the fire to test the discus (*cakra*) of the dramas composed by Bhāsa, the fire could not become a carrier of the *Svapnavasavādattā.*'[35] Here we are told how the minister Yaugandharāyaṇa is anxious to secure for king Udayana an extension of his power by marrying him to Padmāvatī, daughter of king of Magadha. It contains six acts and is considered most successful.[36] In the concluding benedictory stanza we are told: 'May our lion-king protect the whole of this earth that extends up to the sea, on whose face the Himālayas and the Vindhyas appear like two ear-rings.'[37] The *Pratijñāyaugandharāyaṇa* (The Drama of Yaugandharayāṇa, Firm to his Promise) is closely connected with the *Svapnavāsavadattā.* Here also the plot is from the *Bṛhatkathā* of Guṇāḍhya. It has four acts and is also styled as a *Prakaraṇa.* The hero of the play is Yaugandharāyaṇa, the minister of Udayana, king of Vatsa. Udayana is brought by trick by Bharatarohaka, the minister of Pradyota Mahāsena of Ujjayinī, with the help of a counterfeit elephant with soldiers inside. Udayana is taken prisoner to the kingdom of Pradyota. Mahāsena was discussing the marriage of his daughter Vāsavadattā when the news of Udayana's capture reached him. Udayana as an expert in the art of playing on the lute, started training Vāsavadattā, and wons her love. When the minister Yaugandharāyaṇa hears this news he gets very worried and takes a vow to rescue the king.[38] He goes to Ujjayinī in disguise as a mad man (*unmattaka*) with his friends and roams about in the palace. Ultimately he succeeds in his strategy which enables him to escape the king with Vāsavadattā. But after he had freed his master from imprisonment he himself was captured by the enemy. King Pradyota appreciated the minister's cleverness and the marriage of Udayana and Vāsavadattā was solemnized.[39]

Bhāmaha, a well-known rhetorician, has criticized the play, pleading that Udayana could never have been deceived by an artificial elephant, and if deceived, his life would have never been spared by the enemy. However, Keith does not agree with this contention.[40]

The *Avimāraka* (The Killer of the Asura Avi) is a play in six acts describing the love affair of an exiled prince Avimāraka. Its plot is derived from the story of the *Bṛhatkathā*. The prince saves Kuraṅgī, the daughter of his maternal uncle Kuntībhoja, from a mad elephant. They fall in love. Through the nurse of the princess a secret union of the couple is arranged in the palace. The entry of the youth in the palace in the guise of a thief exhibits a dramatic skill on the part of the author. But the news leaks out and when it comes to the notice of the guard of the harem, the prince flees. He wants to commit suicide by jumping into fire, but does not succeed. Then he wants to fall from a rock, when a *vidyadhara* gives him a magic ring by which it would be possible for him to have secret meeting with his beloved. In the end everything comes to a happy end with the assistance of sage Nārada. The Vidūṣaka plays an important role in this drama. He is not able to read at all—not even the letter inscribed on a seal,[41] but still he is admired very much by his master as he helps bring about his union with his beloved. Jokingly he says, 'I am a Brāhmaṇa with my sacred thread, and a Buddhist monk by the saffron robe (*rattapaḍa*) and when I put off my garments I turn to be a Jain monk (*samaṇa*).'[42] He is greedy for food and wants to relish it only when it is actually given to him.[43] Still he is the most trusted friend of the hero, who portrays his friend's character saying, 'he is witty in entertainments, a warrior in the battles, a teacher in grief, a violent foe to his enemies and he is my festivity in my heart. What is the use of talking much, he is indeed my other half.'[44] Such a Vidūṣaka is not known elsewhere.

Cārudatta or *Daridra Cārudatta* (The Poor Cārudatta) is another important drama of Bhāsa depicting the realistic life of Cārudatta, a merchant whose generosity has impoverished him. Abhinavagupta (*c.* AD 1000) has twice named the *Svapnavāsavadattā* and mentions the *Cārudatta.* It is in agreement with the *Mṛcchakaṭika* of Śūdraka. Unfortunately it has come down to us only in fragments in four acts without beginning or final verses. The hero Cārudatta meets a harlot Vasantaśenā at a festival, and falls in love with her. She takes refuge in Cārudatta's house where she leaves her ornaments in his care. Later these were stolen by a thief in order to gain the means to purchase the freedom of a slave of the harlot, with whom he was in love. Knowing this, Cārudatta is overpowered with shame. Thereupon his noble wife offers her pearl necklace to be handed over to Vasantasenā to compensate her lost jewels. Vasantasenā accepts the necklace with the excuse to have a chance to see the merchant once more. She hands over the slave girl to the thief and proceeds to Cārudatta's house. Here the play ends abruptly, but it seems as if Cārudatta was accused of theft and that Vasantasenā faces grave danger to herself.

The Language of Bhāsa's Plays

A.B. Keith made a comparative study of Prakrit dialects of Aśvaghoṣa, Bhāsa and Kālidāsa in his valuable *The Sanskrit Drama,* on the basis of which we present our study here.

The Prakrit found in Bhāsa's works is normally Śaurasenī which is noticed in all his plays except the *Dūtavākya.* Māgadhī is found in two different forms in his play; and that may be styled as Ardhamāgadhī. The transitional aspect of his language can be compared on the one hand with Aśvaghoṣa and on the other with Kālidāsa. 'Aśvaghoṣa never softens—save in one instance—hard consonants, but both ट and त are changed into ड and द respectively in Bhāsa. Aśvaghoṣa never omits consonants, but, though this is less often carried out than in Kālidāsa, we find the cases of the loss of क, ग, च, ज, त, द, प, ब, व and य when intervocalic. य itself suffers frequent change to ज, contrary to Aśvaghosa's usage. The change of न initial and medial to ण is regular, while it is unknown to Aśvaghoṣa. The aspirants ख, घ, थ, ध, फ and भ are all often reduced as later to ह, but never in Aśvaghoṣa.'

With regard to conjunct consonants we notice that ज्ञ changes in Bhāsa either to ञ or ण्ण, possibly the latter by error; Aśvaghoṣa has ञ only, Kālidāsa ण्ण. For न्य and ण्य Bhāsa has always ण्ण as against Aśvaghoṣa's ञ्ञ.

The eliding of a consonant, with the compensatory lengthening of the vowel as in दीसादि, is unknown to Aśvaghoṣa, where the omission of the consonants twice occurs but without lengthening; it is frequent in Bhāsa and regular in Kālidāsa. The analogous use of a short vowel and a double consonant to represent a long vowel with a single consonant is unknown to Aśvaghoṣa, but Bhāsa has it in एव्व, एव्वम, जोव्वन, देव, एक्क. On the other hand, like Aśvaghoṣa, for र्य he has य्य only in lieu of Kālidāsa's ज्ज. For the later मेत्त मत्त is always found, and the epenthetic vowel is उ, not इ, in पुरूस and पुरूव is normal.

In inflection we have, in the nominative and accusative plural of neuter stems in अ, आनि in Aśvaghoṣa, आणि in Bhāsa, while both आणि and आइं are followed later. The accusative plural masculine has also, analogously to आनि in the Ardhamāgadhī of the Aśoka inscriptions, आणि, and the locative singular faminine is in आअं, not as later आए. For the later अत्ताणअं we have अत्ताणं. For we Aśvaghoṣa has वयं, Kālidāsa अम्हे; Bhāsa both and वअं. In the genitive plural Bhāsa has both अम्हाअं and the only form later अम्हाणं, while Aśvaghoṣa would doubtless have used अम्हाकं. किस्स is kept for later कीस, and कोच्चि (कच्चिद्) disappears later. The root दर्श is represented by दस्स and दंस, ग्रह by गण्हदि, against the later गेण्हदि, which, however, is found in Aśvaghoṣa. The older form करिअ and गच्छिअ or गमिअ are found in lieu of कदुअ and गदुअ, but the last occurs once. मा is used with the gerund in the sense of अलं.

Many of these peculiarities mark also the Māgadhī, which appears in two slightly varied forms, the first in the *Pratijñāyaugandharāyaṇa* and the *Cārudatta*, the second in the *Bālacarita* and the *Pañcarātra*; in the two latter we have ष and ओ for the श and ए of the former. As in Aśvaghoṣa there is no trace of obedience to the rules of grammarians which require स्ट for Sanskrit ष्ठ or ष्ट, श्च for च्छ, स्क or ह्क for क्ष. For 'I' we find अहके which is an intermediate state between Aśvaghoṣa's अहकं and the later हगे. न्य becomes ण्ण, not ञ्ञ, and the use of य to denote a dropped consonant is not carried out.

'The only passages that can claim to be anything like Ardhamāgadhī are the remarks of Indra in disguise in the *Karṇabhāra*, where the characteristic signs, the use of र, स and ए are found; in the speeches of Muṣṭika and Cāṇūra in the *Bālacarita* we have the use of ल and a locative in अम्मि. A single passage in the *Pañcarātra* suggests Māgadhī Apabhraṃśa, but is probably corrupt.'[45]

A specimen of Śaurasenī from the *Pratijñāyaugandharāyaṇa* (Act. 3):[46]

The Vidūṣaka enters in the disguise of a 'jesting beggar' (*ḍiṇḍika*):[47]

विदूषकः (निरूप्य) भो! देवउळपीढिआए मम मोदअमल्लअं णिक्खिविअ दक्खिणामासआणि गणिअ बंधिअ पडिणिवुत्तो दाणि मोदअमल्लअं ण पेक्खामि। (विचिन्त्य) आ एकमोदअपरितोसितो ण दाव ओळग्गो मं अणुसरदि। उच्चदाए पाआरस्स अगई कुक्कुराणं। अक्खदभत्तदाए अ लोहणीअं पहिआणं। आदु अपि णं खा-आमि। भोदु ओग्गारइस्सं दाव अहं। ही ही बुड्ढो विअ सूअरवत्थी सुद्धवादं एव उग्गिरामि। अहव ळोहिदकच्चाअणीए केरअं मम केरअं त्ति करिअ सिवेण पडिहत्थीकिदं भवे। (निरूप्य) जदि वि एसो बम्हआरी बहुकेहि रूवेहि अविणअं करेदि। भोदु पेक्खिस्सं दाव अहं। भो! एदं खु मम मोदअमल्लअं सिवस्स पादमूले

चिट्ठइ। जाव णं गह्णामि। देहि भट्टा! देहि मे मोदअमल्लअं। भट्टा! तुवं पि मम चोरोसि। अविहा आलिहिदं खु मम मोदअमल्लअं संदावतिमिरेण सुट्ठु ण पेक्खामि। भोदु पमज्जिस्सं दाव अहं। ही ही साहु ले चित्तअर! भाव! साहु! जुत्तलेहदाए वण्णाणं जह जहपमज्जामि, तह तह उज्जलदरं होइ। भोदु उदएण पमज्जिस्सं, कहिं णु हु उदअं? इदं सोहणं सुद्धतडाअं। अहं विअ सिवो वि दाव एदस्सिं मोदअमल्लए णिरासो होदु।

Vidūṣaka: Oh! I had kept my pot of मोदक sweetmeat (मोदअमल्लअं *modaamallaaṃ)*[48] here on the pedestal of the temple (*devakulapīṭhikā*)[49] and after counting the gold coins received as a gift at the completion of a religious rite दक्खिणा-मासआणि (*dakkhiṇa-māsaāṇi*)[50] and having tied them when I returned I did not see my pot मोदअ-मल्लअं (*modaa-mallaam*).[51] (Reflecting) Ah! the man who was satisfied only with one मोदक (*modaka*), hanging on me, has he not followed me एकमोदअ-परितोसिदो मा दाव ओलग्गो मं अणुसरदि (*ekamodaaparitosido mā dāva oḷaggo maṃ aṇusaradi*)![52] This wall on account of its height is not accessible to dogs उच्चदाए पाअरस्स अगई कुक्कुराणम् (*uccadāe pāarassa agaī kukkurāṇaṃ*).[53] The travellers are in possession of provision for a journey therefore they cannot be tempted to take the अक्खद भत्तदाए अलोहणीयम् पहिणाणं pot (*akkhadabhattadāe alohaṇiyaṃ pahiāṇaṃ*)[54] away. Or I myself might have eaten it up! आदु अपि णं खाआमि (*ādu api ṇaṃ khāāmi*).[55] If that is so I shall vomit it भोदु ओग्गारइस्सम् दाव अहम् (*bhodu oggāraissaṃ dāva ahaṃ*).[56] Ah! Ah! like an old boar's bladder I give out only pure wind सुद्धवादं एवं उग्गिरामि (*suddhavādaṃ eva uggirāmi*).[57] Or may be that with the impression that whatever belongs to red कात्यायनी Kātyāyanī पार्वती (Pārvatī) is his, Lord Śiva himself might have laid his hands on it अहवा लोहिककच्चाअणीए केरम् मम केरम् जि करिअ सिवेण पडिहत्थि किदम् भवे (*ahavā lohidakaccāaṇīe keraṃ mama keraaṃ tti karia siveṇa paḍihatthikidaṃ bhave*).[58] (Looking) Though he is practising continence he is behaving insolently in multifarious ways जदि वी एसो बम्हआरी-बहुकेहि रूवेहि अविणअम् करेदि (*jadi vi eso bamhaārī bahukehi rūvehi aviṇaaṃ karedi*).[59] Well, let it be, I shall see. Ah! here is my pot of sweetmeat kept at the base of Lord Śiva's foot एदम् खु मम मोदअ-मल्लअं सिवस्स पाद-मूले चिट्ठइ (*edaṃ khu mama modaamallaaṃ sivassa pādamūle ciṭṭhai*).[60] So I take it. O Lord! give back my pot of sweets. O Master! you are my thief! Oh! it is portrayed on the wall which I was not able to see well due to darkness of my grief अविहा आलिहिदम् खु मम मोदअ-मल्यअं संदाव-तिमिरेण (*avihā ālihidaṃ khu mama modaamallaaṃ saṃdāvatimireṇa....*).[61] Well, I shall clean it. Ah! how nicely it was painted with well-formed letters. The more I clean it the more bright it gets जह जह पमज्जामि तह तह उज्जलदरम् होइ (... *jaha jaha pamajjāmi taha taha ujjaladaraṃ hoi*).[62] Well, I shall clean it with water. Where is the water? Here it is in a spotless pond. Now like me the Lord also will be disappointed with regard to this pot अहं विअ सिवो वि दाव एदस्सिं मोदअ-मल्लए णिरासो होदु (*ahaṃ via sivo vi dāva edassiṃ modaamallae ṇirāso hodu*).[63]

In the Cārudatta (Act 1) Śakāra speaks Māgadhī as follows:

शकारः चिट्ठ चिट्ठ वशंचशेणिए! चिट्ठ किं याशि धावशि पधावशि पक्खलंती, शाहु प्पशीद ण मलीअशि चिट्ठ दावा कामेण शंपदि हि जज्झइ मे शलीलं, अंगाळमज्झपडिदे विअ चम्मखंडे॥

Śakāra: Wait, wait O Vasantasenā! Wait

Why are you going away, running, running fast, stumbling? O fair lady! no one is hitting you, wait a little. Now my body is burning with passion like a piece of leather fallen in fire.

A variety of metres is used in Bhāsa's plays. Keith has dealt with them in his *The Sanskrit Drama* (pp. 123f) and Devadhar in his *Bhāsanāṭakacakra*, Appendix A (pp. 561-7).

The Mṛcchakaṭika *of Śūdraka*

As stated already, the *Mṛcchakaṭika* (The Drama of the Clay-Cart) is a prototype of the *Cārudatta* of Bhāsa. The first four acts of the former are a reproduction with slight changes of the latter.[64] It is an important social drama which differs from others in several respects. In classical dramas, generally the hero is the ideal of virtue and bravery, always invincible, and the heroine a model of beauty and love who moves in aristocratic society. As a contrast to this our play-writer has chosen Cārudatta, a Brāhmaṇa by birth, whose ancestors had amassed a large amount of wealth but who by his extreme generosity has subsequently become penniless. Similarly, Vasantasenā is a courtesan by profession, though virtuous like any other lady of noble society. In this play, unlike others, the emphasis is laid on actual life—theft, chasing, intrigue, knavery, attempt to murder and so on. Since this play comes under the category of a *Prakaraṇa*,[65] whose plot is *laukika* (drawn from real life), it has depicted conditions of contemporary society, including the administration of the government and its laws and particularly the life of courtesans and their social status in ancient India.[66] Here we find the courtesan Vasantasenā, a highly cultured lady, loyal to her lover Cārudatta. She lives in luxury manner with her own elephants and an elephant driver and a retinue of attendants. She is highly respected and treated with reverence in society.

The combination of political and love intrigue makes the play valuable. The play gained popularity on account of its popular narrative theme compared to the stereotyped descriptions and characters of other Indian classical drama. It was held in high esteem and has been staged in European countries.[67] It appears that the old rhetoricians did not consider this work of high value and hence they do not quote illustrations from the *Mṛcchakaṭika*.[68] The most important aspect is the variety of Prakrits in this drama. Here we have 10 acts where there are 30 characters, each one having an individuality not found elsewhere. It has been edited by N.B. Godbole with the *Suvarṇālaṅkaraṇa* of Lallā Dīkshit and the *Vṛtti* or the *Vivṛti* by Pṛthvīdhara (Bombay, 1896).[69] According to Pṛthvīdhara, Śaurasenī is spoken by the following characters: the Sūtradhāra (after he changes into Prakrit from Sanskrit), the Naṭī—the wife of Sūtradhāra, Vasantasenā, her maid-servant Madanikā, her servant Karṇapūraka, her mother, Cārudatta's wife Dhūta, his maid-servant Radanikā, Śodhanaka (balif of the law-court) and Śreṣṭhī or guildsman. Āvantīkā is attributed to two policemen Vīraka and Candanaka, Prācyā is spoken by Vidūṣaka, Māgadhī is attributed to Saṃvāhaka (a professional shampoer, who takes to gambling and afterwards turns to be a Buddhist monk), Sthāvaraka (carriage driver of Śakāra), Kumbhīlaka (servant of Vasantasenā), Vardhamānaka (servant of Cārudatta) and Rohasena (son of Cārudatta).[70] Then Śākārī[71] is spoken by Śakāra[72] or Saṃsthānaka (the brother-in-law of the king and the villain of the Play); Cāṇḍālī[73] is spoken by the two Caṇḍālas and Ḍhakkī[74] by Māthura, the keeper of gambling-house and his fellow-player. Mahārāṣṭrī is not mentioned here. Ardhamāgadhī is not spoken by slaves, *rājaputras* or guildsmen (*śreṣṭhī*) as prescribed in the *Nāṭyaśāstra.* Sanskrit is assigned to the hero, the *Viṭa* (an attendant of Vasantasenā), Āryaka (the royal claimant of the throne of Ujjayanī) and Śarvilaka (the Brāhmaṇa thief who commits a robbery).

As Keith has pointed out, the variety of Prakrits found in the *Mṛcchakaṭika* seems to be intended to illustrate the precepts laid down in the *Nāṭyaśāstra.* As stated, the commentator Pṛthvīdhara has assigned Śaurasenī, Āvantī, Prācyā, Māgadhī, Śākārī, Cāṇḍālī and Ḍhakkī to different characters. This distribution of Prakrits agrees with that of the *Nāṭyaśāstra* which ignores Mahārāṣṭrī.

Pṛthvīdhara has mentioned Śaurasenī, Āvantī and Prācyā together; all of them are characterizɩ d by dental स. Āvantī is said to have स and र and be rich proverbial expressions.[75] The *Nāṭyaśāstra* (17, 48) ascribes Āvantī to *Dhūrtas* which is interpreted as to mean gamblers. Mārkaṇḍeya in his *Prākṛtasarvasva* (11.1), like Kramadīśvara, considers Āvantī a *bhāṣā* and calls it an admixture of Mahārāṣṭrī and Śaurasenī.[76] He rejects it as an independent dialect as it does not have any distinctive characteristics (लक्षणा करणात्). In the *Nāṭyaśāstra* (17.51) also Prācyā is ascribed to Vidūṣaka. Though it is mentioned here separately, it is nothing but Śaurasenī. Mārkaṇḍeya has remarked in his *Prākṛtasarvasva* (10.1) that it is derived from Śaurasenī (प्राच्यासिद्धिः शौरसेन्या 10.1). Śākārī and Cāṇḍālī are classed under Māgadhī as stated earlier. Puruṣottama in his *Prākṛtānuśāsana* (13-15) has treated them under Māgadhī. Ḍhakkī is kept apart and since very few illustrations are found of this dialect, it is difficult to ascertain its exact position. Thus we see that the subdivisions of the dialects noticed by later grammarians can be reduced to two principal dialects, Śaurasenī and Māgadhī.[77]

Here is an illustration of the Śaurasenī dialect spoken by Śodhanaka. He is talking to the judge (*adhikaraṇika*):

शोधनकः जं अज्जो आणवेदि। (इति निष्क्रम्य पुनः प्रविश्य। सास्त्रम्) अज्जा गदम्हि तहिं। राजा पालओ भणदि—जेण अत्थकल्लवत्तस्स कालणादो वसन्तसेणा बावादिदा तं ताइं ज्जेव आहरणाइं गले बंधिअ डिंडिमं ताडिअ दक्खिणमसाणं णइअ सूले भज्जेध त्ति जो कोवि अवरो एरिसं अकज्जं अणुचिट्ठदि सो एदिणा सणिआरदंडेण सासीअदि (Act 10)

Śodhanaka: As your Honour commands. (Exits and returns; with tears in eyes). Gentlemen! I had gone there. But King Pālaka has instructed—Tie those very ornaments around the neck of the person who killed Vasantasenā for the sake of a paltry sum of money; and, beating the drum, lead him to the southern crematorium and have him impaled there. And whosoever commits a similar crime, will meet the same punishment attended with great humiliation.

The author shows his skill in the handling of metre. For details see Keith, *The Sanskrit Drama*, p. 142; Kale, *The Mṛcchakaṭika of Śūdraka*, 1962, Appendix I, pp. 173-6.

The Classical Drama of Kālidās

The most famous Indian dramatist is Kālidāsa and his most famous drama is the *Abhjñānaśākuntala* (The Recognition of Śakuntalā). Kālidāsa is traditionally associated with Vikramāditya, the founder of the Vikrama era, which is one of the titles of Candragupta II (AD 376-415). This drama is considered the masterpiece of the poet. It was first known to Europe through the English translation of William Jones who translated it in 1789 and then it reached Germany through a German translation by G. Forester. After reading it Goethe wrote, 'In case you want to call both the heaven and the earth by a common name, I refer you to *Śakuntalā*.'

The legend that forms the theme of the drama is taken from the

Mahābhārata. The drama contains seven acts. King Duṣyanta goes chasing a deer in the neighbourhood of the forest hermitage where he falls in love with the foster-daughter of the sage Kaṇva, Śakuntalā. She was the illegitimate child of Menakā by the sage Viśvāmitra, whom she had seduced. Śakuntalā confesses her love for the king to two of her friends. The king gives her a ring and both are married by the *gandharva* rite. The king returns to his capital. In the meantime, the sage Kaṇva, who was absent, returns to the hermitage. He comes to know what had happened. He decides to send the now pregnant Śakuntalā to the king. Śakuntalā bids good-bye to her foster-father and her friends and sets out for the capital accompanied by two hermits and an elderly hermit-woman Gautamī. All of them reach the royal court of Duṣyanta. Śakuntala reminds the king of their love, but the king refuses to recognize her. Śakuntalā laments bitterly. She requests Mother Earth to open up so that she could enter her. At this time appears Menakā, her mother in heaven. She takes her daughter with her. At this time appears a fisherman with two policemen. A precious ring was noticed in the stomach of the fisherman's fish. King Duṣyanta recognized the ring which he had given to Śakuntalā. But she was no more present. Finally, once when the King was returning victorious from the battle, he saw a young boy. He was told that the boy was none other than Bharata, the son of Śakuntalā. The lovers were united and it was a happy end.

There is a saying about the drama: 'Among the different types of poetry, the drama is most beautiful; among the dramas the *Śakuntalā* is most beautiful, and in that the Act IV and there too the four stanzas are most beautiful (in which the sage Kaṇva bids farewell to his foster-daughter).'[78] The fourth Act is a model of tender sorrow when Śakuntalā bids farewell to the animals and plants of the hermitage, her foster-father and her dear friends. Even the sage Kaṇva loses control over himself, his heart is afflicted with melancholy, his eyes are filled with tears and his voice gets choked, thinking that his Śakuntalā was leaving for her husband's home. He seeks blessings from heaven and asks favour of the trees and animals of the hermitage. He gives expression to his feelings in the following words: 'She who never attempts to drink water first, when you have not drunk, and who although fond of ornaments never plucks a blossom out of affection for you, whose greatest holiday (highest joy) is the advent of the season of the first appearance of your bloom, that very Śakuntalā now departs for the house of her husband. Let you all permit to go.'[79]

Here the poet excels in depicting the emotions of love, portraying the separation and union of the hero and the heroine. Compared to other works of Kālidāsa this work is considered to be the best.

The next well known drama of Kālidāsa is the *Vikramorvaśī* (The Drama of Winning Urvaśī through Strength) which is also a romantic drama. Like Menakā the nymph Urvaśī falls in love not with a sage but with a mortal king Pururavas. It contains five Acts. The story is as old as the *Ṛgveda*. The nymph Urvaśī, after marrying Pururavas, remarked, 'You must embrace me three times, but never lie with me against my will. Moreover, I must never see you naked.' By a curse of Bharata Muni she has to come down to the mortal world. Indra, however, tones down the curse saying that she would live with Pururavas so long as he does not see the face of his son born from her. Here in the first three Acts Pururavas win the love of Urvaśī, the divine nymph. Then commences the Act IV which tells of misfortune. Urvaśī, angry at her husband for some trivial cause, enters the grove of Kumāra which was forbidden to a woman. As a result she was immediately transformed into a creeper. Now Pururavas overwhelmed with grief of her beloved's separation goes from place to place inquiring about her. He takes the cloud hovering over his head for a demon who has robbed her away. He meets the peacock, the cuckoo, the flamingo, the bee, the elephant,[80] the boar and the antelope, inquiring whether they had seen her. The sorrow of separation is so intense that he dances, sings, cries and ultimately faints. He implores the mountain and inquires whether he had seen her. But the mountain gives no reply except the echo 'seen'. He picks up a magic stone and extends it up to a creeper. He embraces it, and it turns into Urvaśī. Here begins Act V. The king passes quite some time in the happy association with his beloved. The magic stone is carried away by a vulture, which, however, is pierced with the arrow of a young archer. This archer happens to be a Kṣatriya boy, son of Urvaśī and Pururavas. The boy is brought before the king and it is proved that he was a son of Pururavas, born of Urvaśī in secret. Urvaśī is summoned, and admits her parentage. Pururavas is happy but she weeps as soon she would be obliged to part with his company, in accordance with the command of Indra. The king, overpowered with grief of separation from his beloved, is ready to abandon his realm in favour of his son, and to retire to the forest. This critical situation is saved by the appearance of sage Nārada. He comes with a news that a battle was being raged between the gods and the demons and that Indra needs the services of Pururavas army in his fight. In fight, the king is bestowed a boon that he would keep the company of his beloved till the end of his life.

Like the *Abhjñānaśakuntala*, this drama too has several times been translated into German and other European languages, and attempts have been made to adapt it for the stage.

It is a romantic drama in which mortal beings are in active and reciprocal communication with gods. It is full of poetic imagination, depicting tender feelings related to intensity of love. However, Keith is critical about it. According to him, the heroine's love is selfish and the hero is diminished to a diminutive stature in comparison. He lacks in self-restraint and manliness in his opinion. The minor characters also according to him are not handled with great success.[81]

The *Mālavikāgnimitra* (The Drama of Mālavikā and Agnimitra) is the third extant drama of the poet. Here is reflected life at court and harem in the mediaeval period. In this comedy we find more humour, wit and joyousness compared to other two serious dramas. The play is performed at a spring festival at Ujjayini in five acts. It depicts a love drama of the heroine Mālavikā, a Vidarbha princess, and King Agnimitra of Śunga dynasty. Here Mālavikā is being given training in the art of dancing. We are told about the importance of this art:

A harmless sacrifice is the dance,
Enjoyable to the eye: so say the wise:
God Śiva, who has united into one
His own body with that of his consort Umā;
He has divided it into two.
So he dances both violently and calmly.
At the time he dances, there generate
From his dance the manifold activities
In the world: the bliss, the passion, the evil;
The three aspects of the spirit;

And there in the dance

Becomes manifest the singular means of rejoicing,
For all the people of different tastes and inclinations:
What is that? That is nothing but dance.[82]

This drama has also several times been translated into German and other European languages and adapted for German stage.

Here are a few illustrations of Prakrit dialects used in the *Abhijnānaśākuntala*:

The Vidūṣaka speaks in *Śaurasenī*:

विदूषक: एव्वं राअकज्जाणि उज्झिअ एआरिसे आउलप्पदेसे वणचरवुत्तिणा तुए होदव्वं। जं सच्चं पच्चहं सावदसमुच्छारणेहिं संखोहिअ संधिवंधाणं मम गत्ताणं अणीसो ह्मि संवुत्तो। ता पसीद मे एक्काहंपि दाव विस्समी-अदु।

Vudusaka: 'In this way, having abandoned royal duties, you are staying like a forest-dweller in this purturbed region. It is a fact that every day pursuing wild animals, the tissues of my joints are shaken, therefore I have lost control over my body. So kindly be pleased to permit me to rest all by myself. (Act II)

Anusūyā is talking to Śakuntalā, the heroine in *Māgadhī*:

अनसूया: हला सउंदले, अणब्भन्तरा क्खु अम्हे, मदणगदस्स वुत्तंतस्स। किंदु जादिसी इतिहासणिबंधेसु कामअमाणाणं अवस्था सुणीअदि तादिसी ते पेक्खामि।
कहेहि। किं णिमित्तं दे संदावो। विआरं क्खु परमत्थदो अजाणिअ अणारंभो पडिआरस्स।

Anasūyā: O Śakuntale! we are ignorant of the state of mind of those afflicted with the God of Love. But I see your similar state of mind as stated in the legendary compositions. Tell me why you are feeling agitated. Without knowing sickness in reality, it is not possible to have its remedy. (Act III)

Śakuntalā recites in *Mahārāṣṭrī*:

शकुन्तला (वाचयति):
तुज्झ ण जाणे हिअअं मम उण कामो दिवापि रत्तिंपि।
णिग्घिण तवइ बलीअं तुइ वुत्तमणोरहाइ अंगाइं॥

I do not know about you but my heart burns day and night with love. This cruel love's desired object concentrated in you, torments my body. (Act III)

We have seen the forms of Śaurasenī, Māgadhī and Ardhamāgadhī in Aśvaghoṣa's plays which are much older than the forms prescribed by the later grammarians. The Ardhamāgadhī we come across here is different from the Ardhamāgadhī of the Śvetāmbara canonical literature. Similar was the case with Śaurasenī which is different from the dialect used in the Digambara canonical literature. Old Prakrit was gradually changing to Mahārāṣṭrī Prakrit of Hāla's *Sattasaī*, also giving rise to Māgadhī and Śaurasenī of Aśvaghoṣa, Bhāsa and Kālidāsa.

As we have seen, the Ardhamāgadhī dialect is mentioned alongside Māgadhī, Āvantī, Prācyā, Śaurasenī, Bāhlīkā and Dākṣiṇātyā as one of the *bhāṣas*, but again, at another place (17.50) and also in the *Sāhityadarpaṇa* (VI.160, p. 404), it is stated that Ardhamāgadhī is used in drama as the language of menials, *rajāputras* and bankers (चेटानां राजपुत्राणां श्रेष्ठिनां अर्धमागधी). But this dialect is not found in extant Sanskrit drama. As stated already, Mārkaṇḍeya in his *Prākṛtasarvasva* has not accepted Ardhamāgadhī as an independent dialect. In the dramas of Kālidāsa the Prakrits are found in their normal state, Śauraseni for prose and Mahārāṣṭrī for poetry. Here the forms of Prakrits are more or less stereotyped, based on the rules of grammar laid down by Vararuci. In the *Mṛcchakaṭika* of Śūdraka, for example, 11 character speaks Śaurasenī, 5 Māgadhī; Avantikā, Prācyā, Śākārī, Cāṇḍālī and Ḍhakkī are spoken by others; Sanskrit is used only by 6 characters. Out of 377 Sanskrit *ślokas* it contains 99 Prakrit *gāthās*. Needless to say that such a variety of Prakrit dialects is not seen in the later drama of Kālidāsa and others. In these dramas the Māgadhī, the Śaurasenī and the Mahārāṣṭrī speeches dominate. For instance, the police officers and the fisherman in *Śakuntalā* speak Māgadhī; but the king's brother-in-law, who is in-charge of the police and is a faint echo of Śakāra, does not speak in the extant form of the drama, either Śākārī or Māgadhī or Dākṣiṇātyā, but simply Śaurasenī.[83]

Other Dramatists

King Śrīharṣa or Harṣadeva is credited with the authorship of *Ratnāvali, Priyadarśikā* and *Nāgānanda* (The Joy of the Serpents). The first two belong to the category of *Nāṭikā*. Śrīharṣa was the king of Sthāṇīśvara and Kānyakubja and reigned from AD 606 to 648. Compared to early Indian kings, his reign is well documented. The famous poet Bāṇa, patronized by him, has left an interesting account of the event leading to his rise to power. The Chinese pilgrim, Hsün Tsang, who has left a very valuable account of India, was present in India during his reign. The first two dramas of Śrīharṣa are named after their heroines, each having four acts. Their hero is the Udayana, the king of Vatsa, whom Bhāsa has already celebrated in his drama. In the *Ratnāvali* at the time of celebrating the spring-festival in honour of the god of love, the girls sing, dance and are occupied in merry-making. This drama has found favour with the text-books on drama which discuss the technical rules. The *Priyadarśikā* depicts a love story between king Udayana and the princess Āraṇyikā, who is no one else than Priyadarśikā, the daughter of Ḍṛḍhavarman. Here the author introduces a play within a play which is not found in any other drama. A play is arranged to be performed for the queen, in which the marriage of Udayana and Vāsavadattā (the queen) is to be shown. The role of the queen is to be played by Āraṇyikā and that of the king by Manoramā, a female friend of Āraṇyikā. Here is a love-song sung by Āranyikā in Mahārāṣṭrī:

घणबंधणसंरुद्धं गअणं दट्ठूण माणसं एदुं।
अहिलसइ राजहंसो दइअं घेत्तूण अप्पणो वसइं॥

Having noticed the sky captivated by the bond of clouds, the royal swan wishes to take her beloved to its residence, the *Mānasarovara* lake.

The *Nāgānanda* is a *nāṭaka* in five acts which is performed at the festival of Indra. It is a dramatization of a Buddhist legend, the self-sacrifice of Jīmutavāhana, a *vidyādhara* prince, who falls in love with Malayavatī, the handsome daughter of the Siddha king. After the solemnization of the marriage of the hero and the heroine, a violent scene of drinking is introduced. A drunken courtier *Viṭa* enters in a jester-like dress, accompanied by a servant, carrying a cask of wine on his shoulder. He shouts loudly:

णिच्चं जो पिबइ सुरां पिआसंगमं च जो कुणइ।
महदे दो अभिदैवा बलदेवो कामदेवो अ॥

There are only two faultless gods: the Baladeva, who always drink only wine, and the second is Kāmadeva, who unites a man with his beloved.

In the dramas of Śrīharṣa the male characters are few, and the females and the Vidūṣaka speak in Prakrit. Generally, the medium of prose is Śaurasenī and that of poetry Mahārāṣṭrī. However, in the *Nāgānanda* Māgadhī is spoken by Kiṅkara. He commands Śaṅkhacūḍa, the Nāga, to don red garments and sit on a slaughter-house stone so that the Garuḍa will eat him detecting him by his garments (एदं लत्तसुअजुअलं पलिहाय आलुह वज्झसिलं जेण तुमं लत्तंसुअ चिण्णोबलक्खिदं गरूडो गेण्हिअ आहालं करिस्सति।). There is nothing new in the Prakrits of the dramas except that the author has followed the rules of grammar laid down by grammarians.

Bhavabhūti, whose to name is mentioned as a great dramatist after Kālidāsa, belongs to around AD 700. He lived in the court of Yaśovarman of Kannauja, and composed three plays, the *Mahāvīracarita* (The Biography of the Great Hero), the *Mālatīmādhava* (The Drama of Mālatī and Mādhava) and the *Uttararāmacarita* (The Second of the Biography of Rāma). All were staged at the time of the feast of God Kālapriyanātha, identified with Mahākāla of Ujjayinī.

The *Mahāvīracarita*, containing seven acts, deals with the story of Rāma as described in the *Rāmāyaṇa*, using dialogues narrating the main events. The *Mālatīmādhava* containing ten acts, describes a love story between Mālatī, daughter of Bhūrivasu, the minister of the king of Padmāvatī, and Mādhava, son of Devarāta, minister of the king of Vidarbha. The *Uttararāmacarita* which contains seven acts, narrates the story of Sītā, discarded by Rāma, and corresponds to the *Uttarakāṇḍa* of the *Rāmāyaṇa*. Out of these dramas, the first is the hero-drama (*vīrarasa-pradhāna*), the second love-drama (*śṛṅgārarasa-pradhāna*) and third is full of pathos (*karuṇarasa-pradhāna*). It is stated that Bhavabhūti did not come into prominence for his skill in dramatic technique, but for his mastery in the use of Sanskrit language. He has used long compounds in prose dialogue which go to prove that his poems were meant more for reading rather than for staging. As far as the Prakrits are concerned, he has confined himself to the Śaurasenī dialect on the model of his Sanskrit style. At this time the Prakrit dialects were losing their importance and were being mechanically transferred from Sanskrit keeping in mind the rules laid down by Vararuci.

Viśākhadatta (ninth century) is another dramatist, the author of the *Mudrārākṣasa* (The Minister's Signet Ring). It deals with the schemes of the wily Cāṇakya to foil the plots of Rākṣasa, the minister of the last of the Nandas, and to place Candragupta Maurya on the throne. It is a drama of political intrigue and there is no talk of love in the whole book. There is only a single female and she has been assigned a secondary role. Importance is given to polity or *nīti* which may be called the 'heroine' of the drama. The author is well-versed in stage-technique (*nāṭyaśāstra*) as well as the science of polity (*Nītiśāstra*); according to him, both require intelligence. The Sanskrit of the play is classical. Besides Śaurasenī and Mahārāṣṭrī, Māgadhī is also used here; the latter is spoken by the Jain monks, Siddhārthaka and Samiddhārthaka, who are disguised as Caṇḍālas, and a servant and an envoy. As Keith has pointed out, there appear traces of Śaurasenī verses as for persons who use Śaurasenī, it is not necessary to sing in Mahārāṣṭrī; here only male characters use Śaurasenī verses.[84] Bhaṭṭa-Nārāyaṇa is another dramatist whose *Veṇīsaṃhāra* (The Drama of Binding the Lock) has been quoted by a number of rhetoricians in their manuals. Vāmana and Ānandavardhana have cited his works, therefore he belongs to the period of AD 800. The plot of the drama is borrowed from the epic of the *Mahābhārata*. In the gambling scene of the epic Draupadī is being dragged by her hair before the assembly of Duryodhana, one of the Kauravas. She vows never to braid her hair till the humiliation suffered by her is avenged. At this time Bhīma comes to her rescue taking a vow that he will fasten her hair with hands stained with the blood of Duryodhana. Here most of the events occurred in the war are just narrated in the *kāvya*-style. An excess of details of narrative diminish the interest of the play. The style is clear and not lacking in force or dignity. Its language has been more popular than the subject-matter. Regarding Prakrit, mainly Śaurasenī dialect is used, except the speeches of the Rākṣasa and his wife, who speak Māgadhī in the beginning of Act III. Keith has pointed out two versions of this play, the Bengali version as opposed to the Devanāgarī version which has systematically re-written the Prakrit into Śaurasenī.[85]

After Bhavabhūti the quality of Sanskrit drama went on declining. Bhaṭṭa Nārāyaṇa, Murāri and Rājaśekhara and others continued writing plays, but they were more of literary type and were used for reading purposes rather than staging.

Decadence of Sanskrit Drama and Decline of Prakrit Drama

The use of Sanskrit along with the various Prakrit dialects must be assigned to circumstances in which Sanskrit drama grew. These dramas reflect the linguistic conditions of the society in which the early play writers lived.

In order to make Sanskrit drama popular, different characters speaking different types of Prakrit were introduced. This divergence of dialects certainly marks the distinction of men and women and high and low but it does not go beyond that. In fact Sanskrit drama by the tenth century was in a state of decadence. It remained confined to a limited section who had sufficient knowledge to comprehend songs, dances, music and all that which was to be conveyed by the drama. As a result, gradually the gulf between the languages of the drama and that of real life went on widening and the distinction of class implied in the distinction of Prakrit dialects came to be a meaningless convention. Formerly, at the time of Bhāsa and Kālidāsa there was not much difficulty in following the main features of the drama, but now the use of Prakrit dialects suffered to a great extent and they were removed to an inferior position. We notice that

Bhavabhūti never uses Prakrit verse in his dramas, he has confined himself to the use of Śaurasenī, which he employs on the ideal of Sanskrit. Then, Bhaṭṭanārāyaṇa in his *Veṇīsaṃhāra* never uses more forms of Prakrit than he can help. In some works like the *Mahānāṭaka* written mainly in verse, with little prose, there is no Prakrit at all. Sanskrit, on the other hand, with its learned possibilities, became the normal but not natural medium. It was more difficult, though richer and more accommodating to stylistic extravagances. It was more difficult to compose drama in Sanskrit with Prakrit dialects in the tenth century than in the fourth, the reason being that the regional languages were gradually assuming literary form. The scarcity of audience also was responsible for decadence of Sanskrit dramas. As pointed out earlier, as there were no fixed rules for the guidance of Prakrit grammarians, there was no uniformity in the use of Prakrit dialects. The rules laid down in the *Nāṭyaśāstra* did not act as a guideline to the dramatists. Mahārāṣṭrī is unknown to the *Nāṭyaśāstra*, but Dhanañjaya in his *Daśarupa* assigns it to the verses used in a drama, whereas Viśvanātha in his *Sāhityadarpaṇa* confines it to the verses of women. Earlier, Aśvaghoṣa and Bhāsa have no clear evidence of Mahārāṣṭrī dialect at all. In this connection, Pischel has discussed the language of the *Lalitavigraharājanāṭaka* (of poet Somadeva) composed for the glorification of Vigraharāja IV of Ajmer. The fragments of this drama are found in two basalt-plates, discovered in a mosque in Ajmer. In these plates (published by Kielhorn, *IA* XX, 201ff) occur Mahārāṣṭrī, Śaurasenī and Māgadhī dialects; their forms agree with the rules of Hemacandra's Prakrit grammar. 'But', observes Pischel, 'Hemacandra was hardly the authority whose views were honoured by Somadeva.' He adds further, 'Hemacandra prescribes (4.271) the absolutive in -दूण in Śaurasenī, Somadeva has the Mahārāṣṭrī form in -ऊण, Hemacandra recognizes टयेव, whereas Somadeva has the Mahārāṣṭrī ज्जेव; in consonant groups in Māgadhī Somadeva has श्, whereas Hemacandra (4, 289) prescribes स्; the former lays down श्त for र्थ, against स्त of Hemacandra (4, 296, 297).' In his concluding remarks, he says, 'Hence it follows that the absolutive in -ऊण may be an error committed by Somadeva himself; even -दूण may be wrong (584); स्त for र्थ as well may be an error committed in course of transmission inasmuch as in 566, 9 we find यहस्तम्-यथार्थ. But as regards श्ंक् for हक्, स्क could hardly, with Konow, be considered to be a slip on the part of a mason. . . . The presence of the absolutive in -ऊण and the passive Śaurasenī -इज्ज and the Māgadhī इय्य may be a mistake committed by the author himself.'

We notice that later poets often mix up the Prakrit dialects with one another. Even the grammarians have their differences with regard to assigning particular dialects to particular words. Mārkaṇḍeya (17th century) for example, is against recognizing लट्ठि to be Śaurasenī (यष्ट्यां लश्च न स्यात्) but Hemacandra in his Prakrit grammar (1.247) sanctions such a form for Śaurasenī. Rājaśekhara, who boasts of his learning and traces his poetic descent from Vālmīki, 'cannot distinguish accurately Śaurasenī and Mahārāṣṭrī in his drama; in the former we find such forms as लट्ठि for यष्टि, अम्मि in the locative and हिंतो in the ablative singular of अ-stems, and एस for the pronoun....Forms like ढिल्ल equivalent to शिथिल in the Karpūramañjarī show how far the vernaculars had advanced beyond the Prakrits of drama.'[86] It should be noted that both Sanskrit and Prakrit were turning into utterly dead languages and it was least surprising that poets like Rājaśekhara had to learn them putting in great labour. Prakrit which was used in the form of spoken dialects, had taken a literary form. As a result poets like Rāmapāṇivāda, Rudradāsa and others started composing their works after making a study of Vararuci's and Trivikrama's works on grammar. Even to explain the Prakrit passages to the readers, they were rendered into Sanskrit *chāyā* (translation). This practice was normal even in the old manuscripts according to Keith. Rājaśekhara had to explain the Prakrit passages of his *Bālarāmāyaṇa* with the help of Sanskrit *chāyā* which indicates that as early as 900 readers were not able to understand Prakrit without Sanskrit explanation.[87]

Saṭṭaka in Prakrit

Saṭṭaka and *Nāṭikā* are not mentioned in the *Nāṭyaśāstra*, and should be taken as a later development. Perhaps the *Saṭṭaka* came into being with the poet Rājaśekhara. The *Saṭṭaka* differs from *Nāṭikā* in the sense that the former is entirely written in Prakrit, it has no introductory scenes of any kind and the acts are called *Javanaikāntara*. Abhinavagupta in his commentary on the *Nāṭyaśāstra* (*GOS*, Baroda, 1934, Vol. II, p. 407) considers *Saṭṭaka* like a *Nāṭikā*. Hemacandra in his *Kāvyānuśāsana* has stated: 'A *Saṭṭaka* has no introductory scenes like *viṣkambha* and *praveṣaka*, is composed only in one language, not in two, Sanskrit and Prakrit, like a *Nāṭikā*.'[88] According to Śāradātanaya

(1175-1250), *Saṭṭaka* is a type of *Nāṭikā* based on dance; it contains the *Kaiśikī* (graceful manner) and the *Bhāratī vṛttis* (verbal manner) and has no *raudra rasa* (sentiment of fury) and *Sandhi* (contraction). Here we have *Yavanikāntara* instead of *Aṅka*; it is devoid of *chādana* (ignoring offences if useful for one's aims), *skhalna* (blundering) *bhrānti* (confusion) and *nihnava* (obscurity).[89] In the opinion of Viśvanātha, a *Saṭṭaka* is composed completely in Prakrit and it has a prominence of *adbhuta rasa* (sentiment of wonder).[90] Rājaśekhara in his *Karpūramañjarī* (1.6) has stated that a *Saṭṭaka* is represented by a dance and is devoid of *viṣkambhka* and *praveśaka.*[91] He has also called it *prākṛta-bandha* or composed in Prakrit.

The *Karpūramañjarī*, the *Vilāsavatī*, the *Candalehā*, the *Ānanda-sundarī* and the *Siṅgāramanjarī* are the five *Saṭṭakas*, out of which the first is considered the best; the second is not available.

Rājaśekhara, the author of the *Karpūramañjarī*, belonged to a Mahārāṣṭra Kṣatriya family of the Yāyāvaras. He claimed descent from Rāma, he married Avantīsundarī of the Cāhamāna family, a talented wife at whose instance the play was produced and staged for the first time. 'He has a considerable vocabulary of fine words and a fund of quaint conceits both in Sanskrit and Prakrit, which bear out his boast that he is master of languages.'[92] He has also ability to handle elaborate meters in Sanskrit and Prakrit. His *Karpūramañjarī* in all contains 144 Prakrit stanzas in which 17 varieties of metre have been employed; his favourite metres being the Śārdūlavikrīḍita, the Sragdharā, and the Vasantatilakā. He calls himself as an expert in every kind of language (*sarvabhāṣā-catura*) and has a mastery over his language. According to him, the question is of expression and not of the language (*uttiviseso kavvaṃ*).[93] Praising the Prakrit dialect he has stated:

परुसा सक्कअवंधा पाउअवंधो वि होई सुकुमारो।
पुरिसमहिलाणं जेत्तिअमिहंतरं तेत्तिअ मिमाणं॥

'The Prakrit composition is smooth, while the Sanskrit is harsh; the difference between the two is as much as between men and women.'[94] Here we have elaborate descriptions of the spring, the dawn, midday, sunset, the pleasure of the harem, the games, the swing and so on. In the opinion of Keith, 'If poetry consisted merely of harmonious sound, he must be ranked high as a poet.'[95] Rājaśekhara has used a number of proverbs in his *Saṭṭaka.*[96] He has mentioned the names of Hariuḍḍha, Nandiuḍḍha, Poṭṭisa, Hāla and others as best of the poets whose stanzas have been quoted in the *Gāthāsaptaśatī* of Hāla. He has used certain words and expressions in his text which are rarely found elsewhere.[97] As Pischel has pointed out, certain poets did not know how to distinguish between two different dialects and in this connection he has quoted the names of Somadeva, the author of the *Lalitavigraharāja Nāṭaka* and Rājaśekhara. He has pointed out that in the case of the latter, the dialects have been mixed up in certain cases.[98]

The *Vilāsavatī* is another *Saṭṭaka* composed by Mārkaṇḍeya (seventeenth century) which is unfortunately not extant. He has quoted a stanza from this work in his book of grammar.[99] Viśvanātha (fourteenth century) in his *Sāhityadarpaṇa* VI. 277-9 has referred to a *nāṭya rāsaka*, known as *Vilāsavatī*. It contained one act and was accompanied by many *tālas* (beating time) and *layas* (union of song, dance and instrumental music). The *Candalehā* was written by Rudradāsa, pupil of Rudra and Śrīkaṇṭha. He was a resident of Calicut and wrote his work round about 1660. The work contains 4 *Yavanikāntaras* describing the love story of Mānaveda and Candralekhā. The sentiment of love is prominent here. It is similar to the *Karpūramañjarī* in style. Like other *Saṭṭakas* it is also influenced by Sanskrit and is composed on the basis of rules of grammar laid down by Vararuci. The *Ānandasundarī* was composed by Ghanaśyāma (AD 1700) of Maharashtra. He was appointed a minister of Tukkoji I of Tanjore. He was known as *Mahārāṣṭra-cūḍāmaṇi* (The Crown of Maharashtra) and *Sarvabhāṣā-kavi* (Poet of all Languages); also known as *Kaṇṭhīrava*. As Rājaśekhara called himself the third incarnation of Vālmīki so also Ghanaśyāma calls himself the incarnation of Goddess Sarasvatī. He was the author of 64 Sanskrit, 20 Prakrit and 20 works of Bhāsa on drama, poetry, *campu*, grammar, rhetorics, philosophy, etc. He has composed three *Saṭṭakas*, *Baikuṇṭhacarita*, *Ānandasundarī* and one more, of which only the *Ānandasundarī* is available. More or less it is an original drama, not based on the *Karpūramañjarī*. The author has incorporated the *garbha-nāṭaka* (Embryo Drama) in his work, otherwise according to him it would have become ridiculous in the eyes of the audience. The drama consists of 4 *Javanikāntaras*. As during this time Prakrit was no more a spoken dialect, our author like Pāṇivāda, Rudradāsa and others composed his work after mastering the works on Prakrit grammar. A number of Marathi words and expressions also have been used by the author in his composition. Bhaṭṭanātha has written commentary on this *Saṭṭaka.* The *Siṅgāramañjarī* is still another *Saṭṭaka* by Viśveśvara, a resident of Almorah. He belongs to the first quarter of the eighteenth century. In his young age he composed a number of works, amongst which the *nāṭikā* known as *Navamālikā* and the *Saṭṭaka Śṛṅgāramañjarī* are worthy to note. On the basis of the manuscript of this *Saṭṭaka,* A.N. Upadhye, in his learned introduction of the *Candalehā* has presented the story of this work. There is much similarity between the descriptions and other literary forms and expressions between Rājaśekhara's *Karpūramañjarī* and the present work. Both have followed the *Vāsavadattā* of Bhāsa, the *Mālavikāgnimitra* of Kālidāsa and the *Ratnāvali* and *Priyadarśikā* of Śrīharṣa. The *Rambhāmañjarī* was composed by Nayanacandra, the pupil of Prasannacandra. He was formerly a follower of Viṣṇu but later was converted to Jainism. He was a poet in six languages (*ṣaḍbhāṣā*) and clever in entertaining kings. He himself has claimed to as talented as Śrīharṣa and the poet Amaracandra. He considers his work better than the *Karpūramañjarī,* saying that it contains elegance like the works of the poet Amaracandra and as beautiful in indirect speech (*vakrimā*) as the works of Śrīharṣa. But as a matter of fact, in his numerous descriptions he has followed only the *Karpūramañjarī.* This work has 3 *Javanikāntaras* in which the author has also used Sanskrit contrary to convention. He belongs to the fourteenth century. He has also composed the *Hammīra mahākāvya* and other Jain works. This work is important as it contains the forms of literary Marathi.[100] As we have already noted Prakrit remained no more a spoken dialect and playwrights had to depend on the rules of Prakrit grammar laid down by Prakrit grammarians. Consequently the Prakrit used in Sanskrit plays turned to be artificial which needed labour on the part of writers. Consequently the gulf between the popular language and those of learning, went on widening. So the writing of Prakrit *Saṭṭakas* became an exacting task for an average poet.

NOTES

1. नानाभावोपसंपन्नं नानावस्थान्तरात्मकम्।
   लोकानुवृत्तकरणं नाट्यमेतन्मया कृतम्॥ *Nāṭyaśāstra,* 1.111.
2. महानयं प्रयोगस्य समयः समुपस्थितः।
   अयं ध्वजमहः श्रीमान् महेन्द्रस्य प्रवर्तते॥

Read *Indra dhvaja-sampad* (Glory of Indra's Banner), *Bṛh Saṃ* (43; 57) op. cit., 1.54.

3. उत्तमाधममध्यानां नराणां कर्मसंश्रयम्।
हितोपदेशजननं धृतिक्रीडासुखादिकृत्॥ op. cit., 1-112 (translation by M. Ghosh).
4. धर्मोऽधर्मप्रवृत्तानां कामः कामोपसेविनाम्।
निग्रहो दुर्विनीतानां विनीतानां दमक्रिया॥
क्लीवानां धार्ष्ट्यकरणमुत्साहः शूरमानिनाम्।
अबुधानां विबोधश्च वैदुस्यं वैदुषामपि॥ op. cit., 108-9 (translation by M. Ghosh).
5. दुःखार्त्तानां श्रमार्तानां शोकार्तानां तपस्विनाम्।
विश्रामजननं लोके नाट्यमेतद्भविष्यति॥ 1.114
धर्म्यं यशस्यमायुष्यं हितं बुद्धिविवर्धनम्।
लोकोपदेशजननं नाट्यमेतद्भविष्यति॥ 1.115 (translation by M. Ghosh, *The Nāṭyaśāstra Translation*, Vol. I, Chapter I, Calcutta, 1967).
6. न तज्ज्ञानं न तच्छिल्पं न सा विद्या न सा कला।
न स योगो न तत्कर्म नाट्येऽस्मिन् यन्नदृश्यते॥ 1.116
7. ऐश्वर्येण प्रमत्तस्य दारिद्येण प्लुतस्यच।
उत्तमस्यापि पठतः प्राकृतं संप्रयोजयेत्॥ 17.33
8. Ghosh further explains as 'persons in disguise' of different kinds of professional and religious mendicants, etc. He has quoted examples: Indra in the guise of a Brhāmaṇa speaks Prakrit in the *Karṇabhāra* drama ascribed to Bhāsa. Then Virādhagupta in the *Mudrārākṣasa* (II) who assumes the guise of a snake-charmer, is another example. So also are Yaugandharāyana and Rumaṇvān in the *Pratijñāyaugandharāyaṇa* (III) ascribed to Bhāsa.
9. In support, Ghosh gives the following quotation from the *Avimāraka* (V) ascribed to Bhāsa: जदि वत्थं अवणेमि समणओ होमि, i.e. 'if I remove clothes I turn into a Śramaṇa'.
10. *Cakracaras* are mentioned in Jain literature. They are mentioned along with *Pāṇḍuraṅga, Taccannika* (Buddhist) and *Boḍiya* (Digambara Jain) monks in the *Ogha Nir*, 82ff, p. 74 and the *Bṛh Bhā* 1.2627. We are told that the sight of a *Cakracara* ascetic foretold roaming about at random. In the commentary of the *Bṛh Bhā* (1.2886) it is stated that while going on a begging tour they used to carry a *sikkaka*, a loop or swing suspended on a chord. Ghosh, however, has called him a juggler. The pertinent verse in the *Nāṭyaśāstra* is:

    व्याजलिङ्गः; प्रतिष्ठानां श्रमणानां तपस्विनाम्।
    भिक्षुचक्रचराणाञ्च प्राकृतं संप्रयोजयेत्॥ 17-34

11. Here M.M. Ghosh has noted the readings from the Baroda edition of the *Nāṭyaśāstra* as follows: 'Similarly Prakrit should be assigned to Śaiva teachers, lunatics, children, persons possessed of spirits of lower order, women, persons of low birth and hermaphrodites.' (B.XVII.37).

12. बाले ग्रहोपसृष्टे च स्त्रीणां स्त्रीप्रकृतौ तथा।
नीचे मत्ते सलिङ्गे च प्राकृतं पाठ्यमिष्यते॥ 18.35
13. परिव्राण्मुनि शाक्येषु चौक्षेषु श्रोत्रियेषु च।
द्विजा ये चैव लिङ्गस्थाः संस्कृतं तेषु योजयेत्॥ 18.36
14. According to Abhinavagupta's commentary on the *Nāṭyaśāstra*, *Āryabhāṣā* means a language in which Vedic words prevail, M.M. Ghosh, Notes, XVIII.26. The *Atibhāṣā* and *Āryabhāṣā* are possibly dialects of pure Indo-Āryan speech. Bhoja in his *Śṛṅgāraprakāśa* (ed. V. Raghavan, pp. 191ff) takes *atibhāṣā*, *Āryabhāṣā* and *Jātibhāṣās* as *śrauta* (Vedic), *ārṣa* (purāṇik) and *laukika* (literary) speeches respectively, Ghosh, Notes, XVIII.27.
15. In the *Rasārṇavasudhākara* (I.297; ed. *TSS*, 1916), they are enumerated as Śabara, Dramiḷa, Āndhraja, Śakāra, Ābhīra, Caṇḍāla, Vanecara, Keith, *The Sanskrit Drama*, 337n.
16. M.M. Ghosh, *The Nāṭyaśāstra*, p. 48.
17. Ibid., p. 337n.
18. शाबर्यामेवौड्रीयोग्गत्तद्देश्यशौरसेन्यादेः (15.9)
यथाः देवजसोआणंदण कर मइ करुणालेश।
एतिके जमउ अच्छउ इ पिहइ सव्व किलेश॥
19. K.C. Acharya has observed: 'Śabara is even now spoken by some hill tribes in South Orissa. The great Jagannātha cult of Orissa is known to have partly owed its origin to ancient Śabara civilization that was prevalent in the country once upon a time', *Mārkaṇḍeya's Prākṛtasarvasva*, p. 91.
20. प्रयुज्यते नाटकादौ द्यूतादि-व्यवहारिभिः।
वणिग्भिर्हीनदेहैश्च तदाहुष्टक्कभाषितम्॥ *Prākṛta-sarvasva*, 16.1
21. टक्कदेशीय-भाषायां टश्यते द्राविडी तथा।
तत्र चायं विशेषोऽस्ति द्राविडीराहता परं॥ *Prākṛta-sarvasva*, 16.2.
22. Ibid., 16.2.
23. न हि रसाहते कश्चिदव्यर्थः प्रवर्तते। को वा दृष्टान्त इति चेत् उच्यते यथा नानाव्यञ्जनौषधिद्रव्यसंयोगाद्रसनिष्पत्तिः तथा नानाभावोपगमाद्रसनिष्पत्तिः। *Nāṭyaśāstra*, VI, p. 82.
24. *The Sanskrit Drama*, p. 276.
25. Op. cit.
26. धीरोद्धते धीरललिते, धीरोदात्ते तथैव च।
धीरप्रशान्ते च तथा पाठ्यं योज्यं तु संस्कृतम्॥ *Nāṭyaśāstra*, 17.31.
27. Ibid., 280.
28. Ed. Lüders, Berlin, 1911.
29. Winternitz, *A History of Indian Literature*, Vol. III, Pt. I, p. 223.
30. Keith, ibid., 75.
31. Ibid., pp. 86f.
32. Ibid., pp. 85f.
33. Ibid., p. 87.
34. C.R. Deodhara has edited the following plays of Bhāsa in the Poona Oriental Series, 1937: स्वप्नवासवदत्ता, प्रतिज्ञायौगन्धरायण, अविमारक, चारुदत्त, प्रतिमानाटक, अभिषेकनाटक, मध्यमव्यायोग, पञ्चरात्र, दूतवाक्य, दूतघटोत्कच, कर्णभार, उरूभङ्ग; बालचरित.

35. भासनाटकचक्रेऽपि च्छेकैः क्षिप्ते परीक्षितुम्।
स्वप्नवासवदत्तस्य दाहकोऽभून्न पावकः॥ *Sūktimuktāvali* (p. 92).
Keith in *The Sanskrit Drama* (p. 92) refers to another reason. He writes, 'The play itself contains a fire, which was feigned by the minister to permit the possibility of the king's new marriage, and it is only appropriate that, as that fire could not burn the queen, so the fire which tried the play was unable to prevail against it.'
36. However, Keith has pointed out how the plot of the drama is open to criticism, ibid., p. 113.
37. इमां सागरपर्यन्तां हिमवद्विन्ध्यकुण्डलाम्।
महीमेकातपत्राङ्कां राजसिंहः प्रशास्तु नः॥
(Translation after Winternitz, *A History of Indian Literature,* Vol. III, Pt. I, p. 243.)
38. यदि तां चैव तां चैव तां चैवायतलोचनाम्।
नाहरामि नृपं चैव नास्मि यौगन्धरायणः॥
This verse is quoted in the *Āva Cū*, p. 162, also Somaprabhasūri, *Kumārapāla,* I, p. 81.
39. See also the *Āvasyaka-cūrni,* pp. 161f; the *Kathā-Saritsāgara,* II. 12-14); *Kumarapālapratibodha,* pp. 76-83.
40. See Keith, *The Sanskrit Drama,* p. 102.
41. When in the second act the Ceṭī asks the Vidūṣaka to read the letter inscribed on the seal, he replies, 'O Lady, this letter is not found in my book!' (भोदि, एदं अक्खरं मम पुत्थए णत्थि)
42. Viduṣaka is talking to Nalinikā in the 5th Act: जण्णोपवीदेण बम्हणो चीवरेण रत्तपडो। जदि वत्थं अवणेमि समणओ होमि।
43. A dialogue is recorded between Nalinikā and Vidūṣaka in the 5th Act:
44. गोष्ठीषु हास्यः समरेषु योधः शोके गरुः साहसिकः परेषु।
महोत्सवो मे हृदि किं प्रलापै द्विंधाविभक्तं खलु मे शरीरम्॥ 4.21
नलिनिकाः याचेमि अहं। इदो एहि बम्हण।
विदूषकः जदि भोयणं देसि तदो गच्छामि अहं। इट्ठं आअन्तुअस्स भोयणदाणं।
नलिनिकाः एहि मे सव्वाभरणं देमि।
विदूषकः णहिघिदवअणेण पित्तं णस्सदि। मम हत्थगदं करेहि।
Nalinikā: I implore you, do come hither Brāhmaṇa.
Vidūṣaka: If you offer me food, I shall go with you. It is desirable to offer food to a guest.
N: I shall offer you all my jewellery.
V: By mere utterance of the word *ghee* the bile does not disappear. You should give it to me in my hand.
45. Keith, ibid., pp. 121f.
46. This act is played under the title *Mantrāṅkanāṭaka* in modern Kerala by the Cakkayars without knowing its connection with the drama of Bhāsa, Gaṇapati Śāstrī, *Pratimānāṭaka,* Introduction, p. xi.
47. According to C.R. Devadhar, T. Gaṇapati Śastrī explains it as: यो विकृतवेषभाषणादिना जनस्य हास्यं जनयन् भिक्षामर्जयति स उच्यते। डिण्डिकस्य वेषो यस्य सः।

48- For their duplicate meanings see T. Gaṇapati Śāstrī's commentary on
63. the passage.
64. For details see M.R. Kale, *The Mṛcchakaṭika of Śūdraka,* 1962, Introduction, pp. 36-8.
65. Its plot is a creation of the author and the hero is of an inferior social status. He is a Brāhmaṇa, a minister, a great merchant, etc., but never a king or a god. It is defined in the *Sāhityadarpaṇa* (6.224-5, p. 434) as follows:
भवेत् प्रकरणे वृतं लौकिकं कविकल्पितं।
श्रृंगारोंऽगी नायकस्तु विप्रोऽमात्योऽथवा वणिक्।
सापायधर्मकामार्थपरो धीरप्रशान्तक:।
66. For details see Kale, ibid., pp. 58-61.
67. It has been very popular in the Soviet Union, the German Democratic Republic and other countries and has been staged several times.
68. First, this work has been quoted in the *Kāvyaprakāśa.* Vāmana refers (III, 2, 4) to a composition by Śūdraka, and also quotes two passages anonymously, Winternitz, *Sanskrit Literature,* III, Pt. I, 251n.
69. M.R. Kale has brought out another edition of the *Mṛcchakaṭika* with Pṛthvīdhara commentary. This commentary, according to him, is somewhat abrupt and meagre in places, therefore he has made considerable additions wherever he felt them necessary for the elucidation of the text. Preface to 1924 edition.
70. But according to Stenzler (his edition of the *Mṛcchakaṭika*), it is Śaurasenī. Observes Pischel: under such conditions, how little we can rely on the scholasts, *Grammatik,* Art. 42. In his *The Sanskrit Drama* (p. 141) Keith writes: 'Māgadhī ascribed to Rohasena, has been largely converted into Śaurasenī in the manuscripts.'
71. Śākārī is mentioned as a form of Apabhraṃśa (अपभ्रंशपाठकेषु शकारीभाषापाठको राष्ट्रिय:), Pṛthvīdhara, Kale, *The Mṛcchakaṭika of Śūdraka,* Act 1, p. 7 fn. According to Pischel, in certain forms this dialect coincides with Apabhraṃśa hence he justifies Pṛthvīdhara, *Grammatik,* Art. 24. In fact it is a Māgadhī dialect; Mārkaṇḍeya derives it from Māgadhī, as we have seen.
72. He combines the fool and the villain of the worst type, unique in this play. His mannerism of speech causes laughter: (a) He substitutes श for स (e.g. वशंतसेणा for वसंतसेणा), (b) his habit of redundant words (IX.1), (c) his absurd mythology (I.25), (d) his invention of the order of words (e.g. न च्छिनौ वृषभौ। न मृता रज्जव: I, p. 266), Kale, ibid., p. 63.
73. The grammarians and the rhetoricians mention Cāṇḍālī as a separate dialect which according to Mārkaṇḍeya is derived from a mixture of Māgadhī and Śaurasenī. He derives again Śābarī from Cāṇḍālī.
74. It is recognized by Mārkaṇḍeya along with Śākārī, Cāṇḍālī and Śābarī among the dialects of Apabhraṃśa. This dialect seems to be a transitional dialect between Māgadhī and Apabhraṃśa. According to

Pṛthvīdhara: लकारप्राया ढक्कविभाषा संस्कृत प्रायत्वे दन्त्यतालव्य सशकारद्वय युक्ता च, Kale, ibid., I, p.7 fn, i.e. it is characterized by preponderance of ल and by the use of the two sibilants, namely the dental स and palatal श. 'It is to be understood from this that in it, as in Māgadhī, र is changed into ल and श into स which, as well as श remains, however, unchanged in places where it occurs in Sanskrit.' writes Pischel, *Grammatik*, Art. 25.

75. शौरसेन्यवन्तिजा-प्राच्या एतास्तु दन्त्यसकारता। तत्रावन्तिजा रेफवती लोकोक्तिबहुला।
76. आवन्ती स्यात् महाराष्ट्रीशौरसेन्योस्तु संकरात्। (11.1)
77. Also see Keith, ibid., 140-2.
78. काव्येषु नाटकं रम्यं रम्या तत्र शकुन्तला।
    तत्रापि च चतुर्थोऽङ्कस्तत्र श्लोकचतुष्टयम्॥
79. पातुं न प्रथमं व्यवस्यति जलं युष्मास्वपीतेषु या।
    नादत्ते प्रियमण्डनापि भवतां स्नेहेन या पल्लवम्॥
    आद्ये वः कुसुयप्रसूतिसमये यस्या भवत्युत्सवः।
    सेयं याति शकुन्तलेति पतिगृहं सर्वैरनुज्ञायताम्॥ Act. IV
80. Read हउं पइं पुच्छिमि अक्खहि गअवरु ललिअपहारे णासिअतरुवरु।
    दूर विणिज्जिअ ससहरकंती दिट्ठी पिअ पइं संमुह जंती॥
    This play has come down in two recensions, one preserved in northern manuscripts, the other in south Indian manuscripts. The former gives a series of Apabhraṃśa verses contained in Act IV of the play, whereas the latter ignored it. The former is edited by Shankar P. Pandit (Bombay, 1879), the latter by R. Pischel (Berlin, 1875). Still a controversy persists about the authenticity of these verses. According to Keith, these verses are doubtful. He writes: 'The arguments against the authenticity of the verses are partly the silence of the theorists, the fact that the existence in Kālidāsa's time of Apabhraṃśa of the type found is more than dubious, that there is sometimes a degree of discrepancy between the verses and the prose of the drama, and that in many imitations of the scene there are no similar verses'. The *Sanskrit Drama*, pp. 151f.
81. See Keith, ibid., p.156. Translation after Winternitz, *A History . . .*, Vol. III, Pt. I, p. 277.
82. देवानामिदमामनन्ति मुनयः शान्तं क्रतुं चाक्षुषं
    रुद्रेणेदमुमाकृतव्यतिकरे स्वाङ्गे विभक्तं द्विधा।
    त्रैगुण्योद्भवमत्र लोकचरितं नानारसं दृश्यते
    नाट्यं भिन्नरुचेर्जनस्य बहुधाप्येकं समाराधनम्॥ I.4.
83. See Keith, ibid., p. 156.
84. Keith, *The Sanskrit Drama*, p. 212.
85. Ibid., p. 219.
86. Ibid., p. 236.
87. Ibid., p. 337.
88. विष्कंभ-प्रवेशरहितो वस्त्वेक भाषया भवति।
    अ-प्राकृत-संस्कृतया सट्टको नाटिका-प्रतिमः॥
89. Śārdātanaya, *Bhāvaprakāśana*, pp. 244, 255, 269.

90. *Sahityadarpaṇa,* VI. 276, p. 452.
91. सो सट्टओ त्ति भण्णइ जो णाडिआइ अणुइरइ।
    किं उण पवेसविक्खंभंकाइं केवलं ण दीसंति॥
92. S.N. Das Gupta and S.K. Dey, *A History of Sanskrit Literature,* Classical Period, Vol. I, Calcutta, 1962, p. 461.
93. Edited by M.M. Ghosh, *Karpūramañjari,* Calcutta, 1939, I, p. 81.
94. In the opinion of Ghosh, this stanza is spurious as it does not occur in the best manuscript 'W' and a very old MS 'B'; see his notes on 1.6, p. 145.
95. Keith, *The Sanskrit Drama,* p. 236.
96. Such as:
    (a) अहवा हत्थे कंकणं किं दप्पणेण (I, p. 85).
    (b) तुरंगस्स सिग्घत्तणे किं सक्खिणो पुच्छंति (ibid.).
    (c) तं सुवण्णं जं कसवट्टिआए णिव्वहदि (ibid.).
    (d) दक्खारासो ण महुरज्जदि सक्कराए (II, p. 105)
97. Read:
    (a) वक्करकालो (II, p. 100) = prattling.
    (b) टेंटा (I, p. 85) = gambling house. Compare the word टिंटेघर in the *Jñāneśvarī* (Chapter 18) where the commentator explains it as तिवाढ्यावरचे घर, which is not correct 'टिंटेघर' is द्यूतगृह (टिंट=द्यूत), a gambling house.
    (c) कालक्खरिअ (कालाक्षरिक)—one who has learnt how to write letters with black ink, Ghosh, notes, p. 150.
98. See infra, p. 257.
99. पाणअ-गओ भमरो लब्भइ दुक्खं गइंदेसु।
    सुहाअ रज्जं किर होइ रण्णो (5.131)
100. Read:
    जरि पेखला मस्तकावरी केशकलापु।
    तरि परिस्खलिला मयूरांचे पिच्छप्रतापु॥
    जरि नयनविषयु केला वेणीदंडु।
    तरि साक्षाज्जाला भ्रमण (र) श्रेणी दंडु॥
    जरि दृग्गोचरी आला विसाल भालु।
    तरि अर्द्धचन्द्र मंडलु भइला ऊर्णायु जालु॥
    भ्रूजुगलु जाणु द्वैधीकृतकंदर्पचापु।
    नयननिर्जितु जाला खंजनु नि:प्रतापु॥
    मुखमंडलु जाणु शशांक देवताचे मंडलु।
    सर्वांगसुन्दरता मूर्तिमंतुकासु॥
    कल्पद्रुम जैसे सर्वलोक आशाविश्रामु।

    Javanikāntara 1.

8

Grammar, Prosody, Lexicography and Poetics

Grammar

Vyākaraṇa or grammar is considered as one of the important *Vedāṅgas* (limbs of the *Veda*, regarded as auxiliary to the corpus), comprising (a) *Sikṣā* or the science of proper articulation and pronunciation, consisting of the knowledge of letters, accents, quantity, the use of the organs of pronunciation and phonetics; (b) *Chanda* or Metre; (c) *Vyākaraṇa* or linguistic analysis of grammar; (d) *Nirukta* or explanation of difficult (Vedic) words; (e) *Jyotiṣa* or astronomy (or Vedic calendar to fix the most auspicious days for sacrifices); and (f) *Kalpa* or ceremonial.[1] The first two of the *Vedāṅgas* are most important as they are intended to secure the correct reading or recitation of the *Veda*.

In order to preserve the sanctity of Vedic hymns, and to pronounce them correctly with proper accent, to follow the rules of grammar was very essential. Before Pāṇinī, the great Sanskrit grammarian, the language of the *Vedas* was not stabilized and even the learned sages pronounced words wrongfully; they pronounced *Yarvāṇaḥ* and *Tarvāṇaḥ* in place of the correct forms *Yadvānaḥ* and *Tadvānaḥ*. As a result Pāṇinī composed his epoch-making work *Aṣṭādhyāyī* (Eight Chapters). Patañjali wrote his well known *Mahābhāṣya* (Great Commentary) on this work wherein he emphasized the study of grammar. He stated, 'In order to preserve the *Veda*, the study of *vyākaraṇa* is essential. The one who understands the rules regarding the elision (*lopa*), the lengthening (*āgama*) and the substitution (*vikāra*) with the assistance of grammar, can safely guard the *Veda*. And the one who is devoid of the knowledge of grammar, is incapable of viewing a speech though he actually views it, and is incapable of hearing it though he actually hear it.'[2]

Further, coming to the period of rhetoricians, we find that Bhāmaha (AD 700-50) in his *Kāvyālaṃkāra* deals with grammar in relation to poetry pointing out particular words that can be properly used by poets who take delight in *vakrokti.*[3] Here he gives direction to the selection of proper words among many grammatical forms in order to secure melody. He has pointed out that a poet should not use such words which are not sanctioned by usage (*aprayukta*), are unintelligible (*durbodha*), hard (*apeśala*), vulgar (*grāmya*), meaningless (*apārthaka*), or not known (*apratīta*). Then, Rudraṭa (between 825-75) in his *Kāvyālaṃkāra* (V. 35) mentions that a poet must have a thorough knowledge of grammar before attempting *śleṣa* (use of words with double meanings). Rājaśekhara (early tenth century) has praised grammar as superior even to the *Veda.*[4] He has stated that one who uses the proper word attains endless victory in the next world and that by using vulgar speech (*apaśabda*) he fails in correct use of words.[5] Similarly, Hemacandra first composes the *Siddhahema-Sabdānuśāsana* on grammar and then the *Kavyānuśasana* on poetics.

BOOKS ON GRAMMAR IN PRAKRIT

Since Prakrit was a dialect of the people and was spoken differently in different regions, it was not possible to have a uniform Prakrit grammar. As a matter of fact, the development of grammar, prosody, lexicography and poetics took place after the development of literature. Regarding Pali, for instance, it has been observed that 'there was no book of Pali grammar in existence till the time of the three great Pali commentators, namely Buddhadatta, Buddhaghosa and Dhammapāla'. All 'appear to have explained the grammatical construction of the Pali words by the rules of Pāṇinī, quoted *verbatim* in Pali'.[6] The development of Pali grammar is a comparatively late phase of Pali literature, as late as the sixth or seventh century, if not later.[7] The general view of scholars is that the Prakrit grammars that we have were written under the direct influence of Sanskrit grammar. After all, it was necessary to have some grammar to comprehend the vast literature of Prakrit which was growing fast. It is said that like his Sanśkrit grammar Pāṇinī also composed a book on Prakrit grammar, the *Prākṛitlakṣaṇa,* but this is doubtful. Hoernle is of the opinion that it is Caṇḍa's *Prākṛtalakṣaṇa* that has been wrongly attributed to Pāṇinī.[8]

VARARUCI THE OLDEST PRAKRIT GRAMMARIAN

As pointed out earlier, Vararuci belongs to the Eastern school, a tradition alleged to have been followed by Lankeśvara, the author of the *Prākṛtakāmadhenu* and others. The earliest commentaries on the *Prākṛtaprakāśa*[9] are the *Prākṛtamañjarī* in verse by *Kātyāyana*[10] and the *Manoramā* by Kashmirian Bhāmaha (seventh-eighth century). Among other commentaries we have the *Prākṛtasaṃjīvanī* by Vasantarāja (fourteenth-fifteenth century), the *Subodhinī* by Sadānanda and the *Prākṛtapāda* by Nārāyaṇavidyāvinoda. Then we have a commentary by Rāmapāṇivāda of Malabar, the author of the *Kaṃsavaho* and the *Usāṇiruddha*. In this commentary illustrations are provided from the *Gāhāsattasaī*, the *Setubandha*, the *Karpūramañjarī*, the *Kaṃsavaho* and other works. As in order to illustrate the *sūtras* of the *Aṣṭādhyāyī* the poet Bhaṭṭi has composed his *Bhaṭṭikāvya*, also known as the *Rāvaṇavadha*, and in order to illustarate the rules of his *Siddhahema*, Hemacandra has composed his *Dvyāśrayakāvya* also known as the *Kumārapālacarita*, so in order to illustrate the rules of the *Prākṛtaprakāśa* of Vararuci and the *Prākṛtaśabdānuśāsana* of Trivikrama, Kṛṣṇalīlāśuka (thirteenth century) of Kerala has composed *Siricindhakavva* (*Śrīcihnakāvya*) or also known as the *Govindābhiṣeka*.[11] This text deals with the sports of Kṛṣṇa. He has illustrated the forms of Prakrit referred to in the *Prakṛtaprakāśa*.[12] This indicates the popularity of this work. This earliest available work on Prakrit grammar, was probably written in a period when Prakrit was still a living language. The *Prākṛtaprakāśa*[13] describes four dialects, Mahārāṣṭrī, Paiśācī, Māgadhī and Śaurasenī. The existing available edition consists of 12 chapters; the first 9 commented by Kātyāyana, deal with the rules of Prakrit (known as Mahārāṣṭrī). The tenth and the eleventh chapters deal with Paiśācī and Māgadhī dialects respectively.[14] The last, twelfth, chapter dealing with Śaurasenī, is not commented on by Bhāmaha; the existence of this dialect is recognized by the author in X.2 and XI. 2. Vararuci gives 29 rules regarding the characteristics of Śaurasenī and (XII. 32) remarks that in other respects it agrees with Maharaṣṭrı, which shows that he gives prominence to Mahārāṣṭrī and Chapter 12 is an integral part of the work. He considers Sanskrit the basis of Śaurasenī (प्रकृति संस्कृतम्, XII.2).

The *Prākṛtaprakāśa* does not explain all the peculiarities of inscriptional Prakrit language (belonging to the period ranging from the fourth century BC to the fourth century AD). It also does not throw light on the Prakrit of Aśvaghoṣa and that of the classical

Sanskrit dramas, whose manuscripts are much influenced by the traditions established by later Prakrit grammarians. The provincial peculiarities of inscriptional Prakrit were possibly outside its scope.[15]

CAṆḌA'S *PRĀKṚTALAKṢAṆA*[16]

After paying obeisance to Vīra (Mahavira), following the old school (*vṛddha-mata*), the author has composed this work. It consists of 3 *pādas* where the rules of Prakrit are enumerated in 99 *sūtras*. In some cases it also contains a fourth *pāda* where the characteristics of Apabhraṃśa, Paiśācī, Māgadhī and Śaurasenī are described each in one *sūtra*. In the opinion of Hoernle, this work has also treated the Ārṣa dialect. According to some, it is an old tract based on the works of earlier grammarians, whereas others consider it a new composition, perhaps based on Hemacandra.

PRĀKṚTAKĀMADHENU OF LAṄKEŚVARA

Prākṛtakāmadhenu is also known as *Prākṛtalaṅkeśvararāvaṇa.*[17] From its benedictory stanza it appears that the author had composed a detailed study and the present one is only briefly narrated.[18] It consists of 34 *sūtras* describing the characteristics of Prakrit; some are vague and do not convey a clear idea. The eleventh *sutra* prescribes उ in lieu of अ (as घरू for गृह), indicating the tendency of Apabhraṃśa. In the last *sūtra* (34) the use of the word *yoṣit* is accepted in place of *mahilā*. *Lakkhaṇa-vihula* is mentioned as a *Kāvya* written in Gauḍi Prakrit.

SAṂKṢIPTASĀRA OF KRAMADĪSVARA

As Hemacandra wrote his *Siddhahema Sabdānuśāsana* to explain the rules of Sanskrit and Prakrit grammar—(the first seven chapters deal with Sanskrit and the eighth with Prakrit) so has Trivikrama in his *Saṃkṣiptasāra.*[19] The first seven chapters of this work are devoted to Sanskrit and the eighth, known as *Prākṛtapāda*, to Prakrit grammar. There is no other similarity noticed between the works of Hemacandra and Kramadīśvara. The latter (twelfth or thirteenth century) follows Vararuci. There are several commentaries, one written by Kramadīśvara himself; it has an explanation (*vyākhyā*) too. Caṇḍīdevaśarman has written a commentary on *Prākṛtapāda*. Here the author gives a very brief treatment to Prakrit; he mainly deals with

Mahārāṣṭrī and Apabhraṃśa. He also recognizes Māgadhī, Paiśācīka, Ardhamāgadhī and Śabara as forms of Prakrit. He refers to Nāgara, Upanāgara and Vrācaṭa as the three main varieties of Apabhraṃśa.

PRĀKṚTĀNUŚĀSANA[20] OF PURUṢOTTAMA

This work consists of 20 chapters, of which the first two are lacking and the third is incomplete. The first five chapters deal with the characteristics of Prakrit in general; the next three with Mahārāṣṭrī, the ninth with Śaurasenī and the tenth with Prācyā. Prācyā is said to be abounding in commonly current speech (*lokokti-bahula*); its forms are like Śaurasenī. Two other chapters deal with Āvantī and Māgadhī respectively. Like Rāmaśarmā and Mārkaṇḍeya, Puruṣottama (twelfth century) also divides Prakrit into bhāṣā, vibhāṣā, Apabhraṃśa and Paiśācīka. Mahārāṣṭrī, Śaurasenī, Prācyā, Āvantī and Māgadhī dialects are included under bhāṣā; Śākārī, Cāṇḍālī, Śābarī and Ṭakkī, under vibhāṣā; the latter are dealt with in four chapters respectively. There is prominence of क in Śākārī (XIII. 9) and of उद् in Ṭakkī (XVI. 2). The seventeenth and the eighteenth chapters deal with Nāgarika and Vrācaḍa respectively. The Kaikeya Paiśācīka and the Śaurasena Paiśācīka are dealt with in the last two chapters respectively.

THE *PRĀKṚTAKALPATARU*[21] OF RĀMAŚARMĀ TARKAVĀGĪŚA BHAṬṬĀCĀRYA

Rāmaśarmā Tarkavāgīśa who belongs to the seventeenth AD, has composed his work on the model of the *Prākṛtakāmadhenu* of Laṅkeśvara. While explaining the subject matter of his work he has followed verbatim the *Prākṛtānuśāsana* of Puruṣottama. He has written his own commentary on this work.[22] It consists of three *Śākhās*. The first contains ten *Stavakas* which deal with the characteristics of Mahārāṣṭrī. The second *Śākhā* contains three *Stavakas*; the first one deals with Śaurasenī, the second with Prācyā, Āvantī, Bāhlīkī, Māgadhī, Ardhamāgadhī and Dākṣiṇātya. Prācyā was the dialect spoken by jesters (*vidūṣaka*); Āvantī is a mixed dialect of Śaurasenī and Prācyā. Āvantī and Bāhlīkī are spoken by a leader of the city, a doorkeeper, a knave, characters of medium rank, constables and merchants; Māgadhī is spoken by *rākṣasas, bhikṣus, kṣapaṇakas* and others; it has its base in Mahārāṣṭrī and Śaurasenī. Dākṣiṇātyā is intermingled with words (*pada*) from the south, endowed with Sanskrit and other languages; its poetry is sweeter even than nectar.[23] These dialects have been treated under the category of bhāṣā. The third *Stavaka* deals with vibhāṣās: Śākārikā, Cāṇḍālikā, Śābarī, Ābhīrikā and Ṭakkī. Cāṇḍālikā or Cāṇḍālī is an admixture of Śaurasenī and Māgadhī; it is abounding in rustic empressions (*grāmyokti*). Śābarī is derived from Māgadhī. On account of the different variety of characters, Māgadhī is divided into Ābhīrikā, Drāviḍikā, Autkalī, Vanaukasī and Māndurikā; Ābhirikā is derived from Śābarī. We are told that Śākārī, Oḍrī and Drāviḍī though included under Apabhraṃśa, are not considered as such when employed in drama, when they are looked upon as vibhāṣā. The third *Śākhā* which is most important for the study of Apabhraṃśa, deals with Nāgara and Vrācaḍa and Paiśācīka Apabhraṃśa. The last is divided into Kaikaya, Śaurasena, Pāñcāla, Gauḍa, Māgadha and Vrācaḍa.

THE *PRĀKṚTASARVASVA*[24] OF MĀRKAṆḌEYA

Mārkaṇḍeya Kavīndra (greatest among poets) flourished between 1490 and 1565. He was a resident of Orissa and wrote his grammar under the ruler Mukundadeva. He quotes a number of Prakrit works, including his own, from which he has collected material. In the beginning of his work he has expressed his indebtedness to earlier grammarians such as Śākalya, Kohala, Vararuci, Bhāmaha, Vasantarāja and others whose works he has consulted before writing his treatise. He has also referred to Aniruddha Bhaṭṭa, *Bhaṭṭikāvya* Bhojadeva, Daṇḍin, Hariścandra, Bhagīratha Vardhamāna, Kapila, Piṅgala, Rājaśekhara, Vākpatirāja, Saptaśatī, Setubandha, Bṛhatkathā, Śṛṅgārotkarṣa and Gaṇapatākā.

As it is evident from the title '*kavīndra*' Mārkaṇḍeya was not only a grammarian but also had a poetic genius. We have already referred to his *Saṭṭaka*, entitled the *Vilāsavatī.* Besides, he has quoted a Prakrit verse, claiming that it was his own (*idaṃ mama*).[25] There is a Sanskrit epic poem known as the *Daśagrīva-vadha-mahākāvyaṃ*, attributed to Kavirāja-cakravarti Mārkaṇḍeya Miśra. This work has been recently discovered and published by the Orissa Sahitya Akademi, Bhubaneswar, 1959. On the basis of a comparative study of the *Prākṛtasarvasva* and the *Daśagrīva-vadha-mahākavyaṃ*, scholars are of the opinion that both the works are by one and the same writer, and Mārkaṇḍeya Miśra was just the childhood name of Mārkaṇḍeya Kavīndra.[26] That shows our author also was a writer of a *mahākāvya.* The entire text is set in metrical form; the speciality of this work is that here to illustrate the rules a number of illustrations are cited from various authors.

Puruṣottamá, Rāmaśarmā and Mārkaṇḍeya seem to be very close with regard to prescription of rules of grammar. They have divided Prakrit into four categories: bhāṣā, vibhāṣā, Apabhraṃśa and Paiśācīka. They deal with Mahārāṣṭrī first and then with Śaurasenī, Prācyā, Āvantī and Māgadhī, all included under bhāṣā. Mārkaṇḍeya has given more details about Śaurasenī than are found in any other book of grammar. He has drawn a sharp distinction between Śaurasenī and Mahārāṣṭrī. He has also described Apabhraṃśa most accurately.[27] He has dealt with bhāṣā, vibhāṣā, Apabhraṃśa and Paiśācīka. The rules of Mahārāṣṭrī have been described; this part of the book is based on Vararuci's *Prākṛtaprakāśa.* The text also deals with Śaurasenī, Prācyā, Āvantī and Bāhlīkī; and Māgadhī and Ardhamāgadhī. Most of the characteristic features of Āvantī laid down by Mārkaṇḍeya tally with those given in the *Prākṛtakalpataru* (II. 2, 5-10) of Rāmaśarmā[28] and the *Prākṛtānuśāsana* (XI) of Puruṣottama. Like Puruṣottama, Mārkaṇḍeya also considers Āvantī as an admixture of Mahārāṣṭri and Śaurasenī. None of the grammarians except Mārkaṇḍeya illustrates Āvantī and Bāhlīkī. In order to illustrate the former Mārkaṇḍeya has quoted: एस किरादोमअमणुसरंतो वेदस-लआ-गहणंपइट्ठो.[29] Mārkaṇḍeya rejects Bāhlīkī and Āvantī as a separate bhāṣā; he includes the former in the latter. While illustrating Bāhlīkī, he quotes: सलसिलुह-सोलब्भ-णिब्भलो मालुदोवहइ. Here र is replaced by ल, otherwise, it is the same as Āvantī आवन्त्यामेव वाहीकी किंतु रस्यात्र लो भवेत्।[30] Regarding Ardhamāgadhī, it remained no more the speech of the plays; it was dead in course of time and survived only in name. According to Mārkaṇḍeya, it was nothing but a form of Māgadhī, that is not very much different from Śaurasenī; Dākṣiṇātyā, has no special characteristic, and Bāhlīkī belongs to Māgadhī. Ardhamāgadhī, Dākṣiṇātyā and Bāhlīkī being denied the status of a bhāṣā, the remaining five languages, Mahārāṣṭrī, Śaurasenī, Prācyā, Āvantī and Māgadhī, are included in this category. Thus after explaining the characteristics of Māgadhī the author has called Ardhamāgadhī not different from Māgadhī as it is not far from Śaurasenī; therefore he has not dealt with it separately.[31] Further, five dialects are treated under the group of vibhāṣā: Śakarı, Caṇḍalı, Śābarī and Ābhīrī and Ṭakkī. Of these, Śākārī is derived from Māgadhī:[32] it has been called a language spoken by Śakāra in Sanskrit drama. Cāṇḍālī is derived from Māgadhī and Śaurasenī;[33] Śābarī is derived from Cāṇḍālī;[34] at times it owes its origin to Śaurasenī, Māgadhī and Śākārī.[35] Mārkaṇḍeya excludes Auḍrī from the list of vibhāṣā as its peculiarities are found in Śābarī itself, which imitates the language of the Oḍra (Orissa) country, and of Śaurasenī.[36] Ābhīrī, according to Mārkaṇḍeya, is exactly like Śābarī.[37]

Ṭākkī is the language of the Takka country. It is used in a play by gamblers and merchants. It is called a mixture of Sanskrit and Śaurasenī.[38] Hariścabdra takes it to be an Apabhraṃśa, but not a vibhāṣā.[39] Mārkaṇḍeya and Rāmaśarmā identify it with Drāviḍī.[40] The text then deals with Nāgara, Vrācaḍa and Upanāgara Apabhraṃśas. 27 kinds of Apabhraṃśas are recorded here.[41] Vararuci recognizes no Apabhraṃśa dialect. Two *pādas* deal with the characteristics of Paiśācī; it is divided into Kekaya, Śaurasena and Pāñcāla. Quoting the view of others, Mārkaṇḍeya mentions 11 kinds of Paiśācī. He rejects all others except the three mentioned above.

THE WESTERN SCHOOL OF PRAKRIT GRAMMARIANS

The Western School is sometimes called the School of Vālmīki, represented by *Vālmīki Sūtras* which are lost in their original form. Ācārya Hemacandra (1088-1172) is the oldest exponent of this School. In the eighth *adhyāya* of his *Siddhahema*, Hemacandra deals with Ārṣa Prakrit (Ardhamāgadhī), Paiśācī, Cūlikā Paiśācī and Apabhraṃśa.

As this work was dedicated to King Siddharāja of Aṇahillapura it is named as *Siddhahema* or *Siddhahema-śabdānuśāsana*. Several important commentaries have been composed on this. Hemacandra himself has composed a commentary *Tattvaprakāśikā*. On it Udayasaubhāgyagaṇi in turn has written another commentary, *Hemaprākṛtavṛtti-ḍhuṇḍhikā*. Maladhārī Upādhyāya Narendracandrasūri has composed an *Avacūri*. There are numerous other commentaries also on this work.[42]

This work consists of 4 *pādas*. The first 3 and a part of the fourth deal with the general Prakrit or the Ārṣa Prakrit. *Sūtras* IV. 260-86 are devoted to Śaurasenī, the *Sūtras* 287-302 to Māgadhī, the *Sūtras* 303-24 to Paiśācī, the *Sūtras* 325-8 to Cūlikā Paiśācī and lastly the *Sūtras* 329-448 are devoted to Apabhraṃśa dialect. Hemacandra has also provided numerous verb-forms which are designated *dhātvādeśas* or 'root substitutes' (IV.1-259). These are various so-called substitutes for some specific Sanskrit roots. 'Some of these substitutes are pure *Desī* roots while others could be derived from the original Sanskrit by applying rules in VIII i and ii.'[43] Pischel has remarked, 'Here Sanskrit fails miserably in rendering any help, though agreement among the new Indian languages is most rigorous.[44] By employing the expressions such as कश्चित्, केचित्, अन्ये, etc., the author has indicated that there were other grammarians whose work he has utilized. Mostly he has described the characteristics of Māgadhī dialect and here he has dealt with one or two rules to explain Ardhamāgadhī. The portion dealing with Apabhraṃśa is most important. He has given beautiful stanzas (from unknown sources) dealing with *śṛṅgāra*, *nīti* and *vairāgya*. It shows that at the time of Hemacandra there existed an extensive literature in Apabhraṃśa; there might be some stanzas composed by the author himself.[45] This literature is also important from the point of view of development of modern Indian languages such as Hindi, Marathi, Gujarati, Bengali and so on. Hemacandra follows Vararuci in many respects but he also disagrees considerably. He approves of यश्रुति while Vararuci rejects it.[46]

PRĀKṚTĀNUŚĀSANA OF TRIVIKRAMA

Hemacandra is followed by Trivikrama (in the thirteenth century). In his benedictory stanzas in the *Prākṛtānuśāsana*[47] Trivikrama has paid obeisance to God Vīra and has remembered Vīrasena, the well-known writer of the *Dhavalā* commentary on the *Ṣaṭkhaṇḍāgama*, and his pupil Jinasena, the author of the *Adipurāṇa*. He belonged to the Digambara sect. He has called himself an efficient poet. He himself has composed a commentary on his work on grammar. Trivikrama has followed a special type of technical term that he has explained in the beginning of his work. From 1.1.17 in his *vṛtti* to the *sūtras*, he has everywhere verbally followed Hemacandra whom he mentions as his authority. His special contribution can be noticed in certain *sūtras* (e.g. 1.3.106; 1.4.121; 2.1.30; 3.1.132; and 3.4.71) in which he has collected together the words that cannot be regulated according to the rules of grammar. Such words to a great extent belong to the *Deśī* category.[48] Like Hemacandra, Trivikrama has mentioned Ārṣa but has excluded it, like *Deṣya*, from his grammar altogether saying it is of an independent origin without having Sanskrit as its source (रूढत्वात्) and is governed mostly by its own rules (स्वतंत्रत्वाच्चभूयसो).[49] The work consists of 3 *adhyāyas*, each with 4 *pādas*. The first two *adhyāyas*, and the first *pāda* of the third *adhyāya* deal with the rules of Prakrit, the second *pāda* (1-26) of the 3rd *adhyāya* with Śaurasenī; (27-42) with Māgadhī; (43-63) with Paiśācī, and (4-67) with Culika Paiśācī. The third and the fourth *pādas* of the same *adhyāya* explain the rules of Apabhraṃśa which is important as explained above.

PRĀKṚTARŪPĀVATĀRA[50] OF SIṂHARĀJA

Siṃharāja, son of Samudrabandhayajvan, belongs to the fifteenth century. In tradition Vālmīki is said to have been the author of this work. The author has referred to Pūrva (12. 42), Kaumāra (Kātantra) and Pāṇinī (2. 2). The work is based on Trivikrama's *Prākṛtaśabdānuśāsana.* Its six sections are divided into 22 *adhyāyas.* They contain three types of words: some are identical with Sanskrit (*sanskṛta-sama*), others are derived from Sanskrit (*sanskṛta-bhava*) or *Deśī* and neither identical with Sanskrit nor derived from it. The tract deals with Śaurasenī, Māgadhī, Paiśācī, Cūlikā Paiśācī and Apabhraṃśa. It is important for the study of nouns and verbal forms.

ṢAḌBHĀṢĀCANDRIKĀ[51] OF LAKṢMĪDHARA

Lakṣmīdhara, also known as Lakṣamaṇasūri, was a resident of Āndhra. He has composed the *Ṣaḍbhāsācandrikā* on the basis of Trivikrama's *Prākṛtavyākaraṇa-vṛtti.* It is called *Ṣaḍbhāṣācandrikā* as it deals with the details of six dialects: Prakrit (Mahārāṣṭrī), Śaurasenī, Māgadhī, Paiśācī, Cūlikā Paiśācī and Apabhraṃśa. The author considers Hemacandra, Trivikrama and Bhāmaha as his *gurus* and has based his treatment on their works. He says Prakrit originated in the country of Maharashtra, in support of which he has quoted poet Daṇḍin. In his self-composed commentary on his work he has ascribed this dialect to women and the low class of people (verses 32-3). Paiśācī and Cūlikā Paiśācī are ascribed to Rākṣasas, Piśācas and the low class of people (verse 35). The countries of Pāṇḍya, Kekaya, Bāhlīka, Siṃgha, Nepāla, Kuntala, Sudheṣṇa, Bhoja, Gāndhāra, Haiva and Kannojana are included under Piśāca (29-30). Apabhraṃśa is ascribed to Ābhīras and others which was considered unfit for poetic expression. The author has quoted Daṇḍin in support of his statement (31). He has dealt with Apabhraṃśa in detail though like Hemacandra he has not quoted Apabhraṃśa couplets to illustrate the rules prescribed by him.

PRĀKṚTAMAṆIDĪPA OF APPAYADIKSITA

The *Prākṛtamaṇidīpa*[52] of Appayadikṣita is also known as *Prākṛtamaṇidīpikā.* The author was a devotee of Śaivism and has written many important works such as the *Śivārkamaṇidīpikā* on Śaiva religion. He belongs to the later sixteenth century. He mentions

Trivikrama, Hemacandra, Lakṣmīdhara, Bhoja, Puṣpanātha, Vararuci, the *Vārtikārṇava-Bhāṣya* and Appayajvan as his authorities. According to him, the *Vārtikārṇava-Bhāṣya* has given too many details, which may be difficult for a common student to grasp, therefore he has composed his work in brief. Śrinivāsagopālācārya has written a commentary in Sanskrit. Pischel is very critical of this work and remarks, 'it is nothing better than an incomplete extract from Trivikrama, devoid of all its merits' (Art. 41).

PRĀKṚTĀNANDA OF PANDIT RAGUNĀTHA

Pandit Raghunātha, son of poet Jyotirvit Sarasa, belonged to the eighteenth century. His *Prākṛtānanda*[53] contains 419 *Sūtras*. As Siṃharāja's *Prākrtarupāvatāra* is based on Trivikrama's *Prākṛta-śabdānuśāsana*, so this tract is on the *Prākṛtaprakāśa* of Vararuci. The first chapter deals with nouns and the second with verbal roots.

OTHER WORKS ON PRAKRIT GRAMMAR

1. Śubhacandrasūri (VS 1605=AD 1548), known as the sovereign of six languages (*Ṣaḍbhāṣācakravartin*), having followed Hemacandra, has composed the *Cintāmaṇi* in three chapters. Like the south Indian Vikramadeva and Siṃharāja he begins his grammar with a number of *Saṃjñāsūtras* (a *Sūtra* which teaches the meaning of a technical term).[54]

2. Śrutasāgara (AD 1518) has composed the *Audāryacintāmaṇi*. It contains six chapters.[55]

3. Samantabhadra is said to have written a Prakrit grammar which is not available.

4. Devasundara wrote the *Prākṛtayukti*.[56]

5. Vīrasena, the well-known *Dhavalā*-commentator, has referred to a metrical work on Prakrit grammar by an unknown author. This work was written between the eighth and the twelfth century.[57]

Among others we have:

1. Narasiṃha's *Prākrtaśabdapradīpikā*.

2. Kṛṣṇapaṇḍita's (also known as Śeṣakṛṣṇa) *Prākṛtacandrikā*, composed in verse.[58]

3. Vāmācārya, who calls himself Karañja-kavi-sārvabhauma, has written a commentary on the *Prākṛtapiṅgala*; he has composed the *Prākṛtacandrikā*, a compendium, for beginners.

4. Candraśekhara, father Kavirāja Viśvanātha, composed the *Bhāṣārṇava* according to the *Sāhityadarpaṇa*.

5. Candraśekhara has referred to the *Prākṛtasāhityadarpaṇa*, also known as *Prākṛtasahityaratnākara*, in his commentary on the *Śākuntala* (175, 24, Pischel edition).

6. Lakṣmīdhara in the introduction (p. 4) of his *Ṣaḍbhāṣācandrikā* refers to the following: (i) Bhāmakavi's *Ṣaḍbhāṣācandrikā*, (ii) Durgācārya's *Ṣaḍbhāṣārūpamālikā*, (iii) *Ṣaḍbhāṣāmañjarī*, (iv) Nāgobā's *Ṣaḍbhāṣāsubantādarśa*, (v) *Ṣaḍbhāṣāvicāra*, (vi) Candraśekhara's *Bhāṣārṇava*.[59]

7. Śākalya and Kohala: Mārkaṇḍeya in the introduction of the first *pāda* of his *Prākṛtasarvasva* refers to Śākalya, Bharata, Kohala, Vararuci, Bhāmaha, Vasantarāja and others, saying that he has composed his treatise after studying their works.

(i) Śākalya occupied a prominent place among Prakrit grammarians of ancient India. He has been mentioned as an authority on Prakrit grammar and quoted by Puruṣottama, Rāmaśarmā Tarkavāgīśa and Mārkaṇḍeya at several places. Rāmaśarmā has referred to Śakalya-Māṇḍavya six times and to Śākalya three times. He has quoted a verse from Śākalya from an unknown source which indicates that the author was quite popular. The verse is:

> अता सणेहो वि इता सिणेहो, पक्खे विणेहो चिह्न होति चिण्हं।
> अता सणाणं इता सिणाणं, यहाणं पिसाकल्लमतं वितिण्णं॥ *Prākrtakalpataru*, I.3.

With the separating vowel अ, स्नेह will change into सणेह; with इ into सिणेह; and it may alternatively become णेहो; and चिन्ह will be changed into चिण्ह. With the separating vowel अ, स्नान will be सणाण; and with इ, सिणाण; and it may alternatively be ण्हाण. This is the expressed opinion of Śākalya. Mārkaṇḍeya has quoted Śākalya several times, sometimes in the original *sūtra* and sometimes in his commentary.[60]

(ii) Kohala has been quoted by Mārkaṇḍeya. In the commentary of XII. 1 quoting Kohala's opinion regarding the use of Māgadhī, he writes, 'According to Kohala, Rākṣasas, Bhikṣus, Kṣapaṇakas and the male attendants (*ceṭa*), etc., are supposed to speak in Māgadhī.'[61] P.V. Kane has assigned the date 650-750 to Kohala.[62]

(iii) Mārkaṇḍeya has also referred to some other unknown authorities; they are (a) Aniruddhabhaṭṭa, (b) Bhagīratha Vardhamāna, and (c) Hariścandra. In the commentary (*Sūtra* XII. 38), while illustrating Dākṣiṇātyā, he says that nowhere are its characteristics described, nor illustrations, except by Aniruddhabhaṭṭa whose

Sanskrit verse he has quoted.[63] The opinion of Bhagīratha Vardhamāna has been quoted twice in the *Prākṛtasarvasva* (see XIV. 3 and XVII.13). As we have already noticed, Hariścandra has taken Ṭakkī as an Apabhraṃśa and not as a vibhāṣā (XVI. 2).[64] Mārkaṇḍeya also quotes the authority of Paiṅgalas, the followers of Piṅgala (see V.34; V.106).[65] *Sārasvata-vyākaraṇa* or the *Sarasvatī-prakriyā* is the exposition of the *Sarasvatī sūtra* of an unknown author, Anubhūtisvarūpācārya. The work is written in Sanskrit and though the author is not Jain, this system of grammar was much popular with the Jains. As a result Jains have written several commentaries on it, *Dīpikā* composed by Candrakīrtisūri of the Nāgapurīya Tapāgaccha in vs 1664, and *Śabdārtha-candrikā* by Haṃsavijaya,[66] among them.

Sambandhodyota is recorded as another treatise on grammar by Rabhāṣānandin. The manuscript is preserved in Jaisalmer Bhandar, Nos. 265, 1227.[67]

During the Mughal period Jains have written treatises on Persian grammar and lexicography. Some of the manuscripts are preserved in the L.D. Institute of Indology Library, Ahmedabad.

The *Pārasībhāṣānuśāsana* in five chapters is a manual of Persian grammar written in Sanskrit. It is composed by Vikramasiṃha, son of Madanpāl Ṭhakkura and pupil of Ānandasūri.[68] A short note on this treatise has been published in the *Woolner Commemoration Volume.*

EUROPEAN SCHOLARS AND THE STUDY OF PRAKRIT GRAMMAR

Richard Pischel (1849-1908) was a great German scholar, who for the first time, after studying unpublished Prakrit manuscripts laboriously, published his epoch-making *Grammatik* der *Prakrit-Sprachen* in 1874 from Braslaw. This was translated into English by Subhadra Jha under the title *Comparative Grammar of Prakrit Languages,* published by Motilal Dass in 1957, and into Hindi by Hemchandra Joshi, published by Bihar Rashtrabhasha Parishad, Patna, in 1958. Pischel also edited Hemacandra's *Prākṛtavyākaraṇa,* known as *Siddahema-śabdānuśāsana* and published it in two parts from Halle Amzar in 1877-80. Part one contained the text and a word index, part two its German translation with elaborate notes and a comparative study of the subject. In collaboration with George Bühler, he has also edited the *Deśīnāmamālā* of Hemacandra, published in the *BSS,* 1880 and the *Pāiyalacchīnāmamālā* of Dhanapāla from Göttingen in 1879. Pischel has also worked on Apabhraṃśa. In his 'matarialien zur

Kenntnis des Apabhraṃśa', published in a Göttingen Journal in 1902, p. 46ff; the author has given a critical compilation and a German translation of the Prakrit stanzas composed by well-known Bhoja.

Pischel's work on Prakrit grammar is considered remarkable as at that time most Prakrit literature was not published and whatever was available, was far from critical. Pischel has mentioned the following works in his *Grammatik* (Art. 43):

1. Albert Höfer: *De Prakrita Dialecto libri duo* (The Prakrit Dialects in 2 parts), Berlin, 1836

2. Christion Lassen (1800-76): *Institutiones Linguae Prakriticae, Bonn,* 1837. Quite a good material on Prakrit dialect has been collected in this book. According to Pischel, 'it is an admirable performance. Lassen effected improvements in a very large number of places in the corrupt texts, correctly utilized them and planned the ground work on which the edifice of later research could be raised up.'

3. Nicolaus Delius: *die Radices Prakriticae*, Bonnae ad Rhenum, 1939. Up-till now none of the native grammars and the Prakrit literature had been published.

4. A. Weber (1825-1901) worked on Mahārāṣṭrī, Apabhraṃśa and Māgadhī.

5. Edward Müller worked on Ardhamāgadhī.

6. H. Jacobi (1850-1937) worked on Jain Mahārāṣṭrī. He published his well known selected Mahārāṣṭrī Tales from Devendragaṇi's commentary on the *Uttarādhyayana,* under the title *Ausgewählte Erzählungen in Mahārāṣṭrī,* Leipzig, 1886. It was translated into English by J.J. Meyer, London, 1909. Jacobi translated *Jain Sutras,* Vols. XXII and XLV in the *SBE* Series.

7. E.B. Cowell published his *A Short Indroduction to the Ordinary Prakrit of the Sanskrit Dramas with a List of Common Irregular Prakrit Words*, London, 1875. It is an elementary book, based on Vararuci's *Prakrit Grammar.*

8. Rishikesh (Hrishikesh) Shastri published *A Prākṛita Grammar with English Translations,* Calcutta, 1833, an attempt to rearrange *Prakrit Grammar* on the European pattern.

9. M. Haug (1827-76) published *Vergleichung des Prakrit mit den Romanischen Sprachen* in Berlin in 1869. Here a comparison is made of the rules of phonetic changes between Prakrit and Spanish, Portuguese, French, Italian and other languages.

10. A.F.R. Hoernle has made a general survey of the history of Prakrit Philology. He has worked on the etymology of Prakrit words.

11. Siegfried Goldschmidt published his *Prākṛticae* from Strassburg in 1879.

Prosody

As we have seen, *Chandas* or metrics are an important constituent of the *Veda*, next to grammar. The *Chandas* play a highly important role in symbolism and mysticism of ancient ritual.[69] The *Sāmaveda* (*Sāma* meaning tune or melody) has melodies which were looked upon as possessing magic power. The melodies or harmonial songs or magic songs were supposed to have meant to appease gods and demons. Such songs which took the shape of *Chandas* or metres were thought to have originated in time immemorial.

The *Ṛgveda* or Veda of Praise is a collection of sacred verses called *Ṛcas* recited in praise of a deity. Since these hymns were sung by sages it was essential to employ a metric element to generate the flow of sound with a regulated pattern formed by long and short, and accented and unaccented syllables. Take for instance, the *Saṃhitā*-texts (*Saṃhitāpāṭhas*) and the Word-texts (*Padapāṭhas*). The *Saṃhitā*-texts have been already the works of phoneticians but it came to their recitation, they had to be recited according to the teaching of the *Śikṣā*; thus one had to take recourse to the so-called Word-texts. In that case the individual words appear separate from the phonetic connection in which they are represented in the *Saṃhitā*-texts. For example, the *Saṃhitā*-text त्वम ह्यग्ने is recited as तुअम् हि अग्ने on the ground of metre. But in the Word-text the verse is presented in a complete grammatical analysis.[70] In large number of cases in the *Ṛgveda* the vowels which according to Sanskrit grammar have been always short, are lengthened, apparently only because the metre requires it. For example, the *pāda* अध हि अग्ने (IV.10.2) is lengthened as अधा ह्यग्ने when it comes to recitation.[71]

The Vedic hymns are in various metres, *Gāyatrī* (*gā*–to sing), *Anuṣṭubh*, *Triṣṭubh* and *Jagatī* being the most common and the *Gāyatrī* the oldest in popularity. It has been said, 'One who knows the *Gāyatrī* gains the three worlds.'[72] In Vedic mythology *Gāyatrī* in the form of a bird fetches the *Soma* juice from heaven. The *Anuṣṭubh* became popular in the later Vedic hymns and it was from this popular metre, that there developed the *śloka*, the chief epic metre of later times. This metre was widely used for all kinds of poetry, especially for didactic and narrative verse.[73]

Piṅgala is a very ancient author who has dealt with metres in his *Chandha-Sūtra*[74] in algebraic form. Piṅgala is also called Nāgapiṅgala,[75] perhaps a mystical personality. The names and the number of metres treated by him indicates that there existed a highly developed secular literature before him. The names of numerous metres such as the *Cāruhāsinī* (Beautiful Smile), the *Śaśikalā* (Digit of the Moon), the *Kāmakrīḍā* (Love Sports), the *Vasantotsava* (Spring Festival), the *Aśoka-puṣpa-mañjarī* (Blossom of Aśoka Flowers) and so on indicate that originally they were love-lyrics.[76] Varāhamihira, being a scholar of astronomy, incorporates the subject of prosody into the chapter on *Grahagocarādhyāya*, Transits of Planets. Making a comparison between gems and *śāstras*, he observes: as gems become fit to be worn as ornaments and are highly esteemed, so is the case with the *śāstras* or scientific works, joined together with excellent ideas couched in fine metres.[77] This chapter, according to the author, contains a collection of metres that are pleasant to hear.[78] The commentator Bhaṭṭotpala explaining this verse has stated: 'Numerous teachers have described the characteristics of metres but they are difficult to comprehend and not fit to be heard, whereas Varāhamihira has made them worthy to be heard, to be easily understood, comprehensive and at the same time brief.'[79]

Citing Māṇḍavya, Piṅgala has said: 'Hearing the words of Māṇḍavya, one may not like my statements, but that is not correct. The reason is that men do not love their devout and chaste wives as they do women moving their hips (*jaghana-capalā*, courtesans).'[80] In other words the author is calling his verses more charming like *jaghana-capalā*. Varāhamihira has provided seven varieties of *Āryā*, viz., मुखचपला, जघनचपला, पथ्या, विपुला, वक्त्र, वैतालीय and औपच्छन्दसिक; three varieties of *Daṇḍakas*, viz., चंडवृष्टिप्रयात (प्रपात), वर्णदण्डक and समुद्रदण्डक, and 47 *vṛttas*. He employes numerous metres which are not found in any other work on prosody. He provides a romantic name *Vilāsinī* (104.31) which is found neither in the *Piṅgala* nor in the *Vṛttaratnākara*. He calls *Hariṇī* as *Vṛṣabhacarita* (104.10). *Suvadanā* (104.6), *Śālinī* (104.30) and *Caṇḍavṛṣṭiprayāta* (or *Prapāta*) (impetuous rainfall) are other names of his metres. A work on Prakrit prosody known as the *Prākṛta-piṅgala-sūtra* is ascribed to Piṅgala, but it may a later work.[81]

The old metres were also employed in the Śvetāmbara Jain Ardhamāgadhī canonical literature. As we have seen, German scholars like Jacobi, Leumann, Schubring and Alsdorf have discussed the antiquity of certain canons on the basis of metre. The *Triṣṭubh*, the *Jagati*, the *Vaitālīya*, the *Aupachandasika*, the *Śloka* and the Old *Āryā* (or the *Gāthā*) are considered to be the old metres in which the oldest stratum of the extant canonical works is available. Alsdorf has laid emphasis on the study of metrical investigation in order to ascertain the critical text of the existing canon which contains old textual corruptions, even older than all the Sanskrit commentaries written on the canonical texts. He does not agree with the views expressed by J. Charpentier, in the Preface of his critical edition of the *Uttarādhyayana*, justifying the correctness of the text of the *Sūtras* relying on the authority of Devendragaṇi's commentary. Alsdorf has pointed out that the utter disregard of metre, an invaluable help in textual criticism, has led Charpentier to the above conclusion. He writes: 'Even the oldest and best commentaries are completely unreliable. We are greatly indebted to their traditional knowledge and shall always carefully examine their suggestions; but in countless instances they misunderstand and misinterpret correct ones.'[82] He has given convincing proof in support of his statement by discussing various readings from the text of the *Uttarādhyayana* and the other canonical texts.[83]

THE GĀHĀLAKKAṆA[84]

It is one of the oldest works on Prakrit prosody. As its name indicates, it deals with *Gāthā*, the most popular metre of Prakrit poetry. In the beginning of his work the author has stated that after paying homage to Jinendra Nemi, he is going to define *Gāthā* as he has learned from his preceptors and to distinguish between long and short letters, as they are employed in Prakrit *kāvya*, composed by earlier teachers. The work was composed by Nanditāḍhya in 92 *Gāthās* dealing with the *Gāthā* metre and its derivatives. In two *Gāthās*, 31 and 61, he mentions his own name. In the former, he has shown his disregard for Apabhraṃśa language saying 'as the prostitutes have no real love for their passionate lovers, in the same way, in the sayings of Nanditāḍhya there are no such words as *jiha* (*yarhi*), *kiha* (*karhi*) and *tiha* (*tarhi*)'.[85] In the other *Gāthā*, Nanditāḍhya has enumerated six varieties of the *Gāthā* metre, *Gāha, Gāhā, Vigāha, Uggāha, Gāhiṇī* and *Khandha*.

The author has also dealt with the *Paddaṭikā*, the *Nadanāvatāra* and the *Dohā* with its varieties the *Upadohā* and the *Apadohā*. But it should be noted that these metres belong to Apabhraṃśa and their definitions as well as the illustrations are also composed in Apabhraṃśa, which goes against the statement of the author. Having discussed this and such other points, H.D. Velankar comes to the conclusion that of a total of 92 stanzas, only about 65 seem to have been composed by the author.[86] At one place, in the beginning of the *Gāthā* 76, the author refers to *granthāntara* (another work), stating that the metre *Candāṇaṇa* is also called the *Madanāvatāra*. This verse is clearly borrowed from Virahāṅka's *Vṛttajātisamuccaya*, and the following verse is actually quoted from this work (I.7). Then, verse 56 is identical with the verse of Rājaśekhara's *Karpūramañjarī* (II. 49). Verse 4 is noticed in Bharata's *Nāṭyaśāstra* (XVIII.6). Besides, the verses 16, 74, 78 and 80 are quoted without mentioning the source, in the commentary of the *Sandeśrāsaka* (Bhayani's ed. 1945) as verses 2, 20, 119 and 94 respectively.[87] Velankar has also traced a quotation in the commentary of the *Sandeśrāsaka* in which the name of Nandiṣeṇa occurs. In this quotation we have a definition of the strophic couplet Raḍḍā, but no quotation is found in the present work.[88]

According to Velankar, our author belonged to somewhere around AD 1000 (i) while illustrating the short in Prakrit, he quotes a stanza from Rājaśekhara's *Karpūramañjarī* (II.49) in verse 56; (ii) Hemacandra in his *Chandonuśāsana* (IV.5-9-11) seems to have quoted from the *Gāhālakkhaṇa* (verses 40-2). Muni Ratnacandra, pupil of *Mahākavi* Devānanda, the author of 108 *Prakaraṇas*, has written a commentary on this work. Harṣaṭa, son of Bhaṭṭamukula, was another commentator according to the Jaisalmer Bhandar Catalogue (p. 61).[89]

VṚTTAJĀTISAMUCCAYA[90]

This is a collection of *vṛtta* or *varṇa* (syllables) and *jāti* or *mātrā* (syllabic instants) metres. It is an important and old work on Prakrit prosody belonging to the classical school of poetry. It is a regular treatise on Prakrit metre written in Prakrit verse by Virahāṅka (distinguished by *viraha*), who may have composed the treatise during the period of *viraha* or separation from his beloved. The author was a learned Brāhmaṇa, a scholar of Sanskrit and Prakrit, and addressed his work to his beloved (*dayitā*). He belongs to the period between the sixth and the eighth century.[91] At the outset, he pays obeisance to goddess Sarasvatī and remembers great poet Gandhahastin, his teacher[92] Sadbhāvalāñchana, Piṅgala, and Avalepacihna.[93] He has also remembered Bhujagādhipa,[94] Viṣadhara,[95] Sālāhaṇa (Sātavāhana or Hāla) and *Vṛddhakavi*.[96] The author has compared his intelligence (*buddhi-vibhava*) with the almost invisible woolly growth on the cheeks of a lovely lady.[97] This work is also known as the *Kaisiṭṭhachanda* or the *Kaisiṭṭavṛttajāisamuccaya* as mentioned in the third and sixth colophons.[98]

Gopāla, the son of Cakrapāla, has written commentary on this work. At the outset he pays obeisance to Piṅgala, Saitava, Kātyāyana, Bharata, Kambala and Aśvatara, and declares that he was going to comment on the *Chandoviciti.*[99] (Examination of Metres) composed by Virahāṅka. The commentator has stated that he had to encounter many difficulties in writing the commentary: the scribes had not copied the manuscript correctly, the text was recited by those who were not well trained (*asaṃskṛta*), it had decayed, it was presented differently by different authors; therefore he had to collect different manuscripts and consult authorities and various other texts before writing his commentary. The commentator has quoted various authorities in support of his statements. He has quoted Sanskrit verses or even a *Sūtra*[100] from certain authorities, saying *tathā coktaṃ* or *etadeva uktaṃ.*[101] The commentator has also added a *Gāthā* or two of his own either to complete the sense or to avoid a wrong meaning.[102]

The *Vṛttajātisamuccaya* is one of the earliest works so far known on Prakrit prosody. It consists of six *Niyamas* dealing with several Prakrit metres and even a few Apabhraṃśa ones. In the beginning of Chapter One the author promises to define and illustrate the *Mātrā vṛttas* and the *Varṇa vṛattas.* Here he enumerates certain names of all the Prakrit metres except the 52 kinds of the *Dvipadī.* Chapter Two defines *Dvipadī,* as consisting of 4 *vastukas,* (metres of 4 lines) each followed by a *Gītikā* immediately after it. It is identified with *Gīti* by later prosodists. Chapter Three deals with 52 varieties of *Dvipadī* with illustrations. Chapter Four provides the definition of the chief Prakrit metre, *Gāthā.* It has 26 varieties, including *Skandhaka, Gīti* and *Upagīti.* The *Skandhaka*[103] has 8 *Caturmātrās* in each half with its 31 varieties, the *Gīti* 7 and a 1/2 *Caturmātrās* in each half, and the *Upagīti* 27 *Mātrās* in each half, distributed like the latter half of a *Gāthā.* Then he defines and illustrates 41 *Samacatuṣpadīs,* 11 *Ardhasama Catuṣpadīs,* 1 *Viṣama Catuṣpadīs,* 7 more *Dvipadīs* and 11 strophic metres. The *Khañjaka* and the *Khaṇḍodgata* are regarded as *Sama Catuṣpadīs;* the *Vaitālīya,* the *Aupachandasika* and the *Āpātalikā* are included in the *Ardha Sama Catuṣpadīs.* The *Dvipathaka* and the *Utphullaka* are mentioned as *Sama Dvipadīs* by Virahāṅka; they are included in the *Ardha Sama Catuṣpadīs* by Hemacandra, Svayambhū and others. The author treats the *Gāthā* and the *Gīti* at great length which shows that these metres were popular at his time. He defines strophic couplets such as *Raḍḍā, Mālāśīrṣaka, Adhikākṣarāśīrṣaka, Saṃgataka, Ekaka, Khaḍahaḍaka, Sopānaka* and others. He has referred to the metres *Aḍilla, Ḍhosā, Māgadhikā* and *Mātrā-Raḍḍā*, and we are told that these metres have been the specialities of the Ābhīrī, Māruvāī (Mārvāḍī), Māgadhī and Apabhraṃśa dialects respectively. In fact, as we find in the illustrations given by the author of the first two dialects, Ābhīrī and Māruvāī, they are nothing but the forms of Apabhraṃśa dialect.

Chapter Five defines 50 *Varṇa vṛttas*, and is in Sanskrit. The last chapter deals with six *Pratyayas* or proofs. They are *Prastāra, Naṣṭa, Uddiṣṭa, Laghukriyā, Saṃkhyā* and *Adhvan*. The *Prastāra* or tabular representation of the long and short vowels of a metre is of several varieties. The purpose of the *Naṣṭa* is to find out the unknown (*naṣṭa*) structures (*vṛtta*) of a particular permutation of a given metre, the serial number (*aṅka*) of this permutation in the midst of the whole of its *Prastāra* being given. The *Uddiṣṭa* is opposed to the *Naṣṭa*. Here the structure of the particular permutations given and we have to find out its serial number in the midst of the *Prastāra*. The *Mātrāvṛtta* and the *Varṇavṛtta* of the *Naṣṭa* and the *Uddiṣṭa* are described. The *Laghukriyā* is a process to find either the number of permutations containing a given number of short or long letters in them each, or the *total number* of short or long letters in all the permutations of a *vṛtta* taken together. The *Saṃkhyā* represents the total number of all possible permutations of the metre. The *Adhvan* or the Way is the space required for writing out the letters in a given stanza or in all permutations taken together of a particular metre as the case may be.[104]

THE *SVAYAMBHŪCHANDA*[105]

Svayambhū was a *mahākavi* and *ācārya* of Apabhraṃśa. He has been remembered with respect by Apabhraṃśa poets. He gained popularity by composing a book on prosody, hence he became known as the *Chandacūḍāmaṇi* (Head Jewel of Prosody). Besides being a poet of repute, he also wrote the *Svayambhū-Vyākaraṇa*. It has been said: 'The elephant in rut in the form of Apabhraṃśa, roams about freely only so long as it is not brought under control by the fall of driver's hook in the form of Svayambhū's *Vyākaraṇa* on its head.' He is compared 'with a lion, equipped with terrible jaws in the form of composition of excellent words, difficult to face on account of its claws in the form of prosody and poetics, and endowed with manes in the form of grammar'.[106]

Besides the *Svayambhūchandas* Svayambhū also wrote the *Paumacariu*,[107] related to the story of Rāmakathā or the Jain *Rāmāyaṇa*, the *Riṭṭhaṇemicariu*, related to the story of the *Mahābhārata*, also known as the *Harivaṃśapurāṇa*, and the *Pañcamīcariu* which is not available at present. A number of illustrations of the *Svayambhūchandas* are taken from the first two works as we shall see later. Svayambhū has also drawn upon the works of earlier or contemporary writers of Prakrit and Apabhraṃśa to illustrate the definitions of metres in his *Svayambhūchandas*. Out of these, the names of Ajjadeva (Āryadeva), Ahimāṇaiddha (Abhimānacihna), Isahala (Viṣadhara), Koūhala (Kautūhala), Goinda (Govinda), Caumuha (Caturmukha),[108] Chailla (Cheka), Jiṇaāsa (Jinadāsa), Niuṇa (Nipuṇa), Tiloaṇa (Trilocana),[109] Dhutta (Dhūrta), Pavaraseṇa (Pravarasena),[110] Pālita (Pādalipta),[111] Bhoia (Bhogika), Maūradeva (Mayūradeva), Mūladeva, Rajjautta (Rājaputra), Rāhā (Rādhā),[112] Vapparāa (Vākpatirāja),[113] Vammautta (Varmaputra), Viaḍḍha (Vidagdha), Vijjā (Vidyā),[114] Veāla (Vetāla),[115] Sālāhaṇa (Sātavāhana),[116] Hariesaeva (Harṣadeva),[117] Bhīru, Kaṇhadatta[118] and others.[119]

Svayambhū, who lived between the eighth and the tenth century was widely read. He has mentioned Raviṣeṇa (who completed his *Padmacarita* in AD 677), by whose grace he had been able to grasp the story of Rāma. He has also referred to the five *Mahākāvyas*[120] (*pañca mahāya-kavvu*), Bharata's *Nāṭyaśāstra*, Piṅgala's *Chandaśāstra*, the *Alaṃkāra-śāstra* of Bhāmaha and Daṇḍin,[121] and Indra's *Vyākaraṇa*, Vyāsa's *Mahābhārata*, Bāṇa's *Akṣarāḍambara* (*Kādambarī*) and Siriharisa (Śrīharṣa),[122] in his *Riṭṭhaṇemicariu*.[123] He has also referred to Caumuha, known for his *Paddhaḍiyā* metre, equipped with *Chaḍḍaṇikā*, *Dvipadī* and the *Dhruvaka*.[124] Besides quoting citations of the above-mentioned poets, the author in his *Svayambhūchandas*, has quoted numerous other authors or their works sometimes without mentioning their names.[125] At several places he has cited quotations from his own *Paumacariu* and *Riṭṭhaṇemicariu*. Sometimes it is noticed that certain ascriptions are assigned to some particular authors but in fact they are traced to the works of the author himself. For instance, the verse *bhāi-vioae* (VI. 54.1, p. 73) is ascribed to Caumuha, though it is recorded in the beginning of the 77th *sandhi* of the *Paunacariu*; the verse *paura-juāṇo* is ascribed to Bhoia (Bhogika) but is recorded in the *Gāhāsattasaī* as well as in the *Vajjālagga*; the verse *suhaa gamaṃ tuha virahe* is ascribed to Candana but it is recorded in the *Vajjālagga*; the verse *te ccia suhāa* is ascribed to Viaḍa (Vidagdha), but is recorded in the *Paramātmaprakāśa* of Yogīndu. Then, certain verses are cited under the names of Maūradeva[126] (Mayūradeva) and Rajjaputta (Rājaputra) but are the part and parcel of the author's *Paunacariu*.[127]

The *Svayambhūchandas* is an important manual of Prakrit and Apabhraṃśa metres. It was one of the basic sources of Hemacandra who modelled his *Chandonuśāsana* on this treatise. It has been quoted as an authority on prosody by later writers. The published text is divided into the *Uttarabhāga* and the *Pūrvabhāga.* As we have noticed, the *Pūrvabhāga* was available to the editor only after the *Uttarabhāga* was already printed, hence the reverse order.

The P. contains 6 sections. Section I of which the first 22 pages are not available should be called the *Skandhaka-jāti* instead of the metres of the *Gāthā* class with *Skandhaka, Gāthādi-vidhi*; it deals with 3 varieties, *Gīti, Upagīti* and *Udgīti.* The poet Pravarasena was known for its *Skandhaka* metre. This metre is taken as the base from which the *Gāthā* has been derived,[128] whereas other prosodists including Piṅgala consider *Gāthā* the basic metre. The *Gāthā* is divided into *Gāha, Uggāha, Viggāha, Avagāha* and *Saṃgāha.* Section II is known as *Galitaka-jāti.* It defines and illustrates the basic *Galitaka* and the metres derived from it. Section III is known as the *Khañjaka-jāti* and defines and illustrates several *khñjaka* metres such as *Khaṇḍa, Dvipadī, Adhikākṣarā, Narkuṭaka* and others.[129] A large portion of this Section is missing. Section IV is known as *Śīrṣakāṇi* or the *Śīrṣaka-jāti.* Here the *Dvipadī-khaṇḍa* is illustrated with a citation from Śrīharṣadeva's *Ratnāvali Nāṭikā* and Abhimānacihna, and the *Dvibhaṅgikā* from Abhimānacihna and Vākpatirāja. The concluding part here is missing. Section VI is known as *Māgadha-jāti.* A portion from the beginning is missing. Section VI is known as *Uktādi-vidhi.* Sanskrit *Varṇa Vṛttas* of 26 classes are treated, beginning with the *Ukta* and ending in the *Utkṛti.* A small portion consisting of some metres is missing here.

Coming to the second part, the *Uttarabhāga,* it contains 8 sections. Section I, known as the *Uktādi-vidhi* is the continuation of the sixth section of the *Pūrvabhāga.* It is a long section. While treating the *Varṇa Vṛttas,* the author does not employ the *Varṇa Gaṇas* while defining these metres, but always uses the five *Mātrā Gaṇas* or the five *Aṃśas.* He indicates how by the addition or removal of a letter or a *Gaṇa* from one metre another metre is formed. Here he deals with various metres. He does not mention a *yati* in the middle of a line of a *Varṇa Vṛtta.* He mentions special *Daṇḍakas* which he calls by the name *Mālā* and which contain an indefinite number of *Mātṛkā Gaṇas.* Section II is small and defines 14 *Ardhasama Varṇa Vṛttas* whose equal and similar halves are made up of unequal and dissimilar lines. Section III should be called the *Viṣamam,* though it is known as the *Prākṛtasāra* in the text. As the learned editor has pointed out, the title refers to the essential metres of the Prakrit language, consisting of all the three earlier sections, including those of the *Purvabhāga.*[130] This is against the Apabhraṃśa metres which are treated in the last five sections. The *Viṣama Vṛttas* which are classified as the *Udgatā, Pracupita,* the *Vaktra,* and *Padacaturūrdhva* groups are treated in this section. The last five sections (the fourth to the eighth) deal with the Apabhraṃśa metres. Out of these the Section IV, known as *Utsāhādīni,* deals with *Utsāha, Dvipathaka* or *Dohā* with its varieties, the *Upadohaka* and the *Avadohaka,* the *Mātrā* with all its varieties, the strophic couplets such as the *Raḍḍā,* the *Vadana, Upavadana, Maḍila* and *Aḍila* all enjoying special favour with Apabhraṃśa poets. Towards the end of the section we have the metres known as the *Dhavala* and the *Maṅgala.* Section V is known as the *Ṣaṭpada-jāti* where the metre *Dhruvaka* is defined as consisting of three classes, six-footed, four-footed and two-footed. Section VI is known as *Catuṣpadī-dvipadyaḥ* which deals with the *Catuṣpadī* and the *Dvipadī* metres. Section VII ought to have been called the *Śeṣadvipadyaḥ* and not *Śeṣa-catuṣpadyaḥ* as printed in the text. Section VIII, known as *Utthakkādayaḥ,* is the last one. Here are defined a few more Apabhraṃśa metres as the *Utthakka,* the *Madanāvatāra,* the *Dhruvaka,* seven types of *Chaḍḍanikā,* three types of *Gāthā,* the *Paddhaṭikā* and the *Rāsa.* Here we have the *Sandhi-bandha* or the *Mahākāvya,* employed for narrative poetry, and the *Rāsa-bandha* employed for lyric poetry, along with other miscellaneous metres.

THE CHANDONUŚĀSANA[131]

This is a comprehensive treatise of Sanskrit, Prakrit and Apabhraṃśa prosody, written by Hemacandra. The *Chandośāsana,* which is useful for the study of poetry, was composed after the *Siddhahema-śabdānuśāsana* and the *Kāvyānuśāsana.* Hemacandra composed it in Sanskrit *Sūtras* with a short commentary known as *Chandaścūḍāmaṇi.* For every metre he has provided illustrations which are self-composed and contain the name of the metre illustrated. Here the author uses the particular language to which the metre belongs. Thus he has given an independent status to Prakrit and Apabhraṃśa prosody. He has based his systematic account of the subject on earlier authorities (*pūrvācāryas*) such as Bharata, Piṅgala, Kāśyapa, Sātavāhana, Dhanapāla, Svayambhū, Saitava and others (some of them are unknown). The treatise consists of the following eight *adhyāyas*: (1) *Saṃjñā-adhyāya*, (2) *Samavṛtta-vyāvarṇana*, (3) *Ardhasama-viṣama-vaitālīya-mātrāsamaka-ādi-vyāvarṇana*, (4) *Āryā-galitaka-khañjaka-śīrṣaka-vyāvarṇana*, (5) *Utsāha-ādi-pratipādana*, (6) *Ṣaṭpadī-catuṣpadīśāsana*, (7) *Dvipadī-vyāvarṇana*, and (8) *Prastāra-ādi-vyāvarṇana*. The fourth chapter begins with *Gāthā*[132] which is called *Āryā* in Sanskrit. It is divided into *Pathyā*, *Vipulā*, *Capalā*, *Gīti*, *Upagīti*, and *Udgīti*;[133] they are dealt with their varieties. The other metres defined and illustrated are about 24 *catuṣpadis*, called *Galitakas*; about 35 *Catuṣpadis* called *Khañjakas*;[134] then we come to the *Śīrṣakas*,[135] they include *Dvibhaṅgīs* or *Tribhaṅgīs*, consisting of 2 or 3 stanzas in different metres. It is stated that the *Śīrṣakas* are well known among Magadha bards and are known as the *Ṣaṭpadas* and the *Sārdhachandas*. According to the author, the other strophic couplets formed with *Mātrā*, *Ullāla*, *Dvipadī*, *Vastuka* and *Dohaka* should be included in the *Dvibhaṅgī*, and the *Raḍḍā* will be treated separately in deference to the practice of the elders. At the end of the chapter we have two longer *catuṣpadīs*, *Sama* and *Viṣams Śīrṣakas* in accordance with the practice of the elders.

After dealing with the Sanskrit and Prakrit metres, the fifth *adhyāya* deals with the Apabhraṃśa metres. Here we have the *Rāsakas*, the *Rāsa*, the *Mātrā* with its various types, the strophic *Raḍḍā*, the *Sarvasama Catuṣpadī*, the *Dhavala*[136] with its various types and finally the terms such as the *Dhavala*, the *Maṅgala*, the *Phullaḍaka*[137] and the *Jhambaṭaka*[138] applied to different metres and under different circumstances. The sixth *adhyāya* deals with the *Ṣaṭpadī* and the *Catuṣpadīs*. The *Ṣaṭpadajāti*, the *Upajāti* and the *Avajāti* are defined here, containing 7, 8 and 9 *mātrās* respectively. In the beginning the *Dhruvā* and *Chaḍḍanikā* are explained as being applied to any kind of metre. The *Ṣaṭpadīs* are followed by the 110 *Ardhasama Catuṣpadīs* and 9 *Sarvasama Catuṣpadīs*. The longer and the shorter *Dvipadīs* are defined in the seventh chapter. The last chapter deals with six *Pratyayas* or proofs: *Prastāra*, *Naṣṭa*, *Uddiṣṭa*, *Sarvaikādigalakriyā*, *Saṃkhyā* and *Adhvana* and their various types.

Chandaḥkandali is a work on prosody on Prakrit metres. It is not available and its author is unknown. The commentator of the

Kavidarpaṇa has referred to this work and has given quotations from here:

(i) Definition of मात्रा पंचपदी (मत्तवालिका, मधुरिका, मत्तविलासिनी, मत्तकरिणी and बहुरूवा) (II.28.66-8, p. 33):

(a) मत्तच्चिय बुच्चइ मत्तवालिया दुइयतुरियचरणेसु।
पढम टगणंमि तगणे कयं वि जुगवं अजुगवं वा॥ 66॥

(b) समचरणणिहणाटगणे ते पुव्वकमेण मत्तमहुयरिया।
इय मत्तविलासिणिया सिहिसरपयमुहदुतेसु दुटा॥ 67॥

(c) मत्तकरिणीव एवं सिंहिसर पायेसु टंमि जइ तगणो।
एयासिं मत्ताईण संकरो होइ बहुरूवा॥ 68॥

It is stated that their illustrations should be known from some other work.

(ii) Twenty-four types of षट्पदी are referred to (II.30.71-2, p. 35):

(a) जीइ कलाउ दसाई सत्तर संता य सिहिरसपएसु।
सेसेसु सत्त छपई सा छपई नाम अट्ठविहा॥ 71॥

(b) इय अट्ठहि उवजाई सत्तट्ठाणे कलाहि अट्ठविहा।
नवहि पुणो अवजाई एवं चउवीसहा छपई॥ 72॥

(iii) ध्रुवा, ध्रुवक, घत्ता and छड्डुणिका have been defined (II.30. 73-4, p. 35):

(a) कडवयनिवहो संधी पद्धडियाईहिं चउहिं पुण कडवं।
संधिमुहे कडवंते धुवा च धुवयं च घत्ता वा॥ 73॥

(b) सा तिविहा छपई चउपई य दुपई य तासु पुण दुन्नि।
छचउप्पईओ कडवयनिहणे छडुणियनामावि॥ 74॥

(iv) Four types of चतुःपदी is mentioned (II.30. 75-80, p. 36):

(a) अह चउपईओ चउहा हवंति अंतरसमा तहद्धसमा।
संकिन्ना सव्व समा य तासु तावंतर समाओ॥ 75॥

(b) विसमे सेगा सेगा सत्ताई सोल जाव पत्तेयं।
अट्ठाई जा सत्तरझ सेगा सेगा समे मत्ता॥ 76॥

(c) चंपय कुसुयाइनामियाओ जाईओ हुंति पणपन्ना।
दिसिगहवसुहयरससरसायर-सिरिनयणचंद-भेएहिं॥ 77॥

(d) एआओच्चिय सुमणोरमाइनामाओ वच्चए मुणह।
एवं दहुत्तरसयं चउप्पई अंतरसमाओ॥ 78॥

(e) अंतरसमयच्चिय दुइयतइय पायाण विणिमयंमि कए।
अद्धसमा य दहुतर सयसंखा तेहिं नामेहिं॥ 79॥

(f) दुहि तिहि चउहि वि विसरिसपाएहि विमिस्सियाओ संकिन्ना।
सव्वसमाओ पुण सरीसएहिं सव्वेहिं पाखहिं॥ 80॥

THE KAVIDARPAṆA[139]

This Mirror of Poets is a manual of prosody which deals with the Prakrit and Apabhraṃśa metres, but primarily with the *Mātrāvṛttas.* Unfortunately, the name of the author is not known. In the beginning he declares that having paid his obeisance to God Arihanta, showing favour to the ignorant and following the precepts of the *śāstras,* he was going to deal with three types of metres in Prakrit. The author has referred to various Prakrit and Sanskrit authorities on the subject and has quoted their work by way of illustration which indicates his wide learning.

As pointed out by H.D. Velankar in his Introduction to the treatise (p. ii), Jinaprabha at the end of his commentary on Nandiṣeṇa's *Ajiyasantithava,* mentions the *Kavidarpaṇa* as the source of the definitions of his *chandas.*[140] It is also found that Jinaprabha reproduces some *gāthās* in the beginning of his commentary from the *Kavidarpaṇa.*[141] He wrote this commentary in AD 1308[142] where he has preferred to follow *Kavidarpaṇa* instead of Hemacandra's *Chandonuśāsana.* From this it is inferred that our author belongs to about the thirteenth century. Like its author the name of the commentator is also unknown. Perhaps the commentary was composed not long after the text, as Velankar has suggested.[143]

The author of the text as well as the commentator both give extensive quotations. Some of these are from well known works; some are not available at present; and some are from unknown sources. The author reproduces various illustrations such as those of the *Śrīdhavala* metre from Hemacandra's *Chandonuśāsana,* the *Dvipadikhaṇḍa* from Śriharṣa's *Ratnāvali Nāṭikā,* the *Cūḍāla-dohaka* from Jinasiṃhasūri (the work unknown), the *Dvibhaṅgī* from Sūriprabhasūri (the work unknown) and the *Dvibhaṅgī* from Tilakasūri (the work unknown). Certain names of distinguished personalities have also been referred to in the text. For example, Yaśoghoṣasūri is mentioned as a well known *gaṇadhara,* who was proud of his knowledge and none equalled him in eloquence of speech. At another place Guru Samudrasūri is eulogized and compared with the desire-yielding tree (*kalpavṛkṣa*). The opinion of Ācārya Seyava (Saitava) is quoted that the *Vakra* becomes a *Vipula Vakra* when the seventh letter is short in all the four *pādas.* Besides, the author has mentioned king Bhīmadeva, Kumārapāla and Śākambharīrāja in eulogizing terms. The commentator too makes similar references to Siddharāja, Jayasiṃha and Kumārapāla, praising

Kumārapāla as an unprecedented ruler of his time, and that there was no one like him in the past and no one will be in future.

The commentator quotes a Prakrit stanza from Pādaliptasūri[144] about whom a reference has been made earlier as author of non-existing *Taraṅgavaikahā* and also a collaborator of the *Gāhāsattasaī*. He has also quoted Manoratha's Prakrit stanzas from his unknown work on prosody.[145] The commentator has also verses from the *Chandakandali*. He has quoted grammatical rules from Hemacandra's *Siddhahema* in order to explain Prakrit words and forms occurring in the text.

The unknown commentator was also a scholar of Sanskrit. He has quoted various authors who are considered authorities on prosody and poetry. In the beginning of his commentary, he has quoted Śūra, an authority on Sanskrit metres, who by paying obeisance to Lord Śambhū and remembering Piṅgala Nāganātha, describes three types of metres which give delight to learned people. He refers to *Piṅgala* who gave the name *Āryāgīti* to the metre which is known as *Skandhaka* in Prakrit. At another place, discussing the rules of *yati*, quoting Svayambū,[146] he cites the opinion of Jayadeva and Piṅgala that *yati* is compulsory even in the Sanskrit *varṇa vṛttas*, whereas Māṇḍavya, Bharata, Kāśyapa and Saitava and others do not agree with this view. Trilocanadāsa was another prosodist whose view regarding the *Āryā* and other metres had been cited.

The commentator also gives his own illustrations regarding the varieties of the *Gāthā*, its derivatives, varieties of a *Dvibhaṅgī* or a *Tribhaṅgī*, and so on. Sometimes these varieties are not mentioned in the text by the author himself, and are reproduced from Hemacandra's *Chandonuśāsana* by the commentator. He has given illustrations of different *Vipulās* which are all composed in Sanskrit. Many of them are directly reproduced from Halāyudha's commentary on the *Chandassūtra* of Piṅgala and some are through the medium of Hemacandra's *Chandonuśāsana*.[147]

The *Kavidarpaṇa* contains six *Uddeśas*. The author composes his illustrations like Hemacandra as a general rule to introduce the name of the metre in the illustration itself. *Uddeśa* I is introductory. The threefold division of metre is enumerated: the *Mātrā*, the *Varṇa* and both. Then different kinds of *gaṇas* are enumerated. Rules are laid down regarding the observation of the *yati* in the middle and end of a line. *Uddeśa* II deals with the *Mātrā vṛttas*, simple or strophic, composed in Prakrit or Apabhraṃśa. The *Mātrā vṛttas* are divided into eleven classes as they contain 2, 4, 5, 6, 7, 8, 9, 10, 11, 12 or 16 *pādas* in them. Among the *Dvipadī* metres the author has selected 2 *Ullālas*, called the *Kuṃkuma* and *Karpūra* in the language of bards of Magadha, and the *Mauktikadāma*. Among the *Catuṣpadīs*, the *Gāthā* stands first. It is of three kinds, *pathyā*, *Vipulā* and *Capalā*. The commentator provides additional information about some more kinds of *Gāthās*. Some divisions bear the names of the four castes. The four derivatives of the *Gāthā* are given: *Gīti*, *Upagīti*, *Udgīti* and *Skandhaka*. The commentator adds more derivatives. Then the author defines ten important *Ardhasama Catuṣpadīs* and twenty-one *Samacatuṣpadīs*; the *Dohaka* which forms a part of the former, plays an important role yielding five different derivative metres. Then various classes of *Samacatuṣpadī* are given. All the *Ardhasamas* form a part of Apabhraṃśa language. The metres, the *Vadana* (also known as *Aḍilā* and *Maḍilā*), *Galitaka*, *Vastuvadana*, *Rāsavalaya* and *Utsāha* are treated as Apabhraṃśa metres. Dealing with the *Pañcapadī*, the commentator has quoted verses from the *Chandokandalī*. Six different types of *Ṣaṭpadī* are given; it is called *Ghattā*. On the basis of the *Chandokandalī* the author gives two more names to *Ṣaṭpadī*, *Dhruvā* and *Dhruvaka*. Here verses have been reproduced from Hemacandra's *Chandonuśāsana*.[148] The *Ṣaptapadī* is also known as *Phulla*, for which the commentator has quoted Manoratha. The *Aṣṭapadī*, also known as *Śrīdhavala*, is defined. It has a specific name *Tarala* and is made of a *Dohaka* and *Saṃdoḥjaka*. The *Navapadī* is called *Raḍḍā* by some. The *Daśapadī* is a couplet formed by a *Dohaka* and a *Ghattā*. The *Ekādaśapadī* and the *Dvādaśapadī* both are *Tribhaṅgīs* or Triplets; the former is formed by a *Vastu* and an *Ullāla* and the latter by a *Khaṇḍaka* followed by *Gīti*. The latter has a specific name, *Dvipadīkhaṇḍa*. To illustrate this metre a quotation is cited from Śrīharṣa's *Ratnāvali*. The *Ṣoḍaśapadī* is made of four stanzas in the same metre like the *Paddhaṭikā*. It is called a *Kaḍavaka* and many such *Kaḍavakas* form a *Sandhi* which is equivalent to the *Sarga* in Sanskrit.

The *Uddeśa* III introduces the *Varṇa vṛttas*; they are divided into the *Sama*, the *Ardhasama* and the *Viṣama*. The first is again divided into 26 subdivisions or *Jātīs*.

The *Uddeśa* IV deals with 109 *Varṇa Vṛttas* of the *Sama Catuṣpadī* type, including the *Daṇḍaka*, eight *Ardha Catuṣpadīs* and all the four different groups of the *Viṣama Catuṣpadīs*. It deals with 26 types of *Jāti*, the *Śeṣa Jāti*, the *Daṇḍaka*, the *Ardhasama Vṛtta*, the *Viṣama Vṛtta* and so on.

The *Uddeśa* discusses the *Ubhayachandas* or Mixed Metres which are partly *Varṇa Vṛttas* and partly *Mātrā Vṛttas*. They are eleven in number, headed by *Vaitālīya*. The *Vaitālīya* group consists of three chief metres, *Vaitālīya*, *Aupacchandasika*, and *Āpātalikā*.

The *Uddeśa* VI covers *Pratyaya* or Proof: *Prastāra*, *Naṣṭa*, *Uddiṣṭa*, *Ekādilagakriyā* (*Ekādilaghugurukriyā*), *Saṃkhyā* and *Adhvayoga*, of which he defines only the *Prastāra* and the *Saṃkhyā*.

THE *CHANDOLAKṢAṆA*[149]

We have already referred to the hymn *Ajiyasantithava* (*Ajitaśāntistava*) of Nandiṣeṇa, who has employed 25 different types of metres in his *Stava*. In order to illustrate these metres, Jinaprabha wrote a *Ṭīkā* in AD 1308. This *Ṭīkā* is known as the *Chnadolakṣaṇa* where the definitions of metres are provided. As indicated in the concluding verse,[150] the commentator has used the *Kavidarpaṇa* as a source. Jinaprabha has also reproduced some of the *Gāthās*[151] from the *Kavidarpaṇa* in his work. He has preferred to follow the *Kavidarpaṇa* instead of Hemacandra's *Chandonuśāsana*.

The *Stava* consists of 35 stanzas in which 25 different metres are employed as already stated. These metres contain 8 *Varṇa Vṛttas*, 6 *Sama Catuṣpadi Mātrā Vṛttas*, 4 *Ardhasama Catuṣpadi Mātrā Vṛttas*, 6 *Viṣama Mātrā Vṛttas* and 1 strophic couplet. The 8 *Varṇa Vṛttas* consist of *Śloka* (3), *Āliṅganaka* (5), *Sopānaka* (8), *Khidyitaka* (17; known as *Vaṃśapatrapatita* in the *Kavidarpaṇa*, IV. 84), *Vidyudvilasita* (21), *Kṣiptaka* (24, 25; also known as *Rathoddhatā* in the *Kavidarpaṇa*, IV. 27), *Dīpaka Aḍila* (26 known as *Svāgatā* in the *Kavidarpaṇa*, IV. 28) and the *Nanditaka* (29).[152] Among *Sama Catuṣpadī Mātrā Vṛttas*, we have six types: the *Kisalayamālā* (19; similar to the *Kāmalekhā* of Hemacandra's *Chandonuśāsana*, 4.59 and the *Mālatī* of Virahāṅka's *Vṛttajātisamuccaya*, 3.35), the *Sumukha* (20), the *Ratnamālā* (23; the *Latākusuma* of the *Kavidarpaṇa*, 4.93 and the *Saṅgatā* of the *Vṛttajātisamuccaya*, 3.34 are similar), the *Lalitaka* (32; almost identical with *Galitaka* of the *Kavidarpaṇa*, 2.23), *Vānavāsika* (33; also in the *Kavidarpaṇa*, 2.20) and the *Aparāntikā* (34; also in the *Kavidarpaṇa*, 5.7).[153]

Among *Ardhasama Catuṣpadī Mātrā Vṛttas*, we have four types: the *Māgadhikā* (4 and 6; its definition is quoted from the *Kavidarpaṇa*, 2.18; it is exactly the same as the *vaitālīya* in its constitution), the *Kusumalatā* (15; this is another name of *Aupacchandasika* according to the *Kavidarpaṇa*, 5.2; the *Kusumalatāgṛha* of Hemacandra's

Chandonuśāsana, 6.19.54 is almost identical); the *Bhujaṅgapari raṅgita* (16) and the *Citrākṣarā* (27).[154]

Among the *Viṣama Mātrā Vṛttas*, we have six types: the *Gāthā* (1 and 2, also 35, 36 and 37; we have noted earlier that the verses 1, 2, 2A are identical with the verses of the *Kavidarpaṇa* I.2, II.4 and II.5 respectively), *Saṅgataka* (7), *Rāsālubdhaka* (10), *Rasanandita* (12), *Citralekhā* (13) and *Lalitaka* (18).[155]

The 25th type of metre is the strophic couplet.

Besides these 24 single and 1 strophic metres, Nandiṣeṇa has employed three different kinds of *Nārāca* (14, 18, 31) and three different kinds of *Veḍha* (8, 11, 22) metres in his commentary. The *Nārāca* and the *Veḍhaka* (*Veṣṭaka*) do not belong to the category of metre. Both are rhythmic kinds of prose, undivided into *padās*; they do not contain a definite number of *mātrā* or *varṇa gaṇas*, or short and long letters, but are full of *anuprāsa* and in some cases of rhyming ends of words and compounds.[156]

THE CHANDAḤKOŚA[157]

This work is composed partly in Prakrit and partly in Apabhraṃśa, the stanzas 1-4 and 51-74 are written in Prakrit and 5-50 in Apabhraṃśa. It deals with about 50 metres, most of which are illustrated by Apabhraṃśa stanzas. It refers to Arjuna (or Alhu) and Gosāla (or Gulhu), who are called *kavi* (poet) and their opinion with regard to the rules of prosody is quoted.[158] The author has also quoted Piṅgala[159] and Nāgarāja (nāyāṇaṃ Īseṇa).[160]

Ratnaśekhara, the author of the *Chandaḥkośa*, was a disciple of Vajrasenasūri and successor of Hematilakasūri of the Nāgapurīya Tapāgaccha. He was a contemporary of Ferozshah Tughlaq to whom Tughlaq preached. He was born in 1315, was initiated in 1327 and appointed *ācārya* in 1345. Besides the *Chandaḥkośa* he had also composed the *Sirivālakahā*, the *Guṇasthānakramāroha* with *vṛtti*, the *Laghukṣetrasamāsa*, the *Saṃbohasattari* and the *Guruguṇaṣaṭtṛṃśikā*. Candrakīrti, who was a lineal descendant of Ratnaśekhara and successor of Bhaṭṭāraka Rājaratnasūri, has commented on this work. This treatise was composed in the second half of the fourteenth century and there was a difference of more than two centuries between the author and the commentator.[161]

Here the treatment of the Prakrit and the Apabhraṃśa metres does not seem to be very methodical. Among Prakrit metres, he defines only the *Gāthā* metre with its varieties such as *Pathyā* and its derivatives like *Gīti* and others. 26 varieties of *Gāthā* are mentioned and 4 of them bear the names of the four castes. As stated earlier, the author employes the Apabhraṃśa language in the verses 5 to 50 where the metres defined are those which were mainly used in Apabhraṃśa poetry. In all 45 metres are defined of which 14 are *Varṇa Vṛttas*, 15 *Sama Catuṣpadī Mātrā Vṛttas*, 7 *Ardhasama Catuṣpadī Mātrā Vṛttas*, 2 *Viṣama Catuṣpadī Mātrā Vṛttas* and 7 strophic couplets, both the constituent metres of which are the *Mātrā Vṛttas.* The treatment of these five different classes of metres does not follow any definite method of classification and hence their description has been confused. In the beginning the 8 *Varṇa Vṛttas,* in which 8 *Akṣara Gaṇas* appear singly, are defined. They are the *Somakānta* (4), *Dodhaka* (5), *Mauktikadāma* (6), *Troṭaka* (7), *Bahula* (8), *Bhujaṅga-prayāta* (9), *Kāminīmohana* (known as *Madanāvatāra* in Prakrit prosody) (10), and *Madanākula* (11). The next four *Varṇa Vṛttas* defined are the two *Nārācas,* the *Somakānta* and the *Pañcacāmara* (14-15), and the *Brumila* (16) and the *Mehānī* (44). The next *Varṇa Vṛtta* defined is the *Hakkā* (45) and the last one is the *Nārāca* metre (46).

Among the 15 *Sama Catuṣpadī Mātrā Vṛttas,* we have the *Vijayaka* (19), *Ekāvali* (47), *Laghucatuṣpadī* (40), *Aḍilā* (41), *Maḍilā* (41), *Bhinna Maḍila* (42), *Mālatī* (49), *Paddhaṭikā* (a popular metre in Apabhraṃśa poetry) (36), *Ābhāṇaka* (17), *Roḍaka* (a well known metre endowed with beautiful words of *Deśī Bhāṣā;* also known as *Vastuka;* also as *Rasākula* according to the commentator) (13), *Gīta* (18), *Dvipadī* (35), *Catuṣpadī* (or *Chaupāī*) (37) and the last one *Daṇḍaka* (30). Among 7 *Ardhasama Catuṣpadī Mātrā Vṛttas, Dohā* (21-4) is most important; *Saurāṣṭra* or *Soraṭha* is an inverted *Dohā* in Prakrit (25). If five *mātrās* are added at the end of a *Dohā,* it is called *Cūlikā* (26); if ten *mātrās* are added, it is *Upacūlikā* (27). If the odd *pādas* of a *Dohā* contains 15 *mātrās* instead of the usual 13, and the even *pādas* are of the usual length, it is called *Udgrāhaka* (28). Another *Ardhasama Catuṣpadī* is *Ghattā* whose odd and even *pādas* contain 18 and 13 *mātrās* respectively (43). Then we have *Besara* or *Sphuṭa-Besara* (20). Among the 2 *Viṣama Catuṣpadīs,* we have *Verālaka* (33) and *Cūḍāmaṇi* (48) metres. Then, among the 7 strophic metres (all of which are *Dvibhaṅgīs* or couplets), we have *Ṣaṭpada* or *Chappaya* (12) (also known as *Kāvya* or *Sārdhacchandas* in Hemacandra's *Chandonuśāsana*), IV.79 Commentary, the *Kavidarpaṇa* (2.33) and the *Prākṛta Paiṅgala* (I.120). Another strophic metre is *Rasākula*

(29), then we have *Rāḍhaka,* also known as *Vastu* (34) (it is known as *Raḍḍā* to Virahāṅka (*Vṛttajātisamuccaya,* 4. 31 and the *Prākṛta Paiṅgala,* 1.133ff).[162] The remaining 4 are *Dvibhaṅgī* are *Kuṇḍalika* or *Kuṇḍaliyā* (31), *Kuṇḍalinī* (38), *Candrāyaṇa* (32), *Candrāyaṇī* (39).

The *Chandaḥkośa* as the name indicates is a collection of *Chandas.* Scholars have traced some of its verses in the *Prākṛta-Paiṅgala* and the *Sandeśa-rāsaka* of Addahamāṇa, a Muslim poet of the thirteenth century. In his introduction to the *Chandaḥkośa,* Velankar has pointed out a few similarities between the *Chandaḥkośa* and the *Prākṛta-Paiṅgala,* e.g. the expression गुल्हेकवि एरिस वुत्तउ (12) has been substituted by सेस कइ वत्थु निवुत्तउ in the *Prākṛta-Paiṅgala* (I.107).[163] He has also traced such verses in the *Sandeśarāsaka.* He writes, 'The *Chandaḥkośa* seems to be based upon some *Rāsakabandha* kāvyas or the *Rāsaka*-like, the *Sandeśarāsaka,* composed by Addahamāṇa. Most of the metres employed in this *Rāsaka* poem or the *Rāsabandha kāvya,* including the strophic couplets *Vastu* and *Raḍḍā,* are among those few which have been defined in the *Chandaḥkośa*[164] and the *Prākṛta-Paiṅgala* as well.'[165]

THE *PRĀKṚTA-PAIṄGALA*[166]

This is one of the most important documents of medieval Indian literature for comprehensive treatment of Prakrit and Apabhraṃśa metres. It records not only the definitions of the metres but also gives copious illustrations, some of which have been composed by the author himself. It is a collection of Prakrit and Apabhraṃśa metres selected from a wide range of contemporaneous literature. This work which belongs to the earlier part of the fourteenth century is valuable from the point of view of history and development of the Middle-Indo-Aryan languages in their various regional forms. It is also important from the point of view of development of Apabhraṃśa metres as they were employed by medieval Hindi poets in their compositions. As the work is a record of metres, we come across beautiful stanzas of lyrical poetry pertaining to the *Ādikāla* (early beginning) of Hindi literature. This was an age of bardic poetry when long narrative poems were composed and sung by *cāraṇas* or bards. Our work belongs to this age and in this respect it becomes different from the tradition of Svayambhū and Hemacandra.

In the beginning the author pays obeisance to Piṅgala or Piṅgala-Nāga, the first composer of prosody.[167] Subsequently he is also known as Phaṇīndra Piṅgala, Nāgarāja Piṅgala, or Bhogirāja when stanzas of earlier poets are given under his own name. Emphasizing the importance of metre it is said, 'As a gold weighing scale does not tolerate the minute difference in measuring weight, so is the case with the scale of ears (*śravaṇa-tulā*) which does not tolerate the violation of a metre in recitation. And if an ignorant man recites poetry in the assembly of wise people devoid of its marks (*lakṣaṇa-vihīna*), he is not aware that he is going to cut his own head by his sword.'[168] Here we have citations from Haribrahma, Babbara, Vidyādhara, Jajjala and others and also from the author himself. Besides we have citations from the *Gāhāsattasaī*,[169] Pravarasena's *Setubandha*,[170] Rājaśekhara's *Karpūramanjarī*,[171] Nanditāḍhya's *Gāhālakkhaṇa*,[172] Ratnaśekhara's *Chandaḥkośa*[173] and so on. The author has also referred to the exploits of Hammīra against the *Mlecchas* and against Alāuddin Khilji; a battle between him and the latter was finalized in 1302. While ready to march to the battlefield, Hammīra addresses his beloved, 'O fair lady, leave my feet and beautiful one, hand over the sword to me with a smiling face. After cutting asunder the bodies of the *Mlecchas*, certainly I will see your face once again.'[174]

The language of the *Prākṛta-Paiṅgala* is called as Apabhraṃśa or Avahaṭṭa. The grammarian Mārkaṇḍeya of the Eastern School considers the author of this work a great Apabhraṃśa poet. He has cited quotations from this work in his *Prākṛtasarvasva*. Several commentaries were written on this work: (i) Ravikara alias Śrīpati's *Piṅgala-sāra-vikāśinī*, (ii) Lakṣamīnātha Bhaṭṭa's *Piṅgala-pradīpa* (1600) (iii) Vaṃśīdhara's *Piṅgala-prakāśa* (AD 1642) all of them included in the present edition under Appendix I, II and III respectively. Among other commentaries are (i) Viśvanātha Pañcānana's *Piṅgala-Ṭīkā*, (ii) Kṛṣṇa's *Kṛṣṇīya-vivaraṇa* and (iii) Yādevendra's (also known as Daśāvadhāna Bhaṭṭācārya) *Piṅgala-tattva-prakāśikā* (all published in Śrī Candramohana Ghosha's *Bibliotheca India Series'* edition, 1902). These commentaries certainly indicate the popularity of the work.

The treatise contains two chapters, the first dealing with the *Mātrāvṛttas* and the other with the *Varnavṛttas*. The former includes the *Gāthā-prakaraṇa*, dealing with *Gāhū*, *Gāthā*, *Vigāthā*, *Udgāthā*, *Gāthinī*, *Siṃhinī* and *Skandhaka*; 27 varieties of *Gāthā* are enumerated. Among other metres like *Dohā*, *Rolā*, *Chappaya*, *Aḍillā*, *Pādākulaka*, *Caubolā*, *Culiyālā*, *Soraṭṭhā* and *Āhīra*, are described with their varieties.

A few illustrations can be noted below:

सेर एक जइ पावउँ घित्ता,
मंडा वीस पकावउं णित्ता।
टंकु एक्क जइ सेंधव पाआ
जो हउ रंक सोइ हउ राआ॥ I.130

If I could obtain one *seer* of *ghee*, I can prepare 20 fine loaves of bread and if I can get a few grains of *saindhava* salt (white rock-salt), though I am a poor man, I shall become a *rājā.*

Here is an illustration of *Culiālā* metre:

राआ लुद्ध समाज खल, बहु कलहारिणि सेवक धुत्तउ।
जीवण चाहसि मुक्ख जइ, परिहरु घर जइ बहुगुणजुत्तउ॥ I.169

If the king is voracious, the people are wicked, the wife is quarrelsome and the servants are knavish, O fool! if you want to live, you abandon your home though it may have many virtues.

Here is an illustration of the *Ābhīra* metre:

सुंदरि गुज्जरि णारि, लोअण दीह बिसारि।
पीणपओहरभार, लोलइ मोत्तिअहार॥ I.178

This beautiful lady is *Gurjarī,* who has wide open eyes and the pearl necklace is rolling around her fleshy breasts.

Chapter two defines *Varṇavṛttas,* giving their definitions and illustrations. At the end a list is provided of these metres. Here is an illustration of the *Sārasvatī* metre:

पुत्त पवित्त बहुत्त धणा, भत्ति कुटुंबिणि सुद्धमणा।
हक्क तरासइ भिच्चगणा, को कर बब्बर सग्ग-मणा॥ II.95

The poet Babbara says, if the sons are sinless, there is plenty of wealth, the housewife is of good heart and devoted, and the servants get scared (out of obedience) when called, why should one desire to obtain paradise?

Lexicography

Nirukta or explanation or etymological interpretation of a word is another important *Vedāṅga* after *Vyākaraṇa* and *Chanda.* The oldest lexicographic work carried out in India is recorded in the *Nighaṇṭavas* or Collection of Vedic terms. Due to the passage of time the meaning of these terms was going into oblivion and the scholars were interpreting them at their will. So Yāska (700-500 BC) took up the challenge and in order to interpret the sacred vedic text commented upon the *Nighaṇṭavas*. In his commentary known as *Nirukta*, the author, while interpreting the vedic hymns, has referred to various other writers who have provided contradictory explanations of the text. Yāska himself has presented more than one interpretation of a word. However, as stated in the *Nirukta* (VII. 1-2), this was the first systematic attempt to interpret the Vedic text.

Pāiyalacchīnāmamālā[175] is an important lexicon of Prakrit[176] by Dhanapāla who composed it for his younger sister Sundarī in 972 in Mānkheḍa, in Dhārā. Dhārā was a centre of learning in those days and Dhanapāla held an honourable position in the court of Muñjarāja who was the ruler (*dhārādhīśa*). This is the earliest *kośa* of Prakrit amongst the available ones. As we have seen, Dhanapāla is also the author of the *Ṛṣabhapañcāśikā* (50 verses in praise of Ṛṣabha). Dhanapāla calls his work *Pāiyalacchī* or *Deśī* or *Deśīśāstra*. He has included more *tatsama* and *tadbhava* words than true *deśī* words (according to Bühler, only one-fourth are *deśī*). The author himself has stated: 'He has incorporated in his work all the words commonly used by the Prakrit poets in their compositions.'[177] Unlike Hemacandra's *Deśīnāmamālā*, he simply enumerates the *deśī* words to help the poet, without giving their meanings. Hemacandra in his self-composed commentary on the *Bhidhānacintāmaṇi* has quoted some verses from Dhanapāla which show that besides the above-mentioned work he has also written other treatises not available at present. Here he has referred to Dhanapāla's excellence in *vyutaptti* (etymology), saying *vyutpattr dhanapālataḥ*. Hemacandra has also referring to Dhanapāla several times in his *Deśīnāmamālā*. Since none of the five passages referred to Dhanapāla are found in the *Pāiyalacchī*, scholars are of the opinion that Dhanapāla might have composed some other *kośa* from which these references have been quoted, or perhaps he might have been some other author of the same nomenclature.

The small lexicon consists of 279 *gāthās* in Āryā metre and comprise 998 Prakrit words with their synonyms. For Prakrit studies it is considered as important as the Sanskrit *Amarakośa* of Amarasiṃha.

Deśīnāmamālā[178] (Collection of *Deśī* Words) also known as *Rayaṇāvali* by Hemacandra is another important work on lexicography. Pischel has called it 'extraordinarily essential' for the knowledge of Prakrit. Hemacandra composed this work after his *Siddhahemaśabdānuśāsana* and the *Kāvyanusāśana*.

In the opening verse the author pays obeisance to the speech of Jina (i.e. the Ardhamāgadhī Prakrit) as the origin of all speech (*asesa-bhāsā-pariṇāmiṇī*). In support of his view, in his self-composed commentary he quotes a verse, already quoted in the *Kāvyānuśāsana*, saying that the speech of Jina was understood by gods as divine speech, by human beings as human speech, by Śabaras as Śābarī speech and by the animals as their own speech.[179]

The author has collected *deśī* words after giving a thought to the whole of the science of *deśī* words (*ṇīsesa-desi-parimala-pallavia*). What is a *deśī* word? According to Hemacandra, *deśya* words are those that 'do not appear to have any connection with Sanskrit in accordance with the rules laid down in his grammar (लक्षणे शब्द शास्त्रे सिद्ध हेमचन्द्रनाम्नि ये न सिद्धाः), which though derived from Sanskrit, are not found in that sense in the Sanskrit lexicons, which have changed their meaning in Prakrit, the change not being due to the secondary or metaphorical use of words (*gauṇa-lakkhaṇa*) and which are used in standard Prakrit from times immemorial, are considered as Deśī.'[180] Further, he says: 'If we collect the words from different regions such as Mahārāṣṭra, Vidarbha, Ābhira and others, there will be no end, and a man will not be able to collect them even though he spends the whole life, therefore we have collected only such words which are current in the Prakrit language from time immemorial.'[181]

Here we have to examine how far the definition of *deśī* is applicable to the *deśī* words incorporated in the *Deśīnāmamālā* composed by the author.

A number of words which are designated as *deśī* in this work are traced to Sanskrit origin. Pischel has diminished considerably the number of the *deśī* words recorded in the *Deśīnāmamālā*. The total number of *deśī* words contained here are 3978 arranged alphabetically according to the first sound, of which 100 are *tatsama*, 1,850 disguised *tadbhavas*, 528 doubtful *tadbhavas* and 1500 *deśī*. Out of the 1500 that do not seem to be *tadbhavas*, 800 are found in the modern Indo-Aryan vernaculars in a modified form. The remaining 700 *deśī* words may contain words of non-Aryan origin, if their equivalents are found in non-Aryan languages.[182] Pischel has pointed out numerous *deśī* words which are either associated with Sanskrit or have absolutely nothing to do with Sanskrit: (i) There are words classified as *deśī* which go back to the genuine Sanskrit roots, simply because they do not have closely corresponding Sanskrit words: (a) *pāso* (eye), *pāsaṃ* (*Deśīnāmamālā*, 6.75) is connected with Ardhamāgadhī *pāsai* (*paśyati* in Sanskrit), (b) *Sivvi* (*needle*), *Deśīnāmamālā* (8. 29) is connected with

Sanskrit *sīvyati.* (ii) Certain compound words whose component parts are basically true Sanskrit, yet have a special meaning ascribed to them in Prakrit that is not to be found in Sanskrit: (a) *acchivaḍaṇaṃ* (closing the eye), *Deśīnāmamālā* (1.39) with commentary; *Sattāvīsaṃjoaṇo* (moon), *Deśīnāmamālā* (8.22) *saptāviṃśati-yojana* (not *dyotana*). (iii) The *deśī* words having no Sanskrit root: (a) *joḍaṃ* (constellation), *Deśīnāmamālā* (3. 49), (b) *tuppa* (anointed), connected with Marathi *tūpa* (clarified butter). (iv) *Deśī* words that exhibit some rare phonetic law: (a) *gaharo* (vulture), *Deśīnāmamālā* (2.84), (b) *vihuṃḍuo,* (*Rāhu,* the seizer of the sun and the moon), *Deśīnāmamālā* (7.65)=*vidhuṃtuda* (moon-troubler) (Art. 9).

George Grierson holds the similar views about the *deśī* words. According to him, they are derived from the spoken dialects of other provinces lying round Madhyadeśa, the home of Vedic and classical Sanskrit in which they as provincial words did not find a place. A majority of these words may be called *tadbhavas,* if *tat* is taken in the sense of primary Prakrits instead of Sanskrit, though a few of them may have been borrowed from Muṇḍā and Dravidian. Grierson writes in his *Linguistic Survey of India* (Vol. I, pp. 127-8):

> *Deśya* words included all words which grammarians were unable to refer to Sanskrit, simply through the ignorance of the writers who catalogued them. Modern scholars can refer most of them to Sanskrit like any other *tadbhavas.* A few other are words borrowed from Muṇḍā or Dravidian languages. The great majority are, however, words derived from dialects of the primary Prakrits which were not that from which Classical Sanskrit has descended. They are the true *tadbhavas* although not in the sense given to that word by Indian grammarians in whose philosophy the existence of such ancient dialects was not dreamt of. These *deśya* words were local dialect forms, and as might be expected, are found most commonly in literary works hailing from countries like Gujarat, far away from the natural home of Classical Sanskrit, the Madhyadeśa. For our purpose they may be considered as identical with *tadbhavas.*[183]

Like the *deśī* words, the *dhātvādeśas* or 'root substitutes' also have not originated from Sanskrit. These 'root substitutes' have not been recorded in the *Deśīnāmamālā* as according to the author they were not current in Prakrit. The grammarians Vararuci, Hemacandra, Kramadīśvara and Mārkaṇḍeya provide much space to the *dhātvādeśas* in their grammars. Hemacandra in his *Deśīnamamālā* does not include the *dhātvādeśas,* but incorporates them in his *Siddhahemaśabdānuśāsana* (IV.1-259).[184] Grierson, in his monograph on the Prakrit *dhātvādeśas* (*Memoirs of the Asiatic Society of Bengal,* Vol. VIII,

No. 2, 1924) has classified them into four classes: (1) Those which are identical with the corresponding Sanskrit forms (for example, the root *cal* is identical in both languages), (2) Those which are regularly derived according to the ordinary phonetic rules, from the corresponding Sanskrit forms (for example, the Sanskrit medial ḍa becomes Prakrit *la*; the root *pīḍa* becomes *pīla*); such a root cannot be called an *ādeśa*, as there is no substitution, but only development, (3) Those which cannot be connected with any corresponding Sanskrit roots by any admitted phonetic rule (for example, an *ādeśa* for the Sanskrit root *cal* is *calla*). These are all true *ādeśas*, and a great number of them are borrowed from *deśya* words and cannot be referred to Sanskrit at all, (4) Those which are regularly derived from Sanskrit roots, but which have changed their meaning, and which are therefore, by Prakrit grammarians equated with and substituted for some other Sanskrit root which has a meaning more akin to the acquired meaning of the Prakrit word. Being substitutes they are also included under the category of *ādeśas*.[185]

It can be concluded from what has been said above that in want of sufficient material, it is impossible to decide in what way the Prakrit language grew. Traditionally, Sanskrit is called the basis of Prakrit (here Sanskrit should be taken in the sense of both Vedic, pre-Vedic and Classical Sanskrit). Really speaking, Prakrit and Sanskrit cannot be separated from each other. They are interdependent, there has been mutual borrowing on either side, and they should be viewed as two phases of common origin in linguistic development. George Bühler finds fault with Hemacandra, saying that in spite of his rare knowledge of Sanskrit and Prakrit, of his large literary and numerous assistants, he has mistaken scores of *tadbhavas* and *tatsamas* for *deśī* words, the reasoning being that the passages where the Sanskrit words occurred, were not accessible to him or not present to his mind.[186] Bühler has pointed out, 'If Prakrit *haluaṃ* can be derived from Sanskrit *laghuka* by rule of metathesis (*Siddhahema*, VIII.2.122) why can we not derive *aihārā* from Sanskrit *acirābhā* and yet Hemacandra calls *haluaṃ* as *tadbhava* and *aihārā deśī*?'[187] In this respect, some contradictions also are noted in Hemacandra. For instance, the word *ḍolā* is included among *deśī* words in his *Deśīnāmamālā* but in his *siddhahema* it is derived from Sanskrit *dolā*; similar is the case with *thora*; it is included among *deśī* in his *Deśīnāmamālā* but derived from *sthavira* in the *Siddhahema*. Hemacandra includes words whose Sanskrit equivalents can, by metaphorical use (*lakṣaṇā*), signify the meaning assigned to the

Prakrit word; for example, *gosaṇṇa* (*gosaṃjña*) derived from Sanskrit word *gosaṃjña* in the sense of *balivarda* or a fool. He also includes the following words as *deśī* in his *Deśīnāmamālā* but as *bhāṣā-śabda* in his *Siddhahema,* adding that they are provincial expressions, popular in Mahārāṣṭra, Vidarbha and other regions and should be known from usage: महाराष्ट्रविदर्भादिदेशप्रसिद्धा लोकतोऽवगन्तव्याः *āhittha, lallakka, Viḍḍira, uppehaḍa, maḍapphara, hallapphala,* and so on. It is concluded that neither Hemacandra nor his predecessors strictly follow the definition of *deśī* as formulated in the *Deśīnāmamālā.*[188]

The author has also incorporated here words of non-Āryan origin such as *aṅgutthala* (a finger ring; Persian *angustaī,* Pehlavi *angust,* Zend *angusta*); *uḍido* (a kind of pulse, Tamil *uḷundu,* Kannaḍa *uddu,* Hindu *uḍada*); *koṭṭhala* (a granary, Telugu *koṭṭu*); *cincā* (tamarind, Telugu *cinta,* Marathi *cinca*); *moggaro* (a bud, Telugu *mogaḍa,* Marathi *mogarā*); *pāva* (a snake, Dravidian *pāmu* or *pāvu*);[189] *ummara* (threshold of a house, Tamil ummārapadi); *cikkā* (small, Kannaḍa *cikkā*); *chāṇī* (cowdung, Tamil *Cāṇi*) and so on.[190] M.K. Amrit Rao has pointed out a number of Persian and Arabic words in the *Deśīnāmamālā.*[191]

Another thing to be noted with regard to *deśī* words is that Hemacandra does not consider the verbal substitutes (*dhātvādeśas*) as *deśī*; he includes some of them in his lexicon but says that he has consciously done so in accordance with the practice of previous writers (*pūrvācāryānurodhāt*).[192]

Further, there are certain readings adopted in the text which are not correct on etymological consideration and have been corrected by the editors in the Gloss by supplying critical notes: कुंढयं (I.63) should have been कुंडयं (Telugu *kuṇḍa*); वट्टिवं (VII.40) should have been वट्टियं (Telugu *veṭṭi*); पच्छेणयं (VI.24) should have been पत्थेणयं (=पाथेय); कुडुच्चियं (II.41) should have been कुडुव्विअं or कुडुंविअं, meaning sexual intercourse (सुरत); हत्थिहरिल्लो (VII.64) should have been हच्छिअरिल्लो, meaning dress (वेष).

Further, Pischel in his *Grammatis* (Art. 36) quotes some words from the *Deśīnāmamālā* about which the author is not sure of their correct form:

(a) It is not clear whether it should be अंबसमी or अंबमसी (I.37), meaning cooked grain wet with being kept overnight (स्तीमित पर्युषित कणिका).[193]

(b) अच्छिहरुल्लो or अच्छिघरुल्लो or अच्छिहरिल्लो (I.41), meaning an enemy (द्वेष्यः) or dress (वेषः).[194]

(c) अवडाहिअ or अवडक्किअ (I.47), meaning killed in a well (कूपादौ निहत:) or cried out (उत्क्रुष्टम्).[195]

(d) उत्तुहिअ or उड्डुहिअ or उडुहिअ (I.105), meaning broken (उत्खोटिम्) or the anger of a married girl (ऊढाया: कुपितम्) or the leavings of a married girl (ऊढाया: उच्छिष्टम्).[196]

Whatever it may be, Hemacandra was a versatile scholar. He not only formulated a new system of Sanskrit and Prakrit grammar, a new prosody, a new method of compiling Sanskrit and *deśī* words in his lexicons but also composed important treatises on poetics, logic, yoga and religious poetry. Pointing out the significance of his *Deśīnāmamālā*, Pischel has stated in his *Grammatik* (Art. 36): 'As far as I can see the *Deśīnāmamālā* constitutes an "authority of the first rank".' Hemacandra was an authority on his subject. He has fixed the forms of a number of words which were quoted wrongly by lexicographers, and he has pointed out innumerable inaccuracies of the composers of the *Deśīkośas*.

The *Deśīnāmamālā* is arranged in eight *vargas*, divided according to the initial letter of the words. They contain in order words beginning with the vowels, gutturals, palatals, cerebrals, dentals, labials, semivowels and aspirants. In each section words with one meaning are given first and then those with different meanings. The author has also written his own commentary. Here he has referred to *pūrvācāryas* (the earlier teachers), *eke* (some), *anye* (others), *kaścit* (some), *kecit* (others) and so on, indicating the difference of opinion with regard to the subject.

Hemacandra refers to Abhimānacihna whose *Deśīkośa* was composed in *sūtras* to which he added a gloss with illustrative examples. Udūkhala wrote a commentary on this work, which is not available. Gopāla was another author of *Deśīkośa*, not extant, but quoted several times in the *Deśīnāmamālā*. It was in the form of verses with the meanings of words supplied in Sanskrit. Devarāja was another writer of a metrical *kośa* where like Hemacandra the meanings of *deśī* words are explained in Prakrit; he is not known. Droṇa was another author of a *Deśīkośa*, explaining the words in Prakrit. We have already discussed Dhanapāla and his *Pāiyalacchīnāmamālā* and Pādalipta whose *Deśīkośa* has been referred to by Hemacandra. Rāhulaka is quoted but nothing is known about him. Sīlāṅk is quoted at several places as an author of the *Deśīkośa*. Then Avantīsundarī is quoted but nothing is known about her work. Sātavāhana or

Śālivāhana, also known as Kuntala, Cauracindha, Pūsa or Hāla, the well known author of the *Gāhāsattasaī*, has been also quoted seven times. The *Sārataradeśī* is mentioned in the *Deśīnāmamālā*. Besides, Lalladikṣita, the commentator of the *Mṛcchakaṭika*, quotes from a *deśīkośa*, the *Deśīprakāśa*, and Kranadīsvara in his *Saṃkṣiptasāra* (VIII, p. 47) refers to a *Deśīkośa* named *Deśīsāra* (*Sāradeśī* in 1.47 com).

Besides, we have the following *kośas*:

Prākṛta-lakṣmī by Dhanapāla composed in vs 1029, a Prakrit dictionary containing 279 verses. It is published by the B.B. and Company, Khargate, Bhavnagar, vs 1973. It is also edited by G. Bühler in *Beitrage Zur Kunde der Indoger Sprachen*, Vol. IV, pp. 70ff.[197]

Siddhaśabdārṇava also known as *Ṛjuprājñavyākaraṇa* or *Śabdārṇava* by Sahajakīrti, is a *kośa* containing six chapters with self-composed commentary. Recorded in the *BORI* Collection, III, No. 466.[198]

Sundara-prakāśa by Padmasundara, pupil of Padmameru, is another *kośa* containing five chapters. The manuscript is in the *BORI* Collection, VI, No. 1422, manuscript dated vs 1619.[199]

Among other lexicons we have the following:

Tauruṣkī-nāmamālā also known as *yavana-nāmamālā* by Somamantrīputra. It is a Sanskrit-Persian *kośa*. It contians 153 *ślokas* (calculated at the rate of 32 *akṣaras* per *śloka*). It is incomplete, Folio No. 1 missing. Mahimāsamudra copied it in Samānalakhānaḍerā. The manuscript, written in vs 1706, is preserved in the L.D. Institute of Indology, Library, Ahmedabad.[200]

Phārasī-kośa: the author is not known. It is also incomplete, and in a *guṭakā* form in Sanskrit. It is in good condition, the age being around vs 1950. The manuscripts are in the Institute at Ahmedabad.[201]

MODERN PRAKRIT *KOŚAS*

Abhidhānarājendrakośa,[202] an encyclopedia of Prakrit has been composed by *ācārya* Vijayarājendrasūri in the twentieth century. Ācārya Rājendrasūri was a great scholar of Prakrit and Jainism, who has compiled this seven-volume Encyclopedia, containing sixty thousand words, after a strenuous labour of 15 years. The work was finally completed in Surat. Here the author has explained the meaning of words in Sanskrit, quoting the original references in Prakrit or Sanskrit as the case may be. At several places he has quoted the whole reference. This authentic *kośa* is essential for the study of Śvetāmbara Jain canonical literature and Jainism in general. A commemoration volume in honour of the author entitled *Shrimad Vijayarajendrasuri Smaraka Grantha* was brought out by *Tīrthaṅkara* of Indore in 1957. The author has also composed an abridged form of his work, entitled the *Saddambuhi* (*śabdāmbudhi*), which is not published so far.

Ardhamāgadhīkośa[203] or *Ardhamāgadhī Dictionary* of Śatāvadhānī Muni Ratnacandra is another important *kośa* where words are explained in Sanskrit, Hindi, Gujarati and English together with their gender, number. It contains 4 volumes. Muni Ratnacandra also published an abridged form of this *kośa* under the title *Jaināgama Śabdakośa* in 1926.

Pāiya-sadda-maṇṇavo or *Prākṛtaśabda mahārṇava* (The Great Ocean of Prakrit Words)[204] by Pandit Hargovinddas Trikamchand Sheth, of the University of Calcutta. This *kośa* was compiled by strenuous labour of fourteen years and was published in 1928. Here the meaning of the words is explained in Hindi. Its second edition has been published by the *PTS*, Varanasi, in 1963.

Alpa-paricita-saiddhāntika-śabda-kośa by ācārya Ānandasāgarasūri, is published in 2 volumes.

Poetics

Like *vyākaraṇa*, *chanda* and *kośa*, the *Alaṃkāra śāstra* or the Science of Poetics is also essential to understand and appreciate poetry. *Alaṃkāra-dappaṇa* (*Alaṃkāra-darpaṇa*) is a treatise on Prakrit poetics (vs 116) recorded in the Gesatmere Palm-leaf Collection of MSS. Its author is not known. It contains 134 *gāthās*. The last *gāthā* is as follows:

अच्चंत सुंदरंपि हु निरलंकारं जणम्मि कीरंतं।
कामिणीमुहं व कव्वं होइ पसण्णं पि विच्छायं।।१३४।।

Rājaśekhara considers *Alaṃkāra* very important and as such recognizes it as a constituent of the *Veda*. Poetics deals with the characteristics (*svarūpa*), sentiments (*rasa*), defects (*doṣa*), virtues (*guṇa*), and figure of speech (*alaṃkāra*). There were numerous pundits of poetics in the past whose works have not come down to us and who are remembered only by name. Rājaśekhara in his *Kāvyamīmāṃsā* has divided the science of poetics into 18 *adhikaraṇas*, each of which was taught by a certain teacher. He has mentioned Sahasrākṣa, Auktikamuktigarbha, Suvarṇanābha, Pracetāyana, Citrāṅgada, Śeṣa, Pulastya, Aupakāyana, Pārāśara, Utathya, Kubera, Kāmadeva, Bharata, Nandikeśvara, Dhiṣaṇa, Upamanyu and Kucumāra.[205]

Among the well known exponents of the science of poetics we have Bhāmaha, Daṇḍin, Vāmana, Rudraṭa, Ānandavardhana, Kuntala, Abhinavagupta, Vāgbhaṭa, Ruyyaka, Bhojarāja, Mammaṭa, Hemacandra, Viśvanātha, Appayadīkṣita and Paṇḍitarāja Jagannātha. As we have noted in Chapter 5, in order to illustrate the subject of *alaṃkāra, guṇa, doṣa, vyañjanā* or *rati* they have preferred to cite examples from Prakrit poetry rather than the Sanskrit Kāvya. These citations have been quoted from the *Gāhāsattasaī, Setubandha, Gauḍavaho, Karpūramañjarī, Harivijaya, Viṣamabāṇalīlā* and so on. This indicates that there existed a vast corpus of Prakrit verses; however those quoted in these works are not properly edited and are full of misprints.[206]

We have already referred to the view of poetry by Bhāmaha and Daṇḍin, the two reputed rhetoricians representing the early school of poetics. Although there is an absence of quotations of Prakrit verse in their work, we find that they were authorities on the science of poetics.

BHĀMAHA'S *KĀVYĀLAṂKĀRA*[207]

Bhāmaha was one of the earliest critics to systematize poetic criticism and present it in condensed form. According to him one cannot become a poet only through mastery of rhetoric. He ridicules the knowledge of the *śāstras* in one who is not a poet, as noted above.

The *Kāvyālaṃkāra* consists of 6 *paricchedas* covering 400 verses. The first section deals with the body (*śarīra*) of poetry: words and meaning together are essential for poetry. The second and the third sections deal with the *alaṃkāras*, the *sabdālaṃkāra* (including *lāṭa, anuprāsa* and *yamaka*) and the *arthālaṃkāra*, among which *upamā* is discussed at considerable length. The fourth and the fifth sections deal with the *doṣas* or faults. The last section is devoted to the selection of suitable words among grammatical forms based on melody. Bhāmaha is often quoted by later rhetoricians and is held in high esteem.

DAṆḌIN'S *KĀVYĀDARŚA*[208]

Daṇḍin is also one of the reputed rhetoricians. He has composed his work in verses and in most cases, while explaining the subject matter, he has given his own examples. As we have stated earlier, he lays emphasis on *alaṃkāras* which he considers aids that give charm to poetry. The first *pariccheda* of the *Kāvyādarśa* deals with the body of the poem (*kāvya-śarīra*) which consists of a set of words in a sentence to convey the desired sense. Here the author enumerates four kinds of language, Sanskrit, Prakrit, Apabhraṃśa and the mixed one. Mahārāṣṭrī is called the excellent Prakrit, as it abounds in good sayings. Section two deals with the *arthālaṃkāra*, comprising the natural description, the *upamā* and the *rūpaka*. Section three deals with the *śabdālaṃkāra* which depends on pleasantness of words.

Comparing Bhāmaha and Daṇḍin, in the opinion of Kane, the latter is superior in the sphere of poetic excellence, whereas the former should be given credit as far as precision, logical acumen and clarity of expression is concerned.

VĀMANA'S *KĀVYĀLAṂKĀRASŪTRA*[209]

Vāmana, the author of the *Kāvyālaṃkāra* (AD 800) is the first to classify the subject matter (*artha*) in poetry. What is the immediate purpose and aim of poetry? Vāmana's answer to give delight or aesthetic pleasure. Vāmana belongs to the *Rīti* school as we have seen. According to him, *riti* or style is the soul of poetry and consists in the special arrangement or combination of words and the speciality lies in the possession of *guṇas*.[210] Vāmana has written his own commentary on the *Kāvyālaṃkārasūtra* where he deals with aesthetics and the rules of prosody and grammar.

RUDRAṬA'S *KĀVYĀLAṂKĀRA*[211]

Like Bhāmaha and Daṇḍin, Rudraṭa also belongs to the *alaṃkāra* school. In his work he discusses the principles of *alaṃkāra* in detail. He has also treated other subjects such as *bhāṣā*, *rīti*, *rasa* and *vṛtti* well, but the matter of *alaṃkāra* is his special choice. The *Kāvyālaṃkāra* is divided into 16 *adhyāyas*, containing 734 verses. There are 14 more verses in Chapter 12 dealing with 8 types of *nāyikās*,[212] with their subdivisions numbering 384. But this portion has been declared an interpolation. It begins with the purpose of writing poetry. In subsequent chapters follows the definition of poetry, the five *alaṃkāras* of *śabda*, the four *rītis*, *vakrokti* and *anuprāsa*, five *vṛttis* of *anuprāsa*, and 4 *śleṣas* and their varieties. The author deals with 6 *bhāṣās*: Prakrit, Sanskrit, Māgadha, Paiśāca, Śaūrasenī, and Apabhraṃśa, the last said to possess many varieties pertaining to different regions. The question arises as to why the language Prakrit is headed over other languages. The commentator Namisādhu replies: Prakrit is the natural language of intercourse of all beings of the world and not refined by grammar, rhetoric, etc. Thus, the author has put it at the head of all other languages.[213] Under *Citra-alaṃkāra*, the author has provided an example of *praśanottara* where three answers are given by the same word:

अहिणव-कमल-दलारुणिण माणु फुरत्ति ण केण।
जाणिज्जई तरुणीअणस्स निद्धामण (निद्धारण) अहरेण॥[214] V.32

What is reddish like a fresh lotus flower? *Adhara* (the lip). Who does not spring with dignity? *Adhara* (the one who is inferior). How do we view a young lady? By her *adhara* (lip).

ĀNANDAVARDHANA'S *DHVANYĀLOKA*[215]

The *Dhvanyāloka* also known as the *Kāvyāloka* or *Sahṛdaya-hṛdayāloka*, occupies an important position in the *alaṃkāra-śāstra* like the *Pāṇinī-sūtras* in the *Vyākaraṇa-śāstra* and the *Vedānta-sūtras* in the *Vedāntaśāstra*. Ānandavardhana also known as Ānandatīrtha (AD 860-90) was head of the royal assembly of king Avantivarmā (855-83) of Kashmir. 'This work shows great erudition and critical insight. It is written in a lucid and forceful style and bears the stamp of originality at every page.'[216] It is divided into 3 parts: the first is 129 *Kārikās* (in the first *KM* edition), known as the *dhvanisajñaka*; another is *Vṛtti*, the commentary by the author himself in prose, explaining the *Kārikās*, known as *ālokasajñaka*; and the third is the Examples, most of which are taken from previous authors.

Abhinavagupta has written a commentary, *Locana*, on this work. Another commentary known as *Candrikā* is mentioned[217] but is not available. Besides *Dhvanyāloka*, Anandavardhana is also author of the *Devīśataka*, the *Viṣamabāṇalīlā*,[218] the *Arjunacarita* and the *Dharmottamā* commentary (*vivṛti*) on the *Viniścaya-ṭīkā*. The author has referred to the following works and authors in his composition: the *Madhumathana-vijaya*,[219] the *Viṣamabāṇa-līlā* (his own work in Prakrit,),

Sarvasena (the author of the *Hari-vijaya* in Prakrit)[220] and the *Setu-kāvya*.[221] The author has also quoted his own verses in Sanskrit and Prakrit as illustrations.[222] In order to illustrate examples of रस, भाव, ध्वनि, अलंकार, etc., treated in the *Dhvanyāloka*, the author has quoted 46 Prakrit verses from standard Prakrit poetic works,[223] but some are his own compositions. Ānandavardhana seems to have set the tradition of quoting Prakrit verses freely in Sanskrit poetic works. Later, his commentator Abhinavagupta follows the lead.

As we have seen, Ānandavardhana is an upholder of *dhvani* school according to which the *dhvani* or implied meaning (प्रतीयमान अर्थ) is the real soul of poetry and not the expressed meaning (वाच्यार्थ).

Here are a few verses quoted by the author:

उदित्तर-कआभोआ जह जह थणआ विणंति बालाणम्।
तह तह लद्धावासो व्व मम्महो हिअअमाविसइ॥ III.4, p. 237

Elevated with her dispersed hair as the breasts of a young lady turns big, as if seeing an opportune time, the god of love enters the region of her heart.

चंदमऊहेहिं निसा णलिणी कमलेहिं कुसुम-गुच्छेहिं लया।
हंसेहिं सरय-सोहा कव्व-कहा सज्जणेहिं कीरई गरुई॥ II.50, p. 109

The night with the moon rays, the pond with lotus flowers, the creeper with a cluster of blossom, the autumn with swans and the discourse about poetry looks graceful with virtuous people.

DHANAÑJAYA'S *DAŚARŪPAKA*[224]

The *Daśarūpa* or *Daśarūpaka* is so called as it is concerned with the representation of ten principle classes of plays or *rūpakas*. It is a treatise on dramaturgy based on Bharata's *Nāṭyaśāstra*. As the slow-witted could get confused by reading the scattered text of Bharata, he has explained the meaning of the text briefly.[225] Dhanañjaya, the son of Viṣṇu, who belonged to the court of Muñja of Malawa, composed this work in the late tenth century.

The *Daśarūpaka* has been quoted by various scholars, authors and commentators. It has a commentary *Avaloka* by Dhanika. Dhanika was a poet himself, and has quoted his Sanskrit and Prakrit verses. He has also quoted from his *Kāvyanirṇaya* which is not available at present. In course of time, the commentary of Dhanika was considered an essential part of the original work and as such was given an important status. Subsequently, Bhaṭṭanṛsiṃha, in order to explain the difficult points of the *Avaloka*, composed his *Laghu Ṭīkā*. Among other commentaries, Bahurūpamishra's *Dasarūpaka-dīpikā* can be mentioned. The *Sāhasāṃkīya Ṭīkā* and the *Ṭīkā* of Devapāṇi have not yet seen the light of the day.

The text of the *Daśarūpaka* is divided into 4 *Prakāśas*. The second section deals with the dialect spoken by hero, heroine and the other characters. It is stated: Sanskrit should be spoken by kings, respectable persons, those who are disciplined, female wandering mendicants, the chief queen, the daughters of ministers and harlots. In general, women are supposed to talk in Prakrit, Śaurasenī is spoken by vile characters, and Paiśācī and Māgadhī by those who are very low.[226]

The commentary of Dhanika is full of quotations of verses. Over 330 verses are quoted here which included 20 by the commentator, some of them in Prakrit. About 26 Prakrit verses are from the *Gāhāsattasaī*, the *Ratnāvali*, and the *Karpūramañjarī*.

Here is a verse:

तह दिट्ठं तह भणिअं ताए णिअदं तहा तहासीणम्।
अवलोइअं सअण्हं सविब्भमं जह सवत्तीहिं ॥ II. p. 124

The looking, the talking, the standing and the sitting posture of the *nāyika* is viewed by her co-wives with curiosity and astonishment.

BHOJA'S *SARASVATĪKAṆṬHĀBHARAṆA*[227]

The *Sarasvatīkaṇṭhābharaṇa* is a comprehensive voluminous study of poetics composed by Bhojadeva or Bhojarāja, who reigned in Dhāra from about 1005 to 1054. He himself being a literary genius and author of the *Śṛṅgāraprakāśa*, the *Rāmāyaṇacampū* and many other works.[228] The text consists of 5 *paricchedas*. The first three have a commentary by Ratnadarpeṇa of Ratneśvara composed at the instance of king Rāmsiṃha Deva of Tirhut; the fourth one is commented on by Jagaddhara; the fourth and the fifth are commented upon by Jivanand Vidyasagara Bhattacharya.

In the *maṅgalācaraṇa* Bhojadeva pays homage to the four-fold Goddess of Learning, i.e. *dhvani*, *varṇa*, *pada* and *vākya*. Then he deals with the object of poetry, its characteristic types, 16 *doṣas* of *pāda*, 16 of *vākya* and the same number of *vākyārdha*, the 24 *guṇas* of *śabda*, and the same number of *vākyārdha*. The author deals with 24 *śabdālaṃkāras*, defines and illustrates 24 *arthālaṃkāras*, the figures of both *śabda* and *artha*, *rasas*, *bhāvas*, heroes and heroines. In all the text consists of 643 *kārikās*, some of which have been taken bodily from Daṇḍin's *Kāvyādarśa*, Ānandavardhana's *Dhvanyāloka* and other works. It contains over 1500 illustrations from its predecessor poets and therefore is important from the point of view of the chronology of Sanskrit literature.

Besides citing illustrations from various poets, the author has also referred to poets by name and composition, some of whom are not known. They are Adbhutappuṇya, Abhinanda, Amaru, Ānandavardhana, Daṇḍin, Dhanika, Namisādhu, Nidrādaridra, Pravarasena, Bhallaṭa, Bhāmaha, Mañjīra, Meṇṭha, Vāmana and Vikaṭanitambā.[229]

As stated earlier, the *Sarasvatīkaṇṭhābharaṇa* contains 350 Prakrit verses, of which 113 are quoted from Sātavāhana's *Gāthāsattasaī*.[230] The rest are from the *Setubandha*, and *Gauḍavaho*, the *Vajjālagga*, the *Ratnāvali*, the *Abhijñānaśākuntala*, the *Viṣamabāṇalīlā*, the *Karpūramañjarī*, the *Mṛcchakaṭika*, the *Harivijaya*[231] and many others; some are from unknown sources.

The author lays down the rules of language (*bhāṣā*). He says Sanskrit is spoken by gods and others, Prakrit by Kinnaras, Paiśācī by Piśāca, whereas Māgadhī is spoken by low-class people.[232] Paiśācī, Śaursenī and Māgadhī are different from each other, some use two dialects, and some all three. The inhabitants of Lāṭa, who hate Sanskrit, enjoy listening to the graceful Prakrit and people from Gujarat are delighted to hear their own dialect, the Apabhraṃśa. The last section deals with *rasa* (sentiment). According to his newly propounded theory, *rasa* is essential for good poetry, and *rasa* is generated from *ahaṃkāra* (self-consciousness). This is called the first stage of *rasa*, which gives rise to various feelings or emotions. These are transformed into *sthāyibhāva* (primary feeling), *vyabhicāribhāva* (transitory feeling) and the *sāttvikībhāva* (natural feeling). This stage *ahaṃkāra* is transformed into *rasa*. Therefore Bhoja does not make any distinction between *ahaṃkāra*, *śṛṅgara* and *rasa*. In his opinion impassioned (*śṛṅgārī*) while composing his poetry, the whole world can become full of sentiment (*rasamayaṃ*); if he is devoid of sentiment the world becomes like that.[233]

Here are some citations from the text. The following is an example of a riddle:

मोरुकलावेण बहइ तह णामह सरिणाउ।
उस्सीसा पाअंतिगओ अणुणत्तिहिं जणु णाउ॥[234] I.134, p. 80

The peacock carries spots like the moon in its tail-feather (*kalāva=kalāpa*) (this indicates the moon). The moon has journeyed from east (*ussīsā*=*ucchīrṣaṃ*=the east) to the west (*pāantigao*=*pādāntagate pādāntena*=west) (this indicates that it is dawn). I knew (*ṇāu*=*jñātaḥa*) this while conciliating her (*aṇuṇattihiṃ*=*anunayantyā*). This is uttered by a broken hearted woman whose husband or lover has been guilty of infidelity (*khaṇḍitā*).

A *khaṇḍitā* woman is addressing a red day-lotus flower (*tāmarasī*) as follows:

वल्लहे लहु वोलंतइ एत्तइ पुणु बहु, बलि
किज्जमि तामरसिणि तुज्झ रोसहु थिरहु।
जेण नि(णि)रग्गलु जंपइ किंपि णि (ण) जाव जणु (ण)
ताव हिमेण विसित्ति झत्थि (त्ति) पुलुट्ठतणु ॥[295] (IV. 87, p. 387-8); also *Śṛṅgāra P.*, X, p. 417

O *tāmarasini* (*padminī*=day lotus flower)! your beloved sun will make departure (*volantai*=*vyapakrāmati*) soon and even though it is a wintery long night it will return after a long time. I offer you tribute for your long lasting desperation (this was addressed by a *khaṇḍitā nāyikā* to *padminī*). The careless one is not at all aware of it and in the meantime you will be crumbled with cold and your body will be consumed.

BHOJA'S *ŚṚṄGĀRAPRAKĀŚA*

The *Śṛṅgāraprakāśa* of Bhojarāja is another important work on poetics, and like the *Sāhityadarpaṇa* deals with dramaturgy. It is considered one of the longest works in Sanskrit literature and the biggest on *alaṃkāra-śāstra*. It is edited by G.R. Josyer, containing 4 volumes (Vol. I, Chapters 1-8, 1955; Vol. II, Chapters 9-14, 1963; Vol. III, Chapters 15-24, 1969; Vol. IV, Chapters 25-30 (no year is mentioned) in all covering 1-1242 pages; Coronation Press, Mysore, Chapters 22, 23 and 24 published in 1926. As the editor has pointed out, it has taken full 20 years to complete this strenuous work. Dr. V. Raghavan has brought out another important edition under the title *Bhoja's Śṛṅgāraprakāśa*, published in 1963 from Madras. Here Raghavan has edited and corrected misprints of numerous Prakrit verses cited by Bhoja and has explained them. He has also dealt with other important aspects of the work.

The main purpose of the author is the exposition of *śṛṅgārarasa*, which he considers the best of all the *rasas*. Bhoja has stated: 'As meaning is prominent in speech, implied meaning (*dhvani*) in poetry, fortune among great merit of a beloved, charm in the body of women, so is *śṛṅgāra* in the heart of a man.'[236] Here he explains his new theory of identifying *rasa* with *ahaṃkāra*, *abhimāna* or *śṛṅgāra*. Elaborating his point of view he has stated:

अत्थणिवेसा ण वि तह चित्तविआसं कुणंति सच्चेविआ।
जह उण ते उम्मिल्लंति सुकविवआहिं सुसीसंता॥[237]

A simple utterance of meaning is not seen creating delight in the heart as words spoken by a good poet stimulate it.

Though the *Śṛṅgāraprakāśa* deals with drama and its 64 features, in the opinion of the author, the poet is to be given prominence over the actor (*abhinetā*) and poetry over acting (*abhineya*). Like Bhāmaha, he considers both *śabda* and *arha* essential for poetry.[238]

The text contains 36 *Prakāśas.* Like the *Sarasvatīkaṇṭhābharaṇa* this text also deals with poetics and grammar, including philosophy of language. He gives definitions of *kāvya*, *śabda* and *artha*, and deals with three varieties of Prakrit: *Sahaja*, *Lakṣita* and *Śliṣṭa*. *Sahaja* is of two kinds: *Sanskrita-sama* and *Deśya*. *Lakṣita* is of two kinds: *Mahārāṣṭrī* and *Śaurasenī*. *Śliṣṭa* is of two kinds: *Paiśācī* and *Māgadhī*. Then he deals with *Apabhraṃśa*, which is of three kinds: *Uttama*, *Madhyama* and *Kaniṣṭha*. *Āvantya* and *Lāṭīya* are included under the category of *Uttama* (the best); *Ābhīra* and *Gaurjara* under *Madhyama* (middle), and *Kāśmīra* and *Paurastya* under *Kaniṣṭha* (lowest).[239] The author discusses *vṛttis*, or connotations: *mukhyā* or conventional, *gauṇī* or secondary and *lakṣaṇā* or figurative.[240]

There is a section on the characteristics of drama (*nāṭaka-lakṣaṇa*) and *prakaraṇa*. Then, non-dramatic poetic compositions are described. 24 varieties of *śravya kāvya* are given. *Abhineya śravya* has the same number of varieties. They are आख्यायिका, उपाख्यान, निदर्शन, प्रवह्लिका, मन्थुल्लिका, मणिकुल्या, कथा, परिकथा, खंडकधा, उपकथा, बृहत्कथा, चंपू, पर्वबंध, कांडबंध, सर्गबंध, आश्वासकबंध, संधिबंध, अवस्कंधबंध, काव्यशास्त्र, शास्त्रकाव्य, कोश, संघात, संहिता and साहित्यप्रकाश.

An आख्यायिका is in prose as the *Mādhavikā*, the *Harṣacarita*, etc.; an आख्यान is in verse; it is recited while acting, narrating or singing. In उपाख्यान an episode is narrated to enlighten the readers as we have in the *Nala*, *Sāvitrī* and *Ṣoḍaśarāja-Upākhyānas.* A *Kathā* has no definite form or language, it may be divine or human or both, such as the *Kādambarī* (in prose) and the *Līlāvatī* (in verse).[241] A *Nidarśana* is an illustrative account explained by the activities of animals and other beings as we have in the *Pañcatantra* or similar accounts regarding *dhūrta* (knave), *viṭa* (sensualist) *kuṭṭinī* (bawd), *mayūra* (peacock), *mārjārikā* (cat) and others.[242] A *Prvahlikā* is a type of *śravya kāvya* written half in Prakrit, indicating some dispute between two persons over some important matter in assembly, as in the *Cetaka*, etc.[243] The *Gorocana* and the *Anaṅgavatī* are quoted as examples of the *Kṣudraka-kathā*, known as *Manthullī* or *Manthullikā*.[244] This *śravya-kāvya* which is one of its 24 varieties, is written in Mahārāṣṭrī Prakrit. In this type a priest, a minister or hermit is ridiculed for his unsuccessful undertaking.[245] The above-mentioned works are not available. As in water a certain thing is not visible in the beginning but is sighted later; so is the case with *Maṇikulyā*. Bhoja has cited the *Matsyahasita* as an example of this type. In *Parikathā* a discussion of opponents is heard by those who are desirous of conquest and are clever in narrating a story, like *Śūdraka*.[246] The *Indumatī* is quoted as an example of *Khaṇḍukathā*. Like the *Gorocana* and the *Anaṅgavatī* the *Indumatī*[247] is also lost. It is a small story with no substories. The *Citralekhā* is quoted as an example of *Upakathā*. The *Bṛhatkathā* is marked with *Lambhas*, has a wonderful meaning (*adbhutārhā*), is composed in Paiśācī dialect, has a wide range of subject, and deals with the life of Naravāhandatta.[248] A *Campū* is another form of *Ākhyāyikā*, having *Aṅkas*, divided into *Ucchvāsas*, composed in prose or verse, such as the *Damayantī*, the *Vāsavadattā* and others.[249] The *Mahābhārata* is included among the *Parvabandha*, the *Rāmāyaṇa* in the *Kāṇḍabandha*, the *Hayagrīvavadha* in the *Sargabandha*. The *Āśvāsakabandha* is a Prakrit counterpart of the Sanskrit *Sargabandha Mahākāvya*. The *Setubandha* is cited as an example here; it is composed in pure Prakrit (निबध्यते प्राकृतेन मुद्धेन). The poems of this class such as the *Setubandha*, the *Rāvaṇavihaya* and the *Harivijaya* are composed in the *Mātrāchandas* also called *Skandhaka*.[250] The *Bhīmakāya* and other works are included in the *Avaskandhabandha*. The meaning of the sacred text (*śāstra*) is incorporated here by poets and hence it is called a *Kāvyaśāstra*; the *Bhaṭṭikāvya* and the *Mudrārākṣasa* are cited as examples. The *Śāstrakāvya* is different from the *Kāvyaśāstra* in the sense that in the former the mystery of the poets is incorporated as *rati vilāsa* and the *Kāmandakīya*. The *Kośa* contains a collection of the eloquent sayings such as in the *Saptaśatikā*. A *Saṅghāta* contains a collection of eloquent sayings (*sukti-samudāya*) like the *Vṛndāvana*, the *Meghadūta* and others. A *Saṃhitā* contains scattered episodes compiled at one place, like the episodes of the *Yaduvaṃśa*, *Dilīpavaṃśa*, etc. Last we come to the *Sāhityaprakāśa*, a variety of *śravyakāvya*; it is a magnificent place of all the *vidyās*. Here the author has cited his own work the *Śṛṅgāraprakāśa* as an example.[251]

The Sections 18, 19, 20 and 21 deal with *Dharma-śṛṅgāra-prakāśa*, the *Artha-śṛṅgāra-prakāśa*, the *Kāmaśṛṅgāra-prakāśa* and the *Mokṣa-śṛṇgāra-prakāśa* respectively. The last portion of the Section 25 and the first portion of the Section 27 are lost. Section 26 is completely lost. Sections 28 and 29 consist of *Dūta-viśeṣa-varṇana* and *Dūta-karmopavarṇana*[252] respectively. Section 31 deals with *Pravāsa-varṇana* and the last one 36 with *Saṃbhogāvasthā-prakāśa.*

This work of Bhojarāja is very important for the study of *alaṃkāra-śāstra.* It contains innumerable citations from well known Prakrit and Sanskrit works. As stated earlier, it consists of 1650 Prakrit verses, though they are not properly edited and are full of errors. The work is broken in between and is beyond repair. The author cites illustrations from numerous works such as the *Mārīcavadha,*[253] the *Rāvaṇavijaya,*[254] the *Setubandha,*[255] the *Harivijaya,*[256] the *Indumatī*, the *Ceṭaka*, the *Śūdrakakathā*, the *Kuvalayāśvacarita,*[257] the *Gorocana*, the *Anaṅgavatī*, the *Indulekhā*, the *Cārumatī*, the *Bṛhatkathā*, the *Mālatīmādhava* and many others. We also meet distinguished authors such as Kālidāsa, Śūdraka, Āḍhyarāja, Rājaśekhara, Vijayāṅkā,[258] Vikaṭanitambā[259] and many others. Some of these works and authors are unknown. Nevertheless, it indicates the extensive scholarship of the author. The *Śūdrakakathā* deals with the episode of heroine Harimatī where a parrot carries a love message. Here a Prakrit verse from this work is cited. The *Cārumatī* gives an illustration regarding a pair of Kinnara (*Kinnara-mithuna*). A Sanskrit verse is cited from this work. A *sārikā* bird enlightens Nandana in the *BK* from which a Sanskrit stanza is cited which indicates that a Sanskrit version of this great work was available of Bhoja, different from the Kashimir versions of Kṣemendra and Somadeva as well as the Nepalese version of Budhasvāmin.[260]

RUYYAKA'S *ALAṂKĀRASARVASVA*[261]

Ruyyaka or Rājānaka Ruyyaka, who composed his work some time between 1135 and 1150, was the teacher of mahākavi Maṅkhuka, the *sāndhi-vigrahika* (minister who decides on war and peace) of Rājā Jayasiṃha of Kashmir. It is a standard work of *alaṃkāra* (figures of speech). The author is a staunch advocate of the *dhvani* school and summarizes the views of Bhāmaha, Udbhaṭa, Rudraṭa, Vāmana, the *Vaktroktijīvita*, the *Vyaktiviveka* and the Dhvanikāra Ānandavardhana on the essence of poetry. He has dealt with more *alaṃkāras* than Mammaṭa.

The work is divided into 3 parts: the *Sūtras* written in prose, defining the figures; the *Vṛtti*, the explanation; and the illustrations which are cited from previous works. Jayaratha who belongs to the first quarter of the thirteenth century has composed a learned commentary, *Vimarśiṇī.* Samudrabandha was another commentator, who wrote his commentary at the court of king Ravivarman of Kolamba in Kerala of the thirteenth century. There was still a third commentary, known as *Saṃjīvanī*, composed by Cakravartin.

Ruyyaka has cited 15 Prakrit stanzas as illustrations. Jayaratha in his commentary has cited 38 Prakrit stanzas. The following is cited as an illustration of *ākṣepa-nirūpaṇa*:

सुहअ! बिलंबसु थोअं जाव इमं विरह-काअरं हिअअं।
संठाविऊण भणिस्सं अहवा बोलेसु किं भणिमो ॥ p. 140

O fair one! pause a little, let me put my heart agitated by pang of separation, under subjugation, or better you may go, what shall I talk to you!

MAMMAṬA'S *KĀVYAPRAKĀŚA*[262]

Mammaṭa (AD 1050-1600) was a resident of Kashmir and was educated in Banaras. His *Kāvyaprakāśa* is a comprehensive work on poetics on which numerous commentaries were composed, which indicates the prestige and honour this work enjoyed and the extent to which it has been studied. It is one of the most famous works on poetics. In the words of P.V. Kane, 'It sums up in itself all the activities that had been going on for centuries in the field of poetics, while it became itself a fountain-head from which fresh streams of doctrines issue forth.'[263] Here the treatment of the subject is full and concise. The work is divided into 143 *kārikās*, often called *Sūtras*, covering the whole field of poetics. It consists of 10 *Ullāsas*, comprising as usual 3 parts, the Kārikā, the *Vṛtti* and the *Udāharaṇas*, the whole work is based on his predecessors.

The *Prastāvanā* refers to various authors such as Bhaṭṭalollaṭa, Śrī Śankuka, Bhaṭṭanāyaka, Abhinavaguptācārya, dhvanikāra (Ānandavardhana), Vāmana, Rudraṭa, and Bhaṭṭodbhaṭa. The author has cited 620 illustrations, including 64 Prakrit verses from other writers to illustrate his thesis.

In the beginning of the first *Ullāsa*, explaining the purpose of poetry (*kāvyaprayojana*), he writes that its immediate purpose and aim is aesthetic pleasure. He explains six purposes of poetry:

काव्यं यशसेऽर्थकृते व्यवहारविदे शिवेतरक्षतये।
सद्यः पर-निर्वृतये कान्तासम्मित तयोपदेशयुजे॥ I.1

It generates (i) fame (*yaśas*) as in the case of Kālidāsa, (ii) wealth (*artha*) as in the case of Śrīharṣa, Dhāvaka and others, (iii) knowledge of worldly ways (*vyavahāra*) as in the case of a king who with the assistance of his counsels, teachers, sages and others, is able to look after his subject properly, (iv) removal of ills (*śivetarakṣati*) as removing of ills generated by the sun, peacocks and others, (v) immediate delight (*sadyaḥ para-nirvṛti*) as one feels delighted immediately after listening to a poetic piece, (vi) generating taste as by a beloved (*kāntā-sammitatayā*).[264]

This work also refers to the poetess Śilābhaṭṭārikā of Kashmir and the poetess Vijjikā; a verse is cited from each of them. In the *Praśasti* the author of the commentary *Bālāvabodhinī* has mentioned 45 other commentaries on this work. Some of the commentators referred to are Śrīdhara, Caṇḍidāsa, Devanātha, Bhāskara, Subuddimiśra, Padmanābha, Māṇikyacandra, Someśvara, Sarasvatītīrtha, Jayanta, Viśvanātha (the author of the *Sāhityadarpaṇa*), Rāghava and so on. The oldest commentary is that of Māṇikyacandra (AD 1159) and the most famous one is the *Kāvyapradīpa*, published in the *Pandit*, New Series, Vols. 10-13.[265]

Here is an illustration of *Śleṣokti* (an expression of a double meaning):

महदे सुरसंधम्मे तमवसमासंगमागमाहरणे।
हर-बहु-सरणं तं चित्तमोहमवसर उमे सहसा॥ IX.372 (also cited in the *Sāhitya-darpaṇa*, X.11.

(i) The meaning of Prakrit verse: O the consort of Śiva (*hara-bahu*), you create my interest in my religious duties, you destroy my gloominess, the root cause of going to and fro in the worldly existence (*gamāgamā*), you alone are a refuge to me, be good enough to remove quickly the illusion of mind.[266]

(ii) The meaning of the same (Sanskrit) verse: O the consort of God Śiva (Ume), always protect me by putting my mind in the acquisition of sacred knowledge which is valuable for my life and which is always craved by gods, kindly be good enough to remove the illusion of my mind from time to time which is of prevailing nature.[267]

HEMACANDRA'S *KĀVYĀNUŚĀSANA*[268]

As we know this work on poetics was composed by Hemacandra after his great *Siddhahemaśabdānuśāsana*. The *Kāvyānuśāsana* is an important work on poetics based on Mammaṭa's *Kāvyaprakāśa*. It uses freely the illustrious *Alaṃkāra* works that preceded it. It is a lucid compendium on the subject of poetics. It is divided into 3 parts: the *Sūtras* in prose which constitute the original work; the *Vṛtti* explaining the *Sūtra* is styled as *Alaṃkāracūḍāmaṇi*; the *Udāharaṇa* or illustrations, which explain the *Alaṃkāracūḍāmaṇi* commentary and add illustrations; it is styled as *Viveka*, here the subject matter is extended in detail (*pratanyate*). The work is divided into 8 *adhyāyas*. The first deals with the purpose of poetry (*kāvyatva*) in 25 *sūtras*; the second deals with classification of poetry (58 *sūtras*); the third on flaws (*doṣas*) has 10 *sūtras*; the fourth on qualities (*guṇas*) has 9 *sūtras* (here he follows Mammaṭa); the fifth and the sixth *adhyāyas* deal with six *śabdālaṃkāra* in 8 *sūtras* and 29 *arthālaṃkaras* in 31 *sūtras* respectively; the seventh section deals with *nāyaka*, and is mainly based on Dhanañjaya's *Daśarūpaka*, also on Bharata's *Nāṭyasāstra* and its commentary by Abhinavagupta, it contains 52 *sūtras*; the last section deals with the varieties of poetic compositions in 13 *sūtras*. Thus the work contains 208 *sūtras* in all, dealing with Sanskrit poetics in all its aspects.

The *Kāvyānuśāsana* is known for its wealth of illustrations. The *Alaṃkāracūḍāmaṇi* commentary contains about 740 illustrations, quoting about 67 different authorities and the *Viveka* commentary provides about 624 illustrations, quoting 201 authorities. Thus the total number of quotations the *Kāvyānuśāsana* contains is about 1632. With its large number of quotations and illustrations the work will prove a very useful study for the history of Sanskrit poetics and literature. It was composed in about 1140 during the reign of Jayasiṃh Siddharaja.

It is stated that as far as the *Kāvyānuśāsana* of Hemacandra is concerned, it is not an original work and the author has collected material from different authors of Sanskrit poetics so he should be called a *saṅgrāhaka* and not a creator.[269] In the opinion of P.V. Kane, 'It is a compilation and exhibits hardly any originality.'[270] It borrows wholesale Rājaśekhara's *Kāvyamīmāṃsā*, Mammaṭa's *Kāvya-prakāśa*, Ānandavardhana's *Dhvanyāloka* and Abhinavagupta's commentary on the *Nāṭyaśāstra* and others. He has expressly stated that he has based his views on those of Abhinavagupta and Bharata (. . . श्रीमानभिनवगुप्ताचार्यः। एतन्मतमेव वास्माभिरुपजीवितं वेदितव्यम् [*Viveka*, p. 66]; तेऽस्माभिर्भरतमतानुसारिभिरुपेक्षिताः [*Kāvyānuśasana*, p. 316]). V. Raghavan observes, 'Not only the *gāthās* and Sanskrit verses given as illustrations by Bhoja, but Bhoja's comments thereon are also reproduced completely by Hemacandra in his *Kāvyānuśāsana*. . . . These six conditions and their illustrations are reproduced from the *Śṛṅgāraprakāśa*.'[271] Further, 'Chapter III of Hemacandra's *Kāvyānuśāsana* is almost identical with Chapter VII of Mammata's *Kāvyaprakāśa*. The number and the illustrations of all the flaws (*doṣas*) are the same in the works. In his own commentary, Hemacandra has given additional Ānandavardhana and Mahimabhaṭṭa *rasa-doṣas, avimṛṣṭa-vidheya* and *krama-bhaṅgas*.'[272] Then 'The treatment of *śravya-kāvya* in Chapter VII of *Kāvyānuśāsana* is completely a reproduction of the sections on *guṇas* and *alaṃkāras* of *prabandha* as a whole and the definitions with examples of the type of *śravya-kāvya* given by Bhoja in Chapters XI and XII of the *Śṛṅgāraprakāśa*.'[273] It is also to be noted that on many occasions, Hemacandra happens to adopt even very long passages from his predecessors but he does not care to indicate the source. In his article 'The Sources of Hemacandra's *Kāvyānuśāsana*' (p. 154) V.M. Kulkarni's remark is worth noting: 'Hemacandra's *pratibhā* is more of *bhāvayitrī* and less of *kārayitrī* type.'[274]

Like the *Sarasvatīkaṇṭhābharaṇa* of Ānandavardhana, the *Kāvyānuśāsana* of Hemacandra is also rich in Mahārāṣṭrī Prakrit verses. In order to illustrate the subject matter, Hemacandra has quoted 60 verses in the text and some 20 in the commentary. These verses are given in present author's *Prākṛit-Puṣkariṇī* with Hindi translation.

Hemacandra, besides citing verses in his *Kāvyānuśāsana* from the well known works such as the *Gāhāsattasaī*, the *Setubandha*, the *Karpūramañjarī*, the *Ratnāvali* and others has also cited verses from other important works which are no more extant.

(i) He has quoted a verse from the *Mahumahaṇaviaa* (*Madhumahanaijaya*) of *Vākpatirāja*. This verse लीलादाढग्गुबूढ, etc., is also found cited in Abhinavagupta's *Locana* (the commentary on the *Dhvanyāloka* (III, 15, p. 152) somewhat incorrectly, but it is correctly cited in the *Alaṃkāracūḍāmaṇi* (pp. 81. 181) of Hemacandra.

(ii) (a) Hemacandra has cited another verse from Sarvasena's *Harivijaya* in his *Kāvyānuśāsana* (pp. 79, 74). The verse चूअंकुरावअंस is also found cited in the *Dhvanyāloka* (III, p. 127). (b) He has referred to the *Harivijaya* along with the *Rāvaṇavijaya*, the *Seṭubandha*, the *Śiśupālavadha* and the *Kirātārjunīya* in his commentaries (*Alaṃkāracūḍāmaṇi*, pp. 171, 461; *Viveka*, pp. 458, 459). (c) Another reference to the *Harivijaya* by Hemacandra in his *Kāvyānuśāsana* (p. 121) we come across is when he points out an error on the part of Sarvasena presenting a disproportionate lengthy description of the sea in alliterative verse and that in a situation of *viprelabha rasa.* But as we have seen that Bhoja does not agree with the criticism of Hemacandra. Raghavan has pointed out the likelihood of the alliterative description as an interpolation.

(iii) Hemacandra has referred to the *Rāvaṇavijaya* which is no more available. The verse सयलं चेव णिबंधं, etc., cited in his *Viveka*-335 (p. 334) is also found cited in Bhoja's *Śṛṅgāraprakāśa* (II. 11, supra, p. 229 and note).

(iv) Hemacandra has cited verses from the *Viṣamabāṇalīlā* of Ānandavardhana. This work is also not available.

(a) The verse ताला जायंति गुणा, etc. (*Kāvyānuśāsana*, pp. 209, 233), which seems to be a popular saying, is often quoted in the *Dhvanyāloka* (II. 62), the *Sarasvatīkaṇṭhābharaṇa* (II. 41, p. 143), the *Śṛṅgāraprakāśa* (I.7, p. 227), the *Kāvyaprakāśa* (VIII. 315) and the *Alaṃkārasarvasva*, p. 23).

(b) Another verse तो ताणं सिरि-सहोअर, etc. (*Kāvyānuśāsana*, p. 74, *śloka* 77), is cited in the *Dhvanyāloka* (II, p. 111).

(c) The verse तो ताणं हअच्छाअं, etc. (*Kāvyānuśāsana*, pp. 145, 170) is cited in the *Sarasvatīkaṇṭhābharaṇa* (IV.56; V.24) and the *Setubandha* (II.45).

(d) The verse हुमि अवहत्थिअ-रे हो, etc. (*Kāvyānuśāsana*, pp. 82, 152) is cited in the *Kāvyaprakāśa* (VII. 320), the *Dhvanyāloka* (III.15 and Bālapriyā commentary, p. 346).

(e) The verse जं परिहरिउं तीरइ, etc. cited in the *Kāvyaprakāśa* (VII. 216) is considered a part of the *Viṣamabāṇalīlā*. See supra, p. 232 and note.

As already mentioned, many Prakrit verses cited in Sanskrit texts on rhetorics are currupt. This is more applicable in the case of Bhoja's *Śṛṅgāraprakāśa* (Josyer edition, published from Mysore). V. Raghavan has tried to correct some of these verses in his *Bhoja's Śṛṅgāraprakaśa.* Several scholars have tried to edit a few of these verses. A. Weber has edited about 35 *gāthās* from the works on Sanskrit poetics in his Critical Edition of *Gāthāsaptaśatī: Uber das Saptaśatakaṃ des Hāla.* A.M. Ghatge has corrected 6 Prakrit verses in the footnotes to his article on Mahārāṣṭrī Language and Literature (published in the *JUB*, Vol. IV, May 1936, Pt. 6, pp. 19-70). A.N. Upadhye has corrected one very obscure Apabhraṃśa verse from Dhanika's *Avaloka* on the *Daśarupaka*. V.M. Kulkarni, has corrected several Prakrit verses cited in the *Śṛṅgāraprakāśa*, the *Dhvanyāloka*, the *Abhinavabhāratī* and other works.[275]

VIŚVANĀTHA'S *SĀHITYADARPAṆA*[276]

Viśvanātha Kavirāja, known as a Sanskrit rhetorician of repute, composed his *Sāhityadarpaṇa* (Mirror of Composition) in the fourteenth century. Like Bhoja's *Śṛṅagāraprakāśa* it treats in detail the entire range of poetics and dramaturgy. While discussing the essence of poetry, against the views propounded by Dhvanikāra, Kuntaka, Bhoja and Mammaṭa, he defends his view that sentiment is the soul of poetry (*vākyaṃ rasātmakaṃ kāvyaṃ*). His greatest contribution in the field of poetics is that he presents in the compass of a single work a full and complete treatment of the science of rhetoric in all its branches, including dramaturgy.

The work contains 10 *paricchedas*, dealing with the benefit of poetry (*kāvyaphala*), definition of a *vākya*, definition of *rasa*, the varieties of *kāvya*, importance of *vyañjanā*, *dṛśya-kāvya* (poetry that is to be seen) and *śravya-kāvya* (poetry to be heard), the first is called *rūpaka* to which 272-556 verses are devoted, and with the flaws (*doṣas*), qualities (*guṇas*), *rīti* and *alaṃkāras*.

Viśvanātha was a resident of Utkala, a contemporary of Sultan Alauddin Muhammad Khilji. He was a poet and as he specialized in 18 languages, he was known as *aṣṭādaśa-bhāṣā-vāra-vilāsinī-bhujaṅga* (A Paramour of Prostitute of 18 Dialects). He has mentioned *Praśastiratnāvali* written by him in 16 dialects as an example of *karambhaka* or a piece of poetry in 16 dialects.[277] Viśvanātha has composed various works such as the *Kāvyaprakāśadarpaṇa*, *Candrakalānāṭaka*, *Rāghavavilāsa* and also the *Narasiṃhavijaya*. He quotes his own verses in Sanskrit and Prakrit at every step while illustrating the principles of rhetorics. Very often he quotes from his drama the *Prabhāvatīpariṇaya* and the Prakrit poem the *Kuvalayāśvacarita*.[278]

The *Sāhityadarpaṇa* has 24 Prakrit stanzas, of which a majority are cited from Hāla's *Sattasaī*, some from Śrīharṣa's *Ratnāvali*, some from *Kāvyaprakāśa*, *Daśarūpaka* and *Dhvanyāloka* and some are from unknown sources; some are his own.[279]

JAGANNĀTHA PANDITARĀJA'S *RASAGAṄGĀDHARA*[280]

The *Rasagaṅgādhara* is a standard work on poetics, particularly on *alaṃkāras*. It comes next only to the *Dhvanyāloka* and the *Kāvyaprakāśa* in the field of poetics. The author had a wonderful command of classical Sanskrit. In order to illustrate the subject matter he cites his own examples. He refutes the theory of *dhvani* (implied meaning). According to him, poetry denotes a word expressing pleasant meaning (रमणी यार्थप्रतिपादकः शब्दः काव्यम्).[281] He asserts that *pratibhā* (talent) alone is the source of *kāvya*.

Paṇḍitarāja Jagannātha flourished between 1620 and 1665. The author laments the death of Āsaf, Commander-in-Chief of Shahjahan in his work *Āsafvilāsa*. He also lived in the court of Dārā Shāh, son of Shahjahan, from 1620 to 1660. He was invited to the royal court of Delhi by Shahjahan to teach Sanskrit to his son. Pleased with the scholarship of the poet, Shahjahan conferred on him the title of Paṇḍitarāja. While sojourning in the royal court, he composed the *Jagadābharaṇa*, eulogizing the prince Dārā. Paṇḍitarāja is also author of the *Gaṅgālaharī* and *Bhāminīvilāsa*[282] from which he cites verses in his work. Paṇḍitarāja Jagannātha, being a lyrical poet, sang praise of Gaṅgā in his *Gaṅgālaharī*. It is said that he was in love with Lavaṅgī, Muslim girl, whom he married. One day he sat on the highest step of a *ghāṭa* on the bank of the Gaṅgā and began to recite a prayer in praise of the Gaṅgā. With the completion of each stanza the river water began to rise. At the recitation of the last stanza of his poetry the water reached the last step of the *ghāṭa* where both were seated. His sins as well as that of his consort were washed off and they were drowned in the holy river.

NOTES

1. The order in the Jain tradition is: *Sikṣā, Kalpa, Vyākaraṇa, Chanda, Nirukta* and *Jyotiṣa, Vivāha* (2.1); *Ovā* (38, p. 172).
2. रक्षाणं वेदानामध्येयं व्याकरणम्। लोपागमवर्ण विकारज्ञो हि सम्यग्वेदान्परिपालयिस्यतीति। उत त्वः पश्यन्न ददर्श वाचमृतः त्वः श्रृण्वन्न श्रृणोत्येनाम्। *Nahābhāṣya*, 1.1.1, pp. 20-4; Bhargav Shastri, *Mahābhāṣya*, I, pp. 76, 85, Bombay, 1951.
3. वक्रवाच्यां कवीनां ये प्रयोगे प्रति साधवः।
   प्रयोक्तुं ये न युक्ताश्च तद्विवेकोऽयमुच्यते॥ VI.23
4. आपः पवित्रं प्रथमं पृथिव्यामपां पवित्रं परमं च मन्त्राः।
   तेषां च सामग्र्यजुषां पवित्रं महर्षयो व्याकरणं निराहुः॥ *Kāvyamimāṃsā*, Chap. VI, p. 25.

5. यस्तु प्रयुङ्क्ते कुशलो विशेषे शब्दान्यथावद्व्यवहारकाले।
   सोऽनन्तमाप्नोति जयं परत्र वाग्योगविद्दुष्यति चापशब्दैः॥
   This verse is quoted by Patañjali in his *Mahābhāṣya* (Paspaśāhnika) to show the utility of grammar, op. cit.
6. B.C. Law, *History of Pali Literature*, p. 632. Kaccāyana (not before the eleventh century) has used freely the Kātantra and Pāṇinī; and Moggalāna is influenced by Candra, Keith, *A History of Sanskrit Literature*, p. 436.
7. B.C. Law, op. cit., p. 637.
8. The following verse
   प्रणम्य शिरसा वीरं स्वल्पैर्व्यापिभिरक्षरैः।
   लक्षणं प्राकृतं वक्ष्ये किंचित् वृद्धमतादिह॥
   has been dismissed by Hoernle as a later accretion as introduced by later writers who revised Caṇḍa's original *Prākṛtalakṣaṇa*; V. Raghavan, *Bhoja's Śṛṅgāraprakāśa*, p. 749.
9. The following editions are published:
   (a) E.B. Cowell, with the commentary of Bhāmaha, Hertford, 1854; 2nd edn. with Notes and English translation along with Bhāmaha's Commentary, London, 1868; 3rd edn., 1962; Ram Shastri Telang, with text only, Banaras, 1899.
   (b) With commentaries of Bhāmaha and Kātyāyana and with a Bengali translation by Vasantakumar Sharma Chattopadhyaya, Calcutta, 1914.
   (c) With Vasantarāja's *Prākṛtasaṃjīvanī* and Sadānanda's *Subodhinī*, in 2 parts, Sarasvatibhavana Series, Banaras, 1927.
   (d) P.L. Vaidya, with English translation, Oriental Series, Poona, 1931.
   (e) Udyotana Shastri with the commentary of Bhāmaha, Varanasi, 1940.
   (f) Dinesh Chandra Sarkar, *Grammar of the Prakrita Language* with original text of *Prākṛtaprakāśa* and English translation, University of Calcutta, 1943; revd. edn., Banaras, 1970.
   (g) C. Kunhan Raja with Rāmapāṇivāda's Commentary, Adyar Library, Madras, 1946.
   (h) K.P. Trivedi, with Gujarati translation, Navsari, 1957.
   (i) Jagannath Shastri Hoshing with Hindi translation, Varanasi, 1959.
10. Bhoja has attributed one *Prākṛtalakṣaṇa* to Kātyāyana. It is a work in prose and verse of a varied nature which does not pertain to the available *Prākṛtaprakāśa* of Vararuci, according to Raghavan. In his opinion he may be different from Kātyāyana, the author of the *Vārtikas* on Pāṇinī, *Bhoja's Śṛṅgāraprakāśa*, p. 750.
11. A.N. Upadhye has edited the first chapter of this poetical work in the *Bhāratīya Vidyā* (3.1).
12. Read the following *gāthās*:
    ईसि-पिक्क फल-पाअवे महा
    वेडिसे विअण-पल्लवे वणे।

सो जणो असुइणो अ-पावइं-
गालम्मि लसिओ मिअंगिमो ॥ 1.6
ईस-पक्क-फलए इस-त्थली
वेउसे वअण-पल्लवे हिओ।
सो सणो असिविणो अ-पावअं
गालए महिवणे मुअंगओ ॥ 1.7

the forms ईषत् (=ईसि, ईस), पक्व (=पिक्क, पक्क), स्वप्न (सवण, सिविण), वेतस (=वेअस, वेइस; वइस in प्राकृतप्रकाश), व्यजन (=वअण, विअण, मृदंग (=मअंग, मुइंग), अंगार (=अंगाल, इंगाल), referred to in the प्राकृतप्रकाश (1.3), have been illustrated.

13. The dialects referred to by Vararuci are clearly later than those of Aśvaghoṣa and reflect perhaps material of the third century at earliest. Keith, *A History of Sanskrit Literature*, p. 433.
14. According to some, these two chapters were added to the original work either by Bhāmaha himself or by an unknown grammarian who lived between Katyāyana and Bhāmaha, Dinesh Chandra Sarkar, *Grammar of the Prakrit Language*, p. 5.
15. Dinesh Chandra Sarkar, op. cit., p. 4.
16. A.F. Hoernle, with a critical Introduction and Indexes, Calcutta, 1880; Devakikanta, Calcutta, 1923; Satyavijaya Jain Granthamala, Ahmedabad, 1929.
17. Edited by Manmohan Ghosh along with *Prākṛtkalpataru* of Rāmśarma Tarkavāgīśa, in Appendix II (pp. 170-2). The first edition was published in the *IA*, Vol. VIII, 1946, pp. 37-9.
18. विस्तराद् गदितं पूर्वं संक्षेपादधुनोच्यते।
बालबोधकरं सूत्रं दध्नो यादृङ्.नवोद्धृतम्॥ Introduction to *Sūtra* 1.
19. First of all, Christian Lassen in his work *Institutions Linguae Prakriticae* (Bonn, 1837) has written about it in detail; Nicolaus Delius published *Radices Prakriticae* (Prakrit Roots), Bonn, 1839. It deals with the ancient list of roots ascribed to Pāṇinī and the *Saṃkṣiptasāra* of Kramadīśvara. Rajendralal Mitra published the whole of the *Prākṛtapāda* in the *Bibliotheca Indica*; its new edition from Calcutta, 1889.
20. L. Nitti Dolchi, with French Introduction, Paris, 1938; D.C. Sircar in his *Grammar of the Prakrit Language*, Appendix (Chaps. IX-XX), pp. 106-20, with English translation. These chapters are very important for the study of minor dialects. Manmohan Ghosh in his *Prākṛtakalpataru*, Appendix I, pp. 156-69.
21. E. Hultzsch, Royal Asiatic Society, Hertford, 1909; L. Nitti Dolchi, Paris, 1939; Manmohan Ghosh, Asiatic Society, Calcutta, 1954 together with Introduction, English translation and Notes. It also contains *Prākṛtānuśāsana* (Chaps. III-XX) of Puruṣottama, the *Prākṛtakāmadhenu* of Laṅkeśvara and the *Prākṛtalakṣaṇa* referred to in the *Viṣṇudharmottara* in Appendices I, II and III respectively. A. George Grierson in 'Apabhraṃśa *Stavakas* of Ramaśarmā' laid stress on the importance of this work; this article was published in the *IA*, Vol. 51, 1922. Later he published an excellent critical edition with notes and translation of

different parts of the work: Śākhā I, Chap. VIII (*Dhātvādeśa*) in *Memoirs of the Asiatic Society of Bengal*, No. VIII, 1924; Śākhā II (Bhāṣa and Vibhaṣa) in the *IA*, 1927-8; Śākhā III, Chaps. I-II (Apabhraṃśa) in the *IA*, 1922-3; Chap. III (Paiśācī) in *Sir Ashutosh Mookerjee Silver Jubilee*, Vols. III, Pt. 2, pp. 119-41, Calcutta, 1925. The remaining portion, containing 1-VII and Chap. IX of Śākhā I, has been carefully studied and edited by L. Nitti Dolchi, Paris, 1939.

22. The commentary is important as it quotes numerous Prakrit verses and short sentences from some unknown Prakrit works to illustrate his statement, particularly in the eighth chapter of the first Śākhā, related to *Dhātvādeśa*. Regarding these quotations M.M. Ghosh, the editor of the *Prākṛtakalpataru*, has observed (p. xx): 'One special feature of the Prakrit quotations is that they are mostly on the various exploits of Kṛṣṇa, and quite a number are on his relation with Rādhā and the *gopis* (cowherd maidens).' This shows that there existed earlier Prakrit poems on the exploits of Kṛṣṇa. Elsewhere also we come across quotations from some Prakrit grammars. In the following quotation, for example, the author does not support the view of those grammarians, according to whom *etad* in feminine becomes *esa*, as we see in the passage *lakkhijjae esa gadā Harissa*:

    लक्ष्यानुरोधादिह कश्चिदाह लक्खिज्जए एस गदा हरिस्स।
    स्यादेतत् स्त्रीविषयेऽपि एस नैतन्मतं प्राकृतशासनानाम्॥ I.6.19

    Elsewhere (I.3.18) Rāmaśarmā has quoted the opinion of Śākalya. Puruṣottama has also quoted the following Sanskrit verse polluted by Pāñcāla-Paiśācīka (अशुद्धसंकीर्ण पैशाचिक). This verse is from his own composition (*yathā mama*) which indicates that he has also written other works besides his book on grammar:
    कमला-काम-संलोल-काम-कला-कुल-कोमलालिका:।
    कलिकाल-काल-कलिलं मुञ्चताम् मोहकल्जोलम्॥ III.3.18

23. दाक्षिणात्य-पद-सम्बलितं यत्
    संस्कृतादिभिरभिच्छुरितं च।
    स्वादुसारममृतादपि काव्यं
    दाक्षिणात्यमिति तत् कथयन्ति॥ 2.2.32
    cf. दाक्षिणात्यपदालम्बि संस्कृताङ्गं विजृम्भितम्।
    काव्यं पीयूषनिस्यन्दि दाक्षिणात्यमितीरितम्॥ *Prākṛtasarvasva*, Com. on 12. 38. This verse has been ascribed to Aniruddhabhaṭṭa.

24. S.P.V. Bhaṭṭanāthswamin, Granthpradarshini, Vizagapattam, 1912 (rpt. 1927); K.C. Acharya, Prakrit Text Society, Ahmedabad, 1968.

25. पद्धुमं जीविअसरिच्छा ततो सुहवी तदो पुणो घरिणी।
    चंडि त्ति भणसि एण्हिं ण मुणामि काहे हुवेज्ज चामुंडा॥ VIII.4 Com.

26. K.C. Acharya, Introduction to *Prākṛtasarvasva*, pp. 21-35.

27. Pischel, *Grammatik*, Art. 40.

28. For main common features of Āvantī laid down by Mārkaṇḍeya and

Rāmaśarmā, see K.C. Acharya, *Mārkaṇḍeya's Prākṛtasarvasva*, p. 76.

29. Here किरादो and वेदसो are Śaurasenī, the rest Mahārāṣṭrī. The *Nāṭyaśāstra* (XVIII. 50) assigns it to rogues (*dhūrtās*).
30. Rāmaśarmā's definition of Āvantī or Bāhlīki as the mixture of Śaurasenī and Prācyā is not substantiated by facts either by the author or literature, K.C. Acharya, op. cit., p. 76.
31. शौरसेन्या अदूरत्वादियमेवार्धमांगधी, 12.38.
32. मागध्या: शाकारी (13.1).
33. चांडालीमागधीशौरसेनीभ्यां प्रायशो भवेत् (14.1) Rāmaśarmā (II.3.10) and Puruṣottama call it a corrupt form of Māgadhī (मागधी-विकृति: XIV.1).
34. चांडाल्या: शाबरीसिद्धि: (15.1) Puruṣottama calls it a dialect of Māgadhī (मागधी-विशेष:). (XV.1)
35. तन्मूलेभ्य: क्वचित् क्वचित् (15.2).
36. शाबर्यामिवौड्रीयोगात्तद्देश्यशौरसेन्यादे: (15.9)
37. With the exception that Ābhīrī has इअ and उअ for क्त्वा आभीर्यं प्येवं स्यात् क्त्व इअउऔ-नात्यपभ्रंश: (15.10). Puruṣottama does not recognize Ābhīrī.
38. टाक्की स्यात्संस्कृतं शौरसेनी चान्योन्यमिश्रिते (16.1) अनयो: संकरादित्यथे:। इयं द्यूतकार वणिगादि भाषा।
39. हरिश्चन्द्रस्त्विमां भाषामपभ्रंश इतीच्छति (16.2); almost the identical *sūtra* in the *Prākṛtanusāsana* (XVI.10).
40. तथा चोक्तम्-
    टक्कदेशीय भाषायां दृश्यते द्राविडी तथा।
    तत्र चायं विशेषोऽस्ति द्राविडैरावृता परम्॥ 16.2 Com.
41. Mentioned in the Introduction of the work. The author in the commentary of XVIII.12 quotes to define the following:
    1. टाक्क, 2. तु बहुला मालवी, 3. वाडीबहुला पाञ्चाली, 4. उल्लप्राया वैदर्भी, 5. संबोधनाढ्या लाटी, 6. ईकारो कारबहुला औड्री, 7. सवीप्सा कैकेयी, 8. समासाढ्या गौडी, 9. डकारबहुला कौन्तली, 10. एकारिणी च पाण्ड्या, 11. युक्ताढ्या सैंहली, 12. द्वियुक्ता, कालिङ्गी 13. प्राच्या तद्देशीयभाषाढ्या, 14. यहादिबहुला आभीरी, 15. वर्णविपर्ययात्, कार्णाटी 16. मध्यदेशीया तद्देशीयाढ्या, 17. संस्कृताढ्या च गौर्जरी, 18. रलहम्यांव्यत्ययेन पाश्चात्या, 19. रेफव्यत्ययेन द्राविडी, 20. तकारबहुला वैतालिकी, 21. एओबहुला काञ्ची।
42. More than 60 commentaries are mentioned, *JSBI*, V, pp. 30ff.
43. P.L. Vaidya, *Prakrit Grammar of Hemacandra*, Notes, VIII.1-259, pp. 26f. An alphabetic list of these substitutes is given in Appendix II, pp. 265-73. George Grierson has classified these Prakrit substitutes into four categories, see his Monograph on the Prakrit Dhātvādeśas (*Memoirs of the Asiatic Society of Bengal*, Vol. VIII, No. 2, 1924) which is based on the study of the *Prakṛtakalpataru* (Śākhā I, Chap. VIII); also see Puruṣottama's *Prākṛtānuśasana* (Chap. VII); also Vraruci's, *Prākṛtaprakāśa* (Chap. VIII).
44. In this connection Pischel has dealt with *deśya* or *deśī* class of words consisting of very heterogeneous elements, which have nothing to do with Sanskrit, for which there is no Sanskrit root, Art. 9.
45. Pischel has observed that Hemacandra calls Apabhraṃśa as a uniform language, but from the rules it appears that under the name of this dialect he has included several different dialects; for example ध्रुं, त्रं in place of यत् and तत् respectively (4.360); तुध्र in place of तव (4.372); प्रस्सदि

in place of पश्यति (4. 393); ब्रोप्पिणु, ब्रोप्पि in place of उक्त्वा (4.391); गृहंति, गृण्हेप्पिणु for गृहन्ति and गृहीत्वा respectively (4.341, 394, 438), Art. 28.

46. Here the observation of Pischel is noteworthy. He writes: 'In other respects Hemacandra and Vararuci differ strongly from one another, a thing which, to a great extent, is to be explained by the fact that Hemacandra has taken into consideration also the Śaurasenī of Digambaras, the peculiarities of which the Jains have carried over to Śaurasenī of the dramas with the result that the Śaurasenī texts have become corrupt and later writers have become misled', Art. 22.
47. The first chapter published by Granthpradarshini, Vizagapattam, 1896; the complete work by T. Laddu, 1922; Jagannath Hoshing, the text and the commentary under the title *Prākṛtavyākaraṇa-vṛtti*, Choukhamba Series, Varanasi, vs 2007; P.L. Vaidya with text and the *Vṛtti*, Solapur, 1954.
48. See Pischel, op. cit., Art. 38.
49. देश्यमार्षंच रूढत्वात्स्वतंत्रत्वाच्च भूयसा।
लक्ष्यनापेक्षते तस्य सम्प्रदायो हि बोधकः॥ 7, p. 2.
50. Edited by E. Hultzsch, Royal Asiatic Society, Herttord, 1909.
51. Edited by Kamlashankar Pranshankar Trivedi, *BSS*, 1916.
52. With Śrinivāsagopālācārya's Sanskrit commentary, Oriental Research Institute Publication, University of Mysore, 1954.
53. Raj PG, 1962.
54. See A.N. Upadhye, 'Subhacandra and his Prākṛtavyākaraṇa', *ABORI*, Vol. XIII, pp. 37-8.
55. Bhaṭṭanāthasvāmin has published 3 chapters (pp. 29-44), Vizagapattam (n.d.).
56. See *Jain Granthavali*, a list of handwritten manuscripts, p. 307.
57. See Hiralal Jain, 'Traces of an old Metrical Grammar', *Bhārata Kaumudī.*
58. The 3rd Report of Peterson (pp. 342-8) has given illustrations from this work, Pischel, *Grammatik*, Art. 41; also Amar Publication, Varanasi, 1969.
59. See Pischel, ibid.; D.C. Sarkar, *Grammar of the Prakrit Language*, p. 4.
60. शाकल्यस्यात इन्मते (V.96); होश्च शाकल्यमते स्यात् (IX.109); आदीतौ बहुलं (V.30) commentary; दंसो णिडि. (VII.106) Com.
61. राक्षसभिक्षुक्षपणकचेटाद्या मागधीं प्राहुरिति कोहलः (XII.1) Com.
62. See '*Gleanings* from Abhinavabharati', *K.B. Pathak Comm. Vol.*, pp. 385ff.
63. दाक्षिणात्यपदालम्बि संस्कृताङ्ग; विजृम्भितम्।
काव्यं पीयूषनिष्यन्दि दाक्षिणात्यमितीरितम्॥ (XII.38 Com., p. 132)
64. हरिश्चन्द्रस्त्विमां भाषामपभ्रंश इतीच्छति।
65. (i) सम्बुद्धावोत्वमिच्छन्ति वाऽदन्तस्य तु पैङ्गलाः, p. 54
(ii) . . . इति श्रीमत्पिङ्गलपादैर्दीर्घस्य लघुत्वादेशात्, p. 62.
66. *JRK*, under *Sārasvata-vyākaraṇa*. *JSBI*, V, pp. 55ff has provided details of 23 commentaries. The Jinabhadrasūri Jñāna Bhandār Handwritten

Manuscripts' Catalogue, Vol. II, 1988, pp. 282f contains several MSS with *tikā, dīpikā, vṛtti, artha* and *vyakhyā* of this work.

67. *Jinaratnakośa,* under Sambandhodyota.
68. Ibid.
69. See *Śatapatha-Brāhmaṇa,* VIII.1. 1-2, after Winternitz, *History of Indian Literature,* I, p. 63 fn. Varāhamihira in his *Bṛh Saṃ* deals with the metres which are associated with the planets. The commentator Bhaṭṭotpala refers to a metrical text for explanation in his commentary.
70. See Winternitz, op. cit., p. 283.
71. Batakrisna Ghosh, *Linguistic Introduction to Sanskrit,* Calcutta, 1937, pp. 65, 69, 56.
72. *Bṛhadāraṇyaka-Upaniṣad,* V.15.
73. For other Vedic common metres see A.L. Basham, *The Wonder That Was India,* 1954, pp. 509-12. For Sanskrit Prosody see Apte's *Sanskrit-English Dictionary,* Appendix I where different metres are treated with their definition, the scheme in *Gaṇas* with the *yati* or Caesura and the Examples.
74. Published with commentary, the *Mṛtasaṃjīvanī* of Halāyudha (later tenth century) in the *KVM,* 91, 1908.
75. Piṅgalanāga (104.64) or Nāgarāja (104.55) is mentioned by Bhaṭṭotpala in the commentary of Varāhamihira's *Bṛh Saṃ,* citing his definition of *Vipulā* and *Pathyā* metres.
76. See Winternitz, *History of Indian Literature,* III, Pt. I, 37.
77. प्रायेण सूत्रेण विना कृतानि प्रकाशरन्ध्राणि चिरन्तनानि।
रत्नानि शास्त्राणि च योजितानि नवैर्गुणैर्भूषयितुं क्षमाणि॥ 104.1
78. श्रुतिसुखदवृत्तसंग्रहमिममाह वराहमिहिरोऽतः॥ 104.64
79. बहुभिराचार्यैश्च्छन्दोलक्षणमुक्तं तच्च दुर्विज्ञेयमश्रव्यं च।
वराहमिहिरेण पुनः श्रव्यं सुखबोधं व्यापकं संक्षिप्तमुक्तमिति॥
80. माण्डव्यगिरं श्रुत्वा न मदीया रोचतेऽथवा नैवम्।
साध्वी तथा न पुंसां प्रिया यथा स्याज्जघनचपला॥ 104.3
81. Published with a commentary in the *KVM,* 41, 1894. One *Prākṛta-Piṅgala-Sūtra* was published in the *Bibliotheca Indica,* 1902; also W. Schubring, *ZDMG,* 75, 1921, pp. 97ff.
82. Uttarajjhāya Studies, *IIJ* 6, 1962, pp. 110-11; reproduced in *Ludwig Alsdorf Klein Schriften,* Weisbaden, 1974, pp. 225-6.
83. See the following articles of the author:
    (i) Vāntuṃ āpātuṃ, *S.K. Chatterji Jubilee Volume, Indian Linguistics,* 16, 1955; pp. 21-8; reproduced in *Ludwig Alsdorf Klein Schriften,* pp. 178-85.
    (ii) The Story of Citta and Sambhūta, *S.K. Belvelkar Felicitation Volume,* 1957, pp. 202-8; reproduced in *L. Alsdorf Klein Schriften,* pp. 186-92.
    (iii) Itthipainnā, A Chapter of Jain Monastic Poetry, edited as a Contribution to Indian Prosody, *IIJ* 12, 1958, pp. 249-70; reproduced in *L. Alsdorf Klein Schriften,* pp. 193-270.
    (iv) Namipavvajjā, Contributions to the study of a Jain Canonical

Legend, *Indological Studies in Honour of W. Norman Brown*, 1962, pp. 8-17, reproduced in *L. Alsdorf Klein Schriften*, pp. 215-24.

84. Edited with Introduction (II, pp. xxx-xxxii) and Notes (p. 134 in Appendix I, pp. 87-98) of the *Kavidarpaṇa*, *Raj OIJ*, 1962.

85. जह वेसाण न नेहो जह सच्चं नत्थि कामुयजणस्स।
तह नंदियड्डभणिए जिह तिह किह पाइए नत्थि॥

86. Introduction to *Gāhālakkhaṇa*, pp. xxxi-xxxii.

87. See Velankar, Notes to Appendix I, *Gāhālakkhaṇa*, p. 154. These verses can be compared with the verses I.54, I.125, I.120 and I.152 respectively of the *Prākṛta-Paiṅgala* (Bibliotheca edn.); also see the verses 51, 36, and 35 respectively of the *Chandaḥkośa*, Velankar, Introduction to *Chandonuśāsana*, p. 44, fn 48. According to the commentator Muni Ratnacandra, the verse 57 is taken from the *Rohiṇī-caritra*, 59 and 6 from the *Puṣpadanta-caritra* and the 61 from the *Gāthāsahasra-pathālaṃkāra*.

88. The quotation is as follows:
जासु वियरणि हुंति पयपंच,
पढमं चिय पंनरह,
बीय चारि गारह निरुद्ध(त्त) उ॥
तह तीयइ पंचदह, रडुभेउ जाणहु सु सुद्धउ।
करहिणि मोहिणि मियनणि, राहासेणु(णि) मुणिंदु।
अंतिहि दोहउ जसु हवइ, कवि नंदड्ड भणंति॥ op. cit.

89. See Hiralal Rasikhdas Kapadia, *Pāiya Bhāṣāo are Sāhitya*, p. 62 fn.

90. Edited by H.D. Velankar with his learned Introduction, Indices, Appendices and Brief Notes with Gopāla's Sanskrit Commentary, *Raj OIJ*, 1962.

91. See Velankar, Introduction, p. xxii.

92. सद्भावलाञ्छानं स्वगुरूं, Gopala's commentary.

93. May be identified with Abhimānacihna whose *Deśī* Lexicon (अभिमानचिह्न-सूत्र with *svopajña vṛtti*) has been quoted by Hemacandra in his *D*, Muni Jinavijaya, Preface, p. 3.

94. *Bhujagādhipau kambalāśvatarau*, Commentary (II.8).

95. I. 22; II. 7.

96. *Vṛddhakaviḥ Harivṛddhaiti kecit*, op. cit.

97. कामिन्या उत्तमाया योषित: कपोललक्ष्मणा, गण्डशोभा अवयवेन एदृश: परितनु: बुद्धिविभव:, p. 2.

98. Also known as कइसिद्ध-कविसिद्ध-कृतसिद्ध-छन्दोविचिति-वृत्तजाति-समुच्चय, C.D. Dalal, *A Catalogue of Manuscripts of the Jain Bhandars at Jesalmere*, Baroda, 1923, p. 61.

99. Also referred to by Varāhamihira in his *Bṛh Saṃ* (104.64). Daṇḍin in his *Kāvyādarśa* also has referred to the *Chandovicite*. पद्यं, चतुष्पदं तच्च वृत्तं जातिरिति द्विधा।
छन्दोविचित्यां सकलस्तत् प्रपञ्चो निदर्शित:

100. अत: स आएन्दुंसि र(न) कुर्टक इति, commentary (4.25). *Narkuṭaka* is mentioned as a metre in the *Bṛh Saṃ* (104.52).

101. (a) A Sanskrit verse is quoted (II.6).
(b) Another verse is quoted from Saitava (*Saitavasya vaco*) (IV.108).
(c) Another in the com. (IV.60) which is identical with *Jayadevachandas* (VIII. 12), Velankar, Introduction, p. xxvi.

102. The commentator has amended the original *Gāthās*:
(a) VI.59 and VI.61. In the latter case the commentator's remark is *ayamapi anārṣaḥ pāṭhaḥ* (this text too is not authentic).
(b) In some cases the commentator has incorporated his self-composed *Gāthā* in the original work, e.g. see IV.54. The author's remark is *asmābhir gātheyaṃ racitā* (this *gāthā* is composed by me). At another place (VI.60) he has composed only half a *gāthā*; *anena gāthārdhena sarveṣāṃ adhvayuktirghaṭate.*

103. Svayambhū in his *Svayambhūchandas* regards *Skandhaka* as the basic metre from which he derives the *Gīti* and the *Gāthā*. Velankar, *Chandonuśāsana*, Introduction, pp. 23f.

104. For details see Velankar, *Vṛttajātisamuccaya*, Introduction, pp. x-xxi.

105. Edited by H.D. Velankar with Introduction, Indices, Brief Notes and Appendices together with the Sanskrit text of Rājaśekhara's *Chandaḥśekhara* (Chap. 5 only). The text is divided into two parts: (i) Chaps. 1-8 (pp. 1-102) and (ii) Sections 1-6, known as *Pūrvabhāga*, pp. 103-27. The *Pūrvabhāga* should have appeared first, in the beginning of the text, but as the editor has pointed out, it was available to him only after the concluding part of the text was already printed. This *Pūrvabhāga* is based on a palm-leaf manuscript discovered by Mahāpandita Rahula Samkrityayana in a Tibetan monastery along with numerous Buddhist manuscripts.

106. तावच्चिय सच्छंदो भमइ अवब्भंस-मत्त-मायंगो।
जाव न स्वयंभु-वायरण-अंकुसो तच्छिरे पडइ ॥ 5 ॥
सच्छह-वियड-दाढो छंदोलंकारणहर-दुप्पिच्छो।
वायरण-केसरड्ढो सयंभु-पंचाणणो जयउ ॥ 6 ॥ quoted from the beginning portion of the *Paumacāriu*, Nathuram Premi, *Jain Sahitya*, 1956, p. 211.

107. Edited by H.C. Bhayani with Introduction, Indices and Appendices in 3 parts, *SJS*, Bombay, 1953 and 1960; Translated into Hindi by Devendra Kumar Jain. The first 57 *Sandhis*, consisting of 3 parts (the *Vidyādhara-Kāṇḍa*, the *Ayodhyā-Kāṇḍa* and the *Sundara-Kāṇḍa*), *BJP*, 1957-8.

108. He was well known poet of Apabhraṃśa, earlier than Svayambhū. He was an author of the *Harivaṃsa*, the *Paumacariu* and the *Pañcamīcariu*; none of his works is available. Svayambhū has also written the works bearing the same title. See H.C. Bhayani, *JOI*, Baroda, 7, 3, 1958, p. 218. Here the writer considers Caturmukha's Apabhraṃśa works as the probable source of some epic citations in the Apabhraṃśa section of the *Svayambhūchandas*. Premi has pointed out that the citations referred to under the name of Caturmukha in the *Svayambhūchandas*

(IV.2.1-3; VI.54.1; 63.1; 65.1 and 87.1) are taken from his *Paumacariu* (ibid., p. 209).

109. He is referred to as one of the best poets of Prakrit lyrical poetry in the *Gāhāsattasai.* The following stanza of Trilocana is cited in the *Svayambhūchandas* (I.66.1, p. 29):

अव्वो गिम्हे उण्हा वाआ दिवसअर-किरण-बणदव-भरिआ जलंति दिसामुहा
वासारत्ते दूसंचारा णव-जलअ-जणिअ-जल-वहल-पहा णिरंतर-कद्दमा।
हेमंते ओसद्दीभावा घण-तुहिण-पवण-पडिपहअ-दुमा ण देंति प्रवेसअं
णाहाही कत्तो दे जत्ता अणुहवसु सुहअ सइ सुरअ-सुहं रसाअण-संनिभं॥

110. His citation is from his well known epic the *Setubandha* (III.9), also quoted in the *Sarasvatīkaṇṭhābharaṇa* (IV.162, Bombay edn., 1934) of Bhojarāja.

111. He was one of the best poets responsible for shaping the *Gāhāsattasaī,* (see supra p. 205). The present text has cited the following stanzas under the name of Pālitta:

(i) उअ-पोम्मराअ-मरगअ-संवलिआ णहं-अलाओ ओवरइ।
णह-सिरि-कंठ-ब्भट्ठ व्व कंठिआ कीर-रिंछोली॥ *Pūrva bhāga* (*P*), I.1.4, p. 103 also in *Gāhāsattasaī* (I.75) and the *Chandonuśāsana* (I.10.2).

(ii) वण-महिस-जूह-संभमउ कद्दमु-प्पील-भमिअ-मीण-उलं
आसण्ण-सोस-भीअं हुवइ व जीअं तलाअस्स॥ *P.* I.5.3, p. 106.

(iii) आआस-तलाए णिम्मलम्मि पप्फुल्ल-चंद-कमलम्मि।
मिअ-महुअर-चरण-विहडिअस्स व जोन्हा-रओ फुरइ॥ *P.* I.5.4, p. 106.

112. The poetesses also participated in composing stanzas for the *Gāhāsattasaī.* Here is a citation from her:

मत्त-करिंद-कवोल-मओ-ज्झर-पंक-पसाहण-सामलिआ
दाहिण-मारुअ-मेलविआ-मअ-भेंभलिआ-भसला-वलिआ।
केअइ-केसर-धूसलिआ पसरंत-मणोहर-णीसणिआ
घोलइ कामि-अणो-वरि णज्जइ वम्मह-मुक्क-सरासणिआ॥ I.58.1, p. 25

113. Vākpatirāja is the author of the *Gauḍavaho.* The following incomplete stanza of his p. 25 is cited:

थण-दिण्ण-गरूअ-चंदण-पंगु-अक्खमणंससेसुमासइ-
भर-कुंचिअ-मउअ-सिहो चक्कलिओ तीअ रोमंचो॥
विअलिम्मि x x x x *P.* IV. 2.2, p. 115.

114. See supra (p. 207 and fn.). The following stanza by her is quoted in the text (I.3.1, p. 2):

उद्दंड-कोअणद-कोमल-कोस-कंती
कंता-कुच-ग्गहण-कंटइअ-प्पकोट्ठो।
मित्त-छिआइ-रिउ-चारू विलासिणीणं
सम्माण-दाण-भअ-भोअकरो करो दे॥

115. The following quotation is cited from Vetāla which indicates that he was Jain: 'णिच्चं णमो वीअराआ' एव माइत्ति (I.84.1, p. 40).

116. Sālāhana (Sātavāhana) and Hāla are quoted separately in the text under I.4.2, p. 105 and I.47.2, p. 21 respectively. It is to be noted that the following stanza is ascribed to Sālāhaṇa (I.4.2, p. 105) but it is also recorded in Nanditāḍhya's *Gāhālakkhaṇa* (27):

    थण-दोहडिए भरइ व बाला लाअण्णं-सलिलोहं।
    रमणालवाल-णिग्गअ-रोमावलि-वल्लरि व्व सिंचेइ॥

    Again, in the same Section and on the same page (I.4.1, p. 105) the following stanza is ascribed to Niuṇa (Nipuṇa) though it is recorded in Nanditāḍhya's *Gāhālakkhaṇa* (28):

    जाओ हरइ कलत्तो (त्तं) वड्ढंतो भोअणं हरइ।
    अत्थं हरइ समत्थो पुत्तसमो वेरिओ णत्थि॥

117. हा हिअअ किं विसूरसु, रूअं दट्ठूण परकलत्ताण।
    पात्वेण णवरि लिप्पसि, पावं पाविहिसि तं ण पाविहिसि॥ (I.3.2, p. 105). This stanza is ascribed to Bhīru, but recorded in the *Gāhālakkhaṇa* (26).

118. अप्पिज्जउ जणअसुआ, अणुणिज्जउ, राहओ पअत्तेण।
    आअड्ढिअचाअवरा, जाव ण णिवडंति दुज्जआ रामसरा॥ (I.3.3, p. 105).
    It is ascribed to Kaṇhadatta, though recorded in the *Gāhālakkhaṇa* (29).

119. See Index IV: Index of Authors, pp. 156f.

120. They are *Raghuvaṃśa, Kumārasambhava, Śiśupālavadha, Kirātārjunīya* and *Bhaṭṭi.*

121. See *Paumacariu,* I.3.7-8, I.2. 5-9.

122. Śrīharṣa is known for his skilfulness (*nipuṇatā*) as stated in the beginning of the *Riṭṭha ṇemi cariu* सिरिहरिसें णियणिउणत्तणउ also in the *Svayambhūchandas* (I.171, p. 31): जह (यथा- श्रीहर्षो निपुणः कविरित्यादिः).

123. Pandit Premi has made his observations in his *Jain Sahitya* (pp. 201ff), based on the study of a Bhandarkar Institute MS. Now this work has been edited by Ramsingh Tomar and will be published with introduction by H.C. Bhayani in the *PTS.* The first Kāṇḍa of the work has been published by the *BJP* with Hindi translation by Devendra Kumar Jain; the remaining portion is undertaken by Devendrakumar Shastri and will be published by the *BJP.*

124. *Ritthanemicariu* (I.2-5-9).

125. In his introduction to the *Svayambhūchandas* (p. xvii) Velankar has pointed out that the text contains as many as 60 citations that are quoted without any name attached to them; out of these, 16 refer to the story of the *Rāmāyaṇa* and 7 to the *Mahābhārata* or the *Harivaṃśa;* out of these 16 citations 12 have been traced to Svayambhū's own *Paumacariu.* See Appendix III: *Svayambhūchandas and other Works* (pp. 241f.). Premi has traced some of the stanzas of the *Svayambhūchandas,* about which no reference is made, to the *Paumacariu* of the author, *Jain Sahitya,* p. 206.

126. It is Māuradeva (Matṛdeva) in the Introduction of H.C. Bhayani's *Paumacariu*, Pt. III, p. 40, which is a printing error.
127. See Bhayani's Introduction, pp. 39 fn.39, and 40 for further examples.
128. Also held by Varāhamihira in the *Bṛh Saṃ* (104-54).
129. See Brief Notes of the editor on page 158 where he asks the reader to correct the printed heading of the chapter.
130. For details see H.D. Velankar, Introduction, pp. viii-x.
131. Critically edited with Hemacandra's own commentary *Chandeścūḍāmaṇi* and an anonymous Tippaṇaka *Paryāya* with elaborate Introduction and useful appendices by H.D. Velankar, *SJS* (No. 49), Bombay, 1961. Here the Appendix I provides A Classified List showing the Structure of Sanskrit Metres (pp. 283-321); Appendix II provides a Classified List showing the Structure of Prakrit Metres in 14 Sections (pp. 335-56) as follows:

    I समद्विपदी, II विषमद्विपदी, III समचतुष्पदी, IV अर्धसमचतुष्पदी, V विषमचतुष्पदी, VI पंचपदी, VII षट्पदी, VIII अष्टपदी, IX द्विभंगी, X त्रिभंगी, XI चतुर्भंगी, XII पंचभंगी, XIII अष्टभंगी, and XIV द्वादशभंगी. In *Pariśiṣṭa* I the editor has reproduced the fifth chapter (*sūtras* 39-75) of the *Jānāśrayī*, an old work on Sanskrit metres with English translation. The *Mātrā vṛttas* are defined here under four different headings. Its study is very important for the history of ancient Prakrit prosody (pp. 240ff). Another *Chandonuśāsana* (in Sanskrit) has been composed by Jayakīrti, a Digambara Jain of Kannaḍa region. In the tradition of Piṅgala and Jayadeva it is divided into 8 chapters. The author has used the works of Janāśraya, Jayadeva, Piṅgala, Pūjyapāda, Māṇḍavya and Saitava. He has also referred to the well known Kannaḍa poet Asaga (AD 950) in his composition. Mahākavi Vāgbhaṭal (fourteenth century) has also composed *Chandonuśāsana* in Sanskrit, *JSBI*, V, pp. 133, 137.
132. आर्यैव संस्कृतेतर भाषासु गाथासंज्ञा, IV.1. Com.
133. The आर्या has the following nine subdivisions:
    पथ्या विपुका चपला मुखचपला चघनचपला च।
    गीत्युपगीत्युद्गीतय आर्यागीतिर्नवैव वार्यायाः।
    See Apte, *Sanskrit-English Dictionary*, App. I.
134. The difference between the two is that the गलितक has यमक while the खंजक has only the अनुप्रास. The गलितक devoid of यमक becomes a खञ्जक : गलितकमेवायमकं सानुप्रासं समांह्रि खञ्जकम्॥ 4.49.
135. The *Dhavala* metres can be seen in the sayings of Sātavāhana: धवलानि च सातवाहनोक्तिषु द्रष्टव्यानि, V.32 Com.
136. The prolonged खञ्जक is known as शीर्षकः खञ्जकं दीर्घीकृतं शीर्षकम्॥ IV.84.
137. The songs of demigods: देवगानं फुल्लडकम्॥ V.41.
138. Its sounds have a stream of fragrant water:
    वक्ष्यमाणा गन्धोदकधारैवेयं गानवशाज्झम्बटक संज्ञा लभते॥ V.42.
    (i) Definition of मात्रा पंचपदी (मत्तवालिका, मधुरिका, मत्तविलासिनी, मत्तकरिणी and बहुरूवा) (II.28.66-8, p. 33):

(a) मत्तच्चिय वुच्चइ मत्तवालिया दुइयतुरियचरणेसु।
पढमटगणंमि तगणे कयंवि जुगवं अजुगवं वा॥ 66॥

(b) समचरणणिहणाटगणे ते युज्य कमेण मत्तमहुयरिया।
इय मत्त विलासिणिया सिहिसरपयमुहदुतेसु दुटा॥ 67॥

(c) मत्तकरिणीव एवं सिहिसर पायेसु टंमि जइ तगणो।
एयासिं मत्ताईण संकरो होइ बहुरूवा॥ 68॥

It is stated that their illustration should be known from some other work.

(ii) Twenty-four types of षट्पदी are referred to (II.30.71-2, p. 35):

(a) जीइ कलाउ दसाई सत्तरसंता य सिहिरसपएसु।
सेसेसु सत्त छपई सा छपई नाम अट्ठविहा॥ 71॥

(b) इय अट्ठहि उवजाई सत्तट्ठाणे कलाहि अट्ठविहा।
नवहि पुणो अवजाई एवं चउवीसहा छपई॥ 72॥

(iii) ध्रुवा, ध्रुवक, घत्ता and छड्डुणिका have been defined (II.30.73-4, p. 35):

(a) कडवयनिवहो संधी पद्धडियाईहिं चउहिं पुण कडवं।
संधिमुहेकडवंते धुवा च धुवयं च घत्ता वा॥ 73॥

(b) सा तिविहा छपई चउपई य दुपई य तासु पुण दुन्नि।
छ च उप्पईओ कडवयनिहणे छडुणियनामावि॥ 74॥

(iv) Four types of चतुःपदी is mentioned (II.30.75-80, p. 36):

(a) अह चउपईओ चउहा हवंति अंतरसमा तहद्धसमा।
संकिन्ना सव्वसमा य तासु तावंतरसमाओ॥ 75॥

(b) विसमे सेगा सेगा सत्ताई सोल जाव पत्तेयं।
अट्ठाई जा सत्तरस सेगा सेगा समे मत्ता॥ 76॥

(c) चंपय कुसुमाइनामियाओ जाइओ हुंति पणपन्ना।
दिसिगहवसुहयरससरसायर सिहिनयणचंद भेएहिं॥ 77॥

(d) एआओच्चिय सुमणोरमाइनामाओ वच्चए मुणह।
एवं दहुत्तरसयं चउप्पई अंतरसमाओ॥ 78॥

(e) अंतरसमयच्चिय दुइयतइयपायाण विणिमयंमि कए।
अद्धसमा य दहुतरसयसंखा तेहिं नामेहिं॥ 79॥

(f) दुहि तिहि चउहिवि विसरिसपाएहि विमिस्सियाओ।
सवसमाओ पुण सरीसएहिं सव्वेहिं पाएहिं संकिन्ना॥ 80॥

139. Edited by H.D. Velankar with his learned Introduction, Indices and Brief Notes, together with Nanditāḍhya's *Gāhālakkhaṇa* (Appendix I), Ratnaśekharasūri's *Chandḥkośa* (Appendix II) and the *Chandólakṣaṇa* (Appendix III) by Jinaprabha in his commentary on Nandiṣeṇa's *Ajiyasantithava*; Indene of Metres (in Appendices I, II and III, pp. 80-6 of *Gāhālakkhaṇa, Chandaḥkośa, Chandolakṣaṇa*, 1962.

140. कविदर्पणमुपजीव्य प्रायेण च्छन्दसामिह स्तोत्रे।
स्वपरोप्रकारहेतोरभिदधिरे लक्षणानि मया॥ 35

141. The following *Gāthās* of the *Chandolakṣaṇa* are almost identical with the *Kavidarpaṇa* I.2, II.4, II.5, II.19-20 and V.7 respectively:

(i) नेया मत्ता छन्दे दुतिचउपंचछकला गणा सव्वे ॥
दुतिपंचअट्ठतेरसभेइल्ला कचतटपनामा ॥ 1 ॥
(ii) मुणिटा गुरू तत्थ न जो विसमे छट्ठे उ मज्झका पढमे ।
दूए उ दलंमि लहू छट्ठे सेसं समं गाहा ॥ 2 ॥
(iii) दुइया छट्ठे पढमाउ सत्तमे लाउ कुणह उवरिदले ।
नलहुंमि पंचमे पढमयाउ इह तलदले विरइं ॥ 2A ॥
(iv) टचउक्के न व बारसलहुहिं सा वाणवसियाहोइ ॥ 33 ॥
(v) अडकलरगणो लहुगुरु सव्वेहिं तहवरंतिया होई ॥ 34 ॥

142. Also quoted by Somacandra (AD 1272) in his commentary on the *Vṛttaratnākara*, Velankar, *Chandonuśāsana*, Introduction, p. 41.
143. Ibid.
144. Here is the stanza:

गज्जंते खे मेहा फुल्ला नीवा पणच्चिया मोरा ।
नट्ठो चंदुज्जोओ वासारत्तो हला पत्तो ॥ VIII.7.36, p. 16.

This *Gāthā* is quoted as an illustration of *Sāmānyatodṛṣta* by Bhojarāja in his *Sarasvatīkaṇṭhābharaṇa* (III.154).
145. The following *Gāthās* from Manoratha are quoted:

(i) An illustration of सरलगाढा (गाथा):
महमहइ लच्छिमयकुडयनीवपरिमलभरेण घणसमओ ।
अइभरयपीयसुरसुरहियं व वरतरुणिमुहकमलं ॥ II.8.43, p. 17.
(ii) Definition of फुल्लः जइ मत्तजाईणं उज्जाला हिट्ठयंमि दीसंति ।
ता ताइं सव्वाइं फुल्लयनामेण कहियाइं ॥ II.33.95, p. 42.
(iii) Definition of तरलः
जइ दोहयाण हिट्ठे दीसइ संदोहओ हहं (?) रइओ ।
ता ते सव्वे छंदम्मि तरल नामेण नायव्वा ॥ II.33.96, p. 43.

146. जयदेवपिंगला सक्कयंमि दुच्चिय जइ समिच्छंति ।
मंडव्वभरहकासवसेयवपमुहा न इच्छंति ॥ I.71, p. 31.
147. See Velankar, Introduction, p. v for references.
148. See IV.87.5; IV. 87.4; IV.87.7; IV.87.6; IV.87.9; IV.87.8; IV.87.11; IV. 84.10 respectively.
149. W. Schubring critically edited in the *Zeitschrift fuer Indologi und Iranistik* (*ZII*), 1923, pp. 178-203. Edited with Introduction, Section IV (pp. xliv-li), Appendix III (pp. 111-19) of the *Kavidarpaṇa*, Rajasthan Oriental Research Institute, Jodhpur, 1962.
150. See supra, p. 457, fn. 2.
151. Ibid., fn. 3.
152. For a comparative view of these metres and references, see Velankar, Introduction, pp. xlv-xlvi.
153. For detail see Velankar, Introduction, pp. xlvi-xlvii.
154. Ibid., pp. xlvii-xlviii.
155. Ibid., pp. xlviii-l.
156. L. Alsdorf, 'Der Veḍha in der Vasudevahiṇḍi', *Asiatica: Festschrift*

Friedrich Weller. Zum 65 Geburtstag, Leipzig, 1954, pp. 1-11; reproduced in *Ludwig Alsdorf Klein Schriften*, 1974, pp. 167-77. Writing about the antiquity of the *Vasudevahiṇḍi* text in another article, Alsdorf has pointed out that this work composed in Archaic Jain Mahārāṣṭrī, contains the old *Veḍha* metre; this is an unmistakable sign of great antiquity. 'The Vasudevahindi, a Specimen of Archaic Jain Mahārāṣṭrī,' *BSOS*, Vol. 8, pp. 320-1.

157. Schubring, *ZDMG*, Vol. 75, pp. 97ff, 1922. Edited with Introduction (III, pp. xxxiii-xliii) and Notes (p. 155f) in (Appendix II, pp. 99-110) of the *Kavidarpaṇa, Raj OIJ*, 1962. One *Prākṛta-Chanda-Kośa* (vs 1544) is recorded in the *Raj OIJ* Collection, Pt. I, 1963, p. 284; another in the Pande Luṇkaraṇji Shashtra Bhandar in Jaipur.

158. (a) Arjuna is mentioned as follows:

(i) अज्जुणो जंपए (10), (ii) अल्हु जंपेइ (11), (iii) अज्जुणेण भासिओ (15), (iv) अज्जुणि कहिओ (19), (v) जंपइ अल्हकवि (27), (vi) कविअल्हि उत्त (30), (vii) सुकवि अल्हि राढउ सु उत्तउ (34), (viii) अज्जुणि सुकइ बद्धओ (35), (ix) अज्जुणि वुत्तउ (41).

(b) Gosāla is mentioned as follows:

(i) सुगुल्हु पयंपइ (6), (ii) गुल्हकवि एरिस वुत्तउ (12), (iii) गोसालेण दिट्ठओ (14), (iv) गोसालेण पयासिओ (18), (v) गुल्हु पयंपइ (26), (vi) गुल्ह पयंपइ (29).

Here a reference is made to Sanskrit poets who have a contemptuous attitude towards Apabhraṃśa poetry:
रासाउल छंद जु एह हुइ, काइं कविय डंखहि अलिय।
According to Velankar, the author of the *Gāthākośa* must have reproduced some stanzas in his treatise from their works, Introduction, p. xxxiii.

159. A reference to Piṅgala is made in stanza No. 45 where the मात्रावृत्त is called हक्का. This is called *Catūṣpadi* in the *Prākṛta Paiṅgala* (1.97).
160. See verse No. 4 where a *Varṇa Vṛtta* known as *Somkanta* is defined. It is known as the *Vidyunmālā* both in the *Chandahsūtra* (6.6) and the *Prākṛta Paiñgala* (II.66).
161. H.D. Velankar, Introduction, p. xxxiv.
162. *Rāḍhaka* and *Raḍḍā* seem to be identical, Velankar, Introduction, p. xxxix.
163. For other similarities, compare verses 16, 25, 31, 46, 50 with the verses of *Prākṛta-Paiṅgala* (here the name of Phaṇīndra is mentioned), I.170 (Nāgarāja Piṅgala is mentioned), I.146 (Sukai is mentioned), II.68 and I.141 respectively.
164. The verses Nos. 7, 16; 17, 21, 26, 32 and 41ab; 41cd can be compared with the verses 170-1 (pp. 69-70): here *Nandaṇi* or *Nandiṇi* is substituted for the word *Troṭaka*, 23 (p. 10); 26 (p. 12); 31 (p. 15); 112 (p. 46): here we have *Cūḍillau* instead of *Cūliyāu*; 82 (p. 32); 104 (p. 42); 111 (p. 45); of the commentary of the *Sandeśarāsaka*; Notes on the Appendix II, *Chandaḥkośa*, p. 155.

165. H.D. Velankar, Introduction to *Chandonuśāsana*, p. 44fn.
166. Ed. by Dr. Bholashankar Vyas with Hindi translation, 3 Sanskrit commentaries and Glossary in Part I; the Part II contains an elaborate Introduction in Hindi consisting of philological and prosodial study of the work, *PTS*, Varanasi, 1959 and 1962.
167. *Piṅgalanāgachanda* written in Prakrita and Apabhraṃśa is recorded in the *Raj OIJ*, Pt. II (B), 1965, Appendix, p. 143.
168. जंम ण सहइ कणअ-तुला, तिलतुलिअं अद्ध-अद्धेण।
 तंम ण सहइ सवण-तुला, अवछंदं छंद-भंगेण॥ I.10
 अबुह बुहाणं मज्झे, कव्वं जो पढइ लक्खणविहूणं।
 भू-अग्ग-लग्ग-खग्गहिं, सीसं खुडिअं ण जाणेइ॥ I.11
169. *Jeṇa viṇā ṇa jivijjai* (I.55) is traced in the *Gāthāsattasaī* (IV.464).
170. *Jaṃ jaṃ āṇei giriṃ* (I.74) identical with the *Setubandha* (VIII.43).
171. *Raṇḍā Caṇḍā* (II.107), *Mantaṃ na tantaṃ* (II.115), *Je tīa tikkhacala* (II.151) *je laṅkā giri* (II.187), *jaṃ dhoañjaṇa* (II.189) and *Īsārosa-ppasāda* (II.201) are identical with I.23, I.22, II.5, I.20, I.26 and of the *Karpūramañjarī* respectively.
172. *savvāe gāhāe* (I.57), *jā paḍhama tīa pañcama* (I.65) and *bhamaru bhāmaru* (I.80) are identical (with some variation) with 6, 9 and 88 stanzas of the *Gāhālakkhaṇa* of the *Chandaḥkośa* (12).
173. *gulhakavi erisa vuttau* is substituted by *sesakai vatthu nivuttau* (I.107).
174. मुंचहि सुंदरि! पाअं, अप्पहि हसिऊण सुमुहि! खग्गं मे।
 कप्पिअ मेच्छ सरीरं, पेच्छइ वअणाइँ तुम्ह धुअ हम्मीरो॥ I.71
175. Ed. George Bühler, Götingen, 1879; Gulabchand Lalubhai, Bhavnagar, vs 1973; Pandit Bechardas Jivraj Doshi, Kashiram Jain Granthmala, 1960.
176. *Amarakośa* or *Nāmaliṅgānuśāsana* of Amarasiṃha is the earliest Sanskrit *Kośa.* Numerous commentaries on this work such as by Kṣīrasvāmin, (eleventh century), Vindhyaghaṭīya Sarvānanda (twelfth century) and Rayamkuṭamaṇi (fifteenth century), who used 16 earlier authors, are known. Then the *Abhidhānaratnamālā* of the poet-grammarian Halāyudha and Yādavaprakāśa's *Vaihayantī* can be noted, Keith, *A History of Sanskrit Literature*, p. 413f. The earliest known Pali Buddhist lexicon is the *Abhidhānappadīpikā* by Moggalāna Thera. *Ekakkharakośa* can be added to this. B.C. Law, *A History of Pali Literature*, p. 637.
177. कव्वेसु जे रसड्ढा सद्दा बहुसो कईहि बज्झंति।
 ते इत्थ मए रइया रमंतु हिअए सहिअयाणं॥ 4॥
178. Ed. R. Pischel and G. Bühler, *BSS*, 1880; 2nd edn., 1938; Murlydhar Banerjee, *The Deśīnāmamālā of Hemacandra*, Calcutta, 1931; Edited by P.V. Ramanujaswami, *BSS*, Poona, 1938; Pandit Bechardas Jivaraj Doshi, *Desisaddasaṃgaho* (Pt. I) with Gujarati translation and Notes, Bombay, 1960; H.C. Bhayani, *Studies in Hemacandra's Deśīnāmamālā*, Varanasi, 1966.

179. देवा दैवीं नरा नारीं शबराश्चापि शाबरीं।
तिर्यंञ्चोऽपि हि तैरश्चीं नेनिरे भगवद्गिरम्॥

180. Translation by Pischel:
जे लक्खणे ण सिद्धा, ण पसिद्धा सक्कयाहिहाणेसु।
ण य गउणलक्खणसत्तिसंभवा ते इह णिबद्धा॥ 3॥
(a) लक्षणे शब्दशास्त्रे सिद्धहेमचन्द्रनाम्नि ये न सिद्धाः . . .
तेऽन्यैर्देशीषु परिगृहीता अपि अस्माभिर्न निबद्धाः।
(b) ये च सत्यामपि प्रकृतिप्रत्ययादि विभागेन सिद्धौ संस्कृताभिधानकोशेषु न प्रसिद्धास्तेऽप्यत्र निबद्धाः। . . .
(c) ये च संस्कृताभिधानकोशेष्वप्रसिद्धा अपि गौण्या लक्षणया वालङ्कराचूडामणिप्रतिपादितया शक्त्या संभवन्ति . . .
ते इह देशीशब्दसंग्रहे न निबद्धाः (यथा मूर्खे बइल्लो)

181. देसविसेसपसिद्धीइ भण्णमाणा अणंतया हुंति।
तम्हा अणाइपाइअपयट्टभासा विसेसओ देसी॥ 4॥

182. Art. 9; Murlydhar Banerjee, *The Deśīnāmamālā of Hemacandra*, p. xxxiii.

183. Also see John Beams, *A Comparative Grammar of the Modern Aryan Languages of India*, 1966, p. 12; A.F.R. Hoernle, *A Comparative Grammar of the Gaudian Languages*, 1880, Introduction, pp. xxxix-xl; R.G. Bhandarkar, *Wilson Philological Lectures*, 1904, p. 106; P.D. Gune, *Introduction to Comparative Philology*, 1958, pp. 275f; Murlydhar Banerjee, *The Deśīnāmamālā of Hemacandra*, Calcutta, 1931, pp. xxiv-xxvii; S.R. Chatterji, *Indo-Aryan Hindi*, 1922, p. 92; also 'Pabi, Sanskrit and Prakrit Etymology' by Richard Morris, *Transactions of the 9th International Congress of Orientalists*, Vol. I, 1983.

184. P.L. Vidya has arranged them alphabetically in Appendix II of his *Prakrit Vyākaraṇa*, Poona, 1928. The basic difference between the *Deśī*-words and the *Dhātvādeśas* is that the former are intended to include the non-Āryan and hence non-Indo-European words, whereas the latter cover such elements as are ultimately of Indo-European origin.

185. Really speaking they should not be called *adeśas*.

186. Introduction to the *Pāiyalacchī*, p. 13. Examples are quoted to illustrate this point: *parī*, 'milkpail' is reckoned a *deśī* word (VI. 37) but it is also used in Sanskrit in the same sense; *purilladeva*, '*asura*' is a *deśī* word (VI.55) but is also a Sanskrit word (from *pūrvadeva*) in the same sense; *bambhaṇī*, 'lizard' is reckoned as *deśī* (VI.90) but also signifies the same sense in Sanskrit (in Western part of Uttar Pradesh, in Muzaffarnagar district, a lizard is called '*bāmhaṇī*'). J.C.J.

187. Pischel in his *Grammatik* (Art. 36), under the heading of 'Gross blunder committed by Hemacandra' mentions some words, pointing out his slip: For example, *kaṇṭhadīṇāra* is used in the sense of *vṛtivivara* or 'opening in a fence' (II.24), but elsewhere (VI.67) the same word designates a 'particular ornament' (*ābhūṣaṇa-bhedaḥ*); the word *paero* designates '*vṛtivivara*' (an opening in a fence) along with its other meanings (VI.67). Similarly *poālo* (VI.62) and *vovālo* (VII.79) are

included as two different words, carrying the meaning of a young ox, but really they are one and the same.

188. See P.V. Ramanujaswami, *The Deśīnāmamālā of Hemacandra*, p. 5.

189. 'पाप एव असौ' इति वदन्ति, कुमारिल भट्ट, Tantravārtika, p. 227, see Pandit Bechardas Doshi, *Deśīsaddasaṃgano* (*Rayaṇāvali*) under *pāp*.

190. See P.V. Ramanujaswami's Glossary (pp. 1-92) which includes only such words which Hemacandra considers really *deśī*.

191. See *IA*, xlvi, 1917, p. 33ff; also Sir G. Grierson, *JRAS*, 1919, p. 235.

192. न च धात्वादेशानां देशीषु संग्रहो युक्तः। सिद्धार्थशब्दानुवादपरा हि देशी साध्यार्थपराश्च धात्वादेशाः I.37 Com. P.V. Ramanujaswami, Introduction to his edition, p. 5. In Appendix II (99-118) he has given the index of Verbal Substitutes from the *Deśīnāmamālā* as well as from the *Siddhahema*. The Appendix I (pp. 93-8) provides the words considered as *deśya* by others but as *tadbhavas* by Hemacandra.

193. अंबसमीत्यत्र सकारमकारयोर्व्यत्यये अंबमसीति केचित्पढन्ति। तत्र केषांचिद्भ्रमोऽभ्रमो वेति बहुदृश्वान एव प्रमाणम्।

194. तदेवं ग्रन्थकृद्विप्रतिपत्तौ बहुज्ञाः प्रमाणम्, i.e. even authors differ from one another so the well-informed persons should be the authority.

195. अवडाहिअं अवडक्किअं इत्यन्योन्य पर्यायशब्दावुक्त्वा गजनिमीलिकया गताः। अस्माभिस्तु सारदेशीनिरीक्षणेन विवेकः कृतः (the basis of our observaṭion is the material found in the *Sāradeśī*).

196. तकार संयोगस्थाने डकार संयोगं केचित्पपढन्ति। स च लिपिभ्रम एव इत्यनेकदेशीपरिशीलनेन निश्चितमस्माभिः (the difference between त and ड is due to the scribe's error; we have decided the form after observation of numerous *Deśī* works).

197. *JK* under *Prakrit-lakṣmī*.

198. Ibid.

199. Ibid.

200. Catalogue of Sanskrit and Prakrit MSS Collection by Muniraj Shri Punyavijaya, Pt. II, 1965, Ahmedabad, p. 794f. Ambalal P. Shah refers to Pratāpbhaṭṭa's *Yavananāmamālā* MS is available in the Institute.

201. Muniraj Shri Punyavijaya's above-mentioned collection.

202. Jain Prabhakar Printing Press, Ratlam, vs 1946-60. It has been recently reprinted.

203. Ajmer-Bombay, 1923-32.

204. Calcutta, vs 1985; 2nd edn., Varanasi, 1963.

205. P.V. Kane has referred to Suvarṇanābha, Kucumāra and Nandikeśvara in his notes on the *Sāhityadarpaṇa, Paricchedas* I, II and X (under the title 'History of Sanskrit Poetics', p. 1). The first two appear as teachers of the Sāṃprayogika and Aupaniṣadiaka sections of Erotics in the *Kāmasūtra* and the last has been referred to in the last chapter of the *Nāṭyaśāstra*.

206. A list of Prakrit stanzas quoted in the works pertaining to *alaṃkāra-śāstra* with their meanings in Hindi is published in Appendix II of the author; *Prakrit Sahitya ka Itihas* (pp. 703-84), 1st edn., 1961. The same

list is published in the *Prākrit-Puṣkariṇī,* 1961. It has a *prastāvanā* in Hindi.

207. Ed. K.P. Trivedi, *BSS,* 1909; P.V. Nagnatha Sastry, Delhi, 2nd edn., 1970; Batuknath Sarma and Baladeva Upadhyaya, 1928. Udbhaṭa the author of the *Kāvyālaṃkāra-saṃgraha,* has written a commentary on this work, known as *Bhāmaha-vivaraṇa,* which has been lost.
208. Ed. Rangacharya (with two commentaries), 1910; Belvalkar and Rangacharya Raddi Shastri (with an original commentary, known as *Prabhā vyākhyā*), *BORI,* 1938.
209. Published in *KM,* 1889, *Kāvyālaṃkārasūtra-vṛtti* (with *Vagbhaṭālaṃkāra* and *Sarasvatīkaṇṭhābharaṇa*), published by Anundoram Borooah, Calcutta, 1883; English translation of Vāmana's *Sūtras* and *Vṛtti* in *Indian Thought,* Vols. 3 and 4, 1912; Bombay, 1958; 4th edn., Vanivilasa Press, 1909, trans. G. Jha.
210. रीतिरात्मा काव्यस्य। विशिष्टा पदरचना रीतिः। विशेषो गुणात्मा, *Kavyālaṃkārasūtra,* I.2, 6-8.
211. Published in *KM* with Namisadhu's Commentary (in 1068), 1886; 3rd edn., 1928, edited by Ramchandra Mishra, Varanasi, vs 2017.
212. अधीनपति, वासकसज्जा, अभिसारिका, उत्का,
अभिसंधाता, प्रगल्भा, प्रोषितपतिका, खंडिता।
213. See supra, Chap. I, p. 5.
214. For other Prakrit verses see IV.11-15, 17-21.
215. Published in the *KM* with the commentary *Locana* of Abhinavagupta only on the first three *Udyotas.* The fourth one is printed as an original text without commentary; the 3rd revd. edn., Bombay, 1928. S.K. Dey has edited Abhinava's commentary on the 4th *Udyota* in the *Journal of the Department of Letters,* Calcutta University, Vol. IX, pp. 15-42. The Haridāsa-Granthamālā has brought out another edition without *Locana,* with a modern commentary by Shri Badarinath Sarman, 1937; the *Calcutta Sanskrit Series* has brought out the text without *Locana* with a modern commentary *Avadhāna* by Madhusudan Mishra. Both appear to be the copies of the *Kāvyamālā* edn. The text with the *Locana* and the *Bālapriyā* commentary by Pandit Shri Mahadeva Shastri, Chaukhamba Sanskrit Series, Vidyavilas Press, Varanasi, 1940; edited by Pattabhirama Shastri, Chaukhamba Sanskrit Series, Banaras, 1940.
216. P.V. Kane, ibid., p. 152.
217. In his commentary Abhinavagupta has referred to this work, saying चान्द्रकाकारस्तु पठितः (p. 185).
218. See supra, Chap. 5, p. 232.
219. See supra, p. 226.
220. See supra, p. 227ff.
221. The same as *Setubandha,* see supra, pp. 220-3.
222. After P.V. Kane, ibid., p. 193.
223. About 40 verses are published in author's *Prākṛit Puṣkariṇī.* For an

explanation of these verses see the *Dhvani-gāthā-pañjikā* of Ratnākara, Government Collection of MSS at *BORI* Catalogue, Vol. XII, No. 1821.

224. Ed. F. Hall, Calcutta, 1865; reprinted with an English translation by G.G.O. Hass, Columbia University Indo-Iranian Series (*CUIS*), New York, 1912; NSP, Bombay, 1928 (4th edn.); Varanasi, 1955; with Bahurūpamishra's *Daśarūpaka-dīpikā* by A.N. Pandey, Bharatiya Vidya Prakashan, Varanasi, 1979.
225. व्याकीर्णे मन्दवुद्धीनां जायते मतिविभ्रमः।
तस्यार्थस्तत्पदैस्तेन संक्षिप्य क्रियतेऽञ्जसा I.5
226. पाठ्यं तु संस्कृतं नृणामनीचानां कृतात्मनां।
लिङ्गिनीनां महादेव्या मंत्रिजावेश्ययोः क्वचित् II.63
स्त्रीणां तु प्राकृतं प्रायः शौरसेन्यधमेषु च।
पिशाचात्यन्तनीचादौ पैशाचं मागधं तथा II.64
227. Ed. A. Barooah, Calcutta, 1884; *KM* with the commentary on I-III by Ratneśvara, composed under Rāmasiṃha, and on IV by Jagaddhara; edited by Kedarnath Durgaprasad, Bombay, 1925; 1934; the commentary on the IV and V by Jivanand Vidyasagar Bhattacharya, Calcutta, 1894: Madras University Sanskrit Services, 1937; also in *TSS.*
228. He is credited with having composed 84 works on almost all sciences of medieval India such as the सरस्वतीकंठाभरण, समरांगणसूत्रधार, युक्तिकल्पतरु, श्रृंगारमंजरी, कोदण्डमण्डन and so on.
229. The following verse composed by her has been cited in 3 different forms with certain variations:

किं द्वारि दैवहति के सहकारकेण
संवर्धितेन विषपादप एष पापः।
अस्मिन्मनागपि विकास विकारभाजि
भीमा भवन्ति मदनज्वरसंनिपाताः II.35

also compare the verse on pp. 139, 617 and 625 (1925 edn.); also *Śṛṅgāra P.* XI, p. 449.
230. A list of these Prakrit verses is published by G.A. Jacob putting in great labour (*bhūyasā śrameṇa viracitā*), Introduction, 1925 edn.
231. The verses published on pages 567, 583 and 588 are identifiable with the verses of *Harivijaya* of Sarvasena, *Bhoja's Śṛṅgāraprakāśa* by V. Raghavan, p. 475.
232. देवाद्याः संस्कृतं प्राहुः प्राकृतं किन्नरादयः।
पैशाचाद्यं पिशाचाद्याः मागधं हीनजातयः॥ II.11, p. 122.
233. रसोऽभिमानोऽहङ्कारः श्रृंगार इति गीयते।
योऽर्धस्तस्यान्वयात्काव्यं कमनीयत्वमश्नुते॥ V.1.
श्रृंगारी चेत् कविः काव्यं जातं रसमयं जगत्।
स एव चेदश्रृंगारी नीरसं सर्वमेव तत्॥ V.3.
234. Sanskrit commentary: मयूरो बर्हभारे चन्द्रकं वहति। अनेन संकेतेन चन्द्रनाम लभ्यते। शिरोदेशः उच्छीर्षं। चरणदेशः पादान्तः। उच्छीर्षेण प्राची दिग्लक्ष्यते। 'प्राक् शिरा शयीत' इति वचनात्। अर्थात् पादान्तेन प्रतीची। ततश्च 'प्राच्या प्रतीचिमर्धचन्द्रोगतः' इति प्रात कालोद्भेदो वाक्यार्थः।

235. Sanskrit commentary: हे तामरसिनि पद्मिनि, वल्लभे सूर्ये लघु शीघ्रं व्यपक्रामति उपगच्छति सति हिमसमये रात्रेर्दीर्घत्वात् चिरेण पुनरागच्छति सति तव रोषस्य स्थिरस्य बलिरुपहारोऽहं क्रिये। इति काचित् खण्डिता पद्मिनीमुद्दिश्य वदति। मे न हेतुना निराकुलो जनो यावदेव किमपि न जानाति तावदेव हिमेन विशीर्णा झटिति त्वं दग्धतनुरसि।

236. तात्पर्यमेव वचसि ध्वनिरिव काव्ये सौभाग्यमेव गुणसंपदि वल्लभस्य।
लावण्यमेव वपुषि स्वदतेऽङ्गनायाः श्रृंगार एव हृदि मानवतो जनस्य॥ I. *śloka* 5, p. 1.

237. Vol. I, Chap. I, p. 2 (Josyer edn.).

238. अतोऽभिनेतृभ्यः कवीनैव बहुमन्यामहे, अभिनयेभ्यश्च काव्यमेवेति।
तत्पुनः शब्दार्थयोः साहित्यमामनन्ति; तद्यथा 'शब्दार्थौ सहितौ काव्यम्' इति। ibid.

239. I.3, pp. 102f. Here the examples are cited of each one. The example of Paiśācī given here is almost the same as given by Hemacandra in his *siddhahema* (VIII.4. 326) though in a corrupt form:
पनमथ पनय-पकुप्पित-गोली-चलनग्ग-लग्ग-पति-विंबं।
तससु नख-तप्पनेसुं एकातस-तनु-थलं लुद्दं॥

240. I.6, pp. 204ff.

241. याऽनियमित-गति-भाषा दिव्यादिव्योभयेति वृत्तवती।
कादम्बरीव लीलावतीव सा कथा कथिता॥ II.11, p. 469.

242. निश्चीयते तिरश्चामतिरश्चां वा यत्र चेष्टाभिः।
कार्यमकार्यं वा तन्निदर्शनं पञ्चतन्त्रादिः॥
धूर्त-विट-कुट्टिनीमत-मयूर-मार्जारिकादि यल्लोके।
कार्याकार्य-निरूपणमिह निदर्शनं तदपि॥ Ibid.

243. यत्र द्वयोर्विवादप्रधानमधिकृत्य जायते सदसि।
सार्धप्राकृत-रचित-प्रवह्लिका चेटकप्रभृति॥ Ibid.
Elsewhere (I.3, p. 122) Bhoja has referred to चेटक along with the पञ्चतन्त्र as a work in prose and verse with prose predominating: पद्य प्रधान-गणि तदेव त्रिधा। तत्र सजातीयेन पंञ्चतन्त्र चकेट . . .दौ (चेटकादौ). The विशेष निशीथ चूर्णी of जिनदासगणि महत्तर equates चेटककथा with वसुदेवचरिय as an example of कथा (IV.26).

244. क्षुद्र कथा मन्थुल्ली येह महाराष्ट्रभाषया भवति।
गोरोचनेन कार्या सानङ्‌गवतीव वा कविभिः॥
Here in his *Kāvyānuśāsana* (p. 338) हेमचन्द्र reads प्रेतमहाराष्ट्र्या and मतल्किका instead of मन्थुल्ली but it is wrong, Raghavan, *Bhoja's Śṛṅgāraprakāśa*, p. 823. Elsewhere (I.3, p. 122) Bhoja calls मन्थुल्थी in prose:
आख्यायिकासु (षु) कथासु (षु) मधुमल्लिकादिषु।

245. यस्यामुपहासः स्यात् पुरोहितामात्यतापसादीनाम्।
प्रारब्धानिर्वाहे सापिहि मन्थुल्लिका भवति॥ II.11, p. 469.

246. पर्यायेण बहूनां यत्र प्रतियोगिनां कथाकुशलैः।
श्रूयन्ते शूद्रकवज्जिगीषुभिः परिकथा सा तु॥ II.11, p. 469. It is mentioned by Ānanda vardhana in his *Dhvanyāloka* (Udyota III): खण्डकथा-सकलकथयोः प्राकृतप्रसिद्धयोः कुलकादि-निबंधन भूयस्त्वात्, दीर्घसमासायामपि न विरोधः Raghavan, *Bhoja's Śṛṅgāraprakāśa*, p. 821.

247. Further the *Indumati* is cited as an example of acquisition of a woman (*strī-lābha*) at the occasion of *Svayamvara* of Indumati, ibid., p. 476.

248. लम्भाङ्कितान्द्भुतार्था पिशाचभाषामयी महाविषया।
नरवाहन दत्तादेश्चरितमिव बृहत्कथा भवति॥ II.11, p. 470.

249. आख्यायिकैव साङ्का सोच्छ्वासा दिव्यपद्यगद्यमयी।
सा दमयन्ती-वासवदत्तादिरिहोच्यते चम्पूः ॥ Ibid.
250. XI, p. 470.
251. एतस्मिन् श्रृंगारप्रकाशे सुप्रकाशमेवाशेषशास्त्रसम्पदुपनिषदामखिलकला काव्यौचित्यकल्पना रहस्यानां च सन्निवेशो दृश्यते। ibid.
252. There are numerous references here regarding the *dūta-karma*, the duty of a messenger, carrying love message. If the beloved is beyond approach then a messenger should be sent with the message. 24 *duta-karmas* are described XXVIII, pp. 922ff. In order to fulfil one's objective of love 48 methods are described with citing illustrations from various works. The methods are *dūta-sampreṣaṇa, sandeśa-dāna, dūtānugama, sakhī-vigarhaṇa, dūta-paripraśna, priyā-sandeśa, dūta-vākya, guru-janaśankā, priyābhigama* and so on (XXIX, pp. 949ff).
253. See supra, 5, p. 231.
254. Ibid.
255. Ibid., p. 220.
256. Ibid., p. 227.
257. Ibid., p. 233.
258. Ibid., p. 207.
259. Ibid. See V. Raghavan, 'Sanskrit and Prakrit Poetesses', in *Quarterly Journal of the Mythic Society*, Banglore, Vol. XXV, Nos. 1-3.
260. Raghavan mentions Bhoja quoting a Paiśācī passage from the story of the gambler-pauper *Geṇṭākarāla* (or *ṭeṇṭākarāla* from the *Kaliṅgasenā-lambha, Bhoja's Śṛṅgaraprakāśa*, pp. 842ff. Also see R. Narsimhachariar, 'An Old Sanskrit Version of the Bṛhatkathā', *JRAS*, 1913, pp. 389-90. This version was written by the Gaṅga King Durvinīta of the first half of the sixth century. This is believed to be the source of the Tamil version of the *BK*.
261. T. Ganapati Shastri, *TSS*, 1915.
262. Vāmanācārya's *Bālāvabodhinī* commentary, Poona, 1933 (5th edn.). It has undergone several editions: *BSS*, 1901; Ānandāśrama Series, Poona, 1911; 2nd edn. of the same, 1950; an English translation by Ganganath Jha in the *Pandit*, New Series, Vols. 18-21; revd. edn., Poona, 1936.
263. *Sāhityadarpaṇa of Viśvanātha*, p. 255.
264. Explained in the commentary as follows:
तथा च कान्ता यथा दयितं गुरु-मित्राद्यधीनमपि इतरजन-वैलक्षण्येन कटाक्ष-भुजक्षेपादिना सरसतामापाद्य स्वाभिमुखी-कृत्य स्वस्मिन् प्रवर्तयति, एवं काव्यमपि सुकुमारमतीन् सुखि-स्वभावान् नीतिशास्त्र-पराङ्मुखान् राजकुमारादीन् ललित-पद-कदम्ब-कोप-दर्शित-श्रृंगारादि-रसेन मधुर-पानादिना कटुक-कषायौषध-पान-पराङ मुखान् बालकानिव सदुपदेश-स्वरूप-स्वार्थे प्रवर्तयतीति।
265. For a list of commentaries see Kane, *History of Sanskrit Poetics*, 1951, Index, 388ff.
266. मह देसु रसं धम्मे, तमवसम् आसम् गमागमाहरणे, हर-बहु ! सरणं तं चित्तमोहं अवसरउ मे सहसा।

267. हे उमे! मे महदे आगमाहरणे तं सुरसन्धं स्मासङ्गं अव, अवसरे (च) बहु-सरणं चित्त-मोहं सहसा हर।
268. Published with *svopajña-vṛttis*, known as *Alaṃkāracūḍāmaṇi* and *Viveka*, edited by Rasiklal C. Parikh, with a Foreword by Dr. A.B. Dhruva, Notes in English by A.B. Athavale, Shri Mahavir Jain Vidyalaya, Bombay, 1938; 2nd edn., 1965. Earlier edn. in *KM*, 70, 1901.
269. In this regard, the following statement of Rājaśekhara in his *Kāvyamīmāṃsā* has an interesting reading:

    नास्त्यचौरः कविजनो नास्त्यचौरो वणिग्जनः।
    स नन्दति विना वाच्यं यो जानाति निगूहितं॥

    There is no poet that is not a thief, no merchant that does not cheat, but he flourishes without reproach who knows how to hide his theft. After V.M. Kulkarni, 'Sanskrit Writers on Plagiarism', *Studies in Sanskrit Sāhityāśastra*, Patan, 1983.
270. *The Sāhityadarpaṇa of Viśvanātha, Paricchedas* I, II, X *arthālaṃkaras*, 3rd edn., Bombay, 1951, p. 277.
271. *Bhoja's Śṛṅgāraprakāśa*, p. 708.
272. Ibid., p. 246.
273. Ibid., p. 709.
274. Ibid., p. 154.
275. See V.M. Kulkarni, 'Some Aspects of Prakrit Verses in Alaṃkāra Works', *Studies in Sanskrit Sāhityāśastra*, pp. 155-7.
276. Satyavrat Singh, Choukhamba Vidyabhawana, 1957. It has undergone various editions: edited by E. Röer, with an English translation by J.R. Ballantyne and Pramadādāsa Mitra, Bibl. Ind, 1851-1875; rpt., Varanasi, 1956; P.V. Kane Bombay, 1910; Shivadatta Kaviratna, with the commentary *Rucira*, Bombay, vs 1973; Ramacharana's commentary (written in AD 1700), *NSP*, Bombay; with two commentaries, *Vijñapriyā* of Maheśvara Bhaṭṭa and the *Locana* of Anantadāsa (son of Viśvanātha), Motilal Banarasidass, 1938.
277. करम्भकं तु भाषाभिर्विविधाभिर्विनिर्मितम्।
    यथा मम- षोडशभाषामयी प्रशस्तिरत्नावली॥ VI.337
278. See supra, p. 233.
279. The following Prakrit verses has been cited by Viśvanātha, saying that they were his own compositions: (यथा मम)

    (i) ओवहइ उल्लहइ परिवहइ सअणे कहिं पि।
    हिअएण फिट्टइ लज्जइ खुट्टइ दिट्टीए सा, VII.8
    (ii) यथा ममः पंथिअ, पिपासिओ विअ लच्छीअसि जासि ता किमण्णत्तो।
    ण मणं वि वारओ इध अत्थि घरे घणरसं पिअंताणं॥ IV.6
    (iii) भिसणी-अल-सअणीए निहिअं सव्वं सुणिच्चलं अंगं।
    दीहो णीसासहरो एसो साहेइ जीअइत्ति परं॥ III.192
    (iv) यथा मम-
    एसा कुडिल-घणेण सुचिउर-कडप्पेण तुह णिबद्धा वेणी।
    मह सहि! दारइ डंसइ आअस-जट्ठिव्व कालअइव्व हिअअम्॥ III.167

(v) यथा मम-
कमलेण विअसिएण सुसंजोएंती विरोहिणं ससि-बिंबम्।
करअल-पल्लत्थ-मुही किं सुचिरं सुमुहि! अंतराहिअ-हिअआ॥ III.170

(vi) यथा मम चन्द्रकलायां चन्द्रं प्रति-
जइ संहरिज्जइ तमो घेप्पइ सअलेहिं ते पाओ।
वससि सिरे पसुवइणो तहवि इत्थीअ जीअणं हरसि॥ VI.184

280. Pandit Durgaprasad, *NSP*, VI. 184, Bombay, 1888; published with a commentary in the *KM*, 15, 1889.

281. Page 4.

282. Or 'The Sports of a Beautiful Woman', edited with a Sanskrit gloss by Lakshman Ramachandra Vaidya, Bombay, 1887. In the Introduction, Vaidya gives a list of Jagannātha's works; ed. by Shivarama Mahadeva Paranjape, Poona, 1895, with introduction, English translation and notes; by B.G. Bal, Bombay, 1985, with Sanskrit gloss and English translation; edited critically with his own commentary by Har Dut Sharma, Poona, 1935.

9

Secular Literature[1]

Joisa—Jyotiṣa or Astronomy or Astrology

Jyotiṣa is one of the six *Vedāṅga* texts or the supplementary science of the Veda which consist of phonetics (*sikṣā*), ritual (*kalpa*), grammar (*vyākaraṇa*), etymology (*nirukta*), metrics (*chanda*) and astronomy (*jyotiṣa*).[2] Originally, it seems, *Jyotiṣa* was a particular magical formula for exorcising the evil spirit supposed to possess weapons.[3] Later, it was taken as a science of the movements of the heavenly bodies and divisions of time dependent thereon, a short tract for fixing the days and hours of the Vedic sacrifices.[4] The science of astronomy is called *jyotirvidyā* or *nakṣatravidyā*,[5] or the knowledge of planets *Jyotirjña* or *Jyotirvid*, or an astronomer is one who possesses the knowledge of planets.

Jains to make their religious teachings popular, adopted popular motifs, myths, legends and tales. They incorporated magical practices, superstitious beliefs, popular deities, local customs and dialects as a part of their teaching. They composed secular works not only regarding mathematics, grammar, politics, medicine and so forth but also produced valuable treatises on prognostication, foretelling by casting dice, omens, testing of precious stones, construction of buildings, training of horses and elephants, knowledge of birds and animals, alchemy, archery, and cooking. Jains not only have written numerous treatises on *Jyotiṣa* but it also forms a part of their canonical literature. The *Sūrapannatti*[6] and the *Candapannatti*[7] are part of the *Upāṅga* literature of the Śvetāmbaras and deal with the movements of the sun, the moon and the planets in 20 sections. It is to be noted that the subject matter of one is almost identical with the other. Both have been presented in the form of questions and answers between Gautama Indrabhūti and his teacher Mahavira. Among other canonical works mention may be made of the *Gaṇivijjā*[8] and the *Joisakaraṇḍaka*,[9] both being constituents of the *Paiṇṇā* literature. Both deal with various aspects of astronomy; the former deals with the auspicious and inauspicious day, *karaṇa*, *muhūrta* and so on. Here we come across the word *horā* which indicates the influence of Greeks on Indian astronomy.[10] The latter deals with the subject matter contained in the *Sūra* in brief. Ācārya Pādalipta is said to have written a Prakrit commentary on this work, the excerpts from which have been cited by Malayagiri in his commentary.

It seems there was a vast literature on astronomy and astrology in ancient India. We are told that Alberuni travelled to India in AD 1030 to study Hindu astronomy and culture. He is also reported to have translated the *Bṛhatsaṃhitā* and the *Laghujātaka* of Varāhamihira (*mihira* is 'sun' in Persian, *mitra* in old Indo-Āryan), a renowned scholar of the sixth century. He is said to have obtained a special boon from the sun god, his father Ādityadāsa (Servant of the Sun) being his teacher. His mission was to revive the ancient learning of astronomy and astrology which was fast disappearing at his time. Utpala or Bhaṭṭotpala (tenth century), the commentator of the *Bṛh Saṃ*, has shown respect towards him, calling him an *ācārya* or teacher known for the compilation of works on the science of *Jyotiṣa* (*Jyotiṣa-śāstra-saṃgraha-kṛt*). Varāhamihira refers to various earlier *ācāryas*, on whose teachings are based his works. He refers to *pūrva-śāstra, eke, tajjña, bahānāṃ mataṃ* and so on, interpreted by Utpala as the works of Vṛddha Garga, Parāśara, Kāśyapa, Vajra, Bādarāyaṇa, Asita, Devala and others.[11] It is to be noted that our author acknowledges the greatness of Greek (*yavana*) authors in this science in the following well known verse:

म्लेच्छा हि यवनास्तेषु सम्यक् शास्त्रमिदं स्थितम्।
ऋषिवत्तेऽपि पूज्यन्ते किं पुनर्दैवविद्द्विजः ॥ 2.32

The *Yavanas* are no doubt *Mlecchas*, but this science has found a stable position with them. When even they are honoured as *ṛṣis* (sages), how much Utpala has referred to several authorities on the subject and has quoted extensively from their works. He has quoted Īśvara (LXXVII.II), the author of the *Gandhayukti*, a work on Perfumery in Prakrit which is not available.

He has also mentioned Ṛṣiputra,[12] Garga, Asita, Devala, Nagnajit,[13] Parāśara, Bāhulaka (may be Bāhuka of the Sūya), Bhadrabāhu,[14] Yavaneśvara,[15] Vīrasoma,[16] Samudra (or Sāmudrika),[17] Siddhasena[18] and others.

SOME POPULAR WORKS ON *JYOTIṢA*

We come across certain popular works on the subject which are either separate treatises or form part of a larger text:

1. *Vivāhapaḍala* (*Vivāhapaṭala*): Apparently, there were several studies of the same title. Utpala has referred to two *Vivāhapaṭalas* and is reported to have commented upon them. The *Bṛhajjātaka* (XXIV.16; XXVIII.3) of Varāhamihira has referred to this work.[19] Elsewhere it forms a chapter of the *Bṛhat Saṃhita* (III) and Vindhyavāsin is mentioned as the author of this chapter. *Śāraṅgadhara* was another author who composed the work of the same title in AD 1478, and Pītāmbara yet another, who wrote his in 1522.[20] It is also recorded in the *Raj OIJ Jodhpur Collection*, Pt. II (B), 1965. It was composed in VS 1856: Commentary by Kashinath (VS 1912) and with *Stāvaka*. It is mentioned in the *Niśīthacūrṇi* (13.4362, p. 400) without naming its author. Elsewhere Abhayakuśala or Ubhayakuśala is referred to as the author of the work. It is available in the form of manuscript, containing 130 verses, interspersed with quoted Prakrit stanzas.[21] There are commentaries by several authors: (a) Harṣakīrti's '*Bālāvabodha*', (b) Somasundarasūri's pupil Amaramuni's '*Bodha*', and (c) Muni Vidyānema's '*Artha*' (composed in VS 1873/AD 1657),[22] also *Avacūri* by Kṣemakara.[23]

2. *Agghakaṇḍa* (*Arghakāṇḍa*), also known as *Ṣaṣṭisaṃvatsara-phatāphala*: *Argha* is a technical term in *Jyotiṣa*, meaning a collection of 20 pearls (having the weight of a *dharaṇa*). A king used to fix the price of commodities with the consultation of traders, and this was known as *argha-saṃsthāpana*.[24] The *Nisī Cūr* mentions this work along with the *Vivāhapaḍala*. As the *Vivāhapaḍala* was consulted at the time of a wedding, so was the *Agghakaṇḍa*, to predict the fluctuation of prices of a commodity.[25] The *Bṛh Saṃ* contains a chapter known as *Arghakāṇḍa-adhyāya* (Fluctuation of Prices), consisting of 14 verses. The well known Jineśvarasūri in his *Pañcaliṅgīprakaraṇa* has referred to the *Joisagghakaṇḍāi*.[26] Durgadeva is mentioned as another author of the work. He has also composed the *Ṛṣṭasamuccaya* in AD 1032 in Kumbhanagar (Rajasthan).

3. *Rukkhāyuvveya* (*Vṛkṣāyurveda*): It was an important art of planting or cultivating trees, flowers and fruits in ancient India. It finds mention in the *Arthaśāstra* (2.24) of Kauṭilya. It is mentioned in

Saṅghadāsagaṇi Vācaka's *VH* (p. 56, line 27f), supposed to be based on the tradition of the *BK*. Here in the story of Dhanaśrī, we are told that her husband Samudradatta was expert in the art of *Rukkhāyuvveya*. He was employed by Dhanya, a garden-owner of Girinayara (Girnar). The owner was pleased to see his garden flourished within a short time with all kinds of flowers and fruits. *Vṛkṣāyurveda* is also mentioned in Budhasvāmin's *BKŚS* (5.225), a Nepalese Sanskrit version of the *BK*. We are told that Viśvila, a young artisan of Saurāṣṭra, was expert in this art. He cut down the wood from the forest and manufactured a flying machine out of it. He also manufactured valuable cooking utensils, conducive to health and longevity, in accordance with the rules laid down in this art.[27] The *Bṛh Saṃ* contains a chapter *Vṛkṣāyurveda-adhyāya* (55; Treatment of Trees), consisting of 31 verses. Here ancient sages like Kāśyapa and Parāśara are mentioned, who laid down rules with regard to planting and cultivating trees. Among later works on the subject mention may be made of Kṛṣiparāśara, the *Abhilaṣitārthacintāmaṇi*, the *Viśvavallabha* of Cakrapāṇi Miśra, the *Vṛkṣāyurveda* of Surapāla and the *Upavanavinoda*.[28] Damodara Gupta refers to *Vṛkṣāyurveda* in his *Kuṭṭinīmata* (24). The *Pārijātamañjarī* text inscribed at Dhāra (*Ep. Ind.*, VIII) refers to *Citraprayoga*, denoting the technique of growing different flowers on different trees.[29] The *Vṛkṣacikitsāropaṇādi* was another work dealing with planting of trees.[30] The *Pupphajoṇisattha* (*Puṣpayoniśāstra*), referred to in the *Taraṅgalolā* (152) of Nemicandra-gaṇi dealt with bedding of flowers.[31] There is still another work in Kannaḍa, known as the *Bījāropaṇanakṣatra* or the Proper Constellation for Planting a Seed.[32]

4. The *Laggasuddhi* (the *Lagnaśuddhi*), also known as the *Lagnakuṇḍalikā*.[33] It contains 133 *gāthās* which deal with auspiciousness of the zodiacal signs (*lagna*). The *Lagnaśuddhi-prakaraṇa* is assigned to Haribhadrasūri (vs 1650),[34] and is referred to in the commentary of the *Bṛhat Saṃhitā* (LIII.113, p. 493).

5. The *Aṅgavijjā* (*Aṅgavidyā*):[35] As stated, is a vast literature on astronomy (the science of heavenly bodies) and astrology (practical astronomy, now almost confined to the once-supported art· or science of the influence of the stars on human and terrestrial affairs), dealing with prognostication, augury, divination, fortune-telling, omens and bodily signs. *Aṅga* literary means limbs or gestures. It deals with the science of divination, not through the movement of

stars or constellations or reading the horoscope, but through physical signs and symbols (*aṅga*). The science of divination is quite old. We are told that it is based on the teachings of the early *ācāryas*. The *Aṅgavijjā* is a compiled work by an unknown author. It has been stated that Mahavira himself had taught this work to his disciples and this text was studied in a *gurukula* by those who led the life of celibacy and honoured gods, guests and monks.[36] It formed a part of the *Diṭṭhivāya*, the twelfth *Aṅga* of the Śvetāmbara Jain canonical literature which is no more extant.[37]

The *Aṅga* is considered the most prominent among *aṣṭāṅga-mahānimittas*, consisting of (i) *aṅga* or movements of limbs of the body (ii) *svara* or notes of birds (iii) *lakṣaṇa* or the science of interpreting bodily signs (iv) *vyañjana* or the marks of distinction such as moles, black spots, etc. (v) *svapna* or dreams (vi) *chinna* or rending of clothes (vii) *bhauma* or related to earth, an earthquake (viii) *antarikṣa* or related to sky; various colours and forms of the sky resulting from unnatural phenomena.[38] *Aṅga* is used here in a wider sense, indicating the knowledge of victory and defeat, a king's death or recovery from disease, anarchy, calamity, profit and loss, happiness and misery, life and death, famine, good harvest, drought or good rainfall, loss of wealth or acquiring desired wealth.[39] It is stated that as the sun is most prominent among all appearances so is the *aṅga* among all *nimittas*, and as all the rivers merge into the occean so also all the *nimittas* merge into the *aṅga*, and as the perfect knowledge (*kevalajñāna*) is the highest among all kinds of knowledge, so is the *aṅga* among all other *nimittas*.[40]

The *Aṅgavidyā* also finds mention in Kauṭilya's *Arthaśāstra* (1.11.17). It is described as the science of interpreting the touch of the body by means of which are ascertained events such as a small gain, burning by fire, danger from thieves, the killing of a traitorous person, a gift of gratification, news about happenings in a foreign land and the prediction 'this will happen today or tomorrow' or 'the king will do this'.[41]

The *aṅgavidyā* has also been referred to in the *Manusmṛti* (VI.20) along with the science of *utpāta*, *nimitta* and *nakṣatra*. The science of *nimitta, uppādo, aṅgavijjā, vatthuvijjā, khattavijjā* and *supinapāṭhakas* and *nemittas* are mentioned in the Brahmajāla sutta of the *Dīghe* (translation by Rhys Davids, 16-18). The well known Durgadeva was the author of the *Aṅgavidyāparīksā* (vs 1750).

SIMILARITY BETWEEN THE *AṄGAVIJJĀ* AND THE *BṚHAT SAṂHITĀ*

The *Aṅgavijjā* seems to be a much earlier work than the *Bṛh Saṃ* of Varāhamihira, but both are based on the teachings of the earlier traditions. Varāhamihira is known as *Jyotiṣa-śāstra-saṃgraha-kṛt*, the compiler of work on the science of *Jyotiṣa*. His work is also known as *Aṅgaviniścaya*, which determines the marks of the body. Obviously both are based on the then-existing ancient literature, providing a lot of information with regard to various aspects of social life.

It is significant that the *Bṛh Saṃ* has devoted a chapter entitled *Aṅgavidyā* (Signs of Limbs) containing 44 verses. The commentator Utpala, commenting on this chapter, has cited several quotations from Parāśara which shows that Parāśara was considered an authority on the subject. In the last verse of the chapter the author declares: 'Thus I have explained clearly the science of prognostication of touching the limbs, after carefully examining the treatises on the subject so that the people may attain their cherished object. An intelligent and noble astrologer who knows all this will always be honoured by the kings and the people.'[42]

Another interesting point about this chapter of *Bṛh Saṃ* is that all the 44 verses (except the first, which is interchanged with a somewhat different verse) are identical with the verses printed under the first appendix (*prathamaṃ pariśiṣṭaṃ*) of the *Aṅgavijjā*. The title given to this appendix by late Muni Punyavijaya, the editor, is '*Saṭīkaṃ Aṅgavidyāśāstraṃ*' (the *Aṅgavidyāśāstra* with commentary) with a footnote saying that he found this work to be broken, without a beginning or end, and that he himself had provided this title to the work (ग्रन्थोऽयमाद्यन्तविरहितः खण्डित एव प्राप्तोऽस्ति, अतो नामाप्यस्येदं मत्परिकल्पितमेव ज्ञेयमिति). At the end of the 44th verse the editor has added: 'Further, this work is broken' (अग्रे खण्डितो ऽयं ग्रन्थः). M.R. Bhat, the editor of the *Bṛh Saṃ*, while introducing the chapter Aṅgavidyā writes (p. 432): 'The commentator is of the opinion that this chapter may not be by Varāhamihira himself', but any way (in the opinion of the author J.C.J.) 'the Science of Limbs' does form a part of the contents of the second chapter (II.18) of the *Bṛh Saṃ*.[43]

By making a closer study of these two works we notice much similarity between their contents: even the titles of certain chapters are identical. The *Uppātaṇajjhāo* (53) of the *Aṅgavijjā* is the *Utpātādhyāya* (46) of the *Bṛh Saṃ*, containing 99 verses, the *antalikkha* (*antarikdṣa*) and *bhomma* (*bhauma*) types of *utpāta* are mentioned in both; then we have the *vuṭṭhidārajjhāo* in the *Aṅga* (20) and the

Sadyovarṣaṇādhyaya (28) in the *Bṛh Saṃ*; the *Jattajjhāo* (the military expedition; 47) and the *pavāsajjhāo* (travel; 43) in the *Aṅga* and the *Yogayātra*,[44] also known as *Bṛhadyātrā*, *Bṛhadyogayātrā* or *Mahāyātrā* (march under an auspicious constellation) in Varāhamihira and so on. Besides, there are various kinds of terms and expressions with regard to prognostication, augury, omen, portent, bodily signs, dreams and so forth which are identical in the works of Varāhamihira and the Prakrit Jain secular literature.

Jains also observed certain omens and portents. Auspicious *tithi*, *karaṇa* and *nakṣatra* were taken into consideration while undertaking a journey or going to attend to important work. A Jain monk is prohibited to have *svādhyāya* (religious study) at daybreak (*pūrva-sandhyā*) and evening time (*paścima-sandhyā*); compare the *Sandhyālakṣaṇādhyāya* of the *Bṛh Saṃ* (30), a chapter dealing with the indication at Dawn and Twilight). *Svādhyāya* was prohibited if there was preternatural redness of the horizon (*disādāha*; compare the *digdāha* (glow at the horizon; 31 of the *Bṛh Saṃ*;[45] the earthquake [*bhūmi-kampa*] with the *bhūkampalakṣaṇādhyāya* [32]) in the *Bṛh Saṃ*; a fiery meteor falling from the sky (*ukkā-paḍanaṃ*) with the *ulkālakṣaṇādhyāya* (33) of the *Bṛh Saṃ*; appearance of an imaginary town in the sky (*gandhavva-nagara*) with the *Gandharva-nagara-lakṣaṇa* (signs of aerial city; 36 of the *Bṛh Saṃ*; shower of dust (*paṁsu*) with the *rajo-lakṣaṇa* (38) of the *Bṛh Saṃ*; the conjunction of the evening twilight and the moonlight (जूवग or यूपक)[46] is with the *yūpaka* of the *Bṛh Saṃ*; and a violent gust of wind (*nigghāta*) with the *nirghāta-lakṣaṇādhyāya* (39) of the *Bṛh Saṃ*.[47] Seventy-two *kalās* which incorporate the knowledge of various marks and signs such as distinguishing marks (*lakṣaṇa*) of men, women, horses, elephants, kine, cocks, umbrellas, staves, swords and gems, etc., have been dealt with under the chapters of *puruṣa* (68), *kanyā* (70), *aśva* (66), *hasti* (67), go (61), *kukkuṭa* (63), *chatra* (73), *khaḍga* (50) and *ratna* (80), etc., in the *Bṛh Saṃ*. The *vatthuvijjā* or the science of building, measurement of camps and cities forms another *kalā* which is incorporated under the chapters entitled *Vāstuvidyā* or Architecture (53), containing 125 verses; the *Vṛkṣāyurveda* (55); the *Prāsāda-lakṣaṇa* (56) and the *Vajralepa-lakṣaṇa* (application of hard mortar or cement (57) in the *Bṛh Saṃ*.

Here in the chapter of the *Vāstuvidyā* certain important architectural terms have been explained. About the *nandyāvarta* type of house, we are told that 'It is a house which has verandahs starting from the walls of the halls and going to their respective extremities from left to right, it should have only three doors, leaving off the western one.'[48] Then comes the definition of the *vardhamāna*[49] (53.33), the *svastika*[50] (53.34) and the *rucaka*[51] (53.35) types of mansions, of which the *nandyāvarta* and the *Vardhamāna* are considered to be the best, the *svastika* and the *rucaka* moderate, and the *sarvatobhadra*[52] beneficial for kings, ministers and officials.

Besides architecture, sculpture and town-planning, both works have common topics such as eroticism (*Aṅga* 41; *Bṛhat* 74), lists of gods and goddesses, and various kinds of omens through birds and beasts. Here we have a store of knowledge of various things and objects concerning ancient culture.

The *Aṅgavijjā* is an ancient Prakrit Jain text which like the *Joisakaraṇḍa* is a constituent of the Paiṇṇā literature. Since it is a compilation of the teachings of the early *ācāryas*, it deals with many important subjects, besides the science of prognostication, which are essential to understand life. It contains 60 *adhyāyas* written in Mahārāṣṭrī Prakrit. The various grammatical forms used here are not in consonance with the rules of grammar.[53] In the discussion on gods and goddesses, there is a list of 'foreign goddesses' such as the Apalā (identified with the Greek goddess Pallas Athene), Aṇāditā (the Avestan goddess Anahita), Airāṇī (the Roman goddess Irene), Timisrakeśī (the nymph Themis) and Śālimālinī (the Moon-goddess Selene). Among other non-Jain popular deities we have Śiva, Senāpati Kārtikeya, Vaiśravaṇa, Varuṇa, Skanda, Viśākha, Brahma, Indra, the goddess of crematorium (*śmaśāna*), the goddess of excrement (*varca*), the goddess of the dung-hill (*ukkuruḍika*),[54] and so on. There is also an important list of boats and ships which indicates that maritime trade was carried on by seafaring merchants in those days. The list includes the *koṭṭimba* (identified with cotybmba), *tappaka* (identified with trappaga) and *saṅghāḍa* (identified with the sangar ship), mentioned in the *Periplus of the Erythrean Sea.*[55] One chapter deals with ways to find wealth stored underground, another discusses certain aspects of Jainism, and in the last chapter we are told the ways to gain knowledge of a previous birth.

6. The *Joṇipāhuḍa* (*Yoniprābhṛta*): Like the *Aṅgavijjā* this work is included among the *Paiṇṇā* canonical literature of the Śvetāmbaras. It is significant that this important work is acceptable to both sects, which indicates that this should have been one of the earlier texts composed before the bifurcation of the Jain community. This too

deals with the science of prognostication. It has been referred to by several Śvetāmbara and Digambara texts which shows its popularity. According to tradition, it was composed by Dharasena out of a portion of the *Agrāyaṇīpūrva*, one of the sacred *Pūrva* texts, while residing at Girinagara (Girnar, also known as Ujjayantagiri) in western India. This text was going into oblivion and the author restored it in the *duṣamā*, the fifth era. Originally, it is said to have contained 28,000 *gāthās* (in the *Agrāyaṇīpūrva*).[56]

According to the *Bṛhaṭṭipaṇikā* (written in vs 1556), Dharasena composed this work 600 years after Mahavira (i.e. between the first and the second century AD).[57] The author who was known as *prajñāsramaṇa* (Ascetic of Wisdom) is said to have acquired it as a favour from Goddess Kūṣmāṇḍinī for his two disciples Puṣpadanta and Bhūtabali, who were called from the Āndhra region to be instructed in scriptural knowledge (*śrutajñāna*) which was fast disappearing. This work has been considered with great esteem. It is stated in the *KVLM*: 'The summit of Mount Meru might shake and the current of the river Gaṅgā might go reverse but whatever is told in the *Joṇipāhuḍa* will never go wrong.'[58] *Ācārya* Siddhasena is said to have created magical horses after studying the instructions laid down in this work; buffaloes too are said to have been created by pursuing these instructions.[59] Elsewhere we are told that with the help of these instructions one could fashion the fish and the lion,[60] and also snakes and other animals by infusing certain different types of ingredients. By following these instructions one could also produce gold and jewels.[61] It has been stated that under certain circumstances, if a monk at the time of accepting monkhood, deposited wealth under the earth and later was not able to trace it, he could seek the assistance of the instructions laid down in the work and discover his treasure.[62] Elsewhere it is stated that this work contained magical power and one could conceive the knowledge of *pudgalānubhāga* (fruition of material object).[63] The text is not yet published. The manuscript preserved in the *BORI*, Poona, contains 800 *gāthās*.

Ramala or Pāśaka-vidyā or art of geomancy is used or foretelling events by casting dice. *Ramala* is an Arabic word which means a mode of fortune-telling by means of a dice marked with points. These points give answers to our questions. Obviously this art has been borrowed from the Arabs and various works have been written on the subject.[64] This is also called *Pāśaka-vidyā* (*pāśa* being a particular constellation in astrology).[65] In Jain tradition, the well known *ācārya*

Kālaka is said to have brought the *Ramala* from the Yavana country (Iran). Various works were written by Jains on the subject:

Muni Bhojasāgara (eighteenth century) has written the *Ramala-vidyā.* It is still in manuscript.

The *Ramalaśāstra* has been referred to by Meghavijaya in his *Meghamahodaya,* also known as *Varṣaprabodha,* composed in AD 1678, in mixed Sanskrit and Prakrit.[66]

Various works on *Ramala* have been recorded in the catalogues of manuscripts, which indicates the popularity of this art:

1. *Ramalaśāstra* by Cintāmaṇi Daivajña (nineteenth century), *Raj OIJ Collection,* Pt. II(B), 1965, p. 338.
2. *Ramalaśāstra* by Rāmadeva, son of Kṛṣṇa, son of Rāmarudra (19th century), ibid., p. 340.
3. *Ramalaśāstra,* ibid., appendix, p. 199. The treatise contained a chapter on *śakuna* indicated in the following verse:

   रामो दैवविदां प्रीत्यै पुरोक्तं यवनैर्यथा
   इति आगमशास्त्रे शकुनाध्यायः।

The following titles are mentioned:

1. *Ramalacintāmaṇi* (*Praśnatantram*), vs 1880, *Raj OIJ Collection,* Pt. I, 1963, p. 368.
2. *Ramalajyotiṣa* by Rāmadaivajña, seventeenth century.
3. *Ramalapraśnatantram* by Cintāmaṇi Pandit, vs 1882, ibid.
4. *Ramalasārasaṃgraha,* vs 1871.
5. *Ramalaṃ,* vs 1899, *Raj OIJ Collection,* Pt. II (B), 1965, p. 338.
6. *Ramalanavaratna* by Paramasukha, son of Sītārāma; was composed in vs 1867 at Śivavāṭikā.
7. *Ramalabindu,* nineteenth century.
8. *Ramalasāra* by Śrīpati, son of Lakṣmīnṛsiṃha, vs 1842.
9. *Ramalenduprakāśa* by Rudradhara Tripathi, son of Vālmīki, nineteenth century.
10. *Ramalarahasyasārasaṃgraha* by Bhayadhanjaña Śarman. It contained a chapter *Miśrka-prakaraṇa* as indicated in the following colophon:

    इति भयभञ्जनशर्मकृतौं रमलरहस्ये सारसंग्रहे मिश्रिकप्रकरणं समाप्तम्।

The adaptation of the *Tājika* system also indicates Muslim influence. *Tazi* is a Persian word meaning 'Arabic'. A Śvetāmbara Jain Muni (AD 1464) in his *Pañacaśatīprabandha* (I.75, pp. 40-1), under the title *Tājika-grantha-viracana-saṃbandha,* has provided an account of the composition of the *Tājika-Grantha.* It is said that once the Mughals invaded the region of Gujarat, they caught hold of some people and amongst these was a learned Jain *ācārya.* The *ācārya* was taken to Khurāsān where in course of time he picked up the local language. During his sojourn in the town he made a study of the *Yavanikā-śāstra* on the basis of which he composed the *Tājika-Grantha.* It dealt with the knowledge of past and future but as people were not intelligent enough they were not able to grasp it fully.[67]

Tākijavidyā seems to be quite popular in the eighteenth-nineteenth century; we have numerous manuscripts preserved in the *Raj OIJ Collection,* Pt. I, 1963; Pt. II (B), 1965 and Pt. II (C), 1966:

1. *Tājikaṃ* by Nīlakaṇṭha, son of Ananta, is one of the most important works written in Sanskrit in vs 1840 (AD 1783). Its manuscript is in the *Jodhpur Collection,* Pt. I, 1963, p. 328. The folios of the MS are damaged and discoloured; Nos. 4, 8-10 are missing. It is divided in two parts, the *Saṃjnātantra* and the *Varṣatantra.* The former is difficult to understand (*durūha*) therefore it has been commented upon by Viśvanātha, son of Divākara, in vs 1919[68] (extracts from the commentary are given in the Appendix of the *Jodhpur Collection,* Pt. II [B], 1965, p. 184). The latter, the *Varṣatantra,* was composed in vs 1644(?) (here the last figure is not legible due to the Bombay University Library stamp). The *Tājika-Nīlakaṇṭhī* has several other commentaries (1) composed by Govinda son of Nılakaṇṭha in the twentieth century, perhaps is the same as the *Rasālā Ṭīkā,* referred to on pages 185-7 of the *Jodhpur Collection.*[69] (2) Composed by Mādhava in vs 1860.

2. *Tājikasāra* is another important popular treatise on the subject:

(i) Samarasiṃha of the Prāgvāṭa lineage, son of Kumārasiṃha composed in Sanskrit in the nineteenth century vs. Herein is described the *varsaphala* (the events that are going to take place in the following year) as told in the *Tājika.* The third *tantra* of the treatise has been quoted from the section called *Pṛcchā* of the *Tājikasiddhānta.*[70]
(ii) Haribhaṭṭa was another author who composed it in vs 1805.
(iii) It has a *Tīkā* by Haribhaṭṭa.
(iv) It has an *Artha* by Kusalacanda.
(v) It has an *Udāharaṇa-vṛtti* (elsewhere *Kārikā-vṛtti*) by Sumatiharṣa

(also known as Sāmanta), pupil of Harṣaratna, composed at the time of the reign of King Viṣṇudāsa in vs 1677 at Kharavā (*The Jodhpur Collection*, Pt. I, 1963, pp. 328-30; Pt. II (B), 1965, pp. 272-4).[71]

3. *Tājikasudhānidhi* composed by Nārāyaṇa in vs 1914. A learned Brāhmaṇa, Mādhava, resident of Śrīgrāma of Kāśyapa gotra, was expert in fortune-telling (*sāmudrikajña*). Dādābhāi, his son, was virtuous and no one equalled him in the knowledge of *siddānta*. According to the author, his work is based on the works of Khindhika, Romaka and others.[72]
4. *Tājikapadmakośa* composed in the seventeenth century vs.
5. *Tājikakalpalatā* was composed by Jayarāma in Sanskrit in vs 1826.
6. *Tājikakaustubha* composed by Bālakṛṣṇabhaṭṭa, son of Yādava, in Sanskrit in vs 1833.
7. *Tājikabhūṣaṇa* by Ganeśa Gaṇaka, son of Dhuṇḍhirāja in the nineteenth century vs.
8. *Tājika-Bālāvabodh-Ṭīkā* by Gaṇeśa Gaṇaka, Tikā by Muñjāditya (nineteenth century vs).
9. *Tājikasiddhāntasāra* by Samarasiṃha.
10. *Tājikālaṃkāra* by Sūryadaivajña (vs 1841).

Pāśakevalī or *Pāśakakevalī* or *Pāsā Kevali* is another treatise on the subject. It has been ascribed to Garga, who has been called a great Jain Muni.[73] He has also been referred to by Varāhamihira along with Parāśara and Kāśyapa and by Thakkuarapheru along with Haribhadra, Jauṇa, Varāha and others in his *Jyotiṣasāra*.[74]

Another *Pāśakevali* exists in manuscript. It contains certain technical words such as *adaa, aaya, ayaya*, etc., divided into *a, va, da* and *ya* squares, with the help of which good or bad events are determined.[75] The *Pañcapakṣin* or the *Pañcapakṣijñāna* is another work on divination containing auguries ascribed to Siva by which one is able to foretell the future. Five vowels, *a, i, u, e* and *o* are associated with five birds. The *Pañca-pakṣi-stavaka* in Old Gujarati and the *Pañca-pakṣi-śakunāvali* by Nārāyaṇabhaṭṭa (vs 1840) are recorded in the *Catalogue of Sanskrit and Prakrit Manuscripts*, Pt. III (compiled by Muniraj Shri Punyavijayaji, edited by Pandit Ambalal Shah, L.D. Institute of Indology, Ahmedabad, 1960). Varāhamihira has composed the work under the same title.[76]

Among other manuscripts, the following can be noted. They are preserved in the *Raj OIJ Collection*, Pt. II (B), 1965, pp. 328, 330:

1. *Pañcapakṣipraśna* (vs 1807).
2. *Pañcapakṣiśakunaśāstra* (vs 1924).
3. *Pañcapakṣiśakunaśāstra* with *Ṭīkā* (vs 1831).
4. *Pañcapakṣi-ṭippaṇa* by Kalyāṇakaraṇa Shukla (vs 1908).

Nimitta or Nimitta-śāstra is the science of omens or signs. In Jain tradition it is believed to be a branch of *śrutajñāna* which has been quite popular among Jain monks. It has been mentioned along with *vidyā, mantra* and *cūrṇa*, etc., and is also among the 72 arts. According to the *Daśāsrutaskandha-Cūrṇi*, the *Karmapravāda Pūrva*, one of the 14 *Pūrvas*, dealt with the eight *Mahānimittas*. It is stated that the *Dṛṣṭivāda*, the twelfth *Aṅga* of the Jain canonical literature, contained knowledge of *nimitta*, preached by Mahavira himself.[77]

The *nimitta* has eightfold branches known as *aṣṭāṅgamahānimitta*, already referred to. Under the heading *Aṅgavijjā*, we have dealt with:

(i) *Aṅga* is the first constituent.
(ii) *Svara* is the omen from articulation. Nemicandrasūri in his commentary on the *Uttarā*[78] quotes Prakrit verses regarding *svara*.
(iii) *Lakṣaṇa* or auspicious marks on the body has been elaborately dealt with in the *Aṅgavijjā*. Here the bodily signs have been classified under various categories such as colour, sound, movement, place, collective body and so on.[79] *Sāmudra* (*samudra*) or *Sāmudrika* or marks or spots on the body foretelling good or bad fortune is considered as an offshoot of *Lakṣaṇa* by Udyotanasūri in his *KVLM* where elaborate details are provided in numerous Prakrit verses.[80] Nemicandrasūri in his commentary on the *Uttarā* has cited 18 Sanskrit verses and a Prakrit verse[81] related to the subject. Maladhāri Hemacandra in his *Upadeśamālā-prakaraṇa* has distinguished the characteristics of men and women.[82] Bhavadevasūri in his *Pārśvanāthacarita* expounds the codes of the *Sāmudrika-śāstra*.[83]

A few important Prakrit works can be noted below on the subject:

1. *Karalakkhaṇa*.[84] Its author is not known. It contains 61 *gāthās* dealing with palmistry and the distinguishing marks of men and women. It is also known as *Sāmudrika-śāstra*.
2. *Riṭṭhasamuccaya* (*Riṣṭasamuccaya*):[85] Its author is Durgadeva of the Digambara sect. His teacher's name was

Saṃjayadeva. He completed this work in Kumbhanagara (Kumbhergarh, Bharatpur, Rajasthan) in VS 1089 (AD 1032). It is based on the *Maraṇakaraṇḍiyā*, a work of ancient Jain tradition. Quoting this work as an authority, the author has said: One who does not hear the sound of his own body and does not smell the odour of a lamp (*dīpaka*) is going to survive only for seven days—this has been stated in the *Maraṇakaraṇḍi*.[86]

The work contains 261 *gāthās*, mainly composed in Śaurasenī, dealing with good and bad omens.
The Jodhpur Collection of Manuscripts, Pt. II (B), 1965, p. 212 records सामुद्रिकशास्त्र written in VS 1694 also with *Ṭīkā* and the *Bālāvabodha* by Nṛpati Bhūpati. One सामुद्रिकशास्त्र by Rāmacandragani recorded in the *Jaiselmer Hand-written Manuscripts cat.* II, p. 306.

(iv) *Vyañjana* or foretelling from the marks such as moles, black spots, etc. The *Aṅgavijjā* deals with the distinguished moles and peculiarities of the body and how results could be prognosticated from them. Ordinary human beings are said to possess 32 marks, distinguished persons such as the Baladevas and the Vāsudevas 800, whereas the number is said to have gone up to 8,000 in the case of Cakravartins and the Tīrthaṅkaras.[87]

(v) *Svapna* or interpretation of dreams. The *Viyāhapannatti* devotes a section on dreams where five kinds of dreams are mentioned. The *Aṅgavijjā* deals with auspicious and inauspicious dreams. Before conceiving Mahavira, his mother is said to have had fourteen great dreams. The mother of Gautama Buddha is said to have had a dream that a white elephant was entering her body. This is sculpturally represented on the Bharhut Stūpa. Mahariva is said to have seen ten dreams before attaining omniscience.[88] Nemicandrasūri in his commentary on the *Uttarā* has quoted 14 Prakrit verses on the subject.[89]

Among other works on dreams the following can be mentioned:

1. The *Suniṇasttari* deals with interpretation of dreams in 70 *gāthās*.[90]
2. The *Suniṇaviyāra* by Jinapālagaṇi contains 875 *gāthās*. The work is unpublished.

3. The *Suviṇadāra* has a manuscript in the Patan Jain Bhandar.[91]

(vi) *Chinna* or rending of clothes. It provides favourable or unfavourable predictions after seeing a piece of cloth soiled by black pigment, lampblack or dirt, or gnawed by rats or burnt by fire or cut through or torn at the borders. Nemicandrasūri has quoted 2 Prakrit verses in the commentary of the *Uttarā* (15.7, p. 215a).[92]

(vii) *Bhauma* or terrestrial disturbances such as earthquake. Nemicandrasūri has cited a Sanskrit verse in his commentary on the *Uttarā* (15.7, p. 215a) to explain this phenomenon.[93]

(viii) *Antarikṣa* or atmospheric omens. Good or bad omens can be read from different forms and colours of the sky caused by unnatural phenomena. Sometimes we see an imaginary town (*gandharva-nagara*) in the sky as a result of a mirage.[94]

As indicated earlier, the *Aṣṭāṅgamahānimitta* plays a very important role in the secular literature of the Jains. It forms a part of the *Pūrva* literature. It is stated that the disciples of Pārśvanātha, the twenty-third Tīrthaṅkara, were proficient in the knowledge of the Eight *Mahānimittas*. Makkhali Gosāla, the twenty-fourth Tīrthaṅkara of the Ājīvaka sect, was considered well-versed in the knowledge of *Aṣṭāṅgamahānimittas*. Ārya Kālaka is said to have deputed his disciples to Gosāla in order to acquire knowledge in the science of *nimitta*. Ārya Kālaka himself is said to have gained proficiency in *nimitta* and it is said that he performed a demonstration of his knowledge in the assembly of king Sātavāhana of Paiṭṭhāṇa. Bhadrabāhu II, who has been cited by Utpala in his commentary on the *Bṛh Saṃ* (IX.37), is known as *nimitta-vettā* (learned in *nimitta*). He is said to have composed the *Uvasaggaharathotta* in order to protect the Jain *Saṅgha*, as mentioned earlier. Dharasena, the author of the *Joṇipāhuḍa*, who is accepted by both Digambara and Śvetāmbara sects, is said to have mastered these *Mahānimittas*. Like Vīrasena the author of the *Dhavalā* commentary on the *Ṣaṭkhaṇḍāgama*, Dharasena too pays homage to the *Aṣṭāṅga-mahānimitta-kuśala-jina* in his work.[95] The commentator Abhayadeva in his commentary on the *Sama* has referred to the *Sūtra*, *Vṛtti* and *Vārtika* literature on the Eight *Mahānimittas* where a detailed exposition must have been provided on the subject.[96] Some of the works are given below:

1. *Cūḍāmaṇi* or *Arhaccūḍāmaṇisāra* or *Cūḍāmaṇisāra-śāstra*, also known as *Jñānadīpaka*: It is an important work on *nimitta*. It has been referred to in the *Bṛh Bhā* (1.1313), also Guṇacandragaṇi's *Kahārayaṇakosa* (p. 22af), in Abhayadeva's commentary on the *Ṭhā* (428) and in Laksamaṇagaṇi's *Supāsanāhacariya* (*Prastāva* II, *Samyaktva-praśaṃsā-kathānaka*). It is said that Campakamālā was well-versed in this science and could know in advance the spouse and children to be born to a couple. The *Cūḍāmaṇi* consists of 73 *gāthās.*[97] It is not available.
2. *Chayādāra*: It deals with the interpretation of events by observing shade. It consists of two-page manuscript, covering 123 *gāthās*, preserved in the Patan Jain Bhandar.[98]
3. *Chīñkvicāra*: The prediction of future events is made from one's sneeze. The manuscript is preserved in the Patan Jain Bhandar.[99]
4. *Kālaṇṇāṇa* (*Kālajñāna*): Pādaliptasūri is said to have been the author.[100]
5. *Garuḍasattha* (*Garuḍāśastra*): It is mentioned in Jineśvarasūri's *Kahāṇayakosa* (*Kathākośaprakaraṇa*) in the story of *Nāgadattakathānaka.* It deals with the cure for snake-poison.
6. *Jayapāhuḍa*: It deals with the science of prognostication (*nimitta*). It consists of 378 *gāthās.* It was composed before the tenth century.[101]
7. *Meghamālā*: It consists of 32 *gāthā* dealing with future events on the basis of the movements of constellations and the signs of the rains. The Patan Jain Bhandar has the manuscript.[102]
8. *Nāḍīdāra* (*Nāḍīdvāra*): It deals with particular arteries of human body such as the *iḍā, piṅgalā* and *suṣumnā.* The manuscript is preserved in the Patan Jain Bhandar.[103]
9. *Nāḍīviyāra* (*Nāḍīvicāra*): It deals with good or bad events arising out of the movement of the right or left artery. The manuscript is in the Patan Jain Bhandar.[104]
10. *Nimittadāra* (*Nimittadvāra*): It deals with *nimitta*; the manuscript is available in the Patan Jain Bhandar.[105]
11. *Nimittapāhuḍa* (*Nimittaprābhṛta*): This deals with the *nimittas* such as *kevalī, Jyotiṣa* and *svapna.* It has been referred to in Bhadreśvara's *Kahāvalī* and the commentary on the *Suyā* by Śīlāṅka.[106]
12. *Nimittaśāstra*: It is written by Ṛṣiputra, son of *ācārya* Garga. It consists of 187 *gāthās* dealing with *ākāśa, candra, utpāta, varṣā-utpāta, deva-utpāta-yoga, rāja-utpāta-yoga,* good or bad omens

arising out of a rainbow, the imaginary town (*gandharvanagara*), occurrence of a streak of lightning, or a line of clouds (*meghayoga*). Bhaṭṭotpala, the commentator of the *Bṛh Saṃ*, has referred to Ṛṣiputra in his commentary as stated earlier.[107]

13. *Paṇhavāgaraṇa* (*Praśnavyākataṇa*): This is different from the *Paṇhavāgaraṇa*, the tenth *Aṅga* of the Jain canonical literature. It deals with the questions and answers by a deity appearing in a linen cloth, a mirror, a thumb or an arm. It is referred to in the commentary on the *Ṭhā* by Abhayadeva.[108]
14. *Pipīliyāṇāṇa* (*Pipīlikājñāna*): It predicts good or bad omens arising out of the movement of ants of a particular colour. Its manuscript containing 8 stanzas is available in the Patan Jain Bhandar.[109]
15. *Praṇaṣṭa-lābhādi*: This predicts profit and loss, life and death.[110] The manuscript is in the Patan Jain Bhandar.

Śakunaśāstra or the Art of Omens played a very important role in the life of ancient Indian people. According to tradition it has been handed over right from Indra, Bṛhaspati, Śukra, and sages like Parāśara, Garga and Bhāradvāja. It is stated that king Dravyavardhana who ruled at Ujjain (AD 495-515), wrote a treatise on this subject.[111]

The dictionary meaning of the word *śakuna* is a bird in general, and the knowledge of notes of birds or omens or augury is known as *śakunajñāna*. It was a sort of a hymn or a song sung at festivals to secure good fortune. The *Śakuna-sūkta* or Bird-Hymn is mentioned. *Śakuna-ruta-jñāna* is the knowledge of the notes of birds.[112] There had been a close affinity between birds, animals and tribal people. It was known as totemism which would unite the tribal people in a sympathetic relation with nature. God Śiva is known as Paśupati or Lord of animals. As Nandi is associated with Paśupati so is Garuḍa with Viṣṇu, Haṃsa with Sarasvatī, and Mūṣaka with Gaṇeśa. This affinity was so strong that particular species of animals and birds were associated with superstitious beliefs or were auspicious or inauspicious omens for tribal people.

Śakuna-vidya or the knowledge of notes of birds is considered one of the 72 arts which is necessary to acquire. Varāhamihira in his *Bṛh Saṃ* has devoted several chapters to this topic. They are *Śākunaṃ* (Omens through Birds and Beasts), *Antaracakraṃ* (The Circle of Quarters), *Virutaṃ* (Cries of Birds and Beasts), *Śvacakraṃ* (The Circle of Dogs), *Śivārutaṃ* (The Cries of Jackals), *Mṛgaceṣṭitaṃ* (The

Behaviour of Wild Animals), *Gaveṅgitaṃ* (Intention of Cows), *Aśveṅgitaṃ* (Intention of Horses), *Hasticeṣṭitaṃ* (Attitude of Elephants), *Vāyasavirutaṃ* (Cries of Crows) and *Śakunottaraṃ* (Further Omens). The commentator cites Bhagavān Garga, Ṛṣiputra and Parāśara. Sage Parāśara has dealt with the seasons and their effects on the sexual instincts of different animals. This section contains 80 verses. In one chapter on the Cries of Birds and Beasts in 47 verses, the author has referred to the effect of house-lizard's cry.[113]

Dealing with the chapter on dogs, the commentator has cited references from Parāśara and Garga. The next chapter deals with different forms of cries of jackals.[114] Some chapters are very short, each consisting of only 3 verses. Two chapters deal with the intention of horses and attitude of elephants. One chapter concerns the cries of crows,[115] the next deals with more omens. It is here that the commentator cites 32 verses from the *Akṣarakośa* of Yavaneśvara, as referred to earlier.

Some treatises on Omens are mentioned:

Sauṇaruya (*Sakunaruta*) or the Notes of Birds: It has been mentioned in the *Nandi* (*sūtra* 42) along with the *MBH, Rāmāyaṇa, Kauṭilya, Buddhavacana, Patañjali, Gaṇita, Nāṭaka* and others.[116]

Sauṇadāra (*Śakunadvāra*) or '*Omen-Gate*': This work is catalogued among Jain manuscripts in the Patan Jain Bhandar.

Śakunadvāra is mentioned in the *Bṛh Saṃ.* It is stated, 'If there be two omens called *parigha*[117] which are blasted in action on both sides of a traveller, he would meet with his end. The same two omens situated in their appropriate quarters (right and left) and having pleasant cry and movements are called "Omen-Gates", and lead to the acquisition of wealth or accomplishment of desired object.'[118]

Sāṇaruya (*Śvānaruta*) or Barking of Dogs: It deals with the prediction of events by interpreting the barking of dogs. A treatise of the same title has been noted in the *JRK* and contains 20 *gāthās*.

The following works on *śakuna* may be listed:

1. *Śakunapradīpacūḍāmaṇi* by Upendra, son of Śrīmiśra Lakṣmīdāsa, vs 1799.[119]
2. *Śakunaśāstra* also known as *Śakunasāroddhāra* by Māṇikyasūri, vs 1338.[120]
3. *Śakunaśāstra* (nineteenth century vs), author not known.

4. *Śakunasāra* (nineteenth century VS), author not known.
5. *Śakunāvali* (VS 1910).[121] The MS. available in Jaisalmer Bhandar, *the Jaisalmer Handwritten Manuscripts*, Cat. Vol. II, p. 306.
6. *Śakunarahasya* by Jinadattasūri of Vāyaḍa *gaccha*, author of the *Vivekavilāsa* (VS 1270).[122]
7. *Śakunaratnāvali-kathākośa* by Vardhamanasūri, pupil of Abhayadevasūri.[123]
8. *Khañjanadarśanaphalaṃ* or augury pertaining to sighting the *khañjana* or wagtail bird; composed in Sanskrit in the nineteenth century VS.[124]

There were treatises on prognostication in respect of warlike operaions and various adventures:

Narapati-jaya-caryā or *Narapati-jaya-caryā-śāstra* or *Narapati-jaya-caryā Svarodaya-prakaraṇa* is a work of *Śakunaśāstra* (science of omens). It was composed at Aṇahillapura under the reign of king Ajayapāla of Gujarat (1174-7). It deals with the use of magic diagrams marked with mystic letters as a means of prognostication. In the city of Dhāra there lived a learned Brāhmaṇa named Āmradeva. Narapati was his son, who was expert in the science of omens, clever in *mantra* and *tantra* and possessing knowledge of *Cūḍāmaṇi*. He was *sarvajña* (all knower) in knowledge, respected by royalty and the Goddess of Learning was accomplished to him.[125] It has several commentaries: *Narahari Miśr-ṭīkā* by Narahari,[126] and *Jayalakṣmī-ṭīkā* by Harivaṃśa Mahādeva of the nineteenth century VS[127] are two of them.

Uvassuidāra (*Upaśrutidvāra*): It deals with the interpretation of works. The manuscript containing 3 pages, is catalogued in the Patan Jain Bhandar.[128]

Siddhapāhuḍa (*Sidhaprābhṛta*): It deals with the effect of application of collyrium to the inner coat of eyelids, application of an unguent on the feet (*pādalepa*) and keeping a tablet in the mouth (*guṭikā*).[129]

Vaggakevalī (*Vargakevalī*): It is stated that Vāsukī, a Jain layman of Vārāṇasī, approached *ācārya* Haribhadrasūri, with a copy of this treatise. The *ācārya* is said to have written a commentary on the work, but with the fear that the same might be misused, it was destroyed. This has been stated in the *Kahāvalī* of Bhadreśvarasūri.[130]

Vaddhamānavijjākappa (*Vardhamānavidyākalpa*): Jinaprabhasūri (fourteenth century VS) has eulogized the *Vardhamānavidyā* (magic lore) in 17 *gāthās*. It is stated that one who repeats this *vidyā* 21 times on entering a village, succeeds in accomplishing his work.[131]

Āusattha (Āyuśāstra) or Vejjasattha (Vaidyaśāstra or Āyuvveya (Āyurveda) or the Science of Medicine

Various treatises are mentioned on the subject:

1. *Rukkhāyuvveya* (*Vṛkṣāyurveda*): See supra, pp. 427-8.
2. *Pupphajoiṇsattha* (*Puṣpayoniśāstra*): See supra, p. 428.
3. *Jagatsundarīprayogamālā* was by Yaśaskīrti (Jassaitti) Muni in 1500, has Prakrit stanzas interspersed with Sanskrit and Hindi prose. The *BORI*, Poona has its manuscript. Another MS is available in the Baḍā Mandir, Terah Panthiyān, Shastra Bhandar, Jaipur.[132]

Kālajñāna with a commentary. It was a treatise on Ayurveda, told by Śambhunātha. It predicted death six months in advance.[133]

Atthasattha (*Arthaśāstra*) of Kauṭilya or Caṇakya-Kauṭilya

This is classified as a popular scripture (*laukika śruta*) in the *Nandi* along with the *Mahābhārata*, the *Rāmāyaṇa*, the *Vaiśika*, *Buddhaśāsana*, *Kapila*, *Lokāyata*, and *Patañjali*.[134] The treatise has also been referred to in other Jain texts. The *VH* of Saṅghadāsagaṇi Vācaka has cited a quotation from this work, saying, 'particularly, the growing enemy should be destroyed by employing deceit or a weapon'.[135] Further, Nemicandragaṇi in his *Taraṅgalolā* which is based on Pādalipta's *Taraṅgavaikahā*, has cited a few Prakrit stanzas from the *Atthasattha*, saying 'A secret is disclosed if it goes to a female messenger. A woman discloses a secret when she ought to have kept it hidden.'[136] Then Droṇācārya, a contemporary of Abhayadeva, in his commentary on the *Ogha*, cites a quotation from *Cāṇakya*, saying, 'It is no fault if one does not evacuate excrement and urine.'[137]

Haribhadrasūri in his *Dhuttakkhāṇa* (*Dhūrtākhyāna*) which is different from the one referred to in the *Nisi*,[138] mentions Khaṇḍapāṇā, the author of the *Atthasattha*, one of the five *dhūrtas*, assembled in the city park of Ujjain.[139]

Kāmaśāstra or Treatise on Sexual Love

In order to make their sermons fascinating, Jain authors incorporated erotic tales in their preachings. The *Mayaṇamauḍa* (*Madanamukuṭa*) is said to be written in Prakrit by Gosai Vipra of Mahāpura, situated on the bank of the Sindhu river.[140] It begins with obeisance to *Makaradhvaja* (having a fish on his banner), *Jodhpur Collection*, Pt. II (B), 1965, p. 155.

Vaiśika Śāstra or the Art of Courtesans or Harlotry

This is one of the arts in which courtesans are well-versed. We are told that Dattaka or Dattavaiśika had composed this treatise for the sake of courtesans of Pāṭaliputra. It is stated that once a courtesan tried to seduce Dattaka by employing charms mentioned in the *Vaiśika* but could not succeed. Thereupon she pretended to burn hereself in the fire. Dattaka thought that the courtesan must have been very clever as such a trick was never mentioned in the *Vaiśika*. Dattaka was caught and thrown into the fire, and still he refused to believe the courtesan.[141] *Vaiśika* is mentioned in Bharata's *Nāṭyaśāstra* in the sense of generating specialization in all arts or to have the knowledge of solicitation of prostitutes. One who knows the art of *vaiśika* is supposed to be expert in all arts and crafts; he should be able to captivate the heart of women, be well-versed in the *śāstras*, handsome, heroic, courageous, well-dressed, well-spoken, and expert in the conduct of love affairs. Bhojadeva, pointing out the secret of the *Vaiśika Upaniṣad*, has stated in his *Śṛṅgāramanjarī*: 'As people are frightened of a tiger so prostitutes are of showing true love to their paramour. It is on account of this that a number of paramours have been deceived by prostitutes.'[142] It is stated in the *Vaiśikatantra* that if it is not possible to acquire wealth out of real death, death should be faked.[143] The *Sūya Cū* has cited a quotation saying, 'The mind of women is difficult to conceive.'[144]

Dhaṇuvveya (*Dhanurveda*), Āühaveda (Āyudhaveda) or Archery

Dhanurveda or *Iṣvastra* is included in the 72 arts. It appears that the art of archery was at a highly developed stage in ancient India. It was compulsory for princes to acquire proficiency in this art. Various positions and movements in archery have been mentioned.[145] We come across various terms regarding this art such as *dhaṇupiṭṭha* (the back of the bow), *jīvā* (bow-string), *nhāru* (gut), *isu* (arrow), and *ārāmuha* (awl-tipped arrow).[146] Among *bāṇas* we have *saddavehī* (shooting at a sound without seeing an object),[147] *nāgabāṇa, tāmasa-bāṇa, paumabāṇa, vahnibāṇa, mahāpuruṣabāṇa, mahārudhirabāṇa* and so on; the *tāmasabāṇa* filled the battlefield with darkness.[148] We are told that Ceḍaga (Ceṭaka), the ruler of Vaiśāli and an influential leader of 18 confederate kings (*gaṇarājā*) of Kāsī and Kosala, was a skilful archer, who never missed his aim. His sister Tisalā was the mother of Mahavira.[149] The *Dhanurmaha* (festival of archery) was a special festival in which bowmen demonstrated their skill.[150] We come across various *svayamvara*-marriages when the contestants had to prove their skill in archery by shooting an effigy that stood before them, to win the princess.[151]

Gandhavvaveya (*Gandharvaveda*) or the Art of Music

Like *Dhanurveda*, the *Gandharvaveda* also has been assigned the status of the *Veda*. The word *gandharva* denotes various aspects of music, vocal as well as instrumental. *Naṭṭa* (art of dance), *gīta* (art of singing), *saragaya* (vocal music), *vāditta* (instrumental music), *pukkharagaya* (drum music) and *samatāla* (rhythm in music) are incorporated in the 72 arts, which shows that music was popular in ancient India. In ancient Jain texts we come across details of music, dance and drama. In the *Rāya* we are told about 32 types of dance-drama; actors and actresses are said to have dramatized the life-story of Mahavira, covering his previous life, his descent into womb, childhood, youth, sexual sports, renunciation, penance, attainment of *kevalajñāna* and propagation of his message. Various musical intruments are mentioned.[152] The seven notes (*svaras*) are mentioned in the *Thā.* Gandharvadattā was expert in playing *vīṇā.* In order to get her married a competition was held in Campā in which well-dressed contestants participated from all over to seek the hand of the beautiful maiden. The *gandharvas* are celestial singers inhabiting heaven. Tumburu, Nārada, Hāhā, Hūhū and Viśvavasu were known for their delightful songs.[153] It was a practice to pay homage to Tumburu and Nārada at the beginning of training in playing musical instruments.[154] It is stated that the *Sarapāhuḍa*, a portion of the

14 *Pūrvas*, which is no more extant, dealt with the description of seven notes, their place of origin, names of birds and beasts that utter these notes, and the names of musical instruments that produce them. According to the commentators, as this work is no more extant, the subject matter should be studied from the works of Bharata and Viśākhila which in their opinion are said to be only a part of the *Pūrva* literature.[155] The *Anuyoga* has referred to 7 *svaras* and their characteristics, *grāma* (gamuts), *mūrchanā* (intonation), virtues and defects of singing and so on.[156] The *Anuyoga Cū* has cited 3 Prakrit stanzas on the subject, which shows that there must have been some treatise on music in Prakrit. The author has dealt with 7 *svaras* and 9 *rasas* with illustrations.[157]

Gandhaśāstra or Preparations of Fragrant Substances or Personal Hygiene and Toilet

It constitutes the rules of preparing food (*annavihi*), drink (*pāṇavihi*), dress (*vatthavihi*), toilet (*vilevaṇavihi*), and bed (*sayaṇavihi*). It also incorporates the knowledge of wearing ornaments of silver (*hiraṇṇajutti*), gold (*suvaṇṇa*) and other ornaments (*ābharaṇavihi*); also preparation of powders (*cuṇṇajutti*) and the means of improving the complexion of damsels (*taruṇipaḍikamma*), preparing ornamental designs from leaves (*pattacchejja*) and cutting the links of a chain in consecutive order (*kaḍacchejja*).[158]

The *Gandhaśāstra* is referred to in the *BKŚS* of Budhasvāmin. The *Gandhajuttisattha* (*Gandhayuktiśāstra*) is mentioned in the *Taraṅgalolā* of Nemicandragaṇi.[159] Varāhamihira deals with *Gandhayukti* in his *Bṛh Saṃ.* The commentator Bhaṭṭotpala while commenting on this chapter cites verses from a *Nighaṇṭu* lexicon wherein the meanings of the words employed in the text are explained. He has also cited a Prakrit stanza of the *Gandhayukti* written by Isvara.[160] P.K. Gode has referred to a rare manuscript of the *Gandhavāda* with its Marathi commentary composed between 1350 and 1550.[161]

Dhātuvidyā or Alchemy

This is one of the 64 *kalās* as we have seen. Several methods were employed to turn base metal into gold. Gold obtained by blowing the stone with bellows, was known as *pāṣāṇa-dhātu*; when by moistening copper with mineral fluid, it was known as *rasa*; it was also obtained by blowing a piece of clay with certain application or without it, with bellows, and known as *dhātu-maṭṭiyā.*[162] We come across a mendicant who smearing a piece of black iron with elixir, put it on the burning charcoal and blew it with bellows. This caused the iron to change into gold.[163] *Udyotanasūri* (eighth century) in his *KVLM* has provided some details about the *dhātuvāda.* It is enumerated here as one of the 64 *vijñānas* such as *nimitta, mantra, yoga, añjana, kuhaka* (black magic), *dhātuvāda, yaakṣiṇī-siddhi* and *khatta* (*sainya-vidyā* or military science). The students who resided in the cells (*maṭhas*) were trained in this lore.[164] The art of alchemy was practised in a secluded place of the Vindhya forest. It is said that while practising alchemy one could produce the yellow of gold, white of silver, black of iron and colourless flames of bronze.[165] *Dhātuvāda* is considered a faultless method of acquiring riches.[166] The *Joṇipāhuḍa* is considered the source of the lore.[167] Among other works on the subject, the following can be mentioned:

1. *Dhātūtpatti*: It is written by Ṭhakkura Pherū, son of Śrīcandra of Kannanapur Mahendragarh, in about 1315. Here in 57 *gāthās* is given a description of brass, copper, lead, zink, bronze, mercury, vermilion (*hiṅgulaka*), red lead (*sindūra*), camphor, sandalwood, musk (*mṛganābhi*) and other materials. Here is also given the measurement in terms of *yava, māśā, ṭaṅka* and *tolā.*[168]

2. *Bhūgarbhaprakāśa*: The author Ṭhakkura Pherū deals with the earth containing various precious metals such as copper, gold, silver, vermilion, etc., and what colour and taste will lead to the discovery of a particular metal.[169]

Khanyavāda or *Khanyavidyā* or Mining

The important ores obtained from mines are silver, iron, copper, tin, lead, gold and diamonds. It has been stated in the *KVLM* that the branches of the *mālūra* tree indicate the presence of wealth below. In this connection the author has cited the *Khanyavāda*, saying: 'If there is a tree other than that of the milky juice, one is sure to have some small or big amount of wealth hidden underneath.' This lore helped to discover wealth by digging the earth. Certain *mantras* were enchanted before digging.[170]

RATNAPARĪKṢĀ OR TESTING OF PRECIOUS STONES

The earth is called *ratnagarbhā* (endowed with precious stones, or jewels). The jewels are either five,[171] nine[172] or eighteen. The *Uttarā* (36. 75f) enumerates the follwing *ratnas*:

गोमिज्ज (गोमेद), रुयग (रुचक), अंक, फलिह (स्फटिक), लोहियक्ख (लोहिताक्ष), मरगय (मरकत), मसारगल्ल, भुयगमोयग (भुजगमोचक), इंदनील (इन्द्रनील), हंसगब्भ (हंसगर्भ), पुलक, सोगंधिय (सौगन्धिक), चन्दप्पभ (चन्द्रप्रभा), वेरुलिय (वैडूर्य), जलकंत (जलकान्त or चन्द्रकान्त) and सूरकंत (सूर्यकान्त).[173]

The *Arthaśāstra* (II.11.29) devotes a chapter to *Kośa-praveśya-ratnaparīkṣā* (the examination of precious articles received into the treasury). Here are described various *ratnas* such as the सौगंधिक (a variety of ruby), वैडूर्य (lapis lazuli), इन्द्रनील (sapphire), शुद्धस्फटिक (pure crystal); they are known as *maṇis* or gems (29-32). Then we have विमलक, सस्यक, अंजनमूलक, पित्तक, सुलभक, लोहिताक्ष, मृगाश्मक, ज्योतीरसक, मालेयक, अहिच्छत्रक, etc., known as subsidiary types of gems (*antarajātayah*). The sources (*yoni*) and the colours (*varṇa*) of *vajra* (diamonds) are mentioned. It is stated that a diamond which is big, heavy, capable of bearing blows, with symmetrical points, capable of scratching a vessel, revolving like a spindle and brilliantly shining, is excellent (*praśasta*). And that whose points are lost, which is without edges and defective on one side is bad (*apraśasta*). *Pravāla* (coral) which comes from Ālakanda (Ālasāndra) and from Vivarṇa (of the Yavana-dvīpa), and which is red and of the colour of the lotus, is excellent, with the exception of that which is eaten by insects and which is bulging in the middle.

Varāhamihira in his *Bṛh Saṃ* has devoted four chapters, *Ratnaparikṣā, Muktālakṣaṇaṃ Padmarāgalakṣaṇaṃ,* and *Marakata-lakṣanam,* to the quality, variety, weight, price and the source of *ratnas.* He mentions twenty-two varieties, of which the diamond (वज्र), pearl (मुक्ता), ruby (पद्मराग), and emerald (मरकत) are considered most important. The twenty-two varieties of gems are (80.4-5):

वज्र (diamond), इन्द्रनील (sapphire), मरकत (emerald), कर्केतर (agate), पद्मराग (ruby), रूधिर (blood-stone), वैदूर्य (or वैडूर्य) (beryl or lapis lazuli), पुलक (amethyst) विमलक, राजमणि (royal gem), स्फटिक (crystal), शशिकान्ता (moon-gem), सौगन्धिक (a variety of ruby), गोमेद (opal or zircon), शंख (conch), महानील (azure stone), पुष्पराग (topaz), ब्रह्ममणि (brahma-gem), ज्योतीरस, सस्यक, मुक्ता (pearl) and प्रवाल (or विद्रुम) (coral).

The author has pointed out that since a jewel endowed with good qualities ensures good luck and one with bad qualities disaster (*aniṣṭa*), it is advisable to examine the fortune (of kings) depending on good or bad jewels.[174] At times different authorities are cited in this connection. It is stated that according to some, a woman wishing to beget a son should never wear diamonds, but in the opinion of the author, diamonds that are triangular (*śṛṅgāṭaka*), trigonal (*tripuṭaka*) and like the coriander seed (*dhānyaka*) or the buttocks (*śroṇinibha*) are productive of good results. Pearls got from pearl-oysters (*śuktija*) are considered the best. Eight sources of the best pearls are mentioned; Siṃhalaka (Ceylon) is the best. The presiding deities over different varieties of pearl are referred to. We are told that those who wear these extremely valuable pearls obtain sons, wealth, popularity and renown, their disease and grief disappear and their desires are fulfilled. Further, the author praises an excellent ruby and mentions its price according to weight. According to him these prices are based on the standard as laid down by ancient seers (*pūrvācāryaiḥ samuddiṣṭaṃ*).

Ratnaparīkṣā BY ṬHAKKURA PHERŪ

Ṭhakkura Pherū, the Jain treasurer of king Alauddin and Qutbuddin of Delhi, composed the *Ratnaparīkṣā* in 132 Prakrit stanzas in AD 1315 for the sake of his son Hemapāla. This tract is based on the earlier works of Suramiti, Agastya and Buddhabhaṭṭa.[175] It deals with verification, such as the place of origin, shape, colour, variety, quality, defect, and price. The author has dealt with nine *ratnas*. By adding seven more to this number there are sixteen *ratnas* in all, which are divided into *mahāratnas* and *uparatnas*. The *vajra* is found in Śūrpāraka, Kaliṅga, Kośala and Mahārāṣṭra; the *muktāphala* and the *padmarāgamaṇi* in Siṃhala, Tumbara and other countries; the *marakatamaṇi* in Malaya mountain and Barbara country; the *indranīla* in Siṃhala; the *vidruma* in Vindhya ranges, Cīna, Mahācīna, and Nepāla; and the *lahasuniyā*, the *vaiḍūrya* and the *sphaṭika* in Nepāla, Kashmir, and other countries. It has been stated that the good *ratnas* provide good health, long life, wealth and respect; they protect us from snakes, wild beasts, flood, fire and lightning, and cure wounds and disease. The examiner of *ratnas* was called *Māṇḍalika*. Persian *ratnas* have been described. The varieties of *Padmarāgamaṇi* are mentioned, *cunnī* being one of them. The extremely dark *mānika* was known as *cippaḍiyā* and *hīrā* (diamond) was known as *phāra*; this name is prevalent even now.

Dravyaparīkṣā[176] or the Science of Coins by Ṭhakkura Pherū

Composed in AD 1318, this treatise contains 149 Prakrit stanzas dealing with the verification of different types of precious stones—their prize, weight, substance, name and the place of origin. *Cāsaṇiya* (*Cāsanī*) and the purification of gold, silver and other metals employed for coins are described, as also prices of the coins. One chapter describes various coins such as *khurāsānī Mudrā, vikramārka mudrā, gurjarī mudrā, mālavī mudrā, nalapura mudrā, jālandharī mudrā, ḍhillikā, mahamūda sāhī, caukaḍiyā, pharīdī, alāuddīnī, mominī, alāī, mulatānī, mukhtalaphī* and *sirāzī.*

This treatise is an important source for coinage of the fourteenth century. The author is said to have composed this work after examining coins minted in the royal mint of Delhi.

Vāstusara[177] or the Science of Architecture by Ṭhakkura Pherū

The science of architecture or house-building is very ancient. Varāhamihira devotes three chapters in his *Bṛh Saṃ: Vāstuvidyā, Prāsāda-lakṣaṇa* and *Pratimā-lakṣaṇa* to it. They deal with architecture, description of temples and of idols respectively. The author has cited various authorities such as Garga, Parāśara, Bṛhaspati, Viśvakarman, Bhāradvāja and others. Towards the end of the chapter on temples, the author states that he has derived the material from sages like Garga, Manu, Vasiṣṭha, Maya and Nagnajit. In the chapter on idols also he has quoted Naganajit and Vasiṣṭha as authorities on the subject. The author has provided a delightful description of the image of Viṣṇu to be made for worship.

Ṭhakkura Pherū composed this treatise in VS 1372 (AD 1315). It contains 158 Prakrit *gāthās* wherein the section *gṛhavāstu-prakaraṇa* contains *bhūmi-parīkṣā, bhūmi-sādhanā, bhūmi-lakṣaṇa, māsaphala, nīva-niveśa-lagna, gṛha-praveśa-lagna,* and *sūryādi-grahāṣṭaka.* The 54 *gāthās* deal with *bimba-parīkṣā-prakaraṇa* and 68 with *prāsāda-prakaraṇa.*

Porāgama or *Sūdaśāstra* or *Annasaṃskāraśāstra* or the Art of Cooking

The *Porāgama* is mentioned in the *VH.* The *Sūdaśāstra* which has been ascribed to Bhīmasena finds reference in the *BKŚS* it is also known as the *Annasaṃskāraśāstra* (XVI.60). Elsewhere it is stated that the art of cooking depends on the knowledge of medicine and in order ot acquire this knowledge people used to travel to the country of Yavana (Greece). King Nala, the husband of Damayantī, is said to have been expert in preparing delicious dishes out of the heat of sun-rays.[178]

Assasatta (*Aśvaśāstra*) or Knowledge of Horses

Horses were considered very important in ancient India and cavalry an important part of the four-fold army (*cāturaṅgiṇī*). The *Arthaśāstra*, describing the functions of cavalry, has stated that horses are specially useful for guarding advance positions, protecting the treasury and commissariat, cutting off the enemy's supply, delivering attacks against the enemy's forces and pursuing a retreating foe. Varāhamihira in his *Bṛh Saṃ* (*Aśvalakṣaṇa*) provides characteristics of horses. The sage Śālihotra is considered a great authority on the subject. Śrīharṣa in the first chapter of his *Naiṣadhīyacarita*, while describing King Nala's steed, makes his observations on the subject. Bhaṭṭotpala, while commenting on the above chapter, cites authorities like Parāśara and Vararuci.

Various species of horses are referred to in ancient Jain literature. The *Samarā* of Haribhadra refers to Vāhlīka, Turuṣka, Kamboja and Vajjira horses. The *KVLM* of Udyotanasūri, besides 18 species of horses, refers to Vollāha,[179] Kayāh and Serāha horses, perhaps Arabic names, introduced by Arab horse-traders. Hemacandra in his *Abhidhānacintāmaṇi* has provided a list of horses.[180] However, he seems to be ignorant of their identification and has considered them of Sanskrit origin. Besides, there were other species of horses such as the *ākīrṇa*, the *kanthaka*,[181] *galita, aśva, aśvatara, ghoṭaka, pañcapuṇḍra* (bearing white marks at five places).[182] Horses were great assets to a king. They bore special names such as Jaladhikallola, Kamalāmelā, Sphuliṅgamuha (emitting sparks of fire), Vallabha, Haṃsavilambita and so on.[183] Several treatises have been composed by Śālihotra on horses.

Hatthisikkhā (*Hastisikṣā*) or the Art of Training Elephants

Since elephants had an important place in the army and were used on royal occasions, their training was considered most valuable. Maladhāri Hemacandrasūri in his *BHBH*, while enumerating 72 arts, has mentioned *hasti-sikṣā* along with *Bharata, Kāmaśāstra, Dhanurveda, turaga-sikṣā, dhātuvāda, lakṣaṇa* (characteristics of men, women, etc.), *aṅgavidyā* and so on. In the *Ṭhā* the elephant is considered as one of the seven jewels, the *senāpati* (general), *gṛhapati* (steward), *vardhakī* (architect), *purohita* (priest), *strī* (wife), *hasti* (elephant) and *aśva* (horse).

Several species of elephants have been mentioned in ancient Jain texts. The *Nāyā* has dealt with the characteristics of an elephant. The best of the species was seven hands in height, nine in width, and measured ten hands in the middle;[184] it was well equipped in seven parts of the body such as foot and tail. It was gentle, having the right measure with its head raised, and provided a comfortable seat. Its back resembled a boar, its cavity of abdomen was raised up and fleshy, its abdomen was hanging; it had a long trunk, long lips and its back appeared like the rear part of a bow. It was equipped with a well-contracted rightly measured body, with a closely knit measured tail, with full handsome feet like a tortoise, white-coloured, spotless, glossy and with harmless nails.[185]

Four kinds of elephants mentioned are the *bhadda* (bhadra), *manda, miya* (mṛga) and s*aṃkiṇṇa* (*saṃkīrṇa*). They have been classified according to their seasonal uses, physical strength, sharp or slow intelligence and their ability to attack others. Out of these the first was supposed to be the best; it attacked with its teeth. The *manda* was so called as it was slow in the endurance and speed; it made an attack with its trunk.[186] The *miya* species of elephant was timid and depressed and it made an attack with its lips. The last one (also known as *miśra*), belonged to the lowest category. It was thin in appearance and nature and attacked with its whole body.[187] There were special trainers of elephants. Ditches were dug to catch them. They were made to fall in deep ditches and made to starve.[188] They were made to lift logs of wood, small pieces of stones, bells, jujubes and mustard seeds. The *gandhahastin* or a scent-elephant was the best species; it was a valuable possession of Vāsudeva Kṛṣṇa. The Secanaka (the Sprinkler) was elephant of King Śreṇika for which a great battle ensued between Kūṇika on one side and Halla and Vihalla on the other. Udāyin and Bhūtānanda were two other elephants possessed by Kūṇika. The elephant Nalagiri was considered one of the four precious possessions of King Pradyota of Ujjayanī. Bhadrāvatī belonged to Udayana, who successfully carried away Vāsavadattā on its back from Ujjayani to Kosambī.[189] Several treatises were composed on the subject. One Durlabharāja, a Jain layman, composed

Hasti-parīkṣā, also known as *Gajaprabandha* or *Gajaparīkṣā* in AD 1158.[190]

The *Pālakapya-gajāyurveda* by Pālakapya Muni was in the form of a dialogue between king Romapāda of the Aṅga region and the sage Pālakapya. The treatise is preserved in the Jodhpur Collection of Manuscripts, Pt. I, 1963, p. 147.[191] It begins with *Sri Śāradāyai namaḥ*. The work is available up to 2nd *Sthāna* only. Keith has referred to *Mātaṅgalīlā* in Sanskrit by Nārāyaṇa (*TSS* 10, 1910).[192]

Mṛgapakṣi-śāstra or the Knowledge of Animals and Birds

Like treatises on horses and elephants there were compositions on other animals and birds. Varāhamihira wrote on characteristics of cows (*golakṣaṇa*), horses (*aśvalakṣaṇa*), cocks (*kukkuṭa*), tortoises (*kūrma*), goats (*chāga*) and so on. Dealing with the characteristics of cows, the author has stated that he had gathered information from Parāśara, who was a teacher of Bṛhadratha. Besides Parāśara, the commentator has cited Śālihotra in support of his statement. In the chapter on dogs the commentator cites Garga as an authority on the subject. Explaining the characteristics of cocks, tortoises and goats, the commentator again mentions the authority of Garga. In fact horses, elephants, bulls, dogs, cocks, tortoises and goats were nourished by royalty in ancient India. Often these animals were used in sports.

Caurakarma or *Coravidyā* or the Art of Stealing

A regular art in ancient India, this has been ascribed to various schools headed by Skanda, Kanakaśakti, Bhāskarānandi and Yogācarya. Skanda or Kumāra Kārtikeya was considered a deity of thieves, who were known as Skandaputra (Son of Skanda).[193] Before making departure for committing robbery, the robbers used to pay obeisance to Kharapaṭa, Prajāpati, Sarvasiddha, Bali, Śambara, Mahākāla and Kātyayānī, the mother of Kārtikeya.[194]

Mūladeva is considered as the arch-thief of Hindu fiction. He is supposed to have composed a manual of thieving entitled *Steyaśāstra* or *Steyasūtra*.[195] Various stories of Mūladeva are mentioned in Jain literature. In the *Nisī Bhā* and *Cū* and in the *Dhuttakkhāṇa* of Haribhadrasūri Mūladeva is shown in the company of Kaṇḍarīka, Elāṣāḍha, Śaśa and Khaṇḍapāṇā. Mūladeva is depicted as a crest-jewel of rogues expert in hypocrisy and knavery. Kṣemendra in his *Kalāvilāsa* has stated that when a merchant in order to get his son trained in the art of knavery (*dhūrtavidyā*)[196] visited Mūladeva, who was surrounded by pupils, explaining them the significance of *dambha* (practising hypocrisy). Various types of thieves and robbers are mentioned. Those who committed theft of horses, elephants, jewellery and kidnapped the inmates of the royal harem were the worst; those who robbed cows, buffaloes, made breaches in the wall and kidnapped maid-servants were of the second category; and those who in order to obtain food and drink robbed wayfarers and picked the purses of people belonged to the third category.[197]

Elaborate descriptions of robbers occur in the Jain canonical literature. They seemed to have been very powerful and even the royal army found it difficult to suppress them and control them. They used to move in groups, well equipped with *gomukhī* sword, bow and arrow and quiver. They were in possession of various charms, spells and incantations. They entered a city with a pomp, declaring that anyone trying to stop them must face dire consequences. They recited spells to open locks (known as *tālodghāṭinī vidyā*) and opened doors by sprinkling water over them which they carried in their waterbag (*udakabasti*). In order to find out whether anyone in the house was asleep or not, they blew their *kākalī* instrument. They also carried various useful things like measuring string, a cover for a burning lamp, a small box containing bees to be let out to extinguish lights in the house (*bhramara-karaṇḍaka*) and so on.

Thieves lived in their settlements called *corapalli*, situated in unapproachable mountain-ravines, surrounded by bamboo hedges, a trench or a mountain waterfall. Details are provided of numerous ring-leaders of robbers in Jain canonical literature. Vijaya of Siṃhaguhā was very cruel, expert in hitting an invisible object by mere sound and the foremost warrior in brandishing the sword. He gave refuge to adulterers, pick-pockets, thieves and undesirable persons. He terrorized people, broke into their houses, plundered property, took captives and tortured them.[198] Rohiṇeya is mentioned as another robber in the *Vya Bhā*. After his father died, his mother advised him to carry on with the profession of his father. At the time of committing the first theft, she waved her hand on his head, lit a lamp with seven wicks, put a mark on his forehead, and offered him blessings. Later, like the robber Aṅgulimāla of the Buddhists, he accepted Jain monkhood.[199]

APPENDIX

Catalogues of Manuscripts dealing with Secular Literature

There are various publications of Catalogues of Jain manuscripts preserved in various Bhandars. Some of them are as follows:

1. Among Western scholars G. Bühler was the first to undertake the survey of the Grantha Bhandars. His First Report covers the MSS surveyed during 1870-1, known as *Collection of 1870-1*; II *1871-2*; III *1872-3*; IV *1873-4*; V *1874-5*; VI *1875-6*; VII *1877-8*; VIII *1879-80.* All of them have been published by Bombay Government Central Press, 1880.

2. A list of famous palm-leaf manuscripts in the Śāntinatha Temple at Cambay. These are the MSS listed and described in the *First Report of Dr. Peterson.* This collection is preserved at the *BORI*, Poona, known as *Collection A of 1882-1883*; II *Report, 1883-4*; III *Report, 1884-5*; IV *Report, 1886-92*; V *Report, 1892-5*; VI *Report, 1895-8.*

3. *A Descriptive Catalogue of the Berlin MSS*, prepared by A. Weber in two volumes.

4. *A Catalogue of Sanskrit and Prakrit Manuscripts*, Muniraj Shree Punyavijayaji's Collection, Part I, compiled by Muniraj Shree Punyavijayaji, edited by Pandit Ambala P. Shah, L.D. Institute of Indology, Ahmedabad, 1965.

5. *A Catalogue of Sanskrit and Prakrit Manuscripts*, Muniraj Shree Punyavijayaji's Collection, Part III, compiled by Muniraj Shree Punyavijayaji, edited by Pandit Ambala P. Shah, L.D. Institute of Indology, Ahmedabad, 1968.

6. *A Catalogue of Jaisalmer Jain Bhandar Manuscripts*, edited by C.D. Dalal and Pandit Lachandra M. Gandhi, Gaikwar Oriental Series, Baroda, 1923.

7. *Grantha Sūci of Jaisalmer Bhandar*, edited by Muni Punyavijaya, published by L.D. Institute of Indology, Ahmedabad, 1972.

Jinabhadrasūri Jñānabhandara-Jaisalmer Handwritten Manuscripts, Cat., Vol. II, compiled by inmates of Seva Mandir Raoti, Jodhpur, 1988.

8. *Jain Granth Bhandars in Jaipur and Nagpur*, edited by Prem, University of Rajasthan, Jaipur, 1978.

Besides, the following important Bhandars can be added to the list: Śāstra Bhandars of Delhi, Jain Grantha Bhandars of Agra, Grantha Bhandar of Sonipat, Amar Granthālaya Indore, and Jain Grantha Bhandar of Surat.

The following Bhandars in south India, contain Jain manuscripts in Tamil, Telugu, Kannada as well as Malayalam: Śāstra Bhandar Jain Maṭha Mūḍbidrī, Vīra Bāṇī Bilās Jain Siddhata Bhavan Mūḍbidrī, Jain Maṭha Kārkal, Ādinātha Grantha Bhandar Aliyoor, and Siddhānta Basti Mūḍbidrī (see Dr. Dastoorchand Kasliwal, *Jaina Grantha Bhandaras in Rajasthan*, Shri Digambar Jain Atishaya Kshetra Shri Mahavirji, Jaipur, 1967).

The following are treatises on Jain secular literature, based on the *Kośa*:

1. *Akāladantakappa* a work on Jyotiṣa; mentioned in the *Jain Granthāvali*, p. 364.

2. *Āyajñānatilaka* composed by Vosaribhaṭṭa at Aṇahilawāḍa. It is an astronomical work in 750 *gāthās*, divided into 25 chapters. The author was a pupil of Digambara Ācārya Dāmanandin. He has composed his own commentary on the work. The word *āya* is mentioned in the *Bṛhatsaṃhitā* of Varāhamihira in the sense of eleventh lunar mansion. Here the answer to a question is obtained through 8 symbols such as smoke, a lion, an elephant, a donkey, a dog, a bull and a crow. Malliṣenasūri (VS 1100=AD 1043), pupil of Jinasena, has referred to Bhaṭṭavosari in his Sanskrit work *Āyasadbhāva* (*JSBI*, V, pp. 222f). See *A Report of a Tour in Search of Sanskrit MSS* by R.G. Bhandarkar: The Collection of 1884-7.

3. *Ulluṇṭhavādimukhakīlaka* an astrological work, composed by Abhayacandra Upādhyāya, pupil of Ānandrāja of the Kharatara *gaccha*. It consists of 123 *gāthās*.

4. *Kararekhālakṣaṇa*, an astrological work, dealing with the lines on the palm. It contains 59 *gāthās*.

5. *Koṣṭhakacintāmaṇi* is composed by Śīlasiṃha, pupil of Devaratnasūri, successor of Jayānandasūri of the Āgama *gaccha*. The author has written an auto commentary in Sanskrit. The word *koṣṭhaka* occurs in the *Bṛh Saṃ*. Here figures are allotted to certain squares (*koṣṭhaka*) and if counted either of the four sides, the total is the same. The author has also dealt with hundreds of *yantras*, mystical diagrams supposed to possess occult powers. The manuscript is catalogued in the Kielhorn's Collection of 1881-2. The L.D. Institute of Indology Ahmedabad possesses a manuscript of the original work along with a commentary, consisting of 101 pages; written in the sixteenth century.

6. *Nāthapustikā* deals with magic practices in 1397 *gāthās*. It is composed by Khelawāḍī Māhūya (*Bṛhat-ṭippanikā*, No. 596). But in the *Jain Granthāvali* (p. 355) the *Khelawāḍī* is a separate work composed by Māhūya, which is not correct, according to Velankar.

7. *Candrārkīpaddhati* is an astrological work. *Cantrārkki-Turkātājaka* with com. is recorded in the *Jaisalmer cat.*, Pt. II, p. 296.

8. *Joisacakkavicāra* (*Jyotiṣacakravicāra*) deals with *Jyotiṣa*. It is composed by Vinayakuśala and is mentioned in the *Jain Grathāvali*, p. 347.

9. *Mantramahodadhi* is composed by Durgadeva, a well known Digambar Jain writer. It deals with magic formulae in 36 *gāthās*.

10. *Mṛgapakṣiśāstra* is an important Sanskrit treatise written by Haṃsadeva, a protege of King Śauṇḍadeva. It is in a two parts, containing 1712 stanzas in Anuṣṭup metre. It is a 'rare work' on zoology and its manuscript is preserved in the palace library of Trivandrum.[200] Divided into 36 sections, it deals with the nature, habits, types, young ones, sport, conception, food habits, and lifespan of 225 animals and birds. Here we have a lively description of a lion, elephant, horse, cow, bull, swan, crane, cuckoo, pigeon, tiger, goat, deer, hawk, rhinoceros, buffalo, camel, sheep, dog, crow, monkey, jackal, cat and rat. The author is said to have lived in the thirteenth century.

11. *Sūtakavicāra* deals with the impurity caused by child-birth (*sūtaka*). The manuscript is preserved in 11 different Bhandars in Surat.

12. *Suvarṇasiddhistotra* by Acārya Pādalipta deals with the process of acquiring gold by artificial means.

13. *Hastalakṣaṇavicāra* deals with the lines on the palm; composed by Harṣakirti.

14. *Pārasībhāṣānuśāsana* is a manual of Persian grammar written in Sanskrit. It contains five chapters and is composed by Vikramasiṃha, son of Madanpal Ṭhakkur, pupil of Ānandasūri.

The following manuscripts are noted in the *Catalogue of Sanskrit and Prakrit Manuscripts*, compiled by Muniraj Shri Punyavijayaji, edited by Pandit Ambala P. Shah, Pt. I, Ahmedabad, 1965; also 1969:

Dakṣiṇāvartaśaṅkhakalpa is a work on *Āyurveda* (vs 1736)
Solasvapnavicāra (vs 1650)
Kararekhālakṣaṇapañcāśikā (vs 1750). It is available up to the 73rd *gāthā*.

Nāsikāuicaāra deals with omens (vs 1450); composed by Muni Khemamūrti, pupil of Jñānacandrasūri of Bṛhadgaccha. The MSS is damaged; was copied it at Bidarnagar at the time of Mahmūdrāj Sūratrāṇa's reign.

Pañcavākyaśakunavicāra-yantra (vs 1796).

Pallī-patana-vicāra (vs 1650) deals with prognostication by observing the fall of house-lizards on the person.

Pallivicāra (vs 1750).

Pallīvicāra; *Gṛhagodhāvicāra*; *Kṛkalāsavicara* (vs 1650).

Pallīśaraṭa patana-vicāra (vs 1850).

Paśupakṣi-śakunāvalī (vs 1650).

Bhramara-phalāphala-vicāra-prakaraṇa (vs 1650).

Madhukara-maṇi-parīkṣā (vs 1650).

Mātṛkā-praśna-sakunāvali (vs 1650) deals with a diagram written in character in which a magical power is ascribed (*mātṛkā*).

Mātṛkā-śakunāvali (vs 1650).

Aṅga-sphuraṇa-vicāra-prakaraṇa (vs 1750).

Danta-parīkṣā-kalpa (vs 1750).

Nāḍi-parīkṣā (vs 1850); from Ramavinoda.

Pipīlikā-lakṣaṇa (vs 1950).

Pipīlikā-vicāra (vs 1950).

Bhaḍḍali-grantha (vs 1550) deals with foretelling the future (*bhaḍḍara*). MS of Bhaḍalivācaka by Bhaḍali is available in Jaisalmer Handwritten Manuscripts: Cat. II, p. 300.

Bhaḍali-vākya (vs 1650).

Bhūmi-lakṣaṇa-gāthā (vs 1950).

Mṛtyu-jñāna-parijñāna (vs 1686).

Catalogue of Sanskrit and Prakrit MSS in the Rajasthan Oriental Institute Jodhpur, Pt. I, edited by Muni Jinavijaya, Jodhpur, 1963.

Pallī-saraṭa-śānti-vidhānaṃ (nineteenth century vs) in Sanskrit.

The Raj OIJ Collection, Pt. II (A), 1964.

Gāthākośa by Vīracandra, pupil of Yaśascandrasūri (eighteenth century vs).

Pallī saraṭa patana-śānti-vidhānaṃ by Garga (1844 vs) in Sanskrit

Rasa-vilāsa by Pṛthvi Sukavi, pupil of Abhayasūri (eighteenth century vs).

The Raj OIJ Collection, Pt. II (B), 1965.

Āya-praśna-grantha (nineteenth century vs) in Sanskrit.

Praśna-jñāna by Utpala Bhaṭṭa (1794 vs).

Puruṣa-parīkṣā by Vidyādhara kavi (nineteenth century vs).

Hasta-rekhā-prakaraṇa (nineteenth century VS).

Hasta-saṃjīvanaṃ by Meghavijayopādhyāya (nineteenth century VS).

Hikamata-prakāśa composed in Sanskrit and Persian (nineteenth century VS).

The Jaisalmer Handwritten Manuscripts Catalogue, Vol. II, 1988.

Gāngā Telī Kathā (p. 268).

Ciḍiyā kā Vyāha Va Agagosa (p. 270).

Taule Bhole Kā Śloka (p. 270).

Majalisa (p. 272).

Kaṅkātu Bhātaṇa Sambandha (p. 278).

WORKS IN MANUSCRIPT

The importance of handwritten manuscripts was high in early days when there was no printing press. People used to copy them and distribute them to far-off places and this was considered a meritorious deed. It is stated that king Kumarapāla, the successor of Siddharāja of Gujarat, employed several hundred scribes to make copies of the scriptures and distribute them all over India. The well known minister Vastupāla, the builder of the famous temple of Neminatha at Ābu, was once a governor of Cambay (Khambat), installed a *Jñānabhaṇḍār* (storehouse of knowledge) at the cost of 18 lakh rupees. As a devout Jain he himself copied manuscripts, some of them preserved even to this day in the Śāntinātha Bhaṇḍāra of the same city.

Several thousand manuscripts have been preserved in these Bhaṇḍāras and not all of them belong to subjects related to Jainism. Many are Buddhist and Vedic works that are rare and not found elsewhere. These manuscripts are related to various secular topics such as medicine, astrology, astronomy, music, sculpture, architecture, art of love, polity, logic, metre, lexiçography, grammar, poetry, rhetoric, magic (*mantra-śāstra*) and so on. Theses valuable manuscripts have to be preserved with great care from damage or destruction as they were prepared with enormous difficulty. They had to be protected from water, fire, thieves and particularly from rats.[201] Jain teachers have declared the *Jñāna-pañcamī*, the fifth day of the bright half of the month of Kārtika, as a festival day so that devotees may pay homage to the *Śāstras* (holy books), clean, dust and copy them themselves, and induce others to do the same.

Bhaṇḍāras or collections of manuscripts were common in Gujarat, Saurashtra, Kaccha, Marwar, Mewar, Punjab, Uttar Pradesh and south India and possessed several hundred thousands of handwritten manuscripts. We are told that the Bhaṇḍāras of Gujarat, Saurashtra and Kaccha alone had at minimum 5 to 7 lakh manuscripts.[202] Most important Bhaṇḍāras were located in Cambay, Jaisalmer and Patan. Outside India we have them in Berlin, London, Oxford, Vienna, Strasbourg and other places. Among scholars who have catalogued these manuscripts are A. Weber, Peter Peterson, Kielhorn, G. Bühler, R.G. Bhandarkar, C.D. Dalal, L.B. Gandhi, Dvivedi, H.D. Velankar, Muni Jinavijaya, Muni Punyavijaya, Muni Vijayakumudasūri, H.R. Kapadia, K. Bhujabali, Kasturchand Kasaliwal and others. The Bhaṇḍāra at Cambay was visited by Peterson several times and the result was the publication of his Reports in several volumes. A list of famous palm-leaf manuscripts in the Śāntinātha Temple at Cambay was published in the *First Report of Dr. Peterson.* This collection is preserved at the Bhandarkar Institute in Pune, known as *Collection of 1882-1883.* Then followed the subsequent Reports as we have seen. Muni Punyavijayaji has also prepared a catalogue of palm-leaf manuscripts of the Śāntinātha Jain Mandir of Cambay which has been published by the Orienal Institute of Baroda, Pt. I (1961) and Pt. II (1966). Jaisalmer has ten Jñāna Bhaṇḍāras, out of which the Jinabhadrīya Bhaṇḍāra has a collection of most important palm-leaf manuscripts.[203] This section contains rare works not available elsewhere. These manuscripts were also catalogued in Shridhar R. Bhandarkar's Reports 1904-5 to 1905-6, published in 1909. The Catalogue of Jaisalmer by Muni Punyavijaya covers all the palm-leaf manuscripts and numerous paper manuscripts; they are published in the L.D. Series in Vol. 36, 1972. An excellent account of collection of manuscripts at Cambay, Jaisalmer and Patan, particularly Jaisalmer, has been published in the *Schubring Felicitation Volume,* Hamburg, 1952 under the title *Neues von alten Jaina-Bibliotheken* (New Light on Ancient Jaina Libraries). This important article for the first time informed us of the valuable work carried on by Muni Punyavijayaji for preservation of manuscripts. Valuable Jaina manuscripts are also available at Patan Jain Bhaṇḍāra. C.D. Jalal has catalogued the manuscripts in Patan Jain Bhaṇḍāra, of which Pt. I describes only palm-leaf manuscripts published in the Gaikwad Oriental Series, 1937; Pt. II contains paper manuscripts. Peterson also describes the palm-leaf and paper manuscripts of Patan in his *Fifth Report* (1892-5). The *Catalogue of Manuscripts in the Shri Hemachandracharya Jain*

Jñānamandira, Patan, Pt. I carries a description of paper manuscripts preserved in 13 collections.

Besides Jñānabhaṇḍāras at Cambay, Jaisalmer and Patan, there existed numerous Bhaṇḍāras, of which the following are worth mentioning:

1. *Catalogue of Manuscripts Preserved in the Limbdi Jain Jñānabhaṇḍāra*, edited by Muni Chaturvijayaji, Bombay, 1928.[204]

2. Kielhorn's Collection of MSS, known as *Collection of 1881-1882*.

3. G. Bühler has handled thousands of manuscripts. His observations are included in his *Indische Palaeographie*, Strassburg, 1896 (translated into English under the title Indian palaeography, Calcutta, 1962). His second Collection, known as the *Collection of 1871-1872* is published under *A Catalogue of Collections*, Bombay Government Central Press, 1880, as we have seen.

4. Muni Punyavijayaji's *Collection of Sanskirt and Prakrit Manuscripts*, Pt. I (1963), Pt. II (1965), Pt. III (1968), published by L.D. Institute of Indology, Ahmedabad, as referred to above. All his Collections are preserved in the above Institute.

5. Muni Jinavijayaji has edited a *Catalogue of Sanskrit and Prakrit Manuscripts* in the Rajasthan Oriental Institute, Jodhpur, Pt. I (1963); Pt. II (A) (1964); Pt. II (B) (1965); and Pt. II (C) (1966).

6. H.R. Kapadia has edited *Descriptive Catalogue of MSS in the Government MSs Library*, Bhandarkar Oriental Research Institute, Poona, Vol. XVII, Pt. I (1935); Pt. II (a), 1936; Pt. III, 1940; Pt. IV; Vol. XVIII, Pt. I (1952). He has also published various articles in the 'manuscriptology' in the *ABORI* and in the *JUB*, Bombay.[205]

7. Kasturchand Kasliwal has published *Jain Grantha Bhaṇḍāras in Rajasthan*, Jaipur, 1967.

8. Kasturchand Kasliwal has also published *Rajasthan ke Jain Śāstra Bhaṇḍāro kī Grantha-sūci* in 5 parts, Pt. V pub. in 1972, Digambara Jain Atiśaya Kṣetra, Mahavirji, Jaipur.[206]

9. Rai Bahadur Hiralal, *Catalogue of Sanskrit and Prakrit MSS in Central Provinces of Berar*, Nagpur, 1926.

10. *Catalogue of Sanskrit and Prakrit MSS in the Library of India Office*, London.

11. H.D. Velankar, *Descriptive Catalogue of the MSS in Bombay Branch of Royal Asiatic Society* in 4 vols., 1925, 1928, 1930.

12. *Jinaratnakośa* in 2 vols. by H.D. Velankar, Poona, 1944. Here the list of Jain works and their authors is given alphabetically. Various important Jain Catalogues have been utilized for its compilation.

13. K. Bhujabali Shastri, *Praśastisaṃgraha*, Arrah, 1942.

14. H.D. Velankar, *A List of MSS Preserved in the GOI*, Baroda, 1933.

15. A List of MSS kept at the Pannalal Jain Sarasvati Bhavan, Bhuleshvar, Bombay. It contains a list of MSS in various Digambara Jain Bhandars throughout India. So far 5 Reports have been published.

16. *Catalogue of MSS in the Calcutta Sanskrit College*, Vol. X, 1909.

17. *A Catalogue of MSS in the Panjab Jain Bhandars*, Pt. I compiled by Banarsi Das Jain, Lahore, 1939.

18. K.L. Janert, *An Annotated Bibliography of the Catalogues of Indian MSS*, Pt. I, Wiesbaden, 1965.

19. A. Guerinot, *Essai de Bibliographie Jaina*, Paris, 1906.

20. *Bṛhaṭṭipanikā* is an old list of Jain works at Patan, Cambay, Broach, etc. (not Jaisalmer), in vs 1440 (AD 1383) by a Jain monk; published in the Jain Sahitya Saṃśodhaka, I, 2, Poona, 1925.

21. *Jain Granthavali*, a catalogue of Jain works was prepared on the basis of the *Bṛhaṭṭippanikā* in vs 1965, published by the Jain Śvetāmbara Conference, Bombay, 1909.

22. Pandit Kailashchandra Jain Siddhantashastri mentions 3 hand-lists of Digambar Jain works now preserved in the Library of the Syadvada Mahavidyalaya, Banaras. The list is prepared by Baba Dulichand in vs 1926. He came from Phaltan (Maharashtra) and after travelling thrice throught India collected about 800 MSS. This list is published in the Jain Siddhanta Bhaskara, Arrah (vs 1995, pp. 219-33). The collection has been catalogued by K. Kasliwal in his *Rajasthan ke Jain Śāstrabhaṇḍāro kī Sūci*, Pt. IV, Jaipur, 1962.

23. *Jain Siddhant Bhawan Granthavali*, in 2 vols., cataloguing 2020 important works in Sanskrit, Prakrit, Apabhramsa and Hindi, 1987.

24. *Kannaḍa-prāntīya Tāḍapatrīya Grantha Sūci* contains a list of some palm-leaf manuscripts in Kannada script in the Jain Matha of Moodbidri and Karkal, *BJP*, Kashi, 1948.

25. *Catalogue of the Jaina Manuscripts at Strasbourg* by Chandrabhal Tripathi, 1975.

Inscriptional Prakrit

Inscriptional Prakrit is very important from the point of view of chronology. Such inscriptions are widely scattered all over India and range from about the middle of the third century BC to the end of the fourth century AD. Inscriptional Prakrit was centuries earlier than the schools of Prakrit grammar; the dialects or the dialectal variations recorded in these inscriptions represent living forms of speech current in different regions in those days. Our linguistic history begins with the inscriptions of Aśoka, the Mauryan emperor of Magadha, who reigned between 277 and 261 BC. His inscriptions are scattered throughout western, southern, central and eastern India. They are inscribed in Pali, some in Brahmi and others in Kharoshti script. These earliest inscriptions are very important for the study of Middle Indo-Aryan dialects.

From the Jain point of view the Prakrit inscription of Hāthigumphā by Khāravela, a great patron of Jainism, who belonged to about the middle of the first century BC is important. The inscription was inscribed in Brahmi script at Udayagiri hill near Bhubanesvara. Compared to Aśoka's inscriptions there seems to be a better flow of language in these inscriptions, which indicates the richness of the dialect. It describes the thirteen years of the reign of Khāravela. Then inscriptions come from eastern India but do not really represent eastern dialects like Magadhi. There is another inscription, of King Vāsiṣṭhīputra Pulumāvi, in Nasik; it belongs to AD 149. Here we are told about excavation of a cave by the chief queen Gautamī Balaśrī, the mother of Śātakarṇī. Various selections of Jain inscriptions have been published. Some of the important ones are A. Guerini's *Reporter the Epigraphy Jaina* (1908), containing inscriptions from 242 BC to AD 1866; Puranchand Nahar's *Jain Lekha-Saṅgraha* in 3 parts (1915, 1927 and 1929), containing the inscriptions of the Śvetāmbaras; Hiralal Jain, *Jain Silālekha-saṃgraha* (Pt. I), 1928; Vijayamurti Shastri, Pts. II and III (based on Guerini's list; Vidyadhar Joharpurkar, Pt. IV (1961); they contain the Digambara inscriptions. To this list can be added Jinavijaya's *Prācīna Jain Lekha-saṃgraha* in two parts; Jayantavijaya's *Arbuda Prācīna Likha-saṃdoha*; Vijayadharmasūri's *Prācīna Jain Lekha-saṃgraha*, and others.

NOTES

1. Secularism is defined as the view that consideration of the present well-being of mankind should predominate over religious considerations in civil affairs or public education, *The Heritage Illustrated Dictionary of the English Language*, edited by William Morris, New York, 1975.
2. Compare the following 14 subjects of study (*vijjaṭṭhāṇa*) in Devendragaṇi's *Uttarā* Com.: 4 *Vedas*, 6 *Vedāṅgas*, *Mīmāṃsā*, *Nyāya*, *Purāṇa* and *Dharma-śāstra* (*Sū.* 40f); also *Viyāha*, 2.1.
3. *MW.*

4. Ibid., the same idea is expressed in the *Jambu.* Com., p. 2.
5. *Das* 8.5.
6. See supra, p. 83. Published with Malayagiri commentary, *AGS, NSP,* Bombay, 1919; J.F. Kohl, text in Roman script, Stuttgart, 1937; A. Weber, *Über die Sūryaprajñapti* (an essay), 1868; R. Shamshastri, an abridged translation of the work in *the Quarterly Journal of the Mythic Society,* Banglore, XV, 138-47; XVI, 201-12, under the title 'A Brief Translation of Mahāvīra's Sūryaprajñapti'; G. Thibaut, *On the Sūrprajñapti, JASB,* 1880, il, 107ff, 181ff; the author has based his treatment of the subject on Malayagiri's commentary; W. Schubring, *The Doctrine of the Jainas,* p. 101. Also see a recent publication on *Jaina Astronomy* by Sajjan Singh Lishk, Vidyasagar Publications, 1987, reviewed in the columns of *Sunday Review, The Times of India,* 18 September 1988.
7. Winternitz remarks that originally this text was most probably preceded the *Sūra* and was a separate work, *History of,* II, 457.
8. Ed. W. Schubring, Kleina Schriften, pp. 137-41.
9. *RKŚS,* Ratlam, 1928.
10. *Horā* is a Greek word, meaning 'an hour'. In Portuguese '*hora*' (*ho* is pronounced as *o*) conveys the same meaning. It is the 14th part of an *ahorātra.* It is used by Varāhamihira in his *Bṛh Saṃ* (I.9; II, 3, 6, 18; XXXIV. 11; XCVI.1). *Horā-śāstra* is horoscopy or the astrological science; *horāvid* is one who is versed in horoscopy. Candrasena, a Digambara *ācārya,* in his unpublished *Kevalajñānahora* had defined *horā* in the following verse:

    होरा नाम महाविद्या, वक्त्व्यं च भवद्धितम्।
    ज्योतिर्ज्ञानिकरं सारं भूषणं बुध-पोषणम्॥ *JSBI,* Pt. V, p. 182.

    It is a great science (*mahāvidyā*), it must be treated for the welfare of all of you. It imparts the knowledge of astrology; it is an excellent ornament and it leads to the prosperity of wise people.

11. Ṭhokkurapherū (AD 1315) in his *Jyotiṣasāra* mentions हरिभद्र, नरचन्द्र, पद्मप्रभसूरि, जउण (यवन), वराह (वराहमिहिर), लल्ज, पराशर and गर्ग on whose works he has based his composition. असित and देवज are referred to in the *Isibhāsiya* as well as in the *Sūya* (3.4-2, 3, 4, pp. 94a-95). In the *Sūya* असित, देवल, द्वीपायन, पराशर, बाहुक and others are said to have attained liberation. In the *Ovā* (38) पराशर and द्वीपायन are counted among Brāhmaṇa *Parivrājakas.*
12. Mentioned as son of Ācārya Garga and the author of the *Nimittaśāstra,* translated into Hindi by Parkrit Lalaram Shastri, Solapur, 1941.
13. Referred to in the *Ova* (38) as one of the Kṣatriya *parivrājakas.* These *parivrājakas* were supposed to have possessed knowledge of the four *Vedas, Itihāsa, Nighaṇṭu, Ṣaṣṭhitantra, Gaṇita, Sikṣā, Kalpa, Vyākaraṇa, Chanda, Nirukta* and *Jyotiṣa.*
14. Cited in the commentary of the *Bṛh Saṃ* (IX.37). Meghavijaya in his *Varṣaprabodha* (also known as *Meghamahodaya*) has cited some Prakrit

verses under the name of Bhadrabāhu, which indicates that he had composed a work on *Nimitta*. H.R. Kapadia, *Pāiya Bhāsāo ane Sāhitya*, p. 168. According to Vijayavimalagaṇi, the commentator of the *Gacchāyārapaiṇṇā*, Bhadrabāhu and Varāhamihira were brothers, and after making a study of the *Candapaṇṇatti* and other Jain canonical works, he is said to have composed his *Vārāhīsaṃhitā* or the *Bṛh Saṃ* as it is called. It is difficult to say how far this statement can be treated as authentic.

15. He must have been a Yavana teacher. Utpala in his commentary on chapter 19 (*Graha-varṣa-phalādhyāya*=Planetary Years and Effects) has referred to this teacher several times; also 96.13; 98.17; 104.7, 10, 24, 53, 60. He has composed the *Akṣarakośa* in 32 verses which has been commented upon by Utpala (96.13, pp. 848-58). Yavaneśvara has translated the *Yavana-Jātaka* (its manuscript has been preserved in Nepal) from Greek in AD 169 which was probably reproduced in verses by Sphūrtidhvaja, a century later; Winternitz, *A History of*, III, Pt. II, p. 658.
16. Author of 'Elephant's Treatment', M.R. Bhat, Introduction to *Bṛhat-saṃhitā*, p. xxxviii.
17. It is a science of human physiognomy. Utpala is said to have been adept in this science, M.R. Bhat, ibid., p. xli. Udyotanasūri (eighth century) in his *KVLM* has referred to *Samudraśāstra* or *Sāmudrika* as an offshoot of *Lakṣaṇa*, see author's *PNL*, p. 145.
18. Utpala has cited him in his commentary (21.5). He seems to be the Jain teacher skilled in magic art, different from the well known Siddhasena Divākara. It is said that Ācārya Siddhasena was capable of creating magic horses following the instructions laid down in the *Joṇipāhuḍa* (see further). For other similar references see M.R. Bhat, ibid., p. xxxviii.
19. See M.R. Bhat, ibid., p. xiv.
20. *JSBI*, Pt. V, p. 189.
21. Ibid.
22. Ibid., p. 194.
23. *The Jaisalmer Handwritten Manuscript's Catalogue*, Vol. II.
24. कुर्वीत चैषां (वणिजां) प्रत्यक्षमर्घसंस्थापनं नृप, *Manusmṛti*, 8.402.
25. इमं दव्वं विक्कीणाहि इमं वा कीणाहि।
26. *Arghyakāṇḍa* also available in Sanskrit. It was composed by Hemaprabhasūri, pupil of Devendrasūri in the eighteenth century (*Raj OIJ Collection*, Pt. I, 1963, p. 362); also recorded in the *Raj OIJ Collection*, Pt. II(B), 1965, p. 324, composed in VS 1942; also in the *Raj OIJ Collection*, Pt. II(C), p. 136, composed in the nineteenth century.
27. Also see the author's *The Vasudeva*, pp. 615, 629n.
28. M.R. Bhat, ibid., p. 527.
29. V.S. Agrawala, *Bṛhatkathāślokasaṅgraha—A Study*, p. 309n.
30. *MW*.

31. The *Kusumalatā dhyāya* (Chap. 29) of the *Bṛhatsaṃhita* also deals with prognostics from flowers and creepers.
32. See *Kannaḍa Prāntīya Tāḍapatrīya Grantha-Sūci*—A Catalogue of Jain Maṭha of Mūḍabidrī, Jain Maṭha of Kārkal and Ādinātha Grantha-bhaṇḍāra of Abyoor, etc., *BJP*, 1944.
33. Ed. Upādhyāya Kṣamāvijayagaṇi, Bombay, 1938.
34. There is a similar work entitled *Diṇasuddhi* (*Dinaśuddhi*) by Ratnaśekhara Sūri dealing with the auspiciousness of the day; editor and publisher the same as above.
35. Edited by Punyavijaya with the Introduction of Motichand in English and *bhūmikā* of V.S. Agrawala in Hindi, *PTS*, 1957. It is also known as *Yogavidhi*, H.R. Kapadia, *Govt. Collection of Mss*, *BORI*, Vol. XVII, Pt. 1, p. 322.
36. तेण चाऽधीयता अंगं वसया गुरुकुलम्मि य॥
    सुची सुचिसमायांरो बंभचारी जितिंदिओ।
    अच्चए य जहासत्तिं देवताऽतिथि-साहवो॥ 3.36-7, p. 5
37. *Aṅgavijjā*, 1.1.
38. अंगं 1 सरो 2 लक्खणं 3 च वंजणं 4 सुविणो 5 तहा।
    छिण्णं 6 भोम्मं 7 अंतलिक्खाए 8 एमेव अट्ठ आहिया॥ *Aṅgavijjā*, 1.1, p. 1
    The order differs in different works: The *Sama* (29.477) has: भौम, उत्पात, स्वप्न, अन्तरिक्ष, अंग, स्वर, व्यंजन, लक्षण, The *Ṭhā* (8-608) has उत्पात, निमित्त, मंत्र, आख्यात (आइक्खिय) चिकित्सा, कला, आवरण (वास्तुविद्या), अज्ञान, मिथ्याप्रवचन and the *Uttarā* (15.7) has the following: छिन्न, स्वर, भौम, अंतरिक्ष, स्वप्न, लक्षण, दंड, वास्तुविद्या, अंगविकार, स्वरविजय।
39. जयं पराजयं वा राजमरणं वा आरोग्गं वा रण्णो आतंकं वा उवद्दवं वा मा पुण सहसा वियागरिज्ज णाणी। लाभाऽलाभं सुहदुक्खं जीवितं मरणं वा सुभिक्खं दुब्भिक्खं वा अणावुट्ठिं सुवुट्ठिं वा धणहाणिं अज्झप्पवित्तं वा कालपरिहाणं अंगहियं तत्तत्थ णिच्छियमई सहसा उ ण वागरिज्ज णाणी। *Aṅgavijjā*, II.18-20
40. Ibid., I.4-7, p. 1.
41. . . . अङ्गविद्यया शिष्य संज्ञाभिश्च कर्माण्यपि जनोऽवसितान्यादिशेत्-अल्पलाभं अग्निदाहं चोरभयं दूष्यवधं तुष्टिदानं विदेशप्रवृत्ति-ज्ञानं, 'इदमद्य श्वो वा भविष्यति, इदं वा राजा करिष्यति'। इति।
42. इति निगदितमेतद् गात्रसंस्पर्श-लक्ष्म, प्रकटमभिमताप्त्यं वीक्ष्य शास्त्राणि सम्यक्।
    विपुलमतिरुदारो वेत्ति यः सर्वमेतन्नरपति-जनताभिः पूज्यतेऽसौ सदैव॥ 5.1.44.
    A manuscript of *Aṅgavidyā* is recorded in the *Raj OIJ*, Pt. I, 1963, p. 296. It is stated here that the author's work is based on the instructions awarded by Nārada:
    अंगविद्यां प्रवक्ष्यामि नारदेन च यत्कृतम्।
    अंगदर्शनमात्रेण ज्ञायते च शुभाशुभम्॥
43. However, Pandit Ambalal P. Shah says that the *Āṅgavidyāśāstra* is a separate work by an unknown author (*JSBI*, v, p. 218) which does not seem to hold good.
44. It had a commentary of Sūryadeva Somasuta of Naidhruva *gotra*. Kern had edited 9 chapters of this work. Now the entire work has been published, edited by J.L. Shastri, *IAIB*, p. 27, M.R. Bhat, Intr., p. xiv.
45. नभः प्रसन्नं विमलानि भानि प्रदक्षिणं वाति सदागतिश्च।
    दिशा च दाहः कनकावदातो हिताय लोकाय सपार्थिवस्य॥

46. It is a particular conjunction of the class *ākṛti-yoga* (i.e. when all the planets are situated in the 1st, 2nd, 3rd and 4th houses), *MW.* The term is explained in the *Āva-Cū* (II.221) as follows:
संझप्पभा चंदप्पभा य जेण जुगवं भवंति तेण जुवगो। सा य संझप्पभा चंदप्पभा वरिता फिडंति न नज्जति, सुक्क-पक्ख पाडिवगादिसु तिसु दिणेसु, संझच्छेदे य अणज्जमाणे, कालवेलं न मुणंति अतो तिण्णि दिणे पादोसियं कालं न ग्रेण्हंति, तेसु तिसु दिणेसु पादोसियं सुत्तपोरिसिं न करेति।

47. Also, *Nisi Bhā* 19. 6088-6117; *Āva Cū,* II, pp. 217-41, the section on the *asajjhāyanijjutti* in the *gāthās* is identical, except that the *Niryukti* and the *Bhāsya gāthās* are mixed up. Also *Mūlācāra* (5.77-9):
दिसदाह-उक्कपडणं, विज्जु चडुक्कासणिदं धणुगं च।
दुग्गंध सज्झदुद्दिणं, चंदग्गह, सूर-राहु-जुज्झं च॥
कलहादि-धूमकेदू धरणी-कंपं च अब्भ-गज्जं च।
इच्चेवमाइ बहुया सज्झाए वज्जिदा दोसा॥
While commenting on the *Bhūkampa-lakṣaṇādhyaya* (32), the commentator Bhaṭṭotpala has cited the following verses from Garga:
निर्घातोल्का-मही-कम्पाः स्निग्ध-गंभीर-निःस्वनाः।
मेघा स्तनित-शब्दाश्च, सूर्येन्दु-ग्रहणे तथा॥
परिवेषेन्द्रचापं च गन्धर्वनगरं तथा।
मण्डलैरेव बोद्धव्याः शुभाशुभ-फलप्रदाः॥ 23॥

48. नन्द्यावर्तमलिन्दैः शाला कुड्यात् प्रदक्षिणान्त गतैः।
द्वारं पश्चिममस्मिन् विहाय शेषाणि कार्याणि॥ (LIII.32)
The *nandyāvarta,* the *vardhamāna* and the *svastika* are incorporated among 8 lucky *aṣṭamaṅgala.* They are: *svastika, śrīvatsa, nandyāvarta, vardhamāna, bhadrāsana, kalaśa, darpaṇa* and *matsyayugma* (*Nāyā,* I.32; *Jīvā* [142]; *Ovā* [32]). The 8 auspicious marks are carved in the *Mathura* art. *Svastika vardhamān* and *nandyāvarta* are referred to in the *Mahābhārata.* The *Tiloyapaṇṇatti* (*adhikara* 4) of Yativṛṣabha has recorded the following 8 *maṅgalas: bhṛṅgāra, kalaśa, darpaṇa, vyajana, dhvajā, chatra, camara* and *supratiṣṭha.* Compare the following lists provided in Brahmanic works:

(a) मृगराजो वृषो नागः कलशो व्यजनं तथा।
वैजयन्ती तथा भेरी दीप इत्यष्ट मङ्गलम्॥

or

(b) लोकेऽस्मिन्मङ्गलान्यष्टौ ब्राह्मणो गौर्हुताशनः।
हिरण्यं सर्पिरादित्य आपो राजा तथाष्टकम्॥

In the Mathura inscriptions, Ara, the eighteenth *Tīrthaṅkara,* is known as Nāndyāvarta (*arahato Nāndiāvatasa pratimā*), W. Schubring, *The Doctrine of the Jainas,* 49. In the *Aṅguttaranikāya-Aṭṭhakathā* (I.265), it is a large fish. In the *Mahābhārata,* it is a kind of diagram. In the *Jīvā,* it is a mansion.

49. It is a kind of house having no entrance on the south in the *Bṛh Saṃ.* Abhayadeva in his commentary on the *Ovā* (31) has explained the term as follows: an earthenware vessel (शराव) or a man being carried on one's

shoulder (स्कन्धारोपित पुरूष) or the five *svastikas* (स्वस्तिक पंचक) or a particular mansion (प्रासाद विशेष).

50. A mansion or a temple of a particular form in the *Bṛh Sam.* It is also a kind of mystical cross or mark made on persons or things to bring good luck.
51. A building or temple having terraces on three sides and closed only on the north in the *Bṛh Saṃ.*
52. A building having continuous galleries around in the *Bṛh Saṃ.*
53. See Punyavijaya Muni, Preface of *Aṅgavijjā.*
54. See author's *PNL*, pp. 123-5.
55. Ibid., pp. 172f.
56. अग्गेणिपुव्व-निग्गय-पाहुड-सत्थस्स मज्झयारम्यि।
किंचि उद्देसदेसं धरसेणो वज्जियं भणइ॥
गिरिउज्जिंत-ठिएण पच्छिमदेसे सुरट्ठ-गिरिनयरे।
बुड्डंतं उद्धरियं दूसमकाल प्पयावंमि॥ योनिप्राभृत, प्रथम खण्डे
अट्ठावीस-सहस्सा गाहाणं जत्थ वन्निया सत्थे।
अग्गेणिपुव्व-मज्झे संखेवं वित्थरे मुत्तुं॥ ibid., चतुर्थखण्डप्रान्ते Hiralal Rasikdas Kapadia, *Āgamonu Digdarshan*, pp. 234-5.
57. योनिप्राभृतं वीरात् छाटसेनम्, *Jain Sāhityasaṃśodhaka*, Pariśiṣṭa 1, 2.
58. अविचलइ मेरु-चूला सुर-सरिया अवि वहेज्ज विवरीया।
ण य होज्ज किंचि अलियं जं जोणीपाहुडे रइयं॥
59. *Niśī Cū*, 4.1804, p. 281; *Bṛh Bhā*, 1.2681.
60. *Prabhāvakacarita*, 5.115-27.
61. *Viśeṣā Bhā*, 1775, Com. by Hemacandrasūri; *Vinodakathāsaṅgraha* (also known as *Kathākośa*), 46.
62. For further explanation see *Vyava Bhā*, 5.89; *Niśī Cū*, 10.3066, p. 111; *Bṛh Bhā*, 11.557-74.
63. जोणिपाहुडे भणिद-मंत-तंत-सत्तीओ पोग्गलाणुभागो त्ति घेत्तव्वो। Hiralal Jain, Introduction to *Saṭkhaṇḍāgama*, p. 30.
64. The following Sanskrit works are mentioned:
रमल ग्रन्थ, रमलचिन्तामणि, रमलतत्त्वसार, रमलतन्त्र, रमलनवरत्न, रमलपद्धति, रमलप्रश्न, रमलप्रश्नतन्त्र, रमलभूषण, रमलयन्त्रिका, रमलरहस्य, रमल-रहस्य-सार-संग्रह, रमलशास्त्र, रमलसार and others, *MW* under the entry 'ramala'.
65. Ibid., under '*Pāṣa*'.
66. Published by Bhagvandas Jain, Jaipore, H.D. Velankar, *JK* under '*Varṣaprabodha*'.
67. Keith has mentioned Nīlakaṇṭha's *Tājika* in two parts, the *Saṃjha Varṣatantra.* This treatise was written in 1587 and exists in various manuscripts and editions, *A History of Sanskrit Literature*, p. 534.
68. दुरूहः, इति संज्ञातन्त्रस्यटीकां व्यवधत्, Appendix, p. 185.
69. श्रीनीलकण्ठ ज्योतिर्वित्-सूनु गोविन्द ज्योतिर्विदरचिता रसालाभिधा संज्ञाविवेक विवृतिः समाप्तिमगमत्।
70. प्रायो न जातकफले चिरप्रयोज्ये मितः स्फुरति पुंसाम्।
तेनाऽत्र हायनफलं प्रकाश्यते ताजिकप्रोक्तं॥
इति प्राग्वाटान्वयकुमारसिंहात्मजेन समरसिंहेन ताजिकसिद्धान्तात्

पृच्छोद्देशोद्धृतस्तृतीयतन्त्रः सम्पूर्णः। इति श्रीशिवकृतताजिकतन्त्रत्रयः समाप्तः Jodhpur collection, Pt. I, 1963, p. 152 .

71. For *Tājika-grate-bhāva-phala, Tājika-bhūṣana, Tājika-sāra,* see *Jaisalmer Handwritten Manuscripts, Cat.*, Vol. II, p. 298.

72. श्रीग्रामोद्भवकश्यपान्वयनिधिः सामुद्रिकज्ञः सुधीः।
श्रीमान् माधवसंज्ञको द्विजवरो विघ्नेश-सेवारतः।
दादाभाईति तस्मादजनि गुणगणैः पूरितस्तत्त्ववेत्ता, सिद्धान्तानां चकास्ता मुनिजनविदित स्तत्समः कोऽपि नान्यः ॥ ३ ॥
तस्माल्लब्धवरः परोपकृतये नारायणोऽहं ब्रुवे, तार्त्तीयैक सुधानिधिर्गणितवित् तुष्ट्यै चमत्कारिकम्।
श्रीमान् खिंधिक-रोमकादिरचितात् संगृह्य सारं परं, यस्य ज्ञानलवेन मुख्यपदवीं प्राप्नोति निःसंशयम् ॥ ४ ॥
The Jodhpur Collection, Pt. I, 1963, pp. 152-3.

73. जैन आसीद् जगद्वन्द्यो गर्गनामा महामुनिः।
तेन स्वयं निर्णीतं यत् सत्याशाऽत्र केवली ॥
एतज्ज्ञानं महाज्ञानं जैनर्षिभिरुदाहृतम्।
प्रकाश्य शुद्धशीलाय कुलीनाय महात्मभिः ॥ ibid., p. 220.

74. Rajasthan Prāchya Vidya Pratishthan, Jodhpur, 1961. Keith has mentioned two treatises under the title *Pāśakevalī,* preserved as Pts. IV and V of the Bower manuscript in bad Sanskrit with many signs of Prakritic influence. The language of this work is of peculiar character, being popular Sanskrit, heavily affected by Prakritism; perhaps the fourth century, Horenle, *Bower Manuscript,* pp. 84ff. J.E. Schroter refers to *Pāśakevalī* (1900). Later tracts are known, ascribed to Garga, which shows the knowledge of the term *horā* which postulates the period of Greek influence, *A History of Sanskrit Literature,* p. 534.

75. See *JSBI,* V, p. 220, *Caturakṣara-pāśakevali* (vs 1622) is recorded in the *Raj OIJ Collection,* Pt. I, 1963, p. 362.

76. See M.R. Bhat, Introduction to *Bṛhatsaṃbhitā,* p. xv. The *Pañcapakṣī* or the *Pañcapakṣi-śāstra* is mentioned as the name of several works on astrology. These works had several commentaries, *MW.*

77. *Aṅgavijjā,* I.8-12, pp. 1f.

78. सज्जं रवइ मऊरो, कुक्कुडो रिसहं सरं।
हंसो रवइ गंधारं, मज्झिमं तु गवेलए ॥ १ ॥
तथा-
सज्जेण लहइ वित्तिं, कयं च न विणस्सइ।
गावो-पुत्ता य मित्ता य-नारीणं होई वल्जहो ॥ २ ॥
रिसहेण उ ईसरियं, सेणावच्चं धणाणि य ॥ इत्यादि।

79. See Varāhamihira's *Bṛh Saṃ* (Chaps. 68 and 70 on *Puruṣa-lakṣaṇa* and *Kanyā-lakṣaṇa* respectively). The origin of the science of characteristics of men is traced to the deity Śiva, one of his numerous names being Samudra, and to a sage of the same title. According to another tradition, Samudra was Viṣṇu, hence this lore is known as *Sāmudra-śāstra.* The human body is also called *samudra* as it is imprinted with lines. There is a short treatise ascribed to Prahlāda in Kannaḍa, M.R. Bhat, Introduction to the chapter *Purusa-lakṣaṇam,* p. 599. The commentator Utpala has cited Ṛṣiputra, Garga, Samudra, and Prahlāda in support of his

statements. He has also quoted from the *Prahlādasāmudrika*. On pages 634-6 he has summarized some main principles from this work.

80. Pages 129.8-131, 23; *Sāmudrika* is also mentioned in Guṇacandragaṇi's *Kahārayaṇakosa*, pp. 34a, 50.
81. चक्खुसिणेहे सुहिओ, दंतसिणेहे च भोयणं मिट्ठं।
 तय-णेहेण य सोक्खं नह-नेहे होइ परमधणं॥ १॥ 15.7, p. 216.
82. *Indriya-jaya-dvāra* (431-59).
83. 595-630; also Bloomfield, *The Life and Story*, p. 158.
84. Ed. Prafulla Kumar Modi, *BJP*, Kashi, 1954 (2nd edn.).
85. Ed. A.S. Gopani, *SJS*, Bombay, 1945.
86. न हु सुणइ स-तणु-सद्दं, दीवय-गंधं च णेव गिण्हेइ।
 जो जियइ सत्त-दियहे इय कहियं मरणकंडीए॥ 139॥
87. *Nisī Cū*, 13. 4292.
88. See author's *LAI*, 1984, pp. 196f.
89. 8.13, pp. 129af. These verses have been compared by J. Charpentier with those of the *Svapnacintāmaṇi of Jagaddeva*, *Uttarā*, Notes, 310f.
90. *RKŚS*, Ratlam, 1929, included in *Siripayaraṇasaṃdoha*.
91. *JRK*.
92. अंजण-खंजण-कद्दम-लित्ते, मूसग-भक्खिय अग्गि-विदड्ढे।
 तुन्निय-कुहिय-पज्जवलीढे होइ विवागु सुहो असुहो वा॥ १॥
 देवेसु उत्तमो लाभो, माणुस्सेसु य मज्झिमो।
 आसुरेसु च गेलन्नं मरणं जाण रक्खसे॥ २॥

 The *Bṛh Saṃ* contains a chapter on the *Vastracchedalakṣaṇam* (71) which deals with the omens from slits of governments. The following verse describes the effects of the slits or status of garments:

 लिप्ते मषी-गोमय-कर्दमाद्यैश्छिन्ने प्रदग्धे स्फुटितेच विन्द्यात्।
 पुष्टं नवेऽल्पाल्पतरं च भुक्ते पापं शुभं चाधिकमुत्तरीये॥ 71.14

 When a cloth is stained with ink, cow-dung, mud or any such thing, when it is cut, burnt or torn, one should know the effects, whether good or bad, will be full, if the cloth is new; moderate, if used for a short time; and almost nil, if it is old. These effects are greater in the case of upper clothes.

 Here the commentator cites Parāśara, explaining at length the effects of damages done to sandals (*upānaha*).
93. शब्देन महता भूमिर्यदा रसति कम्पते।
 सेनापतिरमात्यश्च, राजा राष्ट्रं न पीड्यते॥ १॥
94. कपिलं सस्यघाताय, माञ्जिष्ठं हरणं गवाम्।
 अव्यक्तवर्णं कुरूते, बलक्षोभं न संशयः॥ २॥
 गन्धर्वनगरं स्निग्धं सप्राकारं सतोरणम्।
95. सौम्यां दिशं समा श्रित्य, राज्ञस्तद्विजयङ्करम्॥ २॥ 9.72 (1949).
96. 29.47; also see *Aṅgavijjā*, 1.1; *Sūya*, 12.9; *Ṣaṭkhaṇḍāgama*, *Dhavalā*, IX.72 (1949); *Āva Ṭī*, p. 660 by Haribhadra; *Piṇḍa Nir.* Com., 408. However in the *Ṭhā* (8.608) they are considered as sinful treatises

(*pāpa-śruta*); the *Uttarā* (15.7) enumerates them as छिन्न, स्वर, भौम, अंतरिक्ष, स्वप्न, लक्षण, दंड, वास्तुविद्या, अंगविकार and स्वरविजय. A Jain monk is prohibited to practise them.

97. See *PNL*, pp. 147f.
98. *JSBI*, V, p. 204.
99. Ibid., p. 205.
100. Muni Punyavijayaji informed me that it was another name of *Jyotiṣkaraṇḍa.*
101. *SJS*, 1958.
102. *JSBI*, V, p. 205.
103. *JSBI*, V, p. 204.
104. Ibid., p. 205.
105. Ibid., p. 204.
106. See professor Hiralal Rasikdas Kapadia, *Pāiyabhāshā ane Sāhitya*, pp. 167f.
107. Translated by Pandit Lalaram Shastri, published by Vardhamana Parshvanatha Shastri, Solapur, 1941.
108. 10.485a. It contains 450 *gāthās.* A palm-leaf manuscript of the work is catalogued in the Patan Jain Bhandar. It has several commentaries, *JSBI*, V, p. 203.
109. *JRK.*
110. *JSBI*, V, p. 205.
111. See *Śākunaṃ* (86) of *Bṛh Saṃ*, pp. 757f.
112. *Sarva-bhūta-ruta* (the notes of all beings) is mentioned in the *Mūlasarvāstivāda* of *Vinayavastu*, p. 32. The language of fish, donkey, ram, ants, crow, jackal, dog and lizard was understood, see *PNL*, p. 73 and note.
113. Udyotanasūri in his *KVLM* (184.14) has referred to *giroliyāruta* (chirping of a household lizard) along with *śivā-ruta* (howling of jackals) and *kākaruta* (notes of a crow). The *Gṛhagodhā-vicāra* and the *Kṛkalāsavicāra* (vs 1650) are mentioned in the *Catalogue of Sanskrit and Prakrit MSS*, Pt. III, p. 960, compiled by Muniraj Shri Punyavijayaji, Ahmedabad, 1969.
114. Śīlavatī, an expert in interpreting the language of birds and animals, gave a surprise to her father-in-law by comprehending the notes of a she-jackal and a crow, see *Kumāravālapaḍiboha*, 3.6; *Āva Cū*, 562, after *PNL*, p. 73.
115. *Kākaruta* is mentioned in Maladhāri Rājaśekhara's *BHBH*, I, 83. *Vāyasa-vidyā* is referred to in the *Arthaśāstra* (13.1.9).
116. Almost an identical list is in the *Anuyoga.*
117. Two birds flying on each side of a traveller, *MW.*
118. क्रियादीप्तौ विनाशाय यातुः परिघसञ्ज्ञितौ ॥ ५१ ॥
    तावेव तु यथाभागं प्रशान्तरुतचेष्टितौ ।
    शकुनौ शकुनद्वारसञ्ज्ञितावर्थसिद्धये ॥ ५२ ॥

119. इति श्री शाकुलवर्द्धन-श्री वाचस्यतिसुपुत्र-श्रीमिश्र लक्ष्मीदासात्मजोपेन्द्र विरचिते शकुनप्रदीपचूडामणौ सप्तमोध्याय: । *Jodhpur Collection*, 1965, p. 200.
120. *JSBI*, V, p. 197.
121. *Jodhpur Collection*, Pt. II(B), 1965, pp. 340, 342.
122. *JSBI*, V, p. 197. Published under the title *Śakunaśāstra* with translation by Pandit Hiralal Hansaraj, Jamnagar, 1899.
123. *JSBI*, V, 198.
124. *Jodhpur Collection*, op. cit., p. 326.
125. Ibid., p. 194; also Keith, *History of Sanskrit Literature*, p. 534.
126. इतिश्री नरहरि विरचिते स्वरोदयरीकायां समाप्तं, *Jodhpur Collection*, 1965, p. 194.
127. *Jodhpur Collection*, 1965, pp. 326, 328.
128. *JSBI*, V, p. 204.
129. Ibid., pp. 205f.
130. Ibid., p. 206.
131. Published by Dahyabhai Mohokamlal, Ahmedabad along with *Bṛhathrīṅkārakalpavivaraṇa*, n.d.
132. *JSBI*, V, pp. 233f. Among Sanskrit works, the following can be mentioned:

    (i) *Puṣpāyurveda* by *ācārya* Samantabhadra. 18,000 species of flowers have been described. It is not available.
    (ii) *Kalyāṇakāraka* by Pūjyapāda, not available, translated by Jedyaddaḷa Somanātha in Kannaḍa in the twelfth century.
    (iii) *Kalyāṇakāraka* by Ugrāditya, pupil of Śrīnandi. The author has referred to Pūjyapāda, Samantabhadra, Pātrasvāmin, Siddhasena, Daśarathaguru, Meghanātha, Siṃhasena and other *ācāryas*. According to the author, his work is based on the *Aṣṭāṅgasamgraha* of Samantabhadra. Published with Hindi translation, Sakharam Nemchand Granthamala, Solapur, 1940.
    (iv) *Nāḍīparīkṣā* by Pūjyapāda, mentioned in the *GRK*.
    (v) *Rasacintāmaṇi* by Anantadevasūri, not available.
    (vi) *Nighaṇṭukośa* by Amṛtanandi, contains an exposition of 22,000 medical words from the Jain point of view.
    (vii) *Aṣṭāṅgahṛdaya-vṛtti* by Pandit Āśādhara. It is based on Vāgbhaṭa's *Aṣṭāṅgahṛdaya*, a well known treatise on *Āyurveda*. The author has called his commentary *Udyota*; completed in vs 1296.
    (viii) *Siddhāntarasāyanakalpa* by Samantabhadra. In order to explain the terminology contained in this treatise, Amṛtanandi has composed his *Nighaṇṭukośa*, as stated above. It is not available.
    (ix) *Merudaṇḍatantra* by Gummaṭadeva Muni.
    (x) *Yogaratnamālā-vṛtti* by Guṇākarasūri. This commentary has been composed in vs 1296 on Nāgārjuna's *Yogaratnamālā*.
    (xi) *Yogaśata-vṛtti* by Pūrṇasena. The original text is written by Vararuci.
    (xii) *Yogacintāmaṇi* by Harṣakīrtisūri, pupil of Candrakīrtisūri.

According to the author, this treatise is based on the works of Ātreya, Caraka, Vāgbhaṭa, Suśruta, and others. It is also known as *Vaidyakasāra-saṃgraha*; was completed in about vs 1660.

(xiii) *Vaidyavallabha* by Muni Hastiruci. It contains 8 chapters.

(xiv) *Dravyāvali-nighaṇṭu* by Muni Mahendra.

(xv) *Siddayogamālā* by Siddharṣi Muni.

(xvi) *Rasaprayoga* by Somaprabha *ācārya*.

(xvii) *Āyruvedamahodadhi* by Suṣeṇa.

(xviii) *Cikitsotsava* by Haṃsarāja.

(xix) *Nāḍivicāra*, the author unknown. Its manuscript is in the Patan Jain Bhandar.

(xx) *Nāḍīcakra* and *Nāḍīsamcārajñāna*: The authors are not known. It has been referred to in the *Bṛhaṭṭippaṇikā*.

(xxi) *Nāḍīnirṇaya*: The author is not known. It contains 41 verses. The manuscript consists of 5 pages.

(xxii) *Jayaparājaya*: The author Jayaratnagaṇi, pupil of Bhāvaratna, an *ācārya* of Pūrṇimā-pakṣa, composed this treatise in vs 1662.

(xxiii) *Sārasaṃgraha*: Published by Jain Siddhant Bhavan, Arrah, under the title *Akalaṅkasaṃhitā*. The author has cited the authority of Suśruta, Vāgbhaṭa, Harītamuni, Rudradeva and others.

See *JSBI*, V, pp. 226-36, under *Ayurveda*.

133. कालज्ञानकलायुक्तं शंभुनाथेन भाषितम्।
मासैः षड्भिरप्येवं जायते मृत्युरोगिणाम्॥ *Jodhpur Collection*, Pt. I, 1963.

134. 42, 193a; *Aṇuoga*, 40f; *Nisī Cū*, 11.10.

135. अत्थसत्थे य भणियं—विसेसेण मायाए सत्थेण ण हन्तव्यो अप्पणो विवड्ढमाणो सत्तु।

136. तो भणइ अत्थसत्थंमि वण्णियं सुयणु! सत्थयारेहिं।
दूती परिभवदूती न होइ कज्जस्स सिद्धकरी॥
एतो हि मंतभेओ दूतीओ होज्ज कामनेमुक्का।
महिला मुंचरहस्सा रहस्सकाले न संठाइ॥
आभरणमवेलायां नीणंति अवि य घेघति चिंता
होज्ज मंतभेओ गमणविघाओ अनिव्वाणी॥ (853-5).

137. चाणक्कए वि भणियं: जइ काइयं न वोसिरइ तो अदोसो त्ति (*Gāthā*, 418, p. 152).

138. *Pit gāthā*, 294-6.

139. *Ākhyāna* 5. It is to be noted that Somadevasūri (tenth century) composed his *Nītivākyāmṛta* based on the *Arthaśāstra*. As Cāṇakya had composed his *Arthaśāstra* for the guidance of King Candragupta, so did Somadevasūri his *Nītivākyāmṛta* for King Mahendra and similar was the case with Hemacandra who composed his *Laghu Arhannīti* based on his *Bṛhadarhannītiśāstra*, in verses for Kumārapala of Gujarat. Haribala has written a Sanskrit commentary on the *Nītivākyāmṛta* where he has cited the views of other authors. Neminātha has written a commentary in Kannaḍa in the twelfth or thirteenth century on this work which seems to have been based on the Sanskrit commentary. The manuscript is catalogued in the Karkal Jain Hostel (see Nathuram Premi, *Jain Sahitya*, 1956, p. 185.

140. Hiralal Rasikdas Kapadia, *Pāiya Bhāshāo ane Sāhitya*, p. 184. *Madanakamaratna* by Pūjyapāda is mentioned as another treatise in Sanskrit verses. Out of handwritten 64 pages, the remaining 52 pages deal with sexual love, *JSBI*, V, p. 227. The *Haramekhala*, a treatise on subjugation by means of spells, etc., is mentioned in the commentary of the *Samavāyāṅga* (29) by Abhayadeva.
141. *Sūya* Com. 4.1.24. Dattaka is mentioned as an author of the *Vaiśika* in the *Kuṭṭinimata* (504) of Dāmodara. The *Kāmasutra* contains a chapter on *Vaiśuika*; also see *Lalitavistara*, pp. 156f; *Mṛcchakaṭika*, 1, p. 2.
142. यद् व्याघ्रादिव प्रेम्ण: सावधानतया सर्वदा एवं आत्मा रक्षणीय: । तत्र रागवशात् बहवो भुजंगा वेश्याभिर्विप्रलब्धा: Ed. Kalpalata Munshi, *SJS*, Bombay, 1959.
143. See Jagdishchandra Jain, *Women in Ancient Indian Tales*, Delhi, 1987, p. xiii. Read the story 'The Faked Death of Kāmalatā' told in the *Kumāravālapaḍiboha* by Somaprabhasūri. For its English version see *Women in Ancient Indian Tales*, pp. 48-52.
144. दुर्विज्ञेयो हि भाव: प्रम दानाम—quoted from the *Vaisikatāntra*, p. 140.
145. आलीढ, पच्चालीढ, सीहासण and मंडलावत्त are mentioned in Jinesvarasūri's *Kathākośaprakaraṇa* (p. 24); also see *The Vasudeva*, pp. 352f.
146. Devendragaṇi, *Uttarā* Com., 4, p. 89.
147. *Nāyā*, 18, p. 208.
148. See *LAI*, pp. 102f. The effect of *nāgabāṇa* is described in the following verse:

    चित्रं श्रेणिक ! ते बाणा भवन्ति धनुराश्रिता: ।
    उल्कारूपाश्च गच्छन्त: शरीरे नागमूर्तय: ॥
    क्षणं बाणा: क्षणं दण्डा: क्षणं पाशत्वमागता: ।
    आकरा ह्यस्त्रभेदास्ते यथाचिन्तितमूर्तय: ॥
149. See *LAI*, pp. 454f, pp. 99f.
150. A.D. Pusalkar, *Bhāsa—A study*, Lahore, 1940, p. 440f.
151. *PNL*, p. 142 धनुर्वेद-वीरचिनचमणि-परिच्छेद in Sanskrit is mentioned *Jodhpur Collection*, Pt. II(B) 1965, p. 212; written in vs 1769.
152. See *LAI*, pp. 244-7 and for their identification.
153. *Vasudevahiṇḍi*, 130, 21-2, *The Vasudeva*, pp. 665f.
154. *VH*, 127, 10; *The Vasudeva*, p. 214.
155. *Thā*, 7.553; *Jīvā* Com. 3.193af; *Anuyoga*, 127 *LAI*, pp. 243f.
156. Here is cited the 128th *Sūtra* of the *Ṭhā* containing *Svaramaṇḍalasūtra* (p. 553) *verbatim*.
157. Ibid. Among other treatises, the *Saṅgītaratnākara* of Śāraṅgadeva (thirteenth century AD), the *Saṅgītadarpaṇa* of Dāmodara and the *Rāgavibodha* of Somanātha are mentioned in Sanskrit. They deal with *rāgas* or musical modes, including 50 pieces of author's own compositions for lute with notation. A.B. Keith, *A History of Sanskrit Literature*, p. 466.
158. See *LAI*, under 72 *Kalās*, p. 228. Note the following 64 *kalās* enumerated in the *Śaivatantra* (Tārānātha Tarkavācaspati's Dictionary):

गीतम्, वाद्यं, नृत्यं, नाट्यं, आलेख्यं, विशेषकच्छेद्यं, तण्डुल-कुसुमबलि-विकाराः, पुष्पास्तरणं, दशन-वसनांग-रागः, मणि-भूमिका-कर्म, शयनरचनं, उदक-वाद्यं, उदक-घातः, चित्रायोगाः, माल्य-ग्रन्थन-विकल्पाः, केश-शेखरापीड-योजनं, नेपथ्य-योगाः, कर्ण-पत्र-भङ्.गाः, गन्धयुक्तिः, भूषण-योजनं, इन्द्रजालं, कौचुमार-योगाः, हस्त-लाघवम्, चित्र-शाकपूप-भक्ष्य-विकार-क्रिया, पानक-रस-रागासव-योजनं, सूची-वाप-कर्म, वीणा-डमरूक-सूत्र-क्रीडा, प्रहेजिका, प्रतिमा, दुर्वचकयोगाः, पुस्तक-वाचनं, नाटकाख्यायिका-दर्शनं, काव्य-समस्या-पूरणं, पट्टिका-वेत्र, वाण-विकल्पाः, तर्कू-कर्माणि, तक्षणं, वास्तु-विद्या, रूप्य-रत्न-परीक्षा, धातुवादः, मणि-राग-ज्ञानं, आकर-ज्ञानं, वृक्षायुर्वेद-योगाः, मेष-कुक्कुर-लावक-युद्ध-विधिः, शुक-सारिका-प्रलापनं, उत्सादनं, केश-मार्जन-कौशलं, अक्षर-मुष्टिका-कथनं, म्लेच्छितक-विकल्पाः, देश-भाणा-ज्ञानं, पुष्प-शकटिका-निमित्त-ज्ञानं, यन्त्र-मातृका, धारण-मात्रिका, सम्पात्यं, मानसी-काव्य-क्रिया, क्रिया-विकल्पाः, छलितक-योगाः, अभिधान-कोश-च्छन्दो-ज्ञानं, वस्त्र-गोपनानि, द्यूत-विशेषः, आकर्षण-क्रीडा, बालक-क्रीडनकानि, वैनायिकीनां विद्यानां ज्ञानं, वैजयिकीनां विद्यानां ज्ञानं.

159. Also mentioned in the *VH* (51, 3); *Mṛcchakaṭika* (VIII.13) and *Lalitavistara* (See E.G. Thomas' article in the *Bulletin School of Oriental Studies* VI, pp. 515-17).

160. ओल्लम्मि ओल्लओ जो दिज्जइ बेह इति सो भणिओ।
बोहो उण जो चुण्णो चुण्णविणि अच्छगंधो सो॥ 77.11 com.
The mixing together of two liquids is known as *vedha* (piercing) while that of two powders as *bodha* (expansion).

161. *Studies in Indian Literature History*, I.

162. *Nisī Bhā*, 13. 4313; Devendragaṇi, *Uttarā Ṭīkā*, 4, 83; *Das Cu*, 1, 44.

163. *VH*, 146, 22f; *The Vasudeva*, 670f.

164. 150.17f; 151, 1-5.

165. 195.12f *Dhātuvāda* is also called *narendra-kalā* (*narinda-kala*), 197.16.

166. अत्थस्स उण उवाया दिसिगमणं होइ मित्तकरणं च
णरवरसेवा कुसजत्तणं च माणप्पमाणेसुं॥
धातुव्वाओ मंतं देवयाराहणं च केसिं च।
सायरतरणं तह रोहणम्मि खणणं वणिज्जं च॥
णाणाविहं च कम्मं विज्जासिप्पाइं णेयरूवाइं।
अत्थस्स साहयाइं अणिंदियाइं च एयाइं॥ 57, 24-7

167. 196, 32; 197, 6; *Daś*, 1, 44.

168. Included in the *Ratnaparīkṣādi Saptagrantha-saṃgraha*, Rājasthān Prācyavidya—pratiṣṭhāna, Jodhpur, 1961. The following are the seven treatises: *Yugapradhāna Catuṣpadī*, *Gaṇitasāra*, *Vāstusāra*, *Jyotiṣasāra*, *Ratnaparīkṣā*, *Dravyaparikṣā*, and *Dhātūtpatti*.

169. Rājasthān Pracyavidyāpratiṣṭhāna, Jodhpur, 1961.

170. Such as णमो इंदस्स णमो धरणिंदस्स, णमो धणयस्स, णमो धण-पालस्स (104, 31-2).

171. They are नीलक, वज्जक, पद्मराग, मौक्तिक and प्रवाल; or सुवर्ण, रजत, मुक्ता, राजावर्त, and प्रवालक, Apte, *Sanskrit-English Dictionary*.

172. मुक्ता, माणिक्य, वैडूर्य, गोमेद, वज्र, विद्रुम, पद्मराग, मरकत and नीज ibid.

173. Also see *Paṇṇa*, 1.17; *Jīvā*, III.69; *Nisī Bhā*, 2.1031; *Daś Cū*, 212; also *Divyāvadāna* (XVIII, p. 229); *Milindapañha*, p. 118. The *Paramatthadīpanī*, the commentary on the *Udāna* (p. 103) gives the follwing list of gems:
वजिर, महानील, इंदनील, मरकत, वेलूरिय, पदुमराग, फुस्सराग, कक्केतन, फुलक, विमल, लोहितांक, फलिक,

पवाल, जोतिरंग, गोमुत्तक, गोमेद, सोगंधिक, मुत्ता, संख, अंजनमूल, राजावह, अमतब्बाक, पियक and ब्राहणी. Also see Agastimata's list in the *Les Lapidaires Indiens* by Louis Finot, Paris, 1896, p. 137.

174. रत्नेन शुभेन शुभं भवति नृपाणामनिष्टमशुभेन।
यस्माददत: परीक्ष्यं दैवं रत्नाश्रितं तज्ज्ञै: ॥ 80.1
The author is told by a Maharashtrian lady of a practice prevailing in Maharashtra that a diamond was not to be sold to the buyer directly. The piece was to be kept with a third party for some time and observe good or bad omen if even used. Later on it was sold.

175. *Agastimata*, the *Ratnaparikṣā* of Buddhabhaṭṭa and the *Navaratna Parikṣā* of Nārāyaṇa Paṇḍita are mentioned by Keith, *A History of Sanskrit Literature*, p. 465.

176. Published along with the *Dhatūtpatti*, Vaishali Prakrit Institute, Vaishali, 1976.

177. Also published by Chandan Sagar Jñānabhaṇḍāra, Vejalpur, vs 2002.

178. *Kathākośa* in Sanskrit by an unknown author, composed after the last quarter of the eleventh century, translated by C.H. Tawney into English in 1895.

179. A chest-nut coloured horse with a light mane and tail, *MW*.

180. Also see Someśvara's *Mānasollāsa*; Jayadatta's *Aśvavaidyaka*; *Aśvaśāstra*, Tanjore, 1952; Durlabharāja's *Turaṅgaprabandha* (vs about 1215), not available. The *Jodhpur Collection*, Pt. II (B), p. 240 has referred to Nakula's *Śālihotṛa* (*Aśva cikitsā*) with *ṭīkā*; Keith refers to Gaṇa's *Aśvavaidyaka* or *Aśvāyurveda* and Bhoja's *Śābihotra* (in 138 verses), dealing with the care of horses and their diseases, ibid.

181. See *Uttarā*, 11.16; *Ṭhā*, 4.327; *Dhammapada-Aṭṭhakathā*, I.85.

182. *LAI*, p. 97.

183. Ibid., p. 98 for *Mallikākṣa* type of horse, he has cited the following *gāthā*:
उज्जू अकिसणकन्ती, तारंते ई समल्लिआ कुसुमे।
भाविज्जइ अच्छीइं जाणं ते मल्जिआ-अच्छा॥ (61.14)

184. The description is identical with the *Arthaśāstra* (2, 31, 11):
सप्तारत्निरुत्सेधो नवायामो दश परिणाह: प्रमाणश्चत्वारिंशद्वर्षो भवत्युत्तम: cf. the following verse of Parāśara cited in the commentary of the *Bṛh Saṃ* (67.4) by Utpala:
परिणाहो दशसमो नवायाम: स उच्छ्रय:।
सप्त ज्येष्ठप्रमाणस्य नागस्य समुदाहृत: ॥

185. The commentator of the *Bṛh Saṃ* (67.7) has cited the following verse of Parāśara:
विंशत्यष्टौ दश नखा: स्थिरा: कर्मसमाहिता:।
गजानां पूजिता: पादा ये च स्युरकचाविला: ॥
An elephant should have at least 18 and not more than 20 nails.

186. In the *VH* (the *Pauma-lambha*-8) is mentioned the *manda* elephant, who was trumpeting like a dark cloud, decorated with a covering, variegated with the designs of lotuses, was chained in a golden rope

and was producing sound from a pair of jingling bells, p. 355.

187. See *Ṭhā*, 4.281; *Nāyā*, 1, p. 39; *Arthaśāstra*, 2.31.18; *Bṛh Saṃ*, *Hastilakṣaṇa* (67.1-10). The *Sammohavinodinī*, the commentary on the *Vibhaṅga* (p. 397) gives the following ten species of elephants: कालावक, गंगेय्य, पंडर तंब, पिंगल, गंध, मंगल, हेम, उपोसथ and छद्दन्त.

188. Maladhāri Hemacandra, *BHBH*, p. 83.

189. *LAI*, pp. 95f.

190. *Jain Granthāvali*, p. 361.

191. अंगदेशेस्वभूच्छ्रीमान् रोमपादो महीपतिः।
गजारोहणशक्रेव धृतबुद्धिर्जितश्रमः ॥ ७ ॥

192. *History of Sanskrit Literature*, p. 465.

193. Śūdraka, *Mṛcchakaṭika* (III).

194. See Bhāsa, *Cārudatta* (III); *Avimāraka* (III). In the *Mattavilāsaprahasana* (p. 15) Kharapaṭa is called the composer of *Cauraśāstra*; also Bloomfield, 'The Art of Stealing', *AJP*, Vol. 44, pp. 98f.

195. Keith has referred to the *Ṣaṇmukhakalpa* (Haraprasada, Report I, p. 8) consisting of knowledge of magic for thieves, ibid., p. 465.

196. *Dhūrtasamāgama prahasana* by Jyotirīśvara, composed in vs 1933 is recorded in the *Jodhpur Collection*, Pt. II (B), 1965, p. 148.

197. *Nisi Bhā*, 21. 3650-2.

198. *Nāyā*, 18, pp. 208-9 ff; *LAI*, pp. 84f.

199. See *LAI*, pp. 83-6.

200. Ambalal P. Shah informs that a manuscript of this work was available to Shri Raghavacharya of Madras, who presented it to the Maharaja of Travancore. Dr. K.C. Woodgot a copy made of this work and took it to the U.S.A. Shri Sundarācharya published its English translation in 1925. The original work is not yet published, *JSBI*, Vol. V, p. 250 footnote.

201. The following verse is mentioned in the beginning of the manuscripts:
उदकानलचौरेभ्यो मूषकेभ्यो हुताशनात्।
कष्टेन लिखितं शास्त्रं यत्नेन परिपालयेत्॥

202. Jñāna bhandāro nī Samṛddhi, *jñānāñjali*, Munī Shri Puṇyavijayaji Commemoration Volume, 1919, p. 7. (in Gujarati).

203. 'Jeselmer ane tenā Prāchīn Jain Jñānabhanḍāro', a Radio talk recorded by Muni Puṇyavijayaji on 15.7.1965 from Ahmedabad, Baroda Radio Station, published in the *Jñānāñjali*, pp. 53-7.

204. See 'Liṃbaḍi Jñānabhanḍārnu Avalokan' (in Gujarati) by Muni Puṇyavijayaji, *Jñānāñjali*, pp. 17-38.

205. See *Catalogue of the Jains Manuscripts at Strasbourg* by C.B. Tripathi, p. 8, n. 36.

206. The compiler is said is have handled more than 50,000 Prakrit MSS in various Bhandars of Rajasthan.
Khindaka is the Arabic astronomer Alkindi.

10

A General Survey

Prakrit (*prāk-kṛtaṃ*) is a natural dialect of the people whereas Sanskrit is so called as it is refined or polished. As explained by Nami Sadhu, 'Prakrit is the speech easily intelligible to children, women and others and the source of all other speeches. It is of homogenous character like rain water falling from the clouds; the same speech specialized by refinement is later differentiated into Sanskrit and other speeches.' Prakrit and Sanskrit are sister languages, there is no contradiction between them but instead they are complementary to each other. Both are important as they possess abundant literature depicting social and cultural life of Indian people.

As Māgadhī or Ardhamāgadhī was a spoken dialect of Magadha, Mahavira and Buddha, in order to have a direct contact with the people, preferred to preach in this dialect. Both did not believe in supremacy of caste or race and did not differentiate between man and man; their religious or moral preaching was meant for all. The religion preached by Mahavira was known as *nigganṭha dhamma* (*nirgrantha dharma*; religion of non-attachment), and he emphasized on cessation of worldly activities by means of practising self-restraint. He preached the doctrine of 'Do not do unto others what you do not like to yourself.' He exhorted his followers to 'realize that you are your own friend, why are you then looking for a friend outside yourself?' and 'you should keep control over yourself, only then you will be relieved of suffering'. He exhorted them saying 'All beings are like you, they like pleasure and shun pain, they avoid destruction; life is dear to them, they like to live long; to all life is dear, therefore their life should be protected.' In order to illustrate his point he had taken recourse to numerous examples, anecdotes and tales of animals and human beings. *Nigganṭha-Nāta-putta* Mahavira taught his fundamental principles to his disciples, who in return put them in the form of *Sūtras*, also known as *Āgama*, *Śruta*, *Siddhānta* or *Pravacana*. This sacred literature of the Jains is known as *Duvālasaṅga* (*Dvādaśāṅga*) *Gaṇi-piṭaka* or *Pravacana-veda*, comprising twelve *Aṅgas*. The

Digambaras too believe in twelve *Aṅgas*; their names have been mentioned in literature; they form a part of the *Aṅgapraviṣṭa*; the *Aṅgaba-hya* being divided into fourteen parts. The *Dṛṣṭivāda*, the twelfth *Aṅga*, according to the Śvetāmbaras is lost, whereas according to the Digambaras, only a portion of this work has remained in the form of the *Chakkhaṇḍāgama* of Puṣpadanta and Bhūtabali and the *Kasāyapāhuḍa* of Guṇadhara. Besides these twelve *Aṅgas*, the twelve *Upāṅgas*, the ten *Paiṇṇas* (*Prakīrṇakas*), the six *Chedasūtras*, the two Individual Texts and the four *Mūlasūtras*—in all 45 *Āgamas* (barring the *Dṛṣṭivāda*) have been admitted in the Śvetāmbara tradition.

This Āgamic literature was further explained by illustrious teachers by way of *Nijjutti* (*Niryukti*), *Bhāsa* (*Bhāṣya*), *Cuṇṇi* (*Cūrṇi*) and *Vṛtti* or commentaries. This literature, like the Buddhist canonical literature, in the words of B.C. Law,

> developed under the aegis of religion which was destined to be a great civilising influence in the East, highly ethical in tone, dignified in the forms of expression, dramatic in setting, direct in narration, methodical in argument and mechanical in arrangement. This wealth of literary output was shown forth in its lucidity and grandeur in the garb of a new literary idiom having a place midway between the Vedic Sanskrit on one hand and classical Sanskrit on the other.

The Āgamic literature along with its vast exegetical literature contains vast information regarding historical, geographical, economic, linguistic, social and cultural aspects of ancient Indian people.

The Śvetāmbara Jain canonical literature was composed in Ardhamāgadhī, also known as Ārṣa or the dialect spoken by *ṛṣis* or sages which can be compared with Sanskrit and is called *deva-bhāṣā* or the divine language. Unfortunately, we have no ways of knowing the exact nature of this dialect which was spoken at the time of Mahavira, nearly 2,500 years ago. Vararuci, the author of the *Prākṛta-prakāśa* (sixth century), is the first grammarian of Prakrit but as he does not deal with Ardhamāgadhī, we do not get any information from him about the dialect. We first come across Ardhamāgadhī or Ārṣa in Hemacandra's Siddhahema but here this dialect is not included among the six major dialects mentioned by the author. Though Ardhamāgadhī and Ārṣa are treated as identical, the author seems to differentiate between the two in certain respects. Like the Śvetāmbaras, in the Digambara tradition also the Āgamic literature, the *Dvādaśāṅga*, was composed by the *gaṇadharas*, the chief disciples of Mahavira.

In course of time, due to long-lasting famine, according to tradition, as the monks were not able to hold the teachings of the Master in totality, it was thought necessary to hold a congregation of learned monks so that the Jain Canon could be preserved. Several such meetings were convened, the first being in Pāṭaliputra about 160 years after Mahavira's *nirvāṇa,* under the leadership of Sthūlabhadra, in about 367 BC; this was followed by Mathura convention after about 827 years after Mahavira's *nirvāṇa,* under the leadership of Ārya Skandila, in about AD 300 (and after about 840 years after Mahavira's *nirvāṇa* or AD 313 according to the followers of Nāgārjuna); then, simultaneously, another convention was held at Valabhi under the leadership of Nāgārjuna. A final council of learned Jain monks was convened 980 (or 993) years after Mahavira, in about AD 453 or 466, under the leadership of Devardhigaṇi Kṣamāśramaṇa at Valabhi. This council was important as it was here that a reconciliation was made between the different versions of Ārya Skandila and Nāgārjuna, giving preference to the former. Moreover, the canonical texts were put to writing in this council.

It appears that in spite of the utmost efforts on the part of the learned Jain monks, the canonical texts could not be preserved in true form. The later commentators such as Śīlāṅka, Abhayadeva, Malayagiri and others have specifically pointed out that they had different versions of the canonical texts before them, a number of readings had become corrupt and therefore beyond the grasp of the intellect. Since the ancient traditions were lost and the texts remained full of inaccuracies and contradictions, it was not possible to render faithful explanations. Yet the commentators have advised the readers not to be confused and read the text faithfully.

Under the circumstances, there is no wonder that the Digambaras disowned the canonical texts of the Śvetāmbaras, declaring that they had been lost beyond repair and could not be restored. However, the Yāpanīyas, who flourished in large number in south, admitted the existence of the Āgamic literature, some even cited it as authority and wrote commentaries on it. Whatever it may be, there is no uniformity in the extant canonical texts, their compilation belongs to different periods though a few of them can be traced to the period of Mahavira himself. However, to ascertain the period of this literature, various factors such as form, style, modulation, structure, content and of course the language have to be taken into consideration. As far as language is concerned, it cannot be a deciding factor as the orthography of manuscripts often differs according to region. Besides, there must have been numerous changes in the language of the Canon based on the teachings of Mahavira, during the course of all these long years. We also notice very many changes in the original Ardhamāgadhī, the language of the canonical texts, as it was being transformed gradually into Maharashtri Prakrit. This can be easily said with regard to the rules concerning *ya-śruti, na ṇa, anusvāra-anunāsika* and so on. While explaining the rules of Prakrit grammar, Hemacandra and other grammarians, instead of laying down permanent rules, have referred to the expressions such as *kvacit, prāyaḥ, vā* and so on. This only shows that there had been no uniformity and homogeneity in Prakrit.[1]

However, it is to be noted that though there have been alterations and modifications in the canonical texts from time to time, the material they contain is very valuable as it comprehends subject matter concerning the origin, growth and development of Jainism. This literature enables us to understand the basic principles of Jainism laid down by Mahavira. The Digambaras refused to believe in the authenticity of this literature and so suffer a good deal. Under the circumstances, they had to fall back on the ancient works of the Yāpanīyas such as the *Bhagavatī Ārādhanā* of Śivārya and *Mūlācārya,* also known as the *Ācārāṅga* of Vaṭṭakera, besides the works of Kundakunda, who seems to belong to a later period, the third or the fourth century AD. They also claimed that the Mūḍabidrī texts known as the *Chakkhaṇḍāgama* and the *Kasāyapāhuḍa,* which are said to have constituted a part of the *Dṛṣṭivāda,* have survived in the form of the sacred scriptural texts. But looking to the language, style and contents of these texts, as far as their antiquity is concerned, they do not stand in comparison with the simplicity of style and the archaic language of some of the extant canonical texts of the Śvetāmbaras.

Apart from dogmatic doctrinal literature contained in the Ardhamāgadhī Canon of the Śvetāmbaras, Prakrit has also contributed a good deal in the sphere of narrative literature in Maharashtri. Narrative literature or story-telling is the best way to express one's ideas effectively and forcefully. India has a long tradition of story-telling. The *Baḍḍakahā* or the *Bṛhatkathā* by Guṇāḍhya which was full of 'wonderful meaning', unfortunately is no more extant. As time passed, Ardhamāgadhī was being replaced by Maharashtri; a more flexible popular dialect. The Jain monks who were supposed to be well acquainted with local customs and usages and who were drawn from a cross section of the society, had to be well-versed in all sorts of popular tales and anecdotes, religious, moral, humorous and adventurous. In order to preach religious sermons they travelled from place to place and by their oratory and power of elocution impressed their audience. Undoubtedly, this was a great contribution towards the growth and development of Indian narrative literature. Listening to a story, in ancient India, was considered a meritorious deed. It is said to have fulfilled the desired object and the narrator as well as the listener of the story became free from sin. It helped in purging of emotions and relieved a person from fatigue and wearisomeness. There have been various types of stories such as the stories related to *dharma* (righteousness), *artha* (attainment of wealth) and *kāma* (desire for sensual pleasure), stories pertaining to wit and humour, to wise people, artless simple fools, rogues, scoundrels, prostitutes, bawds and so on. It has been stated that by listening to such tales, a man becomes alert and is able to guard himself against the clutches of rogues and scoundrels. The character of fools, debauchers, imposters, swindlers and liars is exposed through such tales.

Jain authors have always been in search of good stories from whatever source, though they ended in predominance of religious or moral teaching. They were aware that people were more keen to listen to love stories and much less tedious didactic stories. They were aware that if people's attention were to be drawn towards religious tales, some 'sugar-coated pill' had to be administered. It is stated that under such circumstances, like a physician who administers his health-restoring bitter medicine to an unwilling patient under the pretext of the medicine of his liking, in the same way, a virtuous story should be told under the pretext of a love story. Various such works such as the *Taraṅgavaikahā* by Pādaliptasūri, a court-poet of Hāla and a contemporary of the celebrated poet Guṇāḍhya, the *Naravāhanadattakahā*, the *Malayavatī*, the *Magadhasenā*, the *Vasudevacariya*, the *Ceṭakakathā* and many others can be mentioned here. The *KVLM* by Udyotanasūri, though called a religious story, is compared to a newly wedded bride in form and beauty and should be read most attentively, says the author.

Like the *kāma-kathā*, Jain writers also emphasized on the *artha-kathā* (attainment of worldly prosperity by acquiring wealth). It is stated that without wealth a virtuous life is not possible and without virtuous life there is no happiness. How can one bestow charity without money, and how a poor man can satisfy his basic needs? Moreover, without money how could one lead an independent life, one had to hang on others even for trifling things. In Prakrit Jain literature we come across various sons of merchants who, in spite of the fact that their forefathers had left them huge amounts of wealth, proposed to travel abroad to earn. A man was applauded only if he offered charity out of his own self-earned money, otherwise he was looked down upon as a thief, who wanted to earn generosity just hanging on his father's money. Here we read thrilling narratives of daring merchants, who, in order to acquire wealth passed through inaccessible mountains, rivers, wild forests, deserts and had to undertake perilous sea-journeys. The Prakrit Jain works, including the *Nāyā*, the *Āvā*, the *Uttarā-Tīkā*, the *VH*, the *Samarā*, the *KVLM*, the *Kahāṇayakośa*, the *Nammayāsundarīkahā*, the *Sirivālakahā* and others provide detailed accounts of trading merchants, who in order to acquire wealth, travelled to far-off countries.

In all these stories, as indicated, there is a tinge of morality. In order to make them popular, various symbolic forms are employed. The parable of 'The Man in the Well', the metaphor of roads (*mārga*), the personification of anger (*krodha*), vanity (*māna*), deceit (*māyā*), greed (*lobha*) and infatuation (*moha*) are characterized by introducing Caṇḍasoma, Mānabhaṭṭa, Māyāditya, Lobhadeva and Mohadatta respectively—with a biographical sketch of these characters. At places are introduced the painted scroll depicting the *saṃsāra-cakra* (the wheel of worldly existence), including exciting scenes representing people suffering from diseases, lying on their cots in a helpless disabled state; the wife, relations and friends crying and lamenting, the relatives carrying the bier to the burning ground and lighting the pile of wood in the crematorium. Elsewhere, a Chain of Destruction is depicted where more powerful living beings are shown to act in a cruel manner towards weaker ones. To make the narration more effective and forceful, various literary forms such as the *praśnottara*, *pāda-pūrti*, *vakrokti*, *vyājokti*, *ślesokti*, *gūḍha-uttara*, *gūḍha-caturtha-pāda*, *prahelikā*, *samasyā-pūrti*, *madhya-uttara*, *bahi-uttara*, *ekālāpa*, and *gata-pratyāgata* are employed.

Jain authors have also preserved numerous works directly aimed at edification or religious or moral instructions, known as *aupadeśika* or didactic literature. Herein they emphasized charity, austerities, purity of conduct, self-restraint, discipline, devotion to religious study and so on leading to renunciation of worldly objects and tranquillity of mind. It is stated that in order to understand and appreciate this literature one has to prepare one's mind by cultivating the feeling of renunciation, otherwise just as a mouse has nothing to do with wealth and a crow with a golden necklace, so too the study of this literature will not be of any use. In order to make the subject lively, didactic verses, pithy sayings, riddles and so on were incorporated in the literature. Some works were composed for the enlightenment of slow-witted simple people directing them towards ritual practices. Various tales such as those of eminent pontiffs, virtuous men and women, kings and royal officers, masters and slaves are introduced to explain the teachings of Mahavira. Here the emphasis is laid on *ṣaṃvega* or the desire for emancipation, without which, it is said, the long practice of austerities, observance of conduct for a long time and the study of holy scriptures repeatedly is of no avail. In order to direct a person to right conduct, didactic teachings are provided, citing examples of birds, animals, insects, trees, plants, medicine, sugar, sugar cane juice, molasses, water-pond and also a desire yielding tree (*kalpa-taru*).

There is a vast biographical literature too in Prakrit. The *Tisaṭṭhi-salākā-purusa-cariya* (*Triṣaṣṭi-śalākā-puruṣa-carita*) incorporates the life-histories of Tīrthaṅkaras, Cakravartins, Baladevas, Vāsudevas and Prativāsudevas. It contains the legends of Rāma and Kṛṣṇa based on the Jain *Rāmāyaṇa* and the Jain *Mahābhārata* respectively. Here we get accounts of Rāma, Lakṣamaṇa and Sītā, the kidnapping of the latter, the battle between Rāma and Rāvaṇa, five Pāṇḍavas, Draupadī, King Nala and his queen Damayantī and many others. This literature contains the life-history of ascetic heroes who having undergone extreme physical torture are said to have attained *mokṣa*; learned patriarchs, renowned kings and rulers who tried their utmost to spread the tenets of Jain religion; royal ministers who got the Jain statues and Jain temples constructed enthusiastically; leading merchants who donated wealth for the cause of the spread of Jainism; outstanding authors and eminent women who successfully safeguarded their virtue and fought for the security of their country. The *VH* which provides the life-history of Vasudeva and the *Paumacariya* which provides the life-history of Rāma give an account of the Harivaṃśa lineage, though in Jain tradition its origin, like the removal of the *garbha* of Mahavira and the achievement of emancipation of Malli, is included among the ten wonders of the world. Among others the *Pāsanāhacariya*, the *Mahāvīracariya*, the

Supāsanahacariya, the *Rayaṇacūḍācariya*, the *Kumma-puttacariya*, the *Kaṇhacariya*, the *Davayantīcariya*, the *Sīyācariya*, and *Vijayacanda-kevalicariya* can be mentioned. The tendency of writing biographical accounts of great personalities gained popularity and the tradition continued in Sanskrit, Apabhraṃśa, Kannaḍa, Tamil, Old Hindi, Rajasthani and Old Gujarati.

Jains also composed the *Kathākośa* or Treasury of Tales, consisting of numerous interesting stories pertaining to religious and moral teaching. The narratives contained here are generally taken from the earlier material. Some authors composed their own narrative also. Generally this literature was composed during the eleventh and twelfth centuries. Here the *Kahāṇayakosa* (*Kathākośa-prakaraṇa*) by Jineśvarasūri, the *Ākhyānamaṇikośa* (or the *Kathāmaṇikośa*) by Nemicandrasūri, the *Kahārayaṇakosa* (the *Kathāratnakośa*) by Guṇacandragaṇi, the *Kumāravālapaḍiboha* (the *Kumārapa-la-pratibodha*), the *Dhammakahāṇayakosa* (the *Dharmakathānakakośa*) by some unknown author, the *Kahāvali* (the *Kathāvali*) by Abhaya-devasūri's pupil Bhadreśvara, the *Kathāsamāsa* (or *Upadeśamālā*) by Jinabhadra and various others can be mentioned. In Sanskrit Hariṣena's *BKK*, Hemacandra's *TSP*, the *Kathākośa* by Prabha-candra, the *Kathakośa* by Nemidatta, the *PKK* by Rāmacandra Mumukṣu and others can be recorded. Then, besides the *Vaḍḍāra-hane* in Old Kannaḍa prose, there are several other works preserved in the Moodbidri, Kārkal and Śravaṇa Beḷgoḷ Jain Bhandars in the form of manuscripts.

Bhāmaha stated in the eighth century that as there is no charm without grace, and no light without moon, so there is no skill in speech without poetry. After religious and narrative literature in Prakrit we come to poetical composition. Gradually Ardhamāgadhī was being replaced by Maharashtri Prakrit. Daṇḍin has called this a dialect *par excellence*, containing a jewel-mine of beautiful sayings. Due to its tenderness, elegance and charm, it was considered suitable for lyrical poetry. Phonetically also it was most appropriate for the purpose as by dropping consonants it assumed a delicate form. The Prakrit grammarians took advantage of this developed situation, consequently, after describing the chief characteristics of this dialect, they just mentioned a few rules of the rest of the dialects, stating: 'शेषं महाराष्ट्रीवत'. Since Prakrit was a dialect spoken by the masses, it was considered to have a better emotional appeal than the artificial Sanskrit. It is said that the oldest love-songs were composed in Prakrit and it possessed the major portion of Indian lyric poetry. Jayavallabha, the author of the *Vajjālagga*, an important work on anthology, and its commentator Ratnadeva have pointed out the significance of this very important literary dialect. The commentator has stated that though he is well-versed in Sanskrit, he has, looking to the general interest of the people in erotic poetry, written this commentary in Prakrit verse. The author, pleading that Prakrit is more suitable for love poetry, argues: since it is a spoken dialect by common people, it is within their reach and hence it surpasses Sanskrit. He observes: 'If it is true that Prakrit poetry is charming, full of melodious words, dear to the heart of young ladies and characterized with erotic sentiment, who would like to read Sanskrit?' Further, 'If one does not know how to read and listen to Prakrit poetry, he should feel ashamed of talking of love.'

It is most significant that the well known rhetoricians, while illustrating the merits of excellent poetry, instead of selecting illustrations from Sanskrit, drew from Prakrit. Ānandavardhana, the propounder of the *dhvani* school, Abhinavagupta, the author of the *Locana*, an elaborate commentary on the *Dhvanyāloka*, Dhanañjaya, the author of the *Daśarūpaka*, Bhojarāja, the well known author of the *Sarasvatīkaṇṭhābharaṇa* and *Sṛṅgāraprakāśa*, Mammaṭa, the author of the *Kāvyaprakāśa*, Hemacandra, the author of the *Kāvyānuśāsana* and others have given extensive quotations from Prakrit literature in their compositions. Bhojarāja, according to whom the *śṛṅgāra-rasa* (the erotic sentiment), is most dominant in poetry, cites as many as 1650 *gāthās* in his *Śṛnagāraprakāśa* and 350 in his well known *Sarasvatīkaṇṭhābharaṇa*, a compilatory work of great dimension. These citations are from the celebrated compositions such as the *Gāhākosa* or the *Gāhāsattasaī* of Hāla, the *Vajjālagga* of Jayavallabha, the *Setubandha*, also known as the *Rāvaṇavaho* or *Dasamuhavaho* of Pravarasena, the *Gauḍavaho* of Vappairāa or Vākpatirāja, the *Harivijaya* of Sarvasena (not available), the *Marīcavadha* and the *Rāvaṇavijaya* which has been composed only in Āśva-sakabandha metre.

In this connection the *Amaruśataka* of Amaru, one of the most well known Indian Sanskrit lyric poets and the *Āryāsaptaśati*, written on the model of the *Gāhāsattasaī*, of Govardhana, a court-poet of Lakṣamaṇasena and contemporary of famous Jayadeva, are relevant as important lyrical compositions, depicting most delicate and tender sentiments of love. Eulogizing the lyrical stanzas of the former,

Ānandavardhana has remarked that each of the stanzas here conveys such a sentiment that it appears like an independent work in miniature. Needless to say this work has been immensely influenced by Prakrit lyric poetry. Govardhana who is known for his eulogy on Prakrit poetry, has stated: 'As Balarāma has raised the river Yamunā, the daughter of Kalinda to the sky, in same way, for the first time, he has carried over to Sanskrit by force the type of poetry that usually was found elegant expression in Prakrit.'

The *Gāhākosa* or the *Gāhāsattasaī* is a collection of 700 Prakrit lyrical verses, these being *muktakas* or isolated stanzas without any interconnection, each complete and with a charm of its own. The renowned Bāṇabhaṭṭa, Udyotanasūri, Govardhana, Rudraṭa, Mammaṭa, Vāgbhaṭa and many others have envisaged profound appreciation for this anthology. It has been stated that Sātavāhana or Hāla has made an excellent collection of 700 stanzas out of one crore. These beautiful lyrical stanzas were composed in different metres and *alaṃkāras*, are full of meaning, and abound in figurative speech. This Prakrit anthology had several recensions and 18 commentaries were written on it, which is sufficient to indicate its popularity. It is no wonder that the Prakrit lyrical poetry had gained such a high stature in the first and second century AD. Since the *Gāhāsattasaī* is a compiled work, it contains the poetical stanzas of the renowned poets of Prakrit including Guṇāḍhya, Aṇiruddha, Avantivamma, Hariuḍḍha (Harivṛddha), Poṭṭisa, Pālitta (Pādalipta), Īsāṇa, Bhoja, Naravāhana, Dāmodara, Trilocana and many others. Many of them are unknown and we have no approach to their works. We also come across the names of distinguished women poets such as Revā, Śaśiprabhā, Rohā, Girisutā, Guṇamugdhā and others. Elsewhere we meet Vikaṭanitambā, Vijjā or Vijjakā, Śilābhaṭṭārikā, Prabhudevī, Subhadrā and others whose excellent poems are cited in various works, including the *Subhaṣitas*.

Like the *Gāhāsattasaī*, the *Vajjālagga* is another rich collection of lyrical stanzas in Maharashtri Prakrit. The citation of its stanzas by various rhetoricians in their works indicates its popularity. Its verses are also quoted in Sanskrit drama. Two-thirds of this poetic work fall in the category of *kāma* (love). The *Setubandha*, the *Gauḍavaho* and the *Līlāvai* are *mahākāvya* or epic, of which the first two have followed the great Sanskrit poet Bhavabhūti and here we notice the high-flown artificial style of Sanskrit poetry. Both are full of metaphors, puns, alliteration and long compounds. Daṇḍin has referred to the

Setubandha as an example of Maharashtri written in elegant style. Vākpatirāja, the author of the *Gauḍavaho,* was a disciple of Bhavabhūti. Since the work is an example of ornate poetry, the author has employed various *alaṃkāras* in his composition. The *Mahumahaviaa* (*Madhumatha-vijaya*) is another important poetical work of Vākpatirāja which unfortunately is not available. Abhinavagupta and Hemacandra have cited illustrations from it in the *Locana* and the commentary of the *Kāvyānuśāsana* respectively. The *Harivijaya* by Sarvasena is an important epic poem, describing the city, the mountain, the sunset, the march of the hero Hari (Kṛṣṇa) for battle, and his conquest. Ānandavardhana and Kuntaka have equated him with Kālidāsa as far as his graceful and delicate style is concerned. This poetical composition which is lost to us, seems to have been quite popular with Sanskrit rhetoricians. Bhojadeva in his *Sarasvatīkaṇṭhābharaṇa* and *Śṛṅgaraprakāśa* has cited numerous stanzas from this work. Hemacandra in his commentaries of the *Kāvyānuśāsana* has made a reference to this work along with the *Rāvana-vijaya, Setubandha, Siśupāla-vadha, Kirātārjunīya* and others. In the *Avantīsundarī,* the author is said to be a king. The *Mārīca-vadha,* dealing with the killing of Mārīca, was a poetical work of which nothing is known. The work has been cited by Bhoja, Abhinavagupta and Hemacandra. It was a type of *rāga-kāvya* and was sung in *ḍhakka* (or *ḍakka*) *rāga,* according to Hemacandra. The *Rāvaṇa-vijaya* has been referred to by Hemacandra, as pointed out. It is regarded as equal to the *Harivijaya* and the *Setubandha.* It is known for its description of a hero and his vehicle, an elephant, a horse, a *garuḍa* bird and so on according to Bhoja. The *Visamabāṇalīlā* of Ānandavardhana is not available like many other important works on the subject. This work deals with love on the model of the *Gāhāsattasaī* and is also designated as *Ānandakathā.* The author has cited several stanzas from this work in his *Dhvanyāloka.* At one place, citing a reference from this work, he has compared the words of good poets with the sports of good ladies. The poet Mammaṭa in his *Kāvyaprakāśa* and Hemacandra in the commentary on the *Kāvyānuśāsana* have quoted from this work. The *Kuvalayāśvacarita,* containing the story of the adventures of Kuvalayāśva, was composed by Kavirāja Viśvanatha, the author of the *Sāhityadarpaṇa.* He has cited a Prakrit stanza from this work in his *Sāhityadarpaṇa* which is not available. The *Līlāvai* by Kouhala is another poetic work which was composed at the request of his wife in *Marahaṭṭa desī-bhāsā.* The author ends his text by addressing his beloved, 'One who reads or listens to this poem daily does not suffer from the pang of separation of her lover.'

Nāṭaka or drama is considered most graceful of all poetry. The *Āatyaveda* which is known as the fifth *Veda* is also designated as the *Nāṭyaśāstra.* It was the science of dance or mime in ancient India which played an important role in life. In Greece the word drama is derived from *dran* which means to do or to act; without deed or action on the stage no piece of poetry can be called a drama. In Greek mythology, Dionysius is considered the god of wine and in order to invoke the deity various games and sports were arranged in his honour and it was from that time that the Greek drama was initiated. In the Vedic ritual texts various ceremonies were held which can be designated a type of drama. In ancient India Brahman is said to have created the art of drama 'related to good, bad and indifferent which produces courage, amusement and bestows counsel'. The *vidūṣaka* plays an important role here. He is supposed to be a good-humoured companion and confidential friend of the king or the hero of the play, and his business is to excite mirth.

In the *Nāṭyaśāstra* of Bharata Sanskrit is spoken by high class people; a king, a hero, a harlot, a *śrotriya* (conversant in the sacred learning), a Brahmana and so on, whereas Prakrit is assigned to children, persons of lower order, women, or lunatics. This clearly shows the class distinction with regard to language and culture. In other words, it seems learning and culture were reserved for the higher ranks, Brahmanas and ruling Ksatriyas. That reflects the aristocratic nature of Indian dramatic art. It is significant that to make the Sanskrit drama interesting and related to real life, it was not enough to depict only aristocratic characters, but create entertainment and make the play popular, the playwright had to introduce other characters. In fact a drama is associated with real life which should be believable to the audience. The story of life is to be depicted with force and vividness and for that Prakrit has contributed a good deal to make Sanskrit drama triumphant. The use of a variety of dialects spoken by different characters is significant in this respect as it helped a great deal in the development of Sanskrit dramas. Here we find the real harmony and concord between Sanskrit and Prakrit where they are complimentary to each other and assist in one another's development.

Maharashtri, Śaursenī, Māgadhī, Paiśācī and Apabhraṃśa are the important dialects that occur in Sanskrit drama. Vararuci, the earliest Prakrit grammarian, refers to only Prakrit (known as Maharashtri), Paiśācī, Māgadhī and Śaurasenī. It is to be noted that these dialects had ceased to be the spoken languages since long, therefore in the existing Prakrit literature, including Sanskrit dramas, they have to be understood as quite different from originally spoken dialects. In course of time, the Prakrit dialects, like Sanskrit, attained a standardized literary form and lost touch with day to day life.

Aśvaghoṣa (first century AD) is the earliest known playwright in Sanskrit. The discovery of fragments of palm-leaf of his drama in Turfan has proved that the technique of drama was fully developed in the first century AD; the drama was divided into acts in which a *vidūṣaka* was made to play an important role. The Prakrit dialects employed in his dramas are Śaurasenī, Māgadhī and Ardhamāgadhī and it is significant that the forms of these dialects are much older than found in classical Sanskrit drama. These old forms are certainly very important for the study and development of the Middle-Indo-Āryan. The Ardhamāgadhī dialect, for instance, employed here is quite different from the dialect of the sacred literature of Jains. So is the case with Śaurasenī and Māgadhī which are older than the dialects used by the later Prakrit grammarians. The archaic features of these dialects used by Aśvaghoṣa are compared with Palī and the dialects of older inscriptions.

Bhāsa is an important playwright of the third century who has composed a number of plays, including the *Cārudatta*, a pattern for the *Mṛcchakaṭika*. Kālidāsa, Bāṇa and Rājaśekhara have lauded him as a poet and Vākpatirāja has treated him with favour. The Prakrit dialect used by Bhāsa in his plays normally is Śaurasenī except his *Dūtavākya*, which is without Prakrit. The Māgadhī used by him is in two varied forms, one in the *Pratijñāyaugandharāyṇa* and the *Cārudatta* and the other in the *Bālacarita* and the *Pañcarātra*. The transitional aspect of his language can be compared on the one hand with Aśvaghoṣa and on the other with Kālidāsa. There is a variety of metres used in his plays.

The *Mrcchakaṭika* of Śūdraka (fifth century) is an important social drama unlike the other classical Sanskrit dramas and deals with real life. According to the *Nāṭyaśāstra* tradition, a hero (*nāyaka*) is supposed to be equipped with various characteristics. He should be *dhīrodātta*, *dhīroddhata*, *ḍhiralalita*, and *dhīra-praśānta*. He always comes out victorious, knows no defeat and never faces death. In the same way, a heroine is always a model of beauty, charm and grace. In contrast to this laid down tradition, Cārudatta, the hero, is a Brahmana by birth and though coming from a rich family, becomes penniless. He has to face numerous hurdles, unlike the heroes of classical plays. Similarly Vasantasenā, the heroine, is a highly virtuous lady but a concubine by profession. Cārudatta is her lover whom she loves most intensely. This is not a play like other classical plays of Sanskrit, portraying stereotyped life of various characters. It is important from the point of view of study of Prakrit dialects, including the minor ones. There are as many as 30 characters, mostly speaking Prakrit, each having his/her individuality. Prominence is given to Śaurasenī and Māgadhī Prakrits, Sanskrit being assigned only to a few characters.

Kālidāsa (fourth century) is famous for his play, the *Abhijñāna-śākuntala.* Here we notice the use of Prakrit dialects in their usual normal forms. Generally, Śaurasenī is used for prose and Maharashtri for poetry. The *vidūṣaka* speaks in Śaurasenī but Śakuntalā the heroine in Maharashtri and the fisherman in Māgadhī. Here the use of Prakrit dialects seems to have taken a stereotyped form which is based on the rules laid down by Prakrit grammarians. The language of Kālidāsa abounds in compounds and was naturally influenced by classical Sanskrit.

Thereafter we do not notice any new trend in Sanskrit dramas. As a matter of fact, by the tenth century there has been a state of decadence and declination. Bhavabhūti (AD 700) who had a mastery over Sanskrit language, uses long compounds. His plays are confined to Śaurasenī which he models on Sanskrit style. In fact, now the Prakrit dialects were more or less mechanically transformed from Sanskrit, they lost their independent identity and were written according to the rules of grammar laid down by Vararuci and others. Bhaṭṭanārāyaṇa (before the eighth century) in his *Veṇīsaṃhāra* uses few Prakrit forms, and in the *Mahānāṭaka,* which is written mainly in verse, never uses any Prakrit. There was a wide gulf now between the Prakrit dialects and the reality of life, therefore it remained confined to a limited section of the audience. Linguistic distinctions that had strengthened class distinctions, terminated into a meaningless convention. In this manner, the Prakrit turned into an artificial dialect and acquired an inferior position. On the other hand, Sanskrit became richer, abundantly furnished and elaborately decorated in style, but at the same time went beyond the reach of a common man. It became difficult to compose Sanskrit drama with a variety of Prakrit dialects and like Sanskrit, Prakrit gradually assumed literary form.

Rājaśekhara (about the ninth century), the renowned author of the *Karpūramañjarī*, who has shown his skill of composing 144 Prakrit stanzas of his work, employing 17 varieties of metres, is considered a great scholar of Prakrit of his time. He was so fond of Prakrit that he discarded Sanskrit and preferred to compose his *saṭṭaka* in Prakrit. But it should be noted that as Prakrit remained no more a spoken language, it was a laborious task to prepare a composition in that dialect. In course of time, people started studying Prakrit with its Sanskrit *chāya* Rājaśekhara himself has explained the Prakrit passages of his work *Bālarāmāyaṇa* with the help of Sanskrit *chāyā*. Moreover, as Prakrit dialects were getting outdated, poets and playwrights were not able to distinguish one dialect from the other. Rājaśekhara has also introduced vernacular words such as *ḍhilla* (from *śithila*) which indicates that Prakrit was being replaced by vernaculars dialects in Sanskrit dramas helped a great deal in its growth and development. This went on for 1500 years beginning with the Christian era. This period reflects the linguistic position of the society in which the Sanskrit drama grew. But as Prakrit remained a spoken dialect, definite rules of grammar could not be framed, consequently it continued to change from region to region and was ultimately lost in oblivion.

Vyākaraṇa (grammar), *chanda* (prosody), *kośa* (lexicography) and *alaṃkāra* (poetics) are essential for the study of language and literature. A certain word must be pronounced properly with proper accent. The *Vedas* are considered sacred by Brahmaṇas and their sacredness was tried to be preserved by reciting the vedic hymns precisely. This purpose could be served by *sikṣā* or the science of proper articulation and pronunciation which provides the knowledge of letters, accents, quantity, the use of organs of pronunciation and phonetics. There must not be any kind of imperfection as far as pronunciation of *akṣara, mātrā, pada, svara, vyañjana, sandhi, refa* (the letter *ra*), *bala* (the accent), *sāma* (melody) and *santāna* (the harmony of words in continuation of recitation) are concerned. It was believed that the slightest imperfection with regard to these would cause immense loss to the reciter of the sacred text. Those who had command over poetics have also laid stress on the study of *vyākaraṇa* because, according to them, it is by the study of grammar that a poet can use the proper word to convey the desired idea. Vararuci of the eastern group seems to be the earliest grammarian (sixth century) of Prakrit. He is followed by Laṅkeśvara, Kramadīśvara, Puruṣottama, Rāmaśarmā Tarkavāgīśa Bhaṭṭācarya and Mārkaṇḍeya.

Puruṣottama (twelfth century) divided Prakrit into bhāṣā. Ramaśarmā Tarkavāgīśa (seventeenth century) follows Puruṣottama. The author in his self-composed commentary on his work cites numerous Prakrit verses and sentences which are related to the narration of *dhātvādeśa*. Kavīndra Mārkaṇḍeya (1490-1565) was not only a grammarian of repute but also a poet of genius. He is writer of the *Vilāsavatī*, a *saṭṭaka*, and also the *Daśagrīva-vadha-mahākāvya*, a Sanskrit epic. Mārkaṇḍeya has provided more details about Śaurasenī compared to other grammarians. He has also dealt with Apabhraṃśa accurately. According to him, Ardhamāgadhī is a type of Māgadhī which is not far from Śaurasenī. It appears that in the time of our author Ardhamāgadhī became a dead language and remained only in name. Mārkaṇḍeya is the only author who provided illustrations of Āvantī and Bālhīkī; according to him, the latter is included in the former.

Dākṣiṇātyā has no characteristics of its own and Bālhīkī is nothing but a form of Māgadhī according to the author. Ābhīrī is as good as Śābarī therefore it has no separate existence according to him. Like Rāmaśarmā he identifies Ṭakkī with Drāviḍī. He has recorded 27 varieties of Apabhraṃśa whereas Vararuci has no place for Apabhraṃśa dialect.

Ācārya Hemacandra (1088-1172) is the oldest exponent of the western school of Prakrit grammarians. He adds Cūlikā Paiśācī and Apabhraṃśa to Maharashtri, Paiśācī, Māgadhī and Śaurasenī, the division of languages accepted by the eastern school. Hemacandra too does not accept the division of bhāṣā, vibhāṣā, Apabhraṃśa and Paiśācika, Ardhamāgadhī, being a form of Māgadhī, is rejected by the Eastern school, whereas Hemacandra mentions Ardhamāgadhī or Ārṣa, though in his Prakrit grammar while discussing the rules of Māgadhī, he refers to a rule of Ardhamāgadhī casually. According to the tradition, the language of the older Jain *Sūtras* was Ardhamāgadhī, which should be considered identical with Ārṣa. Vararuci as we have seen, out of 12 chapters has devoted 9 to Prakrit (Maharashtri). He prescribes rules with regard to Śaurasenī and remarks that in other respects it agrees with Maharashtri. In the same way, Hemacandra deals with Prakrit, which he calls Ārṣa. Here he discusses rules related to Śaurasenī with the remark in the last *sūtra* that the remaining should be understood like Prakrit. Hemacandra disagrees with Vararuci in certain points such as *ya-śruti*, the use of *na* and *ṇa*, *anunāsika* and *anusvāra* and so on. Vararuci does not accept

Apabhraṃśa as a separate dialect. Hemacandra has provided numerous verb-forms or *dhātvādeśas* in Prakrit. His portion of Apabhraṃśa is most important. Trivikrama (thirteenth century), Siṃharāja (fifteenth century), Lakṣmīdhara and Appayadīkṣita (sixteenth century) are the followers of the western school. It is to be noted that Trivikrama excludes Ārṣa from his list of Prakrit dialects while Siṃharāja, Lakṣmīdhara and Appayadīkṣīta take no notice of it.

There were other grammarians of Prakrit, who are less known or altogether unknown. As we have seen Mārkaṇḍeya has referred to certain grammarians, whose opinions he has quoted. Lakṣmīdhara also has referred to certain Prakrit works on grammar. However, one thing is common with these grammarians: all consider Maharashtri (which is designated as Prakrit in some cases) the principal Prakrit, and its chief characteristics with regard to phonology and morphology are described in detail. The remaining dialects are then given as exception to the general rules holding for Maharashtri, and respectively for the following dialects described. Regarding the variety of rules of Prakrit grammar, S.M. Katre has observed in his *Prakrit Languages and Their Contribution to Indian Culture* (p. 32): The differentia of grammatical rules are indications of an artificial canalising of probable tendencies, exaggerating the minor idiosyncracies of the different languages with which they deal. It is the same tendency which makes Mārkaṇḍeya record 27 varieties of Apabhraṃśa or the 11 varieties of Paiśācī.

Next to grammar, comes prosody or *chanda*, important since time immemorial. *Chanda* originates from song which is sung. Melodies, harmonial songs, or magic songs as they were called, were supposed to appease gods and demons. The *Sāmaveda* is said to have possessed powerful melodious songs which created magic power. Piṅgala or Piṅgalanāga or Phaṇīndra-piṅgala or Nāgarāja-piṅgala or Bhogirāja is said to have been the first composer of *chandas.*

As stated, the oldest stratum of the Śvetāmbara canonical texts were composed in old metres. The pro-canonical literature also accepted popular metres. Later important works were composed to explain Prakrit metres. The *Gāhālakkhaṇa* seems to be one of the oldest works written by Nanditāḍhya to explain the *gāthā* metre, the most popular in Prakrit poetry. The author has no love for the Apabhraṃśa dialect. Mahakavi Muni Ratnacandra has written a commentary on this treatise. The *Vṛttajāti-samuccaya* (Collection of

Vṛtta and *Jāti* Metres) by Virahāṅka is another important work on old prosody. The work is also known as *Kaisiṭṭhachanda* or *Kaisiṭṭhavṛttajāti-samuccaya.* The author is non-Jain and was a scholar of Sanskrit and Prakrit. He has mentioned the names of great poet Gandhahastin, his teacher Sadbhāvalāñchana, Piṅgala, Avalepacihna, Bhujagādhipa, Viṣadhara, Vṛddhakavi and others. Gopala, the commentator, has referred to Piṅgala, Saitava, Kātyāyana, Bharata, Kambala, and Aśvatara. As the text was corrupt, the commentator faces many difficulties in writing. The *Svayambhū-chandas* by Mahākavi Svayambhū is another important treatise of prosody. The author was a well-read scholar, proficient in various branches of learning. He cites quotations from numerous works and the works of his own which indicates the wide learning on the part of the author. This treatise is an important manual of Prakrit and Apabhraṃśa metres on the model of which is based the *Chandonuśāsana* of Hemacandra.

The *Chandonuśāsana* by Hemacandra is a comprehensive work on Prakrit, Sanskrit and Apabhraṃśa prosody. He wrote this work in the form of Sanskrit *sūtras* with a short commentary. This treatise is based on the study of Bharata, Piṅgala, Kāśyapa, Sātavāhana, Dhanapāla, Svayambhū, Saitava and others. Here the author has provided illustrations of every metre, containing the name of the metre. The *Chandaḥkandali* (The Flower of Prosody) by an unknown author is another treatise on the subject, but not extant. But the anonymous commentator of the *Kavidarpaṇa*, has cited a number of quotations from it. The *Kavidarpaṇa* is an important manual of prosody, dealing with Prakrit and Apabhraṃśa metres. Unfortunately, neither the name of the author nor its commentator is known. From the benedictory verses (*maṅgalācarṇan*) we know that he was Jain and his work is based on various *śāstras* of Prakrit and Sanskrit on the subject. His citations from various authoritative works is proof of his wide learning. The author of the *Kavidarpaṇa* as well as its commentator both make extensive quotations from various works on the subject.

The commentator has also given his own illustrations. We have already referred to *Chandolakṣaṇa, Ajiyasantithava* of Nandiṣeṇa. The author Nandiṣeṇa has employed 25 different metres in his *Stava.* In order to illustrate these metres Jinaprabha has written a *Tīkā* known as *Chandolakṣaṇa* in 1308 on this important work. Then, the *Chandaḥkośa,* partly composed in Prakrit and partly in Apabhraṃśa is written by Ratnaśekhar, pupil of Vajrasenasūri. He was a contemporary of Pherozshah Tuglak and was conferred the title of an *ācārya* in 1345. The *Prākrta-paiṅgala*, is an important document of the medieval period. This work is very important for making a comparative study of Prakrit and Apabhraṃśa metres. Numerous copious illustrations are provided here by the author to illustrate the metres. As this work belongs to the earlier part of the fourteenth century it is important for the history and development of Middle-Indo-Āryan languages. A number of Apabhraṃśa metres were borrowed from this work by medieval Hindi poets.

After *vyākaraṇa* and *chanda* comes *kośa* or lexicon, which is a collection of words chosen skilfully. In order to secure melody, the poets have to choose words and expressions to signify the desired meaning for which the *kośa* is very helpful. However, compared with Sanskrit lexicons, Prakrit seems to be very poor.

The *Pāiya-lacchī-nāmamālā* by poet Dhanapāla is the earliest *kośa* of Prakrit which he composed in 972. The work is also designated as *Deśī* or *Deśī-śāstra* by the author. He has incorporated such words which are abound in sentiment (*rasāḍhya*) and generally used by Prakrit poets. 'Let these words give pleasure to the good-hearted people full of love (*shṛdaya*)', he asserts. Dhanapāla was known for his etymology (*vyutpatti*). He has been cited by Hemacandra in his *Abhidhāna-ciñtamaṇi* and the *Deśīnamāmālā*. The *Deśīnāmamālā*, also known as the *Rayaṇāvali* is a very important work of Hemacandra on lexicography. But as Pischel has pointed out, a number of words here which are designated as *deśī* have been traced to Sanskrit origin. This study is considered as an 'authoritative work of the first rank'. His contribution is that he has fixed the forms of numerous words which were quoted wrongly by lexicographers and has pointed out innumerable inaccuracies in the works of *deśīkośas* of various writers. Hemacandra has written his own commentary on this work. Here he has referred to earlier teachers with their difference of opinion with regard to a particular topic. Besides, he has mentioned different writers of various *deśīkośas*. He has also quoted authors who still remain unknown. Among other *kośas*, mention may be made of *Sundara-prakāśa* by Padmasundara, *Tauruṣkī-nāmamālā* or *Yavana-nāmamālā* (Sanskrit-Persian) by Somamantrīputra and the *Phārasī kośa* (author unknown) written in Sanskrit. Among other *kośas*, compiled in modern times, are *Abhidhānarājendra-kośa* by Ācārya Rājendrasūri, a seven-volume encyclopaedic work, *Ardhamāgadhī-kośa* or *Ardhamāgadhī Dictionary* by Śatāvadhānī Muni Ratnacandra in four volumes. The *Pāiya-sadda-mahaṇṇaco* (*Prākṛta-śabdamahārṇava*) by Pandit Hargovinddas Trikamchand Sheth, Calcutta, 1928 (revised edition, Varanasi, 1963); *Alpa-paricita-saiddhantika-śabda-kośa* by Ācārya Anandsagarasūri, in two volumes.

Alaṃkāra or Poetics: As *vyākaraṇa* is essential to understand the language correctly, *chanda* to bring about melody in poetry, *kośa* to make a selection of words with the desired meaning, so is *alaṃkāra* to embellish poetical passage. Pointing out the significance of *alaṃkāra*, the author of the *Alaṃkara-dappaṇa*, a treatise on Prakrit poetics, still in manuscript form, has compared *kāvya* with the face of most beautiful lady; as she looks devoid of lustre without adornment, so is *kāvya* which lacks brightness without *alaṃkāra*.

We have already referred to the well known rhetoricians who have made a good contribution in the field of poetics propounding their own theory of *kāvya*. Amongst them, Ānandavardhana, the propounder of the *dhvani* theory, was an erudite scholar and lover of Prakrit. He seems to be the first to set the tradition of citing Prakrit verses freely to illustrate the subtleties of Sanskrit poetics. Since the author was a poet himself, he has cited illustrations from his own work in Prakrit. His *Visamabāṇalīlā*, also known as *Ānandakathā*, is unfortunately no more extant. The poetic work dealt with love on the model of the *Gāhāsattasaī*. The work is said to have contained the conversation of cupid with a youth where the former is said to have conquered the three worlds by defeating the *asuras*. The author has also referred to other important Prakrit poetic works such as the *Mahumaha-viaa* (*Madhumatha-vijaya* or The Conquest of Viṣṇu) of Vākpatirāja, the *Hari-vijaya* of Sarvasena and the *Setubandha* of Pravarasena which are considered profound and have been cited by many reputed scholars of poetics. Abhinavagupta, the commentator of the *Dhvanyāloka*, has also cited a number of Prakrit verses in his commentary *Locana*. Dhananjaya (974-96) is known for his *Daśarūpaka* which deals with ten principle types of plays. He has quoted 26 Prakrit stanzas from various important works. Dhanika, his own brother, has written a commentary on his work, known as *Avaloka*. Dhanika was a poet himself and has added his own verses besides the Sanskrit and Prakrit verses from other authors. His commentary is full of quotations including about 26 stanzas from well known Prakrit works. King Bhoja or Bhojarāja reigned in Dhara from about 1005 to 1054 and was a prolific writer, said to have been the author of 84 works dealing with almost all the sciences of medieval India. His *Sarasvatīkaṇṭhābharaṇa* is a comprehensive voluminous study of Sanskrit poetics. He was so fond of Prakrit poetry that in order to illustrate the particulars of poetics, he has incorporated 350 Prakrit stanzas. Some of these are from unknown sources. He has also referred to certain names of poets, some of them unknown. Bhojarāja's other important work is the *Śṛṅgāraprakāśa.* The text is fragmentary and as far as the Prakrit portion is concerned, full of errors. V. Raghavan brought out an edition under the title *Bhoja's Śṛṅgāraprakāśa* in 1963. He has cited 1650 Prakrit stanzas, the biggest number ever cited in any other work of Sanskrit *Alaṃkāra-śāstra.* This work contains various references of various authors and their works such as the *Cetaka,* the *Pañcatantra,* the *Kṣudraka-kathā,* the *Gorocana,* the *Anaṅgavatī,* the *Indumatī* the *Setubandha,* the *Rāvaṇa-vijaya,* the *Hari-vijaya,* the *Abdhi-mathana* by Caturmukha, the *Bhīmakāya,* the *Mārīcavadha,* the *Kuvalayāśvacarita,* the *Śūdraka-kathā,* the Sanskrit version of the *Bṛhatkathā* and so on.

Jain writers have also numerous works on secular literature with a popular appeal, which attracted common people. It also appealed to people and they came over to Jain religion.

Joisa or *Jyotiṣa* (astronomy, the science of the movements of the heavenly bodies, or astrology, the science of the influence of the stars on human and terrestrial affairs) was very popular in ancient India. It is stated that Alberuni arrived here in AD 1030 in order to learn Hindu astronomy and culture. As far as Jains are concerned, *jyotiṣa-vidyā* or the science of astronomy formed a part of their canonical literature. The renowned Jain preceptor Acārya Kālaka is said to have brought this science from the country of Yavana (Irana). Muni Bhojasāgara is said to have been taken to Khurāsāna, Persian city, from Gujarat where he mastered this science and composed his Ramalavidyā based on the *Yavanikāśāstra.* Various works on *jyotiṣa* were composed by Jain authors, the most prominent being *Vivāhapaṣala* which was consulted at the time of a wedding. Varāhamihira has mentioned it. Vindhyavāsin is said to have the author of this work. It seems to be different from the *Vivāhapaṣala* of the Jains. The *Agghakaṇḍa* (*Arghakāṇḍa*) was consulted for determining the price of saleable commodity. The *Bṛh Saṃ* contains a chapter, the *Arghakāṇḍa-adhyāya.* The *Aṅgavijjā,* a very important work on the subject, dealt with the science of divination from physical signs and symbols (*aṅga*). The science of divination is quite ancient and Mahavira is said to have taught it to his disciples. The *aṅga* or movements of the limbs of the body is considered most prominent among the *Aṣṭāṅgamahānimtta* or the Eightfold Branches of *Nimitta* or prognostication. We are told that there had been a vast literature on this branch of knowledge with the *Sūtra*, the *Vṛtti* and the *Vārtika* where detailed exposition was provided on the subject. The *Aṅgavidyā* is mentioned in the *Arthaśāstra*, the *Manusmṛti*, the *Dīghanikāya* of the Buddhists and the *Bṛh Saṃ* of Varāhamihira. Various topics of the *Aṅgavijjā* bear almost the identical titles, as those of the *Bṛh Saṃ*. The *Laggasuddhi* (*Lagnaśuddhi*) is another such work which deals with zodiacal signs (*lagna*). The *Lagnaśuddhi* is referred to in the commentary of the *Bṛh Saṃ* by Utpala. The *Joṇipāhuḍa* (*Yoniprābhṛta*) is admitted in the Śvetāmbara as well as the Digambara traditions. The work has been composed by Dharasena, known as *Prajñāśramaṇa*.

Ramala or *Ramala-vidyā* or *Pāśakavidyā* (*pāśa* being a particular constellation in astronomy) or the Art of Geomancy is foretelling events by casting dice. This art was received by Indians from Arabs. As pointed out earlier, Muni Bhojasāgara composed the *Ramalavidyā* which he learnt in the country of Yavana. The *Ramala-śāstra* has been referred to by *Meghavijaya* in his Meghamahodaya which was composed in 1678. Various other works on this subject were written by Jains, which are preserved in manuscript forms in Jain Bhandars. *Śakunaśāstra* or the Art of Omens holds a very important place from ancient times in the life of Indian people. The word *śakuna* generally means a bird and the knowledge of notes of birds and animals it is known as *Śakunajñāna*. Varāhamihira has devoted several chapters on the topic, on which the commentator Utpala has cited Bhagavān Garga, Ṛṣiputra and Parāśara as authorities. The commentator cites 32 verses from the *Akṣarakośa* of Yavanācārya; the work is not available. A treatise known as *Sāṇuruya* (*Śvānuruta*) or the Barking of Dogs is catalogued in the Jain Manuscripts of Patan Jain Bhandar. Elsewhere the *Giroliyā-ruta*, the *Śivā-ruta*, the *Kāka-ruta*, the *Gṛha-godhikā-vicāra* and *Kṛkalāsa-vicāra* are mentioned. Most of the works on the subject are in manuscript.

Āusattha (*Āyuśāstra*) or *Vejjasattha* (*Vaidyaśāstra*) or *Āyuvveya* (*Āyurveda*) or the Science of Medicine is considered the science and art of life. It was a great healing art of ancient India, occupying a better position even than the *Vedas*. The *Vedas* provided happiness in future whereas by practising *Āyurveda* one could achieve happiness in this world by acquiring wealth and honour for oneself and giving life to those who are affected with disease and illness. Various treatises on the subject were written in Prakrit. This science of medicine was applicable not only for the welfare of human beings but also for the growth and nourishment of trees and plants. The *Rukkhāyuvveya* (*Vṛkṣayurveda*) or art of planting or cultivating trees played an important role in ancient India in the sphere of ecology. The *Bṛh Saṃ* contains a chapter the *Vṛkṣāyurvedaadhyāya* where the commentator has referred to the ancient sages Kāśyapa and Parāśara as authorities. The *Pupphajoṇisattha* (*Puṣpayoniśāstra*) dealt with the budding of flowers. The *Kusumalatā-adhyāya* is a chapter in the *Bṛh Saṃ.* The seeds were planted in the proper season in the field. The *Bījāropaṇa-nakṣatra,* a treatise in Kannaḍa has prescribed the rules for planting of seeds in appropriate constellation. The *Atthasattha* (*Arthaśāstra*) in Prakrit is referred to in various Jain works of antiquity. The *Mayaṇamauḍa* (*Madanamukuṭa*) was composed by Gosai Vipra in Prakrit. The *Vasiyasattha* (*Vaiśikaśāstra*) or the Art of Courtesans provided knowledge of solicitation of prostitutes. *Dhaṇuvveya* (*Dhanurveda*) or Archery was highly advanced in the ancient period and heroism was invariably associated with this art. *Dhaṇuvveya* and *Īsattha* (*Īṣvastra*) are included in the seventy-two arts. Like *Āyurveda* and *Dhanurveda, Gandharvaveda* also is said to have the status of the *Veda.* In Jain tradition the *Sara-pāhuḍa,* dealt with a description of *svaras* (musical notes). The *Gandhaśāstra* dealt with the preparation of fragrant substances. The *Bṛh Saṃ* contains a chapter on *Gandhayukti.* According to the commentator this work was written by Īsvara, from which a Prakrit stanza has been cited. The *Dhātu-vidyā* (Alchemy), the *Khanya-vidyā* (Mining) and the *Ratna-parīkṣā* (Test of Precious Stones) are mentioned. Varāhamihira has devoted four chapters on the subject where the details of precious stones are discussed in detail. A *ratna* was considered an omen. The *Ratnaparīkṣā* was written by Thakkuarapheru (fourteenth century). His other work was *Vāstusāra* or the Science of Architecture which deals with the building of houses. Varāhamihira has devoted three chapters on the subject, dealing with architecture and description of temples and idols. According to the author the material has been drawn from ancient writers including Nagnajit and Vasiṣṭha. Then we have *Porāgama, Sūdaśāstra* or *Anna-saṃskāra-śāstra* or the Art of Cooking; the *Assa-sattha* (*Aśvaśāstra*), the Knowledge of Horses; the *Hatthi-sattha* (*Hasti-śāstra*), the Art of Training Elephants; the *Caurakarma* or *Coravidyā,* the Art of Committing theft; the *Dhūrtavidyā,* the Art of knavery and so on. Many of these works are still in the form of manuscripts lying unpublished in Jain Bhandars. The publication of these valuable works will throw flood of light on social and cultural history in India.

RESUMÉ

In recent times the study of Prakrit has been neglected for some reason or the other. There has been no regular provision for the study of Prakrit in universities or educational institutes in India. Even in earlier days, at the time of Rājaśekhara we find that Prakrit could not hold its own to remain a living language and its progress more or less came to standstill. Readers used to understand Prakrit with the help of Sanskrit. Even the Prakrit passages of Sanskrit drama were printed along with the Sanskrit rendering in the footnote. As Prakrit no more remained a spoken tongue, the authors had to put in hard-labour to compose their treatises in Prakrit. As the study of Prakrit was diminishing day by day, there were few scholars who could follow the language correctly. Consequently, the Prakrit stanzas contained in the works of *Alaṃkāraśāstra* by way of illustrations, were printed wrongly and in some cases it becomes difficult to make head or tail of the text.

Mahavira and Buddha in order to reach a simple common man, preferred to preach their sermons in the local dialect of Magadha. They did not choose Sanskrit, the refined and polished language of highly educated people. Mahavira preached in Māgadhī or Ardhamāgadhī, explaining to his disciples what true religion was and how could one get rid of one's worldly suffering. Mahavira explained the principle of non-violence in mind, speech and deed. He explained the theory of *karma* and denounced caste, declaring that one is great or small by one's own deeds and not by birth. His religion was meant for one and all, men and women, so called touchables and untouchables. Mahavira's teachings were compiled in the *Āgamas.* In the course of time it was not possible to retain all that was preached by the Master, hence arose the need to convene councils of learned monks.

Needless to point out that during this long period of a thousand years there must have been considerable changes not only in the language, but also in the contents of the sacred literature. It is for this reason that the later commentators find themselves at a loss to explain the true meaning of the canonical texts. They have cited different versions of the texts and in absence of an authentic version they have shown their inability to offer authoritative interpretations.

As far as Ardhamāgadhī is concerned, there is no uniformity about its use. The Prakrit grammarians like Vararuci do not mention it at all. This dialect as employed in the Sanskrit dramas is quite different from that of the Śvetāmbara canonical texts. The Ardhamāgadhī dialect of Aśvaghoṣa differs from the dialect employed in orthodox classical Sanskrit dramas. Here we come across older forms of the dialect; the rules of grammar are not correctly followed here. Looking to certain similar changes, the dialect of Old Ardhamāgadhī is considered more akin to Old Māgadhī and the dialect of Aśoka's pillar inscriptions. No doubt, as far as the subject matter, the grammatical forms and the use of metres are concerned, a certain portion of the canonical text is quite old and can be compared with the Palī Canon of the Buddhists, yet the Āgamic literature has undergone several redactions and from time to time the regional dialects have infiltrated the original text.

The same thing can be said about Śaurasenī, the dialect of the extant canonical text of the Digambaras. Like the Ardhamāgadhī employed by Aśvaghoṣa, his Śaurasenī also is much older than the one employed in later classical Sanskrit drama as well as the Digambara Śaurasenī canonical texts.

However, looking to the contents, the subject matter, the magnitude and the archaic forms of the dialect, the extant canonical text of the Digambaras seems to be younger. Here we notice homogeneity of forms of language and absence of the *deśī* words unlike the Ardhamāgadhī canonical text of the Śvetāmbaras. It is also to be noted that as due to influence of the south-western dialect, there were changes in the original Ardhamāgadhī canonical dialect, in the same way the original Śaurasenī dialect has undergone considerable change due to the influence of the western speech. It also intermingled with Ardhamāgadhī. Though according to the Digambaras, the sacred literature is lost beyond recovery, a certain portion of the *Dṛṣṭivāda* is available in the form of the *Chakkhaṇḍāma Sutta* and the *Kasāyapāhuḍa* in Śaurasenī. Among other important works in Śaurasenī are Yativṛṣabha's *Tiloyapaṇṇatti*, Śivārya's *Bhagavatī Ārādhanā*, Vaṭṭakera's *Mūlācāra*, the works of Kundakunda and so on. Of these the *Bhagavatī Ārādhanā* and the *Mūlācāra* are important as the contents and even some Prakrit *gāthās* of both are identical with the canonical texts of the Śvetāmbaras. Aparājitasūri, the commentator of the *Bhagavatī Ārādhanā*, has also written a commentary on the *Daśavaikālika Sūtra* and has cited canonical texts in support of his statement. Similarly, the author of the *Mūlācāra*, also known as the *Ācārāṅga Sūtra*, besides dealing with the six essential duties (*saḍāvaśyaka*), has supported the view of emancipation of women (*strī-mukti*), not favoured by the Digambaras. Both texts of antiquity can be useful for making a comparative study of the Digambara and Śvetāmbara dogmas, analysing the conditions under which the split occurred.

The Śvetāmbaras who tried to preserve their sacred literature, developed it by adding commentaries and explanations by way of *nijjtti, bhāsa, cuṇṇi* and *ṭīkā*. In order to make the exegetical literature delightful, various fascinating popular tales and anecdotes were inserted. Certainly this helped a lot in the development of Prakrit literature.

The Śvetāmbaras and the Digambaras also composed independent treatises regarding the teachings of Jainism, including philosophy, the theory of *karma*, conduct of laymen (*śrāvakācāra*), rules for monks and nuns, rituals, cosmology, cosmography and so on. All these valuable works helped a good deal in the development of Prakrit literature.

The narrative literature of Prakrit is another milestone in the growth and development of Prakrit literature. In place of the Brahmanic traditional (*paurāṇika*) literature abounding in mythological narration, Jain writers tried to present a novel outlook towards life. They depicted the life of common people, with all their aspirations, hopes, desires, disappointment, happiness and sorrow. Here we come across the notable scenes of utmost poverty, quarrelsome women, adventurous merchants, sea-journeys, love affairs, prostitutes, bawds, feats of robbery, propitiation of deities, achievement of magic lore and so on. Jain writers were in search of popular stories so that they could make their sermons fascinating. Some of these stories were related to presence of mind, ready wit, creating bewilderment, generating humour, riddles and puzzles and questions and answers. They also compiled numerous *kathākośas* (treasury of tales), comprising collections of stories not only in Prakrit but also in Sanskrit, Apabhraṃśa, Kannaḍa, Old Gujarati, Old Hindi and so on. The purpose of these stories was not just to create entertainment, but it is stated that those who are desirous of highest good should possess the knowledge of good conduct (*cāritra*) for which it is necessary to read the tales of fools and knaves and prostitutes and bawds so that one may guard oneself from the grip of the bad people. Jain narrative literature is a storehouse of popular stories, fables, fairy tales, tales of animals, a number of which stand comparison with world story literature. The vast narrative literature composed in Maharashtri Prakrit has certainly contributed a great deal to the development of Prakrit literature. Some of the notable works written by the Śvetāmbaras are the *Taraṅgavaikahā* by Pādalipta, the *Vasudevahiṇḍi* by Saṅghadāsagaṇi Vācaka, the *Majjhimakhaṇḍa* by Dharmasebagaṇi Mahattara, the *Samarāiccakahā* and the *Dhuttakkhāṇa*, both by Haribhadra, the *Kuvalayamālā* by Udyotana-sūri, the *Kahāṇayakosa* by Jineśvarasūri, the *Akkhāṇamaṇikosa* by Devendragaṇi, the *Kahārayaṇakosa* by Guṇacandragaṇi, the *Kumāravālapaḍiboha* by Somaprabha; the *Uvaesamālā* by Dharma-dāsagaṇi, the *Uvaesapada* by Haribhadra, the *Dhammovaesa-mālā-vivaraṇa* by Jayasiṃhasūri and the *Bhavabhāvanā* by Maladhāri Hemacandra. The Digambara authors preferred to write more in Sanskrit, Apabhraṃśa, Kannaḍa, Old Gujarati, Old Rajasthani and Old Hindi. Some of the prominent compositions are the *Yaśastilakacampū* by Somadevasūri, the *Bṛhatkathākośa* by Hariṣeṇa, the *Kathākośa* by Prabhācandra, the *Kathākośa* by Nemidatta, the *Kathākośa* by Śrīcandra (Apabhraṃśa), the *Vaḍḍārāhane* (Old Kannada), and the *Puṇyāsravakathākośa* by Nāgarāja (Old Kannaḍa, based on Sanskrit version). A number of such works are preserved in the Bhandarkar Oriental Research Institute, Poona, the Jain Matha of Moodbidri, Karkal and Śravaṇabeḷgoḷ.

Where poetry is concerned, Prakrit comes into its own. Since it was a dialect of common people it could create a better emotional appeal in the minds of readers. Though the principles of Jainism are based on renunciation, relinquishing worldly pleasures and retirement from life, an ordinary man was hardly convinced with dry teachings full of moral virtue and righteousness. He wanted something thrilling that could appeal to his emotions. Under the circumstances, Jains were obliged to compose romantic love stories. Jayavallabha, the author of the *Vajjālagga*, has declared that though he is well-versed in Sanskrit poetry, looking to the erotic-mindedness of people he has decided to compose his work in Prakrit. The admirers of Prakrit poetry have asserted that if this poetry is charming, full of melody, dear to the hearts of young maidens and characterized with erotic sentiment, who would like to read Sanskrit poetry? The majority of the stanzas of the *Gāhāsattasaī* contain erotic material. As already stated, Poet Bhoja who considers the erotic sentiment (*śṛṅgāra*), as the only sentiment which dominates in poetry, has cited more than a thousand stanzas from the works of Prakrit lyrical poetry in his *Śṛṅgāraprakāśa.*

As this literature was very important from the point of view of poetic grace, it has exercised a good deal of influence on later poetical works such as the *Amaruśataka* of Amaru, the *Āryāsaptaśatī* of Govardhana, the *Bihārī-satasaī* of Bihārī, *Ṣatasaiyā* of Dayārāma, the *Dalapata-satasaī* of Dalapatarām and others. Prakrit poetry can be called the highest landmark in the development of Prakrit literature.

As we have seen in Sanskrit dramas, a variety of Prakrit dialects is employed to make the drama popular. On the whole, the outlook of the Sanskrit dramas seem to be aristocratic, where the important status is assigned to the hero who is either a king, a royal sage or a god who happens to appear in human form. The *vidūṣaka* is his constant companion and makes him laugh and consoles him at the time of distress. To make the drama realistic, Prakrit dialects were introduced, different characters speaking different dialects. Sanskrit is assigned to the Brahmanas and Kṣatriya or ruling class, and the chief queen, whereas Prakrit is allocated to ascetics, hermits, women, children and low class people. It is stated that a woman should not make an attempt to speak in Sanskrit as it looks odd like the sound '*su su*' of a cow in whose nostrils a new rope has been tied.

The *Mṛcchakaṭika* of Śūdraka is the only extant social drama. Here the hero Cārudatta, a Brahman by birth, has become a penniless because of his excessive generosity. The part of heroine is assigned to Vasantasenā, a courtesan by profession. Since the play is drawn from real life, the contemporary life of the time is depicted. Here we come across the government administration, the life of courtesans, their social status, intrigues, knavery, attempt to murder, theft and so on. The heroine is a highly respected lady who is treated with great reverence, who is loyal in her love to Cārudatta. There are 30 characters in the play who speak various dialects, including the minor ones such as Āvantī, Prācyā, Śākārī, Cāṇḍālī and Ḍhakkī. Here we notice the use of Prakrit dialects more than Sanskrit. The use of a variety of Prakrits seems to be intended to illustrate the rules laid down in the *Nāṭyaśāstra.* Gradually, the gulf between the language of the drama and the real life of people widened, as a result the Sanskrit dramas were confined only to a limited section of the audience.

Coming to the tenth century we do not see progress in the drama literature. Bhavabhūti, for instance, a great Sanskrit poet, bases his Śaurasenī on the model of Sanskrit. It was difficult to write Sanskrit drama with Prakrit dialects and distinguish between Śaurasenī and Maharashtri. Both Sanskrit and Prakrit had come to be almost the dead languages and one had to put in a great labour in writing a Sanskrit drama. Thus when the playwrights lost contact with Prakrit, authors like Rāmapāṇivāda, Rudradāsa and others were obliged to write their works after making a study of Vararuci and Trivikrama. Whatever it may be, the employment of Prakrit in Sanskrit dramas was a great achievement of Prakrit which helped a good deal to bring Sanskrit drama closer to life.

Treatises on Prakrit grammar were written under the direct influence of Sanskrit grammar. Vararuci is considered to be the oldest grammarian of Prakrit and Hemacandra wrote his grammar in the twelfth century. A poet should also possess thorough knowledge of metrics so that he can employ the rich variety of metres in his composition. It seems there existed a highly developed variety of metres in ancient India; they were employed in love-songs to eulogize beautiful ladies. Jain authors employed varieties of metre in praise of God Jina. The study of the lexicon too was essential for a poet so that he chose the rarest possible words in his composition to convey the appropriate meaning. Similarly, in order to acquire knowledge of the variety of figures of speech it was essential to have a thorough knowledge of *alaṃkāraśāstra.* As Prakrits were simple spoken languages, writers in Palī and Prakrit did not feel the necessity of writing treatises on poetics. Perhaps Hemacandra is the only one who wrote on grammar, prosody, lexicography and poetics with authority.

Jains also contributed a good deal in the sphere of secular literature. At times Jain monks had to encounter difficult situations when they had to take recourse to magical practices, science of medicine, science of prognostication, astrology and other popular sciences. Ācārya Bhadrabāhu, Kālaka, Khapuṭa, Vajra, Pādalipta, Viṣṇukumara, Akalanka, Samantabhadra and many other renowned teachers are cited as examples who are highly esteemed by Jains. Of their works, a few are published, though the majority remain in manuscripts in Jain Bhandars; they are recorded in various important catalogues prepared by scholars.

Thus we see that during a period of 2,200 long years Prakrit literature passed through various stages: geographical, historical, political, social, and cultural, and turned into a full-fledged literary language. This literature of vast magnitude is a perennial source for reconstructing the literary and cultural history of India. Middle Indo-Āryan is a very important link between the Old Indo-Āryan and the New Indo-Āryan, between the past and the present. It inspires us to study India's past with its present in a correlated manner so that one is able to study the past in the light of the present and vice versa. The time has come for the study of Prakrit dialects in all their aspects and in historical perspective, on a broad national level. Such a study will be of vital importance for a comprehensive understanding of the plentiful and inexaustible heritage of India. Prakrit literature is an essential part of Indian people—their religion, ritual, customs, way of living and thinking. Thousands of important manuscripts are lying unpublished in various Jain Bhandars in the north and the south and they need immediate attention. The study of Prakrit language and literature needs vitalization and reorientation. It should be made compulsory for students of Indian languages, comparative religion, and ancient Indian history and culture. In order to make it popular, selections of thought-provoking stories and delightful pieces of poetry should be published. An Encyclopedia or Treasury of Prakrit tales and a critical Prakrit dictionary are urgent needs of the day.

NOTE

1. A few incongruities in the sacred literature can be noted down here:

(i) There is no systematic life-story of Mahavira like that of Gautama Buddha in the Buddhist Canon; controversy regarding his place of *nirvāṇa*; his being transplanted from the fetus of a Brahman lady to that of a Kṣatriyāṇī by Hariṇegameṣi. Who was he?—a commander-in-chief of Indra, or a demon with the head of a ram, supposed to seize or injure children (as referred to in the *Atharvaveda*)? What is meant by the term '*naigameṣāpahṛta*'? It has been explained as a disease of pregnancy caused by bodily wind known as *nāgodara*, king of decay of the fetus in the womb, in the *Caraka* and the *Suśruta*. This episode of '*garbha-haraṇa*' is enumerated as one of the Ten Wonders in the canonical text. There are differences of opinion about Mahavira's marriage. Whether Mahavira had a daughter, named Anavadyā (or Priyadarśanā)? Was she given in marriage to Jāmāli, the son of Mahavira's sister Sudarśanā? Both these episodes are not mentioned in the biography of Jāmāli referred to in the *Viyāha*. Difference of opinion also exists about Mahavira's *acelakatva* (nudity). As for his undergoing of intense suffering at the hands of residents of the Lāḍha region—is it an exaggeration of facts at the hands of the devotees?

(ii) There is a difference of nomenclature of 24 Tīrthaṅkaras in the *Viyāha*. The Tīrthaṅkara Ara is called Nandyāvarta in the Mathura inscriptions.

(iii) Was Malli a man or a woman? Like the *garbha-haraṇa* of Mahavira, the emancipation of Malli as a woman is also enumerated as one of the Ten Wonders.

(iv) The life-history of Pārśvanātha appears to be the prototype of that of Mahavira. We are told nothing special about Pārśvanātha, except the dialogue between Keśī and Gautama which we come across in the *Uttarā*.

(v) The life of Keśī, the followers of Pārśvanātha, described in the *Rāya*, is applicable to other disciples of Mahavira (as well as narrated in the *Ovāiya*).

(vi) In the *Jambu*, Ṛṣabha, the first Tīrthaṅkara, is known under various titles such as *Vajja-pāṇi* (Indra in the *MBH*), *Purandara* (Indra in the *Ṛgveda*), *Śatakratu* (Indra in the *Śatapatha Brāhmaṇa* and *MBH*), *Sahasrākṣa* (Indra in the *Ṛgveda*), *Maghavā*, *Pākaśāsana*, *Śūla-pāṇi* and *Vṛṣabha-vāhana* and so on.

(vii) Here the heavenly damsels arriving to celebrate the birth-festival of Ṛṣabha are not all damsels; some of them signify the names of *tithis* (lunar day), of Durgā, nymphs, Indra's daughters, and the heavenly cars.

(viii) Among eleven *gaṇadharas* of Mahavira, Indrabhūti and Sudharma are most prominent, the rest seem to be their prototypes.

(ix) In the earlier text, the *Ācārāṅga*, the characteristics of the soul are described on the pattern of the *Upaniṣadas*: neither big, nor small (*na dīhe na hrasse*), but by later writers the soul is known as 'measuring one's own body' (*sva-deha-parimāṇa*).

(x) There is no mention of *Dharmāstikāya* and *Adharmāstikāya* in earlier Jain texts.

(xi) Out of seven *Tattvas* and nine *Padārthas*, only *Saṃvara* gets a prominent place in the *Ācārāṅga*. Here the emphasis is on the release of the soul from the bondage of *karma*.

Index